Halides of the Transition Elements

Halides of the Second and Third Row Transition Metals

Halides of the Transition Elements

is a series of three volumes consisting of
the present title together with the following

**Halides of the Lanthanides and Actinides
by D. Brown**

and

**Halides of the First Row Transition Metals
by J. H. Canterford and R. Colton**

Halides of the Transition Elements

Halides of the Second and Third Row Transition Metals

J. H. Canterford
and
R. Colton

Department of Inorganic Chemistry,
University of Melbourne,
Parkville, Victoria.

A WILEY-INTERSCIENCE PUBLICATION
John Wiley & Sons Ltd.
London New York Sydney

546.62
H13
71430
October, 1970

Printed in Northern Ireland by The Universities Press

Preface

The last few years have seen a great increase in interest in the chemistry of the second- and third-row transition elements. No doubt the scarcity of the elements, and consequently their high price, delayed development to some extent, but the realization that their chemistry is markedly different from that of the first-row transition elements has strongly stimulated research.

It is remarkable that, despite the obvious interest in these elements, there is no other book that deals only with the chemistry of these elements as a group. Although we have restricted our treatment to only the halide chemistry, we believe this is sufficient to illustrate the general features of the chemistries of these elements.

The treatment has been strictly limited to halides, oxide halides, complex halides, and complex oxide halides. Simple adducts of the halides with donor molecules have not been examined in detail, but references are made to relevant papers in the sections on reactions of the halides.

Apart from the first three review chapters, all the chapters have been treated in a uniform way. Briefly, each chapter is divided into two sections, one on halides and oxide halides, and the other on complexes. Within each division the compounds are treated in decreasing oxidation states and within each oxidation state the order is invariably fluorides, chlorides, bromides, and finally iodides. The available data for each compound are presented in a well defined order. We realise that this type of treatment may lead to some monotony, but we hope the advantages of being able to rapidly find the required data for a particular compound outweigh the disadvantages. All temperatures are in degrees celcius unless specified otherwise.

The bibliography for the main text is complete to the end of 1966. All additional material available to us up to March 1968 is briefly outlined in Addenda at the end of most chapters.

There has been a formal course of the chemistry of the second- and third-row elements at the University of Melbourne for five years, and this book is written in such a way that it may serve as the basis of such courses elsewhere. At the same time, we have attempted to give sufficient detail for the book to be useful to research workers.

Our sincere thanks are offered to several of our colleagues for numerous discussions, to Miss H. Hampel for her assistance, and to the Chemistry Department Librarian, Miss I. M. Rennie, for her unfailing assistance in obtaining inaccessible journals. Special thanks are offered to Dr. T. A. O'Donnell who read the manuscript and made many constructive suggestions, and to our publishers for their co-operation in allowing us to add the Addenda at the galley-proof stage.

Grateful acknowledgment is made to the following publishers and societies for permission to reproduce illustrations.

Book or Journal	Publisher	Figure
Inorg. Chem.	American Chemical Society	3.1, 3.2, 3.3, 3.4, 3.6, 3.7, 3.8, 3.9, 3.12, 3.13, 3.15, 3.16, 3.20, 3.23, 5.3, 5.4, 7.4, 7.5, 2.1
J. Am. Chem. Soc.	American Chemical Society	3.14, 5.7, 10.4, 10.5, 11.3
J. Appl. Phys.	American Institute of Physics	7.1, 10.2
J. Less Common Metal.	Elsevier Publishing Co. Amsterdam.	3.17, 3.18, 3.19
Nature	McMillan Journals Ltd.	3.5, 7.3
Chem. Ind.	Society of Chemical Industry	4.2
Acta Cryst.	International Union of Chrystallography	4.3, 5.1, 5.2, 5.6, 5.9, 6.1, 8.2, 10.6, 11.1, 11.2
Acta Chem. Scand.	Munksgaard	5.10, 5.11, 5.12, 5.13
J. Inorg. Nucl. Chem.	Pergamon, Oxford	7.2, 8.1
Z. Anorg. Allgem. Chem.	Barth, Leipzig	9.1
Chem. Commun.	The Chemical Society	10.3

J. H. C.
R. C.

University of Melbourne,
Victoria, Australia.
March 1968.

Contents

Contents

Contents

Chapter 1

Fluorides

Much of the major progress in transition-metal fluorine chemistry has been made since 1950, much of the stimulus being gained from the requirements of atomic energy programmes. Many of the advances could not have been made without the spectacular development of new constructional materials and the ready availability of elemental fluorine. In some cases, such as the preparation and characterization of the hexafluorides of the platinum group, special techniques are essential because of the extreme reactivity of the compounds, particularly towards moisture. Indeed, some techniques are so specialized and advanced that they are available only to a few groups of workers.

Whilst there is no doubt that Otto Ruff was the founder of transition-metal fluorine chemistry and that he achieved remarkable success with very limited experimental facilities, it is nevertheless true that much of the work by Ruff and his coworkers is in error and needs to be reinvestigated and extended with the use of modern techniques. Partial hydrolysis of his products frequently led Ruff to incorrect formulation of his compounds and incorrect assessment of their physical and chemical properties; the classic example of this was the formulation of the yellow volatile solid osmium hexafluoride, as the octafluoride[1].

Considerably more experimental work has been reported on the preparation and characterization of binary fluorides, particularly the volatile fluorides, than on oxide fluorides. Indeed, there has been no systematic study of the oxide fluorides at all, mainly owing no doubt to the fluorine chemists' desire to work in an oxygen-free system. However, although oxide fluorides are usually carefully avoided since they normally arise as impurities due to the presence of air or moisture in the system, Edwards and coworkers[2] have shown by structural studies that they merit more attention than they have received in the past.

A similar situation arises with the complex salts, although considerably less work has been reported on the complex fluorides than on the binary fluorides. Even less has been reported on the complex oxide fluorides.

Binary fluorides and complex fluorides of the second- and third-row transition metals in high formal oxidation states are readily prepared for those elements towards the left of the Periodic Table; but, as the atomic number of the metal increases in each series, the higher oxidation states become more difficult to attain. Furthermore, compounds in a higher oxidation state tend to become more reactive with increasing atomic number across each series.

MANIPULATION OF FLUORINE AND FLUORIDES

The manipulation of elemental fluorine and the more reactive fluorides probably presents some of the most challenging practical difficulties encountered in inorganic chemistry.

The volatile fluorides are handled most conveniently in vacuum systems, and extreme care must be taken if Pyrex glass is to be used as the construction material, since traces of moisture are sufficient to begin a cyclic hydrolysis process which can lead to complete loss of the compound. Further, some of the more reactive fluorides react directly with glass even after it has been dried most rigorously; in such cases it is essential that some other constructional material be used. It should be noted that it is necessary to make a deliberate choice of materials of construction and sometimes it is in fact advantageous to use a combination of the various construction materials available.

A full account of materials available for handling reactive fluorides and for construction of vacuum lines and ancillary equipment has recently been given by Canterford and O'Donnell[3].

Generally, the non-volatile fluorine compounds must be handled by dry box techniques, and usually the normal chemical techniques used for air or moisture sensitive compounds are sufficient.

GENERAL PREPARATIVE TECHNIQUES

Binary Fluorides

There is no doubt that, when applicable, direct fluorination of the heated metal in a flow system is the most convenient and efficient method of preparation. Typical examples of compounds prepared by this method are niobium and tantalum pentafluorides[4], technetium[5] and osmium[6] hexafluorides, and silver difluoride[7]. This method of preparation normally produces the fluoride with the metal in its highest oxidation state although, for the more reactive fluorides, special techniques are required. Two such special techniques have been used. Pressures of fluorine higher than one atmosphere and elevated temperatures must be used to prepare pure samples of rhenium heptafluoride[8] and osmium heptafluoride[9]. For the preparation of the hexafluorides of ruthenium[10], rhodium[11] and platinum[12], the metal in the form of wire or powder is heated electrically in fluorine until it begins to burn; the metal is situated very close to a surface cooled by liquid nitrogen, so that there is immediate quenching of any decomposition reactions of the hexafluoride. Even with this technique some lower fluorides are usually obtained as side products, and the hexafluorides are purified by vacuum distillation.

The more reactive halogen fluorides have been used with certain metals and certain oxides to produce fluorides of the transition metals. Once again the highest stable fluoride is usually obtained, although the initial product is often an adduct which must be thermally decomposed to give the transition-metal fluoride. Typical examples of the use of halogen fluorides are the preparation of rhenium hexafluoride by the action of chlorine trifluoride on rhenium at 300° [13], zirconium tetrafluoride by the action of bromine trifluoride on zirconium at elevated temperatures[14] and molybdenum hexafluoride by the action of iodine pentafluoride on molybdenum trioxide[15]. If possible, it is preferable to avoid use of the halogen fluorides because of the tendency to form adducts; and with bromine trifluoride in particular, the product is often contaminated with free bromine which is difficult to remove.

Lower fluorides are frequently prepared by reduction of higher fluorides using the metal itself. Examples are the reduction of niobium pentafluoride by niobium at about 350° to give niobium tetrafluoride[16,17] and the preparation of molybdenum pentafluoride by reduction of molybdenum hexafluoride by molybdenum in a flow system at 400° [18]. Alternative reagents for the reduction of certain higher fluorides are also frequently used and some examples are given in Table 1.1.

TABLE 1.1

Preparation of Lower Fluorides

Higher Fluoride	Product	Reductant	Conditions	Ref.
NbF_5	NbF_4	Phosphorus	Sealed tube, 350°	17
MoF_6	MoF_5	PF_3	Room temperature	19
WF_6	WF_4	C_6H_6	Bomb, 110°	20
ReF_6	ReF_5	$W(CO)_6$	Room temperature	21
RuF_5	RuF_3	Sulphur	Sealed tube, 200°	22
OsF_6	OsF_5	Iodine	Excess of OsF_6 in IF_5 solution	23
PdF_3	PdF_2	SeF_4	Reflux	24

An alternative procedure for the preparation of lower fluorides is the thermal disproportionation of higher fluorides. This is particularly applicable to the disproportionation of pentafluorides to the corresponding hexafluoride and tetrafluoride. All pentafluorides except those of niobium and tantalum decompose in this manner.

Halogen exchange reactions involving anhydrous hydrogen fluoride and other fluorine compounds are of limited applicability but they have been used to prepare some compounds, as shown in Table 1.2.

TABLE 1.2

Preparation of Fluorides by Halogen Exchange

Reagents	Conditions	Product	Ref.
$ZrCl_4$ and HF	Flow system, $300°$	ZrF_4	25
$NbCl_5$ and HF	Room temperature	NbF_5	26
$MoBr_3$ and HF	Flow system, $600°$	MoF_6	27
WCl_6 and HF	Room temperature	WF_6	28
$NbCl_5$ and AsF_3	Reflux	NbF_5	29

Halogen exchange with anhydrous hydrogen fluoride is to be avoided if possible, since the extremely pure hydrogen fluoride required for this reaction is very difficult to prepare[30]. Commercial hydrogen fluoride must *not* be used since it normally contains water which leads to hydrolysis. In addition, any oxide halide in the starting material will at best be converted into an oxide fluoride.

There are, of course, a number of specific methods of preparation of individual compounds, but these are discussed in the appropriate chapters.

Oxide Fluorides

Frequently oxide fluorides have been prepared as impurities by the fluorination of metals coated with an oxide film although, surprisingly, fluorination of an oxide is not widely used for deliberate preparation of these compounds. A mixture of oxygen and fluorine may be passed over the heated metal in a flow system, typical examples being molybdenum and tungsten oxide tetrafluorides[31] and osmium oxide pentafluoride[32]. However, in this type of reaction, the relative proportions of oxygen and fluorine are often quite critical. For example, passing a 1 : 2 mixture of fluorine and oxygen over heated osmium metal gives osmium trioxide difluoride[33], whereas a 2:1 fluorine–oxygen mixture gives osmium oxide pentafluoride[32]. This is a good example of the greater tendency of oxygen than of fluorine to force the transition metal to exhibit a higher oxidation state.

It is an indication of the apparent lack of interest in oxide fluorides that there is no other preparative method of general applicability, although some highly specific preparations have been reported. These are discussed in the appropriate chapters.

Complex Fluorides

The formation of complex fluorides of transition metals in water or aqueous hydrogen fluoride is of limited applicability. The only complex fluorides that can be prepared in aqueous solutions are the hexafluoro-metallates(IV) of ruthenium[34], osmium[35], iridium[35] and platinum[36], which are formed by the interaction of water and the corresponding hexafluoro-metallate(V). There are, however, several other hexafluorometallates(IV) that are stable towards hydrolysis, but they are prepared by non-aqueous methods. For example, potassium hexafluoro-technetate[37] and -rhenate(IV)[38] have been prepared by reaction of the other hexahalo-technetates and -rhenates(IV) with potassium hydrogen fluoride in the melt. The products may be purified by recrystallization from hot water.

Complex fluorides of zirconium[39], hafnium[39], niobium[40] and tantalum[41] may be prepared by interaction of the transition-metal fluoride and alkali-metal fluoride in aqueous hydrogen fluoride solution; however, strict control of the relative concentrations of all the reactants is necessary to obtain a specific complex. With niobium it is possible to obtain complex oxide fluorides by this method using dilute hydrogen fluoride solutions[42].

Various complex fluorides of zirconium[43,44], hafnium[45], niobium and tantalum[46-48] may be prepared by fusing the transition-metal fluoride with alkali-metal fluorides in the correct proportions in an inert atmosphere. This method is naturally not readily applicable to complex fluorides derived from the more volatile transition-metal fluorides.

Peacock and coworkers have made extensive use of iodine pentafluoride and liquid sulphur dioxide as solvents for the preparation of a large number of complexes of molybdenum, tungsten, technetium and rhenium in various oxidation states. The general method is the reaction of the transition-metal hexafluoride, or for molybdenum and tungsten the hexacarbonyl, with alkali-metal halides in an excess of solvent. A few representative examples are given in Table 1.3.

It is important to note that, when reduction is possible, great care must be exercised in using the correct proportions of the reactants to form a pure product. In cases where reduction cannot occur, it is advisable to use a small excess of the volatile transition-metal fluoride to facilitate purification of the complex fluoride. The choice of alkali-metal halide is important, since reduction is far more likely to occur with an iodide.

TABLE 1.3

Preparation of Complex Fluorides in Non-aqueous Solvents

Reactants	Solvent	Product	Ref.
KF and MoF_6	IF_5	K_2MoF_8	49
MI and MoF_6 (M = K, Rb or Cs)	IF_5	$MMoF_6$	49
KF and MoF_6	SO_2	K_3MoF_8	49
NaI and MoF_6	SO_2	Na_2MoF_6	50
KI and WF_6	IF_5	K_2WF_8	51
MCl and TcF_6 (M = Na, K, Rb or Cs)	IF_5	$MTcF_6$	5
MI and ReF_6 (M = Li, Na, K, Rb or Cs)	SO_2	$MReF_6$	52
KI and $W(CO)_6$	IF_5	K_2WF_8	51
KI and $Mo(CO)_6$	IF_5	K_3MoF_8	49

One of the most useful methods of preparing complex fluorides of metals of the platinum group, and also of silver and gold, is by passing fluorine or chlorine trifluoride over a complex chloride. Alternatively, an intimate mixture of a binary halide, or even the metal itself, and the appropriate amount of an alkali-metal halide can be heated in the fluorinating atmosphere or refluxed in an excess of bromine trifluoride. Some representative examples are given in Table 1.4.

TABLE 1.4

Preparation of Complex Fluorides by Anhydrous Reactions

Reactants	Fluorinating Agent	Product	Ref.
M_2PdCl_6 (M = K, Rb or Cs)	F_2	M_2PdF_6	53
$MAuCl_4$ (M = K or Cs)	F_2	$MAuF_4$	53
MCl and $RuCl_3$ (M = K, Rb or Cs)	F_2	$MRuF_6$	54
MCl and $RhCl_3$ (M = K, Rb or Cs)	F_2	M_2RhF_6	55
MX and Ru (M = K, Cs or Ag; X = Cl or Br)	BrF_3	$MRuF_6$	34
MBr and $OsBr_4$ (M = Na, K, Cs or Ag)	BrF_3	$MOsF_6$	35
CsCl and $RhCl_3$	BrF_3	Cs_2RhF_6	56
K_2PtCl_6	ClF_3	K_2PtF_6	57
Au and KCl	BrF_3	$KAuF_4$	58
Au and Ag	BrF_3	$AgAuF_4$	58

Complex Oxide Fluorides

No general method of preparation of complex oxide fluorides of the second- and third-row transition metals has so far been developed, but this is probably merely a reflection of the lack of interest in this class of compound.

BINARY FLUORIDES

Binary fluorides of the second- and third-row transition metals span oxidation states VII to I, but the most important and most extensively studied fluorides are those in oxidation states VI and V. It will become apparent that the chemistry of fluorides in the lower oxidation states has in general been neglected and certainly merits further investigation.

Hexafluorides

The hexafluorides of the second- and third-row transition metals form a well-defined group of compounds which display systematic variations in physical and chemical properties. The changes in physical properties throughout the series are not large, but they have a pronounced effect on chemical properties. The resultant variation in chemical properties ranges from the inert character of tungsten hexafluoride to the remarkable reactivity of platinum hexafluoride. Tungsten hexafluoride has been used as a solvent for NMR studies of other volatile fluorides[59]; both molybdenum and tungsten hexafluoride dissolve iodine readily *without reaction*[60], and tungsten hexafluoride undergoes halogen exchange only with the *most powerful* halogenating agents[61]. The extreme reactivity of platinum hexafluoride is typified by its ability to oxidize molecular oxygen[62] and xenon[63], and its fluorinating power is demonstrated by the formation of bromine pentafluoride from bromine trifluoride at room temperature[12].

The difference between the first-row and the second- and third-row transition elements has been frequently stated, but it has often been inferred or stated that the second- and third-row transition elements have quite similar physical and chemical properties. It has now been established that there is a gradual divergence of physical and chemical properties between the two transition series, going from left to right across the Periodic Table. These trends are beautifully demonstrated by the hexafluorides; in general, the hexafluoride of a second-row element is less stable and hence more reactive than that of the corresponding third-row element and these differences increase towards the right of the Table. The combination of these two major trends leads one to expect that the hexafluorides of the second transition series to the right of the Periodic Table should be exceedingly reactive substances. Indeed, it seems almost certain that palladium hexafluoride should not exist under normal conditions, and even rhodium hexafluoride is an extraordinarily unstable reactive compound[11].

The ease of preparation of the hexafluorides and their thermal stabilities are further evidence for these trends. Thus, molybdenum and tungsten hexafluorides are readily prepared, and, with the tungsten compound, even halogen exchange between tungsten hexachloride and a number of fluorine compounds is sufficient to produce it[28,64]. The difficulty of preparation of the hexafluorides increases towards the right of the Periodic Table and for ruthenium, rhodium and platinum hexafluorides special techniques are necessary, as described earlier in this chapter. The hexafluorides of molybdenum, tungsten, technetium, rhenium, osmium and iridium appear to be quite stable thermally at room temperature, whereas those of ruthenium, rhodium and platinum are thermally unstable, decomposing to fluorine and a lower fluoride. The order of decreasing stability and decreasing ease of formation of the platinum-group metal hexafluorides has been given as[65]: $OsF_6 > IrF_6 > PtF_6 > RuF_6 > RhF_6$. One would expect a thermally unstable hexafluoride to show greater chemical reactivity than a thermally stable hexafluoride.

It is our intention to attempt to correlate chemical and physical properties of the hexafluorides on the basis of these trends.

Physical properties. The hexafluorides are all volatile compounds which have been shown to be monomeric in the vapour phase. As a group, the hexafluorides are characterized by extremely short liquid ranges as shown in Table 1.5.

TABLE 1.5

Melting and Boiling Points of the
Hexafluorides

Compound	M.p.	B.p.	Ref.
MoF_6	$17.4°$	$34.0°$	66, 67
WF_6	$2.0°$	$17.1°$	67, 68
TcF_6	$37.4°$	$55.3°$	69
ReF_6	$18.5°$	$33.7°$	8
RuF_6	$54°$	a	10
OsF_6	$32.1°$	$45.9°$	6
RhF_6	$\approx 70°$	a	11
IrF_6	$43.8°$	$53.6°$	67
PtF_6	$61.3°$	$69.14°$	12

a The thermal instability of these compounds makes a determination of their boiling points very difficult.

A remarkable feature of the hexafluorides is the fact that the compounds of the third-row elements are *more* volatile than the corresponding second-row hexafluorides. This phenomenon is quite inexplicable in terms of the conventional ideas of the relationship between molecular weight and volatility. However, Bradley[70] has pointed out that, in pairs of molecules that are essentially identical except for the atomic number of the central metal atom, the heavier molecules may in fact be the more volatile. Bradley quoted as specific examples molybdenum and tungsten hexafluorides, as well as alkoxides of zirconium and hafnium. The apparent anomolous order of boiling points arises because the intermolecular forces are almost identical on the periphery of the molecules and it is the entropy term which becomes predominant at elevated temperatures. This effect is common to all the transition-metal hexafluorides. Furthermore, in each transition-metal series, as in a homologous series, the melting and boiling points of the hexafluorides tend to increase uniformly, as shown in

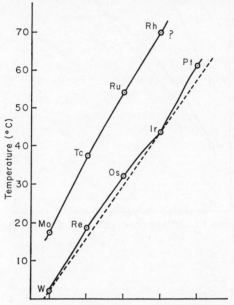

Figure 1.1   Melting points of the hexafluorides.

Figures 1.1 and 1.2. In both melting and boiling points there is an irregularity at iridium hexafluoride, which may be due to errors in the measurements but is more likely to be a real effect. Its cause is not immediately clear, but iridium hexafluoride has a d^3-configuration and should therefore be a regular octahedron, whereas other hexafluorides are known to exhibit Jahn–Teller distortions[71–74].

Finally, the divergence between the two transition series is shown in Figure 1.3 where the difference in melting points of the corresponding second- and third-row hexafluorides are plotted as a function of atomic number. There is some doubt as to the exact melting point of rhodium hexafluoride[11], but, apart from the rhodium hexafluoride–iridium hexafluoride pair, there is a linear increase in the difference between the melting point of a second-row hexafluoride and that of its third-row analogue across the Periodic Table.

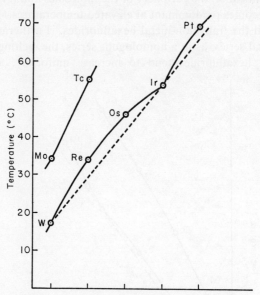

Figure 1.2   Boiling points of the hexafluorides.

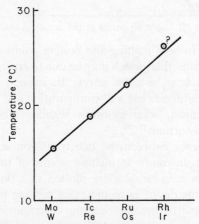

Figure 1.3   Differences in melting point between second- and third-row
hexafluorides.

Without exception the hexafluorides undergo a solid-phase transition from a low-temperature orthorhombic form to a high-temperature cubic form. The transition temperatures and the known heats of transition are given in Table 1.6. The volume change associated with the solid-phase

TABLE 1.6

Transition Temperatures and Heats of Transition

Compound	Transition Temperature	ΔH *trans* kcal mole^{-1}	Ref.
MoF_6	$-8.7°$	1.960	67
WF_6	$-8.2°$	1.400	67
TcF_6	$-5.3°$	1.827	69
ReF_6	$-3.45°$	2.027	8
RuF_6	$2.5°$	—	10
OsF_6	$-0.4°$	1.970	67
RhF_6	$\sim7.0°$	—	11
IrF_6	$0.4°$	1.700	67
PtF_6	$0.0°$	2.14	12

transition is quite large and precautions are necessary when allowing solid hexafluorides to warm up from low temperatures. The cubic form is the least dense and there have been occasions when hexafluorides collected in cooled conventional glass traps have shattered the apparatus on warming. To overcome this problem it is advisable to use traps of large diameter fitted with internal cold fingers. The change in volume is typified by molybdenum hexafluoride and the densities of both forms of the solid are given in Table 1.7[75].

TABLE 1.7

Density of Solid Molybdenum
Hexafluoride

Temp. (°K)	Modification	Density (g/cm³)
77.16	Orthorhombic	3.519
173.83	Orthorhombic	3.393
237.0	Orthorhombic	3.27
278.0	Cubic	2.88

The heats of transition of the third-row transition series are shown in Figure 1.4. Once again there is a marked deviation for iridium hexafluoride which in this case is clearly outside the experimental error. The shape of the curve is reminiscent of the well-known plots of atomic radii, etc.[76,77], for the first-row transition elements. We suggest that the curve

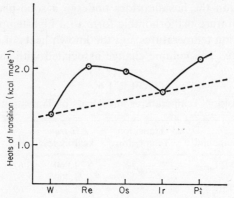

Figure 1.4   Heats of transition of solid hexafluorides.

reflects the known spherical character of tungsten and iridium hexafluorides and the known Jahn – Teller distortions in the hexafluorides of
rhenium, and osmium[72].

The infrared spectra of all the hexafluorides have been recorded in the
vapour phase and have been interpreted on the basis of octahedral symmetry, but in fact Jahn – Teller distortions are apparent in several of the
compounds. The fundamental modes of vibration which have been derived
from the observed spectra by consideration of the overtone and combination bands are given in Table 1.8.

The a_{1g} (ν_1) mode is the completely symmetrical vibration and may be
taken as the frequency closest to a measure of the bond strength. This is
because the vibration does not change the symmetry of the molecule and
does not involve any movement of the heavy central metal atom.

TABLE 1.8

Infrared Spectra of the Hexafluorides (ν in cm^{-1})

Compound	ν_1	ν_2	ν_3	ν_4	ν_5	ν_6	Ref.
MoF_6	741	643	741	262	312	122	78
WF_6	772	672	712	258	316	215	79
TcF_6	705	551	748	265	255	?	80
ReF_6	755	596	715	257	246	193	71
RuF_6	675	573	735	275	262	?	73
OsF_6	733	632	720	268	252	220	72
RhF_6	634	595	724	282	269	192	73
IrF_6	696	643	718	276	260	205	81
PtF_6	655	601	705	273	242	211	72

The positions of the a_{1g} stretching frequencies are plotted as a function of atomic number in Figure 1.5. It is clear that the frequency, and hence the bond strength, drops markedly with an increase in atomic number in each transition series. This sequence fits exactly with the chemical reactivity of the hexafluorides, as will be discussed below.

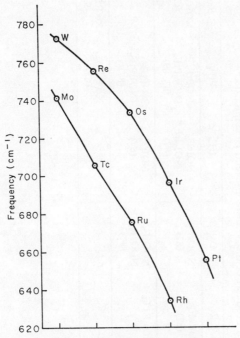

Figure 1.5 Metal–fluorine stretching frequencies (a_{1g} mode) in the hexafluorides.

These trends in stability can be readily understood if it is assumed that some π-bonding occurs in the hexafluorides by donation of fluorine p-electrons into the orbitals of the metals, as well as the normal σ-donation. As the number of electrons in the metal t_{2g} orbitals increases across the series, the π-bonding effects will decrease, resulting in decreasing stability. The π-bond effects would be expected to be greater in the third-row than in the second-row transition metals and this is confirmed in Figure 1.5. Fluorine-to-transition-metal π-bonding has recently been unambiguously demonstrated by Dyer and Ragsdale[82,83] in a ^{19}F NMR study of a series of titanium tetrafluoride–nitrogen-base adducts.

On the basis of physical properties, there should be a steady decrease in chemical stability, and hence an increase in chemical reactivity, in each

TABLE 1.9
Reaction Products of the Transition-Metal Hexafluorides[a]

Reactant	WF_6	MoF_6	ReF_6	OsF_6	IrF_6	PtF_6	RuF_6	RhF_6
NO	n.r. (87, 88)	$NOMoF_6$ (88)	$NOReF_6$ (87)	$NOOsF_6$ (87)	$NOIrF_6$ $(NO)_2IrF_6$ (87)	$NOPtF_6$ $(NO)_2PtF_6$ (87, 89)	$NORuF_6$ (62)	—
NOF	$NOWF_7$ $(NO)_2WF_8$ (87, 90)	$NOMoF_7$ (90)	$(NO)_2ReF_8$ (87)	$NOOsF_7$ $NOOsF_6$ (87)	$NOIrF_6$ (87)	$NOPtF_6$ $(NO)_2PtF_6$ (87)	—	—
Xe	n.r.	n.r.	n.r.	n.r.	n.r.	$Xe(PtF_6)_x$ (63)	$Xe(RuF_6)_x$ (91)	$Xe(RhF_6)_x$ (91)

[a] n.r. = no reaction

series with increasing atomic number. It is difficult to decide *a priori* the relative reactivities of the second- and third-row hexafluorides because of the differences in size, ionization potential and π-bonding between the two series. However, it is expected that a second-row hexafluoride would be more reactive than its corresponding third-row analogue. As noted above, the thermal stabilities and ease of preparation of the platinum-group metal hexafluorides follow the expected trends.

Chemical properties. It is becoming increasingly clear that much of the early literature on the chemical reactivity of the transition-metal hexafluorides is suspect. For example, molybdenum and tungsten hexafluorides have long been regarded as being very reactive and almost identical in chemical as well as in physical properties[84,85]. It is now known that there is a marked difference between the reactivities of these two hexafluorides, the tungsten compound being virtually inert as a fluorinating agent and even in halogen-exchange reactions[61]. The reactions of the hexafluorides with carbon disulphide very clearly demonstrate that both hexafluorides are quite weak fluorinating agents. Tungsten hexafluoride does not react with carbon disulphide, but molybdenum hexafluoride reacts slowly with it to produce bis(trifluoromethyl) disulphide[61]. This is to be compared with the complete rupture of the carbon–sulphur bond by stronger fluorinating agents such as chromium pentafluoride[61] and uranium hexafluoride[86]; in these reactions, carbon tetrafluoride and sulphur hexafluoride are formed. There are two major reasons why much of the early literature on this subject is suspect. The first is the extreme sensitivity of the hexafluorides to moisture; far too often chemical reactivity has been confused with ease of hydrolysis and, indeed, the only reaction in which the chemical reactivities of molybdenum and tungsten hexafluorides are similar is their reaction with moisture. The second is the practical difficulties in handling and analysing these compounds; for example, it now appears certain that the product formulated as osmium octafluoride by Ruff and Tschirch[1] was a mixture of osmium hexafluoride and hydrogen fluoride. The reaction of the hexafluorides of platinum, rhodium and ruthenium with glass obviously makes a study of the chemical reactivities very difficult without specialized techniques[3,65].

It is somewhat difficult to establish an exact order of chemical reactivity of the transition-metal hexafluorides because so far few reagents have been used with all the compounds. However, the relative reactivities of the hexafluorides with nitric oxide, nitrosyl fluoride and xenon clearly demonstrate the general order of reactivity, although naturally there are minor variations with the different reagents. The products of reaction of each of these compounds with the hexafluorides are given in Table 1.9.

Nitric oxide does not react with tungsten hexafluoride, but reduction occurs with the hexafluorides of molybdenum, rhenium, osmium and ruthenium since infrared evidence shows the presence of the NO^+ group. With iridium and platinum hexafluorides there is further reduction to the quadrivalent state. With nitrosyl fluoride the trend is even more pronounced; molybdenum, tungsten and rhenium hexafluorides react but show no reduction; osmium shows partial reduction to osmium(v), and with iridium the reduction to iridium(v) is quantitative. Platinum hexafluoride forms two complexes, one containing platinum(v) and the other platinum(iv).

Xenon reacts only with the thermally unstable, very reactive hexafluorides[91].

The same trends in reactivity can be seen from a consideration of the reactivity of the hexafluorides towards chlorine trifluoride and bromine trifluoride. Molybdenum and tungsten hexafluorides may be prepared by the action of these reagents on the metals[27,92], and rhenium hexafluoride has been prepared by using chlorine trifluoride[13]. Thus, these hexafluorides do not react with chlorine trifluoride or bromine trifluoride. On the other hand, platinum hexafluoride is reduced by both chlorine trifluoride[93] and bromine trifluoride[12]. Presumably ruthenium and rhodium hexafluorides would react in a similar fashion. The remaining hexafluorides do not appear to be formed by the action of these reagents on the metals.

O'Donnell and Stewart[61] have examined the relative reactivities of molybdenum and tungsten hexafluorides in detail towards a wide range of reagents. With the appropriate reagents, either reduction to lower fluorides or mere halogen exchange has been shown to occur more rapidly with molybdenum hexafluoride than with tungsten hexafluoride. These comparative results, which confirm the trends noted above, are treated in detail in Chapter 6.

In conclusion, it appears that there is a clear and distinct correlation between physical and chemical properties of the transition-metal hexafluorides, although it is highly desirable that further chemical studies on the comparative reactions of these compounds be made.

Pentafluorides

The pentafluorides of the second- and third-row transition metals form an interesting series, but it is not possible to consider the series as a whole, as with the hexafluorides, because there are three distinct structural types. Naturally, the structural properties have a great influence on both physical and chemical properties.

The pentafluorides of all the second- and third-row elements from niobium and tantalum to platinum are known with the exception of tungsten pentafluoride and palladium pentafluoride. The non-existence of tungsten pentafluoride is surprising and is discussed in Chapter 6. On the other hand, the trend in stability of the pentafluorides of the second-row transition metals lead us to expect palladium pentafluoride to be very unstable.

The pentafluorides are all polymeric in the solid state. They melt to give viscous liquids, thereby suggesting that some association persists in the liquid, although there is often a colour change on melting which may indicate a change in the degree of polymerization. Niobium and tantalum

TABLE 1.10

Melting and Boiling Points of the Pentafluorides

Compound	M.p.	B.p.	Ref.
NbF_5	80.0°	234.9°	96
TaF_5	95.1°	229.0°	96
MoF_5	67°	214°	31
TcF_5	50°	—	97
ReF_5	48°	221.3°	31
RuF_5	86.5	227°	98
OsF_5	70°	226°	31
RhF_5	95.5°	—	99
IrF_5	104°	—	100
PtF_5	80°	—	62

pentafluorides have been examined in detail and the results confirm the polymeric nature of the melt[94]. In the vapour phase, however, those pentafluorides that have been examined in detail all appear to be mono-meric[31,95]. It is interesting to note the very large liquid range of all the pentafluorides (Table 1.10), which reflects the necessity of breaking several intermolecular bonds to give a monomeric vapour from a polymeric liquid. The contrast with the *extremely* short liquid ranges of the hexafluorides is especially noteworthy.

With the exception of the niobium and tantalum compounds, the penta-fluorides are thermally unstable, but because of the three distinct structural types there is no regular progression of thermal stability as observed with the hexafluorides. The boiling points reported in Table 1.10 are for most cases extrapolated from vapour-pressure data at comparatively low tem-peratures. All the thermally unstable pentafluorides disproportionate to the corresponding hexafluoride and tetrafluoride.

Structures. Edwards, Peacock, and their coworkers have examined the structures of the pentafluorides of niobium, tantalum[101], molybdenum[18], ruthenium and osmium[102] by single crystal X-ray diffraction techniques. They have shown that these pentafluorides form two distinct types of tetramer and, from preliminary structural data, that technetium and rhenium pentafluorides form yet a different type of polymeric lattice[2]. Bartlett and coworkers have shown that the pentafluorides of rhodium, iridium and platinum are all isostructural with ruthenium penta-fluoride[99,100,103].

The distribution of the three structural types, A, B and C, between the pentafluorides of the second- and third-row transition series and also of vanadium and chromium, which fall into the general scheme, is shown in Table 1.11.

TABLE 1.11

Distribution of Structures of the Pentafluorides

VF_5	CrF_5	—				
NbF_5	MoF_5	TcF_5	RuF_5	RhF_5	—	
TaF_5	—	ReF_5	OsF_5	IrF_5	PtF_5	
A		*B*		*C*		

Structure A: The structure adopted by niobium, tantalum and molyb-denum pentafluorides consists of a tetramer formed by fluorine-bridged metal atoms arranged almost at the corners of a square, as shown in Figure 1.6. The major feature to be noted is that the M–F–M bridges are almost *linear* and the metal and bridging fluorine atoms are in a planar arrangement. Each metal atom is octahedrally coordinated, but the fluorine atoms above and below the plane of the metal atoms are slightly

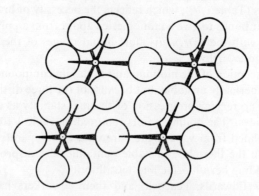

Figure 1.6 An idealized representation of structure A.

displaced towards the centre of the square. This is presumably an electro-static effect resulting from the greater repulsion from the terminal fluorine than from the bridging fluorine, since the respective metal–fluorine bond distances are significantly different. For example, in niobium penta-fluoride, the niobium–fluorine terminal bond distance is 1.77 Å whereas the niobium–fluorine bridging distance is 2.07 Å.

Structure B: The structure adopted by vanadium, chromium, techne-tium and rhenium pentafluorides has been inferred by showing that these

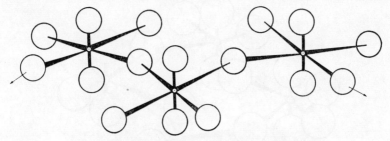

Figure 1.7 An idealized representation of structure B.

compounds have a slightly distorted form of the molybdenum oxide tetrafluoride structure, which itself has been characterized by a single crystal X-ray diffraction study by Edwards and coworkers[2].

The basic structure is shown in Figure 1.7 and consists of infinite chains of octahedrally coordinated metal atoms, the octahedra being joined by sharing corners in the *cis* positions.

Structure C: The structure adopted by the remaining pentafluorides is based on a tetrameric unit similar to that in structure A, but the fluorine bridges are non-linear and this results in a marked distortion of the arrange-ment of the metal atoms into a rhombus, rather than a square. However, the eight atoms forming the cyclic unit remain coplanar with alternate fluorine atoms projecting into and out of the rhombus as shown in Figure 1.8.

It is our belief that the distribution of the structures adopted by the pentafluorides may be explained on the basis of slight fluorine-to-metal π-bonding of the type previously discussed for the hexafluorides.

In structure A, adopted by the pentafluorides of niobium, tantalum and molybdenum, the fluorine bridges are linear, suggesting that some π-bonding is occurring. Since only ligand-to-metal π-bonding is possible, these are the most favourable cases for π-bonding since here the number of d-electrons on the metal is only one or zero.

The chain structure B, adopted by vanadium, chromium, technetium and rhenium pentafluorides, shows some evidence that π-bonding may still occur on a reduced scale, although this suggestion must be made with caution since detailed information about the pentafluorides themselves is not yet available. However, for molybdenum and rhenium oxide tetrafluorides, the angles at the bridging fluorine atom are 151° and 139°, respectively, suggesting that the effects of π-bonding decrease from molybdenum to rhenium. It is significant that vanadium and chromium

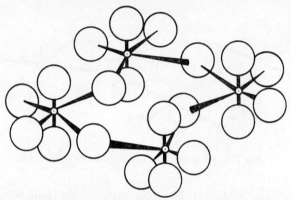

Figure 1.8   An idealized representation of structure C.

pentafluorides both adopt this structure rather than structure A, but this can be rationalized when it is realized that these elements would not be expected to be so amenable to π-bonding with fluorine and that structure A is stabilized by π-bonding.

Finally, it is clear that in structure C the bridging fluorine atoms adopt a tetrahedral configuration with two lone pairs and that no π-bonding occurs in the cyclic unit. This is exactly in accord with the expected trends in fluorine-to-metal π-bonding, since these elements towards the right of the Periodic Table contain several electrons in the t_{2g}-orbitals which would tend to preclude the weak p_π-donation from fluorine.

It is most interesting that a self-consistent explanation of the observed trends in the stabilities of the hexafluorides and the structures of the pentafluorides can be given in terms of weak π-bonding from fluorine to metal. The only well-proved case of such π-bonding is for the titanium tetrafluoride adducts, but, in fact, greater π-bonding would be expected for the hexafluorides and pentafluorides of the second- and third-row transition metals because of the higher formal charge on the metal. Nevertheless, it must be stressed, that so far there is no direct proof that such π-bonding occurs.

Very little systematic work has been reported on the chemical reactivities of the pentafluorides as a series, although some study has been made of individual compounds[4,36,99]. However, there is little doubt that the order of reactivity is similar to that observed for the hexafluorides, increasing with increasing atomic number in each series.

Tetrafluorides

The tetrafluorides of the second- and third-row transition metals, as a series, are poorly characterized, although some individual members such as the tetrafluorides of zirconium, niobium and platinum have been well studied. The tetrafluorides have been prepared by a wide variety of methods and there is no general procedure that can be used for all members of the series. Direct fluorination of the metal in a flow system gives the tetrafluorides for zirconium[104] and rhodium[105], but thermal dispropor- tionation of certain pentafluorides[31,36] and reduction of a higher fluo- ride[16,17,106] are the most common methods.

The structures of only zirconium[107] and niobium[16,17] tetrafluorides have been established beyond doubt. Palladium[108] and platinum[36] tetrafluorides are structurally similar to each other, and it has been suggested that they have a structure similar to that of uranium tetrachloride[109].

There has been no systematic study of the chemical properties of the heavy transition-metal tetrafluorides.

Trifluorides

The "trifluorides" of the heavy transition metals form a fairly complete series, but it has recently become apparent that some of the compounds claimed as trifluorides are in fact non-stoichiometric oxide fluorides. Schafer and coworkers[16,110] have shown that the so-called niobium and tantalum trifluorides are oxide fluorides of the general formulae MO_xF_{3-x}, where, for niobium at least, x covers a very wide composition range. Obviously this situation arises because of the very similar size of the oxide and the fluoride ion, and analogous examples may be found with other transition metals. Support for this conjecture comes from the apparent non-stoichiometric platinum oxide fluoride formed when fluorine is passed over a heated mixture of metallic platinum and powdered glass[36]. This compound, of formula PtO_xF_{3-x}, was shown by X-ray diffraction tech- niques to be isomorphous with the other platinum-group metal trifluo- rides[36]. In addition, "palladium trifluoride," which Bartlett and Rao[108] have shown to be palladium(II) hexafluoropalladate(IV) (see Chapter 10), is also isomorphous with the other platinum-group metal trifluorides. It appears, therefore, that a full reinvestigation of this group of compounds is necessary.

Similar doubts exist as to the authenticity of the so-called molybdenum trifluoride. It has been prepared by two different routes, and the products were rather dissimilar in their physical properties. This anomaly is discussed in detail in Chapter 6.

Gold trifluoride is the only trifluoride for which a single-crystal X-ray diffraction study has been reported. Bartlett and coworkers[111] found that gold trifluoride is hexagonal and the structure is a fluorine-bridged polymer involving *cis*-bridging groups in a square-planar arrangement about the gold atom.

COMPLEX FLUORIDES

The complex fluorides and complex oxide fluorides are dominated by the chemistry of the transition metals in oxidation states V and IV, although complexes between oxidation states VIII and III are known.

Hexafluorometallates(v)

Kemmitt, Russell and Sharp[112] have made a very extensive survey of the structures adopted by the hexafluorometallates(v). They found that there are only four basic structural types and the distribution of these are summarized, together with additional more recent data[5,91,99], in Table 1.12.

TABLE 1.12

Structural Types of the ABF_6 Compounds

B	A						
	Li	Na	Ag	K	Tl	Rb	Cs
Nb	R_1	C	T	T	R_2	R_2	R_2
Ta	R_1	C	T	T	R_2	R_2	R_2
Mo	R_1	C		T	R_2	R_2	R_2
W	R_1	C		T		R_2	R_2
Tc		R_1		R_2		R_2	R_2
Re	R_1	C		T		R_2	R_2
Ru	R_1	R_1	T	R_2	R_2	R_2	R_2
Os	R_1	R_1	T	R_2		R_2	R_2
Rh							R_2
Ir	R_1	R_1	T	R_2		R_2	R_2
Pt				R_2		R_2	R_2

R_1 = rhombohedral $LiSbF_6$ type
C = cubic $NaSbF_6$ type
T = tetragonal $KNbF_6$ type
R_2 = rhombohedral $KOsF_6$ type

The rhombohedral lithium hexafluoroantimonate(v) structure may be considered to be a slightly distorted sodium chloride type lattice. The hexafluoroantimonate(v) ion is a regular octahedron. This is the characteristic structure for compounds with small cations. The cubic sodium hexafluoroantimonate(v) structure is equivalent to the sodium chloride structure. The tetragonal potassium hexafluoroniobate(v) structure is closely related to the caesium chloride structure with slightly distorted NbF_6 octahedra. Finally, the potassium hexafluoroosmate(v) structure, which only occurs with the larger cations, contains distorted OsF_6 octahedra.

It is clear from the Table that it is the cation which is the dominating influence in deciding the lattice adopted by the hexafluorometallates(v). The distribution of the structural types among these complexes has been discussed in detail by Kemmitt and coworkers[112].

The infrared-active metal–fluorine stretching frequencies of a number of hexafluorometallates(v) have been recorded (see Table 1.13), but it is to be noted that this is ν_3 and not the completely symmetrical a_{1g}-mode; so the frequencies do not indicate the relative bond strengths. These results have been compiled by Peacock and Sharp[113].

TABLE 1.13

Infrared Stretching Frequencies (cm^{-1}) of Some
Hexafluorometallates(v)

Anion	Frequency	Anion	Frequency
NbF_6^-	580	TaF_6^-	580
MoF_6^-	623	WF_6^-	594
TcF_6^-		ReF_6^-	627
RuF_6^-	640	OsF_6^-	616
RhF_6^-		IrF_6^-	667

Hexafluorometallates(iv)

The hexafluoro anions of the heavy transition metals in oxidation state iv form an extensive series. They may be prepared by a variety of wet or dry methods since they are often resistant to hydrolysis. With the exception of some of the zirconium and hafnium salts (see Chapter 4) all these complexes contain discrete MF_6 anions, and their lattices differ only in the packing arrangements[114]. Some hexafluorometallates(iv) are known to occur in more than one polymorphic modification, thereby indicating that energy differences between alternative structures are small. Details of the distribution of the major structural types have been collated by Sharpe[114] and Peacock[115].

TABLE 1.14

Infrared Stretching Frequencies (cm^{-1}) of Some
Hexafluorometallates(IV)

Anion	Frequency	Anion	Frequency
TcF_6^{2-}	574 (ref. 37)	ReF_6^{2-}	541
RuF_6^{2-}	581	OsF_6^{2-}	548
RhF_6^{2-}	589	IrF_6^{2-}	568
PdF_6^{2-}	602	PtF_6^{2-}	583

The infrared-active metal–fluorine stretching frequencies have been observed for most hexafluorometallates(IV) by Peacock and Sharp[113] and are summarized in Table 1.14. Although these frequencies cannot be used in any quantitative sense, it should be noted that they are considerably lower than the corresponding hexafluorometallate(V) frequencies, in accord with the lower formal charge on the metal.

REFERENCES

1. O. Ruff and F. W. Tschirch, *Ber.*, **46**, 929 (1913).
2. A. J. Edwards, G. R. Jones and B. R. Steventon, *Chem. Commun.*, **1967**, 462.
3. J. H. Canterford and T. A. O'Donnell, in *Technique of Inorganic Chemistry* (Eds. H. B. Jonassen and A. Weissberger), Interscience, Vol. 7 (1968).
4. J. H. Canterford and T. A. O'Donnell, *Inorg. Chem.*, **5**, 1442 (1966).
5. D. Hugill and R. D. Peacock, *J. Chem. Soc.*, **1966**, A, 1339.
6. B. Weinstock and J. G. Malm, *J. Am. Chem. Soc.*, **80**, 4466 (1958).
7. H. von Wartenberg, *Z. anorg. allgem. Chem.*, **242**, 406 (1939).
8. J. G. Malm and H. Selig, *J. Inorg. Nucl. Chem.*, **20**, 189 (1961).
9. O. Glemser, H. W. Roesky, K. H. Hellberg and H. W. Werther, *Chem. Ber.*, **99**, 2652 (1966).
10. H. H. Claassen, H. Selig, J. G. Malm, C. L. Chernick and B. Weinstock, *J. Am. Chem. Soc.*, **83**, 2390 (1961).
11. C. L. Chernick, H. H. Claassen and B. Weinstock, *J. Am. Chem. Soc.*, **83**, 3165 (1961).
12. B. Weinstock, J. G. Malm and E. E. Weaver, *J. Am. Chem. Soc.*, **83**, 4310 (1961).
13. N. S. Nikolaev and E. G. Ippolotov, *Doklady Akad. Nauk SSSR*, **134**, 358 (1960).
14. A. Chretien and B. Gaudreau, *Compt. Rend.*, **248**, 2878 (1959).
15. N. S. Nikolaev and V. F. Sukhoverkhov, *Bul. Inst. Politeh Isai (NS)*, **3**, 61 (1957).
16. H. Schafer, H. G. Schnering, K. J. Niehues and H. G. Nieder-Vahrenholz, *J. Less-Common Metals*, **9**, 95 (1965).
17. F. P. Gortsema and R. Didchenko, *Inorg. Chem.*, **4**, 182 (1965).

18. A. J. Edwards, R. D. Peacock and R. W. H. Small, *J. Chem. Soc.*, **1962**, 4486.
19. T. A. O'Donnell and D. F. Stewart, *J. Inorg. Nucl. Chem.*, **24**, 309 (1962).
20. H. F. Priest and W. C. Schumb, *J. Am. Chem. Soc.*, **70**, 3378 (1948).
21. G. B. Hargreaves and R. D. Peacock, *J. Chem. Soc.*, **1960**, 1099.
22. E. E. Aynsley, R. D. Peacock and P. L. Robinson, *Chem. Ind. (London)*, **1952**, 1002.
23. G. B. Hargreaves and R. D. Peacock, *J. Chem. Soc.*, **1960**, 2618.
24. N. Bartlett and J. W. Quail, *J. Chem. Soc.*, **1961**, 3728.
25. *U.S. Pat.* 2,602,725 (1952).
26. O. Ruff and E. Schiller, *Z. anorg. allgem. Chem.*, **72**, 329 (1911).
27. H. J. Emeleus and V. Gutmann, *J. Chem. Soc.*, **1949**, 2979.
28. O. Ruff and F. Eisner, *Ber.*, **38**, 742 (1905).
29. L. Kolditz and G. Furcht, *Z. anorg. allgem. Chem.*, **312**, 11 (1961).
30. M. E. Runner, C. Balog and M. Kilpatrick, *J. Am. Chem. Soc.*, **78**, 5183 (1956).
31. G. H. Cady and G. B. Hargreaves, *J. Chem. Soc.*, **1961**, 1568.
32. N. Bartlett, N. K. Jha and J. Trotter, *Proc. Chem. Soc.*, **1962**, 277.
33. M. A. Hepworth and P. L. Robinson, *J. Inorg. Nucl. Chem.*, **4**, 24 (1957).
34. M. A. Hepworth, R. D. Peacock and P. L. Robinson, *J. Chem. Soc.*, **1954**, 1197.
35. M. A. Hepworth, P. L. Robinson and G. J. Westland, *J. Chem. Soc.*, **1954**, 4269.
36. N. Bartlett and D. H. Lohmann, *J. Chem. Soc.*, **1964**, 619.
37. K. Schwochau and W. Herr, *Angew. Chem. Intern. Ed. Engl.*, **2**, 97 (1963).
38. R. D. Peacock, *Chem. Ind. (London)*, **1955**, 1453.
39. H. Bode and G. Teufer, *Z. anorg. allgem. Chem.*, **283**, 18 (1956).
40. H. Bode and H. von Dohren, *Acta Cryst.*, **11**, 80 (1958).
41. J. L. Hoard, W. J. Martin, M. E. Smith and J. F. Whitney, *J. Am. Chem. Soc.*, **76**, 3820 (1954).
42. J. L. Hoard and W. J. Martin, *J. Am. Chem. Soc.*, **63**, 11 (1941).
43. C. J. Barton, W. R. Grimes, H. Insley, R. E. Moore and R. E. Thoma, *J. Phys. Chem.*, **62**, 665 (1958).
44. G. D. Robbins, R. E. Thoma and H. Insley, *J. Inorg. Nucl. Chem.*, **27**, 559 (1965).
45. H. R. Hoekstra and J. J. Katz, *J. Am. Chem. Soc.*, **71**, 2488 (1949).
46. J. S. Fordyce and R. L. Baum, *J. Chem. Phys.*, **44**, 1159 (1965).
47. J. S. Fordyce and R. L. Baum, *J. Chem. Phys.*, **44**, 1166 (1965).
48. A. Mukhatar and R. Winand, *Compt. Rend.*, **260**, 3674 (1965).
49. G. B. Hargreaves and R. D. Peacock, *J. Chem. Soc.*, **1958**, 4390.
50. A. J. Edwards and R. D. Peacock, *Chem. Ind. (London)*, **1960**, 1441.
51. G. B. Hargreaves and R. D. Peacock, *J. Chem. Soc.*, **1958**, 2170.
52. R. D. Peacock, *J. Chem. Soc.*, **1957**, 467.
53. R. Hoppe and W. Klemm, *Z. anorg. allgem. Chem.*, **268**, 364 (1952).
54. E. Weise and W. Klemm, *Z. anorg. allgem. Chem.*, **279**, 74 (1955).
55. E. Weise and W. Klemm, *Z. anorg. allgem. Chem.*, **272**, 211 (1953).
56. B. Cox, D. W. A. Sharp and A. G. Sharpe, *J. Chem. Soc.*, **1956**, 1242.
57. I. I. Chernyaev, N. S. Nikolaev and E. G. Ippolitov, *Doklady Akad. Nauk SSSR*, **132**, 378 (1960).

58. A. G. Sharpe, *J. Chem. Soc.*, **1949,** 2901.
59. N. Bartlett, S. Beaton, L. W. Reeves and E. J. Wells, *Can. J. Chem.*, **42,** 2531 (1964).
60. T. A. O'Donnell, unpublished observation.
61. T. A. O'Donnell and D. F. Stewart, *Inorg. Chem.*, **5,** 1434 (1966).
62. N. Bartlett and D. H. Lohmann, *J. Chem. Soc.*, **1962,** 5253.
63. N. Bartlett, *Proc. Chem. Soc.*, **1962,** 218.
64. O. Ruff, F. Eisner and W. Heller, *Z. anorg. allgem. Chem.*, **52,** 256 (1907).
65. N. Bartlett, in *Preparative Inorganic Reactions* (Ed., W. L. Jolly), Vol. 2, Interscience, New York, 1965.
66. T. A. O'Donnell, *J. Chem. Soc.*, **1956,** 4681.
67. G. H. Cady and G. B. Hargreaves, *J. Chem. Soc.*, **1961,** 1563.
68. E. J. Barber and G. H. Cady, *J. Phys. Chem.*, **60,** 505 (1956).
69. H. Selig and J. G. Malm, *J. Inorg. Nucl. Chem.*, **24,** 641 (1962).
70. D. C. Bradley, *Nature*, **174,** 323 (1954).
71. H. H. Claassen, J. G. Malm and H. Selig, *J. Chem. Phys.*, **36,** 2890 (1962).
72. B. Weinstock, H. H. Claassen and J. G. Malm, *J. Chem. Phys.*, **32,** 181 (1960).
73. B. Weinstock, H. H. Claassen and C. L. Chernick, *J. Chem. Phys.*, **38,** 1470 (1963).
74. M. S. Child and A. C. Roach, *Mol. Phys.*, **9,** 281 (1965).
75. D. W. Osborne, F. Schreiner, J. G. Malm, H. Selig and L. Rochester, *J. Chem. Phys.*, **44,** 2802 (1966).
76. F. A. Cotton and G. Wilkinson, *Advanced Inorganic Chemistry*, 2nd ed., Wiley, New York, 1966.
77. L. E. Orgel, *Introduction to Transition Metal Chemistry*, Wiley, New York, 1960.
78. B. Weinstock and G. L. Goodman, *Advan. Chem. Phys.*, **9,** 197 (1965).
79. T. G. Burke, D. F. Smith and A. H. Nielsen, *J. Chem. Phys.*, **20,** 447 (1952).
80. H. H. Claassen, H. Selig and J. G. Malm, *J. Chem. Phys.*, **36,** 2888 (1962).
81. H. C. Mattraw, N. J. Hawkins, D. R. Carpenter and W. W. Sabol, *J. Chem. Phys.*, **23,** 985 (1955).
82. D. S. Dyer and R. O. Ragsdale, *Chem. Commun.*, **1966,** 601.
83. D. S. Dyer and R. O. Ragsdale, *Inorg. Chem.*, **6,** 8 (1967).
84. N. V. Sidgwick, *The Chemical Elements and Their Compounds*, Oxford Univ. Press, London, 1950, p. 1034.
85. A. B. Burg, in *Fluorine Chemistry* (Ed. J. H. Simons), Vol I, Academic Press, New York, 1950, p. 112.
86. T. A. O'Donnell, D. F. Stewart and P. W. Wilson, *Inorg. Chem.*, **5,** 1438 (1966).
87. N. Bartlett, S. P. Beaton and N. K. Jha, *Chem. Commun.*, **1966,** 168.
88. J. R. Geichman, E. A. Smith, S. S. Trond and P. R. Ogle, *Inorg. Chem.*, **1,** 661 (1962).
89. F. P. Gortsema and R. H. Toeniskoetter, *Inorg. Chem.*, **5,** 1217 (1966).
90. J. R. Geichman, E. A. Smith and P. R. Ogle, *Inorg. Chem.*, **2,** 1012 (1963).
91. N. Bartlett and N. K. Jha, in *Noble Gas Compounds* (Ed. H. H. Hyman), University of Chicago Press, Chicago, 1963.
92. N. S. Nikolaev, Y. A. Buslaev and A. A. Opalovskii, *Zh. Neorg. Khim.*, **3,** 1731 (1958).

93. F. P. Gortsema and R. H. Toeniskoetter, *Inorg. Chem.*, **5**, 1925 (1966).
94. F. Fairbrother, K. H. Grundy and A. Thompson, *J. Chem. Soc.*, **1965**, 761.
95. S. Blanchard, *J. Chim. Phys.*, **62**, 919 (1965).
96. F. Fairbrother and W. C. Frith, *J. Chem. Soc.*, **1951**, 3051.
97. A. J. Edwards, D. Hugill and R. D. Peacock, *Nature*, **200**, 672 (1963).
98. J. H. Holloway and R. D. Peacock, *J. Chem. Soc.*, **1963**, 527.
99. J. H. Holloway, P. R. Rao and N. Bartlett, *Chem. Commun.*, **1965**, 306.
100. N. Bartlett and P. R. Rao, *Chem. Commun.*, **1965**, 252.
101. A. J. Edwards, *J. Chem. Soc.*, **1964**, 3714.
102. J. H. Holloway, R. D. Peacock and R. W. H. Small, *J. Chem. Soc.*, **1964**, 644.
103. N. Bartlett, F. Einstein, D. F. Stewart and J. Trotter, *Chem. Commun.*, **1966**, 550.
104. H. M. Haendler, S. F. Bartram, R. S. Becker, W. J. Bernard and S. W. Bukata, *J. Am. Chem. Soc.*, **76**, 2177 (1954).
105. O. Ruff and E. Ascher, *Z. anorg. allgem. Chem.*, **183**, 193 (1929).
106. J. H. Holloway and R. D. Peacock, *J. Chem. Soc.*, **1963**, 3892.
107. R. D. Burbank and F. N. Bensey, *U.S.A.E.C. Report*, K-1280 (1956).
108. N. Bartlett and P. R. Rao, *Proc. Chem. Soc.*, **1964**, 393.
109. R. C. L. Mooney, *Acta Cryst.*, **2**, 189 (1949).
110. H. Schafer and H. G. Schnering, *Angew. Chem.*, **76**, 833 (1964).
111. F. W. B. Einstein, P. R. Rao, J. Trotter and N. Bartlett, *J. Chem. Soc.*, **1967**, A, 478.
112. R. D. W. Kemmitt, D. R. Russell and D. W. A. Sharp, *J. Chem. Soc.*, **1963**, 4408.
113. R. D. Peacock and D. W. A. Sharp, *J. Chem. Sov.*, **1959**, 2762.
114. A. G. Sharpe, in *Advances in Fluorine Chemistry*, Vol I, Butterworths, London, 1960.
115. R. D. Peacock, in *Progress in Inorganic Chemistry* (Ed. F. A. Cotton), Interscience, New York, 1961.

Chapter 2

Chlorides, Bromides and Iodides

Examination of the information available for the chlorides, bromides and iodides of the second- and third-row transition metals shows that it is markedly different from that available for fluorides. Considering the number of fluorides of these elements, a large amount of physical data is available, but for the compounds of the other halogens most of the information is on preparative techniques. This is partly due to the fact that the chlorides, bromides and iodides generally occur in lower oxidation states than the fluorides, particularly towards the right of the Periodic Table, with a consequent decrease in volatility, thus making the measurement of many physical properties very difficult.

The bonding between these transition metals and the halogen atoms has not been closely studied in detail. However, when a complete survey is made of the physical and chemical properties of these compounds, particularly complex chlorides and bromides, it appears that the trends in physical and chemical properties can be best rationalized on the basis of some back-donation from partly filled metal t_{2g} orbitals to the empty d-orbitals of the halogen.

Because of the difficulties involved, there have been spectacular advances in the technology of handling fluorine and volatiles fluorides. However, there has been no necessity for such advances for the other halides. Halogen compounds are usually prepared by techniques such as sealed-tube reactions and flow systems that have been familiar for many years. The only real advance in preparative techniques is the thermal-gradient method, which combines the best features of both the methods mentioned above. The thermal-gradient technique, which will be described later, is particularly suited to the preparation of halides which readily dispro-portionate.

Among the binary halides, the stability of the highest formal oxidation states show the same trends as were noted for the fluorides, the stability gradually decreasing towards the right of the Periodic Table. However, the ability of the other halogens to force a metal to exhibit its highest oxidation state is not as high as that of fluorine. For example, the highest fluorides are obtained for the elements of Groups IV to VI inclusive and for rhenium, but chlorine forms only molybdenum pentachloride and rhenium hexachloride. The effects are further shown by considering particular elements: the highest halides formed are, for molybdenum, the hexafluoride, pentachloride, tetrabromide and triiodide, and for rhenium the heptafluoride, hexachloride, pentabromide and tetraiodide. These trends are not so clearly defined among complex halides, although it is true that towards the right of the Periodic Table hexafluorometallates(v) are common whereas the other halogens form hexahalometallates(iv). The elements of Groups IV and V seem particularly reluctant to form complex bromides and iodides.

GENERAL PREPARATIVE TECHNIQUES

Many binary halides and oxide halides of these transition metals are susceptible to hydrolysis, particularly the covalent compounds in high oxidation states. This means that the majority of preparations and manipulations must be carried out under strictly anhydrous conditions. Volatile compounds are most conveniently handled in vacuum systems, and involatile compounds must be handled in a dry box. A few of the more reactive compounds, such as molybdenum and rhenium pentachlorides, react with dry oxygen, so for these compounds a nitrogen- or argon-filled dry box is essential. With the exception of a few compounds in a lower oxidation state, the majority of complex halides may be handled in the open laboratory, at least for short periods.

Possibly the most widely used preparative technique in the field of binary halides and oxide halides is the flow system. Although at first sight this method is very simple, it is capable of producing significantly different products by subtle variation of such conditions as temperature, flow rate, dilution with inert carrier gases, etc. In order to obtain the best results in systems where a variety of products is possible, considerable experience in the use of flow systems is necessary. For example, molybdenum pentachloride has been known for over a hundred years and has always been described as a green-black crystalline solid[1]. However, it is now known that the green colour is due to the presence of molybdenum oxide tetrachloride as an impurity, the oxygen being derived from an oxide film on the molybdenum metal: the pure pentachloride is a jet-black crystalline solid[2].

In the chlorination of oxides, one would normally expect that, the higher the temperature of chlorination, the greater the extent of chlorination. This is generally true in sealed-tube reactions, but it is often not so in flow systems. As a specific example, let us consider the action of carbon tetrachloride vapour on heated niobium pentaoxide in a flow system. At 650–700°, a mixture of niobium pentachloride and niobium oxide trichloride is obtained[3] but, in marked contrast, a quantitative yield of niobium pentachloride is obtained if the same reaction is carried out at only 200°[4]. The explanation of this apparent paradox lies in the lower involatility of the oxide trichloride than of the pentachloride. At low temperatures, the oxide trichloride, which is undoubtedly formed as an intermediate in the reaction, is not sufficiently volatile to sublime out of the hot zone and is therefore available for further chlorination. On the other hand, at the higher temperature, the equilibrium vapour pressure of the oxide trichloride is quite high and much of it therefore escapes from the reaction zone before it can be fully chlorinated.

Sealed-tube reactions have been used for the preparation of binary bromides and iodides directly from the elements; but the widest application of sealed-tube reactions has been to halogenation of oxides and to interaction of two compounds of the transition metal. Aluminium halides, particularly the iodide, have been treated extensively with transition metal oxides, and the reaction is efficient because of the high lattice energy of aluminium oxide and the fact that aluminium triiodide is frequently the only volatile compound in the system.

The interaction of carbon tetrachloride and oxides in a sealed tube has also been widely used. The disadvantage of this method is that fairly high temperatures are required, and considerable pressures of carbon tetrachloride and phosgene vapours are produced, thus making an explosion likely. Indeed, Tyree and coworkers[5] recommend that the tube containing the reactants be placed in a metal bomb which itself contains the correct quantity of carbon tetrachloride to equalize the pressure within the glass tube. A further disadvantage of a sealed-tube reaction at elevated temperatures is that a thermally unstable compound cannot be prepared.

In a sealed-tube reaction, such as the interaction of carbon tetrachloride and an oxide, the extent of halogenation usually increases with increasing temperature. For example, with tungsten trioxide and carbon tetrachloride at 250° the oxide tetrachloride is formed[6], whereas at 400° the hexachloride is the predominant product[5,7].

A very elegant modification of the simple sealed-tube reaction is the thermal-gradient technique which has been fully exploited by Schafer and his coworkers. Basically, the apparatus consists of a long evacuated tube which is usually divided into compartments by constrictions. The least volatile reactant is heated to a high temperature at one end of the tube, and the more volatile reactant is heated to a temperature that generates a vapour pressure sufficiently high to cause reaction. The centre portion of the tube is maintained at a temperature intermediate between those of the two ends, and the temperatures are adjusted so that the product sublimes from the hottest zone to the centre compartment.

The diffusion of gases in a good thermal gradient is such that the equilibrium conditions in the tube strongly favour formation of the required product, and removal of the product as a solid phase drives the

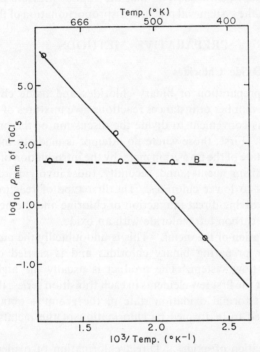

Figure 2.1 Variation, with temperature, of log vapour pressure of $TaCl_5(g)$ over (A) $TaCl_4(s)$ and (B) $TaCl_5(s, l)$.

reaction to completion. In addition, if, as is often the case, the product is a compound that tends to undergo thermal decomposition into one or both of the reactants, the decomposition can be minimized by careful control of the temperature gradient. This is well illustrated by the preparation of tantalum tetrachloride from tantalum metal and tantalum pentachloride, which has been described by McCarley and Boatman[8]. Tantalum tetrachloride tends to disproportionate into the pentachloride and the trichloride, but the decomposition can be eliminated completely by careful control of the temperature. The situation is summarized in Figure 2.1, where the vapour pressure of tantalum pentachloride itself and the equilib-rium dissociation pressure of tantalum pentachloride over the solid tetrachloride are plotted as a function of temperature. It is seen that the vapour pressure of tantalum pentachloride from tantalum tetrachloride exceeds that of tantalum pentachloride itself at temperatures above the intersection of the vapour pressure plots (280°). Thus, in order to obtain pure tantalum tetrachloride, it is essential that the centre compartment of the tube be kept below 280°, so that the vapour pressure of tantalum pentachloride in the system will preclude disproportionation of the product.

PREPARATIVE METHODS

Chlorides and Oxide Chlorides

Methods of preparation of binary chlorides and oxide chlorides are similar and in a number of instances reactions give mixtures of both types of product. It is convenient to divide the discussion of the preparations into two classes. First, those where no attempt is made to influence the final oxidation state of the transition metal by the introduction of additional reducing or oxidizing agents; and, secondly, those involving reduction of higher chlorides to lower chlorides. The first type of reaction includes preparations involving direct interaction of chlorine and the heated metal or oxide and of carbon tetrachloride with an oxide.

Direct chlorination of the metal. This is undoubtedly the method most widely used for preparing binary chlorides and is carried out almost invariably in a flow system. The product is usually the highest stable chloride and, for the first few elements in each transition series, the chloride with the highest formal oxidation state of the group is obtained. The products reported to be formed by chlorination of the metals are given in Table 2.1.

Direct chlorination of oxides. Direct chlorination of oxides has been well investigated for the transition metals of Groups IV to VII inclusive, but only slightly studied for the remaining Groups. It is interesting that the elements of the early Groups give the binary chlorides in this reaction, but those of the later Groups form oxide chlorides. The products obtained from this type of reaction are given in Table 2.2.

An interesting point emerging from Table 2.2 is the use of carbon with niobium pentaoxide to effect complete conversion of the oxide into the pentachloride, the oxygen being removed through the formation of phos-gene. As will be noted later, carbon tetrachloride is a very efficient reagent for converting oxides into binary chlorides because it too can remove oxygen effectively.

TABLE 2.1

Products Formed by Chlorination of the Metal

Metal	Product	Temp.	Ref.
Zr	$ZrCl_4$	Elevated	9
Hf	$HfCl_4$	Elevated	9
Nb	$NbCl_5$	300–350°	10
Ta	$TaCl_5$	300–350°	10
Mo	$MoCl_5$	Elevated	2
W	WCl_6	600°	11, 12
Tc	$TcCl_6 + TcCl_4$	Elevated	13
Re	$ReCl_6 + ReCl_5$	Elevated	14, 15
Ru	$RuCl_3$	600°	16
Os	$OsCl_4$	550–600°	17
Rh	$RhCl_3$	300–800°	18
Ir	$IrCl_3$	600°	19
Pd	$PdCl_2$	600°	18
Pt	$PtCl_4$	Elevated	20
Au	$AuCl_3$	200°	21

For elements beyond Group V the product formed by chlorinating the oxide is always an oxide chloride. This is partly due to the volatility of the oxide chlorides, since in a flow system they are rapidly removed from the hot reaction zone. This explanation is supported by the fact that in a static system chlorinating agents such as thionyl chloride, which are weaker than elementary chlorine, can convert the same oxides completely into binary chlorides.

Reaction of carbon tetrachloride with oxides. At elevated temperatures carbon tetrachloride is a very powerful chlorinating agent for transition metal oxides. Frequently, because of the formation of phosgene, chlorination proceeds further than with chlorine itself. However, the effect is no

TABLE 2.2

Products Obtained by Direct Chlorination of Oxides

Oxide	Product	Temperature	Ref.
ZrO_2	$ZrCl_4$	Elevated	9
HfO_2	$HfCl_4$	Elevated	22
Nb_2O_5	$NbCl_5 + NbOCl_3$	500–700°	23, 24
Nb_2O_5 and C	$NbCl_5$	280–300°	25
MoO_3	MoO_2Cl_2	650°	2
MoO_2	MoO_2Cl_2	350–550°	26, 27
WO_2	WO_2Cl_2	500–550°	28
TcO_2	$TcOCl_4 + TcOCl_3$	Elevated	15, 29
ReO_3	ReO_3Cl	160–190°	30
OsO_2	$OsOCl_4$	Elevated	31

doubt enhanced by the fact that the reactions are usually carried out in a sealed tube, thus precluding escape of the volatile oxide chlorides.

The products obtained from the interaction of carbon tetrachloride and transition metal oxides are given in Table 2.3.

As noted in the introduction, the choice of temperature for flow system reactions is sometimes critical, as shown by the niobium pentaoxide–carbon tetrachloride reaction.

TABLE 2.3

Products Obtained by the Action of Carbon Tetrachloride on Oxides

Oxide	Product	Conditions	Ref.
ZrO_2	$ZrCl_4$	Flow system, elevated temp.	9
Nb_2O_5	$NbCl_5 + NbOCl_3$	Flow system, 650–700°	3
Nb_2O_5	$NbCl_5$	Flow system, 200–225°	4
		Sealed tube, 270–300°	32
Ta_2O_5	$TaCl_5$	Sealed tube, 300–400°	5, 32
MoO_3	$MoCl_5$	Bomb, 400°	5
MoO_2	$MoCl_4$	Sealed tube, 250°	6
WO_3	$WOCl_4$	Sealed tube, 250°	6
WO_3	WCl_6	Bomb, 400°	5, 7, 12
WO_2	WO_2Cl_2	Sealed tube, 250°	6
Tc_2O_7	$TcCl_4$	Bomb, 400°	5
Re_2O_7	$ReCl_5$	Bomb, 400°	5

When the highest chloride is thermally unstable, for example technetium hexachloride, this chloride is not formed by the high-temperature sealed-tube method. In general, thermally unstable chlorides must be prepared in a flow system to allow them to be rapidly removed from the hot reaction zone. The only exceptions to this statement are chemical transport and the thermal-gradient preparations as described above.

Reaction of other chlorinating agents with oxides. Binary chlorides and oxide chlorides have been prepared by the action of several other chlorinating agents on the transition metal oxides. Thionyl chloride is a moderately powerful chlorinating agent, but frequently the final product is an oxide chloride. However, if the oxide chloride can be left in thionyl chloride solution, further chlorination often proceeds slowly. An important advantage of the use of thionyl chloride is that no steps are necessary to exclude moisture, since thionyl chloride reacts with the moisture, the products being volatile and thus easily removed from the reaction system. Aluminium chloride has been used as a chlorinating agent in a few cases, and here the driving force is the large lattice energy of aluminium oxide.

Some typical examples of the action of these chlorinating agents on transition metal oxides are given in Table 2.4. Variable amounts of niobium pentachloride and niobium oxide trichloride are obtained from the niobium pentaoxide–aluminium trichloride reaction, because of the interaction of the pentaoxide with the pentachloride to form the oxide trichloride. However, tantalum oxide trichloride is thermally unstable, giving tantalum pentaoxide and pentachloride, so that only tantalum pentachloride is produced.

TABLE 2.4

Miscellaneous Preparations of Chlorides and Oxide Chlorides

Oxide	Reagent	Product	Conditions	Ref.
Nb_2O_5	$SOCl_2$	$NbCl_5$	Flow system, 100–150°	33
Nb_2O_5	$AlCl_3$	$NbCl_5 + NbOCl_3$	Sealed tube, 230–400°	34
Ta_2O_5	$SOCl_2$	$TaCl_5$	Flow system, > 150°	33
Ta_2O_5	$AlCl_3$	$TaCl_5$	Sealed tube, 200°	34
NbO_2	$AlCl_3$	$NbCl_4$	Sealed tube, 290°	35
MoO_3	$SOCl_2$	$MoOCl_4$	Reflux	36
WO_3	$SOCl_2$	$WOCl_4$	Reflux	2
ReO_2	$SOCl_2$	$ReCl_4$	Reflux	37
OsO_4	$SOCl_2$	$OsOCl_4 + OsCl_4$	Reflux	38, 39

Miscellaneous preparations of oxide chlorides. There are several methods available for the preparation of oxide chlorides which, whilst not so general as the preceding methods, may in particular cases prove to be the most convenient. Typical examples are the action of a mixture of chlorine and oxygen on heated osmium metal to give the oxide tetrachloride, and the action of oxygen on technetium tetrachloride to give technetium trioxide chloride. A fairly general method, which may be included here, is the interaction of an oxide and a chloride of the same metal to give oxide chlorides. Most of these methods suffer from the disadvantage that a mixture of products is obtained. A number of examples are given in Table 2.5.

It will now be clear that a number of general preparative methods of binary chlorides and oxide chlorides of the transition metals in their higher oxidation states are available. In many cases careful consideration of the physical properties and thermal stability of the compound required will suggest the most efficient method.

Reactions that involve reduction to lower binary chlorides also fall into distinct groups, depending on whether the reductant is the transition metal itself, or an additional reagent such as aluminium. In the latter case, of course, it is necessary to separate the required product from the aluminium trichloride.

TABLE 2.5

Miscellaneous Preparations of Oxide Chlorides

Reactants	Products	Conditions	Ref.
Mo and Cl_2/O_2	MoO_2Cl_2	Flow system	2
Os and Cl_2/O_2	$OsOCl_4$	Flow system	40
$NbCl_5$ and O_2	$NbOCl_3$	Flow system	25, 41, 42
$TcCl_4$ and O_2	TcO_3Cl	Flow system	43
$ReCl_3$ and O_2	$ReOCl_4 + ReO_3Cl$	Flow system	43, 44
$ReCl_6$ and O_2	ReO_3Cl	Gentle heat, flow system	14
Nb_2O_5 and $NbCl_5$	$NbOCl_3$	Thermal gradient, 350–210°	23, 45
Nb_2O_5 and $NbOCl_3$	Nb_3O_7Cl	Sealed tube, 600°	46
Ta_2O_5 and $TaCl_5$	$TaOCl_3$	Flow system, 600°	47
WO_3 and WCl_6	$WOCl_4$		48
MoO_3 and $MoCl_3$	$MoOCl_2$		49
Re_2O_7 and $ReCl_5$	$ReOCl_4 + ReO_3Cl$	Gentle heat	50
$NbCl_5 \cdot Et_2O$	$NbOCl_3$	Thermal decomp., 90°	42, 51
$TaCl_5 \cdot Et_2O$	$TaOCl_3$	Thermal decomp., 65°	42

Reduction of higher chlorides with the metal. Preparation by reduction of higher chlorides with the transition metal itself is restricted to Groups IV and V, where it has been used with great success. Two general procedures have been employed; either the simple sealed-tube technique or the thermal-gradient method, in which the reducing metal is maintained at a high temperature and the volatile chloride is heated to produce a workable vapour pressure. The comparatively involatile chloride in the lower oxidation state crystallizes in the central part of the tube. Some typical preparations by these two methods are given in Table 2.6. It will be noted that, while the conditions required for reduction of zirconium and hafnium tetrachlorides are very similar, tantalum pentachloride is significantly more difficult to reduce than its niobium analogue.

Reduction of higher chlorides with aluminium. Aluminium is a more powerful reducing agent than most of the heavy transition metals, and

TABLE 2.6

Preparation of Lower Chlorides by Reduction of Higher Chlorides
with the Appropriate Metal

Chloride	Product	Conditions	Ref.
$ZrCl_4$	$ZrCl_3$	Bomb, 500°	52, 53
		Thermal gradient, 700–330°	54
$HfCl_4$	$HfCl_3$	Bomb, 500°	53
$NbCl_5$	$NbCl_4$	Sealed tube, 380°	51, 55
		Thermal gradient, 400–250°	56–58
$TaCl_5$	$TaCl_4$	Sealed tube, 630°	59
		Thermal gradient, 630–280°	60

higher chlorides of the transition metals are usually reduced under comparatively mild conditions by this reagent. The use of aluminium as a reducing agent appears to have been restricted to those elements towards the left of the Periodic Table. This is probably because most of the chlorides of the later elements tend to be readily reduced to the metal (see below). Some typical reductions with aluminium are given in Table 2.7.

TABLE 2.7

Reduction of Higher Chlorides with Aluminium

Chloride	Product	Conditions	Ref.
$ZrCl_4$	$ZrCl_3$	Bomb, 300°	61
$NbCl_5$	$NbCl_4$	Sealed tube, 300°	62
$TaCl_5$	$TaCl_4$	Sealed tube, 400°	63, 64
WCl_6	WCl_4	Thermal gradient, 475–225°	65

Thermal decomposition of higher chlorides. Apart from the chlorides of the elements of Groups IV and V, the highest chlorides of the transition metal elements tend to be thermally unstable with respect to loss of chlorine. In some cases the products are lower chlorides, but in others the metal is the only product obtained. In some cases, for example, rhenium trichloride, thermal decomposition of a higher chloride represents the only practical method of preparing the compound in a low oxidation state. It is interesting that the structures of the resultant lower chlorides, when known, are all polymeric, often with strong metal–metal bonding. The thermal decomposition products of a number of chlorides are shown in Table 2.8.

TABLE 2.8

Thermal Decomposition of Chlorides

Chloride	Product	Conditions	Ref.
$MoCl_5$	$MoCl_3$	High temperature	66
WCl_6	WCl_5	At boiling point	67
$TcCl_6$	$TcCl_4$	At room temperature	13
$ReCl_5$	$ReCl_3$	At boiling point	15
$RuCl_3$	Ru	650°	68
$OsCl_4$[a]	$OsCl_3$	470°	17
$OsCl_3$	Os	470°	17
$RhCl_3$	Rh	High temperature	69
$IrCl_3$	Ir	775°	19
$PdCl_2$	Pd	600°	70
$PtCl_4$	$PtCl_2$	350°	71–73
$PtCl_4$	Pt	400°	71
$AuCl_3$	AuCl	160°	74
AuCl	Au	350°	74

[a] Must be carried out under a small pressure of chlorine.

Thermal disproportionation and related reactions. It is characteristic of many intermediate chlorides of the elements of Groups IV, V and VI that they undergo thermal disproportionation to a higher chloride and either a lower chloride or the metal itself. The reaction is invariably carried out in a sealed tube, the end containing the starting material being heated and the other end kept sufficiently cool to condense the more volatile higher chloride.

The reverse of thermal disproportionation is interaction of a chloride in a high oxidation state and one in a low oxidation state, to give a compound of intermediate oxidation state. These reactions are carried out in conventional sealed tubes or, alternatively, in a thermal gradient. Some typical examples of both types of reaction are given in Table 2.9.

TABLE 2.9

Thermal Disproportionation and Related Reactions

Reactants	Products	Conditions	Ref.
$ZrCl_3$	$ZrCl_4 + ZrCl_2$	400–500°	52, 53, 75
$ZrCl_2$	$ZrCl_4 + Zr$	Higher temperatures	76
$HfCl_3$	$HfCl_4 + HfCl_2$	Above 400°	53
$NbCl_4$	$NbCl_5 + NbCl_3$	250–500°	77, 78
$TaCl_4$	$TaCl_5 + TaCl_3$	340°	79
$MoCl_3$	$MoCl_4 + MoCl_2$	500°	80
$MoCl_2$	$MoCl_4 + Mo$	500–600°	81
WCl_4	$WCl_5 + WCl_2$	High temperature	80, 82
$NbCl_5 + NbCl_3$	$NbCl_4$	Thermal gradient, 280–180°	35
$TaCl_5 + TaCl_3$	$TaCl_4$	Sealed tube, 320°	63
$MoCl_5 + MoCl_3$	$MoCl_4$	Sealed tube, 250°	83

Hydrogen reduction of higher chlorides. Hydrogen reduction in a flow system was one of the earliest methods of preparation of lower chlorides of these transition metals. This method is seldom used nowadays because of the difficulty of controlling the composition of the final product. However, reduction of volatile chlorides in hydrogen by an electrodeless gas discharge has been applied to the preparation of some lower chlorides, as shown in Table 2.10.

TABLE 2.10

Hydrogen Reduction Reactions

Reactant	Product	Conditions	Ref.
$ZrCl_4$	$ZrCl_3$	Electrodeless discharge, 200°, 3 mm H_2	84
$NbCl_5$	$NbCl_4 + NbCl_3$	Flow system, 450°	35
$TaCl_5$	$TaCl_4$	Gas discharge	85
$MoCl_5$	$MoCl_3$	125°, H_2 at 450 lb/in.^{2}	83
WCl_6	WCl_5	400°	86

Lower oxide chlorides. There are two general methods of reducing oxide chlorides to oxide chlorides in a lower oxidation state. The first involves interaction of an oxide and the highest chloride or oxide chloride, usually in presence of a reducing agent. The reductant may be the transition metal itself, hydrogen or aluminium. The reactions are invariably carried out by either conventional sealed-tube reactions or thermal-gradient techniques. Typical examples are given in Table 2.11.

TABLE 2.11

Reduction of Oxide Chlorides

Reactants	Product	Conditions	Ref.
Nb_2O_5, $NbCl_5$ and H_2	$NbOCl_2$	Thermal gradient, 500–400°	46
Nb_2O_5, $NbOCl_3$ and H_2	$NbOCl_2$	Thermal gradient, 500–400°	46
Nb_2O_5, $NbCl_5$ and Nb	$NbOCl_2$	Sealed tube, 360°	46
Ta_2O_5, $TaCl_5$ and Ta	$TaOCl_2$	Sealed tube, 450°	46
$TaCl_5$, SiO_2 and Ta	$TaOCl_2$	Sealed tube, 500°	46
MoO_3, $MoCl_5$ and Mo	$MoOCl_2$	Thermal gradient	49
$WOCl_4$ and Al	$WOCl_3$	Sealed tube, 100–140°	87

The second general method of preparing oxide chlorides in a lower oxidation state is by thermal decomposition of higher oxide chlorides, but it appears that, so far, this type of reaction is restricted to the preparation of oxide trichlorides. These reactions will be discussed in detail later, but typical examples are given in Table 2.12.

TABLE 2.12

Thermal Decomposition of Oxide Chlorides

Initial Oxide Chloride	Product	Conditions	Ref.
$MoOCl_4$	$MoOCl_3$	At boiling point	2
$TcOCl_4$	$TcOCl_3$	Gentle heat	43
$OsOCl_4$	$OsOCl_3$	Gentle heat	38

Bromides and Oxide Bromides

The distinction between preparative methods for binary bromides and oxide bromides is much more pronounced than for the corresponding chlorine compounds. Only in a few cases are binary bromides formed from transition metal oxides.

Bromides have not been so well studied as chlorides, but it is clear that the same general preparative procedures are applicable. Direct bromination of the metal usually requires higher temperatures than the corresponding chlorination, and frequently the product contains the metal in a lower oxidation state than in the chloride prepared in an analogous manner. Direct bromination is usually carried out in a flow system, with nitrogen as a carrier gas; but, with bromine, sealed-tube reactions are feasible and have been carried out in a few cases.

Reaction of carbon tetrabromide with the metal oxide is useful but carbon tetrabromide is not such a strong halogenating agent as carbon tetrachloride. In no case is a binary bromide obtained, and higher temperatures are required for oxide bromides than for oxide chlorides.

Direct bromination of the metal. The products obtained by direct bromination of the transition metals are given in Table 2.13.

TABLE 2.13

Bromides Formed by Direct Bromination of the Metal

Metal	Product	Conditions	Ref.
Nb	$NbBr_5$	Flow system, 500–550°	10, 88
Ta	$TaBr_5$	Flow system, 500–550°	10, 88
Mo	$MoBr_3$	Flow system, 450°	89
	$MoBr_2$	Flow system, 650–700°	90
W	WBr_6	Flow system, gentle heat	91
	WBr_5	Flow system, 450–500°	67
Re	$ReBr_5$	Flow system, 500°	92
Ru	$RuBr_3$	Bomb, 450–500°	93, 94
Os	$OsBr_4$	Sealed tube, 450°	95
Pd	$PdBr_2$	Flow system	96
Pt	$PtBr_4$	Flow system	96
Au	$AuBr_3$	Flow system, 150°	96

The thermal instability of some of the higher bromides is nicely demonstrated by the fact that low-temperature bromination favours the formation of, say, tungsten hexabromide, whereas reaction at higher temperatures gives the pentabromide. It is known that tungsten hexabromide is thermally decomposed to the pentabromide at about 200°.

It is obvious that, apart from the Group V metals, the differences between the elements of the two transition series are quite pronounced and that invariably a higher bromide is obtained for the third-row element than for the corresponding second-row element.

Preparation of bromides from oxides. The preparation of binary bromides from oxides is mainly restricted to the elements of Groups IV and V, although the action of carbon tetrabromide on tungsten trioxide

TABLE 2.14

Preparation of Binary Bromides from Oxides

Oxide	Reagent	Product	Conditions	Ref.
ZrO_2 and C	Br_2	$ZrBr_4$	Flow system, 580°	97
HfO_2 and C	Br_2	$HfBr_4$	Flow system, 700–800°	98
Ta_2O_5 and C	Br_2	$TaBr_5$	Flow system, above 460°	42, 99
Nb_2O_5	$AlBr_3$	$NbBr_5$	Sealed tube, 200°	34
Ta_2O_5	$AlBr_3$	$TaBr_5$	Sealed tube, 200°	34
Nb_2O_5	CBr_4	$NbBr_5$	Sealed tube, 370°	100
Ta_2O_5	CBr_4	$TaBr_5$	Sealed tube, 200°	101

does give some hexabromide, together with oxide bromides. The preparations which have been reported are given in Table 2.14.

A number of interesting features are shown in Table 2.14. Tantalum oxide tribromide is thermally unstable, decomposing to the pentaoxide and the pentabromide[42]; this results in the formation of only the pentabromide when bromine is passed over a heated intimate mixture of tantalum pentaoxide and carbon. The analogous reaction with niobium pentaoxide gives thermally stable niobium oxide tribromide. Similarly, the interaction of carbon tetrabromide and tantalum pentaoxide in a sealed tube proceeds to the pentabromide at only 200°, but at this temperature the analogous reaction with niobium pentaoxide gives the oxide tribromide: it is necessary to raise the temperature to 370° to prepare niobium pentabromide.

Direct bromination of oxides. With the exceptions of zirconium, hafnium and tantalum noted above, bromination of an oxide yields oxide bromides. The reported reactions of this type are given in Table 2.15

TABLE 2.15

Direct Bromination of Oxides

Solid reactants	Gaseous reactants	Product	Conditions	Ref.
Nb_2O_5 and C	Br_2	$NbOBr_3$	Flow system, 540°	42, 102
WO_2	Br_2	WO_2Br_2	Sealed tube, 460°	103
TcO_2	Br_2	$TcOBr_3$	Flow system	104
$KReO_4$	Br_2	ReO_3Br	Flow system	105
ReO_3	Br_2	ReO_3Br	Flow system	106
Re_2O_7	Br_2	ReO_3Br	Flow system	107
ReO_2	Br_2	$ReOBr_4$	Flow system	92
Mo	Br_2 and O_2	MoO_2Br_2	Flow system	2
W	Br_2 and O_2	WO_2Br_2	Flow system	2
Re	Br_2 and O_2	$ReOBr_4$	Flow system	92

TABLE 2.16

Miscellaneous Preparations of Oxide Bromides

Reactants	Product	Conditions	Ref.
Nb_2O_5 and CBr_4	$NbOBr_3$	Sealed tube, 200°	100, 101
Ta_2O_5 and CBr_4	$TaOBr_3$	Sealed tube, 200°	101
WO_3 and CBr_4	WO_2Br_2	Sealed tube, 200°	108
	$WOBr_4$	Sealed tube, 470°	103
$NbBr_5$ and O_2	$NbOBr_3$	Flow system, 160°	42
$TaBr_5$ and O_2	$TaOBr_3$	Flow system, 200°	42
Nb_2O_5 and $NbBr_5$	$NbOBr_3$	Thermal gradient	45
$NbBr_5 \cdot Et_2O$	$NbOBr_3$	Thermal decomp., 112°	42
$TaBr_5 \cdot Et_2O$	$TaOBr_3$ (impure)	Thermal decomp., 74°	42

together with the products of the similar reaction involving passage of a bromine–oxygen stream over the heated metal.

The remaining general methods that have been applied to the preparation of oxide bromides are similar to those described above for oxide chlorides; they are summarized in Table 2.16.

The best method of preparing the thermally unstable tantalum oxide tribromide is by interaction of the pentabromide and oxygen. Reaction between tantalum pentaoxide and tantalum pentabromide in a sealed tube in a temperature gradient does *not* proceed. The effect of temperature on the composition of the final product obtained is clearly shown by the reaction of carbon tetrabromide with tungsten trioxide in a sealed tube.

Lower bromides have been prepared by methods analogous to those used for the chlorides.

Reduction of higher bromides with the metal. Reduction with the metal is a very useful way of preparing lower bromides, and some of the reported preparations are given in Table 2.17.

TABLE 2.17

Reduction of Higher Bromides with the Appropriate Metal

Bromide	Product	Conditions	Ref.
$ZrBr_4$	$ZrBr_3$	Sealed tube, 485°	53, 109
$HfBr_4$	$HfBr_3$	Sealed tube, 500°	53
$NbBr_5$	$NbBr_4$	Thermal gradient, 410–350°	56, 110, 111
$NbBr_5$	$NbBr_3$	Sealed tube, 500°	111
$TaBr_5$	$TaBr_4$	Thermal gradient, 620–310°	112
$TaBr_5$	$TaBr_3$	Thermal gradient, 620–380°	112
$TaBr_5$	$TaBr_{2.5}$	Thermal gradient, 620–450°	112
WBr_5	WBr_4	Thermal gradient, 630–340°	113

The effect of temperature on the products obtained by reduction of niobium and tantalum pentabromides is apparent from the Table. At comparatively low temperatures the tetrabromides are obtained, but at higher temperatures the tetrabromide disproportionates to the pentabromide and the tribromide. At still higher temperatures tantalum tribromide itself disproportionates, forming hexameric $TaBr_{2.5}$ and the pentabromide. Since an excess of tantalum pentabromide is present in the tube, the dissociation of the tribromide can only occur when its dissociation pressure is greater than the pressure of pentabromide already in the tube. This allows ready control of the composition of the reaction product.

Miscellaneous preparations of bromides. Reduction of higher bromides with aluminium and hydrogen has also been reported for a number of cases, as shown in Table 2.18.

TABLE 2.18

Reduction of Higher Bromides

Bromide	Reductant	Product	Conditions	Ref.
$ZrBr_4$	Al	$ZrBr_3$	Sealed tube, 450°, H_2 atm.	114
$HfBr_4$	Al	$HfBr_3$	Sealed tube, 450°, H_2 atm.	98
$TaBr_5$	Al	$TaBr_4$	Thermal gradient, 550–250°	8, 115
WBr_5	Al	WBr_4	Thermal gradient, 475–240°	65
$ZrBr_4$	H_2	$ZrBr_3$	Electrodeless gas discharge	84
$NbBr_5$	H_2	$NbBr_3$	Flow system, 500°	110, 116
$TaBr_5$	H_2	$TaBr_3$	Flow system, 200–700°	110, 117, 118

The lowest bromides of the elements of Groups IV and V are usually prepared by the thermal disproportionation of bromides in an intermediate oxidation state, as shown in Table 2.19.

Thermal decomposition has been used as a method of preparation of a number of bromides in different oxidation states. A higher or lower bromide may be formed, together with bromine or the transition metal

TABLE 2.19

Thermal Disproportionation of Bromides

Initial bromide	Products	Conditions	Ref.
$ZrBr_3$	$ZrBr_4 + ZrBr_2$	350°	53, 114
$HfBr_3$	$HfBr_4 + HfBr_2$	350°	53, 98, 114
$NbBr_4$	$NbBr_5 + NbBr_3$	450°	111
$TaBr_4$	$TaBr_5 + TaBr_3$	500°	85, 112, 119
$TaBr_3$	$TaBr_5 + TaBr_{2.5}$	Sealed tube, 220–450°	110, 112

itself. A few bromides decompose completely to the elements, no intermediate bromides being isolated. Some typical examples are given in Table 2.20.

It is interesting to compare the action of heat on molybdenum tetrachloride and molybdenum tetrabromide. The chloride disproportionates to give the pentachloride and the trichloride. However, molybdenum pentabromide is unknown, and molybdenum tetrabromide dissociates to

TABLE 2.20

Thermal Decomposition of Bromides

Initial bromide	Products	Conditions	Ref.
$ZrBr_2$	$ZrBr_4 + Zn$	Above 400°	98
$HfBr_2$	$HfBr_4 + Hf$	Above 400°	98
$MoBr_4$	$MoBr_3 + Br_2$	High temperature	120
$MoBr_2$	$MoBr_4 + Mo$	900°	120
WBr_6	$WBr_5 + Br_2$	200°	113
$ReBr_5$	$ReBr_3 + Br_2$		92
$RuBr_3$	$Ru + Br_2$	Above 450°	94
$OsBr_4$	$OsBr_3 + Br_2$	350°	95
$PtBr_4$	$PtBr_2 + Br_2$	300°	121
$PtBr_2$	$Pt + Br_2$	Above 400°	121

give the tribromide and bromine, strongly suggesting that, if the pentabromide could be prepared, it would be found to be thermally unstable.

Iodides and Oxide Iodides

There has been comparatively little study of iodides as a group. In general, iodides tend to stabilize lower oxidation states of the transition metals, and it is only for Groups IV and V that iodides of the transition elements in their maximum oxidation state are obtained. Oxide iodides are restricted to niobium and tantalum.

Direct interaction of iodine and the metal. This method is of fairly limited application since a number of the transition metals do not react with iodine. The preparations of this type that have been reported are given in Table 2.21.

Preparation of iodides by means of aluminium triiodide. In reactions with transition metal oxides or chlorides, aluminium triiodide is a very powerful and convenient reagent for the preparation of binary iodides. Chaigneau, in particular, has used this method to advantage with a number of elements. The large lattice energy of aluminium oxide is of

TABLE 2.21

Direct Interaction of Iodine and the Metal

Metal	Product	Conditions	Ref.
Zr	ZrI_4	Flow system, 400°	61
Hf	HfI_4	Sealed tube, high temperature	122
Nb	NbI_5	Flow system, 600°	123, 124
		Sealed tube, 270°	125
Ta	TaI_5	Flow system, above 700°	124, 126, 127
		Sealed tube, 340–370°	128
Mo	MoI_3	Sealed tube, 300°	129
Pt[a]	PtI_4	Sealed tube, 150–250°	130, 131
Au	AuI	Sealed tube, 120°	132

[a] Best reaction conditions are stoichiometric quantities and as low a temperature as possible because of the thermal instability of PtI_4.

great importance in assisting the reaction to proceed. The reactions are invariably carried out in a sealed tube and some examples are given in Table 2.22.

Niobium pentaiodide is thermally unstable and interaction of niobium pentaoxide and aluminium triiodide gives only niobium triiodide and niobium oxide triiodide[134].

TABLE 2.22

Preparation of Binary Iodides by Means of
Aluminium Triiodide

Reactant	Product	Conditions	Ref.
ZrO_2	ZrI_4	400°	133, 134
$ZrCl_4$	ZrI_4	330°	135
$HfCl_4$	HfI_4	330°	135
$NbCl_5$	NbI_5	300°	136
Ta_2O_5	TaI_5	230°	133, 134
$TaCl_5$	TaI_5	410°	136
MoO_3	MoI_2	230°	133
MoO_2	MoI_2	230°	133

Lower iodides. Thermal dissociation of a higher iodide is the usual method of preparing iodides in a lower oxidation state, although a few examples of reduction with the metal itself have been reported, as shown in Table 2.23.

Oxide iodides. The formation of oxide iodides is restricted to niobium and tantalum and the methods of preparation are given in Table 2.24.

TABLE 2.23

Preparation of Lower Iodides

Reactants	Products	Conditions	Ref.
$ZrI_4 + Zr$	ZrI_3	Sealed tube, 300–500°	53, 137, 138
$HfI_4 + Hf$	HfI_3	Sealed tube, 400°	53
$TaI_5 + Ta$	TaI_4	Sealed tube, above 325°	8, 115, 128
ZrI_3	$ZrI_4 + ZrI_2$	Above 325°	139
NbI_5	NbI_4	Sealed tube, 270°	140, 141
NbI_4	$NbI_5 + NbI_3$	430°	140
MoI_3	MoI_2	100°	142
ReI_4	ReI_3	Sealed tube, 350°	143
PtI_4	PtI_3	200°	131
PtI_3	PtI_2	270°	130, 131

TABLE 2.24

Preparation of Oxide Iodides

Reactants	Product	Conditions	Ref.
Nb_2O_5, Nb and I_2	$NbOI_3$	Thermal gradient, 400–275°	144
	NbO_2I	Sealed tube, 475°	145
	$NbOI_2$	Thermal gradient, 500–450°	144
Nb_2O_5 and AlI_3	$NbOI_3$	Sealed tube, 230–300°	134
Ta_2O_5, Ta and I_2	$TaOI_3$	Sealed tube, 500°	145

Complex Chlorides and Oxide Chlorides

It is convenient to consider complex chlorides and oxide chlorides together, as the same general preparative methods can be applied for both types of compounds. Three general methods of wide applicability can be identified. The transition metal chlorides are treated with an alkali-metal halide in the melt or, alternatively, with an alkali metal or quaternary ammonium halide in hydrochloric acid or a non-aqueous solvent. Here no attempt is made to control the oxidation state of the final product. The third method involves reduction of a compound of the transition metal in a higher oxidation state with a variety of reducing agents in hydrochloric acid.

Preparations in the melt. Niobium is the only metal for which complex oxide chlorides have been prepared in the melt. The method has been quite widely applied to the preparation of complex chlorides in lower oxidation states, but it should be noted that in these reactions rigorous exclusion of oxygen is essential. The reactions which have been reported are given in Table 2.25.

TABLE 2.25

Preparation in Alkali-metal Chloride
Melts (M = alkali metal)

Reactant	Product	Ref.
$ZrCl_4$	M_2ZrCl_6	146–150
$HfCl_4$	M_2HfCl_6	147–149
$NbCl_5$	$MNbCl_6$	146, 149, 151
$TaCl_5$	$MTaCl_6$	146, 149, 151
$NbOCl_3$	M_2NbOCl_5	152–154
	$MNbOCl_4$	152, 153, 155
$NbCl_4$	M_2NbCl_6	156–158
$TaCl_4$	M_2TaCl_6	159, 160
$TaCl_3$	M_2TaCl_5	161
WCl_6	$MWCl_6$	12
$MoCl_5$	M_2MoCl_6	162–164
WCl_5	$MWCl_6$	12
$ReCl_5$	M_2ReCl_6	165

The elements of Groups IV and V invariably give complexes with the metal in the same oxidation state as in the original chloride, but the elements of Groups VI and VII often give complexes of lower oxidation state with the evolution of chlorine.

Preparations in hydrochloric acid solution. The chlorides of zirconium, palladium, platinum and gold give complex chlorides in hydrochloric acid solutions of alkali-metal chlorides. It appears also that lower chlorides of the elements of Groups VI and VII also give chloro complexes, although often of a polymeric nature. The more familiar higher chlorides of the elements of Groups V, VI and VII react with hydrochloric acid to give complex oxide chlorides, and indeed this represents one of the best methods of preparing these salts. Particularly for those elements towards the left of the Periodic Table, it is often advantageous to saturate the solution with hydrogen chloride gas to prevent hydrolysis reactions. Addition of alkali-metal chloride leads to the isolation of well-defined compounds. Some typical examples are given in Table 2.26.

Reactions in non-aqueous solvents. These reactions can be conveniently divided into two types. The first involves the use of inert solvents, which merely allow interaction of the parent binary chloride or oxide chloride with a suitable chloride. The cation is usually a quaternary ammonium derivative for solubility reasons. A few typical reactions are given in Table 2.27. The influence of the solvent on the products obtained from molybdenum pentachloride clearly reflects the great reactivity of this halide.

TABLE 2.26

Complex Chlorides and Oxide Chlorides from Hydrochloric Acid Solution

Chloride	Product	Ref.
$ZrCl_4$	M_2ZrCl_6	166
$NbCl_5$	M_2NbOCl_5	167–169
$TaCl_5$	M_2TaOCl_5	170
$MoCl_5$	M_2MoOCl_5	171, 172
WCl_5	M_2WOCl_5	171
$ReOCl_4$	M_2ReOCl_6	50
$ReCl_5$	M_2ReOCl_5	173
Re_3Cl_9	$M_3Re_3Cl_{12}$	174, 175
$PdCl_2$	M_2PdCl_4	176
$PtCl_2$	M_2PtCl_4	176
$AuCl_3$	$MAuCl_4$	176

TABLE 2.27

Preparations in Non-aqueous Solvents
R = quaternary ammonium derivative;
M = alkali metal

Halide	Product	Solvent	Ref.
$WOCl_4$	$RWOCl_5$	$CHCl_3$	177
$MoCl_5$	$RMoCl_6$	CH_2Cl_2	178
$MoCl_5$	$RMoOCl_4$	SO_2	171
WCl_5	$RWOCl_4$	SO_2	171
$MoCl_5$	M_2MoCl_6	SO_2	179
$ReOCl_4$	$RReOCl_5$	$CHCl_3$	180

TABLE 2.28

Preparations in Thionyl Chloride

Reagent	Product	Ref.
$ZrCl_4$	R_2ZrCl_6	184
$NbCl_5$	$MNbCl_6$	182
$TaCl_5$	$MTaCl_6$	182
WCl_6	$MWCl_6$	183
$WOCl_4$	$RWCl_6$	181
NH_4TcO_4	$(NH_4)_2TcO_2Cl_4 \cdot SOCl_2$	104
$ReOCl_4$	R_2ReCl_6	185
NH_4ReO_4	$(NH_4)_2ReO_2Cl_4 \cdot SOCl_2$	185

The second type of reaction in non-aqueous media involves the use of chlorinating solvents. Almost all the work reported has been done with thionyl chloride, and only this solvent will be discussed here.

Adams and his coworkers[181] made very extensive use of thionyl chloride to prepare complex chlorides of many transition metals from the readily available hydrated oxide of the metal. Usually a quaternary ammonium cation is used for solubility reasons, but Bagnall and his coworkers[182,183] have used mixtures of iodine monochloride and thionyl chloride to prepare alkali-metal salts. Some typical preparations are given in Table 2.28.

Reduction reactions in hydrochloric acid solution. Probably the most general method of preparation of complex chlorides and oxide chlorides is by the reduction of an oxide, or an oxygen complex, of the transition metal in concentrated hydrochloric acid. Both chemical and electrolytic reductions have been carried out. Some typical examples are given in Table 2.29.

TABLE 2.29

Preparation of Complex Chlorides by Reduction

Starting material	Reductant	Product	Ref.
Mo(VI) in HCl	N_2H_4	$MoOCl_5^{2-}$	186
	HI	$MoOCl_5^{2-}$	187–189
	Electrolytic	$MoCl_6^{3-}$	81, 190, 191
	Electrolytic	$MoOCl_5^{2-}$	192, 193
W(VI) in HCl	$H_2C_2O_4$	$WOCl_5^{2-}$	194
	Electrolytic	$WOCl_5^{2-}$	195
	Sn	$W_2Cl_9^{3-}$	196, 197
	Electrolytic	$W_2Cl_9^{3-}$	198
Tc(VII) in HCl	HCl alone	$TcCl_6^{2-}$	199
	HI	$TcCl_6^{2-}$	200
$TcCl_6^{2-}$ in HCl	Zn	$Tc_2Cl_8^{3-}$	201
Re(VII) in HCl	HI	$ReCl_6^{2-}$	202, 203
	H_3PO_2	$Re_2Cl_8^{2-}$	204, 205
Ru(VIII) in HCl	HCl alone	$RuCl_6^{2-}$	206
$RuCl_6^{2-}$ in HCl	$H_2C_2O_4$	$RuCl_5^{2-}$	207
	Electrolytic	$RuCl_4^{2-}$	208
Os(VIII) in HCl	HCl alone	$OsCl_6^{2-}$	209
	$FeCl_2$	$OsCl_6^{2-}$	210
$IrCl_6^{2-}$ in HCl	$H_2S, H_2C_2O_4$	$IrCl_6^{3-}$	176
$PdCl_6^{2-}$ in HCl	Pd	$PdCl_4^{2-}$	211
$PtCl_6^{2-}$ in HCl	N_2H_4	$PtCl_4^{2-}$	212
	H_2S	$PtCl_4^{2-}$	176

Oxidation in hydrochloric acid solution. As shown in Table 2.30, few examples have been reported of the oxidation of lower-valent complex chlorides in hydrochloric acid solution to complex chlorides of a higher oxidation state.

TABLE 2.30

Oxidation in Hydrochloric Acid Solution

Starting material	Oxidant	Product	Ref.
$ReOCl_5^{2-}$	Air	$ReOCl_6^{2-}$	173
$RuCl_5^{2-}$	Cl_2	$RuCl_6^{2-}$	207, 213
$RhCl_6^{3-}$	Cl_2	$RhCl_6^{2-}$	214, 215
Pd and HCl	Cl_2	$PdCl_6^{2-}$	18, 96
Pt and HCl	Cl_2	$PtCl_6^{2-}$	18, 96

Complex Bromides and Oxide Bromides

Bromine tends to stabilize lower oxidation states of the transition metals in complex bromides. Hence there are no complex bromides of the elements of Groups IV and V. Complex oxide bromides are few.

Complex bromides have not been prepared from melts, probably because of their inherent instability. Almost all preparations have been carried out in hydrobromic acid solution from binary chlorides or bromides, oxides, and, most frequently, chloro complexes which form the corresponding bromides by simple halogen exchange. Some typical examples are given in Table 2.31.

TABLE 2.31

Preparation of Complex Bromides in
Hydrobromic Acid Solution

Reactant	Product	Ref.
$NbBr_5$	$NbOBr_5^{2-}$	216
$MoCl_5$	$MoOBr_5^{2-}$	171
WCl_5	$WOBr_5^{2-}$	171
$TcCl_6^{2-}$	$TcBr_6^{2-}$	200
$ReCl_6^{2-}$	$ReBr_6^{2-}$	43, 200
ReO_2	$ReBr_6^{2-}$	217
RuO_4	$RuBr_6^{2-}$	218
OsO_4	$OsBr_6^{2-}$	219
$OsCl_6^{2-}$	$OsBr_6^{2-}$	220
$PdBr_4^{2-}/Br_2$	$PdBr_6^{2-}$	176, 221
$PdCl_4^{2-}$	$PdBr_6^{2-}$	222
$PtCl_4$	$PtBr_6^{2-}$	222
$AuBr_3$	$AuBr_4^{-}$	223, 224

Complex Iodides

The methods of preparation of complex iodides are similar to those for complex bromides but, even more so than for the bromides, they are restricted to the elements to the right of the Periodic Table. Some typical examples are shown in Table 2.32.

TABLE 2.32

Preparation of Complex Iodides in Hydriodic Acid
Solution

Reagent	Product	Ref.	Reagent	Product	Ref.
$TcCl_6^{2-}$	TcI_6^{2-}	200	ReO_4^-	ReI_6^{2-}	203, 227
ReX_6^{2-}	ReI_6^{2-}	43, 200	OsO_4	OsI_6^{2-}	228
$OsCl_6^{2-}$	OsI_6^{2-}	225	$IrCl_6^{3-}$	IrI_6^{3-}	229
$PtCl_6^{2-}$	PtI_6^{2-}	176, 226			

STRUCTURES OF HALIDES AND OXIDE HALIDES

Although a considerable number of halides and oxide halides have been examined by X-ray powder diffraction techniques, in comparatively few cases has the stereochemistry been fully established by single-crystal methods.

The niobium pentachloride structure, consisting of dimeric units containing octahedrally coordinated metal atoms (Figure 5.1, p. 154) has been shown to be adopted by the pentachlorides of niobium[230], tantalum[230] and molybdenum[231]. Judged from its physical characteristics and chemical properties, it is likely that rhenium pentachloride also has this structure. The original claim[230] that niobium and tantalum pentabromides were isomorphous with the pentachlorides has been shown to be incorrect[88,232]. Nevertheless, it is possible that the same type of molecular stereochemistry is retained, and that mere differences in the packing arrangement give a different symmetry to the lattice.

The only other structure thought to be of fairly wide general occurrence is the niobium oxide trichloride structure (Figure 5.2, p. 157). This consists of dimeric Nb_2Cl_6 units linked by double chains of niobium–oxygen linkages parallel to the crystallographic axis. The infinite chains reduce the volatility of the compound markedly in comparison with niobium pentachloride.

Although the only compound proved unequivocally by single-crystal X-ray methods to have this structure is the niobium compound, there is some evidence from infrared studies that a number of other oxide tri-halides also adopt this structure. It is interesting that all these compounds are rather involatile. The infrared stretching frequencies[233] are given in Table 2.33.

TABLE 2.33

Metal–Oxygen Stretching Frequencies (cm^{-1}) of Oxide Trihalides

Compound	M–O stretch	Compound	M–O stretch
$NbOCl_3$	767	$NbOBr_3$	732
$MoOBr_3$	810	$WOCl_3$	796
$WOBr_3$	722	$TcOBr_3$	770

A somewhat similar type of structure has been shown to be adopted by tungsten oxide tetrachloride and tetrabromide[234,235]. In this case, planar WX_4 groups are linked in infinite single chains by oxygen bridges. Once again the compounds are comparatively involatile and the metal–oxygen stretching frequency falls in the region usually associated with oxygen-bridged systems. It would appear from their physical properties, and especially from their infrared spectra, that most other oxide tetrahalides contain terminal oxygen atoms, so this structure does not appear to be a common one.

McCarley and coworkers[8,56,65] have shown by X-ray powder diffraction methods that the tetrachlorides of niobium, tantalum and molybdenum, and also the tetrabromides of niobium and tantalum, are isomorphous, although there have been different interpretations of the symmetry of the lattices by other workers (see Chapter 5). None of these tetrahalides is ismorphous with α-niobium tetraiodide, for which single-crystal data are available[236]. This compound (Figures 5.5 and 5.6, pp. 171, 172) consists of infinite chains of NbI_6 units sharing edges, but the niobium atoms are drawn together in pairs, the resulting metal–metal bond causing diamagnetism. The other tetrahalides mentioned above are also diamagnetic, and McCarley[8,56] suggests that their structures are of the same general type but with different packing arrangements.

Other individual structures have been determined, but so far no clear indication of other general types of structure are apparent. These individual structures are discussed in their appropriate chapters.

STRUCTURES OF COMPLEX HALIDES

Although a few individual compounds have been examined by single-crystal techniques, there is no doubt that the complex halides of these elements have been neglected from the crystallographic point of view. The only type of compound examined extensively by X-ray powder diffraction techniques is the alkali-metal hexahalometallates(IV). The chlorides and bromides almost invariably adopt the K_2PtCl_6 structure (Figure 10.4, p. 379), which is essentially a sodium chloride type lattice. It is worth noting that usually the corresponding hexaiodide is not isomorphous, but chemical and spectral evidence suggests that the stereochemistry of the iodo anions is similar to the other halides, and the lattice change is merely due to a change in packing arrangement caused by the large size of iodine. Conversely, the sodium salts often do not have the K_2PtCl_6 structure, presumably for similar reasons.

It appears likely that the interesting μ-oxo-decachlorometallates(IV) and related structures may be more extensive than has been suspected previously. Single-crystal studies on the ruthenium[237] and rhenium[238] compounds serve to confirm the stereochemistry of the complex. There is good evidence that similar compounds of osmium(IV)[38] and tungsten(IV)[239] exist.

STABILITIES OF OXIDE HALIDES

There are a number of oxide chlorides and oxide bromides that are thermally unstable and decompose by loss of a halogen atom. This type of decomposition is particularly common with hexavalent compounds of the type MOX_4, giving oxide halides of the type MOX_3. There are a few examples of technetium and rhenium(VII) compounds decomposing thermally to the trioxide. Some typical examples are given in Table 2.34.

TABLE 2.34

Thermal Decomposition of Some Oxide Halides

Oxide halide	Product	Oxide halide	Product
$MoOCl_4$	$MoOCl_3$	$WOCl_4$	Stable
$WOBr_4$	Stable	$TcOCl_4$	$TcOCl_3$
$ReOCl_4$	Stable	$ReOBr_4$	$ReOBr_3$
$OsOCl_4$	$OsOCl_3$	TcO_3Cl	TcO_3
ReO_3Cl	Stable	ReO_3Br	ReO_3

For Group VII a fair generalization is to equate the stability of technetium chlorides with rhenium bromides. Thus, the stability of technetium oxide tetrachloride is very similar to that of rhenium oxide tetrabromide. It is worth noting that the oxide tetrabromides of both molybdenum and technetium are unknown.

Most of the oxide trihalides are thermally stable, the exceptions being molybdenum oxide trichloride, tantalum oxide trichloride and oxide tribromide, and rhenium oxide tribromide.

It has recently been established, that with only one exception, the thermally stable oxide halides contain bridging oxygen atoms, and the thermally unstable ones contain terminal oxygen atoms[233]. The infrared metal–oxygen stretching frequencies[233] are given in Table 2.35.

TABLE 2.35

Infrared Spectra (cm^{-1}) of Oxide Halides

Oxide halide	Thermal stability	M–O frequency	Oxide halide	Thermal stability	M–O frequency
$MoOCl_4$	Unstable	989, 977	$NbOBr_3$	Stable	732
$WOCl_4$	Stable	875	$MoOCl_3$	Unstable	1007
$WOBr_4$	Stable	824	$MoOBr_3$	Stable	810
$ReOCl_4$	Stable	1031, 1015	$WOCl_3$	Stable	796
$ReOBr_4$	Unstable	1001	$WOBr_3$	Stable	722
$OsOCl_4$	Unstable	997	$TcOBr_3$	Stable	770
$NbOCl_3$	Stable	767	$ReOBr_3$	Unstable	1018

The rhenium compound is the only oxide tetrachloride that apparently has terminal oxygen atoms and yet is thermally stable. Attempts to decompose it by irradiation with ultraviolet light have failed[233]. The structures of tungsten oxide tetrachloride and oxide tetrabromide have been determined[234,235] and contain infinite chains with tungsten–oxygen linkages. A similar type of linkage occurs in niobium oxide trichloride[240], but the structures of the remaining compounds are unknown.

Edwards[241] has suggested that molybdenum oxide trichloride adopts the niobium oxide trichloride structure, but the infrared data do not support this suggestion. However, the metal–oxygen stretching frequencies for most of the oxide trihalides are consistent with this type of structure (Table 2.35).

THERMODYNAMICS

In Figure 2.2 the heats of formation of a number of binary chlorides are plotted. They show rather clearly some of the characteristic trends in the stability of transition metal halides.

It is obvious that the halides of zirconium and hafnium are extraordinarily similar in all oxidation states, but this situation is undoubtedly the exception rather than the rule. For the other two Groups for which sufficient data are available, the chlorides of third-row elements are the more stable in high oxidation states, but the second-row compounds become the more stable in the low oxidation states. Although the elements for which quantitative results are available are limited, there is no doubt that this is a general trend throughout the two transition series.

Figure 2.2 also clearly shows that towards the right of the Periodic Table the stability of the maximum oxidation state of the elements in chlorides

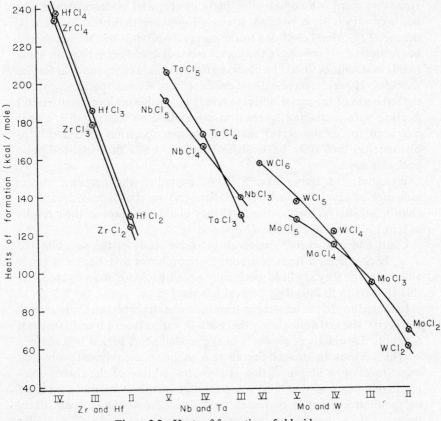

Figure 2.2   Heats of formation of chlorides.

falls rapidly. Even for molybdenum in Group VI, the maximum oxidation state is not stable in the binary chloride, and for no element beyond Group VI is the maximum oxidation state attainable as a binary chloride.

BONDING IN COMPLEX HALIDES

There has been little study of the bonding in the halide complexes of the second- and third-row transition elements, although Cotton and Harris[242]

have recently presented a molecular-orbital treatment of the bonding
scheme in the hexachlorometallates(IV) of some of the third-row elements.
These workers followed previous treatments used to explain the electron
spin resonance spectra of the same complexes, and considered only the
σ-bonds between the metal and chlorine and possible π-interaction between
the filled p-orbitals of chlorine and the partly filled t_{2g}-orbitals of the metals.
However, there is a considerable body of chemical evidence, which has
not been previously correlated, strongly suggesting that back-donation of
the metal t_{2g}-orbital electrons to the empty $3d$-orbitals of chlorine should
be considered. If only ligand-to-metal π-bonding was occurring, the same
trends in stabilities should be observed for these halo compounds as for the
fluorides. However, there is direct evidence from Raman spectroscopy that
the strengths of the metal–chlorine bonds in the hexachlorometallates(IV)
increase with increasing t_{2g}-electron population on the metal[243], and it
has been specifically stated that the Raman spectrum of hexachloro-
platinate(IV) can only be explained on the basis of metal-to-ligand
back-donation.

Westland and Bhiwandker[244-246] have studied the magnetic super-
exchange of several hexachlorometallates(IV) in the diamagnetic hexa-
chloroplatinate(IV) host lattice, and they could only explain their results
in terms of metal-to-chlorine d_π–d_π-bonding.

Chatt and coworkers[247] made an extensive study of the possibility of
d_π–d_π-back-donation from platinum to phosphorus and sulphur ligands
and, although they say little specifically about back-donation to chlorine,
this appears to fit into their general scheme.

In their study of the bonding in transition metal complexes, Craig and coworkers[248] showed quite clearly that back-donation from a transition metal
to empty $3d$-orbitals of elements of the second short period is feasible.

Whilst it must be stressed that there is so far no unequivocal proof that
metal-to-halogen back-donation is a general feature of the chloro complexes of the second- and third-row transition metals, it would be expected
on qualitative grounds that such back-donation would be more likely
than with the first-row transition series. Naturally, a synergic effect, similar
to that accepted in the bonding models for carbonyls, phosphines and
cyanides of the transition metals, can be envisaged.

The chemical and physical evidence which seems to indicate back-donation of electrons is summarized in the following sections.

Thermal Stabilities of Complex Chlorides

The published interpretation of ESR and nuclear quadrupole resonance
(NQR) data has involved some metal–halogen π-bonding, but it has been
assumed that this ligand-to-metal π-bonding was donation of p_π-electrons

of chlorine into the partly filled d-orbitals of the metal, exactly as we have already discussed for fluorine compounds. As noted in Chapter 1, this would result in a gradual *decrease* in the stabilities of the compounds as the t_{2g}-orbital electron population increases, in agreement with the experimental results for fluorides. However, if a double-bonding mechanism involving, first, σ-donation of an electron pair from chlorine, followed by back-donation from the π-orbitals of the metal into the empty d-orbitals of chlorine, then exactly the opposite trends in stability would be expected. That is, there should be an *increase* in stability of the chloro complex as the metal π-electron population increases, because of increased capacity for back-donation.

It is an experimental fact that all complex chlorides and oxide chlorides with a d^0-configuration are thermally unstable with respect to dissociation to the parent halide or oxide halide, whereas the corresponding fluoro complexes are much more stable, as expected. A typical example is the thermal dissociation of potassium hexachloroniobate(v) to niobium pentachloride and potassium chloride at a temperature as low as 300°. On the other hand, the d^1-complex, potassium hexachloroniobate(iv), is thermally stable, melting without decomposition at 782°[156]. It is true that certain halo complexes with electronic configurations other than d^0 may be thermally decomposed, but in no case is the parent transition metal halide liberated. The products of this type of decomposition are the metal, alkali-metal halide and free halogen[18]. In addition, the temperatures required to decompose the complexes typified by M_2OsCl_6 and M_2PdCl_6 are of the order of 600–700°. Some typical thermal stabilities of a number of halo complexes are summarized in Table 2-36.

TABLE 2.36

Thermal Stabilities of Some Halo Complexes

Compound	Stability	Decomposition product	Ref.
ZrF_7^{3-}	Stable at 900°		249
ZrF_6^{2-}	Stable at 600°		250
$ZrCl_6^{2-}$	Decomposes at 400°	$ZrCl_4$	149
$HfCl_6^{2-}$	Decomposes at 450°	$HfCl_4$	149
NbF_7^{2-}	Stable at 730°		251
TaF_7^{2-}	Stable at 770°		252
$NbCl_6^-$	Decomposes at 300°	$NbCl_5$	146, 253
$TaCl_6^-$	Decomposes at 370°	$TaCl_5$	146, 149
$NbCl_6^{2-}$	Stable to 800°		159
$TaCl_6^{2-}$	Stable to 800°		159
$NbOCl_5^{2-}$	Decomposes at 400°	$NbOCl_3$	155
$NbOCl_4^-$	Decomposes at 300°	$NbOCl_3$	155

Infrared and Raman Spectra

As noted in Chapter 1, there is a marked decrease in the a_{1g}-stretching frequency of the metal–fluorine bond in the hexafluoride series for increasing t_{2g}-electron population. The hexachlorometallates(IV) form a similar series of octahedral symmetry, and their Raman spectra have been investigated by Woodward and his coworkers; but unfortunately results are not available for many compounds. Nevertheless, it is quite clear that the trends in the a_{1g}-mode do not follow the same patterns as observed for the hexafluorides.

Woodward and Creighton[254] examined the Raman spectra of the hexachloro-palladate(IV) and -platinate(IV) and the hexabromoplatinate(IV) ions and found in all cases that ν_2 was more intense than ν_1, which is the reverse of the relative intensities usually observed. They suggested that this effect arose somehow from the $(t_{2g})^6$-configuration of the metal atoms, but did not elaborate further. In a later paper, Woodward and Ware[255] showed that the Raman spectrum of K_2PtF_6 was normal and in this paper they made the proposal that the irregular spectra of the chloro and bromo complexes were due to back-donation from the filled t_{2g}-orbitals into empty d_π-orbitals of chlorine.

The a_{1g}-mode has been recorded for the series K_2MCl_6 (where M = Re, Os, or Pt), and Woodward and Ware[255] point out that the force constants of the metal–chlorine bonds increase in this series, whilst for the hexafluorides they decrease in the same series.

Nuclear Quadrupole Resonance

Nakamura and coworkers[256–261] have studied the pure halogen nuclear quadrupole resonance for a number of hexahalometallates(IV) of the third-row transition series. Single lines were observed in all cases for the chloro and bromo complexes, showing that all the halogen atoms were crystallographically equivalent, in agreement with their known K_2PtCl_6 type structure. It is the variation of the resonance frequency and the quadrupole coupling constant across the series which is of interest.

Nakamura and his associates interpreted the quadrupole spectra by the Townes–Dailey procedure[262,264], which is a valence-bond approach to the interaction in simple molecules involving only s- and p-orbitals, particularly organic molecules. It is perhaps debatable whether this simple treatment can be used for complex halides of the heavy transition metals, especially as one of the postulates of the method is that no π-bonding of any type occurs. Very recently, Cotton and Harris[265] have derived a more general formula for quadrupole coupling constants in terms of a molecular-orbital approach, which makes no assumption concerning the amount of p_π–d_π ligand-to-metal bonding.

The interpretation of the quadrupole spectra by Nakamura and co-workers does not appear to be self-consistent. No account is taken of the possibility of d_π–d_π-bonding and any π-bonding is assumed to be of the p_π–d_π type. However, this π-bonding is not treated in the Townes–Dailey method and it is incorporated in the following way. The electron spin resonance spectrum of the hexachloroiridate(IV) anion has been interpreted as evidence that each metal–chlorine bond has about 5% of

TABLE 2.37

Nuclear Quadrupole Resonance Data for
Hexachloro-Metallates(IV)

Compound	Ionic character	σ-bond character	π-bond character
$PtCl_6^{2-}$	0.44	0.56	0
$IrCl_6^{2-}$	0.47	0.48	0.054
$OsCl_6^{2-}$	0.47	0.43	0.108
$ReCl_6^{2-}$	0.45	0.39	0.16
WCl_6^{2-}	0.43	0.35	0.22

π-character (but see below), and the assumption is made that the amount of π-character in the metal–halogen bond increases linearly with the number of holes in the metal t_{2g}-orbitals. Thus, as there cannot be any p_π-donation to Pt(IV) and ESR studies give 5% of π-character in $IrCl_6^{2-}$, the values shown in Table 2.37 are easily obtained. With the further assumption that there is 15% of s-character in chlorine σ-orbitals, the amount of ionic character in the metal–halogen bond is calculated from the expression:

$$|eQ_q| = (1 - i)(1 - s)\,|eQ_q|_{\text{atom}}$$

which was originally derived by Townes and Dailey for simple molecules without π-bonding, such as carbon tetrachloride. In this expression, $|eQ_q|$ is the quadrupole coupling constant (which itself is calculated on the assumption that the quadrupole assymmetry factor is zero), i is the ionic character of the bond, s is the s-character in the halogen orbital and $|eQ_q|_{\text{atom}}$ is the quadrupole constant of the halogen atom. The results obtained in this manner as given in Table 2.37. A basic assumption in the derivation of these values is that there is no π-bonding in hexachloroplatinate(IV), and of course there can be no $p_\pi \rightarrow d_\pi$ halogen–metal bonding. Hence a gradual decrease in bond order from tungsten to platinum should be observed, and the greatest π-bonding and strongest metal–halogen bond should be found in hexachlorohafnate(IV). However, it is an experimental fact that the bond orders increase, at least from rhenium to platinum. Also the Raman spectra indicate the presence of d_π–d_π-back-bonding, and hexachlorohafnates(IV) are the least stable hexachlorometallates(IV). Under these circumstances the charge distributions calculated above appear to be suspect.

The electronegativity differences between these metals and chlorine are too small to account for the large ionic character of the bonds as calculated. Ionic characters of the order of 20% would be more appropriate.

Electron Spin Resonance

The electron spin resonance of the hexachloroiridate(IV) anion (low spin d^5) shows hyperfine structure which can only be accounted for by the interaction of the single unpaired electron with the chlorine nuclei[266–268]. This was explained on the basis of $p_\pi \rightarrow d_\pi$ chlorine-to-metal interaction, forming bonding and antibonding π-molecular orbitals with the unpaired electron in the antibonding orbitals. The relative energies of the orbitals were such that the antibonding orbital was predominantly a metal orbital, but had a sufficient halogen component to allow some delocalization of the unpaired electron to the halogens.

It was estimated from the hyperfine structure that the unpaired electron is about 26% delocalized on to the halogens, giving approximately 4.5% of π-character to each iridium–chlorine bond. The amount of delocalization can also be calculated from the observed value of g, again assuming the same bonding scheme, but this method gave 34% of delocalization. The discrepancy of about 25% was unexplained[266]. It is possible that the anomaly can be removed if d_π–d_π-delocalization on to chlorine is involved, in which case about 30% of five electrons is delocalized, giving roughly 25% of π-character to each iridium–chlorine bond. If this value were used, more reasonable values for the ionic component of the bond would be deduced from nuclear quadrupole measurements.

If only $p_\pi \rightarrow d_\pi$-delocalization is involved in the metal–chlorine bonds, then the amount of delocalization would be expected to increase from iridium to tungsten, and the hyperfine splitting due to chlorine should become more pronounced. However, exactly the opposite effect is observed, since no hyperfine structure could be observed in the electron spin resonance spectrum of the hexachlororhenate(IV)[269] and oxopentachloromolybdate(V)[270] ions.

REFERENCES

1. F. A. Cotton and G. Wilkinson, *Advanced Inorganic Chemistry*, Interscience, New York, 1966.
2. R. Colton and I. B. Tomkins, *Australian J. Chem.*, **18**, 447 (1965).
3. S. A. Shchukarev, E. K. Smirnova, T. S. Shemyakina and A. N. Ryabov, *Russ. J. Inorg. Chem.*, **7**, 626 (1962).
4. O. Ruff and F. Thomas, *Z. anorg. allgem. Chem.*, **156**, 213 (1926).
5. K. Knox, S. Y. Tyree, R. D. Srivastava, V. Norman, J. Y. Bassett and J. H. Holloway, *J. Am. Chem. Soc.*, **79**, 3387 (1957).
6. E. R. Epperson and H. Frye, *Inorg. Nucl. Chem. Letters*, **2**, 223 (1966).
7. S. A. Shchukarev, G. I. Novikov, A. V. Suvorov and A. K. Baev, *Zhur. Neorg. Khim.*, **3**, 2630 (1958).
8. R. M. McCarley and J. C. Boatman, *Inorg. Chem.*, **2**, 547 (1963).
9. W. B. Blumental, *The Chemical Behaviour of Zirconium*, Van Nostrand, New Jersey, 1958.
10. K. M. Alexander and F. Fairbrother, *J. Chem. Soc. Suppl.*, **1949**, S223.
11. M. H. Lietzke and M. L. Holt, Inorg. Syn., **3**, 163 (1950).
12. I. V. Vasil'kova, N. D. Zaitseva and P. S. Shapkin, *Russ. J. Inorg. Chem.*, **8**, 1237 (1963).
13. R. Colton, *Nature*, **193**, 872 (1962).
14. R. Colton, *Nature*, **194**, 374 (1962).
15. W. Geilmann, F. W. Wrigge and W. Biltz, *Z. anorg. allgem. Chem.*, **214**, 248 (1933).
16. J. M. Fletcher, W. E. Gardner, E. W. Hooper, K. R. Hyde, F. H. Moore and J. L. Woodhead, *Nature*, **199**, 1089 (1963).
17. N. I. Kolbin, I. N. Semenov and Y. M. Shutov, *Russ. J. Inorg. Chem.*, **8**, 1270 (1963).
18. F. Puche, *Ann. Chim. (Paris)*, **9**, 233 (1938).
19. W. E. Bell and M. Tagami, *J. Phys. Chem.*, **70**, 3736 (1966).
20. L. Wohler and S. Streicher, *Ber.*, **46**, 1591 (1913).
21. L. Capella and C. Schwab, *Compt. Rend.*, **260**, 4337 (1965).
22. I. V. Vinarov and N. P. Kromova, *Khim. Prom. Nauk Tekhn. Zhur.*, **1963**, 32.
23. H. Schafer and F. Kahlenberg, *Z. anorg. allgem. Chem.*, **305**, 326 (1960).
24. P. Sue, *Compt. Rend.*, **208**, 814 (1939).
25. P. Sue, *Bull. Soc. Chim. France (Memoirs)*, **6**, 831 (1939).
26. R. L. Graham and L. C. Hepler, *J. Phys. Chem.*, **63**, 727 (1959).
27. H. M. Neumann and N. C. Cooke, *J. Am. Chem. Soc.*, **79**, 3026 (1957).
28. A. V. Komandin and D. N. Tarasenkov, *J. Gen. Chem., USSR*, **10**, 1337 (1940).
29. C. M. Nelson, G. E. Boyd and W. T. Smith, *J. Am. Chem. Soc.*, **76**, 348 (1954).
30. C. J. Wolf, A. F. Clifford and W. H. Johnston, *J. Am. Chem. Soc.*, **79**, 4257 (1957).
31. R. Colton and R. H. Farthing, *Australian J. Chem.*, in the press.
32. H. Schafer and C. Pietruck, *Z. anorg. allgem. Chem.*, **267**, 174 (1951).
33. H. Funk and W. Weiss, *Z. anorg. allgem. Chem.*, **295**, 327 (1958).
34. M. Chaigneau, *Compt. Rend.*, **243**, 957 (1956).

35. H. Schafer, C. Grosser and L. Bayer, *Z. anorg. allgem. Chem.*, **265**, 258 (1951).
36. R. Colton, I. B. Tomkins and P. W. Wilson, *Australian J. Chem.*, **17**, 496 (1964).
37. D. Brown and R. Colton, *Nature*, **198**, 1300 (1963).
38. R. Colton and R. H. Farthing, *Australian J. Chem.*, in the press.
39. P. Machmer, *Chem. Commun.*, **1967**, 610.
40. M. A. Hepworth and P. L. Robinson, *J. Inorg. Nucl. Chem.*, **4**, 24 (1957).
41. Y. Saeki and T. Matsushima, *Denki Kagaku*, **32**, 667 (1964).
42. F. Fairbrother, A. H. Cowley and N. Scott, *J. Less-Common Metals*, **1**, 206 (1959).
43. R. Colton, unpublished observations.
44. O. W. Kolling, *Trans. Kansas Acad. Sci.*, **56**, 378 (1953).
45. H. Schafer, F. Schulte and R. Gruehn, *Angew. Chem.*, **76**, 536 (1964).
46. H. Schafer, E. Sibbing and R. Gerken, *Z. anorg. allgem. Chem.*, **307**, 163 (1961).
47. H. Schafer and E. Sibbing, *Z. anorg. allgem. Chem.*, **305**, 341 (1960).
48. S. A. Shchukarev, G. I. Novikov, A. V. Surorov and V. K. Maksimov, *Russ. J. Inorg. Chem.*, **4**, 935 (1959).
49. H. Schafer and J. Tillack, *J. Less-Common Metals*, **6**, 152 (1964).
50. A. Bruckl and K. Ziegler, *Ber.*, **65**, 916 (1932).
51. A. Cowley, F. Fairbrother and N. Scott, *J. Chem. Soc.*, **1958**, 3233.
52. H. L. Schlafer and H. W. Willie, *Z. anorg. allgem. Chem.*, **327**, 253 (1964).
53. E. M. Larson and J. J. Leddy, *J. Am. Chem. Soc.*, **78**, 5983 (1956).
54. B. Swaroop and S. N. Flengas, *Can. J. Chem.*, **42**, 1495 (1964).
55. C. H. Brubaker and R. C. Young, *J. Am. Chem. Soc.*, **74**, 3690 (1952).
56. R. E. McCarley and B. A. Torp, *Inorg. Chem.*, **2**, 540 (1963).
57. H. Schafer and L. Bayer, *Z. anorg. allgem. Chem.*, **277**, 140 (1954).
58. H. Schafer and C. Pietruck, *Z. anorg. allgem. Chem.*, **266**, 151 (1951).
59. P. Frere, *Ann. Chim. (Paris)*, **7**, 85 (1962).
60. H. Schafer and F. Kahlenberg, *Z. anorg. allgem. Chem.*, **305**, 178 (1960).
61. G. W. Watt and W. A. Baker, *J. Inorg. Nucl. Chem.*, **22**, 49 (1961).
62. *German Pat.* 903,034 (1954).
63. H. Schafer and L. Grau, *Z. anorg. allgem. Chem.*, **275**, 198 (1954).
64. S. A. Shchukarev and A. R. Kurbanov, *Izv. Akad. Nauk Tadzh. SSR, Otd. Geol. Khim. i Tekhn.-Nauk*, **1962**, 56.
65. R. E. McCarley and T. M. Brown, *Inorg. Chem.*, **3**, 1232 (1964).
66. R. Colton and R. L. Martin, *Nature*, **207**, 141 (1965).
67. R. Colton and I. B. Tomkins, *Australian J. Chem.*, **19**, 759 (1966).
68. W. E. Bell, M. C. Garrison and U. Merten, *J. Phys. Chem.*, **64**, 145 (1960).
69. U. Merten, W. E. Bell and J. D. Hale, *U.S.A.E.C. Report* T.A. 2512 (1961).
70. M. A. Oranskaya and N. A. Mikailova, *Russ. J. Inorg. Chem.*, **5**, 5 (1960).
71. J. Krustinsons, *Z. Elektrochem.*, **44**, 537 (1938).
72. S. A. Shchukarev, M. A. Oranskaya and T. S. Shemyakina, *Zh. Neorg. Khim.*, **1**, 17 (1956).
73. V. P. Kazakov and B. I. Peshchevitskii, *Radiokhimiya*, **4**, 509 (1962).
74. S. A. Shchukarev, M. A. Oranskaya and V. M. Tsintsius, *Zh. Neorg. Khim.*, **1**, 881 (1956).

75. *U.S. Pat.*, 2,953,433 (1960).
76. K. Uchimura and K. Funaki, *Denki Kagaku*, **33**, 163 (1965).
77. H. Schafer and K. D. Dohmann, *Z. anorg. allgem. Chem.*, **300**, 1 (1959).
78. H. Schafer, *Angew Chem.*, **67**, 748 (1955).
79. A. R. Kurbanov, A. V. Suvorov, S. A. Shchukarev and G. I. Novikov, *Russ. J. Inorg. Chem.*, **9**, 289 (1964).
80. S. A. Shchukarev, G. I. Novikov, I. V. Vasil'kova, A. V. Suvorov, N. V. Andreeva, B. N. Sharupin and A. K. Baev, *Russ. J. Inorg. Chem.*, **5**, 802 (1960).
81. S. Senderoff and A. Brenner, *J. Electrochem. Soc.*, **101**, 28 (1954).
82. S. A. Shchukarev, G. I. Novikov and N. V. Andreeva, Vestn. Leningr. Univ., **14**, *Ser. Fiz. i Khim.*, 120 **1959**.
83. D. E. Couch and A. Brenner, *J. Res. Nat. Bur. St.*, **63A**, 185 (1959).
84. I. E. Newnham and J. A. Watts, *J. Am. Chem. Soc.*, **82**, 2113 (1960).
85. V. Gutmann and H. Tannenberger, *Monatsh. Chem.*, **87**, 2769 (1956).
86. W. Biltz and C. Fendius, *Z. anorg. allgem. Chem.*, **172**, 385 (1928).
87. G. W. A. Fowles and J. L. Frost, *Chem. Commun.*, **1966**, 252.
88. R. F. Rolsten, *J. Phys. Chem.*, **62**, 126 (1958).
89. C. Durand, R. Schaal and P. Souchay, *Compt. Rend.*, **248**, 979 (1959).
90. K. Lindner and H. Helwig, *Z. anorg. allgem. Chem.*, **142**, 180 (1925).
91. H. A. Schaffer and E. F. Smith, *J. Am. Chem. Soc.*, **18**, 1098 (1896).
92. R. Colton, *J. Chem. Soc.*, **1962**, 2072.
93. S. A. Shchukarev, N. I. Kolbin and A. N. Ryabov, *Russ. J. Inorg. Chem.*, **5**, 923 (1960).
94. S. A. Shchukarev, N. I. Kolbin and A. N. Ryabov, *Vestn. Lenigr. Univ.*, **16**, *Ser. Fiz. i Khim.*, 100 (1961).
95. I. N. Semenov and N. I. Kolbin, *Russ. J. Inorg. Chem.*, **7**, 111 (1962).
96. N. V. Sidgwick, *The Chemical Elements and Their Compounds*, Oxford Univ. Press, London, 1950.
97. S. S. Berdonosov, A. V. Lapitskii, L. G. Vlasov and B. G. Berdonosova, *Russ. J. Inorg. Chem.*, **7**, 753 (1962).
98. W. C. Schumb and C. K. Morehouse, *J. Am. Chem. Soc.*, **69**, 2696 (1947).
99. W. K. van Haagen, *J. Am. Chem. Soc.*, **32**, 729 (1910).
100. S. A. Shchukarev, E. K. Smirnova, I. V. Vasil'kova and N. I. Borovkova, *Russ. J. Inorg. Chem.*, **7**, 625 (1962).
101. M. Chaigneau, *Compt. Rend.*, **248**, 3137 (1959).
102. W. M. Barr, *J. Am. Chem. Soc.*, **30**, 1668 (1908).
103. S. A. Shchukarev and G. A. Kokovin, *Russ. J. Inorg. Chem.*, **9**, 849 (1964).
104. R. Colton and I. B. Tomkins, *Australian J. Chem.*, in the press.
105. R. Colton and G. Wilkinson, *Chem. Ind.* (*London*), **1959**, 1314.
106. E. Amble, F. L. Miller, A. L. Schawlaw and C. H. Townes, *J. Chem. Phys.*, **20**, 192 (1952).
107. A. Bruckl and K. Ziegler, *Monatsh. Chem.*, **53**, 329 (1933).
108. M. Pourand and M. Chaigneau, *Compt. Rend.*, **249**, 2568 (1959).
109. H. L. Schlafer and H. Skoludek, *Z. anorg. allgem. Chem.*, **316**, 15 (1962).
110. S. S. Berdonosov, A. V. Lapitskii and L. G. Vlasov, *Russ. J. Inorg. Chem.*, **7**, 1125 (1962).
111. H. Schafer and K. D. Dohmann, *Z. anorg. allgem. Chem.*, **311**, 139 (1961).

112. H. Schafer, R. Gerken and H. Scholz, *Z. anorg. allgem. Chem.*, **335**, 96 (1965).
113. R. E. McCarley and T. M. Brown, *J. Am. Chem. Soc.*, **84**, 3216 (1962).
114. R. C. Young, *J. Am. Chem. Soc.*, **53**, 2148 (1931).
115. R. E. McCarley and J. C. Boatman, *Inorg. Chem.*, **4**, 1486 (1965).
116. C. H. Brubaker and R. C. Young, *J. Am. Chem. Soc.*, **73**, 4179 (1951).
117. S. S. Berdonosov, A. V. Lapitskii and L. G. Vlasov, *Vestn. Mosk. Univ. Ser. II, Khim.*, **18**, 57 (1963).
118. R. C. Young and T. J. Hastings, *J. Am. Chem. Soc.*, **64**, 1740 (1942).
119. S. S. Berdonosov and A. V. Lapitskii, *Russ. J. Inorg. Chem.*, **9**, 152 (1964).
120. I. V. Vasil'kova, A. E. Efimov and B. Z. Pitirimov, *Khim. Redkikh. Elementov, Leningr. Gos. Univ.*, **1964**, 44.
121. S. A. Shchukarev, T. A. Tolmacheva, M. A. Oranskaya and L. V. Komandroskaya, *Zh. Neorg. Kkim.*, **1**, 8 (1956).
122. B. Krause, A. B. Hook, F. Wawner and H. Rosenwasser, *Anal. Chem.*, **32**, 1210 (1960).
123. D. M. Chizhikov and A. M. Grin'ko, *Russ. J. Inorg. Chem.*, **4**, 444 (1959).
124. K. M. Alexander and F. Fairbrother, *J. Chem. Soc.*, **1949**, 2472.
125. R. F. Rolsten, *J. Am. Chem. Soc.*, **79**, 5409 (1957).
126. F. Korosy, *Technikai Kurir*, **9**, 81 (1938).
127. F. Korosy, *J. Am. Chem. Soc.*, **61**, 838 (1939).
128. R. F. Rolsten, *J. Am. Chem. Soc.*, **80**, 2952 (1958).
129. J. Lewis, D. J. Machin, R. S. Nyholm, P. Pauling and P. W. Smith, *Chem. Ind. (London)*, **1960**, 259.
130. G. R. Argue and J. J. Banewicz, *J. Inorg. Nucl. Chem.*, **25**, 923 (1963).
131. S. A. Shchukarev, T. A. Tolmacheva and G. N. Shavutskaya, *Russ. J. Inorg. Chem.*, **9**, 1351 (1964).
132. A. Weiss and A. Weiss, *Z. Naturforsch.*, **11b**, 605 (1956).
133. M. Chaigneau, *Bull. Chim. Soc. France*, **1957**, 886.
134. M. Chaigneau, *Compt. Rend.*, **242**, 263 (1956).
135. L. A. Nisel'son, M. V. Teslitskaya and T. A. Shvedova, *Russ. J. Inorg. Chem.*, **7**, 502 (1962).
136. L. A. Nisel'son and I. V. Petrusevich, *Russ. J. Inorg. Chem.*, **5**, 120 (1960).
137. F. I. Busol, *Zhur. Fiz. Khim.*, **33**, 799 (1959).
138. J. D. Fast, *Z. anorg. allgem. Chem.*, **239**, 145 (1938).
139. F. R. Sale and R. A. J. Shelton, *J. Less-Common Metals*, **9**, 64 (1965).
140. J. D. Corbett and P. W. Seabaugh, *J. Inorg. Nucl. Chem.*, **6**, 207 (1958).
141. P. W. Seabaugh and J. D. Corbett, *Inorg. Chem.*, **4**, 176 (1965).
142. F. Klanberg and H. W. Koholschutter, *Z. Naturforsch.*, **15b**, 616 (1960).
143. R. D. Peacock, A. J. E. Welch and L. F. Wilson, *J. Chem. Soc.*, **1958**, 2901.
144. H. Schafer and R. Gerken, *Z. anorg. allgem. Chem.*, **317**, 105 (1962).
145. H. Schafer and L. Zylka, *Z. anorg. allgem. Chem.*, **338**, 309 (1965).
146. I. S. Morozov and A. T. Simonich, *Russ. J. Inorg. Chem.*, **6**, 477 (1961).
147. I. S. Morozov and S. In'Chzhu, *Russ. J. Inorg. Chem.*, **4**, 307 (1959).
148. I. S. Morozov and S. In'Chzhu, *Russ. J. Inorg. Chem.*, **4**, 1176 (1959).
149. I. Zvara and L. K. Tarasov, *Russ. J. Inorg. Chem.*, **7**, 1388 (1962).
150. R. L. Lister and S. N. Flengas, *Can. J. Chem.*, **43**, 2947 (1965).
151. I. S. Morozov, B. G. Korshunov and A. T. Simonich, *Zh. Neorg. Khim.*, **1**, 1646 (1956).

152. S. A. Shchukarev, E. K. Smirnova and I. V. Vasil'kova, *Vestn. Leningr. Univ.*, **18**, *Ser. Fiz. i Khim.*, 132 (1963).
153. S. A. Shchukarev, T. S. Shemykina and E. K. Smirnova, *Russ. J. Inorg. Chem.*, **9**, 304 (1964).
154. E. K. Smirnova and I. V. Vasil'kova, *Vestn. Leningr. Univ.*, **19**, *Ser. Fiz. i Khim.*, 164 (1964).
155. I. S. Morozov and V. A. Krokhin, *Russ. J. Inorg. Chem.*, **8**, 1244 (1963).
156. B. G. Korshunov and V. V. Safonov, *Russ. J. Inorg. Chem.*, **6**, 285 (1961).
157. V. V. Safonov, B. G. Korshunov and Z. N. Shevtsova, *Russ. J. Inorg. Chem.*, **7**, 1021 (1962).
158. E. K. Smirnova and I. V. Vasil'kova, *Vestn. Leningr. Univ.*, **20**, *Ser. Fiz. i Khim.*, 161 (1965).
159. N. I. Kopylov, S. S. Novoselov, L. A. Yuzbak and A. A. Kashaev, *Russ. J. Inorg. Chem.*, **9**, 763 (1964).
160. V. V. Safonov, *Russ. J. Inorg. Chem.*, **10**, 359 (1965).
161. V. V. Safonov, B. G. Korshunov, Z. N. Shevtsova and S. I. Bakum, *Russ. J. Inorg. Chem.*, **9**, 914 (1964).
162. A. I. Efimov, L. P. Belorukova and A. M. Ryndina, *Russ. J. Inorg. Chem.*, **8**, 605 (1963).
163. A. I. Efimov, I. V. Vasil'kova, E. K. Smirnova, N. D. Zaitseva, T. S. Shemyakina and I. L. Perfilova, *Khim. Redkikh Elementov Leningr. Gos. Univ.*, **1964**, 38.
164. I. V. Vasil'kova and A. I. Efimov, *J. Gen. Chem. USSR*, **32**, 2699 (1962).
165. H. V. A. Briscoe, P. L. Robinson and C. M. Stoddart, *J. Chem. Soc.*, **1931**, 2263.
166. J. E. Drake and G. W. A. Fowles, *J. Less-Common Metals*, **3**, 149 (1961).
167. H. Funk, W. Weiss and K. P. Roethe, *Z. anorg. allgem. Chem.*, **301**, 271 (1959).
168. N. P. Lipatova and I. S. Morozov, *Russ. J. Inorg. Chem.*, **10**, 231 (1965).
169. R. F. Weinland and L. Storz, *Ber.*, **39**, 3057 (1906).
170. J. Dehand, J. Guechais and R. Rohmer, *Bull. Soc. Chim. France*, **1966**, 346.
171. E. A. Allen, B. J. Brisdon, D. A. Edwards, G. W. A. Fowles and R. G. Willaims, *J. Chem. Soc.*, **1963**, 4649.
172. W. Wardlaw and H. W. Webb, *J. Chem. Soc.*, **1930**, 2100.
173. R. Colton, *Australian J. Chem.*, **18**, 435 (1965).
174. W. T. Robinson, J. E. Fergusson and B. R. Penfold, *Proc. Chem. Soc.*, **1963**, 116.
175. J. A. Bertrand, F. A. Cotton and W. A. Dollase, *Inorg. Chem.*, **2**, 1166 (1963).
176. *Nouveau Traité de Chimie Minerale* (Ed. P. Pascal), Masson, Paris, **1966**, A, 1631.
177. G. W. A. Fowles and J. L. Frost, *J. Chem. Soc.*, **1966A**, 1631.
178. B. J. Brisdon and R. A. Walton, *J. Inorg. Nucl. Chem.*, **27**, 1101 (1965).
179. E. A. Allen, D. A. Edwards and G. W. A. Fowles, *Chem. Ind. (London)*, **1962**, 1026.
180. B. J. Brisdon and D. A. Edwards, *Chem. Commun.*, **1966**, 278.
181. D. M. Adams, J. Chatt, J. M. Davidson and J. Geratt, *J. Chem. Soc.* **1963**, 2189.
182. K. W. Bagnall and D. Brown, *J. Chem. Soc.*, **1964**, 3021.

183. K. W. Bagnall, D. Brown and J. G. H. Du Preez, *J. Chem. Soc.*, **1964**, 2603.
184. S. S. Sandhu, B. S. Chakkal and G. S. Sandhu, *J. Indian Chem. Soc.*, **37**, 329 (1960).
185. K. W. Bagnall, D. Brown and R. Colton, *J. Chem. Soc.*, **1964**, 3017.
186. J. P. Simon and P. Souchay, *Bull. Chim. Soc. France*, **1956**, 1402.
187. P. Klason, *Ber.*, **34**, 148 (1901).
188. I. Nordenskjold, *Ber.*, **34**, 1572 (1901).
189. E. Wendling, R. Rohmer and R. Weiss, *Compt. Rend.*, **256**, 1117 (1963).
190. W. R. Bucknall, S. R. Carter and W. Wardlaw, *J. Chem. Soc.*, **1927**, 512.
191. K. H. Lohmann and R. C. Young, *Inorg. Syn.*, **4**, 97 (1953).
192. R. G. James and W. Wardlaw, *J. Chem. Soc.*, **1927**, 2145.
193. F. Foerster and E. Fricke, *Angew. Chem.*, **38**, 458 (1923).
194. O. Collenburg, *Z. anorg. allgem. Chem.*, **102**, 247 (1918).
195. O. Collenburg and A. Guthe, *Z. anorg. allgem. Chem.*, **134**, 317 (1924).
196. H. B. Jonassen and S. Cantor, *Rec. Trav. chim.*, **75**, 609 (1956).
197. O. Olsson, *Ber.*, **46**, 566 (1913).
198. H. B. Jonassen, A. R. Tarsey, S. Cantor and G. F. Hetfrich, *Inorg. Syn.*, **5**, 139 (1957).
199. R. H. Busey, *U.S.A.E.C. Report*, ORNL 2782 (1959).
200. J. Dalziel, N. S. Gill, R. S. Nyholm and R. D. Peacock, *J. Chem. Soc.*, **1958**, 4012.
201. J. D. Eakins, D. G. Humphreys and C. E. Mellish, *J. Chem. Soc.*, **1963**, 6012.
202. F. Kraus and H. Steinfeld, *Chem. Ber.*, **64**, 2552 (1931).
203. F. Kraus and H. Dahlmann, *Chem. Ber.*, **65**, 877 (1932).
204. F. A. Cotton, N. F. Curtis, B. F. G. Johnson and W. R. Robinson, *Inorg. Chem.*, **4**, 326 (1965).
205. F. A. Cotton and C. B. Harris, *Inorg. Chem.*, **4**, 330 (1965).
206. S. Forcheri, V. Lungagnani, S. Martini and G. Sibona, *Energ. Nucl.* (*Milan*), **7**, 537 (1960).
207. J. L. Howe, *J. Am. Chem. Soc.*, **49**, 2381 (1927).
208. G. A. Rechnitz, *Inorg. Chem.*, **1**, 953 (1962).
209. L. L. Larson and C. S. Garner, *J. Am. Chem. Soc.*, **76**, 2180 (1954).
210. F. P. Dwyer and J. W. Hogarth, *Proc. Roy. Soc. N.S. Wales*, **84**, 194 (1951).
211. *British Pat.*, 879,074 (1959).
212. N. G. Klyuchnikov and R. N. Savel'eva, *Zhur. Neorg. Khim.*, **1**, 2764 (1956).
213. J. L. Woodhead and J. M. Fletcher, *U.K.A.E.A. Res. Report*, R-4123.
214. F. P. Dwyer, R. S. Nyholm and L. E. Rogers, *Proc. Roy. Soc. N.S. Wales*, **81**, 267 (1947).
215. F. P. Dwyer and R. S. Nyholm, *Nature*, **160**, 502 (1947).
216. A. Sabatini and I. Bertini, *Inorg. Chem.*, **5**, 204 (1966).
217. G. K. Schweitzer and D. L. Wilhelm, *J. Inorg. Nucl. Chem.*, **3**, 1 (1956).
218. J. L. Howe, *J. Am. Chem. Soc.*, **26**, 942 (1904).
219. R. Gilchrist, *J. Res. Nat. Bur. St.*, **9**, 279 (1932).
220. A. Gutbier, *Ber.*, **46**, 2098 (1913).
221. A. Gutbier and A. Krell, *Ber.*, **38**, 2385 (1905).
222. E. Biilmann and A. C. Anderson, *Ber.*, **36**, 1565 (1903).

223. H. Stammreich and R. Forneris, *Spectrochim. Acta*, **16**, 363 (1960).
224. A. Sabatini, L. Sacconi and V. Schettino, *Inorg. Chem.*, **3**, 1775 (1964).
225. J. E. Fergusson, B. H. Robinson and W. R. Roper, *J. Chem. Soc.*, **1962**, 2113.
226. G. A. Shagisultanova, *Russ. J. Inorg. Chem.*, **6**, 904 (1961).
227. H. V. A. Briscoe, P. L. Robinson and A. J. Rudge, *J. Chem. Soc.*, **1931**, 3218.
228. E. Fenn, R. S. Nyholm, P. G. Owston and A. Turco, *J. Inorg. Nucl. Chem.* **17**, 387 (1961).
229. J. W. Mellor, *A Comprehensive Treatise on Inorganic and Theoretical Chemistry*, Longmans, London, 1936.
230. A. Zalkin and D. E. Sands, *Acta Cryst.*, **11**, 615 (1958).
231. D. E. Sands and A. Zalkin, *Acta Cryst.*, **12**, 723 (1959).
232. S. S. Berdonosov, A. V. Lapitskii, D. G. Berdonosova and L. G. Vlasov, *Russ. J. Inorg. Chem.*, **8**, 1315 (1963).
233. J. H. Canterford, R. Colton and I. B. Tomkins, *Australian J. Chem.*, in the press.
234. H. Hartung, *Z. Chem.*, **4**, 232 (1964).
235. H. Hess and H. Hartung, *Z. anorg. Chem.*, **344**, 157 (1966).
236. L. A. Dahl and D. L. Wampler, *Acta Cryst.*, **15**, 903 (1962).
237. A. McL. Mathieson, D. P. Mellor and N. C. Stephenson, *Acta Cryst.*, **5**, 185 (1952).
238. J. C. Morrow, *Acta Cryst.*, **15**, 851 (1962).
239. R. Colton and G. G. Rose, *Australian J. Chem.*, in the press.
240. D. E. Sands, A. Zalkin and R. E. Elson, *Acta Cryst.*, **12**, 21 (1959).
241. D. A. Edwards, *J. Inorg. Nucl. Chem.*, **25**, 1198 (1963).
242. F. A. Cotton and C. B. Harris, *Inorg. Chem.*, **6**, 376 (1967).
243. L. A. Woodward and M. J. Ware, *Spectrochim. Acta*, **20**, 711 (1963).
244. A. D. Westland, *Can. J. Chem.*, **38**, 1800 (1960).
245. A. D. Westland and N. C. Bhiwandker, *Can. J. Chem.*, **39**, 2353 (1961).
246. A. D. Westland and N. C. Bhiwandker, *Can. J. Chem.*, **39**, 1284 (1961).
247. J. Chatt, L. A. Duncanson and L. M. Venanzi, *J. Chem. Soc.*, **1955**, 4456.
248. D. P. Craig, A. Maccoll, R. S. Nyholm, L. E. Orgel and L. E. Sutton, *J. Chem. Soc.*, **1954**, 332.
249. I. M. Sheiko, R. V. Chernov and V. S. Kikhno, *Ukr. Khim. Zh.*, **27**, 469 (1961).
250. P. A. Polishchuk, *Russ. J. Inorg. Chem.*, **9**, 80 (1964)
251. H. Schafer, H. G. Schnering, K. J. Niehues and H. G. Nieder-Vahrenholz, *J. Less-Common Metals*, **9**, 95 (1965).
252. V. I. Konstantinov and P. H. Ts'ui, *Russ. J. Inorg. Chem.*, **8**, 23 (1963).
253. T. S. Shemyakina, E. K. Smirnova, T. I. Popova and V. M. Kuptsova, *Russ. J. Inorg. Chem.*, **9**, 1291 (1964).
254. L. A. Woodward and J. A. Creighton, *Spectrochim. Acta*, **17**, 594 (1961).
255. L. A. Woodward and M. J. Ware, *Spectrochim. Acta*, **19**, 775 (1963).
256. D. Nakamura, Y. Kurita, K. Ito and M. Kubo, *J. Am. Chem. Soc.*, **82** 5783 (1960).
257. K. Ito, D. Nakamura, Y. Kurita, K. Ito and M. Kubo, *J. Am. Chem. Soc.*, **83**, 4526 (1961).
258. D. Nakamura, K. Ito and M. Kubo, *J. Am. Chem. Soc.*, **84**, 163 (1962).

259. K. Ito, D. Nakamura, K. Ito and M. Kubo, *Inorg. Chem.*, **2**, 690 (1963).
260. R. Ikeda, D. Nakamura and M. Kubo, *J. Phys. Chem.*, **69**, 2101 (1965).
261. R. Ikeda, D. Nakamura and M. Kubo, *Bull. Soc. Chem. Japan*, **36**, 1056 (1963).
262. C. H. Townes and B. P. Dailey, *J. Chem. Phys.*, **17**, 783 (1949).
263. B. P. Dailey and C. H. Townes, *J. Chem. Phys.*, **23**, 118 (1955).
264. B. P. Dailey, *Discussions Far. Soc.*, **19**, 255 (1955).
265. F. A. Cotton and C. B. Harris, *Proc. Nat. Acad. Sci. U.S.*, **56**, 12 (1966).
266. J. Owen, *Discussions Far. Soc.*, **19**, 127 (1955).
267. J. H. E. Griffiths and J. Owen, *Proc. Roy. Soc.*, **226A**, 96 (1954).
268. J. H. E. Griffiths, J. Owen and I. M. Ward, *Proc. Roy. Soc.*, **219A**, 526 (1953).
269. R. O. Rahn and P. B. Dorain, *J. Chem. Phys.*, **41**, 3249 (1964).
270. H. Kon and N. E. Sharpless, *J. Phys. Chem.*, **70**, 105 (1966).

Chapter 3

Cluster Compounds

In recent years there has been a remarkable growth of knowledge about, and a continuing interest in, metal–metal bonding. Owing to their comparatively large sizes, atoms of the second- and third-row transition elements have been particularly prominent in this connexion. One type of metal–metal interaction which has received an enormous amount of attention in the last few years has been the formation of the so-called cluster compounds. For the purposes of this chapter, we define a cluster compound as a discrete unit containing at least three transition-metal atoms in which strong metal–metal bonding is present. This definition excludes entities such as the $[Re_2Cl_8]^{2-}$ ion, although this is held together solely by metal–metal bonds; compounds of this type are discussed in chapter 7. Cluster compounds are, of course, not confined to halide chemistry; they have been found in oxide and alkoxide systems, and are particularly common among organometallic compounds of the transition metals. However, these classes are outside the scope of this book and the reader is referred to more general discussions of clusters such as the comprehensive review by Cotton[1].

Cluster compounds have a curious history. It has been known for a considerable time that some of the lower halides of niobium and tantalum contain cations of the type $[M_6X_{12}]^{2+}$ and that molybdenum dihalides are hexameric, containing $[Mo_6X_8]^{4+}$ cations. These clusters, however, attracted little attention for many years, possibly partly because, when anhydrous, they are insoluble and rather intractable.

In 1963 the trimeric nature of the $Re_3Cl_{12}^{3-}$ ion was discovered and since that time a large number of rhenium compounds have been shown to be trimeric. At the same time there has been more intensive study of the previously known cluster systems. Although the three major types of cluster to be considered in this chapter are the rhenium trimers and the hexamers of the niobium and molybdenum groups, other systems such as the platinum halides and clusters of the type M_3Cl_8 are known, and no doubt others will be discovered.

Schafer and Schnering[2] have introduced a convenient notation to describe the structures of cluster compounds. For example, hexameric molybdenum dichloride is written as $[Mo_6Cl_8]Cl_2Cl_{4/2}$, which indicates that the compound consists of a basic Mo_6Cl_8 cluster with two terminal chlorine atoms and four bridging chlorine atoms; each bridging atom is shared between two clusters, filling the six coordination sites on the Mo_6Cl_8 unit. Nb_3Cl_8 is written as $[Nb_3Cl_4]Cl_{6/2}Cl_{3/3}$, indicating a Nb_3Cl_4 core with six chlorine atoms each bridging between two clusters and three chlorine atoms each bridging between three Nb_3Cl_4 units, thus giving the overall stoichiometry of Nb_3Cl_8.

TRINUCLEAR RHENIUM COMPOUNDS

A considerable number of compounds containing a triangular cluster of rhenium atoms in the trivalent state is now known. Almost all the structural work on this interesting class of compounds has been done either by Cotton and his group or by Penfold, Fergusson, and their coworkers.

The basic unit is undoubtedly the Re_3X_9 group (where $X = Cl$ or Br). In this unit each rhenium atom has one coordination site vacant and usually further ligands are found coordinated in this position. These ligands may be terminal halogen atoms, as in $[Re_3Cl_{12}]^{3-}$, inter-cluster bridging atoms as in rhenium trichloride, or normal donor ligands such as phosphines or pyridine. The New Zealand group has beautifully demonstrated that not all the terminal positions need be occupied, and that when vacancies occur there is a significant distortion of the metal triangle.

Probably the most impressive structure in this series is that of rhenium trichloride where the clusters themselves are arranged in groups of six. Rhenium trichloride is undoubtedly the parent compound of this whole class, and indeed all the trinuclear rhenium clusters are prepared directly from the trihalides. However, we believe the structural principles involved in these compounds are most easily illustrated by first considering the monomeric anionic clusters.

Preparations and Structures

Caesium tri-μ-chlorononachlorotrirhenate(III). The compound with the empirical formula $CsReCl_4$ is prepared by mixing hydrochloric acid solutions of caesium chloride and rhenium trichloride. It was the first trinuclear rhenium(III) cluster to be examined by X-ray diffraction techniques, and its structure was reported independently and almost simultaneously by both of the groups who have dominated this field[3-5].

The crystals are orthorhombic with $a = 14.06$, $b = 14.00$ and $c = 10.69$ Å. The space group is *Ama*2 and there are twelve formula units in the cell. The compound is trimeric and should be formulated as $Cs_3[Re_3Cl_{12}]$.

The structure of the anion is shown in Figure 3.1. It consists of an equilateral triangle of rhenium atoms, each pair being bridged by a

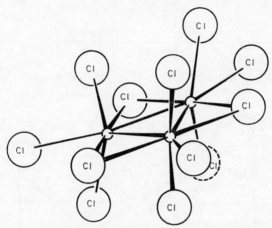

Figure 3.1 Perspective view of the $[Re_3Cl_{12}]^{3-}$ anion. Large circles represent chlorine atoms, small circles represent rhenium atoms.

chlorine atom in the plane of the metal triangle. Also in this plane there is a terminal chlorine on each rhenium atom; the orientation of this non-bridging chlorine–rhenium bond is directly away from the centre of the metal triangle. The remaining two non-bridging chlorines bonded to each rhenium atom are placed symmetrically above and below the plane of the metal triangle. Although it is not a crystallographic requirement, the $[Re_3Cl_{12}]^{3-}$ anion has D_{3h} symmetry within experimental error.

The important dimensions in the trinuclear cluster are given in Table 3.1, these values being taken from the refined data of Cotton's group.

TABLE 3.1

Dimensions in the $[Re_3Cl_{12}]^{3-}$ Anion

Distance	Value (Å)
Re–Re	2.477
Re–Cl (bridge)	2.39
Re–Cl (terminal, in plane)	2.52
Re–Cl (terminal, out of plane)	2.359

There are several important features to note in this structure. The rhenium–rhenium distance is very short compared with the interatomic distance in rhenium metal (2.65 Å), suggesting that strong metal–metal bonding contributes to the stability of the system: this will be discussed further in the section on bonding in these clusters. The bridging rhenium–chlorine and the terminal out-of-plane rhenium–chlorine bonds appear to

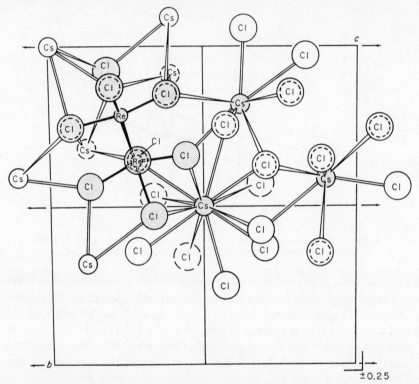

Figure 3.2 A projection of the crystal structure of $Cs_3Re_3Cl_{12}$ showing the packing of the ions.

be normal in length, but the bonds to the terminal chlorine atoms in the plane of the metal triangle are distinctly longer. This suggests somewhat weaker bonding to these chlorine atoms, an idea confirmed by chemical reactions to be described below.

The manner in which the anions are packed in the lattice is shown in Figure 3.2.

Caesium   tri-μ-bromononabromotrirhenate(III).   The   salt   of   empirical formula $CsReBr_4$ has only been briefly mentioned as being one of the products of the interaction of caesium bromide and rhenium tribromide in hydrobromic acid solution[6]. It is orthorhombic with $a = 11.1$, $b = 14.60$ and $c = 14.6$ Å. The space group and cell dimensions are similar to those of $Cs_3Re_3Cl_{12}$ and it is assumed to be isostructural with this compound[7].

Tetraphenylarsonium tri-μ-chlorooctachlorotrirhenate(III). The compound $[(C_6H_5)_4As]_2Re_3Cl_{11}$ is prepared by adding tetraphenylarsonium chloride to a solution of rhenium trichloride in ethanol saturated with gaseous hydrogen chloride[8]. The crystal structure has been determined

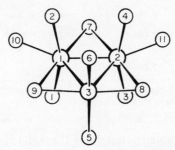

Figure 3.3 An idealized drawing of the $[Re_3Cl_{11}]^{2-}$ anion. Thick circles represent Re and thin circles Cl atoms.

by Penfold and Robinson's X-ray diffraction studies of a single crystal. The compound is triclinic with $a = 12.01$, $b = 26.22$, $c = 9.87$ Å, $\alpha = 88.5°$, $\beta = 66.2°$ and $\gamma = 105.4°$. The space group is $P\bar{1}$ and there are two molecular units in the cell.

The structure of the anion is shown in Figure 3.3. The basic unit is the same as in the $[Re_3Cl_{12}]^{3-}$ ion, except that one of the terminal in-plane chlorine atoms is absent. The halogen-deficient rhenium atom causes a slight, but significant, distortion of the triangular framework as shown by the variation in the metal–metal distances:

Re(1)–Re(2)	2.483 Å
Re(2)–Re(3)	2.431 Å
Re(3)–Re(1)	2.438 Å

There are also some differences in the angle between the two terminal chlorines on each rhenium as shown in Table 3.2. The remaining internuclear distances in this cluster are normal for rhenium(III) clusters and they are compared with those from other clusters in Table 3.2.

Although there is no crystallographic requirement of symmetry for the anion, it does possess C_{2v} symmetry within the limits of experimental error.

TABLE 3.2

Comparison of Rhenium Trinuclear Cluster Distances and Angles

Compound	Re–Re	Re–X bridge	Re–X t.o.p.	Re–X t.i.p.	Re–X–Re bridge	X–Re–X terminal
$Cs_3Re_3Cl_{12}$	2.477	2.39	2.359	2.52		
$(Ph_4As)_2Re_3Cl_{11}$	2.483 2.435[a]	2.35	2.30	2.56	63°	158° 153°[a]
$Cs_2Re_3Br_{11}$	2.496 2.433[a]	2.55	2.47	2.72	59.4° 56.7°[a]	159.7° 133.7°[a]
Re_3Br_9 (in $M_2Re_4Br_{15}$)	2.46	2.55	2.45	—	58.0°	155°
Re_3Cl_9	2.489	2.46	2.29 2.40[b]	2.66[b]	60.7° 62.4°	162.9°[b] 157.8°
$Re_3Cl_9[P(C_6H_5)(C_2H_5)_2]_3$	2.48	2.39	2.36	—		

t.o.p. = terminal, out-of-plane. t.i.p. = terminal, in-plane.
[a] Involves halogen-deficient rhenium atoms.
[b] Involved in inter-cluster bridging.

There is a plane of symmetry containing the metal atoms and the bridging chlorines, and another at right angles to the first, containing Re(3) and chlorines(5), (6) and (7) (Figure 3.3).

The packing of the ions in the crystal lattice is shown in Figure 3.4.

Caesium tri-μ-bromooctabromotrirhenate(III). The similar compound $Cs_2Re_3Br_{11}$ was prepared simply by mixing hydrobromic acid solutions of caesium bromide and rhenium tribromide[6].

The crystal structure of this compound has been determined by Elder and Penfold[9]. The anion, $Re_3Br_{11}^{2-}$, has a configuration similar to that of $Re_3Cl_{11}^{2-}$; there is similar distortion of the metal triangle, but in this case the closing of the angle between the two out-of-plane bromine atoms on the bromine-deficient rhenium is far more pronounced. Usually this angle is in the range 155–160° for the non-deficient rhenium atom (see Table 3.2), but in this compound it is reduced to 133°.

The packing of the anions in $Cs_2Re_3Br_{11}$ is shown in Figure 3.5.

Tri-μ-bromoheptabromotrirhenates(III). These compounds have been isolated by adding the bromide of large cations, such as triphenylarsonium or caesium, to solutions of rhenium tribromide in hydrobromic acid[6].

An excess of pyridine reacts with $[(C_6H_5)_3PH]Re_3Br_{10}$ to give $Re_3Br_9(py)_3$, but with smaller amounts of pyridine the complex $[(C_6H_5)_3PH]Re_3Br_{10}(py)_2$ may be obtained. There is no direct structural evidence available so far to prove that these compounds contain trinuclear clusters, but very strong evidence to this effect is provided by the method of preparation, the

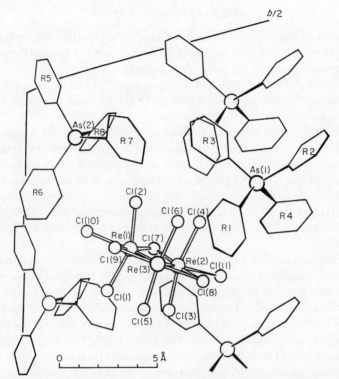

Figure 3.4 The crystal structure of [(C₆H₅)₄As₂]Re₃Cl₁₁ viewed perpendicular to (OO1) showing the environment of the anion.

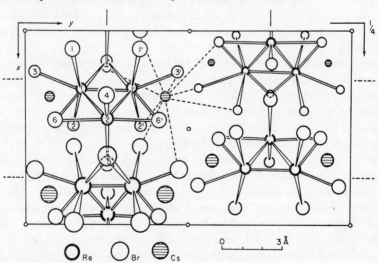

Figure 3.5 The Cs₂Re₃Br₁₁ structure as viewed down the c-axis.

similarity of their spectra to those of established clusters (to be discussed below) and the fact that $[(C_6H_5)_3PH]Re_3Br_{10}$ is a 1:1 electrolyte in nitrobenzene and has half the calculated molecular weight[6].

The unit-cell parameters tentatively assigned[6] to $CsRe_3Br_{10}$ have since been shown[7] to belong to $Cs_3Re_3Br_{12}$, the error arising because a number of products are formed in the reaction.

Trirhenium tri-μ-bromohexabromide. Reaction[10] of the bromides of several large cations such as quinolinium, pyridinium or tetraethylammonium with rhenium tribromide in hydrobromic acid leads to compounds of the type $M_2[Re_4Br_{15}]$. These are difficult to obtain pure because, as will be shown below, they contain rhenium atoms in oxidation states III and IV. If no oxidation occurs, complexes of the type $M_2Re_3Br_{11}$ are obtained; on the other hand, the extent of oxidation must be strictly controlled.

A single-crystal X-ray diffraction study has revealed a remarkable structure, consisting of equal numbers of discrete trirhenium tri-μ-bromohexabromide units, Re_3Br_9, and hexabromorhenate(IV) ions, together with quinolinium cations[10]. The Re_3Br_9 groups are the final stage of the gradual loss of the in-plane terminal bromine atoms. In this case, all the rhenium atoms are halogen-deficient and the metal triangle reverts to a regular configuration. There is, however, a significant decrease in the metal–metal distance compared with that in the non-deficient clusters (see Table 3.2). It should be carefully noted that the Re_3Br_9 group occurring in this compound is not the same as the Re_3X_9 groups occurring in rhenium trichloride and tribromide; in the latter compounds there are inter-cluster bridging halogens and, as a result, none of the rhenium atoms is halogen-deficient.

Rhenium trichloride. Rhenium trichloride is prepared by thermal decomposition of rhenium pentachloride in a nitrogen stream[11]. Two forms of rhenium trichloride may be prepared, which differ in their magnetic properties, although X-ray powder diffraction patterns are identical for the two forms[12]. The crystal structure of the high-temperature form of rhenium trichloride has been determined by Cotton and Mague[13,14]. The compound is hexagonal with $a = 10.33$ and $c = 20.36$ Å. The space group is $R\bar{3}m$ and there are eighteen formula units in the cell.

The structure contains no halogen-deficient rhenium atoms. The in-plane terminal chlorines, and one of the out-of-plane chlorine atoms on each rhenium atom are used to bridge to a neighbouring cluster. Thus, there is no discrete Re_3Cl_9 entity in the structure. The Re_3Cl_9 cluster in rhenium trichloride is shown with part of one of its neighbours in Figure 3.6. The unit is joined to the next cluster by bridging through its in-plane chlorine, $Cl_{(4)}$, and by one of its out-of-plane chlorines, $Cl_{(1)}$. The other two rhenium atoms are likewise bound to adjoining clusters by means of $Cl'_{(1)}$, $Cl''_{(1)}$, $Cl'_{(4)}$ and $Cl''_{(4)}$. It should be noted that the $Cl_{(1)}$ in one cluster is the $Cl_{(4)}$ of its neighbour and *vice versa*. The $Cl_{(2)}$ set of terminal halogens is not used in any inter-cluster bridging. So, for the first time,

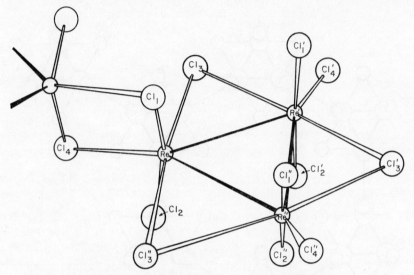

Figure 3.6　The Re_3Cl_9 cluster in rhenium trichloride.

the two out-of-plane halogens are not equivalent. This type of inter-cluster bridging results in the formation of infinite lamina perpendicular to the *c*-axis. A section of one of these is shown in Figure 3.7.

Most of the dimensions of the Re_3Cl_9 unit are very similar to those of the other trinuclear rhenium clusters and the actual values are given in Table 3.2. The important modifications to the usual arrangement are the different environments of the out-of-plane halogens and the marked increase in the already long bond distance from rhenium to the in-plane halogen. Thus it may be concluded that one of the bonds to each inter-cluster bridging chlorine atom is very long and hence presumably rather weak. This is in accord with the observed solubility of rhenium trichloride in donor solvents. As will be shown below, the spectra of these solutions provide very strong evidence that the Re_3Cl_9 unit is retained; presumably the compound exists in solution as $Re_3Cl_9(solvate)_3$ with the solvate molecules in the in-plane terminal positions. Many adducts of rhenium trichloride of the general type $Re_3Cl_9 \cdot L_3$ (where L is a donor molecule) have been prepared, and in one case the structure has been determined and confirms the above suggestion.

Solutions of rhenium tribromide show a spectrum quite similar to that of rhenium trichloride, suggesting the presence of Re_3Br_9 clusters; but the halides are not isomorphous[15].

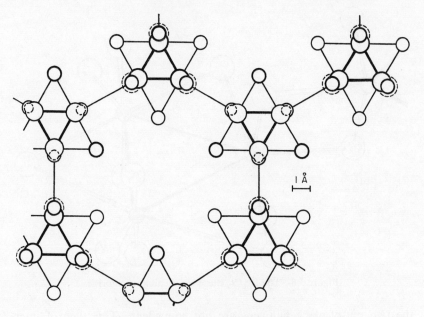

Figure 3.7   A section of the Re_3Cl_9 lattice.

The remarkable stability of the trinuclear unit in both rhenium trichloride and rhenium tribromide has been demonstrated by mass-spectrometric examinations[16,17]. The more detailed study by Buchler and his coworkers[16] showed that the parent ion, $Re_3X_9^+$, was by far the greatest peak in the mass spectrum. Furthermore, although there is a considerable difference in the heats of formation of rhenium trichloride and tribromide (-189 kcal mole^{-1} and -118 kcal mole^{-1}, respectively), their heats of sublimation are almost identical at 48 kcal mole^{-1}, suggesting that the intercluster bonding is similar in the two compounds. The fact, noted above, that the compounds are not isostructural may be merely a reflection of different packing arrangements in the two compounds.

Tris(diethylphenylphosphine) tri-μ-chlorohexachlorotrirhenium(III).   The compound of empirical formula $ReCl_3 \cdot P(C_6H_5)(C_2H_5)_2$ is readily prepared by mixing hot solutions of the phosphine and rhenium trichloride in dimethylformamide and allowing the mixture to cool slowly[18].

The crystal structure has been determined by Cotton and Mague[19]. The crystals are cubic with $a = 20.53$ Å with space group *Pa*3. The compound is trimeric and the structure consists of the usual triangular arrangement of rhenium atoms. The phosphines occupy the terminal in-plane positions as shown in Figure 3.8. The interatomic distances are given in Table 3.2.

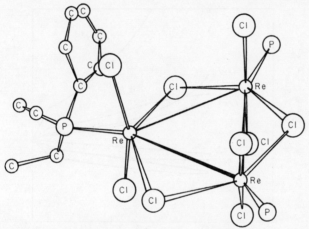

Figure 3.8   A perspective view of the $Re_3Cl_9[P(C_2H_5)_2C_6H_5]_3$ molecule.

The corresponding bromo compound is isomorphous with it and so may be assumed to have the same structure.

Bonding

The bonding in the rhenium trinuclear clusters has been discussed by Fergusson and coworkers[20] in terms of valence-bond theory. Martin and Colton[21] have given an elementary treatment of the system by the molecular-orbital approach, but Cotton and Haas[22] have provided the most detailed treatment of the system so far reported, also using the molecular-orbital approach. Although it is true that all three treatments explain the strong metal–metal bonding in the clusters, only the description by Cotton and Haas makes any attempt to place the treatment on a semiquantitative basis.

Cotton and Haas[22] note that each metal atom in every metal cluster is in a slightly distorted square-planar arrangement, and that it is merely different arrangements of these units which lead to the different stereochemistries found in clusters. Furthermore, they point out that each metal atom in each cluster is able to coordinate one additional ligand. They therefore assume that in the rhenium cluster the metal uses its $6s$, $6p_x$, $6p_y$ and $5d_{x^2-y^2}$ orbitals to bond to the four chlorine atoms around the metal (for a typical example, see Figure 3.6). They then make the assumption that the p_z- and d_{z^2}-orbitals on the metal atoms do not hydridize and that the orbital directed to the centre of the triangle is d_{z^2}. Obviously this assumption cannot be completely true, but Cotton and Haas show that it has no drastic effect on the final molecular-orbital distribution. The three d_{z^2}

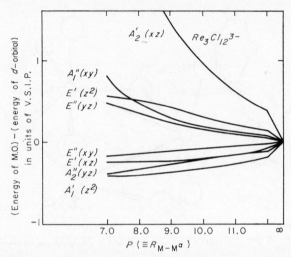

Figure 3.9   Molecular-orbital energy-level diagram for an M_3X_{12} system.

metal orbitals interact to form the σ-framework of the triangle, and the remaining d-orbitals (d_{xy}, d_{yz}, d_{zx}) interact to form the π-system. It should be noted that any π-interaction with the bridging halogen atoms is ignored.

The resultant molecular-orbital diagram is shown in Figure 3.9 where the orbital separations are plotted as a function of the metal–metal interaction. It will be seen that the molecular orbitals fall nicely into two groups, the bonding and the antibonding orbitals, independently of the strength of the metal–metal interaction. In the rhenium(III) trimers there are twelve metal electrons which just fill the bonding molecular orbitals, thus giving a natural explanation of the diamagnetism of the system. Since there are twelve bonding electrons between three metal contacts the bond order between the metal atoms is two.

Other Rhenium(III) Trimeric Complexes

A considerable number of rhenium(III) complexes have been prepared by direct interaction of the appropriate ligand with the trihalide in an inert solvent. Some of these complexes were prepared before the trimeric nature of the halides themselves was established, and it was therefore not realised that the adducts could be trimeric. Although direct structural evidence is not yet available for these compounds, it is apparent from their chemical reactions, and particularly from their absorption spectra (see below), that they are all trimeric. A few of these compounds are given in Table 3.3: this list is not exhaustive and merely serves to illustrate the wide variety of ligands that may substitute rhenium trichloride without destroying the trinuclear cluster. The corresponding bromide compounds are known in most cases.

TABLE 3.3

Trinuclear Rhenium Compounds

Compound	Colour	Ref.
$Re_3Cl_9[(C_6H_5)_3P]_3$	Purple	23
$Re_3Cl_9(C_5N_5N)_3$	Green	23
$Re_3Cl_9[(C_6H_5)_3PO]_3$	Red	23
$Re_3Cl_9[(C_6H_5)_2SO]_3$	Brown	23
$Re_3Cl_9(CH_3CN)_3$	Purple	24
$Re_3Cl_9(bipy)_{1.5}$	Purple	24
$Cs_3Re_3Cl_9(NO_3)_3$	Red	25
$[Re_3Cl_3(CNS)_9]^{3-}$	Brown green	26

Most of the rhenium(III) clusters can be considered to be derived either from the $[Re_3Cl_{12}]^{3-}$ ion by exchange of the labile in-plane halogen atoms, or by cleavage of the inter-cluster bridges in rhenium trichloride itself. That this is reasonable has been demonstrated by Robinson and Fergusson[26] who studied the rate of exchange of chlorine atoms in the $[Re_3Cl_{12}]^{3-}$ anion in hydrochloric acid solution labelled with ^{36}Cl. They showed that three chlorine atoms in $[Re_3Cl_{12}]^{3-}$ exchange rapidly, six others exchange more slowly, and the remaining three are completely inert to exchange. These three types of chlorine atom in $[Re_3Cl_{12}]^{3-}$ are readily identified as the in-plane halogens, the terminal out-of-plane halogens and the bridging halogens, respectively.

In almost all their reactions, rhenium trichloride and rhenium tribromide give derivatives that retain the trinuclear arrangement, although there are a few circumstances under which the clusters are degraded. Cotton and Lippard[27] have shown that rhenium tribromide may be oxidized in hydrobromic acid merely by heating it for some time on a water bath with free access of air. The nature and proportions of the products that may be isolated depend rather critically upon the nature of the cations added to the system. However, in general, the products are salts of the monomeric hexabromorhenate(IV) anion and the oxotetrabromorhenate(V) anion.

Bailey and McIntyre[28] have examined the spectrum of rhenium trichloride in certain melts. They found it to be stable in molten dimethyl sulphone, but in the presence of added chloride ion partial breakdown to the octachlorodirhenate(III) ion, $[Re_2Cl_8]^{2-}$, occurred. This is the only method so far reported of converting a rhenium(III) trimer into a corresponding member of the dimer series. On the other hand, in the LiCl–KCl eutectic melt, rhenium trichloride disproportionates to rhenium metal and the hexachlororhenate(IV) anion[28].

Spectra

It is not yet possible to give a full assignment to the visible spectra of the rhenium(III) complexes. However, all those cluster compounds examined so far show two bands in the visible region of the spectrum. Usually these bands occur between 500 and 550 mμ and between 750 and 800 mμ. Their relative intensities are somewhat variable but are usually in the range 2:1 or 3:1, respectively, for the chloro complexes. The intensity of the band at 550 mμ in the bromo complexes is difficult to assess as it usually appears as a shoulder on a large charge-transfer band[23].

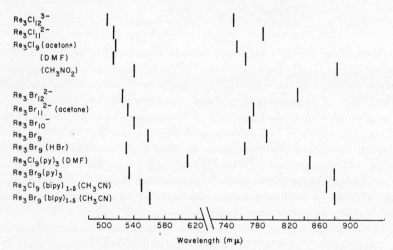

Figure 3.10 Characteristic absorption spectra of some rhenium(III) clusters.

The positions of the two major bands for a number of rhenium trinuclear clusters are given in Figure 3.10, from which several general points can be seen. The position of the band at about 800 mμ is more variable than that of the band at shorter wavelengths. There is a definite trend in the positions of the bands in the series $[Re_3Br_{12}]^{3-}$, $[Re_3Br_{11}]^{2-}$ and

$[Re_3Br_{10}]^-$, but the position of the low-energy band of the Re_3Br_9 group in the $[Re_4Br_{15}]^{2-}$ compounds does not follow this trend. The two thiocyanato complexes, $[Re_3Cl_3(CNS)_9]^{3-}$ and $[Re_3Cl_3(CNS)_8]^{2-}$, show enormous shifts of both bands towards longer wavelengths, the bands occurring at about 600 and 970 mμ[26]. A similar, but much smaller, shift is also observed for a few other complexes such as the pyridine and nitrile compounds. It can be reasonably suggested that in these complexes some interaction is occurring between the π-systems of the metal and the ligands.

Possible Analogous Trinuclear Systems

There is no reason to suppose that trinuclear compounds of the type just discussed need be restricted to rhenium(III). There are a few other systems whose magnetic and spectral properties can be best explained on the basis of structures containing trinuclear clusters, but it must be stressed that so far direct structural evidence is not yet available for these compounds.

Rhenium tetrachloride. Rhenium tetrachloride is prepared by the action of thionyl chloride on pure rhenium dioxide[29]. The compound prepared in this way is amorphous and thermally unstable. Its magnetic susceptibility is anomalously low[30] and has lately been rationalized on the basis of a trinuclear structure[21]. Rhenium(IV) has a d^3-configuration, so if a trinuclear cluster, Re_3Cl_{12}, of the same geometry as $[Re_3Cl_{12}]^{3-}$ is envisaged, the same molecular orbital scheme (Figure 3.9) can be used. The nine electrons will occupy $(A_1')^2$, $(A_2'')^2$, $(E')^4$ and $(E'')^1$, giving, as a result, one unpaired electron per trimer, or $\frac{1}{3}$ electron per rhenium atom. The magnetic moment of rhenium tetrachloride is in fact 1.00 B.M. ($\frac{1}{3}$ of the "spin only" value for a single electron) per rhenium atom, independent of temperature[21]. Additional support for the trinuclear suggestion comes from the fact that in aqueous solution exactly one quarter of the total chlorine is readily hydrolysed: it is necessary to use alkali fusion to release the total chlorine content. Both of these facts are compatible with a stable trinuclear structure with labile in-plane terminal halogen atoms.

It was noted above that the metal–metal distances in all the rhenium(III) clusters fall in a very narrow range. If a crystalline rhenium(IV) cluster compound could be obtained, there should be a significant increase in the metal–metal bond distance as there is less π-bonding available in the d^3-system.

Molybdenum trichloride. Molybdenum trichloride is another system where it is possible that trinuclear clusters may occur. Klemm and Steinberg[31] measured the magnetic moment of this compound many years ago and found a value slightly in excess of 1 B.M. This result has recently been confirmed[32] and, after due account has been taken of a temperature-independent term, the magnetic moment is in fact 1 B.M. per molybdenum atom over the temperature range 90–300°K. Once again the magnetic evidence can be interpreted on the basis of a trinuclear cluster.

It is important to compare this conclusion with the results of Schnering and Wohrle[33] who showed by an X-ray diffraction study that molybdenum trichloride contains pairs of molybdenum atoms. However, it is to be noted that this material, prepared by thermal decomposition of the tetra-chloride, was virtually diamagnetic, with a molar susceptibility of only 19×10^{-6} cgs at room temperature. The paramagnetic molybdenum trichloride referred to above was prepared by the thermal decomposition of molybdenum pentachloride in a nitrogen stream, exactly the method used to prepare trimeric rhenium trichloride. It is well known that halides of many heavy transition metals are polymorphic, the structure obtained depending on the mode of preparation. The two sets of conflicting data given above need not necessarily be mutually exclusive.

The mixed halide $Mo_2Cl_3F_6$. The evidence put forward by Stewart and O'Donnell[34] to substantiate the claim that this compound contains tri-nuclear clusters of metal atoms is better than that available for any other compound except the rhenium(III) clusters.

They found that $Mo_2Cl_3F_6$ is formed whenever molybdenum hexa-fluoride reacts at room temperature with chlorides such as phosphorus trichloride, carbon tetrachloride or silicon tetrachloride. It is also readily formed by treating molybdenum pentachloride with molybdenum hexa-fluoride or anhydrous hydrogen fluoride[34]. The orange solid could be sublimed unchanged at 80°, but at higher temperatures it decomposed to give molybdenum trichloride and molybdenum hexafluoride.

Two types of structure could be envisaged from the empirical formula, one involving octahedral coordination of each molybdenum atom and three chlorine bridges, a structure of the same type as that of the $[W_2Cl_9]^{3-}$ ion. An alternative formulation would be ionic, for example, $(MoCl_3)^+(MoF_6)^-$. Conductance measurements in acetonitrile showed the compound to be ionic; furthermore, a most impressive experiment showed that electrolysis in a three-compartment cell gave half the molybdenum and all the chlorine in the cathode compartment, and half the molybdenum and all the fluorine in the anode compartment. Thus the structure of the compound would seem to be as written above.

The infrared spectrum of the compound in acetonitrile solution showed a strong band at 630 cm^{-1}, attributed to the stretching frequency of the hexafluoromolybdate(v) ion. This value may be compared with that of 623 cm^{-1} found for potassium hexafluoromolybdate(v)[35].

The cation $MoCl_3^+$ does not seem likely to occur as a mononuclear species, and the magnetic evidence is not compatible with this structure. If such a structure existed, the magnetic moment of $Mo_2Cl_3F_9$ should be about 2.45 B.M. *per molybdenum atom.* In fact the magnetic moment[34], both in the solid over a temperature range, and also in acetonitrile solution, is 1.67–1.73 B.M. This is exactly the value to be expected if the cation is trimeric and the compound is $(Mo_3Cl_9^{3+})(MoF_6^-)_3$. From the molecular-orbital diagram for rhenium(III) clusters (Figure 3.9), the electronic configuration of the cation would be $(A_1')^2 (A_2'')^2 (E^1)^2$; the two unpaired electrons would result in a magnetic moment *per molybdenum* of 1.64 B.M. Inclusion of the paramagnetism of the anions, with a spin-only value for the d^1-configuration, would increase the magnetic moment of the compound to 1.68 B.M. per molybdenum atom[34].

Tungsten pentachloride and pentabromide. Klemm and Steinberg[31] found that both these halides had anomalously low magnetic moments, of the order of 1 B.M. in marked contrast to the value of about 1.7 B.M. for molybdenum pentachloride. It has recently been confirmed that molybdenum pentachloride does in fact obey a Curie law with a magnetic moment of 1.70 B.M., independent of temperature[36], and that the magnetic moments of both tungsten pentahalides are exactly 1 B.M. per tungsten atom[37]. Molybdenum pentachloride is known from an X-ray diffraction study to be dimeric, but the structures of the tungsten pentahalides are unknown.

The fact, that the magnetic moment is exactly one-third of an electron per tungsten atom, and that freshly prepared solutions of the halides in acetonitrile are conducting, lead to the suggestion[37] that the compounds should be formulated as trinuclear clusters, $[W_3X_{12}]^{3+}3X^-$. If this is correct the electronic configuration of the trinuclear cluster would be $(A_1')^2 (A_2'')^1$, resulting in one unpaired electron per trimer.

Trinuclear molybdenum(II) compounds. Anderson and Sheldon[38] prepared a series of complexes of molybdenum(II) by the action of hydrochloric acid on molybdenum(II) acetate. Addition of the appropriate cations gave salts which they formulated as $K_6Mo_3Cl_{12}$, $(NH_4)_7Mo_3Cl_{13}\cdot H_2O$ and $Cs_8Mo_4Cl_{16}$. However, no conclusive evidence of the trimeric nature of these species was presented, and it is tempting to compare the formation of the first complex, $K_6Mo_3Cl_{12}$, from molybdenum acetate, which is known to be dimeric with an effective quadrupole bond, with the formation of the dimeric $[Re_2Cl_8]^{2-}$ ion from the similar rhenium(III) chloroacetates[39,40]. It appears unlikely that mere dissolution of molybdenum acetate in hydrochloric acid would rupture the quadrupole bond, and it is possible that $K_6Mo_3Cl_{12}$ should be formulated as $K_4Mo_2Cl_8$, which is of course analytically identical with the original formulation and would be exactly analogous to the rhenium complexes.

General remarks. It is interesting that the possible trimeric species discussed in this last section all show absorption spectra in the visible region that are remarkably similar to those of the rhenium(III) clusters, as may be seen from Table 3.4. There is also an interesting trend in the

TABLE 3.4

Absorption Spectra of Possible Clusters

Compound	Electronic configuration	Absorption maxima (cm^{-1})	Solvent
Re_3Cl_9	d^4	11,300, 18,500	Nitromethane
		13,300, 19,400	Acetone
Mo_3Cl_9	d^3	13,150, 19,100	(Reflectance)
$[Mo_3Cl_9]^{3+}$	d^2	14,100, 21,500	Acetonitrile
$[W_3Cl_{12}]^{3+}$	d^1	13,100, 22,200	Acetonitrile

resistance to hydrolysis of the supposed trimers from the rhenium(III) clusters, which are stable towards hydrolysis, to the tungsten(V) halides which are extremely reactive towards moisture. Such a decrease in hydrolytic stability is exactly the behaviour expected for systems with decreasing metal–metal bonding.

TRINUCLEAR NIOBIUM AND TANTALUM COMPOUNDS

Compounds of the general formula $Nb(Ta)_3X_8$ have been prepared. Schafer and coworkers[41,42] prepared Nb_3Cl_8 by the thermal decomposition of niobium tetrachloride. The compound is hexagonal with $a = 6.74$ and $c = 12.27$ Å[42]. The structure is shown in Figure 3.11 and consists of an equilateral triangle of niobium atoms, each pair of metal atoms being

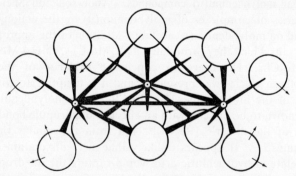

Figure 3.11　The structure of Nb_3Cl_8. Small circles represent Nb, large circles represent Cl atoms.

bridged by a chlorine atom; but the bridges are below the plane of the triangle of metal atoms. A fourth bridging atom above the triangle is shared between the three metal atoms. The remaining halogen atoms are all involved in inter-cluster bridging, some being shared between two clusters and others between three. On Schafer's notation, the compound may be described as $[Nb_3Cl_4]Cl_{6/2}Cl_{3/3}$. Of necessity, there must be at least one unpaired electron per trimer unit and Schafer and Schnering[2] have reported a magnetic moment of 1.86 B.M. per Nb_3Cl_8 molecule.

The structure of the remaining compounds of this type have not been determined by single-crystal studies, but they are likely to be of the same type as Nb_3Cl_8. From X-ray powder diffraction studies, it has been shown[43] that Nb_3Br_8 is hexagonal with $a = 7.227$ and $c = 12.93$ Å. The methods of preparation of these compounds will be discussed in Chapter 5.

HEXAMERIC NIOBIUM AND TANTALUM COMPOUNDS

The hexameric species of the general type $Nb(Ta)_6X_{14}$ have been known for a considerable time and their hexameric structure was suspected quite early. By the use of X-ray scattering from solutions of some of these compounds, Pauling and coworkers confirmed that in solution they exist as the hexameric cations $[M_6X_{12}]^{2+}$. More recently it has been shown that the hexameric unit of metal atoms is also the basic unit in the solid compounds.

A major difficulty in the study of this class of compound has been the lack of systematic and efficient methods of preparation. At present it is still not possible to formulate in a general way the conditions necessary to ensure cluster formation and many of the preparations are of a somewhat *ad hoc* nature.

A recent discovery is that the niobium and tantalum cluster ions of the type $[M_6X_{12}]^{2+}$ can undergo one- or two-electron oxidation. This has considerably widened the potential scope of the chemistry of these systems and already has led to a better understanding of their spectral and magnetic properties.

A considerable amount of work has been done on the visible and infrared spectra of these systems. This is best understood in terms of the structures of the compounds, which will therefore be discussed first. It may be noted that some of this spectral work preceded the structural determinations and led to specific predictions concerning the structures of the complexes which were subsequently confirmed.

Preparations and Structures

The compounds of the general types Nb_6X_{14} and Ta_6X_{14} may be considered to be the parent compounds of the series. They are often isolated from aqueous solutions as the heptahydrates, $M_6X_{14} \cdot 7H_2O$, which may be heated to give the anhydrous halides. More recently, the anhydrous halides have been prepared by reduction of higher halides. The compounds formulated as M_6X_{15} are closely related to the M_6X_{14} series.

The principle methods of preparation of the niobium and tantalum hexamers are given in Table 3.5.

TABLE 3.5

Preparation of Hexameric Niobium and Tantalum Halides

Compound	Method	Ref.
$Nb_6Cl_{14} \cdot 7H_2O$	$NbCl_5$ with Na/Hg at red heat. Extract with water and crystallize.	44
	$NbCl_5/Cd$ at 300°, extract with water, precipitate CdS and recrystallize.	45
$Ta_6Cl_{14} \cdot 7H_2O$	$TaCl_5$ with Na/Hg at red heat. Extract with water and crystallize.	46
$Ta_6Br_{14} \cdot 7H_2O$	$TaBr_4$ with Na/Hg at red heat. Extract with HBr and crystallize.	47
Ta_6Cl_{14}	$TaCl_5/Al$, temperature gradient, 400–200°	48
Ta_6Br_{14}	$TaBr_5/Al$, temperature gradient, 450–280°	48
Ta_6I_{14}	TaI_5/Al, temperature gradient, 475–300°	48
	TaI_5/Ta, temperature gradient, 630–575°	49
$Ta_6I_{14} \cdot 7H_2O$	TaI_5/Ta at red heat, extract with water and crystallize	50
Nb_6F_{15}	NbF_5/Nb above 700°	51
Ta_6Cl_{15}	$TaCl_5/Ta$, temperature gradient, 630–470°	52
Ta_6Br_{15}	Thermal decomposition of $TaBr_3$ or $TaBr_4$	53

Some of the early preparations of hexameric niobium and tantalum species were incorrectly formulated, but they have been included in Table 3.5 with amended formulation, because the preparative methods are still useful.

Several of the lower halide systems of niobium and tantalum have recently been subjected to systematic study. The phase diagrams of the tantalum–bromine and tantalum–iodine systems are given in Figure 3.12 and Figure 3.13. The niobium–iodine system is much simpler than the corresponding tantalum system and it contains no hexameric species. It is therefore given as Figure 5.4 in the section on niobium iodides.

$[M_6X_{12}]^{2+}$ **cations.** Chapin[47] demonstrated over fifty years ago that the product obtained by the reduction of tantalum bromides with sodium amalgam probably contained the $[Ta_6Br_{12}]^{2+}$ cation. He showed that the overall formula of the material is $Ta_6Br_{14} \cdot 7H_2O$ and that only one-seventh of the bromine can be precipitated from the green solutions of the complex by silver nitrate, or replaced by repeated evaporation with hydrochloric acid. It was also demonstrated that the bromide ions could be replaced

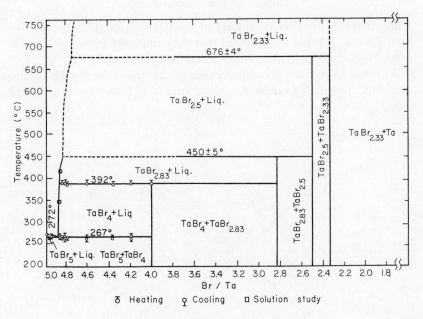

Figure 3.12 The tantalum–bromine phase diagram.

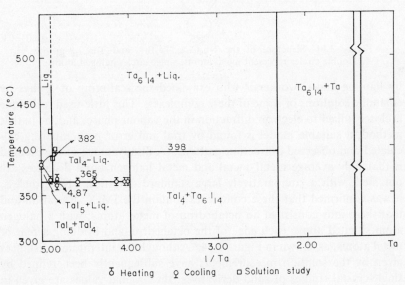

Figure 3.13 The tantalum–iodine phase diagram.

with other ions, to give complexes of the type $[Ta_6Br_{12}]X_2$, where $X =$ OH, Cl, etc. Chapin also showed that the compound previously formulated by Chabrie[46] as $TaCl_2 \cdot 2H_2O$ was in fact $[Ta_6Cl_{12}]Cl_2 \cdot 7H_2O$.

As noted above, the first direct evidence that the lower halides of niobium and tantalum possessed unusual structural features was provided

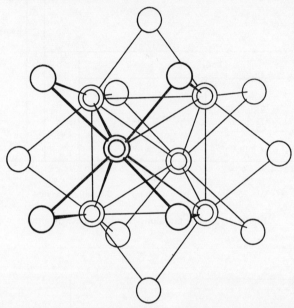

Figure 3.14 Structure of the Nb_6Cl_{12}, Ta_6Br_{12} and Ta_6Cl_{12} groups.
Double circles represent metal atoms, single circles halogen atoms.

by Pauling and coworkers[54] who examined the scattering of X-rays by ethanolic solutions of some of these complexes. This little-used technique is closely allied to electron diffraction in the vapour phase, and, as in that method, a suitable model is found by trial and error by comparing calculated and observed diffraction patterns. A disadvantage of the method is that only average metal–metal and metal–halogen bond distances are obtained, with a comparatively large standard deviation. Nevertheless, it was confirmed that these complexes contain the $[M_6X_{12}]^{2+}$ cation and that these ions consist of an octahedron of metal atoms, with a halogen atom situated above each edge of the octahedron and bridging a pair of metal atoms, as shown in Figure 3.14. Although the interatomic distances given by the solution measurements have subsequently been refined by single-crystal studies of solid derivatives, the original values are given in Table 3.6.

TABLE 3.6

Internuclear Distances (Å) in $M_6X_{12}^{2+}$ Ions in Solution

Compound	Metal–metal	Metal–halogen
$Nb_6Cl_{12}^{2+}$	2.85	2.41
$Ta_6Cl_{12}^{2+}$	2.88	2.44
$Ta_6Br_{12}^{2+}$	2.92	2.62

The structure of $Ta_6Cl_{14}\cdot 7H_2O$. Spectral studies, to be described below, suggested that there is some distortion of the metal octahedron in $Ta_6Cl_{14}\cdot 7H_2O$. This has been confirmed by a single-crystal X-ray diffraction study by Burbank[55]. The crystals were found to be trigonal, with $a = 9.36$ and $c = 8.80$ Å. The space group is $P\bar{3}1m$ and there is one molecular unit in the cell. The basic structure consists of $Ta_6Cl_{14}\cdot 4H_2O$ units, with the Ta_6 octahedron elongated along one axis to give a bipyramidal polynucleus as shown in Figure 3.15. The distance between metal atoms Ta(1) and Ta(1)′ is 4.92 Å and between Ta(2) and Ta(2)′ is 3.94 Å, giving a very large difference of nearly one Angstrom unit[55]. Twelve

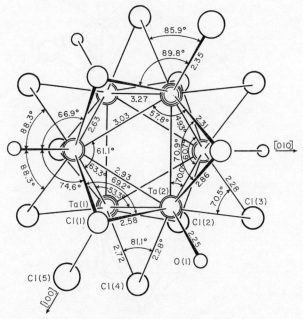

Figure 3.15 The structure of the $Ta_6Cl_{14}\cdot 4H_2O$ unit.

chlorine atoms are at positions approximately on the perpendicular bi-
sectors of the bipyramid edges, to give Ta_6Cl_{12}. The twelve chlorine atoms
themselves form a polyhedron with six approximately rectangular faces
and twelve triangular faces. The remaining two chlorine atoms and four
water molecules complete the coordination spheres of the tantalum atoms,
the chlorine being situated *trans* with respect to the metal octahedron.
These six terminal groups in turn form an elongated bipyramid enclosing
the complex ion.

The $Ta_6Cl_{14} \cdot 4H_2O$ units are arranged in layers perpendicular to the
trigonal axis of the crystal with alternate layers containing three molecules
of water, to give the overall composition $Ta_6Cl_{14} \cdot 7H_2O$. Burbank[55] found
considerable disorder in the crystal and suggested that this occurs during
crystal formation to allow maximum hydrogen bonding in the structure.

Anhydrous halides. The compound Nb_6Cl_{14} has been examined by
Schafer and coworkers[56]. The crystals are orthorhombic with $a = 12.252$,

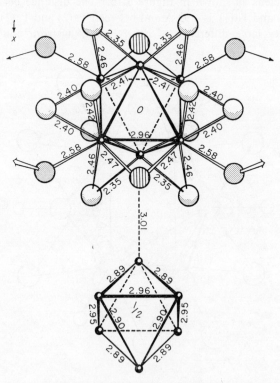

Figure 3.16   The basic unit in Nb_6Cl_{14}.

$b = 11.019$ and $c = 13.494$ Å. The structure consists of the basic Nb_6Cl_{12} unit with the sixth octahedral coordination positions of four niobium atoms in a plane occupied by halogen atoms which each bridge to a neighbouring cluster. The basic unit is shown in Figure 3.16; the clusters are arranged in infinite sheets joined by the bridging halogens. Contact between the layers is limited to the interaction of niobium atoms not bonded to bridging halogens, as shown in Figure 3.16.

The structure of Ta_6I_{14} has also been examined by Schafer and his coworkers[49] and it is of the same general type as that of Nb_6Cl_{14}. The crystals are orthorhombic with $a = 14.445$, $b = 12.505$ and $c = 15.000$ Å.

The basic unit of Ta_6I_{14} is shown in Figure 3.17, where also the important

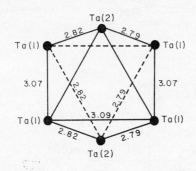

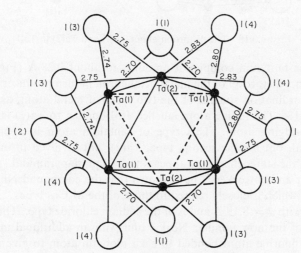

Figure 3.17   The structure of the Ta_6I_{12} group.

internuclear distances are given. The inter-cluster bridging iodine atoms, not shown in the Figure, are bonded to the remaining coordination sites of the metal atoms designated Ta(1). The octahedron of tantalum atoms exhibits a much more pronounced flattening than does the niobium octahedron in Nb_6Cl_{14}. In the latter compound the difference between the two types of niobium–niobium distances is about 0.07 Å (see Figure 3.16),

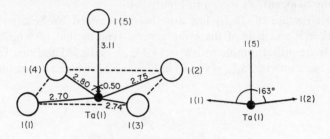

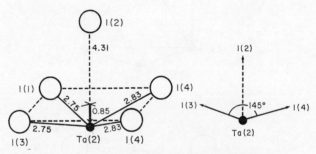

Figure 3.18   The distortion about Ta(1) and Ta(2) in Ta_6I_{14}.

but in the tantalum complex it amounts to about 0.28 Å (Figure 3.17). The distinct distortion of the metal octahedron in turn produces distortion in the coordination spheres of the two types of metal atom, as shown in Figure 3.18. The iodine atom labelled I(5) bonded to Ta(1) is the inter-cluster bridging atom. This type of tantalum atom is approximately octahedral, but for the second type, Ta(2), not involved in inter-cluster bonding, the stereochemistry appears to be square-pyramidal.

Schafer and coworkers[51] have shown that the compound Nb_6F_{15} has a structure which is closely related to those of the M_6Cl_{14} types. The lattice is cubic, with $a = 8.19$ Å and is of the sodium chloride type. The structure consists of the now familiar Nb_6F_{12} unit with an additional inter-cluster bridging fluorine atom bonded to each niobium atom to give an infinite three-dimensional lattice. The basic unit is shown in Figure 3.19, and the most important feature of the cluster is that the octahedron of metal atoms is regular.

The question of distortion of the metal octahedron in these systems will be discussed in the section on bonding, but it is convenient to note here that, as Burbank[55] has pointed out, there appears to be a general structural principle involved. In the solid state, two points are clear. First, all additional ligands occupy the vacant octahedral sites of the metal atoms, and higher coordination of the metal has not been observed. Secondly,

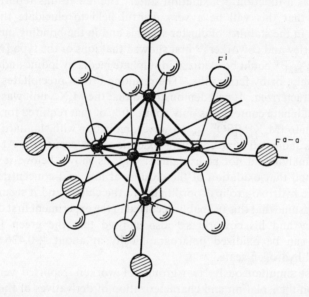

Figure 3.19   Schematic representation of the structure of Nb_6F_{15}.

the distortions of tantalum octahedra are more pronounced than the corresponding niobium distortions. From the few examples examined in detail so far, it appears that the following generalizations hold:

four additional negative ligands cause flattening of the octahedra;

two negative and four neutral groups cause elongation of the octahedra; and

six additional negative groups cause a regular octahedron.

For the oxidized species $[M_6X_{12}]^{4+}$ (see below) Robin and Kuebler[57] again found no spectral evidence for distortion in the niobium clusters, but for tantalum clusters they observed reversed intensities in the splittings compared with $[Ta_6X_{12}]^{2+}$ and suggested that in this case the octahedron is flattened.

Oxidation of Niobium and Tantalum Clusters

It has recently been discovered that both the niobium and tantalum hexameric clusters can be oxidized with retention of the cluster unit. Conversely, the oxidized forms can be conveniently reduced to the usual oxidation state. These compounds represent the first cluster system showing a number of stable oxidation states. This will provide an opportunity to examine the spectra, magnetic properties and structures of the clusters as a function of oxidation state. The few results reported so far indicate that this will be a very fruitful field to elucidate the factors involved in the stability of cluster systems and in the bonding mechanism.

McCarley and coworkers[58] first showed that ions of the type $[Nb_6X_{12}]^{2+}$ and $[Ta_6X_{12}]^{2+}$ could be oxidized in sulphate media by iodine and chlorine, respectively, or by ferric salts. The resulting brown precipitates were not fully characterized. It was demonstrated that the M_6X_{12} unit was retained, but the sulphate content was only about 80% of that required for complete oxidation to $[M_6X_{12}^{4+}][SO_4^{2-}]_2$. However, reduction with standard stannous solutions indicated that complete oxidation had occurred. At the time this anomaly could not be explained; but, as shown below, it has since been found that oxidation of the clusters at low acid concentrations can introduce hydroxo groups coordinated to the cluster and it seems reasonable to assume that this probably occurred in the experiment first described. McCarley and his coworkers[58] also showed that the green $[M_6X_{12}]^{2+}$ clusters can be oxidized polarographically at about $+0.426$ v on the standard hydrogen scale.

Almost simultaneously, two groups of workers reported very similar results on the isolation and characterization of derivatives of the oxidized hexameric niobium and tantalum clusters.

Mackay and Schneider[59] and McCarley and his group[60] each isolated species of the types $[(C_2H_5)_4N]_n[Nb_6Cl_{12} \cdot Cl_6]$ where $n = 2$, 3 or 4. Although no structural work has yet been reported, it seems certain that the anion in each compound is Nb_6Cl_{18} containing the basic Nb_6Cl_{12} unit with an additional chlorine atom filling the final octahedral coordination site on each niobium atom.

The green complex with $n = 4$, that is, $[(C_2H_5)_4N]_4Nb_6Cl_{18}$, contains niobium in the same oxidation state as the parent halide Nb_6Cl_{14}, and indeed it is isolated by adding tetraethylammonium chloride to a refluxed solution of Nb_6Cl_{14} in ethanol saturated with hydrogen chloride[59,60]. The compound with $n = 2$, which is also green, corresponds in oxidation state to the product, which as described above, was formed by chlorine oxidation of Nb_6Cl_{14} in sulphate media. The salt can be isolated after chlorine oxidation of Nb_6Cl_{14} in ethanol saturated with hydrogen chloride. It was noted, however, that at low hydrogen chloride concentrations it was possible to isolate salts with some hydroxide ion and a deficiency of chloride ion. The brown compound with $n = 3$ is prepared by oxidizing Nb_6Cl_{14} in ethanolic hydrogen chloride solution with oxygen, and then adding the cation[59,60]; it is paramagnetic, with a magnetic moment of 1.67 B.M. independent of temperature; this corresponds to one unpaired electron per hexamer unit[60]. The ESR spectrum gave $g = 1.95$; 55 peaks are expected in the hyperfine structure of a hexameric cluster due to the $\frac{9}{2}$ nuclear spin of ^{93}Nb (100% abundance) and 49 of these were observed[59].

Bonding

To date, the most comprehensive examination of the bonding in $[M_6X_{12}]^{2+}$ clusters is the treatment by Cotton and Haas[22] based on molecular-orbital calculations, although earlier treatments have been given by Gillespie[61] using the valence-bond method and by Duffey and coworkers[62] using the molecular-orbital approach.

The basic procedure in the treatment by Cotton and Haas closely parallels that already described for the rhenium trimers. A basic assumption is that each metal is surrounded by a square-planar arrangement of halogens. The only data available at the time were the results of the X-ray scattering experiments with $[M_6X_{12}]^{2+}$ ions in solution. In the context of the subsequent structural work on solid compounds described above, it is clear that the simple treatment is not adequate and a more detailed treatment which can accommodate the distortions of the metal octahedra is required.

Nevertheless, the bonding scheme derived by Cotton and Haas is sufficient to illustrate the basic properties of these systems. After forming σ-bonds to the four halogen atoms about each metal, the remaining metal orbitals were considered by standard group-theoretical procedures and the appropriate overlap integrals were computed. The resulting molecular-orbital energy diagram is shown in Figure 3.20 where the orbital separation is plotted as a function of the metal–metal interaction. As with the rhenium trimer case, it is seen that the energy levels clearly fall into bonding and antibonding groups, together with an approximately nonbonding T_{2g}-orbital, and this pattern is independent of the metal–metal interaction. It should be noted[22] that because of configurational interaction, which is ignored in the treatment, the $T_{2g}(xz, yz)$-orbital is more strongly bonding, and the $T_{2g}(xy)$-orbital is more strongly antibonding, than shown in Figure 3.20.

There are sixteen electrons to be accommodated in the energy levels shown in Figure 3.20 and it is obvious that they occupy

$$(A_{1g})^2(T_{1u})^6(A_{2u})^2(T_{2g})^6,$$

although the order of the levels depends on the magnitude of the metal–metal interaction. Since there are twelve metal–metal contacts in a regular octahedron of metal atoms, the system is electron-deficient with an average

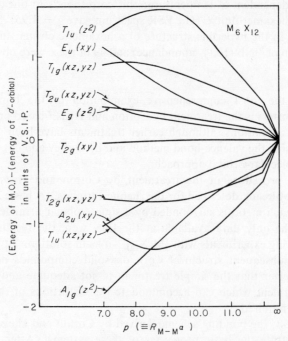

Figure 3.20   Molecular-orbital energy diagram for an M_6X_{12} system.

bond order of only $\frac{2}{3}$. It may be the electron deficiency that is responsible for the distortions in the metal octahedra, since so far no similar effects have been noted in the molybdenum hexameric series which are not electron-deficient. However, this suggestion must be viewed with some caution, since few structures of the molybdenum clusters have been investigated and, by analogy with niobium and tantalum, the likelihood of distortion should be greater in tungsten clusters. So far few tungsten compounds have been studied by structural methods.

Despite the original claim that they were paramagnetic[63], the anhydrous halides M_6X_{14} are diamagnetic. This, together with the observed paramagnetism of $[Nb_6X_{12}]^{3+}$ and the observed diamagnetism of $[Nb_6X_{12}]^{4+}$, is satisfactorily explained[22] on the molecular-orbital scheme on the basis that the highest filled orbital in Nb_6Cl_{14} is A_{2u}.

The halides M_6X_{15} should, of course, be paramagnetic with one un-paired electron per hexamer, since they are entirely equivalent to $[M_6X_{18}]^{3-}$, but so far no detailed study of their magnetic properties has been reported.

It has been suggested by Schafer[2] and by Robin and Kuebler[57] that, at least in a formal way, the Ta_6X_{14} clusters contain two oxidation states of tantalum. The four metal atoms associated with the inter-cluster bridging halogens may be considered to be in oxidation state II and the remaining two tantalum atoms in oxidation state III, giving the overall oxidation state of 2.33. Nb_6F_{15} which contains a regular octahedron of niobium atoms is considered[51] to contain only trivalent metal atoms, whilst $[Ta_6X_{12}]^{4+}$ is thought[57] to contain two tantalum atoms in oxidation state II and four in oxidation state III.

TABLE 3.7

Characteristic Infrared Patterns for Hexameric Niobium
and Tantalum Clusters (cm^{-1})

$[Nb_6Cl_{12}]^{2+}$	340–345	276–290	220–250	144–150
$[Nb_6Br_{12}]^{2+}$	270–280	200–210	170–180	145
$[Ta_6Cl_{12}]^{2+}$	320–330	230–235	175–190	140–145
$[Ta_6Br_{12}]^{2+}$	225–230	175–182	130–145	96–107

The infrared spectra of a considerable number of niobium and tantalum cluster compounds have been investigated by Boorman and Straughan[64]. Although no definite assignment of the bands could be made, it was found that each type of cluster had a characteristic pattern of absorptions which can be used diagnostically to investigate the presence of cluster groups. The absorption patterns are shown in Table 3.7.

HEXAMERIC MOLYBDENUM AND TUNGSTEN SPECIES

Molybdenum forms an extensive series of compounds based on its dihalides, particularly the dichloride. Although the tungsten systems have not been intensively studied, there seems no doubt that they are similar. All these compounds consist of a hexameric unit, $[M_6X_8]$, containing an octahedron of metal atoms, similar to that found in the niobium and tantalum hexameric species, but in this case the halogen atoms are situated above each face of the metal octahedron, thereby bridging three metal atoms. The detailed structures are discussed below, but it may be com-mented at this stage that each metal atom is surrounded by an approximate square of halogen atoms, as in the clusters discussed above (p.79). Once again, there is one octahedral coordination site vacant and available for additional ligand coordination on each metal atom. The simple spatial

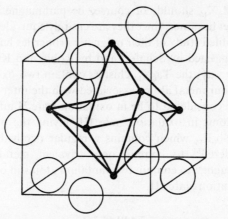

Figure 3.21   Idealized geometry of the $[M_6X_{12}]^{2+}$ cation.

relationships between the two types of hexameric clusters can be readily related to a cube as shown in Figures 3.21 and 3.22.

There is usually a 4+ charge on the M_6X_8 cluster, giving a formal oxidation state of II to each metal atom, so it is perhaps not surprising that all the structures of this type so far examined contain regular octahedra of metal atoms. However, in the case of $[W_6Br_8]^{4+}$, Schafer and coworkers have found it possible to obtain a two-electron oxidation, thereby giving a cluster with the same formal oxidation state as $[Ta_6X_{12}]^{2+}$. The important difference is that the metal octahedron in the tungsten compound is regular, unlike the markedly distorted octahedron in the tantulum compound. Whilst it is true that the halogen coordination is different in

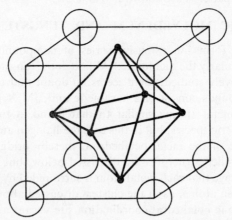

Figure 3.22   Idealized geometry of the $[Mo_6X_8]^{4+}$ cation.

the two clusters, it would be surprising if this difference could induce such a profound structural effect. The only other difference between the clusters is the strength of the metal–metal bonds. In the tantalum case, as pointed out above, there are only sixteen metal d-electrons for twelve metal–metal contacts, giving an average bond order of approximately $\frac{2}{3}$. In the tungsten cluster there are twenty-four electrons, just sufficient to give an average metal–metal bond order of 1. It may be the electron-deficient character of the tantalum cluster which causes the distortion, possibly leading to the formation of multicentre bonds between several metal atoms.

Preparations and Structures

The preparations of the molybdenum and tungsten dihalides are described in detail in Chapter 6. The usual method is either thermal decomposition of a higher halide[65-67] or direct halogenation at sufficiently high temperatures to decompose any higher halides which might be formed[68-71]. Molybdenum dibromide and diiodide have been prepared by fusing the appropriate lithium halide with molybdenum dichloride in a vacuum[72].

As long ago as 1872, Atterburg[69] showed that molybdenum dibromide must be polymeric since only one-third of the halogen could be readily replaced. On the basis of this evidence he suggested that it should be formulated as $[Mo_3Br_4]Br_2$, and he isolated the complexes with ionic bromide replaced by hydroxide, fluoride, etc. Apparent confirmation for this formulation was obtained by Lindner and coworkers[68] on the basis of molecular-weight determination.

Brosset[73] first demonstrated the hexameric nature of molybdenum dichloride derivatives in 1945. The complex previously formulated[68] as $[Mo_3Cl_4(H_2O)_2](OH)_2 \cdot 6H_2O$ was shown to be either

$$[Mo_6Cl_8](OH)_4 \cdot 14H_2O \text{ or } [(Mo_6Cl_8)(OH)_6]2H_3O \cdot 10H_2O,$$

and, in view of more recent work described below, the latter formulation is the more likely. The yellow crystals were found to be rhombohedral with $a = 9.49$ Å and $\alpha = 105.96°$, probable space group $R\bar{3}m$ with a single molecular unit in the cell.

Brosset[74] quickly confirmed the basic structural features by examining the structure of the complex formulated[68] as $[Mo_3Cl_4 \cdot 2H_2O]Cl_2 \cdot 2H_2O$. The crystals are tetragonal with $a = 9.06$ and $c = 28.04$ Å and in fact contain the $[Mo_6Cl_8]Cl_4 \cdot 2H_2O$ group.

Subsequently, Brosset[75] showed by X-ray scattering techniques that the complex acid formulated as $HMo_3Cl_7 \cdot 4H_2O$, dissolved in ethanol, contains the $[Mo_6Cl_8]^{4+}$ unit, and Vaughan[76] showed that the complex salt

$(NH_4)_2[Mo_6Cl_8]Cl_6 \cdot H_2O$ also contains the $[Mo_6Cl_8]^{4+}$ group. All these structures consist of the basic Mo_6Cl_8 unit shown in Figure 3.22 with additional ligands coordinated to the vacant coordination sites of the six metal atoms.

It is only very recently that Schnering and coworkers[2] established that molybdenum dichloride itself has the same hexameric structure, and full crystallographic details are not yet available. This structure consists of the basic Mo_6Cl_8 unit, with two terminal chlorine atoms attached to the molybdenum atom *trans* to each other, and the coordination sites of the remaining four coplanar molybdenum atoms are occupied by chlorine atoms which form bridges to neighbouring clusters. The structure is therefore infinite in two dimensions, giving a layer lattice.

Schafer and coworkers[77,78] have shown that the action of bromine on tungsten dibromide, W_6Br_{12}, gives W_6Br_{16}. The crystals are orthorhombic with $a = 14.60$, $b = 14.28$ and $c = 12.11$ Å and there are four molecular units in the cell. The structure contains a $[W_6Br_8]^{6+}$ cation; there are terminal bromine atoms attached to four of the tungsten atoms and the stoichiometry is completed by two linear Br_4^{2-} groups which form bridges between the clusters. This remarkable compound is therefore formulated in Schafer's notation as $[W_6Br_8]Br_4[Br_4]_{2/2}$. Its magnetic properties have not been reported so far, but it should contain two unpaired electrons per cluster (see below).

A most interesting compound, Nb_6I_{11}, has been prepared by Schafer and his group[78] by the interaction of niobium and niobium pentaiodide at 1000° or, alternatively, by the thermal decomposition of Nb_3I_8 in an atmosphere of argon. The crystals are orthorhombic with $a = 11.30$, $b = 15.32$ and $c = 13.55$ Å. The structure consists of the $[Nb_6I_8]^{3+}$ cation, which has the same geometrical configuration as the molybdenum and tungsten hexameric species. The remaining coordination site on each niobium atom is occupied by an iodine which forms a bridge to an adjacent cluster unit, thus giving a three-dimensional infinite lattice. This compound is the first to be reported showing characteristics of the two types of hexameric species so far described. It is the only cluster containing niobium or tantalum that adopts the geometry hitherto characteristic only of molybdenum and tungsten. The geometry of the bridging groups is similar to that found in Nb_6F_{15}, and so far the corresponding molybdenum and tungsten compounds have not been reported.

Bonding

The first attempt to explain the bonding in the $[M_6X_8]^{4+}$ unit was made by Duffey and coworkers[62], but the most detailed discussion of the bonding has been given by Cotton and Haas[22]. As for the other clusters, it is assumed that the metal atom is surrounded by an approximate square of bridging halogen atoms. An atomic orbital from each metal atom is directed towards the centre of the metal octahedron and participates in metal–metal bonding and there is one remaining coordination site on each metal atom vacant and available for ligand coordination. The molecular-orbital scheme is given in Figure 3.23. There are twenty-four electrons

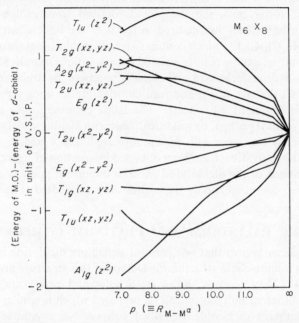

Figure 3.23 Molecular-orbital energy diagram for an M_6X_8 system.

and these are nicely accommodated in the five bonding molecular orbitals. Since there are twelve metal–metal contacts, the bond order is approximately one.

The highest bonding molecular orbital is a triply degenerate T_{2u} orbital, so that with a two-electron oxidation of $W_6Br_8^{4+}$ to $W_6Br_8^{6+}$ there should be two unpaired electrons per cluster unit unless spin-pairing occurs via the Br_4^{2-} bridging groups.

Infrared Spectra

The infrared spectra of a number of hexameric molybdenum and tungsten clusters have been examined by Clark and his group[79] and by Cotton and his group[80]. From the results of the latter it appears that the metal–metal stretching vibration of the molybdenum clusters occurs at about 230 cm^{-1} and is relatively independent of the nature of the halogen atoms involved in the cluster.

Chemical Reactions

Molybdenum dichloride is soluble in hydrochloric acid and from these solutions a considerable number of derivatives of the $Mo_6Cl_8^{4+}$ group have been prepared. Now that it is known that molybdenum dichloride itself contains this cluster unit, the compounds derived from molybdenum dichloride can be entirely rationalized in terms of the basic cluster unit. The anion $[(Mo_6Cl_8)Cl_6]^{2-}$, which contains a terminal chlorine atom on each molybdenum atom, can be readily isolated from solutions of molybdenum dichloride in hydrochloric acid. Sheldon[81,82] showed by tracer experiments with ^{36}Cl that six of the fourteen chlorine atoms were very labile and the remaining eight quite inert. The labile chlorine atoms can be replaced by hydroxyl groups, by mild treatment with alkali, or by bromide or iodide ions, by treatment with the appropriate halogen acid.

Various other derivatives have been obtained by reaction of ligands with ethanolic solutions of the dichloride[83-36]. The important point to note is that in all these compounds only six ligands are coordinated to the basic $Mo_6Cl_8^{4+}$ unit.

HEXAMERIC PALLADIUM AND PLATINUM COMPOUNDS

It has long been known that one form of palladium dichloride is polymeric with an infinite-chain structure[87]. Details of this structure are given in Chapter 10. Very recently, however, Schafer and coworkers[88] have shown that a different polymorph can be prepared which is similar to the hexameric platinum dichloride described below. No crystallographic details of the structure of this form of palladium dichloride are yet available.

A single-crystal X-ray diffraction study of platinum dichloride prepared by the transport method has shown that the halide is in fact hexameric[89]. The crystals are trigonal with $a = 13.11$ and $c = 8.59$ Å. The structure[89], shown in Figure 3.21, consists of discrete Pt_6Cl_{12} units, similar in their geometry to the $Nb_6X_{12}^{2+}$ units except that the platinum atoms are in an *exact* square-planar configuration with the four near-neighbour chlorine atoms. The platinum–platinum distance is 2.36 Å and the platinum–chlorine bond length varies between 2.34 and 2.39 Å.

ADDENDA

Rhenium Trinuclear Cluster Compounds

By the interaction of rhenium tribromide and silver arsenate in acetone solution, followed by extraction with dimethyl sulphoxide (DMSO), Cotton and Lippard[90] were able to isolate the complex $Re_3Br_3(AsO_4)_2(DMSO)_3$. The absorption spectrum of this complex was similar to those of other rhenium(III) trinuclear compounds, and the infrared spectrum above 400 cm^{-1} was consistent with a structure containing the planar Re_3Br_3 unit with an AsO_4 group above and below the plane of the trinuclear core. Three of the oxygen atoms of each AsO_4 group are each bonded to one rhenium atom in the core, so that they effectively occupy the positions of the out-of-plane chlorine atoms in the $[Re_3Cl_{12}]^{3-}$ structure (Figure 3.1, page 71). The DMSO molecules are thought to occupy the terminal in-plane positions. At present, this most interesting structure is based on indirect evidence but, if substantiated by structural studies, it will be the first example of yet another variant of cluster-compound structures.

Niobium and Tantalum Hexameric Cluster Compounds

McCarley and his coworkers[91] have made further preparative studies of hexameric niobium compounds. The interaction of niobium pentachloride and aluminium powder in a thermal gradient of 450–300° led to the formation of "niobium trichloride," and when heated to 500° this compound gave Nb_3Cl_8. The corresponding bromide could be prepared directly by reduction of niobium pentabromide with zinc at 550°[91].

Studies were also made of the chemical reactivity of Nb_3Cl_8. It was found to react with potassium chloride at 600–900° according to the equation

$$5Nb_3Cl_8 + 14KCl \rightarrow 3K_2NbCl_6 + 2K_4Nb_6Cl_{18}$$

This reaction is of interest as it is one of the few well-established reactions for interconverting a trimeric cluster compound into one containing a hexameric unit. This hexameric compound and also the corresponding bromo-compound were synthesized directly from niobium pentachloride at 800–900° according the equation

$$14NbCl_5 + 20KCl + 16Nb \rightarrow 5K_4Nb_6Cl_{18}$$

These hexameric compounds are obviously analogous to the quaternary ammonium salts of the same anion described on page 96.

Field and Kepert[92] have shown that Nb_6Cl_{14} in dilute hydrochloric acid reacts with a number of donor molecules such as dimethyl sulphoxide and triphenylphosphine oxide to give complexes of the type $[(Nb_6Cl_{12})Cl_2 \cdot L_4]$.

$Nb_6Cl_{15} \cdot 7H_2O$ and its tantalum analogue have been further characterized by means of X-ray powder diffraction, magnetic, and solubility studies[93].

Molybdenum and Tungsten Cluster Compounds

Hartley and Ware[94] have examined the Raman and infrared spectra of $H_2[Mo_6Cl_8]X_6 \cdot 8H_2O$ (where X = Cl, Br, or I), both in the solid phase and in solution. Their results are summarized in Table 3.8.

The action of liquid chlorine on tungsten dichloride leads to the formation of black $[W_6Cl_{12}]Cl_6$. Only two-thirds of the total chlorine was found to be removed by silver nitrate titration[95]. The X-ray diffraction results could be interpreted on the basis of either a hexagonal cell with

TABLE 3.8

Raman and Infrared Spectra (cm^{-1}) of $H_2[Mo_6Cl_8]X_6 \cdot 8H_2O$

X = Cl	X = Br	X = I	Assignment	X = Cl	X = Br	X = I	Assignment
			RAMAN				
92	60	44	t_{2g}	236	160	117	a_{1g}
179	134	109	e_g	247	249	247	t_{2g}
195	195	184	t_{2g}	310	279	247?	e_g
215	216	215	e_g	318	318	318	a_{1g}
225	—	150	t_{2g}?	402	356	318?	a_{1g}
			INFRARED				
221	167	132					
247	232	229					
330	305	295	t_{1u}				
351	360	357					
232	—	—					
294	226	325					

$a = 14.91$ and $c = 8.45$ Å or a rhombohedral cell with $a = 9.05$ Å and $\alpha = 110.8°$.

Sheldon and co-workers[96] prepared a series of compounds formulated as $[Mo_3X_{13}]^{7-}$, $[Mo_3X_{12}]^{6-}$, and $[Mo_3X_{11}]^{5-}$ by the action of concentrated hydrochloric acid on molybdenum(II) acetate, followed by the addition of an appropriate halide.

Three of the salts were examined by X-ray powder diffraction techniques and found to be tetragonal with the following unit cell parameters[97]:

$$K_6Mo_3Cl_{12} \qquad a = 16.02 \text{ Å} \qquad c = 12.18 \text{ Å}$$
$$(NH_4)_7Mo_3Cl_{13} \cdot H_2O \quad a = 17.16 \text{ Å} \qquad c = 14.0 \text{ Å}$$
$$Rb_7Mo_3Cl_{13} \cdot H_2O \qquad a = 17.2 \text{ Å} \qquad c = 14.6 \text{ Å}$$

REFERENCES

1. F. A. Cotton, *Rev. Pure Applied Chem.*, **17**, 31 (1967).
2. H. Schafer and H. G. Schnering, *Angew. Chem.*, **76**, 833 (1964).

3. W. T. Robinson, J. E. Fergusson and B. P. Penfold, *Proc. Chem. Soc.*, **1963**, 116.
4. J. A. Bertrand, F. A. Cotton and W. A. Dollase, *J. Am. Chem. Soc.*, **85**, 1349 (1963).
5. J. A. Bertrand, F. A. Cotton and W. A. Dollase, *Inorg. Chem.*, **2**, 1166 (1963).
6. J. E. Fergusson and B. H. Robinson, *Proc. Chem. Soc.*, **1964**, 189.
7. M. Elder and B. R. Penfold, *Nature*, **205**, 276 (1965).
8. B. R. Penfold and W. T. Robinson, *Inorg. Chem.*, **5**, 1758 (1966).
9. M. Elder and B. R. Penfold, *Inorg. Chem.*, **5**, 1763 (1966).
10. F. A. Cotton and S. J. Lippard, *Inorg. Chem.*, **4**, 59 (1965).
11. W. Geilmann, F. W. Wrigge and W. Biltz, *Z. anorg. allgem. Chem.*, **214**, 248 (1933).
12. D. Brown and R. Colton, *Australian J. Chem.*, **18**, 441 (1965).
13. F. A. Cotton and J. T. Mague, *Proc. Chem. Soc.*, **1964**, 233.
14. F. A. Cotton and J. T. Mague, *Inorg. Chem.*, **3**, 1402 (1964).
15. F. A. Cotton and S. J. Lippard, *J. Am. Chem. Soc.*, **86**, 4497 (1964).
16. A. Buchler, P. E. Blackburn and J. L. Stauffer, *J. Phys. Chem.*, **70**, 685 (1966).
17. K. Rinke and H. Schafer, *Angew. Chem.*, **77**, 131 (1965).
18. J. Chatt and G. A. Rowe, *J. Chem. Soc.*, **1962**, 4019.
19. F. A. Cotton and J. T. Mague, *Inorg. Chem.*, **3**, 1094 (1964).
20. J. E. Fergusson, B. R. Penfold, M. Elder and B. H. Robinson, *J. Chem. Soc.*, **1965**, 5500.
21. R. L. Martin and R. Colton, *Nature*, **205**, 239 (1965).
22. F. A. Cotton and T. E. Haas, *Inorg. Chem.*, **3**, 10 (1964).
23. F. A. Cotton, S. J. Lippard and J. T. Mague, *Inorg. Chem.*, **4**, 508 (1965).
24. F. A. Cotton and R. A. Walton, *Inorg. Chem.*, **5**, 1802 (1966).
25. J. H. Hickford and J. E. Fergusson, *J. Chem. Soc.*, **1967**, A, 113.
26. B. H. Robinson and J. E. Fergusson, *J. Chem. Soc.*, **1964**, 5683.
27. F. A. Cotton and S. J. Lippard, *Inorg. Chem.*, **4**, 1621 (1965).
28. R. A. Bailey and J. A. McIntyre, *Inorg. Chem.*, **5**, 1940 (1966).
29. D. Brown and R. Colton, *Nature*, **198**, 1300 (1963).
30. D. Brown and R. Colton, *J. Chem. Soc.*, **1964**, 714.
31. W. Klemm and H. Steinberg, *Z. anorg. allgem. Chem.*, **227**, 193 (1936).
32. R. Colton and R. L. Martin, *Nature*, **207**, 141 (1965).
33. H. G. Schnering and H. Wohrle, *Naturwiss.*, **50**, 91 (1963).
34. D. F. Stewart and T. A. O'Donnell, *Nature*, **210**, 836 (1966).
35. R. D. Peacock and D. W. A. Sharp, *J. Chem. Soc.*, **1959**, 2762.
36. R. Colton and I. B. Tomkins, *Australian J. Chem.*, **18**, 447 (1965).
37. R. Colton and I. B. Tomkins, *Australian J. Chem.*, **19**, 759 (1966).
38. I. R. Anderson and J. C. Sheldon, *Australian J. Chem.*, **18**, 271 (1965).
39. F. A. Cotton, N. F. Curtis, B. F. G. Johnson and W. R. Robinson, *Inorg. Chem.*, **4**, 326 (1965).
40. F. A. Cotton, C. Oldham and W. R. Robinson, *Inorg. Chem.*, **5**, 1798 (1966).
41. H. Schafer and K. D. Dohmann, *Z. anorg. allgem. Chem.*, **300**, 1 (1959).
42. H. G. Schnering, H. Wohrle and H. Schafer, *Naturwiss.*, **48**, 159 (1961).
43. S. S. Berdonosov and A. V. Lapitskii, *Russ. J. Inorg. Chem.*, **10**, 1525 (1965).
44. H. S. Harned, *J. Am. Chem. Soc.*, **35**, 1078 (1913).
45. H. S. Harned, C. Pauling and K. B. Corey, *J. Amer. Chem. Soc.*, **83**, 4815 (1960).

46. R. M. C. Chabrie, *Compt. Rend.*, **144**, 804 (1907).
47. W. H. Chapin, *J. Am. Chem. Soc.*, **32**, 323 (1910).
48. P. J. Kuhn and R. E. McCarley, *Inorg. Chem.*, **4**, 1482 (1965).
49. D. Bauer, H. G. Schnering and H. Schafer, *J. Less-Common Metals*, **8**, 388 (1965).
50. F. Korosy, *J. Am. Chem. Soc.*, **61**, 838 (1939).
51. H. Schafer, H. G. Schnering, K. J. Niehues and H. G. Nieder-Vahrenholz, *J. Less-Common Metals*, **9**, 95 (1965).
52. H. Schafer, H. Scholz and R. Gerken, *Z. anorg. allgem. Chem.*, **331**, 154 154 (1964).
53. H. Schafer, R. Gerken and H. Scholz, *Z. anorg. allgem. Chem.*, **335**, 96 (1965).
54. P. A. Vaughan, J. H. Sturdivant and L. Pauling, *J. Am. Chem. Soc.*, **72**, 5477 (1950).
55. R. D. Burbank, *Inorg. Chem.*, **5**, 1491 (1966).
56. A. Simon, H. G. Schnering, H. Wohrle and H. Schafer, *Z. anorg. allgem. Chem.*, **339**, 155 (1965).
57. M. B. Robin and N, A. Kuebler, *Inorg. Chem.*, **4**, 978 (1965).
58. R. E. McCarley, B. G. Hughes, F. A. Cotton and R. Zimmerman, *Inorg. Chem.*, **4**, 1491 (1965).
59. R. A. Mackay and R. F. Schneider, *Inorg. Chem,*. **6**, 549 (1966).
60. P. B. Fleming, T. A. Doughety and R. E. McCarley, *J. Am. Chem. Soc.*, **89**, 159 (1967).
61. R. J. Gillespie, *Can. J. Chem.*, **39**, 2336 (1961).
62. L. D. Crossman, D. P. Olsen and G. H. Duffey, *J. Chem. Phys.*, **38**, 73 (1963).
63. E. I. Krylov, *Nauchn. Dokl. Vysshei Shkoly, Khim. i Khim. Tekhnol.*, **1958**, 676.
64. P. M. Boorman and B. P. Straughan, *J. Chem. Soc.*, **1966**, A, 1514.
65. G. I. Novikov, N. V. Andreeva and O. G. Polyachenok, *Russ. J. Inorg. Chem.*, **6**, 1019 (1961).
66. S. Senderoff and A. Brennan, *J. Electrochem. Soc.*, **101**, 28 (1954).
67. F. Klanberg and H. W. Kohlschutter, *Z. Naturforsch.*, **15b**, 616 (1960).
68. K. Lindner, E. Haller and H. Helwig, *Z. anorg. allgem. Chem.*, **130**, 209 (1923).
69. M. A. Atterburg, *Bull. Soc. Chim. France*, **18**, 21 (1872).
70. K. Lindner and H. Helwig, *Z. anorg. allgem. Chem.*, **142**, 180 (1925).
71. R. Siepmann and H. Schafer, *Naturwiss.*, **52**, 344 (1965).
72. J. C. Sheldon, *J. Chem. Soc.*, **1962**, 410.
73. C. Brosset, *Arkiv Kemi, Mineral. Geol.*, **A20**, No. 7 (1945).
74. C. Brosset, *Arkiv Kemi, Mineral. Geol.*, **A22**, No 11 (1946).
75. C. Brosset, *Arkiv Kemi*, **1**, 353 (1949).
76. P. A. Vaughan, *Proc. Nat. Acad. Sci. U.S.*, **36**, 461 (1950).
77. H. Schafer and R. Siepmann, *J. Less-Common Metals*, **11**, 76, (1966).
78. H. Schafer. H. G. Schnering, A. Simon, D. Giegling, D. Bauer, R. Seipmann and B. Spreckelmeyer, *J. Less-Common Metals*, **10**, 154 (1966).
79. R. J. H. Clark, D. L. Kepert, R. S. Nyholm and G. A. Rodley, *Spectrochim. Acta*, **22**, 1697 (1966).
80. F. A. Cotton, R. M. Wing and R. A. Zimmerman, *Inorg. Chem.*, **6**, 11 (1967).
81. J. C. Sheldon, *Nature*, **184**, 1210 (1959).

82. J. C. Sheldon, *J. Chem. Soc.*, **1960**, 3106.
83. J. C. Sheldon, *J. Chem. Soc.*, **1960**, 1007.
84. F. A. Cotton and N. F. Curtis, *Inorg. Chem.*, **4**, 241 (1965).
85. J. E. Fergusson, B. H. Robinson and C. J. Wilkins, *J. Chem. Soc.*, **1967**, 486.
86. D. A. Edwards, *J. Less-Common Metals*, **7**, 159 (1964)
87. A. F. Wells, *Z. Krist.*, **100**, 189 (1938).
88. H. Schafer, U. Wiese, K. Rinke and K. Brendel, *Angew. Chem.*, **79**, 244 (1967).
89. K. Brodersen, G. Thiele and H. G. Schnering, *Z. anorg. allgem. Chem.*, **337**, 120 (1965).
90. F. A. Cotton and S. J. Lippard, *J. Am. Chem. Soc.*, **88**, 1882 (1966).
91. P. B. Fleming, L. A. Mueller and R. E. McCarley, *Inorg. Chem.*, **6**, 1 (1967).
92. R. A. Field and D. L. Kepert, *J. Less-Common Metals*, **13**, 378 (1967).
93. B. Spreckelmayer and H. Schafer, *J. Less-Common Metals*, **13**, 122 (1967).
94. D. Hartley and M. J. Ware, *Chem. Commun.*, **1967**, 912.
95. R. Siepman, H. G. Schnering and H. Schafer, *Angew. Chem., Intern. Ed. Engl.*, **6**, 637 (1967).
96. G. B. Allison, I. R. Anderson and J. C. Sheldon, *Australian J. Chem.*, **20**, 869 (1967).
97. W. van Bronswyk and J. C. Sheldon, *Australian J. Chem.*, **20**, 2329 (1967).

Chapter 4

Zirconium and Hafnium

The dominating feature of a consideration of the elements zirconium and hafnium is the unique similarity of their chemistries. This is reflected in the difficulty of separation of the elements; before the advent of ion-exchange chromatography and other modern distribution techniques, their complete separation was the ultimate test of chemical ingenuity.

The chemistry of these elements is characterized by the difficulty of reduction to oxidation states less than the group valence of four. Indeed, no compound of either of these elements in any oxidation state other than four is known in aqueous solution, and most of the solid compounds in lower oxidation states are readily oxidized.

HALIDES

The known halides of zirconium and hafnium are given in Table 4.1. The compounds often referred to as "zirconyl halides" are in fact complex polynuclear compounds and are more appropriately discussed in the section on complex halides.

TABLE 4.1

Halides of Zirconium and Hafnium

Oxidation state	Fluoride	Chloride	Bromide	Iodide
IV	ZrF_4, HfF_4	$ZrCl_4$, $HfCl_4$	$ZrBr_4$, $HfBr_4$	ZrI_4, HfI_4
III	ZrF_3	$ZrCl_3$, $HfCl_3$	$ZrBr_3$, $HfBr_3$	ZrI_3, HfI_3
II	ZrF_2	$ZrCl_2$, $HfCl_2$	$ZrBr_2$, $HfBr_2$	ZrI_2

Oxidation State IV

Zirconium tetrafluoride. This compound has been prepared by a large variety of methods; but these can in general be divided into three classes:

(i) direct fluorination of metallic zirconium or of a number of zirconium compounds;

(ii) halogen exchange from zirconium tetrachloride; and

(iii) thermal decomposition of ammonium fluorozirconates(IV), which may be prepared in aqueous solution.

These methods of preparation are summarized in Table 4.2.

Zirconium tetrafluoride is a white crystalline solid which is readily purified by vacuum-sublimation. Although it is hydrolysed by water, its hydrates can be isolated from aqueous solutions containing high concentrations of hydrogen fluoride.

TABLE 4.2

Preparation of Zirconium Tetrafluoride

Method	Conditions	Ref.
Zr and F_2	Flow system, 420°	1, 2, 3
ZrO_2 and F_2	Flow system, 520°	2, 3
ZrC and F_2	Elevated temp.	4
ZrB_2 and F_2	Elevated temp.	4
Zr and anhydrous HF	Bomb, 225°	5
Zr and BrF_3		3
ZrO_2 and BrF_3		3
$ZrCl_4$ and BrF_3		3
$ZrCl_4$ and anhydrous HF	Flow system, 300°	3, 6
$ZrCl_4$, $POCl_3$ and anhydrous HF		6
$(NH_4)_3ZrF_7$	500°	7, 8, 9
$(NH_4)_2ZrF_6$	500°	8, 9
NH_4ZrF_5	500°	3

Zirconium tetrafluoride exists in two forms, but in only a few instances is a specific reference made to the polymorph being investigated. Chretien and Gaudreau[3] made a systematic study of the conditions necessary to produce specific forms of zirconium tetrafluoride. They found that above 450° the β-form is obtained exclusively. The α-form is obtained under preparative conditions employing temperatures lower than 450°. It changes to the β-form at 450° and, once obtained, the β-form is stable at all temperatures.

There is considerable confusion concerning the structure of zirconium tetrafluoride, possibly due in some measure, to the unrecognized polymorphic character of the compound. Three examinations of X-ray powder diffraction patterns and one single-crystal study each gave monoclinic symmetry, but there is not complete agreement between the parameters of the unit cell, as shown in Table 4.3.

It is clear that the single-crystal work agrees quite closely with the powder data given by Schulze[11]. The powder diffraction data given in reference 12 refer specifically to the β-form, whereas the other data were determined before the polymorphic nature of the compound was known. It is not clear to which form of zirconium tetrafluoride these other data

TABLE 4.3

Unit-Cell Parameters of Monoclinic Zirconium
Tetrafluoride

Method	a (Å)	b (Å)	c (Å)	α	Z	Ref.
Powder	11.69	9.87	7.64	126.1°	12	10
Powder	9.46	9.87	7.64	94.5°	12	11
Powder	15.82	13.73	15.11	106.3°	52	12
Single crystal	9.57	9.93	7.73	94.5°	12	13

refer. However, it has been noted that the two forms give distinctly different diffraction patterns[9,12].

The structure determined by single-crystal techniques by Burbank and Bensey[13] consists of an eight-coordinate square antiprismatic arrangement of fluorine atoms around each zirconium atom. Each fluorine has two zirconium contacts and the average zirconium–fluorine distance is 2.10 Å. The structure is shown in Figure 4.1.

The vapour pressure of zirconium tetrafluoride has been reported a number of times. At first sight the equations which express the variation

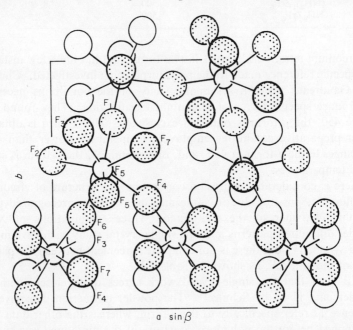

Figure 4.1 Projection of the zirconium tetrafluoride structure along the *c*-axis.

TABLE 4.4

Vapour Pressure of Zirconium Tetrafluoride

Equation: $\log p_{mm} = A - (B/T)$

A	B	Temp. range	Ref.
12.569	11,450	640–905°	14
13.3995	12,376	617–880°	15
12.542	11,360	710–808°	16
12.542	11,310	710–808°	3
13.5571	12,430	408–640°	17
12.150	10,722	440–600°	18

of vapour pressure with temperature appear to differ widely. However, a plot of figures calculated from each of the expressions shows that the discrepancies are not unreasonable. The data are summarized in Table 4.4.

The available thermodynamic data for zirconium tetrafluoride are summarized in Table 4.5. Heat capacities and entropies have been calculated for zirconium tetrafluoride over the temperature range 0–930°.

The infrared spectrum of zirconium tetrafluoride in the vapour phase at 800° has been observed[23]. Tetrahedral symmetry is assumed and adsorptions were observed at 668 cm^{-1} (v_3) and 190 ± 20 cm^{-1} (v_4).

Virtually no chemical property of zirconium tetrafluoride has been reported except its reaction with aqueous hydrogen fluoride. The results

TABLE 4.5

Thermodynamic Data for Zirconium
Tetrafluoride

Property	Value	Ref.
M.p.	912°	16
	932°	19
ΔH_{form}°	−457 kcal mole^{-1}	1
	−456.8 kcal mole^{-1}	20
ΔS_{form}°	81.16 cal deg^{-1} mole^{-1}	20
$\Delta H_{sub, \alpha}$	49.05 kcal mole^{-1}	18
$\Delta H_{sub, \beta}$	52.0 kcal mole^{-1}	16
	52.12 kcal mole^{-1}	3
	55.55 kcal mole^{-1}	21
	56.63 kcal mole^{-1}	15
	56.9 kcal mole^{-1}	17
ΔH_{vap}	37.3 kcal mole^{-1}	16
ΔH_{fus}	14.7 kcal mole^{-1}	16
	15.35 kcal mole^{-1}	19

obtained by various workers are conflicting and it is clear that a large number of compounds exist. The only undisputed conclusion is that the two hydrates $ZrF_4 \cdot H_2O$ and $ZrF_4 \cdot 3H_2O$ can be isolated. Similarly, a wide variety of products has been claimed to result from thermal decomposition of the hydrates. Some of the products reported as resulting from thermal decomposition of the hydrates and as being isolated from aqueous hydrogen fluoride solution are given in Table 4.6. Although many

TABLE 4.6

Miscellaneous Reported Fluoro Compounds of
Zirconium(IV)

Formula	Ref.	Formula	Ref.
$ZrF_4 \cdot 2HF \cdot 0.7H_2O$	24	$Zr_2(OH)F_7$	28
$ZrOF_2 \cdot 2H_2O$	25	$HZrF_5 \cdot 4H_2O$	26
$Zr_4O_3F_{10} \cdot 6H_2O$	26	$Zr_4O_3F_{10}$	27
Zr_4OF_{14}	27	$Zr_3O_2F_8$	27
$Zr_2OF_6 \cdot 2H_2O$	27		

of these compounds cannot be claimed to be well-established, it has been shown by X-ray powder diffraction data that they represent distinct phases[24,29].

Single-crystal X-ray diffraction data[30] of the trihydrate of zirconium tetrafluoride has revealed an interesting dimeric structure with two bridging fluorine atoms, as shown in Figure 4.2. The crystals are triclinic with the following unit-cell parameters: $a = 5.94$ Å, $b = 6.96$ Å, $c = 7.55$ Å, $\alpha = 90.2°$, $\beta = 105.0°$ and $\gamma = 118.9°$. The space group was found to be $P\bar{1}$ with two molecules in the unit cell.

Hafnium tetrafluoride. There is considerably less information available for hafnium tetrafluoride than for its zirconium analogue—a comment common to most compounds of hafnium. This results largely from the difficulty of separating the elements and from the comparative rarity of hafnium.

Hafnium tetrafluoride has been prepared by direct fluorination of the metal[31], the carbide and the boride[32], and by thermal decomposition[33] of ammonium hexafluorohafnate(IV) at temperatures above 500°.

Hafnium tetrafluoride is a white crystalline compound. X-ray powder diffraction data suggest that it is isostructural with zirconium tetrafluoride but, as noted above, there are some discrepancies in the published data for the latter compound. As a result, two interpretations of the diffraction

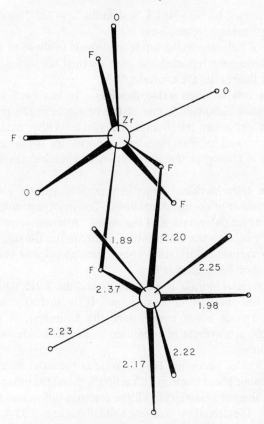

Figure 4.2   The structure of $ZrF_4 \cdot 3H_2O$.

data of hafnium tetrafluoride have been given, each similar to the appropriate zirconium tetrafluoride assignment, namely:

Monoclinic: $a = 9.45$ Å, $b = 9.84$ Å, $c = 7.62$ Å, $\alpha = 94.5°$

(reference 11)

Monoclinic: $a = 11.68$ Å, $b = 9.84$ Å, $c = 7.62$ Å, $\alpha = 126.1°$

(reference 10)

The vapour pressure of hafnium tetrafluoride has been measured over a wide temperature range and is given by the expression[14]:

$$\log p_{mm} = 12.91 - 12{,}460/T \quad (721° \text{ to } 956°).$$

The standard heat, free energy, and entropy of formation of hafnium tetrafluoride have been determined by Hubbard and coworkers[31] by fluorine bomb calorimetry to be -461.4 kcal mole^{-1}, -437.2 kcal mole^{-1} and 81.3 cal deg^{-1} mole^{-1}, respectively.

Hydrates of hafnium tetrafluoride analogous to those of the zirconium compound have been reported and their thermal decomposition has been studied, but the results are confusing[34,35].

Zirconium and hafnium oxide fluorides. It has been claimed[24] that zirconium oxide difluoride is one of the products in the progressive dehydration of zirconium tetrafluoride trihydrate. Other oxide fluorides of both zirconium and hafnium have been reported for the same reaction[35,36], but nothing is known of the constitution or chemical reactions of these compounds.

Zirconium tetrachloride. Zirconium tetrachloride is easily prepared by a large number of chemical reactions. The most convenient laboratory synthesis is direct chlorination of the metal. Alternative procedures used commercially involve the chlorination of zirconium dioxide or zirconium silicate with various chlorinating agents such as sulphur chlorides, phosgene and carbon tetrachloride[37].

Zirconium tetrachloride is a white crystalline solid which is readily purified by sublimation in a vacuum. It is instantly hydrolyzed in water, although at room temperature the hydrolysis is not complete and the stable octahydrate of zirconium oxide dichloride may be isolated from the solution.

The structure of zirconium tetrachloride in the solid state is unknown, but in the vapour phase electron diffraction[38-40] and the infrared spectrum[41] indicate tetrahedral symmetry. All the electron-diffraction studies give a mean value of the zirconium–chlorine bond distance as 2.33 Å. Absorptions were recorded in the infrared spectrum at 421 (v_3), 380 (v_1), 112 (v_4) and 102 cm^{-1} (v_2).

TABLE 4.7

Vapour Pressure of Zirconium Tetrachloride

Equation	Temp. range	Ref.
(Solid) $\log p_{mm} = 11.83 - 5430/T$	230–330°	42
(Solid) $\log p_{mm} = 11.766 - 5400/T$	207–416°	43
(Liquid) $\log p_{mm} = 9.088 - 3427/T$	437–468°	43
(Liquid) $\log p_{mm} = 9.4714 - 3570/T$	438–500°	44

The vapour pressure of zirconium tetrafluoride has been measured twice over the solid and twice over the liquid. The expressions describing the variation of vapour pressure with temperature are given in Table 4.7.

It is clear that the equations giving the vapour pressure over solid zirconium tetrachloride are in very good agreement. However, there appears to be a typographical error in the translation of the original Russian paper by Nisel'son and coworkers[44]. A graphical plot of their results shows that the vapour pressure given by their equation is lower than that given by the equation of Palko and coworkers[43], but the last expression given in Table 4.7 leads to the reverse situation.

TABLE 4.8

Thermodynamic Data for Zirconium
Tetrachloride

Property	Value	Ref.
M.p.	435.5°	45
	437°	43
	438°	44
ΔH°_{form}	−231.9 kcal mole^{-1}	46
	−234.35 kcal mole^{-1}	47
	−234.7 kcal mole^{-1}	48
ΔG°_{form}	−213.4 kcal mole^{-1}	49
ΔH_{sub}	24.7 kcal mole^{-1}	43
ΔH_{vap}	15.7 kcal mole^{-1}	43
	17.1 kcal mole^{-1}	44
ΔH_{fus}	9.0 kcal mole^{-1}	43

Thermodynamic data for zirconium tetrachloride are given in Table 4.8. The quasi-boiling point (vapour pressure = 760 mm) has been reported[44] as 296°. Heat capacities and entropies for zirconium tetrachloride have been calculated[41,50,51] in the following temperature ranges: −21 to 25°, 25–727° and 62–294°.

Very many simple molecular adducts of zirconium tetrachloride have been prepared, with the most varied types of donor atom. Oxygen donor molecules used have included phosphorus oxychloride, tributyl phosphate, thionyl chloride and a large range of ketones, esters, and alcohols. Similarly, a wide range of amines and nitriles have been used as nitrogen donor molecules. A few of the compounds prepared are listed in Table 4.9.

Use of phosphorus oxychloride leads to $ZrCl_4 \cdot POCl_3$ and $ZrCl_4 \cdot 2POCl_3$ simultaneously in solution[57,95]; the 1:1 adduct is associated in solution. It is interesting that phosphorus oxyfluoride and phosphorus oxide chloride difluoride give only the 1:1 adducts under all conditions[57]. The only eight-coordinate adduct of zirconium tetrachloride is the diarsine compound[89,90].

Compounds in which one or more chlorine atoms are replaced have been reported as formed by a number of carboxylic acids[64,96-98], by phenols to give phenoxides[99] and by cyclopentadienylsodium to give bis(cyclopentadienyl)zirconium dichloride[100].

Lithium borohydride and zirconium tetrachloride give zirconium borohydride[101]. Gaseous ammonia reacts with zirconium tetrachloride at high temperatures (>750°) to give a series of nitrides[102]. With fluorosulphuric acid the compound $ZrF_3 \cdot SO_3F$ is formed[103].

TABLE 4.9

Some Molecular Adducts of Zirconium
Tetrachloride

Compound	Ref.
$ZrCl_4 \cdot POCl_3$ and $ZrCl_4 \cdot 2POCl_3$	52–59
$ZrCl_4 \cdot 2(C_4H_9)_3PO_4$	60, 61
$ZrCl_4 \cdot SOCl_2$	58
$ZrCl_4 \cdot 2SeOCl_2$	58
$ZrCl_4 \cdot 2NOCl$	58, 62
Ketones, e.g. $ZrCl_4 \cdot 2(CH_3)_2CO$	63–66
Esters, e.g. $ZrCl_4 \cdot 2CH_3COOC_2H_5$	67–77
Alcohols, e.g. $ZrCl_4 \cdot 2CH_3OH$	78, 79
Nitriles, e.g. $ZrCl_4 \cdot 2CH_3CN$	62, 66, 80–83
Amines, e.g. $ZrCl_4 \cdot phen$	84–88
$ZrCl_4 \cdot 2(CH_3)_2S$	86
$ZrCl_4 \cdot 2Diarsine$	89, 90
Miscellaneous	81, 91–94

Hafnium tetrachloride. The usual laboratory method of preparing this compound is direct chlorination of hafnium metal. The compound has also been prepared from hafnium dioxide by mixing the oxide with molasses, briquetting the mixture and heating it to 800°. The resulting product was chlorinated by means of carbon tetrachloride vapour at 450°. Alternatively, hafnium dioxide can be chlorinated directly at 750°[104].

The structure of solid hafnium tetrachloride is unknown, but electron-diffraction studies have shown it to be a regular tetrahedron in the vapour phase. The mean hafnium–chlorine bond distance was 2.33 Å[40].

The vapour pressure of hafnium tetrachloride has been measured three times, the equations expressing the variation of vapour pressure with temperature being:

$$\log p_{mm} = 11.712 - 5197/T \quad (203\text{--}408°) \quad \text{(reference 43)}$$

$$\log p_{mm} = 11.64 - 5200/T \quad (230\text{--}330°) \quad \text{(reference 42)}$$

$$\log p_{mm} = 12.00 - 5390/T \quad (200\text{--}312°) \quad \text{(reference 105)}$$

TABLE 4.10

Thermodynamic Data for Hafnium
Tetrachloride

Property	Value	Ref.
M.p.	432°	45, 105
	434°	43
ΔH_{form}°	-233.9 kcal mole^{-1}	47
	-236.7 kcal mole^{-1}	106
	-239.0 kcal mole^{-1}	107
ΔH_{sub}	23.8 kcal mole^{-1}	43
	24.6 kcal mole^{-1}	105

These results are not in good agreement; the calculated vapour pressures at 300° are 439.5, 368.1 and 392.6 mm, respectively.

Some thermodynamic values have been calculated from the vapour-pressure measurements and these are given in Table 4.10, together with other available data. Heat capacities and entropies have been calculated[108,109] for hafnium tetrachloride between $-222°$ and 209°.

General reactions of hafnium tetrachloride closely resemble those of its zirconium analogue, although they are naturally far fewer in number. The known reactions are summarized in Table 4.11.

TABLE 4.11

Adducts Formed by Hafnium Tetrachloride

Adduct	Ref.
Nitriles, e.g. $HfCl_4 \cdot 2CH_3CN$	80
Amines, e.g. $HfCl_4 \cdot 2py$	88
$HfCl_4 \cdot 2POCl_3$, etc.	52, 54, 56, 57, 95, 110
Alcohols, e.g. $HfCl_4 \cdot 2CH_3OH$	78, 79
$HfCl_4 \cdot 2Diarsine$	89, 90

Zirconium tetrabromide. Zirconium tetrabromide is best prepared[111,112] by direct bromination of an intimate mixture of zirconium dioxide and carbon at a temperature of about 560°. It is easily purified by sublimation at 250–280°.

The properties of zirconium tetrabromide are in general similar to those of the tetrachloride.

Between 216° and 332°, the vapour pressure of zirconium tetrabromide varies according to the expression[113]:

$$\log p_{mm} = 12.268 - 5945/T.$$

Zirconium tetrabromide melts[45] at 450°; its free energy and heat of formation are -172.5 and -181.6 kcal mole^{-1}, respectively[49]. Nisel'son and Sokolova[114] measured the density of liquid zirconium tetrabromide over a wide temperature range and calculated the critical parameters.

It is reported[111] that zirconium tetrabromide has a cubic lattice with $a = 10.95$ Å and space group $Pa3$.

Several addition compounds of zirconium tetrabromide have been reported; they are of the general types discussed above for zirconium tetrachloride and are summarized in Table 4.12.

TABLE 4.12

Adducts of Zirconium Tetrabromide

Adduct	Ref.
Amines, e.g. $ZrBr_4 \cdot 4N(CH_3)_3$	86–88, 115–117
Nitriles, e.g. $ZrBr_4 \cdot 2CH_3CN$	81, 82, 86
Miscellaneous	118, 119

Zirconium tetrabromide reacts with gaseous ammonia at about 800° to give a series of zirconium nitrides[102]. In liquid ammonia, zirconium tetrabromide appears[120,121] to be reduced by potassium metal to give $Zr(NK)_2 \cdot xNH_3$.

Hafnium tetrabromide. The best method[122] of preparing hafnium tetrabromide is by the action of bromine on an intimate mixture of hafnium dioxide and charcoal at 700–800°.

The variation of the vapour pressure of hafnium tetrabromide over the temperature range 210–317° is given by the expression[113]:

$$\log p_{mm} = 11.697 - 5257/T.$$

Hafnium tetrabromide melts[45] at 424.5° and its heat of formation is given[107] as -200 kcal mole^{-1}.

It is reported that hafnium tetrabromide has a cubic lattice with $a = 10.91$ Å and space group $Pa3$, and that it is isostructural with zirconium tetrabromide[123]. In the vapour phase, an electron-diffraction study gave[123] the mean hafnium–bromine bond length as 2.43 Å, to be compared with a zirconium–bromine distance of 2.44 Å in zirconium tetrabromide.

Whilst one would expect that the general features of the coordination chemistry of hafnium tetrabromide would resemble those of its zirconium analogue, there are no reports so far of such reactions.

Zirconium tetraiodide. A number of interesting methods of preparing zirconium tetraiodide have been reported; and it is noteworthy that the general method applicable to the other halides, that is, passing the halogen over a heated mixture of the dioxide and carbon, does not result in the formation of zirconium tetraiodide[124]. However, it is significant that iodine vapour does react with heated zirconium metal to give the tetraiodide[124]. Zirconium tetraiodide may also be prepared[125,126] by interaction of zirconium dioxide and aluminium triiodide in a sealed tube at 400°. Halogen exchange reactions of zirconium tetrachloride with other iodides, for example, silicon tetraiodide (250°), hydrogen iodide (370°), or, best, aluminium triiodide (370°) also produce zirconium tetraiodide[127].

Zirconium tetraiodide is an orange-red to yellow powder[124] which can be sublimed[128] at 420°. The vapour pressure of solid zirconium tetraiodide over the range 150–230° is given by the expression[128]:

$$\log p_{mm} = 12.03 - 6342/T.$$

Zirconium tetraiodide melts[45] at 500°, and the free energy and heat of formation are -116.6 kcal mole^{-1} and -115.9 kcal mole^{-1}, respectively[49].

Zirconium tetraiodide undergoes an interesting reaction with liquid sulphur dioxide in a sealed tube, giving zirconium disulphite[129]:

$$ZrI_4 + 3SO_2 \rightarrow Zr(SO_3)_2 + 2I_2 + S$$

With gaseous ammonia at room temperature, zirconium tetraiodide forms a series of adducts, $ZrI_4 \cdot xNH_3$, which when heated to 750° give zirconium nitrides[130]. The nitrides may also be prepared[102] by direct interaction of zirconium tetraiodide and gaseous ammonia at 750°. Adducts of zirconium tetraiodide with esters have been reported by Osipov and Kletenik[131].

Hafnium tetraiodide. The action of iodine vapour on heated hafnium metal yields hafnium tetraiodide[132]. Alternatively, halogen exchange between hafnium tetrachloride and aluminium triiodide at 330° may be used[127].

Hafnium tetraiodide is a yellow-orange solid which melts at 449°. An investigation by Stevenson and coworkers[133] has shown that hafnium tetraiodide is polymorphic: at least three forms exist with transitions at 324° and 372°. The vapour pressures for each form are given by the expressions:

α, solid (302–324°) $\log p_{mm} = 19.56 - 10,700/T$

β, solid (325–372°) $\log p_{mm} = 13.97 - 7360/T$

γ, solid (375–405°) $\log p_{mm} = 12.13 - 6173/T$

The corresponding heats of sublimation are given as 48.9, 33.7 and 28.2 kcal mole^{-1}, respectively[133].

It is reported[132] that the structure of an unspecified polymorph of hafnium tetraiodide is cubic with $a = 11.76$ Å and space group *Pa*3.

Oxidation State III

Zirconium trifluoride. It has been reported that zirconium trifluoride is formed when a mixture of hydrogen and anhydrous hydrogen fluoride is passed over zirconium hydride at 750° in a flow system[134]. A less efficient method of preparation is reduction of ammonium hexafluorozirconate(IV) by hydrogen at 650°. The trifluoride is reported to decompose when heated alone above 300°.

Zirconium trichloride. Zirconium trichloride has been prepared from the tetrachloride and a variety of reducing agents under the conditions shown in Table 4.13. Here we may note that zirconium tetrachloride but not hafnium tetrachloride, is reduced by zirconium metal at about 500°. This difference in reactivity has been exploited by Newnham and others in a procedure for obtaining zirconium free from hafnium[137,140,141]. The procedure is to reduce a charge of the hafnium-contaminated zirconium tetrachloride with zirconium. The unchanged tetrachlorides are separated by sublimation, leaving a residue of relatively involatile pure zirconium trichloride.

TABLE 4.13

Preparation of Zirconium Trichloride

Reaction	Conditions	Ref.
Zr and $ZrCl_4$	>500°	135, 136
Zr and $ZrCl_4$	400–500° in a vacuum	137
Zr and $ZrCl_4$	Zr at 700°, $ZrCl_4$ at 330°	138
Al and $ZrCl_4$	300°	124
H_2 gas discharge and $ZrCl_4$	200° and 3 mm H_2	139

Zirconium trichloride is a blue-black solid which becomes brown on exposure to air[138,139]. It dissolves in water with evolution of hydrogen to give initially a brown solution, which becomes colourless quite rapidly as oxidation occurs[136,138].

At temperatures above 400° zirconium trichloride undergoes thermal disproportionation to zirconium dichloride and tetrachloride[135,136,140,141]. Above 650° the only products are zirconium metal and the tetrachloride, because of the thermal instability of zirconium dichloride at these temperatures[140]. The equilibrium dissociation pressure of zirconium tetrachloride over the trichloride has been determined over the temperature range 340–450° and was found to conform to the expression[142]:

$$\log p_{mm} = 11.632 - 6246/T$$

The heat and entropy of dissociation have been calculated to be 30.1 kcal mole^{-1} and 39.1 cal deg^{-1} mole^{-1}, respectively at 298°K[142].

The heat of formation of zirconium trichloride has been estimated to be -172 kcal mole^{-1} [143] or -178.6 kcal mole^{-1} [107], and the entropy of formation[143] as 48 cal deg^{-1} mole^{-1}.

Dahl and coworkers[144] studied the powder diffraction pattern of zirconium trichloride and deduced that this compound had an hexagonal lattice with $a = 6.36$ and $c = 6.14$ Å, but Swaroop and Flengas[145] found a tetragonal lattice with $a = 5.961$ and $c = 9.669$ Å. Zirconium trichloride may prove to be polymorphic, as is common for many transition-metal trichlorides.

The magnetic behaviour of zirconium trichloride is not well understood. The effective magnetic moment is about 0.4 B.M. and it is clear that there are strong antiferromagnetic interactions in the solid[146].

Zirconium trichloride reacts with cyclopentadiene vapour, to give cyclopentadienylzirconium trichloride and dicyclopentadienylzirconium dichloride[147].

Hafnium trichloride. Hafnium trichloride has been prepared[135] by reduction of hafnium tetrachloride with hafnium metal at temperatures between 500° and 700°. At elevated temperatures hafnium trichloride disproportionates to the tetrachloride and the dichloride[135]. The heat of formation of hafnium trichloride has been calculated[107] to be -186 kcal mole^{-1}.

Zirconium tribromide. Zirconium tribromide may be prepared by a variety of methods, all of which are similar to methods described above for preparing the trichloride. Thus zirconium tetrabromide has been reduced with aluminium at 450° in a hydrogen atmosphere[148], in a hydrogen gas discharge at 230° and 4 mm hydrogen[139] or with zirconium metal. The last reaction is interesting because different polymorphs may be obtained under different conditions. At temperatures above 485° the usual blue-black form of the compound is obtained[135,149] but, Schlaefer and Skoludek[149] found that in the temperature range 295–485° dark green needles of zirconium tribromide are formed.

At temperatures greater than 300° zirconium tribromide disproportionates to the dibromide and the tetrabromide[135,148,150]. The equilibrium dissociation pressure of zirconium tetrabromide over zirconium tribromide in the temperature range 320–500° is given by the expression[150].

$$\log p_{mm} = 8.367 - 4671/T.$$

The heat of disproportionation[150] at 412° is 21.2 kcal mole^{-1} and the corresponding entropy is 25.1 cal deg^{-1} mole^{-1}. The heat of formation[107] of zirconium tribromide is -151 kcal mole^{-1}.

The X-ray powder diffraction data[144] for zirconium tribromide suggest that the compound is hexagonal with $a = 6.75$ and $c = 6.31$ Å. It is antiferromagnetic[146].

Zirconium tribromide reacts with cyclopentadiene vapour to give cyclopentadienylzirconium tribromide[147].

Hafnium tribromide. Hafnium tribromide has been prepared by the reduction of the tetrabromide in a hydrogen atmosphere with hafnium metal[135] or aluminium[122]. It is a blue-black solid which reacts with water with the evolution of hydrogen. Like its zirconium analogue, it disproportionates at about 350° to the dibromide and tetrabromide[122,135]. The heat of formation of hafnium tribromide has been reported[107] as -157 kcal mole^{-1}.

Zirconium triiodide. Zirconium triiodide is prepared[135,151-153] by the reduction of the tetraiodide with zirconium metal at temperatures between 300° and 500°. Alternative reducing agents are aluminium[154] or hydrogen in a gas discharge at 290°[139].

Zirconium triiodide is a blue-black solid which disproportionates at high temperatures to the tetraiodide and the diiodide[135,153]. Sale and Shelton[155], however, postulate that the compound $ZrI_3 \cdot ZrI_2$ is formed as an intermediate between 275° and 325°. This intermediate was detected by measuring the equilibrium pressure of zirconium tetraiodide over the solid triiodide. At high temperatures the intermediate decomposes to zirconium tetraiodide and diiodide. The equations describing these processes are:

$$3ZrI_3 \rightarrow ZrI_3 \cdot ZrI_2 + ZrI_4 \quad (275-325°)$$
$$3ZrI_3 \cdot ZrI_2 \rightarrow 2ZrI_2 + 2ZrI_4 \quad (325-400°)$$

The variation of vapour pressure with temperature in the system is given by the expressions:

$$\log p_{mm} = 12.47 - 8700/T \quad (275-325°)$$
$$\log p_{mm} = 37.70 - 26,367/T \quad (325-400°)$$

The corresponding heats of dissociation are 39.9 and 120 kcal mole^{-1} respectively[155]. The heat of formation of zirconium triiodide is reported[107] as -103 kcal mole^{-1}.

Zirconium triiodide has a hexagonal lattice[144] with $a = 7.25$ and $c = 6.64$ Å. It is antiferromagnetic[146,154].

Reaction of zirconium triiodide with cyclopentadiene vapour gives cyclopentadienylzirconium triiodide[147].

Hafnium triiodide. Reduction of hafnium tetraiodide by hafnium metal[135] or aluminium[154] gives hafnium triiodide. This[144] is hexagonal with $a = 7.22$ and $c = 6.59$ Å and is antiferromagnetic[154]. Its heat of formation[147] is -113 kcal mole^{-1}.

Oxidation State II

Zirconium difluoride. Zirconium difluoride has been claimed[156] to result from the action of atomic hydrogen on a thin layer of zirconium tetrafluoride at 350°. It is interesting that there was no evidence for the formation of zirconium trifluoride in this reaction.

Zirconium difluoride is a black, non-hygroscopic solid which, when warmed, ignites in air. At 800° it decomposes to zirconium metal and the tetrafluoride. Zirconium difluoride has an orthorhombic lattice with $a = 4.09$, $b = 4.91$ and $c = 6.56$ Å. Its heat of formation has been given[156] as -224 kcal mole^{-1}.

Zirconium dichloride. Zirconium dichloride is prepared by thermal disproportionation of zirconium trichloride[135,136,140,141]. It has also been made by adding a suspension of sodium metal in paraffin oil to zirconium trichloride in paraffin oil at 100° under nitrogen[157]. Zirconium metal may also be used[158] to reduce the trichloride at 675°.

Zirconium dichloride is a black powder which disproportionates at high temperatures to zirconium metal and the tetrachloride, although some evidence for the intermediate formation of zirconium monochloride has been obtained from studies of the equilibrium pressure of zirconium tetrachloride over solid zirconium dichloride[143].

Estimates of the heat of formation of zirconium dichloride have been -118 kcal mole^{-1} [143] and -124.3 kcal mole^{-1} [107]. It is antiferromagnetic[146].

Hafnium dichloride. Hafnium dichloride has been prepared by thermal disproportionation of hafnium trichloride[135]. Its heat of formation has been reported[107] as -130 kcal mole^{-1}.

Zirconium and hafnium dibromides. Both these dibromides are prepared by thermal disproportionation of the corresponding tribromides[122,135,148]. Both are blue-black solids and the heats of formation are given as -100 and -108 kcal mole^{-1} for zirconium and hafnium dibromides, respectively[107]. At temperatures greater than 400° both dibromides disproportionate to the metal and tetrabromide[122].

Zirconium diiodide. Zirconium diiodide is prepared as a blue-black solid by thermal disproportionation of zirconium triiodide[151,155]. Its heat of formation is given as -68 kcal mole^{-1}.

10

COMPLEX HALIDES AND OXIDE HALIDES

All the complex halides and oxide halides of zirconium and hafnium that have been prepared are compounds of oxidation state IV. It is remarkable that, whilst complex halides of the type MX_6^{2-}, where X is any halogen, exist for most transition metals, bromides and iodides of this type are unknown for both zirconium and hafnium. Although fluoro and chloro complexes of zirconium and hafnium exist, they are considerably less stable thermally than most other complexes of this type. The non-existence of the bromo and iodo complexes cannot be due to steric effects since the Group IV metals form the largest quadrivalent ions in the second- and third-row transition series. It is possible that delocalization of the d-electron density of the metal on to the ligands via a π-bonding mechanism is responsible to a larger extent than previously suspected for the stability of these complexes. Since quadrivalent zirconium and hafnium ions have no d-electrons, this mechanism of ligand stabilization is not available and this situation may account for the low thermal stability of the chloro complexes and the non-existence of hexabromo- and hexaiodo-zirconates(IV) and -hafnates(IV).

Heptafluorozirconates(IV). There are three general ways of preparing heptafluorozirconates(IV), namely: fluorination in the melt of the oxide, carbide or nitride in ammonium or alkali-metal fluorides; direct inter-action at high temperatures of an alkali-metal fluoride with zirconium tetrafluoride; and reactions with aqueous hydrogen fluoride. These, and other methods of a more specific nature, are given in Table 4.14.

TABLE 4.14

Preparation of Heptafluorozirconates(IV)

Method	Conditions	Ref.
ZrO_2 and NH_4HF_2	175–200°	7
ZrO_2 and KBF_4	>600°	159, 160
ZrC or ZrN and NH_4HF_2	Elevated temp.	8
ZrF_4 and MF	Melt	161–163
ZrF_4, MF and aqueous HF	Solution	164
K_2ZrF_6 and KBF_4	Melt	165
$ZrBr_4$ and NH_4F or RbF	In methanol	166, 167

The melting point of sodium heptafluorozirconate(IV) has been reported as 830° [162] and 840° [168], and for the corresponding potassium salt[169] as 921°.

The thermal decomposition of the ammonium salt has been studied in detail by Haendler and coworkers[170], who found that the temperature of decomposition varies with pressure, and the following steps have been identified:

$$(NH_4)_3ZrF_7 \xrightarrow{297°} (NH_4)_2ZrF_6 \xrightarrow{357°} NH_4ZrF_5 \xrightarrow{410°} ZrF_4 \quad \text{(at 760 mm)}$$

The structure of the heptafluorozirconate(IV) anion is not definitely known. It has been frequently stated that in the ammonium, potassium and caesium salts it adopts a pentagonal-bipyramidal arrangement; but, in fact, this conclusion is the result of a series of assumptions and no single-crystal diffraction study has so far been reported to confirm this

TABLE 4.15

Lattice Parameters of the Heptafluorozirconates(IV)

Compound	Symmetry	Unit-cell parameters	Ref.
Na_3ZrF_7	Tetragonal	$a = 5.31$ Å, $c = 10.50$ Å	173
K_3ZrF_7	Cubic	$a = 8.951$ Å	174
$(NH_4)_3ZrF_7$	Cubic	$a = 9.365$ Å	174
Cs_3ZrF_7	Cubic	$a = 9.70$ Å	175

stereochemistry. Potassium and ammonium heptafluorozirconate(IV) have been shown by powder diffraction methods to be isomorphous with the distorted face-centred cubic form of potassium heptafluorouranate(IV)[171]. This in turn has been shown by powder techniques to be isomorphous with potassium dioxopentafluorouranate(IV), and the structure of the latter compound has been unequivocally shown by single-crystal studies[172] to contain a pentagonal-bipyramidal arrangement in the anion. Sodium heptafluorozirconate(IV) is not isostructural with the salts discussed above and, although there is no direct evidence, it has been suggested that in this case the anion adopts a different spatial arrangement. However, it is worth noting that in many series of complex halides the sodium salt adopts a different lattice arrangement although the stereochemistry of the anion remains unchanged.

The lattice parameters of the heptafluorozirconates(IV) are given in Table 4.15.

Potassium heptafluorozirconate(IV) is reported to react with water to give the hexafluorozirconate(IV) anion[159].

Heptafluorohafnates(IV). Although little information is available in the literature it appears that the heptafluorohafnates(IV) may be prepared by the general methods described for their zirconium analogues. For example, they have been prepared by the interaction of hafnium tetrafluoride and alkali-metal fluorides in aqueous hydrogen fluoride solution[176,177]. Potassium heptafluorohafnate(IV) appears[177] to exhibit phase changes at 230° and 430° and melts at 900°.

Only the structure of the sodium salt has been investigated[173] and it appears to be body-centred tetragonal, isomorphous with the corresponding zirconium compound, with $a = 5.31$ Å and $c = 10.50$ Å.

Hexafluorozirconates(IV). Hexafluorozirconates(IV) may be prepared in the melt by fusing the correct proportions of zirconium tetrafluoride and an alkali-metal fluoride[178], or by interaction of zirconium tetrafluoride and an alkali-metal fluoride in aqueous hydrogen fluoride.

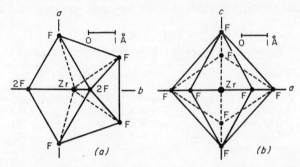

Figure 4.3   Projection of the ZrF_8 polyhedron: (*a*) (00I), (*b*) (0I0).

However, the concentration of free acid must not be too high, otherwise the heptafluoro complexes may be formed[164,179]. Interaction of zirconium dioxide and potassium tetrafluoroborate at less than 600° gives the hexafluorozirconate(IV), but above 600° the heptafluoro compound results[159]. An interesting reaction is that between potassium or caesium fluoride and zirconium tetrabromide in methanol, which yields the corresponding hexafluorozirconates(IV)[166,167]. It is worth noting that with ammonium fluoride it gives the heptafluorozirconate(IV).

The structure of the hexafluorozirconate(IV) anion varies with the nature of the cation. Thus, potassium hexafluorozirconate(IV) does not contain discrete ZrF_6^{2-} units. In fact, the structure consists of ZrF_8 entities formed by sharing four of the eight fluorine atoms around each zirconium atom[180]. The structure of the ZrF_8 polyhedron is shown in Figure 4.3. Lithium hexafluorozirconate(IV) has a hexagonal lattice and does contain ZrF_6^{2-} ions[181]. The rubidium and caesium salts have been shown to have the K_2GeF_6 structure[179], but the structures of the remaining salts are unknown. The lattice parameters of the hexafluorozirconates(IV) are given in Table 4.16.

Novoselova and coworkers[182] studied the stability at high temperatures of potassium hexafluorozirconate(IV) and found the transformations:

$$\alpha \overset{240°}{\rightleftharpoons} \beta \overset{298°}{\rightleftharpoons} \gamma \overset{445°}{\rightleftharpoons} \delta \overset{585°}{\rightleftharpoons} \text{Melt} + K_3ZrF_7$$

The partial conversion of δ-K_2ZrF_6 to a melt and potassium heptafluoro-zirconate(IV) arises because of loss of zirconium tetrafluoride by volatiliza-tion, although in a closed system the reaction is reversible. The earlier results of Yagodin and Tarasov[183] on this system agree in general terms with those of Novoselova although there are differences in the actual transition temperatures quoted.

TABLE 4.16

Lattice Parameters of Hexafluorozirconates(IV)

Compound	Symmetry	Lattice parameters (Å)	Ref.
K_2ZrF_6	Orthorhombic	$a = 6.58, b = 11.4, c = 6.94$	179, 180
Tl_2ZrF_6	Orthorhombic	$a = 13.48, b = 11.67, c = 7.70$	179
$(NH_4)_2ZrF_6$	Orthorhombic	$a = 13.44, b = 11.64, c = 7.72$	179
Li_2ZrF_6	Hexagonal	$a = 4.98, c = 4.66$	181
Rb_2ZrF_6	Hexagonal	$a = 6.16, c = 4.82$	179
Cs_2ZrF_6	Hexagonal	$a = 6.41, c = 5.01$	179

Sheka and Lastochkina[184] studied in detail the hydrolysis of potassium hexafluorozirconate(IV) in aqueous sodium hydroxide and ammonia solution. A large range of complex oxo- and hydroxo-fluoro complexes were postulated as intermediates formed before precipitation of hydrated zirconium dioxide.

Hexafluorohafnates(IV). Hexafluorohafnates(IV) appear to have been prepared only by aqueous methods, similar to those described for the corresponding zirconium salts[179,185,186].

Each of the salts is isostructural with the hexafluorozirconate(IV) for the corresponding cation; their lattice dimensions are in each case almost identical with those of the zirconium salts[179,180]

Hydrolysis of potassium hexafluorohafnate(IV) in aqueous sodium hydroxide and ammonia solution has been studied, and complex inter-mediates similar to those postulated for zirconium have been suggested[187].

Pentafluorozirconates(IV). The pentafluorozirconates(IV) are best pre-pared by fusing equimolar proportions of zirconium tetrafluoride and an alkali-metal fluoride[161–163,178,188–191].

The first report of the variation of vapour pressure with temperature over sodium pentafluorozirconate(IV) suggested that this compound itself was a predominant species in the vapour[163]. The same workers later modified their ideas and postulated a species $NaZr_2F_9$ in the vapour[188]. However, subsequent work by Siderov and coworkers[189,190], using both vapour-pressure measurements and mass spectrometry, showed that $NaZrF_5$ is indeed the predominant vapour-phase species at 600°.

Caesium pentafluorozirconate(IV) has been shown[178] to exhibit a phase transition at 330°, but unfortunately the structure of neither polymorph is known.

A remarkable reaction has been reported between sodium pentafluorozirconate(IV) and aluminium borohydride: it gives zirconium borohydride[191].

Pentafluorohafnates(IV). Pentafluorohafnates(IV) have been prepared both in the melt and in aqueous solution under conditions similar for those described for their zirconium analogues[176,186,191].

No information is available concerning these compounds except that the sodium salt reacts with aluminium borohydride to form hafnium borohydride[191].

Miscellaneous fluorozirconates(IV). Various fluorozirconates(IV) have been reported in melts and aqueous solutions of zirconium tetrafluoride and various alkali-metal fluorides. Little is known about their chemical behaviour and structural characteristics. Typical examples are given in Table 4.17.

TABLE 4.17

Complex Fluorozirconates(IV)

Compound	Properties	Ref.
$NaKZrF_6$		192
$Na_3Zr_4F_{19}$		192
$Na_5Zr_2F_{13}$	Monoclinic; $a = 11.62$, $b = 5.49$, $c = 8.44$ Å, $\beta = 97.7$	161, 192–194
$Na_7Zr_6F_{31}$	Hexagonal; $a = 13.80$, $c = 9.42$ Å	161, 195

Sodium and potassium hexafluorochlorozirconates(IV), M_3ZrF_6Cl, have been prepared by the interaction of hexafluorozirconate(IV) and an alkali-metal chloride in the melt[169,196].

Hexachlorozirconates(IV) and hafnates(IV). The most direct general method of preparing the hexachlorozirconates(IV) and hafnates(IV) is by interaction of the tetrachlorides and alkali-metal chlorides in the melt[197–205]. Hexachlorozirconates(IV) have been isolated by dissolving either zirconium tetrachloride or "zirconyl chloride" in concentrated hydrochloric acid, adding the chloride of a large cation, and finally saturating the solution with gaseous hydrogen chloride[206,207]. Similar reactions have been reported with ethanol[208], acetyl chloride[209], benzoyl chloride[210] and thionyl chloride[211].

The hexachlorozirconates(IV) examined so far all exhibit in the cubic K_2PtCl_6 structure with the following unit-cell parameters:

$$K_2ZrCl_6 \quad a = 10.08 \text{ Å} \quad \text{(reference 200)}$$
$$Rb_2ZrCl_6 \quad a = 10.18 \text{ Å} \quad \text{(reference 212)}$$
$$Cs_2ZrCl_6 \quad a = 10.41 \text{ Å} \quad \text{(reference 212)}$$

Alkali-metal hexachlorozirconates(IV) and hafnates(IV) are thermally unstable, being subject to volatilization of zirconium or hafnium tetrachloride[198,199,204]. The equilibrium vapour-pressure equations are:

$$Na_2ZrCl_6: \quad \log p_{mm} = 14.339 - 10,394/T \quad (540–640°) \quad \text{(reference 199)}$$
$$K_2ZrCl_6: \quad \log p_{mm} = 12.03 - 10,580/T \quad (437–527°) \quad \text{(reference 198)}$$
$$K_2ZrCl_6: \quad \log p_{mm} = 19.826 - 18,380/T \quad (735–804°) \quad \text{(reference 199)}$$
$$K_2HfCl_6: \quad \log p_{mm} = 9.52 - 8850/T \quad (457–587°) \quad \text{(reference 198)}$$

The zirconium–chlorine stretching frequency of the hexachlorozirconate(IV) ion has been given[213] as 293 cm^{-1}.

Zirconium oxide dichloride (zirconyl chloride). Anhydrous zirconium oxide dichloride has been prepared by interaction of zirconium tetrachloride and chlorine monoxide in carbon tetrachloride solution[214]. It was suggested that the complex exists as ZrO^{2+} and $ZrOCl_4^{2-}$ in the solid state, with the anion arranged in infinite chains with zirconium–oxygen linkages[214]. Some confirmatory evidence for this formulation has been obtained from ion-exchange studies in concentrated hydrochloric acid[215]. A strong absorption in the infrared spectrum of the compound at 877 cm^{-1} was assigned to the zirconium–oxygen double-bond frequency of the cation[215].

Solid zirconium oxide dichloride is usually encountered as its octahydrate. This is readily formed by partial hydrolysis of zirconium tetrachloride in aqueous hydrochloric acid solution, or, alternatively, by dissolution of hydrated zirconium dioxide in hydrochloric acid. It is a very stable compound and may be recrystallized from solution.

A single-crystal X-ray diffraction study of zirconium oxide dichloride octahydrate has revealed that it is not a simple compound[216]. The complex is, in fact, tetrameric with a cation of structure $[Zr_4(OH)_8 \cdot 16H_2O]^{8+}$, associated with eight chloride ions. The structure of the cation is shown in Figure 4.4 and consists of a slightly distorted square of zirconium atoms. Each pair of zirconium atoms is bridged by two hydroxo groups above and below the plane of the square, with the eight hydroxo groups forming a cube. Four water molecules are coordinated to each zirconium atom to give an eight-coordinate square antiprismatic stereochemistry to each zirconium atom. The lattice is tetragonal, with $a = 17.08$ and $c = 7.689$ Å, and there are two tetrameric units in the cell[216].

There appears to be some confusion regarding the thermal stability of zirconium oxide dichloride octahydrate. Takagi[217] explicitly states that heating the octahydrate gives no lower hydrate and that complete dehydration occurs at 160–180°. In contrast, Komissarova and coworkers[218] reported that three molecules of water are lost even at 40°, the residue

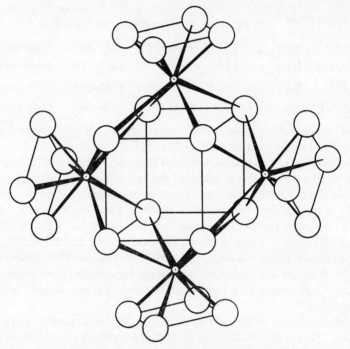

Figure 4.4   Structure of $[Zr_4(OH)_8 \cdot 16H_2O]^{8+}$.

being still soluble in water. This loss of three water molecules is consistent with the structure as described above, since the analytical equivalent of five molecules of water per zirconium atom are coordinated in the complex cation, leaving three molecules of water per zirconium atom less firmly bound in the lattice. Between 80° and 140° further water, as well as some chlorine, is lost and the residue becomes much less soluble in water. At 400° a residue of zirconium dioxide remains. One can rationalize zirconium dioxide as the final dehydration product by envisaging the loss of the four water molecules coordinated to each zirconium atom and condensation of the square of four zirconium atoms into an infinite lattice.

Zirconium oxide dibromide and oxide diiodide octahydrates. Zirconium oxide dibromide octahydrate is isostructural with the corresponding dichloride. The parameters of the tetragonal cell[216] are $a = 17.65$ and $c = 7.95$ Å. The structure of zirconium oxide diiodide octahydrate has not been investigated, and the only chemical information available about this compound is that, when heated, it decomposes according to the equation[219]:

$$2ZrOI_2 \cdot 8H_2O \rightarrow ZrO_2 + ZrI_4 + 16H_2O$$

ADDENDA

Halides

After a careful study of the structure, Gaudreau[220] concluded that there are three crystal modifications of hafnium tetrafluoride and that in general the structural properties of this compound are very similar to those of zirconium tetrafluoride.

The equilibrium vapour pressure of water over $ZrF_4 \cdot 2.8H_2O$ and $ZrF_4 \cdot 2H_2O$ have been measured over the temperature range 20–55° and is given by the expression[221]

$$\log p_{mm} = 10.341 - 2774/T$$

Use of the known heats of solution in dilute hydrofluoric acid allowed the determination of the heats of formation of the monohydrate and the trihydrate as -532.3 and -674.6 kcal mole^{-1}, respectively[221].

It has been shown[222] that zirconium tetrafluoride reacts with donor molecules such as 2,2'-bipyridyl to form what appear to be six-coordinate adducts. Zirconium–fluorine stretching frequencies in the range 453–570 cm^{-1} were recorded.

Kolditz and Degenkolb[223] have prepared zirconium difluoride dichloride by the interaction of $ZrCl_4 \cdot PCl_5$ and the calculated quantity of arsenic trifluoride in arsenic trichloride solution. It is a white solid that is hydrolysed in water. It is insoluble in ether, benzene, and carbon tetrachloride, suggesting that it is perhaps polymeric.

The vapour pressure of zirconium tetrachloride has been measured again; over the temperature range 340–420° the variation with temperature is given by[224]

$$\log p_{mm} = 11.463 - 5193/T$$

The heat of sublimation and fusion for zirconium tetrachloride are given as 23.7 and 14 kcal mole^{-1}, respectively.

The vapour pressure of hafnium tetrachloride has also been reinvestigated and it varies with temperature according to the expression[224]

$$\log p_{mm} = 11.673 - 5148/T$$

over the temperature range 330–410°. Above this temperature the vapour pressure rises sharply and is not a linear function of $1/T$. The heat of sublimation and fusion are given as 23.5 and 18 kcal mole^{-1}, respectively. Clearly the new vapour-pressure equations for both tetrachlorides agree well with those obtained previously.

It has been reported[225] that liquid ammonia reacts with zirconium tetrachloride to give $ZrCl_4 \cdot 8NH_3$ which successively loses ammonia with increasing temperature as shown.

$$ZrCl_4 \cdot 8NH_3 \xrightarrow{145-150°} ZrCl_4 \cdot 6NH_3 \xrightarrow{175-195°} ZrCl_4 \cdot 4NH_3 \xrightarrow{440-460°} ZrCl_4$$

Both zirconium tetrachloride and hafnium tetrachloride react with *o*-phenylenebis(dimethylarsine) to give adducts of the type $MCl_4 \cdot 2D$, as noted previously. It has now been found[226] that in tetrahydrofuran solution the reaction with zirconium tetrachloride is much faster than that with hafnium tetrachloride, and the difference in rates may be used as the basis for a method of separating the elements.

It has now been shown that zirconium tetrabromide can be prepared by the action of boron tribromide on zirconium tetrachloride, at or below room temperature[227]. Both zirconium and hafnium tetrabromide react with *o*-phenylenebis(dimethylarsine) to give eight-coordinate complexes of the type $MBr_4 \cdot 2D$[226]. Zirconium tetrabromide reacts with methylbis(3-dimethylarsinylpropyl)arsine (tas) to give what appears to be the seven-coordinate complex $ZrBr_4 \cdot tas$[228].

In the last year or so the vapour pressure of zirconium tetraiodide has been reported once, and that of hafnium tetraiodide three times. Gerlach and his coworkers[229] found that over the temperature range 120–180° the vapour pressure of zirconium tetraiodide is given by

$$\log p_{mm} = 10.59 - 5730/T$$

In view of the low vapour pressure of zirconium tetraiodide at these temperatures, the agreement with the earlier determination is quite good. In terms of actual vapour pressure, the discrepancy between the two determinations is 3% at 150° and 7% at 180°.

Stevenson and Wicks[230] have again reported their vapour-pressure data for the three polymorphs of hafnium tetraiodide with very slight modifications to the original data. However, Tsirel'nikov and Ioffe[231] have reported values that differ markedly from those of Stevenson and Wicks.

The Russians obtained evidence for only one phase change, which occurred at 332°, and the equations expressing their results are:

$$\log p_{\text{mm}} = 9.051 - 4261/T \quad (275\text{--}332°)$$
$$\log p_{\text{mm}} = 11.619 - 5814/T \quad (332\text{--}395°)$$

Gerlach and his coworkers[229] measured the vapour pressure of hafnium tetraiodide at much lower temperatures, and in the temperature range 120–150° the vapour pressure is given by

$$\log p_{\text{mm}} = 10.93 - 5586/T$$

The controversey over the structure of zirconium trichloride has been resolved. Watts has shown that zirconium trichloride is polymorphic[232]. β-ZrCl$_3$ is hexagonal with $a = 6.382$ and $c = 6.135$ Å, in agreement with the results of Dahl and his coworkers[144]. The structure consists of a distorted close-packed array of chlorine atoms with zirconium atoms occupying one-third of the octahedral holes. Further, it was shown that Swaroop and Flengas[145] were dealing with a modification which has a layer disorder. Watts suggested this was α-ZrCl$_3$, analogous to α-TiCl$_3$.

Hafnium tribromide has been prepared by the reduction of hafnium tetrabromide with aluminium at 470° in a bomb[233].

Fowles and his coworkers[234] have prepared a number of adducts of zirconium trihalides with nitrogen-base ligands such as pyridine, *o*-phenanthroline, and bipyridyl.

Complex Halides

It has been shown that octafluoro complexes of zirconium and hafnium exist. High-temperature phase studies[235] of the potassium fluoride–hafnium tetrafluoride system has shown the existence of potassium octa-fluorohafnate(IV) as a solid phase at 730°.

The existence of octafluorozirconates(IV) has been unequivocally demonstrated by a full structural determination of $Cu_2ZrF_8 \cdot 12H_2O$[236]. The crystals are monoclinic with $a = 15.895$, $b = 9.652$, $c = 11.921$ Å, and $\beta = 121.8°$. The space group is $C2/c$ and there are four molecular units in the cell. The structure contains discrete square anti-prismatic ZrF$_8$ groups with a mean zirconium–fluorine distance of 2.08 Å. Tetra-gonally distorted $Cu(H_2O)_6$ units have copper–oxygen distances of 1.93 and 2.38 Å.

An even more interesting structure has been found[237] for the compound $Cu_3Zr_2F_{14} \cdot 16H_2O$ which is made by the interaction of zirconium tetra-fluoride and copper difluoride in aqueous hydrogen fluoride. The crystals are monoclinic with $a = 10.395$, $b = 10.135$, $c = 10.998$ Å and $\beta = 91.8°$. There are two formula units in the cell and the space group is $P2_1/c$. The structure contains discrete Zr_2F_{14} units in which each zirconium atom is eight-coordinate with a square anti-prismatic arrangement. Two *cis*-fluorine atoms bridge to the other half of the unit, so the two antiprisms share an edge.

Further studies on the preparation of alkali-metal heptafluorozirconates(IV) have been carried out, both in melts[235,238,239], and in aqueous hydrogen fluoride solution[240,241]. The melting point for sodium heptafluorozirconate(IV) was reported[238,239] as 860° and for the potassium salt[235,238] as 923°. Evidence has been presented[242] that in dilute aqueous hydrogen fluoride solution the heptafluorohafnate(IV) ion dissociates to hexafluorohafnate(IV) and fluoride ions. The heat of formation of ammonium heptafluorozirconate(IV) has been determined[243] as -809.2 kcal mole^{-1}.

Studies on the preparation of hexafluorozirconates(IV) and -hafnates(IV) have been continued both in the melt[235,238,239] and in aqueous hydrogen fluoride solution[240,241]. The sodium salt is reported[238,239] to melt at 582° and the potassium salt[235,238] at 608°. The heat of formation[243] of ammonium hexafluorozirconate(IV) is -697.5 kcal mole^{-1} and the compound undergoes a phase transition at 138°. The solubilities of potassium hexafluorozirconate(IV) and -hafnate(IV) in water have been investigated as a function of temperature[244].

The compounds $CuMF_6 \cdot 4H_2O$ (M = Zr and Hf) are isostructural and monoclinic with the identical unit-cell parameters[245], $a = 5.692, b = 10.07$ and $c = 7.560$ Å. The space group is $P2_1/c$ and there are two formula units in the cell. The structure consists of octahedral MF_6 units with planar $Cu(H_2O)_4$ units.

The infrared and Raman spectra of some hexafluorozirconates(IV) and -hafnates(IV) have been examined[242]. The fundamental modes (cm^{-1}) which were characterized are given below.

Cs_2ZrF_6 (solid) $\qquad \nu_1 = 576 \quad \nu_5 = 236$

$(NH_4)_2ZrF_6$ (aq. solution) $\quad \nu_1 = 581 \quad \nu_5 = 238$

Cs_2HfF_6 (solid) $\qquad \nu_1 = 586 \quad \nu_5 = 237$

$(NH_4)_2HfF_6$ (aq. solution) $\quad \nu_1 = 589 \quad \nu_5 = 230$

Alkali-metal pentafluorohafnates(IV) have been prepared in melts[235,238] and the pentafluoroaquozirconates(IV) and -hafnates(IV) from aqueous hydrogen fluoride solutions[240,241,246]. Sodium pentafluorohafnate(IV) melts[238] at 540° and the corresponding potassium salt[238] at 432°. The heat of formation of ammonium pentafluorozirconate(IV) is -581.2 kcal mole^{-1} [243]. This compound is polymorphic and the γ-form is monoclinic with $a = 13.57$, $b = 7.90$, $c = 7.99$ Å and $\beta = 87°$ [243]. The heat of formation of ammonium pentafluoroaquozirconate(IV) was found[246] to be -652 kcal mole^{-1}.

Dutrizae and Flengas[247] have made a thorough study of the thermodynamic properties of some alkali-metal hexachlorozirconates(IV) and

TABLE 4.18

Thermodynamic Properties of Hexachlorozirconates(IV) and -hafnates(IV)

Property	Li$_2$ZrCl$_6$	Li$_2$HfCl$_6$	Na$_2$ZrCl$_6$	K$_2$ZrCl$_6$
M.p.	535°	557°	646°	800°
ΔH_{fus} (kcal mole^{-1})	9.30	8.80	4.00	5.50
ΔS_{fus} (cal deg^{-1}mole^{-1})	10.6	10.9	5.0	5.1
Transition temperature			353°	620°
ΔH_{trans} (kcal mole^{-1})			7.00	4.50
ΔS_{trans} (cal deg^{-1} mole^{-1})			10.9	5.0

-hafnates(IV). The results are summarized in Table 4.18. The measurements were carried out in sealed tubes to prevent volatilization of the tetrachlorides.

The metal–halogen stretching frequencies in some hexachloro- and hexabromozirconates(IV) occur at about 295 and 200 cm^{-1}, respectively[248]. The reflectance spectra of salts of these anions were also recorded and charge-transfer bands were observed[248].

REFERENCES

1. L. M. Nijland and J. Schroeder, *Angew. Chem.*, **76**, 890 (1964).
2. H. M. Heandler, S. F. Bartram, R. S. Becker, W. J. Bernard and S. W. Bukata, *J. Am. Chem. Soc.*, **76**, 2177 (1954).
3. A. Chretien and B. Gaudreau, *Compt. Rend.*, **248**, 2878 (1959).
4. A. K. Kuriakose and J. L. Margrave, *J. Phys. Chem.*, **68**, 290 (1964).
5. E. L. Muetterties and J. E. Castle, *J. Inorg. Nucl. Chem.*, **18**, 148 (1961).
6. *U.S. Patent*, 2,602,725 (1952).
7. C. Decroly, D. Tytgat and J. Gerard, *Energie nucleaire*, **1**, 155 (1957).
8. J. Niemiec, *Compt. Rend.*, **251**, 875 (1960).
9. A. Chretien and B. Gaudreau, *Compt. Rend.*, **246**, 2266 (1958).
10. W. H. Zachariasen, *Acta Cryst.*, **2**, 388 (1949).
11. G. E. R. Schulze, *Z. Krist.*, **89**, 477 (1934).
12. V. Amirthaligam and K. V. Muralidharem, *J. Inorg. Nucl. Chem.*, **26**, 2038 (1964).
13. R. D. Burbank and F. N. Bensey, *U.S.A.E.C. Report* K-1280 (1956).
14. W. Fischer, T. Petzel and S. Lauter, *Z. anorg. Chem.*, **333**, 226 (1964).

15. K. A. Sense, M. J. Snyder and R. B. Filbert, *J. Phys. Chem.*, **58,** 995 (1954).
16. S. Cantor, R. F. Newton, W. R. Grimes and F. F. Blankenship, *J. Phys. Chem.*, **62,** 96 (1958).
17. P. A. Akishin, V. I. Belousov and L. N. Sidorov, *Russ. J. Inorg. Chem.*, **8,** 789 (1963).
18. N. P. Galkin, Y. N. Tumanov, V. I. Tarasov and Y. D. Shishov, *Russ. J. Inorg. Chem.*, **8,** 1054 (1963).
19. R. A. McDonald, G. C. Sinke and D. R. Stull, *J. Chem. Eng. Data*, **7,** 83 (1962).
20. E. Greenberg, J. L. Settle, H. M. Feder and W. N. Hubbard, *J. Phys. Chem.*, **65,** 1168 (1961).
21. K. A. Sense, M. J. Snyder and J. W. Clegg, *U.S.A.E.C. Report* AECD-3708 (1953).
22. C. E. Kaylor, G. E. Walden and D. F. Smith, *J. Am. Chem. Soc.*, **81,** 4172 (1959).
23. A. Buchler, J. B. Berkowitz-Mattuck and D. H. Dugre, *J. Chem. Phys.*, **34,** 2202 (1961).
24. T. N. Waters, *J. Inorg. Nucl. Chem.*, **15,** 320 (1960).
25. I. V. Tananaev, N. S. Nikolaev and Y. A. Buslaev, *Zhur. Neorg. Khim.*, **1,** 274 (1956).
26. N. S. Nikolaev, Y. A. Buslaev and M. P. Gustyakova, *Russ. J. Inorg. Chem.*, **7,** 869 (1962).
27. L. Kolditz and A. Feltz, *Z. anorg. allgem. Chem.*, **310,** 195 (1961).
28. J. Rynasiewicz, *J. Nucl. Mater.*, **12,** 158 (1964).
29. R. L. Wells, *U.S.A.E.C. Report* IDO-14455 (1958).
30. T. N. Waters, *Chem. Ind. (London)*, **1964,** 713.
31. E. Greenberg, J. L. Settle and W. N. Hubbard, *J. Phys. Chem.*, **66,** 1345 (1962).
32. A. K. Kuriakose and J. L. Margrave, *J. Phys. Chem.*, **68,** 2343 (1964).
33. G. von Hevesy and W. Dullenkopf, *Z. anorg. allgem. Chem.*, **221,** 161 (1934).
34. Y. A. Buslaev and N. S. Nikolaev, *Dokl. Akad. Nauk SSSR*, **135,** 1385 (1960).
35. C. E. F. Rickard and T. N. Waters, *J. Inorg. Nucl. Chem.*, **26,** 925 (1964).
36. Y. A. Buslaev, Y. E. Gorbunova and M. P. Gustyakova, *Izvest. Akad. Nauk SSSR, Otd. Khim. Nauk.*, **1962,** 195
37. W. B. Blumental, *"The Chemical Behaviour of Zirconium"*, Van Nostrand, New Jersey, U.S.A., 1958.
38. P. Ehrlich and G. Dietz, *Z. anorg. allgem. Chem.*, **305,** 158 (1960).
39. M. W. Lister and L. E. Sutton, *Trans. Faraday Soc.*, **37,** 393 (1941).
40. V. P. Spiridonov, P. A. Akishin and V. I. Tsirel'nikov, *Zh. Strukt. Khim.*, **3,** 329 (1962).
41. J. K. Wilmshurst, *J. Mol. Spectr.*, **5,** 343 (1960).
42. K. Funaki and K. Uchimura, *Denki Kagaku*, **33,** 167 (1965).
43. A. A. Palko, A. D. Ryon and D. W. Kuhn, *J. Phys. Chem.*, **62,** 319 (1958).
44. L. A. Nisel'son, V. I. Stolyarov and T. D. Sokolova, *Russ. J. Phys. Chem.*, **39,** 1614 (1965).
45. L. A. Nisel'son, *Russ. J. Inorg. Chem.*, **7,** 354 (1962).
46. H. Siemonsen and U. Siemonsen, *Z. Elektrochem.*, **56,** 643 (1952).

47. G. L. Gal'chenko, D. A. Gedakyan, B. I. Timofeev and S. M. Skuratov, *Dokl. Akad. Nauk SSSR*, **161**, 1081 (1965).
48. P. Gross, C. Hayman and D. L. Levi, *Trans. Faraday Soc.*, **53**, 1285 (1957).
49. J. E. Drake and G. W. A. Fowles, *J. Chem. Soc.*, **1960**, 1498.
50. J. P. Coughlin and E. G. King, *J. Am. Chem. Soc.*, **72**, 2262 (1950).
51. S. S. Todd, *J. Am. Chem. Soc.*, **72**, 2914 (1950).
52. E. M. Larsen and L. J. Wittenberg, *J. Am. Chem. Soc.*, **77**, 5850 (1955).
53. V. Gutmann and F. Mairinger, *Monatsh. Chem.*, **89**, 724 (1958).
54. L. A. Nisel'son and B. N. Ivanov-Emin, *Zh. Neorg. Khim.*, **1**, 1766 (1956).
55. D. M. Gruen and J. J. Katz, *J. Am. Chem. Soc.*, **71**, 3843 (1949).
56. I. A. Sheka, *Chem. Zvesti*, **13**, 656 (1959).
57. E. M. Larsen, J. Howatson, A. M. Gammill and L. Wittenberg, *J. Am. Chem. Soc.*, **74**, 3489 (1952).
58. V. Gutmann and R. Himml, *Z. anorg. allgem. Chem.*, **287**, 199 (1956).
59. I. A. Sheka and B. A. Voitovich, *Zh. Neorg. Khim.*, **1**, 964 (1956).
60. A. E. Levitt and H. Freund, *J. Am. Chem. Soc.*, **78**, 1545 (1956).
61. G. P. Nikitina and M. F. Pushlenkov, *Radiokhimiya*, **5**, 456 (1963).
62. R. Perrot and C. Devin, *Compt. Rend.*, **246**, 772 (1958).
63. P. T. Joseph and W. B. Blumenthal, *J. Org. Chem.*, **24**, 1371 (1959).
64. G. Jantsch, *J. prakt. Chem.*, **115**, 7 (1927).
65. L. Wolf and C. Troeltzsch, *J. prakt. Chem.*, **17**, 70 (1962).
66. O. A. Osipov and Y. B. Kletenik, *J. Gen. Chem. USSR*, **31**, 2451 (1961).
67. O. A. Osipov, V. M. Artemova, V. A. Kogan and Y. A. Lysenko, *J. Gen. Chem. USSR*, **32**, 1354 (1962).
68. M. F. Lappert, *J. Chem. Soc.*, **1962**, 542.
69. S. C. Jain and R. Rivest, *Can. J. Chem.*, **42**, 1079 (1964).
70. E. Rivet, R. Aubin and R. Rivest, *Can. J. Chem.*, **39**, 2343 (1961).
71. Y. B. Kletenik, O. A. Osipov and E. E. Kravtsov, *Zh. Obshchei Chem.*, **29**, 11 (1959).
72. W. Wardlaw and D. C. Bradley, *Nature*, **165**, 75 (1950).
73. O. A. Osipov and Y. B. Kletenik, *J. Gen. Chem., USSR*, **29**, 1375 (1959).
74. O. A. Osipov and Y. B. Kletenik, *Zh. Obshch. Khim.*, **27**, 2921 (1957).
75. Y. B. Kletenik and O. A. Osipov, *Izv. Vysshikh Uchebn., Zavedenii, Khim. i Khim. Tekhnol*, **2**, 679 (1959).
76. P. Sartori and M. Weidenbruch, *Angew. Chem.*, **76**, 376 (1964).
77. W. S. Hummers, S. Y. Tyree and S. Yolles, *J. Am. Chem. Soc.*, **74**, 139 (1952).
78. I. A. Sheka and B. A. Voitovich, *Dopovidi Akad. Nauk. Ukr. RSR.*, **1957**, 566.
79. I. A. Sheka and B. A. Voitovich, *Zh. Neorg. Khim.*, **2**, 426 (1957).
80. E. M. Larsen and L. E. Trevorrow, *J. Inorg. Nucl. Chem.*, **2**, 254 (1956).
81. H. J. Emeleus and G. S. Rao, *J. Chem. Soc.*, **1958**, 4245.
82. G. W. A. Fowles and R. A. Walton, *J. Chem. Soc.*, **1964**, 2840.
83. S. C. Jain and R. Rivest, *Can. J. Chem.*, **41**, 2130 (1963).
84. J. E. Drake and G. W. A. Fowles, *J. Chem. Soc.*, **1960**, 1498.
85. G. W. A. Fowles and R. A. Walton, *J. Chem. Soc.*, **1964**, 4330.
86. I. R. Beattie and M. Webster, *J. Chem. Soc.*, **1964**, 3507.
87. G. W. A. Fowles and R. A. Walton, *J. Less-Common Metals*, **5**, 510 (1963).
88. T. C. Ray and A. D. Westland, *Inorg. Chem.*, **4**, 1501 (1965).

89. R. J. H. Clark, J. Lewis and R. S. Nyholm, *J. Chem. Soc.*, **1962**, 2460.
90. R. J. H. Clark, J. Lewis, R. S. Nyholm, P. Pauling and G. B. Robertson, *Nature*, **192**, 222 (1961).
91. R. V. Moore and S. Y. Tyree, *J. Am. Chem. Soc.*, **76**, 5253 (1954).
92. A. Clearfield and E. J. Malkiewich, *J. Inorg. Nucl. Chem.*, **25**, 237 (1963).
93. L. A. Nisel'son and L. E. Larionova, *Russ. J. Inorg. Chem.*, **5**, 83 (1960).
94. W. L. Groeneveld, *Rec. Trav. Chim.*, **71**, 1152 (1952).
95. B. A. Voitovich and I. A. Sheka, *Dopovidi Akad. Nauk Ukr. RSR*, 849 (1958).
96. R. C. Mehrotra and R. A. Misra, *J. Chem. Soc.*, **1965**, 43.
97. R. N. Kapoor, K. C. Pande and R. C. Mehrotra, *J. Indian Chem. Soc.*, **35**, 157 (1958).
98. K. L. Jaura, H. S. Banga and R. L. Kaushik, *J. Indian Chem. Soc.*, **39**, 531 (1962).
99. S. S. Sandhu, J. S. Sandhu and G. S. Sandhu, *Current Sci. (India)*, **29**, 222 (1960).
100. E. Samuel and R. Setton, *Compt. Rend.*, **254**, 208 (1962).
101. W. E. Reid, J. M. Bish and A. Brenner, *J. Electrochem. Soc.*, **104**, 21 (1957).
102. R. Juza, A. Gabel, A. Rabenau and W. Klose, *Z. anorg. allgem. Chem.*, **329**, 136 (1964).
103. E. Hayek, J. Puschmann and A. Czaloun, *Monatsh Chem.*, **85**, 359 (1954).
104. I. V. Vinarov and N. P. Khromova, *Khim. Prom. Nauk-Tekhn. Zhur.*, **1963**, 32.
105. S. In'-Chzhu and I. S. Morozov, *Russ. J. Inorg. Chem.*, **4**, 222 (1959).
106. P. Gross and C. Hayman, *Trans. Faraday Soc.*, **60**, 45 (1964).
107. S. N. Lungu, *Acad. Rep. Populare Romine, Studii Cercetari Fiz.*, **13**, 29 (1962).
108. S. S. Todd, *J. Am. Chem. Soc.*, **75**, 3035 (1953).
109. R. L. Orr, *J. Am. Chem. Soc.*, **75**, 1231 (1953).
110. I. A. Sheka and B. A. Voitovich, *Zh. Neorg. Khim.*, **3**, 1973 (1958).
111. S. S. Berdonosov, A. V. Lapitskii, L. G. Vlasov and D. G. Berdonosova, *Russ. J. Inorg. Chem.*, **7**, 753 (1962).
112. R. C. Young and H. C. Fletcher, *Inorg. Synth.*, **1**, 49 (1939).
113. S. S. Berdonosov, V. I. Tsirel'nikov and A. V. Lapitskii, *Vestn. Mosk. Univ., Ser. II Khim.*, **20**, 26 (1965).
114. L. A. Nisel'son and T. D. Sokolova, *Russ. J. Inorg. Chem.*, **7**, 1382 (1962).
115. S. Prasad and M. Biswas, *Proc. Nat. Acad. Sci. India, Section A*, **34**, 279 (1965).
116. S. Prasad and K. S. Devi, *Proc. Nat. Acad. Sci. India, Section A*, **34**, 282 (1965).
117. S. Prasad and K. Sahney, *Proc. Nat. Acad. Sci. India, Section A*, **29**, 307 (1960).
118. Y. B. Kletenik and O. A. Osipov, *Zh. Obshch. Khim.*, **29**, 423 (1959).
119. S. J. Kuhn and J. S. McIntyre, *Can. J. Chem.*, **43**, 375 (1965).
120. M. Allbutt and G. W. A. Fowles, *J. Inorg. Nucl. Chem.*, **25**, 67 (1963).
121. R. C. Young, *J. Am. Chem. Soc.*, **57**, 1195 (1935).
122. W. C. Schumb and L. K. Morehouse, *J. Am. Chem. Soc.*, **69**, 2696 (1947).
123. S. S. Berdonosov, D. G. Berdonosova, A. V. Lapitskii and L. G. Vlasov, *Russ. J. Inorg. Chem.*, **8**, 277 (1963).

124. G. W. Watt and W. A. Baker, *J. Inorg. Nucl. Chem.*, **22**, 49 (1961).
125. M. Chaigneau, *Bull. Soc. Chim. France*, **1957**, 886.
126. M. Chaigneau, *Compt. Rend.*, **242**, 263 (1956).
127. L. A. Nisel'son, M. V. Teslitskaya and T. A. Shvedova, *Russ. J. Inorg. Chem.*, **7**, 502 (1962).
128. F. R. Sale and R. A. J. Shelton, *J. Less-Common Metals*, **9**, 54 (1965).
129. H. Hecht, R. Geese and G. Jander, *Z. anorg. allgem. Chem.*, **269**, 262 (1952).
130. R. Juza and J. Henders, *Z. anorg. allgem. Chem.*, **332**, 1 (1964).
131. O. A. Osipov and Y. B. Kletenik, *Zh. Obshch. Chem.*, **29**, 2119 (1959).
132. B. Krause, A. B. Hook, F. Wawner and H. Rosenwasser, *Anal. Chem.*, **32**, 1210 (1960).
133. F. D. Stevenson, C. E. Wicks and F. E. Block, *U.S. Bur. Mines Dept. Invest.* No. 6367 (1964).
134. P. Ehrlich, F. Ploeger and E. Koch, *Z. anorg. allgem. Chem.*, **333**, 209 (1964).
135. E. M. Larsen and J. J. Leddy, *J. Am. Chem. Soc.*, **78**, 5983 (1956).
136. H. L. Schlaefer and H. W. Willie, *Z. anorg. allgem. Chem.*, **327**, 253 (1964).
137. I. E. Newnham, *J. Am. Chem. Soc.*, **79**, 5415 (1957).
138. B. Swaroop and S. N. Flengas, *Can. J. Chem.*, **42**, 1495 (1964).
139. I. E. Newnham and J. A. Watts, *J. Am. Chem. Soc.*, **82**, 2113 (1960).
140. V. S. Emel'yanov, A. I. Evstyukhin, I. P. Barinov and A. M. Samonov, *Razdelenie Blizkikh po Svoistram Redkikh Metal*, **1962**, 51.
141. *U.S. Patent*, 2,953,433 (1960).
142. A. J. Turnbull and J. A. Watts, *Australian J. Chem.*, **16**, 947 (1963).
143. K. Uchimura and K. Funaki, *Denki Kagaku*, **33**, 163 (1965).
144. L. F. Dahl, T. I. Chiang, P. W. Seabaugh and E. M. Larsen, *Inorg. Chem.*, **3**, 1236 (1964).
145. B. Swaroop and S. N. Flengas, *Can. J. Phys.*, **42**, 1886 (1964).
146. J. Lewis, D. J. Machin, I. E. Newnham and R. S. Nyholm, *J. Chem. Soc.*, **1962**, 2036.
147. A. F. Ried and P. C. Wailes, *J. Organometl. Chem.*, **2**, 329 (1964).
148. R. C. Young, *J. Am. Chem. Soc.*, **53**, 2148 (1931).
149. H. L. Schlaefer and H. Skoludek, *Z. anorg. allgem. Chem.*, **316**, 15 (1962).
150. H. L. Schlaefer and H. Skoludek, *Z. Elektrochem.*, **16**, 327 (1962).
151. F. R. Sale and R. A. J. Shelton, *J. Less-Common Metals*, **9**, 60 (1965).
152. F. I. Busol, *Zh. Fiz. Khim.*, **33**, 399 (1959).
153. J. D. Fast, *Z. anorg. allgem. Chem.*, **239**, 145 (1938).
154. W. A. Baker and A. R. Janus, *J. Inorg. Nucl. Chem.*, **26**, 2087 (1964).
155. F. R. Sale and R. A. J. Shelton, *J. Less-Common Metals*, **9**, 64 (1965).
156. F. K. McTaggart and A. G. Turnbull, *Australian J. Chem.*, **17**, 727 (1964).
157. *Brit. Patent*, 783,737 (1957).
158. B. Swaroop and S. N. Flengas, *Can. J. Chem.*, **43**, 2115 (1965).
159. P. A. Polishchuk, *Russ. J. Inorg. Chem.*, **9**, 80 (1964).
160. P. A. Polishchuk, *Russ. J. Inorg. Chem.*, **9**, 390 (1964).
161. C. J. Barton, W. R. Grimes, H. Insley, R. E. Moore and R. E. Thoma, *J. Phys. Chem.*, **62**, 665 (1958).
162. R. Winand, *Compt. Rend. Congr. Intern. Chim. Ind.*, *31st*, Liege, **1958**.

163. K. A. Sense, C. A. Alexander, R. E. Bowman and R. B. Filbert, *J. Phys. Chem.*, 337 (1957).
164. V. G. Bambarov, N. V. Demenev and V. M. Polyakova, *Izv. Sibirsk. Otd. Akad. Nauk SSSR*, **1962**, 70.
165. P. A. Polishchuk, *Ukr. Khim. Zhur.*, **30**, 553 (1964).
166. H. M. Haendler, F. A. Johnson and D. S. Crocket, *J. Am. Chem. Soc.*, **80**, 2662 (1958).
167. D. S. Crocket and H. M. Haendler, *J. Am. Chem. Soc.*, **82**, 4158 (1930).
168. N. M. Ch'ang and A. V. Vovoselova, *Vestn. Mosk. Univ., Ser. II, Khim.*, **19**, 37 (1964).
169. I. N. Sheiko, R. V. Chernov and V. S. Kikhno, *Ukr. Khim. Zh.*, **27**, 469 (1961).
170. H. M. Haendler, C. M. Wheeler and D. W. Robinson, *J. Am. Chem. Soc.*, **74**, 2352 (1952).
171. W. H. Zachariasen, *Acta Cryst.*, **7**, 792 (1954).
172. W. H. Zachariasen, *Acta Cryst.*, **7**, 783 (1954).
173. L. A. Harris, *Acta Cryst.*, **12**, 172 (1959).
174. G. C. Hampson and L. Pauling, *J. Am. Chem. Soc.*, **60**, 2702 (1938).
175. G. D. Robbins and J. H. Burns, *U.S.A.E.C. Report* ORNL-TM-310 (1962).
176. B. V. Shchepochkin and N. P. Sazkin, *Tr. Mosk. Khim-Tekhnol. Inst.*, **43**, 55 (1963).
177. B. V. Shchepochkin, N. P. Sazkin and G. A. Yagodin, *Tr. Mosk. Khim.-Tekhnol. Inst.*, **43**, 35 (1963).
178. G. D. Robbins, R. E. Thoma and H. Insley, *J. Inorg. Nucl. Chem.*, **27**, 559 (1965).
179. H. Bode and G. Teufer, *Z. anorg. allgem. Chem.*, **283**, 18 (1956).
180. H. Bode and G. Teufer, *Acta Cryst.*, **9**, 929 (1956).
181. R. Hoppe and W. Dahne, *Naturwiss.*, **47**, 397 (1960).
182. A. V. Novoselova, Y. M. Korenev and Y. P. Simanov, *Dokl. Akad. Nauk SSSR*, **139**, 892 (1961).
183. G. A. Yagodin and V. I. Tarasov, *Russ. J. Inorg. Chem.*, **5**, 967 (1960).
184. I. A. Sheka and A. A. Lastochkina, *Russ. J. Inorg. Chem*, **6**, 954 (1961).
185. B. V. Shchepochkin and N. P. Sazkin, *Russ. J. Inorg. Chem.*, **8**, 664 (1963).
186. N. P. Sazkin, B. V. Shchepochkin and G. A. Yagodin, *Izv. Akad. Nauk SSSR, Ser. Khim.*, 1127 (1965).
187. I. A. Sheka and A. A. Lastochkina, *Russ. J. Inorg. Chem.*, **8**, 1202 (1963).
188. K. A. Sense and R. W. Stone, *J. Phys. Chem.*, **62**, 1411 (1958).
189. L. N. Sidorov, P. A. Akishin, V. I. Belousov and V. B. Shol'ts, *Russ. J. Phys. Chem.*, **38**, 76 (1964).
190. L. N. Sidorov, P. A. Akishin, V. I. Belousov and V. B. Shol'ts, *Russ. J. Phys. Chem.*, **38**, 641 (1964).
191. H. R. Hoekstra and J. J. Katz, *J. Am. Chem. Soc.*, **71**, 2488 (1949).
192. I. M Shieko, V. S. Kikhno and V. I. Mel'nikov, *Ukr. Khim. Zh.*, **29**, 1259 (1963).
193. R. N. Herak, L. M. Manojlovic and S. S. Malacic, *Bull. Boris Kidric Inst. Nucl. Sci.*, **14**, 21 (1963).
194. R. N. Herak, S. S. Malacic and L. M. Manojlovic, *Acta Cryst.*, **18**, 520 (1965).
195. P. A. Agron and R. D. Ellison, *J. Phys. Chem.*, **63**, 2076 (1959).

196. I. N. Sheiko, V. I. Mel'nikov and V. I. Suprunchuk, *Ukr. Khim. Zhur.*, **30**, (1964).
197. I. S. Morozov and A. T. Simonich, *Russ. J. Inorg. Chem.*, **6**, 477 (1961).
198. I. Zvara and L. K. Tarasov, *Russ. J. Inorg. Chem.*, **7**, 1388 (1962).
199. R. L. Lister and S. N. Flengas, *Can. J. Chem.*, **43**, 2947 (1965).
200. R. L. Lister and S. N. Flengas, *Can. J. Chem.*, **42**, 1102 (1964).
201. N. A. Belozerskii and O. A. Kucherenko, *J. Appl. Chem. USSR*, **13**, 1552 (1940).
202. I. S. Morozov and S. In'-Chzhu, *Russ. J. Inorg. Chem.*, **4**, 307 (1959).
203. I. S. Morozov, V. A. Tverskov and G. I. Kurapova, *Russ. J. Inorg. Chem.*, **9**, 1184 (1964).
204. I. S. Morozov and S. In'-Chzhu, *Russ. J. Inorg. Chem.*, **4**, 1176 (1959).
205. I. S. Morozov and B. G. Korshunov, *Zhur. Neorg. Khim.*, **1**, 145 (1956).
206. J. E. Drake and G. W. A. Fowles, *J. Less-Common Metals*, **3**, 149 (1961).
207. G. M. Toptygina and I. B. Barskaya, *Russ. J. Inorg. Chem.*, **10**, 1226 (1965).
208. J. E. Drake and G. W. A. Fowles, *J. Inorg. Nucl. Chem.*, **18**, 136 (1961).
209. K. Goyal, R. C. Paul and S. S. Sandhu, *J. Chem. Soc.*, **1959**, 322.
210. R. C. Paul, K. Chander and G. Singh, *J. Indian Chem. Soc.*, **35**, 869 (1958).
211. S. S. Sandhu, B. S. Chakkal and G. S. Sandhu, *J. Indian Chem. Soc.*, **37**, 329 (1960).
212. G. Engel, *Centr. Min. Geol.*, **1934**, 285.
213. D. M. Adams, J. Chatt, J. M. Davidson and J. Gerratt, *J. Chem. Soc.*, **1963**, 2189.
214. K. Dehnicke and K. U. Meyer, *Z. anorg. allgem. Chem.*, **331**, 121 (1964).
215. D. Naumann, *Z. anorg. allgem. Chem.*, **309**, 37 (1961).
216. A. Clearfield and P. A. Vaughan, *Acta Cryst.*, **9**, 555 (1956).
217. S. Takagi, *J. Chem. Soc. Japan*, **75**, 637 (1954).
218. L. N. Komissarova, V. E. Phyashchev and I. N. Kremenskaya, *Russ. J. Inorg. Chem.*, **5**, 281 (1960).
219. E. Chauvenet and J. Davidowicz, *Compt. Rend.*, **189**, 408 (1929).
220. B. Gaudreau, *Compt. Rend.*, **263C**, 67 (1966).
221. H. Hull and A. G. Turnball, *J. Inorg. Nucl. Chem.*, **28**, 2811 (1966).
222. R. J. H. Clark and W. Errington, *J. Chem. Soc.*, **1967**, *A*, 258.
223. L. Kolditz and P. Degenkolb, *Z. Chem.*, **6**, 347 (1967).
224. N. D. Denisova, E. K. Safronov and O. N. Byetrova, *Russ. J. Inorg. Chem.*, **11**, 1171 (1966).
225. V. P. Orlovskii, N. V. Rudenko and B. N. Ivanov-Emin, *Zh. Neorg. Khim.*, **12**, 2305 (1967).
226. R. J. H. Clark, W. Errington, J. Lewis and R. S. Nyholm, *J. Chem. Soc.*, **1966**, *A*, 989.
227. P. M. Druce, M. F. Lappert and P. N. K. Riley, *Chem. Commun.*, **1967**, 486.
228. G. A. Barclay, I. K. Gregor, M. J. Lambert and S. B. Wild, *Australian J. Chem.*, **20**, 1571 (1967).
229. J. Gerlach, J. P. Krumme, F. Pawlek and H. Probst, *Z. physik. Chem. (Frankfurt)*, **53**, 135 (1967).
230. F. D. Stevenson and C. E. Wicks, *J. Chem. Eng. Data*, **10**, 33 (1965).
231. V. I. Tsirel'nikov and M. I. Ioffe, *Russ. J. Inorg. Chem.*, **11**, 1283 (1966).
232. J. A. Watts, *Inorg. Chem.*, **5**, 281 (1966).

233. H. L. Schlaefer and H. W. Wille, *Z. anorg. allgem. Chem.*, **351,** 279 (1967).
234. G. W. A. Fowles, B. J. Russ and G. R. Willey, *Chem. Commun.*, **1967,** 646.
235. I. N. Shieko, G. A. Bukhalova and V. T. Mal'tsev, *Dokl. Akad. Nauk Ukr.* RSR, **1966,** 782.
236. J. Fischer, R. Elchinger and R. Weiss, *Chem. Commun.*, **1967,** 329.
237. J. Fischer and R. Weiss, *Chem. Commun.*, **1967,** 328.
238. I. N. Shieko, V. T. Mal'tsev and G. A. Bukhalova, *Ukr. Khim. Zhur.*, **32,** 1292 (1966).
239. I. N. Shieko, V. T. Mal'tsev and G. A. Bukhalova, *Dokl. Akad. Nauk Ukr.* RSR, **1966,** 628.
240. I. V. Tananaev and L. S. Guzeeva, *Russ. J. Inorg. Chem.*, **11,** 587 (1966).
241. I. V. Tananaev and L. S. Guzeeva, *Russ. J. Inorg. Chem.*, **11,** 590 (1966).
242. P. A. W. Dean and D. F. Evans, *J. Chem. Soc.*, **1967,** *A*, 698.
243. H. Hull and A. G. Turnball, *J. Inorg. Nucl. Chem.*, **29,** 951 (1967).
244. O. I. Egerev and A. D. Pogorelzi, *Zh. Prikl. Khim.*, **39,** 926 (1966).
245. J. Fischer, A. DeCian and R. Weiss, *Bull. Soc. Chim. France*, **1966,** 2646.
246. H. Hull and A. G. Turnball, *J. Inorg. Nucl. Chem.*, **29,** 2903 (1967).
247. J. E. Dutrizae and S. N. Flengas, *Can. J. Chem.*, **45,** 2313 (1967).
248. R. A. Walton and B. J. Brisdon, *Spectrochim. Acta*, **23A,** 2222 (1967).
249. B. J. Brisdon, T. E. Lester and R. A. Walton, *Spectrochim. Acta*, **23A,** 1969 (1967).

Chapter 5

Niobium and Tantalum

All the possible halides for niobium and tantalum in their pentavalent state are known and these elements are unique in forming pentaiodides. The group valence of five dominates the chemistry of these elements and in general the preparation of compounds in their lower oxidation states involves reduction of the pentahalide. The ease of reduction decreases from iodide to fluoride and, indeed, there is some doubt whether tantalum pentafluoride can be reduced at all.

HALIDES AND OXIDE HALIDES

The known halides and oxide halides of niobium and tantalum are shown in Tables 5.1 and 5.2.

Various oxide fluorides of niobium(v) have been prepared by fusing appropriate mixtures of niobium pentaoxide and niobium dioxide fluoride or by the thermal decomposition of other oxide fluorides. Several oxide chlorides of niobium of more complex stoichiometry than those in Table

TABLE 5.1

Halides of Niobium and Tantalum

Oxidation state	Fluoride	Chloride	Bromide	Iodide
V	NbF_5, TaF_5	$NbCl_5$, $TaCl_5$	$NbBr_5$, $TaBr_5$	NbI_5, TaI_5
IV	NbF_4	$NbCl_4$, $TaCl_4$	$NbBr_4$, $TaBr_4$	NbI_4, TaI_4
III		$NbCl_3$, $TaCl_3$	$NbBr_3$, $TaBr_3$	NbI_3
Non-integral		$NbCl_{2.67}$	$NbBr_{2.67}$	$NbI_{2.67}$
	$NbF_{2.5}$	$TaCl_{2.5}$	$TaBr_{2.5}$	
		$NbCl_{2.33}$		$TaI_{2.33}$

145

TABLE 5.2

Oxide Halides of Niobium and Tantalum

Oxidation state	Fluoride	Chloride	Bromide	Iodide
V	$TaOF_3$ NbO_2F, TaO_2F	$NbOCl_3$, $TaOCl_3$ NbO_2Cl, TaO_2Cl	$NbOBr_3$, $TaOBr_3$	$NbOI_3$ NbO_2I, TaO_2I
IV		$NbOCl_2$, $TaOCl_2$		$NbOI_2$

5.2 may be prepared by thermal decomposition of niobium oxide trichloride.

Oxidation State V

Niobium and tantalum pentafluorides. The best method of preparing these compounds is by direct fluorination of the metals at 200–350° in a flow system[1-4]. Alternatively, chlorine trifluoride may be reacted with the metals, although the removal of the last traces of this reagent from the pentafluorides is difficult[5]. Bromine trifluoride is not a good alternative as a fluorinating agent because stable adducts of the type $MF_5 \cdot BrF_3$ are formed[5,6]. Removal of the bromine trifluoride requires strong heating and indeed only 70% of the coordinated bromine trifluoride was removed from the tantalum pentafluoride adduct at 200°[6].

Other less important methods of preparing niobium and tantalum pentafluorides are summarized in Table 5.3. The classical method of preparing both pentafluorides is the action of anhydrous hydrogen fluoride on the corresponding pentachloride at room temperature[15]. This method, however, should be avoided if possible, since very pure anhydrous hydrogen fluoride is required and any oxide chloride in the pentachloride will at best be converted into an oxide fluoride.

TABLE 5.3

Some Methods of Preparing Niobium and Tantalum
Pentafluorides

Method	Conditions	Ref.
Metal/anhyd.HF	250°, flow system 250°, bomb	7, 8 9
MCl_5 in $AsCl_3/AsF_3$	Reflux	10, 11
Niobium or tantalum carbides or nitrides and anhyd.HF	About 400°	12
K_2NbF_7/AlF_3	800°, sealed tube	13
Nb/SnF_2	375–500°, bomb	14

Both niobium and tantalum pentafluoride are white crystalline solids which are readily purified by vacuum-sublimation. They are rapidly hydrolysed in moist air.

The vapour pressures of the pentafluorides have been measured over wide temperature ranges and the variation with temperature is given by the expressions:

NbF_5: $\log p_{mm} = 8.439 - 2824/T$ (70–230°)   (reference 3)

NbF_5: $\log p_{mm} = 8.372 - 2777/T$ (100–250°)   (reference 4)

TaF_5: $\log p_{mm} = 8.524 - 2834/T$ (80–230°)   (reference 3)

TABLE 5.4

Thermodynamic Data for Niobium and Tantalum Pentafluorides

Property	NbF_5	Ref.	TaF_5	Ref.
M.p.	78.9°	4	95.1°	3
	79.0°	13	97.0°	13
	80.0°	3		
B.p.	233.3°	4	229.0°	3
	234.0°	13		
	234.9°	3		
ΔH°_{form}	−432 kcal mole^{-1}	16	−455.0 kcal mole^{-1}	17
	−433.5 kcal mole^{-1}	17		
ΔG°_{form}	−405 kcal mole^{-1}	16	−428.0 kcal mole^{-1}	17
	−406.2 kcal mole^{-1}	17		
ΔS°_{form}	95.1 cal deg^{-1} mole^{-1}	17	90.4 cal deg^{-1} mole^{-1}	17
ΔH_{vap}	12.9 kcal mole^{-1}	3	13.0 kcal mole^{-1}	3

It is clear by inspection that the two sets of data for niobium pentafluoride are in good agreement.

Thermodynamic data for niobium and tantalum pentafluorides, calculated from the vapour-pressure data and calorimetric measurements are given in Table 5.4. It is worth noting that, like the other pentahalides, tantalum pentafluoride melts at a higher temperature than its niobium analogue but boils at a lower temperature.

Both niobium and tantalum pentafluoride adopt the molybdenum pentafluoride structure (Chapter 1) in the solid state, that is, they form tetrameric units with four metal atoms and four bridging fluorine atoms coplanar. Within experimental error the monoclinic lattices of the two pentafluorides are isodimensional[18] with $a = 9.63$, $b = 14.43$, $c = 5.12$ Å and $\beta = 96.1°$. There are eight formula weights in the unit cell and the space group is $C2/m$. The distance between the metal and a bridging fluorine atom is 2.06 Å and the corresponding distance for the terminal fluorine atoms is 1.77 Å.

The infrared spectrum of solid tantalum pentafluoride has been reported[19]. There are numerous absorptions, the principle ones being found at 253, 515 and 645 cm^{-1}.

The pentafluorides of both niobium and tantalum give dense viscous melts. The variation of density with temperature is given by the expressions:

$$\rho_{NbF_5} = 2.6955 - 2.490 \times 10^{-3}(T - 80) \quad \text{(reference 20)}$$

$$\rho_{NbF_5} = 2.8026 - 9.81 \times 10^{-4}T - 6.16 \times 10^{-6}T^2 \quad \text{(reference 4)}$$

$$(T = 86\text{--}125°)$$

$$\rho_{TaF_5} = 3.8804 - 4.035 \times 10^{-3}T(T - 95) \quad \text{(reference 20)}$$

The viscosities at the melting points are 91.41 and 70.31 centipoises for niobium and tantalum pentafluorides, respectively[20]. Viscosities of this magnitude usually indicate a highly associated liquid and this view is reinforced by the high values of the Trouton constant which are 25.4 (niobium pentafluoride) and 25.9 (tantalum pentafluoride)[20]. There is also evidence of some dissociation in the melt, as judged by electrical conductivities[21]. At the melting points the specific conductivities are 1.63 × 10^{-5} and 1.56 × 10^{-5} for niobium and tantalum pentafluoride, respectively. It has been suggested that a self-ionization mechanism is responsible for the conductivity of the melt[21]:

$$2MF_5 \rightarrow MF_4^+ + MF_6^-$$

Calculation[21] of thermodynamic functions such as the activation energy of molar conductance suggests that in both cases the extent of self-ionization in the melt is less than 1%.

Niobium pentafluoride dissolves in anhydrous ethanol to give, rather surprisingly, a deep purple solution which is highly conducting. The ^{93}Nb NMR spectrum of the solution shows a septet which can be assigned only to the hexafluoroniobate(v) anion[22]. Unfortunately no peak attributable to the cation could be found and it was suggested that an unsymmetrical species with a large field gradient at the central metal atom may be formed. It is clear, of course, that ionization is necessary to form the observed anion from niobium pentafluoride. Some evidence for the tetrafluorotantalum(v) cation has been obtained from ion-exchange and potentiometric studies of solutions of tantalum(v) in perchloric acid–hydrogen fluoride mixtures[23].

The infrared spectrum of niobium pentafluoride in the vapour phase has been recorded by Blanchard[24], who observed strong absorptions at 510,

688, 732 and 748 cm^{-1}. By a comparison with the spectra of other known trigonal-bipyramidal molecules, it was concluded that niobium pentafluoride exists in this form in the vapour phase. It seems reasonable to suppose that the tantalum compound has a similar structure in the vapour phase.

Both niobium and tantalum pentafluoride are readily soluble in bromine trifluoride[6], and at 25° the solubility of the niobium compound is 15.7 g/100 g of solvent[25]. The high solubility of these compounds in bromine trifluoride is due to formation of hexafluorometallates(v), as is confirmed by isolation of many salts of these anions by precipitation reactions[2,6]. The acid strengths of the pentafluorides in anhydrous hydrogen fluoride have been shown to be moderate to high by a variety of qualitative measurements[26,27]. The behaviour of both pentafluorides in aqueous hydrogen fluoride solutions containing from 0 to 100% of hydrogen flouride have been studied by Nikoleav and Buslaev[28,29].

The chemical reactivities of the two pentafluorides are very similar because, as a result of the lanthanide contraction, the metals are similar in size and in electronegativity. Because of this similarity, most studies have been made with niobium pentafluoride only and it has been assumed that tantalum pentafluoride reacts similarly. However, recent studies[1] have shown that niobium pentafluoride is slightly more reactive than the tantalum compound, as indicated by the rate of formation of volatile reaction products; but in all cases both pentafluorides underwent the same type of reaction, that is, no reagent was found which would react with one pentafluoride and not the other[1].

The reduction of niobium pentafluoride to a lower fluoride is difficult to achieve and there is thermodynamic evidence that lower fluorides of tantalum would not be stable at room temperature[30]. Certainly attempts have been made to prepare lower tantalum fluorides but so far without success[1,30]. The lack of oxidizing powder of both pentafluorides is demonstrated by the fact that both form numerous adducts, particularly with organic molecules, whereas a more powerful oxidant would fluorinate the donor molecule or form an adduct with the metal in a lower oxidation state, or both. Some adducts of niobium and tantalum pentafluorides are reported in Table 5.5.

Niobium pentafluoride reacts with liquid ammonia[33] to form a yellow, thermally unstable adduct, $NbF_5 \cdot 2NH_3$. The dissociation pressure of this complex over the range 50–100° is given by the expression:

$$\log p_{mm} = 5.62 - 1270/T$$

and the heat of dissociation was calculated[33] to be 7.87 kcal mole^{-1} at 85°.

Tantalum oxide trifluoride. This compound has been reported to be formed when tantalum pentafluoride vapour reacts with silica at elevated temperatures[36]. No further information is available.

Niobium and tantalum dioxide fluorides. Niobium dioxide fluoride is formed on dissolution of niobium pentaoxide in 48% aqueous hydrogen fluoride[37] or on reaction[13] of niobium pentafluoride with glass at temperatures above 400°. The corresponding tantalum compound is formed by the dissolution of tantalum metal in 48% aqueous hydrogen fluoride[37].

TABLE 5.5

Some Adducts of Niobium and Tantalum Pentafluorides

Adduct	Ref.	Adduct	Ref.
$NbF_5 \cdot O(C_2H_5)_2$	22, 31	$NbF_5 \cdot 2.1SO_3$	2
$NbF_5 \cdot O(CH_3)_2$	31	$TaF_5 \cdot 2.6SO_3$	2
$TaF_5 \cdot O(C_2H_5)_2$	31	$NbF_5 \cdot 2(C_2H_5N)$	2
$TaF_5 \cdot O(CH_3)_2$	31	$TaF_5 \cdot 2(C_5H_5N)$	2
$NbF_5 \cdot S(C_2H_5)_2$	31	$NbF_5 \cdot 1.6$ethylenediamine	33
$NbF_5 \cdot S(CH_3)_2$	31	$TaF_5 \cdot 2XeF_2$	34
$TaF_5 \cdot S(C_2H_5)_2$	31	$NbF_5 \cdot 2(CH_3)_2SO$	35
$TaF_5 \cdot S(CH_3)_2$	31	$TaF_5 \cdot 2(CH_3)_2SO$	35
$NbF_5 \cdot N(CH_3)_3$	22	$NbF_5 \cdot SeF_4$	32
$TaF_5 \cdot SeF_4$	32		

Both dioxide fluorides adopt the cubic rhenium trioxide structure[37], with the oxygen and fluorine atoms randomly distributed in the octahedral positions about the central metal atom. The unit cells have $a = 3.902$ Å (NbO_2F) and 3.896 Å (TaO_2F).

The infrared spectrum of both dioxide fluorides show intense absorptions at about 1000 cm^{-1}, indicating the presence of metal–oxygen double bonds[38].

The thermal decomposition of niobium dioxide fluoride has been studied[39] between 600° and 1200° and it was shown that the compound Nb_3O_7F was formed between 840° and 970°. The final product at high temperatures was niobium pentaoxide.

Miscellaneous niobium(v) oxide fluorides. A number of oxide fluorides of niobium(v) have been prepared by fusing appropriate mixtures of niobium pentaoxide and dioxide fluoride, as shown in Table 5.6. All the structures noted in the Table are modified rhenium trioxide structures.

Niobium and tantalum tetrachloride fluorides. Both niobium and tantalum tetrachloride fluoride are prepared by the action of arsenic trifluoride on a solution in arsenic trichloride of the phosphorus pentachloride adduct with niobium or tantalum pentachloride[10,11]. Both tetrachloride fluorides are extremely hygroscopic yellow powders which are insoluble in non-polar solvents. The tetrachloride fluorides melt at 201° (niobium) and 214° (tantalum) to give golden yellow non-conducting liquids[10,11].

Niobium and tantalum pentachlorides. Many preparative methods for niobium and tantalum pentachlorides have been reported and some of these are summarized in Tables 5.7 and 5.8. In some reactions with

TABLE 5.6
Oxide Fluorides of Niobium(v)

Compound	Structural data	Ref.
Nb_3O_7F	Orthorhombic, $a = 20.67$, $b = 3.83$, $c = 3.927$ Å	40, 41
$Nb_5O_{12}F$	Orthorhombic, $a = 6.15$, $b = 18.29$, $c = 3.92$ Å	40
$Nb_{17}O_{42}F$	Monoclinic, $a = 21.09$, $b = 3.827$, $c = 23.02$ Å, $\beta = 116.2°$	42
$Nb_{31}O_{77}F$	Monoclinic, $a = 37.54$, $b = 3.832$, $c = 21.18$ Å, $\beta = 91.92°$	42

niobium pentaoxide, for example that with aluminium trichloride, a mixture of niobium pentachloride and niobium oxide trichloride is obtained. However, in the corresponding reaction with tantalum pentaoxide, only tantalum pentachloride is obtained. There are indications that tantalum oxide trichloride is thermally unstable. A noteworthy difference between niobium and tantalum is that only for tantalum is a reaction with gaseous hydrogen chloride reported to give the pentachloride. The action of mercurous chloride on niobium and tantalum metal gives niobium trichloride and tantalum pentachloride, respectively[44]. Probably the most convenient method of preparing both pentachlorides is the direct chlorination of the metals.

Niobium pentachloride is a yellow hygroscopic solid, while its tantalum analogue is almost white. It has been suggested that niobium pentachloride exists as two polymorphs in the solid state[43] but this has not subsequently been confirmed. Both pentachlorides are soluble in a variety of inert organic solvents[57–59].

The vapour pressure of niobium pentachloride has been recorded, but there is a scarcity of information on the tantalum compound as shown in Table 5.9.

TABLE 5.7
Preparation of Niobium Pentachloride

Method	Conditions	Ref.
Nb and Cl_2	Flow system, 300–350°	43
Nb_2O_5 and Cl_2	Flow system, >700°	44
Nb_2O_5, C and Cl_2	Flow system, 300–500°	45, 46
Nb_2O_5 and Cl_2 in hexachlorobutadiene	Under reflux	47
Nb_2O_5 and CCl_4	Flow system, 200–225°	48
Nb_2O_5 and CCl_4	Sealed tube, 270–300°	49
Nb_2O_5 and $SOCl_2$	Flow system, 100–150°	50
Nb_2O_5 and $AlCl_3$	Sealed tube, 230–400°	51
NbO_2 and Cl_2	Flow system, 400°	44

TABLE 5.8
Preparation of Tantalum Pentachloride

Method	Conditions	Ref.
Ta and Cl_2	Flow system, 300–350°	43
Ta and HCl gas	Flow system, 350–700°	52–54
Ta and Hg_2Cl_2		55
Ta_2O_5 and $AlCl_3$	Sealed tube, 230–400°	51
Ta_2O_5 and CCl_4	Sealed tube, 300–400°	49, 56
Ta_2O_5 and HCl gas	Flow system, 700°	52
Ta_2O_5 and $SOCl_2$	Flow system, >150°	50
Ta_2O_5 and $NbCl_5$	Sealed tube, elevated temp.	48

TABLE 5.9
Vapour-Pressure Equations for Niobium and Tantalum Pentachlorides

Compound	State	Equation	Ref.
$NbCl_5$	Solid	$\log p_{mm} = 11.51 - 4370/T$	60
		$\log p_{mm} = 11.57 - 4380/T$	61
		$\log p_{mm} = 10.77 - 4010/T$	62
		$\log p_{atm} = 8.629 - 4370/T$	63
	Liquid	$\log p_{mm} = 8.37 - 2870/T$	60
		$\log p_{mm} = 8.43 - 2840/T$	61
		$\log p_{mm} = 7.60 - 2450/T$	62
		$\log p_{atm} = 5.489 - 2870/T$	63
$TaCl_5$	Liquid	$\log p_{mm} = 8.543 - 2865/T$	64

Many thermodynamic data have been accumulated for both penta-chlorides and in general the variation of reported values for a particular property is small. Some of these are listed in Table 5.10.

The densities of liquid niobium and tantalum pentachlorides are given by the expressions[65,66]:

$$\rho_{NbCl_5} = 2.0737 - 3.115 \times 10^{-3}\Delta t + 3.58 \times 10^{-6}\Delta t^2$$
$$(t \text{ from } 204.2° \text{ to } 325°C)$$

$$\rho_{TaCl_5} = 2.6840 - 4.100 \times 10^{-3}\Delta t$$
$$(t \text{ from } 216.2° \text{ to } 305°C)$$

TABLE 5.10

Some Thermodynamic Data for Niobium and Tantalum Pentachlorides

Property	NbCl$_5$	Ref.	TaCl$_5$	Ref.
M.p.	203.4°	64	215.9°	64
	204.2°	65, 66	216.2°	65, 66
	204.7°	49, 60, 63	216.5°	49
	206.0°	67	220.0°	43
	206.8°	68		
	209.5°	43		
B.p.	247.4°	63, 64	232.9°	64
	248.3°	69	234.0°	69
	250.0°	60	239.3°	43
	254.0°	43		
ΔH_{form}° (kcal mole^{-1})	−188.0	70	−205.0	70, 71
	−190.5	63	−205.5	72, 75
	−190.6	71, 72	−206.0	76
	−193.7	73		
ΔS_{form}° (kcal deg^{-1} mole^{-1})	58.6	71	59.4	71
ΔH_{sub} (kcal mole^{-1})	18.3	62	22.7	77
	20.0	43, 60, 61		
ΔH_{vap} (kcal mole^{-1})	11.2	62	13.1	64
	12.6	64	14.9	77
	13.0	61		
	13.1	60		
	13.2	43		
ΔH_{fus}	7.7	43	8.4	43
	9.15	74	9.95	74
$\Delta H_{diss}{}^a$ (kcal mole^{-1})	28.3	60	33.6	77
ΔS_{sub} (cal deg^{-1} mole^{-1})	36.1	62	45.2	77
	38.9	43		
	39.5	60		
	39.8	61		
ΔS_{vap} (cal deg^{-1} mole^{-1})	21.6	62	25.9	64
	24.3	64	29.3	77
	25.1	43, 60		
	25.4	61		
$\Delta S_{diss}{}^a$ (cal deg^{-1} mole^{-1})	47.0	60	31.3	77

^{a} For the reaction: $MCl_5 \rightarrow MCl_4 + \frac{1}{2}Cl_2$

The structure of solid niobium pentachloride has been determined by single-crystal X-ray diffraction measurements[78]. The monoclinic unit cell has the parameters $a = 18.30$, $b = 17.98$, $c = 5.888$ Å and $\beta = 90.6°$. These dimensions are in good agreement with those previously reported from a powder diffraction study[79]. The structure, which is shown in Figure 5.1, consists of dimeric units with bridging chlorine atoms, each niobium atom being surrounded by a distorted octahedron of chlorine atoms. The niobium–chlorine distances are 2.56 Å for bridging chlorines, 2.25 Å

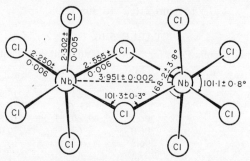

Figure 5.1 Molecular dimensions of the $(NbCl_5)_2$ dimer.

for equatorial positions, and 2.30 Å for the axial positions[78]. Tantalum pentachloride is isomorphous with the niobium compound[78].

In the vapour phase, both pentachlorides have been shown by electron-diffraction studies to be trigonal-bipyramids[80], mean bond lengths being 2.29 Å for niobium pentachloride and 2.30 Å for the tantalum compound.

There has been some confusion as to the constitution of the penta-chlorides in the molten state and in solution. Voitovich and Barabanova[59] suggested, from depression of the freezing point, that both compounds are monomeric in nitrobenzene solution. Gaunt and Ainscough[81] examined the Raman spectrum of solid niobium pentachloride and the infrared spectrum of a carbon disulphide solution. Both spectra were complicated and were interpreted on the basis of trigonal-bipyramidal symmetry, but this work preceded the structure determination of solid niobium pentachloride by Zalkin and Sands[78]. Subsequent evidence has strongly suggested that each pentachloride in fact exists in the dimeric form in both the melt and in solution[82-85].

At very low temperatures tantalum pentachloride forms rather indefinite adducts with liquid ammonia[86]. However, when the reaction is carried out at the boiling point of liquid ammonia[86-88], ammonolysis occurs to give $Ta(NH_2)_2Cl_3 \cdot xNH_3$. When the product is heated to 120°, $Ta(NH_2)_2Cl_3$ itself is obtained[87,88].

Several modes of reaction of niobium and tantalum pentachlorides with amines are possible, depending on the nature of the amine. Thus pyridine, trimethylamine and triethylamine form simple 1:1 adducts (pyridine and triethylamine) or 1:2 adducts (trimethylamine)[89-91]. Replacement occurs when methylamine, dimethylamine or diethylamine react with niobium or tantalum pentachloride, and gives compounds of the types $NbCl_2(NHMe)_3$[90] and $MCl_3(NR_2) \cdot NHR_2$[90-92]. Rather surprisingly, it has been reported[93] that reduction occurs when both niobium

TABLE 5.11

Some Substitution Reactions of Niobium and Tantalum
Pentachlorides

Reactants	Compounds	Ref.
$NbCl_5$ and NaC_5H_5	$(C_5H_5)_2NbCl_3$ and $(C_5H_5)_3NbCl_2$	97
MCl_5 and $(CH_3)_2Zn$	$(CH_3)_3MCl_2$	98
$NbCl_5$ and $LiAlH_4$	$Nb(AlH_4)_x$ (x = 2.5–3.5)	99
$NbCl_5$ and R_2SO	$NbOCl_3 \cdot 2R_2SO$ (R = CH_3 or C_6H_5)	100
MCl_5 and $(C_6H_5)_3PO$	$MOCl_3 \cdot 2(C_6H_5)_3PO$	101
$TaCl_5$ and CH_3CO_2H	$TaCl(OOCCH_3)_4$	102
MCl_5 and $S_2O_6F_2$	$MO(SO_3F)_3$	103
$TaCl_5$ and SO_3F	$TaCl_3(SO_3F)_2$	104

and tantalum pentachlorides react with pyridine and γ-picoline, to give complexes of the type $MCl_4 \cdot 2L$ and with bipyridyl and 1,10-phenanthroline, to give $MCl_4 \cdot L$. This behaviour is to be contrasted with the pyridine reaction noted above. Niobium pentachloride reacts with lithium amides to give compounds of the general formula $Nb(NR_2)_5$ (R = CH_3 or C_2H_5) or $Nb(NR_2)_4$ (R = n-butyl or n-propyl)[94].

Tantalum pentachloride reacts with ammonium chloride at 190° with the evolution of hydrogen chloride. At higher temperatures decomposition of the initial products occurs, to give tantalum dichloride nitride[95,96], as represented by the following equations:

$$2TaCl_5 + 3NH_4Cl \xrightarrow{190°} TaNCl_2 + TaNHCl_3 + NH_4Cl + HCl\uparrow$$

$$TaNCl_2 + TaNHCl_3 + NH_4Cl \xrightarrow{250°} 2TaNCl_2 + NH_4Cl\uparrow + HCl\uparrow$$

Various other substitution reactions of niobium and tantalum pentachlorides are given in Table 5.11.

Niobium and tantalum pentachlorides undergo a large number of addition reactions with donor molecules, both inorganic and organic. In all cases the compounds are simple 1:1 adducts and the majority are presumably octahedral. Some of these adducts are given in Table 5.12.

TABLE 5.12

Some Adducts of Niobium and Tantalum Pentachlorides

Adduct	Ref.
$MCl_5 \cdot POCl_3$	59, 105–109
$MCl_5 \cdot OR_2$ (R = CH_3 or C_2H_5)	54, 110, 111
$MCl_5 \cdot SR_2$ (R = CH_3 or C_2H_5)	110, 112
$MCl_5 \cdot SCl_4$	50
$MCl_5 \cdot PCl_5$	108
$NbCl_5 \cdot (C_6H_5)_3X$ (X = N, P, As, Sb or Bi)	113
$MCl_5 \cdot$ Diarsine	114
$MCl_5 \cdot RCN$ (R = CH_3, C_2H_5 or n–C_3H_7)	84, 115
$MCl_5 \cdot (C_6H_5)_3CCl$	116

Niobium oxide trichloride. A number of methods of preparation of niobium oxide trichloride have been reported and some of these are given in Table 5.13. It is worth noting that several of the methods given in the Table give mixtures of niobium oxide trichloride and niobium pentachloride, thus necessitating the somewhat difficult separation of these compounds by differential vacuum-sublimation.

Niobium oxide trichloride is a white solid which is readily hydrolysed by water. It is thermally unstable, forming niobium pentachloride and niobium pentaoxide[54]. The equilibrium dissociation pressure of niobium pentachloride over solid niobium oxide trichloride is given by the expressions:

$$\log p_{mm} = 17.30 - 9264/T \quad (225–329°) \quad \text{(reference 126)}$$

$$\log p_{atm} = 10.386 - 6290/T \quad (337–397°) \quad \text{(reference 124)}$$

TABLE 5.13

Preparation of Niobium Oxide Trichloride

Method	Conditions	Product(s)	Ref.
Nb_2O_5 and HCl gas	Flow system, 400–700°	$NbOCl_3$	117
Nb_2O_5, C and CCl_4	Flow system, 650–700°	$NbOCl_3$	118
Nb_2O_5, C and Cl_2	Flow system, 500°	$NbOCl_3 + NbCl_5$	46
Nb_2O_5 and Cl_2	Flow system, < 700°	$NbOCl_3 + NbCl_5$	44, 119
Nb_2O_5 and $AlCl_3$	Sealed tube, 230–400°	$NbOCl_3 + NbCl_5$	46, 51, 120
Nb_2O_5 and $SOCl_2$	Flow system, 200°	$NbOCl_3$	121
Nb_2O_5 and $NbCl_5$	Temperature gradient	$NbOCl_3$	68, 119, 122–124
$NbCl_5$ and Ta_2O_5		$NbOCl_3 + TaCl_5$	48
$NbCl_5$ and O_2	400–500°	$NbOCl_3$	45, 46, 125
$NbCl_5 \cdot (C_2H_5)_2O$	Thermal decomp. at 100°	$NbOCl_3$	46, 54

The vapour pressure of niobium oxide trichloride itself is given by the following expressions which have been corrected for the vapour pressure of niobium pentachloride:

$$\log p_{mm} = 13.35 - 6349/T \quad (225\text{--}329°) \quad \text{(reference 126)}$$
$$\log p_{atm} = 10.652 - 6433/T \quad (202\text{--}432°) \quad \text{(reference 127)}$$

Remarkably few thermodynamic results have been reported for niobium oxide trichloride. Its heat of formation has been variously given

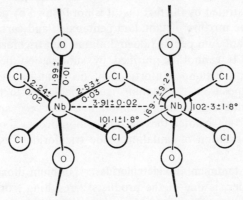

Figure 5.2   Molecular dimensions of niobium oxide trichloride.

as -179.3, -210.2, and -212.2 kcal mole^{-1} [127,119,118]. The heat and entropy of sublimation[119] are 26.1 kcal mole and 44 cal deg^{-1} mole^{-1}, respectively.

The structure of niobium oxide trichloride has been studied by Sands and coworkers[128] by single-crystal X-ray diffraction techniques. They found a tetragonal lattice with $a = 10.87$ and $c = 3.96$ Å. The structure, which is shown in Figure 5.2, consists of chains of dimeric Nb_2Cl_6 units joined by niobium–oxygen linkages so that each niobium atom has approximately octahedral coordination. The bond distances and angles are shown in Figure 5.2.

The infrared spectrum of niobium oxide trichloride shows a strong band at 767 cm^{-1} attributed to the bridging niobium–oxygen stretching frequency[129], and metal–chlorine frequencies[130] at 429, 405 and 295 cm^{-1}.

The only complexes formed by direct interaction with niobium oxide trichloride, apart from complex halides, are $NbOCl_2(\text{Acetylacetone})$[130,131] and $NbOCl_3 \cdot \text{Diarsine}$[114]. Other complexes may be produced indirectly from niobium pentachloride by oxygen abstraction from the ligand as shown in Table 5.11.

Tantalum oxide trichloride. Tantalum oxide trichloride may be prepared by bubbling chlorine monoxide through a carbon tetrachloride solution of tantalum pentachloride at room temperature[132]. Thermal decomposition of $TaCl_5 \cdot (C_2H_5)_2O$ at 65° in a vacuum gives tantalum oxide trichloride[46]. The thermal-gradient method, applied to tantalum pentachloride and tantalum pentaoxide, also leads to the formation of tantalum oxide trichloride[132,133].

The greatest difference between tantalum oxide trichloride and its niobium analogue is the comparative thermal instability of the former. This is well illustrated by the fact that it is not formed by passing chlorine over an intimate mixture of tantalum pentaoxide and carbon[46] or by the interaction of tantalum pentaoxide and aluminium trichloride in a heated sealed tube[51]. It cannot be purified by sublimation because of concomitant decomposition. Unfortunately no quantitative data on the thermal decomposition of tantalum oxide trichloride to the pentaoxide and pentachloride are available, although Dehnicke[132] and Fairbrother and coworkers[46] have noted that decomposition occurs above about 250°. The heat of formation of tantalum oxide trichloride[133] is only -101.3 kcal mole^{-1}.

Niobium and tantalum dioxide chlorides. Niobium dioxide chloride, a pale grey powder, is one of the products[134] resulting from the complex reactions that occur when niobium oxide trichloride is thermally decomposed in an evacuated sealed tube at 350°. The black tantalum analogue has been isolated[52] from the reaction between hydrogen chloride and tantalum pentaoxide above 700°. Tantalum dioxide chloride is stable to at least 1100°.

Triniobium heptaoxide chloride. The compound Nb_3O_7Cl can be prepared[43] by interaction of niobium pentaoxide and niobium oxide trichloride in a sealed tube[135] at 600° or by the thermal decomposition of niobium oxide trichloride[134] at 350°. It is a blue-black solid which is resistant to hydrolysis[135]. It is orthorhombic[136], with $a = 10.88$, $b = 15.53$ and $c = 3.84$ Å.

Niobium and tantalum pentabromides. Numerous methods of preparing niobium and tantalum pentabromides have been reported, as shown in Tables 5.14 and 5.15. Some interesting differences between niobium and tantalum are apparent from the reported preparations of the pentabromides. The action of bromine on an intimate mixture of tantalum pentaoxide and carbon yields the pentabromide; but the corresponding reaction with niobium pentaoxide gives niobium oxide tribromide. The action of mercurous bromide on niobium metal gives niobium tribromide, whereas tantalum yields the pentabromide in the analogous reaction.

TABLE 5.14

Preparation of Niobium Pentabromide

Method	Conditions	Ref.
Nb and Br_2	Flow system, 230–550°	43, 137–139
Nb_2O_5 and $AlBr_3$	Sealed tube, 200°	51
Nb_2O_5 and CBr_4	Sealed tube, 370°	140

Both pentabromides are fairly volatile, yellow-red compounds which are hygroscopic and readily hydrolysed. The vapour pressures of niobium and tantalum pentabromides vary with temperature according to the following expressions:

Solid $NbBr_5$: $\log p_{mm} = 12.52 - 5782/T$ (205–252°) (reference 145)

Liquid $NbBr_5$: $\log p_{mm} = 9.784 - 4347/T$ (252–356°) (reference 145)

Solid $TaBr_5$: $\log p_{mm} = 12.51 - 5546/T$ (180–255°) (reference 145)

Solid $TaBr_5$: $\log p_{mm} = 12.57 - 5650/T$ (200–267°) (reference 146)

Liquid $TaBr_5$: $\log p_{mm} = 8.07 - 3204/T$ (255–344°) (reference 145)

Liquid $TaBr_5$: $\log p_{mm} = 8.17 - 3265/T$ (267–345°) (reference 146)

It is clear that agreement of the two sets of data for tantalum pentabromide is good.

Thermodynamic properties of both pentabromides, calculated from the vapour-pressure measurements and from other experiments, are given in Table 5.16. A curious feature of this Table is the wide range of values given for the melting points of the pentabromides, although there is reasonably good agreement by the various groups of workers about their boiling points. Perhaps this variation is due to impurities in the various samples and illustrates the experimental difficulties involved in handling these readily hydrolysed volatile compounds.

TABLE 5.15

Preparation of Tantalum Pentabromide

Method	Conditions	Ref.
Ta and Br_2	Flow system, 320–550°	43, 54, 138, 141, 142
Ta and HBr	Flow system, 550°	53
Ta and Hg_2Br_2		55
Ta_2O_5, C and Br_2	Flow system, >460°	46, 143
Ta_2O_5 and $AlBr_3$	Sealed tube	41
Ta_2O_5 and CBr_4	Sealed tube, 200°	144

TABLE 5.16

Thermodynamic Data for Niobium and Tantalum Pentabromides

Property	NbBr₅	Ref.	TaBr₅	Ref.
M.p.	254°	145	256°	145
	255°	147	267°	146
	267.5°	43	272°	141
			280°	43
B.p.	361.6°	43	344.0°	145
	365.0°	145	345.0°	146
			348.4°	43
$\Delta H^{\circ}_{\text{form}}$ (kcal mole⁻¹)	−133.9	148	−143.0	148
	−135.2	140	−164.0	71, 76
	−150	71		
$\Delta S^{\circ}_{\text{form}}$ (cal deg⁻¹ mole⁻¹)	73	71	73	71
ΔH_{sub} (kcal mole⁻¹)	26.5	145	25.4	145
			25.8	146
ΔH_{vap} (kcal mole⁻¹)	19.9	145	14.7	145
			14.9	146
ΔH_{fus} (kcal mole⁻¹)			10.9	43, 146
ΔS_{sub} (kcal deg⁻¹ mole⁻¹)	44.1	145	44.0	145
ΔS_{vap} (kcal deg⁻¹ mole⁻¹)	31.6	145	23.8	145
			24.1	146

The variation with temperature of the densities of the liquid pentabromides has been investigated by Nisel'son and Sokolova[147], and the
results obtained are expressed by the equations:

$$\rho_{\text{NbBr}_5} = 3.324 - 2.92 \times 10^{-3}\Delta t + 0.81 \times 10^{-6}\Delta t^2$$

$$(t \text{ from } 255° \text{ to } 410°\text{C})$$

$$\rho_{\text{TaBr}_5} = 3.718 - 3.70 \times 10^{-3}\Delta t + 2.48 \times 10^{-6}\Delta t^2$$

$$(t \text{ from } 268° \text{ to } 413°\text{C})$$

There has been no single-crystal X-ray diffraction study on either
niobium or tantalum pentabromide and there has been some controversy
in the literature on the interpretation of the powder diffraction data.
Zalkin and Sands[78] merely stated that niobium pentabromide was isostructural with niobium pentachloride and they gave the dimensions of the
supposed monoclinic cell. However, subsequent work by Rolsten[137]
and by Berdonosova and coworkers[149] has shown that, in fact, both
pentabromides are orthorhombic and not isostructural with niobium and
tantalum pentachlorides. Furthermore, the lattice parameters of the
orthorhombic cells reported by the latter workers have been supported by
density measurements[137,149]. The reported values are reproduced in
Table 5.17.

TABLE 5.17

Lattice Parameters of Niobium and Tantalum Pentabromides

NbBr$_5$	Zalkin and Sands[78]	Rolsten[137]	Berdonosova *et al.*[149]
Symmetry	Monoclinic	Orthorhombic	Orthorhombic
a	19.2 Å	6.125 Å	6.127 Å
b	18.6 Å	12.92 Å	12.198 Å
c	6.0 Å	18.60 Å	18.55 Å
β	90.0°	—	—
Z	12	8	8
Density (expt.)	—	4.36 g/cc	4.36 g/cc
Density (theor.)	—	4.44 g/cc	4.43 g/cc

TaBr$_5$	Rolsten[137]	Berdonosova *et al.*[149]
Symmetry	Orthorhombic	Orthorhombic
a	6.125 Å	6.155 Å
b	12.92 Å	13.29 Å
c	18.60 Å	18.66 Å
Z	8	8
Density (expt.)	4.99 g/cc	4.99 g/cc
Density (theor.)	5.24 g/cc	5.05 g/cc

Electron-diffraction studies of the vapours of both pentabromides indicate that they are monomeric trigonal bipyramids with mean metal–bromine bond lengths of 2.46 Å in the niobium case and 2.45 Å for tantalum[80]. Vapour-pressure measurements[146] have confirmed the monomeric nature of tantalum pentabromide.

A number of substitution reactions of niobium and tantalum pentabromides have been reported and some of these are given in Table 5.18. Fowles and coworkers[93] found that pyridine reduces both niobium and tantalum pentabromide to the quadrivalent state, giving $MBr_4 \cdot 2C_5H_5N$

TABLE 5.18

Some Substitution Reactions of Niobium and
Tantalum Pentabromides

Reagents	Compound	Ref.
MBr_5 and NaC_5H_5	$(C_5H_5)_2MBr_3$	150
$TaBr_5$ and Ph_2SO	$TaO_2Br \cdot 2Ph_2SO$	100
$TaBr_5$ and Ph_3AsO	$TaOBr_3 \cdot 2Ph_3AsO$	101
MBr_5 and C_5H_5N	$MBr_4 \cdot 2C_5H_5N$	89, 93
MBr_5 and Me_2NH	$MBr_3(Me_2N)_2 \cdot NHMe_2$	92

TABLE 5.19

Some Adducts of Niobium and Tantalum
Pentabromides

Adduct	Ref.
$MBr_5 \cdot OR_2$ (R = CH_3 or C_2H_5)	54, 111
$MBr_5 \cdot SR_2$ (R = CH_3 or C_2H_5)	112
$MBr_5 \cdot$ Diarsine	114
$MBr_5 \cdot RCN$ (R = CH_3, C_2H_5 or n–C_3H_7)	115

but McCarley and coworkers[89] found that only niobium pentabromide is reduced and that tantalum pentabromide forms a simple 1:1 adduct.

A number of other simple 1:1 adducts of both pentabromides with donor molecules have been reported and some of these are listed in Table 5.19.

Niobium oxide tribromide. Although various methods of preparation (summarized in Table 5.20) of niobium oxide tribromide have been reported, several of them are merely incidental to the preparation of the pentabromide. The lack of interest in the oxide tribromide is reflected in the dearth of information regarding its physical and chemical properties.

Niobium oxide tribromide occurs as a fine yellow solid which is readily hydrolysed[139].

The heat of formation of niobium oxide tribromide has been reported[140] as -179.3 kcal mole^{-1}. The only adduct of niobium oxide tribromide reported is $NbOBr_3 \cdot$ Diarsine, and this was isolated by the interaction of the ligand and niobium pentabromide in the presence of traces of water[114].

TABLE 5.20

Preparation of Niobium Oxide Tribromide

Method	Conditions	Ref.
Nb_2O_5, C and Br_2	Flow system, 540°	46, 139
Nb_2O_5 and CBr_4	Sealed tube, 200°	140, 144
Nb_2O_5 and $NbBr_5$	Temperature gradient	123
$NbBr_5$ and O_2	Flow system, 150°	46
$NbBr_5 \cdot (C_2H_5)_2O$	Heat at 112° in a vacuum	46

Tantalum oxide tribromide. Tantalum oxide tribromide follows the trend noted with tantalum oxide trichloride in being much less stable than its niobium analogue, and it has only recently been satisfactorily characterized. It has been prepared in an impure form by thermal decomposition of $TaBr_5 \cdot (C_2H_5)_2O$ at 75° in a vacuum[46] and in a pure form by the action of oxygen on tantalum pentabromide[46] at 200°. Tantalum oxide tribromide is also formed[144] in small amounts by the action of carbon tetrabromide on tantalum pentaoxide in a sealed tube at 200°.

Niobium pentaiodide. Niobium pentaiodide has been prepared by direct interaction of the elements at temperatures greater than 600° in a flow system[151,152] and in a sealed tube[153] at 270°. Interaction of niobium pentachloride and aluminium triiodide in a sealed tube at 300° gives impure niobium pentaiodide[154].

The pentaiodide forms brass-coloured crystals, which are readily hydrolysed with the evolution of hydrogen iodide. It is thermally unstable, decomposing to lower iodides which are described below. The heat and entropy of formation are -102 kcal mole^{-1} and 82 cal deg^{-1} mole^{-1}, respectively.

X-ray diffraction studies have shown that niobium pentaiodide has a monoclinic lattice with $a = 10.58$, $b = 6.58$, $c = 13.88$ Å and $\beta = 109.1°$. There are four formula units in the cell[155].

Pyridine reduces niobium pentaiodide to the quadrivalent state, the adduct $NbI_4 \cdot 2C_5H_5N$ being formed[89].

Tantalum pentaiodide. The methods of preparing tantalum pentaiodide are given in Table 5.21.

TABLE 5.21

Preparation of Tantalum Pentaiodide

Method	Conditions	Ref.
Ta and I_2	Flow system, $>700°$	152, 156, 157
Ta and I_2	Sealed tube, 340–370°	158
Ta_2O_5 and AlI_3	Sealed tube, 230°	159, 160
$TaCl_5$ and AlI_3	Sealed tube, 400–420°	154
$TaBr_5$ and HI	Flow system, elevated temp.	143

Tantalum pentaiodide forms brown crystals, which are hydrolysed by cold water. It reacts slowly with oxygen at room temperature and violently at 400°, to give the pentaoxide[156]. It is insoluble in carbon tetrachloride, paraffins and carbon disulphide, but dissolves in coordinating solvents[156].

The vapour pressure of tantalum pentaiodide has been reported and typical values are[152]:

Solid TaI_5		Liquid TaI_5	
Temp.	Vapour pressure	Temp.	Vapour pressure
320.0°	7.6 mm	500.4°	421.2 mm
402.5°	67.2 mm	518.5°	547.3 mm
478.5°	288.7 mm	531.0°	650.4 mm

TABLE 5.22

Thermodynamic Data for Tantalum
Pentaiodide

Property	Value	Ref.
M.p.	496°	152
B.p.	543°	152
$\Delta H^{\circ}_{\text{form}}$	−117 kcal mole^{-1}	71
$\Delta S^{\circ}_{\text{form}}$	82 cal deg^{-1} mole^{-1}	71
ΔH_{fus}	1.6 kcal mole^{-1}	152
ΔH_{vap}	18.1 kcal mole^{-1}	152
ΔH_{sub}	19.7 kcal mole^{-1}	152

The thermodynamic results reported for tantalum pentaiodide are
given in Table 5.22.

Tantalum pentaiodide is not isostructural with its niobium analogue.
It adopts an orthorhombic lattice[158] with $a = 6.65$, $b = 13.95$ and $c =$
20.10 Å.

With diethyl sulphide, tantalum pentaiodide forms a simple 1:1
adduct[112], but with pyridine reduction takes place[89] to give $TaI_4 \cdot 2C_5H_5N$.

Niobium oxide triiodide. Niobium oxide triiodide has been prepared
by the temperature-gradient method, as shown in Table 5.23.

The oxide triiodide is hydrolysed by moist air and, in contrast to the
dissociation reactions of the other oxide trihalides of niobium and tantalum, it decomposes by loss of iodine to give niobium oxide diiodide[161].

TABLE 5.23

Preparation of Niobium Oxide Triodide

Method	Conditions	Ref.
Nb_2O_5 and NbI_5	Temp. gradient	123
Nb_2O_5, Nb and I_2	Temp. gradient, 400–275°	161
NbO_2I and NbI_5	Temp. gradient	162
Nb_2O_5 and AlI_3	Sealed tube, 230–300°	160

Niobium and tantalum dioxide iodides. Both niobium and tantalum
dioxide iodides have been prepared by interaction of the metallic foil,
iodine and the pentaoxide in a sealed tube at 475° for niobium and at 500°
for tantalum[162].

Oxidation State IV

Niobium tetrafluoride. Niobium tetrafluoride was first prepared by
Schafer and coworkers[13,30] by reducing niobium pentafluoride with the
metal at approximately 350°, using the temperature-gradient technique.

Gortsema and Didchenko[14] found that other reducing agents, such as silicon, phosphorus, boron and iodine, can also be used as reducing agents, although niobium metal is probably the best.

The tetrafluoride is a black non-volatile solid. It is very hygroscopic and it is oxidized by air to niobium dioxide fluoride[14]. It is thermally unstable

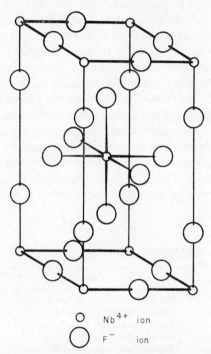

$$\bigcirc \quad Nb^{4+} \quad ion$$

$$\bigcirc \quad F^- \quad ion$$

Figure 5.3 The niobium tetrafluoride unit cell.

and above $400°$ it disproportionates to niobium pentafluoride and $NbF_{2.5}$. The dissociation pressure of niobium pentafluoride is given by the expression[13]:

$$\log p_{atm} = 8.9 - 5500/T$$

X-ray diffraction studies[13,14] show that niobium tetrafluoride crystallizes with the tetragonal stannic fluoride-type lattice with the unit-cell parameters $a = 4.08$ and $c = 8.16$ Å. There are two formula units in the cell, which is shown in Figure 5.3, and the space group is $I4/mmm$.

The two independent groups of workers[13,14] have observed that the magnetic susceptibility of niobium tetrafluoride is of the order of 100–200 × 10^{-6} cgs and is essentially temperature-independent, thus indicating strong interaction between magnetic centres. In view of the postulated crystal structure this interaction must occur *via* the fluorine atoms.

Not one chemical reaction of niobium tetrafluoride has been reported.

Niobium and tantalum tetrachlorides. A large number of preparative methods have been reported for both niobium and tantalum tetrachlorides. The older methods of preparation involved reduction of the pentachloride with reagents such as hydrogen; but in recent years the technique of thermal-gradient synthesis has been applied with great success to the preparation of these compounds. Some of the reported methods for the preparation of niobium and tantalum tetrachlorides are given in Tables 5.24 and 5.25. A number of interesting points are apparent from these Tables. It is clear that tantalum pentachloride is considerably more difficult to reduce than its niobium analogue and indeed this is the basis of a method separation. Schafer and Pietruck[167] found that, whilst niobium pentachloride can be reduced with either niobium or tantalum metal by the thermal-gradient method at comparatively low temperatures (400–200°), tantalum pentachloride cannot be reduced under these conditions. The comparative difficulty of reducing tantalum pentachloride is reflected in the more

TABLE 5.24

Preparation of Niobium Tetrachloride

Method	Conditions	Ref.
$NbCl_5$ and H_2	Flow system, elevated temp. (some trichloride also formed)	163
$NbCl_5$ and Nb	Sealed tube, 380°	163–165
$NbCl_5$ and Al, Fe or Zn	Sealed tube, >300°	163, 165
$NbCl_5$ and Nb	Thermal gradient, 400–250°	163, 166–168
$NbCl_5$ and $NbCl_3$	Thermal gradient, 280–180°	163
$NbCl_5$ and NbO_2	Sealed tube, 290° (some oxide trichloride also formed)	163
NbO_2 and $AlCl_3$	Sealed tube, 290°	163

TABLE 5.25

Preparation of Tantalum Tetrachloride

Method	Conditions	Ref.
$TaCl_5$ and H_2	Gas discharge	169
$TaCl_5$ and Ta	Sealed tube, 630°	170
$TaCl_5$ and Al	Sealed tube, 400°	75, 165, 171–173
$TaCl_5$ and Ta	Thermal gradient, 630–280°	75
$TaCl_5$ and $TaCl_3$	Sealed tube, 320°	171

vigorous conditions required and in the extensive use of more vigorous reducing agents.

Both tetrachlorides are dark volatile solids, which are readily hydrolysed in the atmosphere. They are diamagnetic, indicating interaction between magnetic centres.

Niobium and tantalum tetrachlorides both undergo thermal disproportionation to the corresponding trichlorides and pentachlorides[60,163,171,174].

TABLE 5.26

Thermodynamic Data for Niobium and Tantalum Tetrachlorides

Property	$NbCl_4$	Ref.	$TaCl_4$	Ref.
ΔH°_{form} (kcal mole^{-1})	−166	63	−168.8	75
			−172.6	172
ΔH_{sub} (kcal mole^{-1})	31.4	168	30.2	77
			32.5	75
ΔH_{diss} (kcal mole^{-1})	28.3	60	27.0	77
ΔS_{sub} (cal deg^{-1} mole^{-1})			40.4	77
ΔS_{diss} (cal deg^{-1} mole^{-1})	47	60	48.3	77

The equilibrium dissociation pressure of niobium pentachloride over niobium tetrachloride has been given by the expression[60]:

$$\log p_{mm} = 13.16 - 6190/T \quad (200\text{--}320°)$$

The true vapour pressure of niobium tetrachloride has been determined by Schafer and Bayer[168] by differential pressure measurements made in an atmosphere of niobium pentachloride which prevents disproportionation of the tetrachloride. The expression obtained was:

$$\log p_{mm} = 12.30 - 6870/T \quad (304\text{--}374°)$$

The dissociation pressure of tantalum pentachloride over solid tantalum tetrachloride is given by[171]:

$$\log p_{mm} = 13.2 - 5700/T$$

At temperatures in excess of 800° both tetrachlorides decompose to give the appropriate metal and the pentachloride[165].

Few thermodynamic properties of niobium and tantalum tetrachlorides have been reported, but those available are given in Table 5.26.

The crystal structures of niobium and tantalum tetrachlorides have been investigated by X-ray powder diffraction methods. McCarley and co-workers[166,175] have indexed the diffraction patterns obtained on the basis of an orthorhombic unit cell. They suggest that the two tetrachlorides are isostructural with molybdenum tetrachloride and tungsten tetra-bromide. On the other hand, Schnering and Wohrle[176] and Schafer and coworkers[177] find niobium and tantalum tetrachlorides to be monoclinic. The reported values are given in Table 5.27. McCarley and coworkers[166,175] point out that niobium and tantalum tetrachlorides are not isostructural with α-NbI$_4$ for which single-crystal X-ray diffraction data are available. However, as both tetrachlorides give long, well-oriented crystals, they suggest that niobium and tantalum tetrachlorides consist of long chains, as does α-NbI$_4$, but with a different lattice packing arrangement. If this is correct, it could explain the diamagnetism of the tetrachlorides.

TABLE 5.27

Lattice Parameters of Niobium and Tantalum Tetrachlorides

Compound	Symmetry	Unit-cell parameters	Ref.
NbCl$_4$	Monoclinic	$a = 12.32, b = 6.82, c = 8.21$ Å, $\beta = 134°$	176
TaCl$_4$	Monoclinic	$a = 12.32, b = 6.82, c = 8.21$ Å, $\beta = 134°$	177
NbCl$_4$	Orthorhombic	$a = 8.12, b = 8.88, c = 6.84$ Å	166
TaCl$_4$	Orthorhombic	$a = 8.16, b = 8.92, c = 6.80$ Å	175

Both niobium and tantalum tetrachlorides react with acetonitrile[178] to give complexes of the type $MCl_4 \cdot CH_3CN$. With *o*-phenylenebis-(dimethylarsine) (D) both niobium pentachloride and niobium tetra-chloride[179] give $NbCl_4 \cdot 2D$. Complexes of the types $MCl_4 \cdot 2L$ (L = pyridine or γ-picoline) and $MCl_4 \cdot L$ (L = bipyridyl or *o*-phenanthroline) have been prepared indirectly by interaction of the ligand and the transition-metal pentachloride[93].

Niobium and tantalum oxide dichlorides. Niobium oxide dichloride has been prepared[135] by reaction of niobium pentaoxide with either niobium pentachloride or niobium oxide trichloride in a hydrogen atmosphere in a sealed tube, by using a temperature gradient of 500–400°. An alternative procedure[135] is the interaction of niobium pentaoxide, niobium penta-chloride, and niobium metal in a sealed tube at 350–370°. The corresponding preparation for tantalum oxide dichloride was carried out[135] at 400° to 500°.

Both oxide dichlorides are diamagnetic; they are stable in air at room temperature and resist hydrolytic attack. The heats of formation are -185 and -188 kcal mole^{-1} for niobium and tantalum oxide di-chlorides, respectively[180,181]. Niobium and tantalum oxide dichlorides decompose at elevated temperatures to give complex mixtures of pro-ducts[135].

The niobium compound is monoclinic[176], with $a = 12.79$, $b = 3.93$, $c = 6.70$ Å and $\beta = 105°$.

Niobium and tantalum tetrabromides. Both tetrabromides have been prepared by reduction of the appropriate pentabromide with the metal, using the temperature-gradient method. For niobium[135,166,182] the temperature gradient is about 410–350° and for tantalum[175,183] about 630–300°. Tantalum tetrabromide has also been prepared[138] by the same reaction in a sealed tube at 500°. Interaction of niobium tribromide and gaseous niobium pentabromide in a sealed tube forms niobium tetrabromide[182]. Tantalum tetrabromide is formed by an electrodeless discharge through a gaseous mixture of tantalum pentabromide and hydrogen[169], and this is in contrast to the report[138] that bromides lower than the tetrabromide are formed by reduction of tantalum pentabromide with hydrogen in a flow system. Finally, tantalum tetrabromide may be prepared[141,175] by reduction of tantalum pentabromide with aluminium in a temperature gradient of 500–250°.

Niobium and tantalum tetrabromides are diamagnetic, dark solids which are readily oxidized in air[138,166,182]. Both undergo thermal disproportionation to the corresponding pentabromide and tribromide at elevated temperatures[138,169,175,183,184]. For tantalum tetrabromide, the equilibrium dissociation pressure of the pentabromide over solid tetrabromide is given by[183]:

$$\log p_{atm} = 9.83 - 6145/T$$

From a detailed study of the phase diagram of the tantalum–bromine system, it was concluded[141] that tantalum tetrabromide melts incongruently at 392°.

As with the corresponding tetrachlorides, there is disagreement between different workers on the interpretation of X-ray powder diffraction patterns of niobium and tantalum tetrabromides. McCarley and coworkers[166,175] say they are orthorhombic and isostructural with the corresponding tetrachlorides, whilst Berdonosov and coworkers[185] also found them to be orthorhombic but with quite different unit-cell parameters. The reported values are given in Table 5.28.

Niobium and tantalum tetrabromides and pentabromides react with pyridine and γ-picoline, to give adducts of the type[93,166,175] $MBr_4 \cdot 2L$ and with acetonitrile[178] to form $MBr_4 \cdot CH_3CN$. o-phenylenebis(dimethylarsine) reacts with both niobium tetrabromide and niobium pentabromide[179] to form $NbBr_4 \cdot 2D$

Niobium tetraiodide. Niobium tetraiodide is best prepared by thermal decomposition of niobium pentaiodide in a sealed tube at 270°, the tube being provided with a cooled end to allow deposition of the iodine also formed in the reaction[186,187].

This tetraiodide is a metallic grey solid which is sensitive to moisture. It appears to be trimorphic, although the α to β transition at 348° is characterized by only a small endothermic effect[187]. The α- and the β-phase of niobium tetraiodide give similar X-ray powder diffraction patterns. On the other hand, the β to γ transition at 417° is clearly a phase transformation[187]. In contrast to some of the other niobium and tantalum

TABLE 5.28

Lattice Parameters of Niobium and Tantalum Tetrabromides

Compound	Unit-cell parameters	Ref.
$NbBr_4$	$a = 8.60$, $b = 9.31$, $c = 7.19$ Å, $Z = 4$	166
$NbBr_4$	$a = 7.179$, $b = 12.22$, $c = 12.85$ Å, $Z = 8$	185
$TaBr_4$	$a = 9.58$, $b = 9.30$, $c = 7.21$ Å, $Z = 4$	175
$TaBr_4$	$a = 7.143$, $b = 12.38$, $c = 12.88$ Å, $Z = 8$	185

lower halide systems, the niobium iodide system is simple in that only one phase lower than niobium tetraiodide is observed in the phase diagram, which is shown in Figure 5.4.

All forms of niobium tetraiodide are diamagnetic[187]. In the case of the α-form the reason for this has been clearly established by means of a structure determination by single-crystal X-ray diffraction studies[188]. The orthorhombic lattice was found to have $a = 7.67$, $b = 13.28$ and $c = 13.93$ Å, with eight molecules in the unit cell. The structure is based on a distorted hexagonal close-packing arrangement of iodine atoms with one-quarter of the available octahedral holes occupied by niobium atoms so as to give infinite linear chains of NbI_6 octahedra sharing opposite edges, as shown in Figure 5.5. However, the niobium atoms are shifted from the centres of the octahedra in alternate directions to form pairs of metal atoms 3.31 Å apart, as shown in Figure 5.6. The distances between bridging iodines and niobium atoms are 2.74 and 2.90 Å and the apical niobium to iodine distance is 2.69 Å.

The thermal decomposition of niobium tetraiodide is complex, and the nature of the products depends critically upon the temperature of reaction[186]: at 430° the major reaction is disproportionation to niobium pentaiodide and triiodide, at 540° the metal is obtained, and at intermediate temperatures triniobium octaiodide is a product.

The few chemical reactions which have been reported for niobium tetraiodide, other than its thermal decomposition, are similar to those described for the tetrachloride and tetrabromide. Thus, both niobium

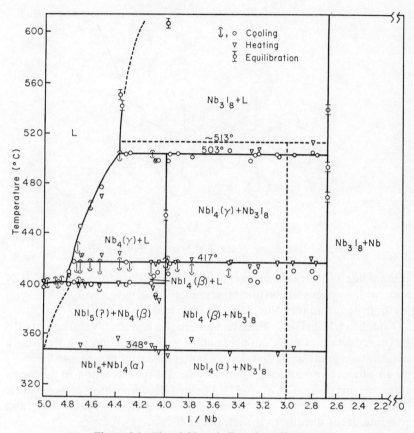

Figure 5.4   The niobium–iodine phase diagram.

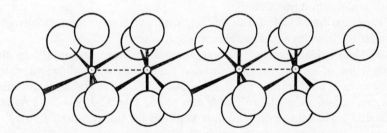

Figure 5.5   Linear chain of NbI_6 octahedra in niobium tetraiodide.

171

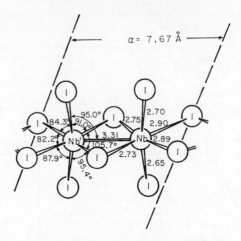

Figure 5.6   Dimensions of the $(NbI_4)_2$ unit in niobium tetraiodide.

pentaiodide and tetraiodide react with pyridine[89,166] to form $NbI_4 \cdot 2C_5H_5N$ and with o-phenylenebis(dimethylarsine)[179] to give $NbI_4 \cdot 2D$. With acetonitrile the adduct $NbI_4 \cdot CH_3CN$ is formed[178].

Tantalum tetraiodide. Tantalum tetraiodide is probably best prepared[175] by the reduction of tantalum pentaiodide with aluminium powder using a temperature gradient of 500–350°. Tantalum metal can be used[141,158,175] as an alternative reducing agent in a sealed-tube reaction at temperatures varying from 325° to 585°. Thermal decomposition of the adduct $TaI_4 \cdot 2C_5H_5N$, formed by interaction of tantalum pentaiodide and pyridine, leads directly to the tetraiodide[175].

It is interesting that reduction of tantalum pentaiodide with tantalum, and thermal decomposition of the tetraiodide adduct, give different forms of tantalum tetraiodide, although neither form appears to be isostructural with α-niobium tetraiodide[175].

Tantalum tetraiodide forms adducts with pyridine[89] and acetonitrile[178] similar to those formed by niobium tetraiodide.

Niobium oxide diiodide. This compound has been prepared[161] by the interaction of niobium metal, niobium pentaoxide and iodine in a sealed tube over a temperature gradient of 500–450°. It is stable in air, diamagnetic, and monoclinic[176] with $a = 15.08$, $b = 3.92$, $c = 7.48$ Å and $\beta = 105°$. No other information is available for this compound.

Oxidation State III

Niobium trifluoride. This compound was reported to be formed in low yield by the action of anhydrous hydrogen fluoride on niobium metal at 225° in a bomb[189] and by the action of a mixture of hydrogen and anhydrous hydrogen fluoride on heated niobium hydride[8,190]. The structure of the blue product was shown by X-ray powder diffraction data to be cubic with the rhenium trioxide-type lattice[189,190].

It was subsequently shown, however, by Schafer and coworkers[13,30] and by Gortsema and Didchenko[14] that "niobium trifluoride," prepared as above, is in fact an oxide fluoride. It has been proposed[13,30] that a series of oxide fluorides of the general formula $Nb[F(O)]_3$ is formed, all having the rhenium trioxide structure, and that a trifluoride completely free from oxygen has not been prepared and is inherently unstable. An alternative interpretation[14] of the data is that the number of anions per cation can be greater than three and that a metal-deficient lattice is formed.

TABLE 5.29

Lattice Parameters of Niobium Oxide Fluorides

Compound	Unit-cell parameter	Ref.
$NbO_{0.99}F_{2.25}$	$a = 3.889$ Å	14
"NbF$_3$"	$a = 3.890$ Å	189
"NbF$_3$"	$a = 3.895$ Å	190
NbO_2F	$a = 3.902$ Å	37
$NbO_{1.65}F_{1.39}$	$a = 3.906$ Å	14

A major difficulty which has no doubt contributed to the confusion surrounding the identity of the products described above, is the fact that oxygen and fluorine are almost identical in size, which makes the X-ray powder diffraction data non-definitive with regard to chemical composition. This is well illustrated by a comparison of the lattice parameters of several niobium oxide fluoride phases shown in Table 5.29.

Tantalum trifluoride. There is reason to suppose that claims to the preparation of tantalum trifluoride are erroneous, for the same reasons as for its supposed niobium analogue; but at present there are not sufficient data available to be definite on this point. The product claimed as tantalum fluoride was prepared either by the interaction[189] of tantalum metal and anhydrous hydrogen fluoride in a bomb at 225° or by passing a mixture of hydrogen and anhydrous hydrogen fluoride over the metal[8] at 300°. The grey product is cubic, with the rhenium trioxide structure, and its unit cell is almost identical with that of tantalum dioxide fluoride:

"TaF$_3$" $a = 3.90$ Å (reference 189)

"TaF$_3$" $a = 3.901$ Å (reference 191)

TaO_2F $a = 3.896$ Å (reference 37)

Schafer and coworkers[30] have attempted to prepare authentic lower trifluorides of tantalum withough success and they have concluded that pure lower fluorides of tantalum are thermodynamically unstable.

Niobium trichloride. The various preparative methods for niobium trichloride are summarized in Table 5.30.

TABLE 5.30

Preparation of Niobium Trichloride

Method	Conditions	Ref.
Nb and Hg_2Cl_2	Elevated temp.	55
Decomp. of $NbCl_4$	250–500°	174, 192
$NbCl_5$ and H_2	146°, thermal decomp. of initial product	192
$NbCl_5$ and H_2	Flow system, 400–500°	8, 45, 193
$NbCl_5$ and H_2	Electrodeless gas discharge	169
Nb and HCl	Flow system, elevated temp.	193

A very detailed study of the niobium–chlorine system by Schafer and Dohmann[192] has shown that stoichiometric $NbCl_3$ is only one composition in a homogeneous phase extending from Cl:Nb ratios of 2.69:1 to 3.13:1. It has been suggested that perhaps this wide composition range is best considered as a variation in the relative amounts of Nb(IV) and Nb(II) in the phase[192].

The heat of formation of niobium trichloride has been given[63] as -139 kcal mole^{-1}.

Tantalum trichloride. Tantalum trichloride has been prepared by the reduction of tantalum pentachloride with aluminium in a sealed tube at 350–400°. The initial product, tantalum tetrachloride, was then thermally decomposed to give the required trichloride[173]. Tantalum trichloride can be prepared[177] directly by reduction of the pentachloride, using tantalum metal under a temperature gradient of 600–365°.

Tantalum trichloride is thermally unstable, disproportionating above 340° according to the equation[194]:

$$3TaCl_3 \rightarrow 2TaCl_2 + TaCl_5$$

The dissociation pressure of tantalum pentachloride is given by

$$\log p_{mm} = 12.815 - 9173/T$$

The heat and entropy of dissociation were found to be 41.9 kcal mole^{-1} and 58.6 cal deg^{-1} mole^{-1}, respectively[194]. The heat of formation of tantalum trichloride[75] is -130.5 kcal mole^{-1}.

Niobium tribromide. Niobium tribromide has been prepared by reduction of the pentabromide with hydrogen at 500° in a flow system[138,193] or with niobium metal in a sealed tube[182] at 400–500°. The action of hydrogen bromide on niobium metal at 425° in a flow system yields a mixture of the pentabromide and tribromide[193].

Niobium tribromide is a dark solid[193] which may be sublimed in a vacuum at 400°. Schafer and Dohmann[192] have shown that $NbBr_3$ is only part of some homogeneous phases with Br:Nb limits of 2.67:1 to 3.03:1.

Tantalum tribromide. Tantalum tribromide has been prepared by the reduction of tantalum pentabromide with hydrogen[138,142,195] and with tantalum metal in a temperature gradient[142,183] of 620–320° or in a sealed tube[138] at 280°.

There are two distinct possible mechanisms for the interaction of tantalum pentabromide and tantalum; they can be expressed by the equations

$$\left.\begin{array}{l} TaBr_5 + Ta \rightarrow TaBr_4 \\ TaBr_4 + Ta \rightarrow TaBr_3 \end{array}\right\} \text{Mechanism A}$$

or

$$\left.\begin{array}{l} TaBr_5 + Ta \rightarrow TaBr_4 \\ 2TaBr_4 \rightarrow TaBr_5 + TaBr_3 \end{array}\right\} \text{Mechanism B}$$

By using tantalum pentabromide labelled with a known specific activity of ^{182}Ta, Berdonosov and Lapitskii[184] were able to distinguish between these two possible mechanisms since the tantalum tribromide produced by the two reactions should have a specific activity of 60% or 80% of that of the original pentabromide according to which mechanistic path is taken. The fact that the final product had 78.6% of the specific activity of the original pentabromide strongly supports mechanism B.

Above 220° tantalum tribromide is thermally unstable, disproportionating according to the equation:

$$3TaBr_3 \rightarrow TaBr_5 + 2TaBr_2$$

but at higher temperatures the decomposition is[183]:

$$5TaBr_3 \rightarrow TaBr_5 + 4TaBr_{2.5}$$

The equilibrium dissociation pressure of tantalum pentabromide for the latter mode of disproportionation is given by the expression:

$$\log p_{atm} = 9.83 - 6821/T.$$

Niobium triiodide. Niobium triiodide is probably best prepared[186,187] by controlled thermal decomposition of niobium pentaiodide, first to the tetraiodide at 270° and then to the triiodide at 430°. It has also been claimed[151] that niobium and iodine in the correct proportions react at elevated temperatures in a sealed tube to produce the triiodide. Niobium pentaoxide reacts with aluminium iodide in a sealed tube at 230–300° to give a mixture of niobium oxide triiodide and niobium triiodide and the products can be separated by sublimation[160].

Niobium triiodide is probably not a thermodynamically stable phase and it does not appear in the niobium–iodine phase diagram (Figure 5.4). It decomposes[187] slowly and irreversibly at about 513° into an iodine-rich liquid and Nb_3I_8. X-ray powder diffraction patterns for niobium triiodide have been interpreted[187] on the basis of a hexagonal cell with $a = 6.61$ and $c = 6.82$ Å.

Tantalum triiodide. McCarley and Boatman[175] claimed to have prepared tantalum triiodide by interaction of tantalum pentaiodide and tantalum metal over a temperature gradient of 585–530°. However, in a later study[141] of the complete phase diagram of the tantalum–iodine system, they found that tantalum triiodide is not an equilibrium phase and suggested that the material they previously described as the triiodide was a mixture of tantalum tetraiodide and Ta_6I_{14}. It appears, therefore, that there is no evidence for the existence of tantalum triiodide.

Miscellaneous lower halides of niobium and tantalum. A number of well-defined lower halides of both niobium and tantalum have been reported. All of them are polymeric. A few contain trimeric clusters of the metals, but the majority contain hexameric clusters of niobium or tantalum. The detailed chemistry of these interesting compounds is given in Chapter 3, but the modes of preparation for the better established compounds of this type are given in Table 5.31.

TABLE 5.31

Preparation of Some Lower Halides of Niobium and Tantalum

Compound	Method	Conditions	Ref.
Nb_3Cl_8	Decomp. of $NbCl_4$		192
Nb_3Br_8	Decomp. of $NbBr_4$		182
Nb_3I_8	Thermal decomp. of higher iodides	525–600°	187, 196
Ta_6Br_{17}	Decomp. of $TaBr_4$	435°	141
Nb_6F_{15}	NbF_5 and Nb, or decomp. of NbF_4	Sealed tube, >700°	13
Ta_6Cl_{15}	$TaCl_5$ and Ta	Temp. gradient, 630–470°	177
Ta_6Br_{15}	Decomp. of $TaBr_4$	250°	141
Ta_6Br_{14}	Ta_6Br_{15} and Ta	640°	141

COMPLEX HALIDES AND OXIDE HALIDES

Complex halides and oxide halides of niobium and tantalum are mainly restricted to oxidation states V and IV. As was pointed out in Chapter 2, most complexes of niobium(v) and tantalum(v) are thermally unstable, yielding the appropriate halides or oxide halides at quite low temperatures. A great deal of quantitative information is available on these systems, but relatively little is known about the chemistry of the complexes.

Oxidation State V

Nonafluorotantalate(v). Potential measurements[23] in the system Ta(v)/HF/HClO₄ provide some evidence for the existence of the nonafluoro-tantalate(v) ion, TaF_9^{4-}. However, no solid compound containing this anion has been isolated.

Octafluoroniobates and -tantalates(v). Both octafluoro anions are formed in potassium fluoride–metal pentafluoride melts[197,198]. Sodium octafluorotantalate(v) has been prepared by crystallization from a hydrogen fluoride solution containing four moles of sodium fluoride per mole of tantalum pentafluoride[199].

A single-crystal X-ray study[199] of sodium octafluorotantalate(v) has revealed a monoclinic lattice with $a = 11.52$, $b = 5.38$, $c = 11.21$ Å and $\beta = 120.9°$. The structure of the anion, which is shown in Figure 5.7, consists of a distorted square Archimedian antiprism in which the

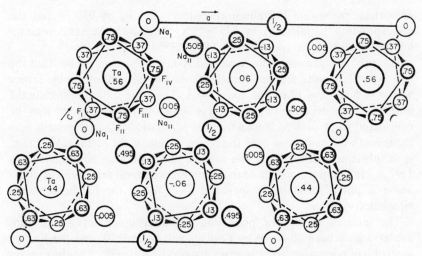

Figure 5.7 The square-antiprismatic structure of the TaF_9^{4-} anion in sodium octafluorotantalate(v).

average tantalum to fluorine bond distance is 1.98 Å. No structural data are available for the octafluoroniobate(v) salt.

Melting points of 760° for potassium octafluoroniobate(v)[198], and 776° [200] or 780° [197] for the corresponding tantalum compound, have been reported.

Heptafluoroniobates(v) and -tantalates(v). Both heptafluoro anions are prepared in melts of alkali-metal fluoride and the appropriate transition-metal pentafluoride[19,201]. Heptafluorotantalates(v) have also been prepared from aqueous hydrogen fluoride solutions[202]. Both anions are

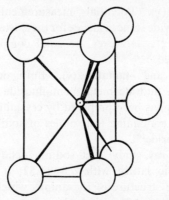

Figure 5.8   Structure of the heptafluoroniobate(v) anion.

colourless, potassium heptafluoroniobate(v) melting at 730° [13] and the corresponding tantalate(v) at 775° [200,203]. Potassium heptafluorotantalate(v) shows a phase transition at 741° [200,203].

Hoard[204] has shown by single-crystal X-ray diffraction studies that the two potassium salts are isodimensional, having an orthorhombic lattice with $a = 5.85$, $b = 12.67$ and $c = 5.80$ Å. There are four molecules in the unit cell. The structure of the anion is shown in Figure 5.8 and may be considered to be derived from a trigonal-prismatic MF_6 arrangement with the seventh fluorine atom over the centre of one of the rectangular faces, with subsequent distortion. The average metal–fluorine bond distance is 1.97 Å. It is important to note that the stereochemical arrangement of the anion is not a pentagonal bipyramid as is found for the heptafluoro-zirconate(IV) anion.

The infrared spectra of potassium heptafluoroniobate(v) and -tantalate(v) have been observed by Fordyce and Baum[19,201], and the Raman spectrum of potassium heptafluoroniobate(v) by Keller[205]. The absorptions observed are noted in Table 5.32.

The ammonium salts of the heptafluoro anions react[206] with ammonia gas at 700° to give either NbN or Ta_3N_5.

Hexafluoroniobates(v) and -tantalates(v). Although both hexafluoroniobates(v) and hexafluorotantalates(v) may be isolated from aqueous hydrogen fluoride solutions[207,208] and from melts of an alkali-metal fluoride and the transition-metal pentafluorides[19,209], the best method reported involves the use of bromine trifluoride[6]. This reagent acts upon

TABLE 5.32

Infrared and Raman Bands (cm^{-1})
of Heptafluoroniobates(v) and
-tantalates(v)

K_2NbF_7, infrared	K_2NbF_7, Raman	K_2TaF_7, infrared
	782w	
631w	630vs	631w
549vs		535vs
470vs		
330m	388m	
306m		315vs
		285vs
		265m

w = weak, m = medium,
vs = very strong.

mixtures of the metal pentaoxide with alkali-metal fluorides, chlorides, bromides or carbonates to give the appropriate salt. Both sodium hexafluoroniobate(v) and -tantalate(v) have been isolated[210] as products from the reaction between sulphur tetrafluoride, the metal pentaoxide and sodium fluoride in a bomb at 350°.

A single-crystal X-ray study of potassium hexafluoroniobate(v) has revealed that the lattice contains discrete NbF_6^- ions[208]. These are slightly distorted from a perfect octahedron, as shown in Figure 5.9, with a mean niobium to fluorine bond length of 2.14 Å. This value is rather larger than usual for niobium(v)–fluorine bond lengths[208]. The lattice parameters deduced from X-ray diffraction patterns for this compound and for a number of other hexafluoroniobates(v) and -tantalates(v) are given in Tables 5.33 and 5.34.

The metal–fluorine stretching frequency occurs at 580 cm^{-1} in potassium hexafluoroniobate(v)[213] and at 580 cm^{-1} [213] or 582 cm^{-1} [19] for the tantalum analogue, which also shows[19] absorptions at 220, 232, 245, 480 and 720 cm^{-1}.

Oxohexafluoroniobates(v) and -tantalates(v). Ammonium and potassium salts of the oxohexafluoroniobate(v) and -tantalate(v) anions have been prepared by the following unusual reaction sequence. A methanolic solution of niobium or tantalum bromide is prepared by adding bromine to a suspension of the metal. Addition of ammonium or potassium fluoride leads to the isolation of the oxohexafluoroniobates(v) and -tantalates(v)[214]. Potassium oxohexafluoroniobate(v) has been prepared by

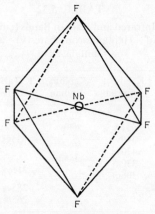

Figure 5.9   The slightly distorted NbF_6^- octahedron.

dissolving niobium pentafluoride in an aqueous solution containing an excess of potassium fluoride[215]. The corresponding tantalum salt was isolated after the controlled hydrolysis at room temperature of tantalum pentafluoride, which had been dissolved in a lithium fluoride–potassium fluoride melt[209].

X-ray powder diffraction patterns of several oxohexafluoroniobates(v) and -tantalates(v) show that they all form cubic lattices, and the suggestion has been made by Williams and Hoard[216] that the anions are isostructural with the heptafluorozirconate(iv) anion and not with the heptafluoroniobate(v) anion. The lattice parameters of several of these salts are given in Table 5.35.

The metal–oxygen double-bond stretching frequency occurs at 921 cm^{-1} for potassium oxohexafluoroniobate(v)[217] and at 888 cm^{-1} for the corresponding tantalum salt[209].

Oxopentafluoroniobate(v). Potassium oxopentafluoroniobate(v) has been isolated as its monohydrate by addition of niobium pentafluoride to an aqueous solution of potassium fluoride at room temperature[215], or to a dilute hydrofluoric acid solution containing some potassium fluoride[205].

TABLE 5.33
Lattice Parameters of Some Hexafluoroniobates(v)

Compound	Lattice type	Lattice parameters	Ref.
$LiNbF_6$	Rhombohedral; $LiSbF_6$ type	$a = 5.473$ Å, $\alpha = 58.09°$	211
$NaNbF_6$	Cubic; $NaSbF_6$ type	$a = 8.28$ Å	211, 212
$AgNbF_6$	Tetragonal; $KNbF_6$ type	$a = 4.968$ Å, $c = 9.551$ Å	211
$KNbF_6$	Tetragonal	$a = 5.18$ Å, $c = 10.05$ Å	207, 208
$TlNbF_6$	Rhombohedral; $KOsF_6$ type	$a = 5.142$ Å, $\alpha = 96.37°$	211
$RbNbF_6$	Rhombohedral; $KOsF_6$ type	$a = 5.14$ Å, $\alpha = 96.4°$	207, 211
NH_4NbF_6	Rhombohedral; $KOsF_6$ type	$a = 5.19$ Å, $\alpha = 96.10°$	207
$CsNbF_6$	Rhombohedral; $KOsF_6$ type	$a = 5.32$ Å, $\alpha = 95.8°$	207, 211

TABLE 5.34
Lattice Parameters of Some Hexafluorotantalates(v)

Compound	Lattice type	Lattice parameters	Ref.
$LiTaF_6$	Rhombohedral; $LiSbF_6$ type	$a = 5.479$ Å, $\alpha = 58.05°$	211
$NaTaF_6$	Cubic; $NaSbF_6$ type	$a = 8.28$ Å	211, 212
$AgTaF_6$	Tetragonal; $KNbF_6$ type	$a = 4.990$ Å, $c = 9.634$ Å	211
$KTaF_6$	Tetragonal; $KNbF_6$ type	$a = 5.20$ Å, $c = 10.05$ Å	207, 208
$TlTaF_6$	Rhombohedral; $KOsF_6$ type	$a = 5.148$ Å, $\alpha = 96.34°$	211
$RbTaF_6$	Rhombohedral; $KOsF_6$ type	$a = 5.14$ Å, $\alpha = 96.4°$	207, 211
NH_4TaF_6	Rhombohedral; $KOsF_6$ type	$a = 5.18$ Å, $\alpha = 96.07°$	207
$CsTaF_6$	Rhombohedral; $KOsF_6$ type	$a = 5.32$ Å, $\alpha = 95.80°$	207, 211

TABLE 5.35
Lattice Parameters of Some Oxohexa-fluoroniobates(v) and -tantalates(v)

Compound	Lattice parameter	Ref.
K_3NbOF_6	$a = 8.88$ Å	214
	$a = 8.95$ Å	216
$(NH_4)_3NbOF_6$	$a = 9.31$ Å	214
K_3TaOF_6	$a = 8.87$ Å	209
	$a = 8.90$ Å	214
$(NH_4)_3TaOF_6$	$a = 9.31$ Å	214

The oxopentafluoroniobate(v) is reported to be monochlinic and iso-morphous with potassium hexafluorotitanate(IV) monohydrate, but no unit-cell parameter was given[215]. It was concluded that discrete $NbOF_5^{2-}$ ions exist in the solid, and support for this supposition is given by infrared and Raman studies[205]. The metal–oxygen double-bond stretching fre-quency[217] occurs at 927 cm^{-1}.

Under certain conditions of preparation, potassium oxopentafluoro-niobate(v) can be isolated as the adduct $K_2NbOF_5 \cdot KHF_2$. This compound is monoclinic with $a = 8.82$, $b = 14.02$, $c = 6.82$ Å and $\beta = 86.6°$, and it has been shown[215] to contain discrete $NbOF_5^{2-}$ ions and not $NbOF_7^{4-}$ ions.

Miscellaneous complex oxofluoroniobates and -tantalates(v). A number of oxofluoroniobates(v) and -tantalates(v) have been isolated by fusion of the transition-metal pentaoxide with an alkali-metal fluoride or by the controlled hydrolysis of complex fluorides.

Potassium trioxofluoroniobate(v), K_2NbO_3F, has been prepared[218] by fusing an equimolar mixture of potassium carbonate and niobium penta-oxide with a large excess of potassium fluoride at 750°; X-ray powder diffraction techniques have shown[218] it to have a tetragonal K_2NiF_4 structure with $a = 3.956$ and $c = 13.670$ Å.

Potassium pentaoxofluorodiniobate(v) and -ditantalate(v), KNb_2O_5F and KTa_2O_5F, have been isolated after mixing equimolar proportions of potassium fluoride and the transition-metal pentaoxide and heating to 900°. Both compounds are tetragonal and the unit cell parameters are[219]: KNb_2O_5F $a = 12.632$ Å, $c = 3.950$ Å; KTa_2O_5F $a = 12.569$ Å, $c = 3.961$ Å.

When lithium fluoride and niobium pentaoxide are mixed in the pro-portions 1:3 and heated to between 800° and 1200° the compound $LiNb_6O_{15}F$ is formed[220]. A single-crystal X-ray diffraction study[221] has shown the lattice to be orthorhombic, with unit-cell parameters $a = 16.64$, $b = 3.96$ and $c = 8.89$ Å. The lattice is a three-dimensional network, and the basic building unit is shown in Figure 5.10. It will be noted that it contains one niobium atom with distorted pentagonal-bipyramidal coordination and five niobium atoms in distorted octahedra. All of the light atoms are bridging and the lattice structure in two dimensions is shown in Figure 5.11. The fluorine atoms are distributed randomly throughout the lattice. The lithium salt is reported to decompose at 1300° according to the equation[220]:

$$3LiNb_6O_{15}F \rightarrow NbOF_3 + 3LiNb_3O_8 + 4Nb_2O_5$$

The corresponding sodium salt, $NaNb_6O_{15}F$, has been prepared[222] in an analogous manner and it is also orthorhombic with $a = 3.949$,

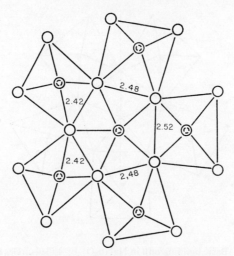

Figure 5.10   The basic building unit in $LiNb_6O_{15}F$. Small circles represent niobium, double circles represent oxygen.

$b = 10.192$ and $c = 14.721$ Å. The basic building unit is shown in Figure 5.12 and it is clear that it is similar to that found in the corresponding lithium salt, but the stereochemistry of the central seven-coordinate niobium atom is regular[222]. This results in a change in the relative dispositions of the outer octahedra and thus leads to a different lattice packing arrangement, as shown in Figure 5.13.

Hexachloroniobates(v) and -tantalates(v). Hexachloroniobates(v) and hexachlorotantalates(v) are usually prepared by fusing the transition metal pentachlorides with the appropriate alkali-metal chloride[223–229].

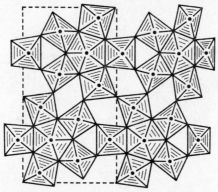

Figure 5.11   Crystal structure of $LiNb_6O_{15}F$.

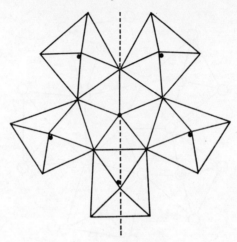

Figure 5.12   Basic building unit in $NaNb_6O_{15}F$. Filled circles are niobium atoms.

An alternative method is to mix the alkali-metal chloride or quaternary ammonium chloride with the pentachloride in a non-aqueous solvent. Iodine monochloride[230], thionyl chloride[231] and mixtures of these two solvents[231] have been used.

The hexachloroniobates(v) are yellow, the hexachlorotantalates (v) are white. The compounds are easily hydrolysed in moist air and in aqueous solution.

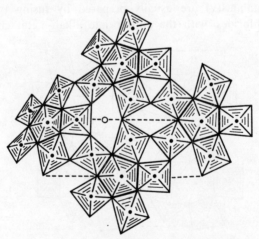

Figure 5.13   Crystal structure of $NaNb_6O_{15}F$.

The complexes are thermally unstable, the hexachloroniobates(v) beginning to decompose at about 300° and the tantalates(v) at about 370°. In both cases the metal pentachloride is evolved[223,228]. The equilibrium dissociation pressures of the pentachlorides over the complexes are given by the following equations:

NaNbCl$_6$ $\log p_{mm} = 11.80 - 5000/T$ (reference 223)

NaNbCl$_6$ $\log p_{mm} = 7.65 - 4300/T$ (225–300°)   (reference 232)

KNbCl$_6$ $\log p_{mm} = 8.22 - 6050/T$ (340–450°)   (reference 232)

NaTaCl$_6$ $\log p_{mm} = 9.15 - 4030/T$ (reference 223)

KTaCl$_6$ $\log p_{mm} = 8.36 - 4820/T$ (200–340°)   (reference 226)

Thermodynamic data for the hexachloroniobates(v) and -tantalates(v) are given in Table 5.36. The heats of formation of these complexes show

TABLE 5.36

Thermodynamic Data for Hexachloroniobates(v) and -tantalates(v)

Property	Compound	Value	Ref.
ΔH_{form}	NaNbCl$_6$	-1.9 kcal mole^{-1}	233, 234
(from MCl and	KNbCl$_6$	-6.7 kcal mole^{-1}	233, 234
Nb(Ta)Cl$_5$)	RbNbCl$_6$	-12.5 kcal mole^{-1}	233, 234
	CsNbCl$_6$	-24.4 kcal mole^{-1}	233, 234
	NaTaCl$_6$	-4.0 kcal mole^{-1}	234, 235
	KTaCl$_6$	-9.9 kcal mole^{-1}	234, 235
	RbTaCl$_6$	-17.6 kcal mole^{-1}	234
	CsTaCl$_6$	-28.0 kcal mole^{-1}	234
ΔH_{diss}	KTaCl$_6$	22.0 kcal mole^{-1}	226

two interesting trends. For either transition metal, the heat of formation increases markedly as the size of the alkali-metal increases, and for the corresponding pairs of salts the hexachloroniobate(v) is always less stable than its tantalum analogue. Morozov and coworkers[225] have shown that the relative values of the free energies of decomposition of the sodium salts confirms the greater stability of the tantalum compound.

A characteristic feature of most of the hexachloroniobates(v) and hexachlorotantalates(v) is that they are polymorphic. The melting points and transition temperatures of some of these complexes are given in Table 5.37.

The hexachloroniobates(v) all show a characteristic absorption band between 333 and 336 cm^{-1} in their infrared spectra[231,239] and the corresponding tantalates(v)[231] at about 320 cm^{-1}

It is remarkable that not even an X-ray powder diffraction study of the structures of any of the hexachloroniobates(v) and -tantalates(v) has been reported. No chemical properties have been reported either.

TABLE 5.37

Melting Points and Transition Temperatures of Some Hexachloroniobates(v) and -tantalates(v)

Compound	M.p.	Ref.	Transition temp.	Ref.
NH_4NbCl_6	304°	228		
$NaNbCl_6$	430°	223	247°	236
	444°	236	256°	238
$KNbCl_6$	396°	67, 236	187° and 334°	67, 236
NH_4TaCl_6	295°	228		
$NaTaCl_6$	470°	223, 225	223°	237
	484°	237	232°	225
$KTaCl_6$	410°	237	185° and 320°	237
$CsTaCl_6$	540°	227	294°	227

Oxopentachloroniobates(v). There are two general methods of preparing oxopentachloroniobates(v), namely, interaction of niobium oxide trichloride and an alkali-metal chloride in the melt[240–244] and addition of an alkali-metal chloride to a solution of niobium pentachloride in concentrated hydrochloric acid[245–247]. It is interesting that sodium chloride and niobium oxide trichloride do not react in the melt[241,243].

The oxopentachloroniobates(v) are yellow crystalline solids, which are stable in dry air. Under normal atmospheric conditions the potassium salt is rapidly hydrolysed, but the rubidium and the caesium salt may be handled fairly easily[246].

The oxopentachloroniobates(v) are thermally unstable and evolve niobium oxide trichloride. The equilibrium dissociation pressures of niobium oxide trichloride are given by the following expressions:

K_2NbOCl_5　　$\log p_{mm} = 6.99 - 4352/T$　(460–700°)　(reference 241)

K_2NbOCl_5　　$\log p_{mm} = 7.141 - 6456/T$　(470–520°)　(reference 243)

Rb_2NbOCl_5　　$\log p_{mm} = 6.66 - 4590/T$　(515–740°)　(reference 241)

Cs_2NbOCl_5　　$\log p_{mm} = 7.05 - 5180/T$　(600–780°)　(reference 241)

The thermodynamic data available for the oxopentachloroniobates(v) are given in Table 5.38.

TABLE 5.38

Thermodynamic Data for Some Oxopentachloroniobates(v)

Property	Compound	Value	Ref.
M.p.	K_2NbOCl_5	486°	240, 244
		500°	241
	Rb_2NbOCl_5	570°	241
		616°	240, 242
	Cs_2NbOCl_5	634°	242
		640°	241
		642°	240
Transition temp.	Rb_2NbOCl_5	588°	242
	Cs_2NbOCl_5	584°	242
ΔH_{diss} (kcal mole^{-1})	K_2NbOCl_5	19.9	241
	Rb_2NbOCl_5	21.0	241
	Cs_2NbOCl_5	23.7	241
ΔS_{diss} (cal deg^{-1} mole^{-1})	K_2NbOCl_5	18.8	241
	Rb_2NbOCl_5	17.3	241
	Cs_2NbOCl_5	19.1	241

The oxopentachloroniobates(v) crystallize with a cubic K_2PtCl_2-type lattice with the following unit-cell parameters[129,240,248,249]:

K_2NbOCl_5 $a = 9.815$ Å; Rb_2NbOCl_5 $a = 10.01$ Å;

$(NH_4)_2NbOCl_5$ $a = 9.95$ Å; Cs_2NbOCl_5 $a = 10.24$ Å.

The infrared spectra of rubidium and caesium oxopentachloroniobates(v) have been studied in detail by Sabatini and Bertini[250] and the absorptions and their assignments are given in Table 5.39.

Oxopentachlorotantalates(v). Very little information is available about the oxopentachlorotantalate(v) ion; presumably most workers have

TABLE 5.39

Infrared Bands (cm^{-1}) of Rubidium and
Caesium Oxopentachloroniobates(v)

Rb_2NbOCl_5	Cs_2NbOCl_5	Assignment
930	928	Nb=O stretch
339	330	Nb–Cl stretch
327	320	Nb–Cl stretch
231	231	Nb–O rock
219	217	Nb–O rock
180	180	Cl–Nb–Cl def
167	168	Cl–Nb–Cl def
87	87	Cl–Nb–Cl def

assumed that the chemistry of these complexes will be virtually identical with that of their niobium analogue. Alkali-metal oxopentachloro-tantalates(v) may be prepared by dissolving tantalum pentachloride in concentrated hydrochloric acid and then adding an alkali-metal chloride[251].

Peroxopentachloroniobates and -tantalates(v). Rohmer and co-workers[248,251] have prepared a series of peroxopentachloroniobates(v) and -tantalates(v) by digestion of the corresponding oxopentachloro compound in concentrated hydrochloric acid with hydrogen peroxide. After digestion, the yellow solutions were cooled and saturated with gaseous hydrogen chloride. The yellow crystalline complexes, $M_2Nb(Ta)O_2Cl_5$, slowly separated. These niobium and tantalum complexes are indistinguishable by X-ray powder diffraction patterns from the more common oxopenta-chloro compounds. The easiest method of distinguishing the two series of salts is by a study of their infrared spectra. The peroxo compounds shown double peaks in the regions 860–900 cm^{-1} and 565–600 cm^{-1}, whilst the oxopentachloro compounds shown a single absorption at about 930 cm^{-1}.

Oxotetrachloroniobates(v). These compounds have been prepared from melts by using equimolar amounts of alkali-metal chlorides and niobium oxide trichloride[241–243]. There is some disagreement as to whether the sodium salt can be prepared[241,243].

The oxotetrachloroniobates(v) are thermally unstable, decomposing with loss of niobium oxide trichloride to give the oxopentachloro-niobates(v). Equilibrium dissociation pressures have been determined as follows:

$NaNbOCl_4$ $\log p_{atm} = 8.077 - 5376/T$ (315–380°) (reference 243)

$KNbOCl_4$ $\log p_{atm} = 9.253 - 6808/T$ (370–417°) (reference 243)

$\log p_{mm} = 12.10 - 6530/T$ (300–420°) (reference 241)

$RbNbOCl_4$ $\log p_{mm} = 11.10 - 5830/T$ (340–450°) (reference 241)

$CsNbOCl_4$ $\log p_{mm} = 7.65 - 3640/T$ (370–430°) (reference 241)

For the rubidium and caesium salts there is disagreement in the literature as to whether the compounds melt, or decompose before melting. A few thermodynamic data are given in Table 5.40.

Oxopentabromoniobates(v). These may be prepared in an analogous manner to the corresponding oxochloro complexes; that is, niobium pentabromide is dissolved in concentrated hydrobromic acid containing an alkali-metal bromide. They are less stable than their chloro analogues.

TABLE 5.40

Thermodynamic Data for Some
Oxotetrachloroniobates(v)

Property	Compound	Value	Ref.
M.p.	$NaNbOCl_4$	430°	244
	$KNbOCl_4$	428°	241
		440°	244
	$RbNbOCl_4$	526°	242
	$CsNbOCl_4$	455°	242
Decomp. temp.	$RbNbOCl_4$	402°	241
	$CsNbOCl_4$	347°	241
ΔH_{diss} (kcal mole^{-1})	$KNbOCl_4$	29.9	241
	$RbNbOCl_4$	26.7	241
	$CsNbOCl_4$	16.7	241

Sabatini and Bertini[250] have recorded the infrared spectrum of caesium oxopentabromoniobate(v) and assigned the absorptions as in Table 5.41.

TABLE 5.41

Infrared Bands (cm^{-1}) of Caesium
Oxopentabromoniobate(v)

Absorption	Assignment
977vs	Nb=O stretch
241b	Nb–Br stretch
211w	Nb–O rock
202w	Nb–O rock
140w	Br–Nb–Br def
111m	Br–Nb–Br def

w = weak, m = medium,
vs = very strong, b = broad.

Oxidation State IV

Dioxofluoroniobates(IV). Salts of the dioxofluoroniobate(IV) anion have been prepared by Ruedorff and Krug[252] by heating equimolar mixtures of niobium dioxide and an alkali-metal fluoride to just below the melting point, in a hydrogen atmosphere.

The results of X-ray powder diffraction studies are given in Table 5.42.

All these salts are very weakly paramagnetic, indicating interaction between magnetic centres.

Hexachloroniobates(IV) and -tantalates(IV). These compounds are prepared by interaction of the alkali-metal chloride and the transition-metal tetrachloride in the melt in the absence of air[178,253–258]. Very little is known of the chemical and physical properties of these compounds except that they appear to be thermally stable and easily oxidized by

14

TABLE 5.42

Lattice Parameters of Dioxofluoroniobates(IV)

Compound	Lattice symmetry	Unit-cell parameters
$LiNbO_2F$	Hexagonal	$a = 5.15, c = 13.87$ Å
$NaNbO_2F$	Orthorhombic	$a = 5.51, b = 5.52, c = 7.82$ Å
$KNbO_2F$	Cubic	$a = 4.01$ Å

air and in water. Melting points and polymorphic transformation temperatures are given in Table 5.43.

The potassium, rubidium and caesium salts of both transition metals are reported to exhibit the cubic K_2PtCl_6 structure[178,255], but lattice parameters are available only for the hexachloroniobates(IV). These are: K_2NbCl_6 $a = 9.960$ Å, Rb_2NbCl_6 $a = 10.046$ Å, and Cs_2NbCl_6 $a = 10.319$ Å.

Oxidation State III

Pentachlorotantalates(III). Safonov and coworkers[259] have studied the interaction of alkali-metal chlorides and tantalum trichloride in the absence of air. They isolated the thermally stable, red pentachlorotantalates(III). The known properties are given in Table 5.44. No compound formation could be detected in the sodium chloride–tantalum trichloride system[259].

TABLE 5.43

Melting Points and Transition Temperature of Some Hexachloroniobates(IV) and -tantalates(IV)

Compound	M.p.	Ref.	Transition temp.	Ref.
Na_2NbCl_6	582°	253, 258	365°	253, 258
K_2NbCl_6	782°	253, 258	548°	258
Rb_2NbCl_6	802°	254		
Cs_2NbCl_6	822°	254		
K_2TaCl_6	732°	257		
Rb_2TaCl_6	756°	256	322°	256
Cs_2TaCl_6	796°	256	352°	256

TABLE 5.44

Properties of Pentachlorotantalates(III)

Compound	M.p.	Transition temp.
K_2TaCl_5	560°	263°
Rb_2TaCl_5	642°	360°
Cs_2TaCl_5	710°	346°

ADDENDA

Halides and Oxide Halides

It has been confirmed[260] that niobium dioxide fluoride decomposes at about 700° according to the equation

$$4NbO_2F \rightarrow Nb_3O_7F + NbOF_3$$

The heat of decomposition was found to be 30.8 kcal mole^{-1}.

Tantalum dioxide fluoride has been prepared by dissolving tantalum pentaoxide in aqueous hydrogen fluoride, evaporating the mixture to dryness, and heating the resultant solid to 300° [261]. When equimolar proportions of tantalum dioxide fluoride and tantalum pentaoxide are heated to between 800° and 1300° a single orthorhombic phase results, with $a = 16.690$, $b = 3.935$, and $c = 8.915$ Å, which was assumed to be Ta_3O_7F.

The thermal decomposition at 850° of TaO_2F proceeds by a different path to that of its niobium analogue[261]:

$$7TaO_2F \rightarrow 2Ta_3O_7F + TaF_5$$

The Ta_3O_7F produced in this reaction is a different modification to that described above. It is orthorhombic (U_3O_8 type) with $a = 6.478$, $b = 10.496$, and $c = 3.907$ Å. However, when heated to 1350° it is transformed into the modification described above[261].

The crystal structure of tantalum tetrachloride fluoride has been determined[262]. The unit cell is tetragonal with $a = 12.71$ and $c = 7.84$ Å. There are eight molecules in the unit cell. Rather surprisingly the compound is of the same type as tantalum pentafluoride itself, being tetrameric with bridging fluorine atoms giving cis-$TaCl_4F_2$ octahedra each sharing two corners. The angle at the fluorine atom is 88.7° and the average tantalum–chlorine bond distance is 2.29 Å.

The vapour pressures of niobium and tantalum pentachlorides have been investigated again. Schafer and Poleit[263] give the following expressions:

Solid $NbCl_5$ (77–110°)

$$\log p_{atm} = 19.3779 - 3.2204 \log T - 5353/T - 7649/T^2$$

Solid $TaCl_5$ (77–110°)

$$\log p_{atm} = 19.422 - 3.220 \log T - 5347/T - 7649/T^2$$

The calculated heats and entropies of sublimation are:

	$NbCl_5$	$TaCl_5$
ΔH_{sub} (kcal mole^{-1})	22.8	22.8
ΔS_{sub} (cal deg^{-1} mole^{-1})	46.2	46.4

New values for the heat of formation are -190.65 kcal mole^{-1} for niobium pentachloride[264] and -205.22 kcal mole^{-1} for the tantalum compound[265]. Both values agree well with earlier determinations.

The far-infrared spectra of both niobium and tantalum pentachloride have been investigated[266]. The observed bands were at the following positions (cm^{-1}):

NbCl$_5$	395s, br	345s	306m	243m	215m
TaCl$_5$	395s	365s, br	340s	245m	226m

Hart and Meyer[267] made a detailed study of the niobium pentachloride–niobium pentaoxide system. There was no indication of the formation of Nb$_3$O$_7$Cl and the only oxide chloride formed as a solid was niobium oxide trichloride.

It has been shown[268] that both niobium and tantalum pentachloride react with triphenylphosphine oxide to give first the 1:1 adduct, but, if an excess of phosphine oxide is present, then the well-established oxygen abstraction reaction occurs to give oxide trichloride adducts.

The heat and entropy of formation of niobium oxide trichloride has been given[269] as -212.7 kcal mole^{-1} and 31.1 cal deg^{-1} mole^{-1}, respectively. The heat and entropy of sublimation are reported[269] to be 28.1 kcal mole^{-1} and 46.2 cal deg^{-1} mole^{-1}.

A number of 1:1 adducts of niobium oxide trichloride have been prepared with nitrogen-base ligands[270,271] and alcohols[272]. The complexes appear to be polymeric.

Tantalum oxide trichloride has been prepared by the interaction of tantalum pentachloride and antimony trioxide in a chlorine stream at 180–250° [273]. It has been shown that the thermal decomposition of tantalum oxide trichloride to tantalum pentaoxide and tantalum pentachloride occurs in two stages[273]:

$$\text{at } 300° \quad 2TaOCl_3 \rightarrow TaO_2Cl + TaCl_5$$
$$\text{at } 540° \quad 5TaO_2Cl \rightarrow 2Ta_2O_5 + TaCl_5$$

Niobium pentabromide has been prepared by the action of boron tribromide on niobium pentachloride[274]. Schafer and Heine[275] determined the heat of formation of niobium pentabromide as -134.6 kcal mole^{-1} in good agreement with earlier values. A re-examination[276] of the electron-diffraction patterns of both niobium and tantalum pentabromide confirmed the trigonal bipyramidal symmetry and gave mean bond lengths of 2.45 Å and 2.44 Å for the niobium and the tantalum compound, respectively, in excellent agreement with the earlier values.

The controversy over the structure of niobium pentabromide is becoming more involved. Dorschner and Dehand[277] examined mixtures of biobium pentachloride and niobium pentabromide by X-ray diffraction techniques. They obtained a complete range of solid solutions and the regular variation of the unit-cell parameters with composition strongly suggested that the compounds are isomorphous, thus supporting the original claim by Zalkin and Sands[78]. It is clear that a single crystal X-ray study of niobium pentabromide is necessary to clarify the situation.

The far-infrared spectra of both niobium and tantalum pentabromide have been examined[266]. The spectra are similar to those of the corresponding pentachlorides and were consistent with D_{2h} symmetry for the metals. Bands were observed at (cm^{-1}):

NbBr$_5$	385w	360w	296s	269s	250s	206m
TaBr$_5$	385m	350m			240s	213s

Adducts of the type NbOBr$_3 \cdot$L have been prepared where L is bipyridyl and *o*-phenanthroline[278]. With acetylacetone the complex NbOBr(Acac)$_2$ was obtained which showed a band in its infrared spectrum at 755 cm^{-1} attributed to a Nb–O–Nb system.

Niobium pentaiodide has been prepared from the elements[275] in a thermal gradient of 450–200°. The heat of formation of niobium and tantalum pentaiodide have been determined[275] as −64.6 kcal mole^{-1} and −70 kcal mole^{-1}, respectively, values which do not agree with those previously reported.

Niobium pentachloride is reduced by phosphorus in a sealed tube at 165° to give niobium tetrachloride, but tantalum pentachloride is not reduced even at 220° [279]. Niobium tetrachloride has also been prepared by the interaction of niobium pentachloride and stannous chloride[280] in a stream of argon at 220°.

Similarly, niobium oxide dichloride has been prepared by the reduction of niobium oxide trichloride by stannous chloride at 450°. Niobium oxide dichloride is reported[280] to be stable to 550°, but above this temperature it decomposes according to the equation

$$2NbOCl_2 \rightarrow NbOCl_3 + NbOCl$$

Diamagnetic adducts of the type NbCl$_4 \cdot$L have been prepared[281] with triethylamine and NNN'N'-tetramethylethylenediamine.

The magnetic moments of both niobium and tantalum tribromide are reported[282] to be 1.0 BM.

Complex Halides and Oxide Halides

Brown and Walker[283] have refined the structure of potassium hepta-fluoroniobate(v) by means of a neutron-diffraction study. The general conclusions are the same as those reached by Hoard[204] by X-ray diffraction techniques. The refined unit-cell parameters are $a = 5.846$, $b = 12.693$, and $c = 8.515$ Å. The niobium–fluorine bond distances, corrected for thermal motion, vary from 1.940 to 1.978 Å.

Interesting information has been obtained on the fluoro anionic species present in solutions of tantalum in hydrofluoric acid solutions, by using infrared and Raman spectroscopy[284]. In 24M-hydrogen fluoride almost all the tantalum is present as hexafluorotantalate(v) but between 3M and 11M, both hexafluorotantalate(v) and heptafluorotantalate(v) are present. In solutions only 0.5M in hydrofluoric acid, the same two anions are present, together with a third unidentified species. In solutions containing no free hydrogen fluoride, but 5.4M in ammonium fluoride, the predominant species was heptafluorotantalate(v). In no case was octafluoro-tantalate(v) observed in aqueous solution.

The interaction of niobium pentaoxide and nitrosyl chloride in bromine trifluoride leads to the formation of white $NO^+NbF_6^-$. Tantalum behaves in a similar manner[285]. Both salts are cubic and isodimensional with $a = 10.22$ Å.

TABLE 5.45

Lattice Parameters of Some Complex Fluorides

Parameter	$K_2NbOF_5 \cdot H_2O$	$CuNbOF_5$	$K_2Nb(O_2)F_5 \cdot H_2O$	$K_2Ta(O_2)F_5 \cdot H_2O$
a	6.241 Å	5.576 Å	8.840 Å	8.846 Å
b	6.197 Å	9.96 Å	8.821 Å	8.938 Å
c	17.935 Å	7.537 Å	26.97 Å	9.217 Å
β	95.0°	103.5°	102.1°	97.2°
Space group	$P2_1/c$	C_2 or Cm	C_2 or Cm	$P2_1/c$
Z	4	2	12	4

Weiss and his coworkers[286,287] have examined the crystal structures of a number of oxopentafluoroniobates(v) and peroxopentafluoroniobates(v) and -tantalates(v). All of the compounds are monoclinic and the results are summarized in Table 5.45.

An electron-diffraction study[288] of anhydrous potassium oxopentafluoro-niobate(v) gave a tetragonal unit cell with $a = 6.12$ and $c = 8.98$ Å. The space group was found to be $P4/nmm$ and there are two molecules in the cell. The $NbOF_5$ group was found to be bipyramidal with C_{4v}

symmetry. The internuclear distances were calculated to be

$$Nb-O \quad 1.68 \text{ Å}$$
$$Nb-F \quad 2.06 \text{ Å} \ (\times 1)$$
$$Nb-F \quad 1.84 \text{ Å} \ (\times 4)$$

Further complex oxofluoro salts of niobium(v) have been prepared[289] by the interaction at high temperature of sodium fluoride and niobium pentaoxide. The structure of these compounds have been examined by X-ray diffraction techniques.

Nitrosyl chloride reacts with both niobium pentachloride and tantalum pentachloride to give 1:1 adducts[290]. The compounds are electrolytes in acetonitrile and infrared spectroscopy shows a strong absorption at about 2160 cm^{-1}, both pieces of evidence suggesting that the compounds should be formulated as $NO^+[(Nb, Ta)Cl_6]^-$.

Furlani and Zinato[291] prepared quaternary ammonium hexachloro- and hexabromoniobates(v) from the pentahalides in thionyl chloride or thionyl bromide. Charge-transfer bands were observed, but were the same as those found for the pentahalides themselves and for the oxopenta-haloniobates(v).

Oxopentahaloniobates(v) have been prepared by treating a quaternary ammonium halide with the appropriate niobium pentahalide in absolute alcohol[291]. Alkali-metal oxopentachlorotantalates(v) have been prepared[273] by the interaction of a hexachlorotantalate(v) with antimony trioxide in a chlorine stream at 150–500°. A variation of this method leads to the formation of the alkali-metal oxotetrachlorotantalates(v)[273]. These compounds are thermally unstable, like their niobium analogues, but because of the thermal instability of tantalum oxide trichloride they decompose in a different manner:

$$2MTaOCl_4 \rightarrow MTaO_2Cl_2 + TaCl_5 + MCl$$

The melting points of potassium, rubidium and caesium oxotetrachloro-tantalates(v) are 625°, 675°, and 700°, respectively. The equilibrium dissociation pressures of tantalum pentachloride over the salts are given by the expressions:

Solid $KTaOCl_4$	$\log p_{mm} = 6.99 - 4912/T$	
Solid $RbTaOCl_4$	$\log p_{mm} = 7.18 - 5238/T$	
Solid $CsTaOCl_4$	$\log p_{mm} = 8.69 - 7230/T$	
Liquid $KTaOCl_4$	$\log p_{mm} = 4.17 - 2400/T$	
Liquid $RbTaOCl_4$	$\log p_{mm} = 3.75 - 2030/T$	
Liquid $CsTaOCl_4$	$\log p_{mm} = 4.77 - 3400/T$	

Nitrosyl chloride reacts with niobium oxide trichloride[290] to give $NO^+NbOCl_4^-$ and it has been confirmed that sodium oxotetrachloroniobate(v) exists[292].

Wendling[293] has reported crystallographic data on some peroxopentachloroniobates(v) and -tantalates(v). They are all cubic with the K_2PtCl_6 type structure. Unit-cell parameters are

	$M_2Nb(O_2)Cl_5$	$M_2Ta(O_2)Cl_5$
M = NH_4	9.90 Å	9.92 Å
M = Rb	10.02 Å	9.98 Å
M = Cs	10.24 Å	10.25 Å

Hexabromoniobates(v) and -tantalates(v) have been prepared[294] by the interaction of the transition-metal pentabromide with a quaternary ammonium bromide in anhydrous acetonitrile. The niobium compounds show a single niobium–bromine stretch at $240\ cm^{-1}$, but the tantalum compounds always gave two peaks at $210–230\ cm^{-1}$, suggesting a possible tetragonal distortion of the $TaBr_6$ group.

Caesium hexachloroniobate(iv) and -tantalate(iv) have been prepared by the interaction of the correct proportions of the pentachlorides and caesium chloride in the presence of phosphorus[279]. Alternatively, caesium hexachlorometallate(v) may be used as the starting material. The preparation of violet hexachlorotantalates(iv) by the interaction of tantalum tetrachloride and alkali-metal chloride in the melt has been confirmed[295]. Further, it was reported that they give blue solutions which are reasonably stable if the solution is saturated with gaseous hydrogen chloride[295]. Confirmation of this observation comes from the reported direct preparation of the niobium salts in this medium by the interaction of niobium tetrachloride and alkali-metal chloride[280]. New lattice parameters have been reported for some of the hexachlorometallates(iv); in some cases the symmetry of the tantalum compound is not the same as that previously reported, but this is probably merely a reflection of the known polymorphic tendencies of this type of compound. The cubic salts are of the K_2PtCl_6 type.

$(NH_4)_2NbCl_6$	Cubic	$a = 9.24$ Å	(reference 280)
Rb_2NbCl_6	Cubic	$a = 10.25$ Å	(reference 280)
Cs_2NbCl_6	Cubic	$a = 10.31$ Å	(reference 280)
K_2TaCl_6	Tetragonal	$a = 9.01, c = 12.43$ Å	(reference 295)
Rb_2TaCl_6	Tetragonal	$a = 10.67, c = 9.07$ Å	(reference 295)
Cs_2TaCl_6	Cubic	$a = 10.32$ Å	(reference 295)

Rubidium and caesium oxotetrachloroniobates(IV) have been reported briefly for the first time[280]. They were prepared by reduction of the corresponding oxopentachloroniobate(V) with stannous chloride in an argon stream at 450–550°.

Alkali-metal pentachloroniobates(III) have been prepared for the first time by Safonov and coworkers, by the interaction of niobium trichloride

TABLE 5.46

Properties of Some Pentachloroniobates(III)

Compound	Melting point	Transition temperature	Ref.
Na_2NbCl_5		362°	296, 297
K_2NbCl_5	718°	590°	296, 297
Rb_2NbCl_5	753°		298
Cs_2NbCl_5	762°		298

and alkali-metal chloride in the melt. A few properties of these complexes are given in Table 5.46. All of the salts are hydrolysed in air, but the resistance towards hydrolysis increases with the size of the cation.

REFERENCES

1. J. H. Canterford and T. A. O'Donnell, *Inorg. Chem.*, **5**, 1442 (1966).
2. H. C. Clark and H. J. Eméleus, *J. Chem. Soc.*, **1958**, 190.
3. F. Fairbrother and W. C. Frith, *J. Chem. Soc.*, **1951**, 3051.
4. J. H. Junkins, R. L. Farrar, E. J. Barber and H. A. Bernhardt, *J. Am. Chem. Soc.*, **74**, 3464 (1952).
5. N. S. Nikolaev and V. F. Sukhoverkhov, *Bul. Inst. Politeh. Iasi* (NS), **3**, 61 (1957).
6. V. Gutmann and H. J. Eméleus, *J. Chem. Soc.*, **1950**, 1046.
7. A. P. Brady, O. E. Meyers and J. K. Clauss, *J. Phys. Chem.*, **64**, 588 (1960).
8. H. J. Eméleus and V. Gutmann, *J. Chem. Soc.*, **1950**, 2115.
9. E. L. Muetterties and J. E. Castle, *J. Inorg. Nucl. Chem.*, **18**, 148 (1961).
10. L. Kolditz and G. Furcht, *Z. anorg. allgem. Chem.*, **312**, 11 (1961).
11. L. Kolditz, C. Kuerschner and U. Calov, *Z. anorg. allgem. Chem.*, **329**, 172 (1964).
12. *U.S. Patent*, 3,056,649 (1962).
13. H. Schafer, H. G. Schnering, K. J. Niehues and H. G. Nieder-Vahrenholz, *J. Less-Common Metals*, **9**, 95 (1965).
14. F. P. Gortsema and R. Didchenko, *Inorg. Chem.*, **4**, 182 (1965).
15. O. Ruff and E. Schiller, *Z. anorg. allgem. Chem.*, **72**, 329 (1911).
16. O. E. Meyers and A. P. Brady, *J. Phys. Chem.*, **64**, 591 (1960).
17. E. Greenberg, C. A. Natke and W. N. Hubbard, *J. Phys. Chem.*, **69**, 2089 (1965).
18. A. J. Edwards, *J. Chem. Soc.*, **1964**, 3714.

19. J. S. Fordyce and R. L. Baum, *J. Chem. Phys.*, **44**, 1159 (1965).
20. F. Fairbrother, K. H. Grundy and A. Thompson, *J. Chem. Soc.*, **1965**, 761.
21. F. Fairbrother, W. C. Frith and A. A. Woolf, *J. Chem. Soc.*, **1954**, 1031.
22. J. V. Hatton, Y. Saito and W. G. Schneider, *Can. J. Chem.*, **43**, 47 (1965).
23. L. P. Varga and H. Freund, *J. Phys. Chem.*, **66**, 21 (1962).
24. S. Blanchard, *J. Chim. Phys.*, **62**, 919 (1965).
25. I. Sheft, H. H. Hyman and J. J. Katz, *J. Am. Chem. Soc.*, **75**, 5221 (1953).
26. A. F. Clifford, H. C. Beachell and W. M. Jack, *J. Inorg. Nucl. Chem.*, **5**, 57 (1957).
27. D. A. McCaulay, W. S. Higley and A. P. Lien, *J. Am. Chem. Soc.*, **78**, 3009 (1956).
28. N. S. Nikolaev and Y. A. Buslaev, *Russ. J. Inorg. Chem.*, **4**, 84 (1959).
29. Y. A. Buslaev and N. S. Nikolaev, *Russ. J. Inorg. Chem.*, **4**, 210 (1959).
30. H. Schafer and H. G. Schnering, *Angew. Chem.*, **76**, 833 (1964).
31. F. Fairbrother, K. H. Grundy and A. Thompson, *J. Chem. Soc.*, **1965**, 765.
32. R. D. Peacock in *Progress in Inorganic Chemistry* (ed. F. A. Cotton), Vol. 2, Interscience, New York, 1960.
33. R. G. Cavell and H. C. Clark, *J. Inorg. Nucl. Chem.*, **17**, 257 (1961).
34. A. J. Edwards, J. H. Holloway and R. D. Peacock, *Proc. Chem. Soc.*, **1963**, 275.
35. F. Fairbrother, K. H. Grundy and A. Thompson, *J. Less-Common Metals*, **10**, 38 (1966).
36. H. Schafer, D. Bauer, W. Beckmann, R. Gerken, H. G. Nieder-Vahrenholz, K. J. Niehues and H. Scholz, *Naturwiss.*, **51**, 241 (1964).
37. L. K. Frevel and H. W. Rinn, *Acta Cryst.*, **9**, 626 (1956).
38. Y. A. Buslaev, Y. Y. Kharitonov and S. M. Sinitsyna, *Russ. J. Inorg. Chem.*, **10**, 287 (1965).
39. S. Andersson and A. Astrom, *Acta Chem. Scand.*, **19**, 2136 (1965).
40. S. Andersson and A. Astrom, *Acta Chem. Scand.*, **18**, 2233 (1964).
41. S. Andersson, *Acta Chem. Scand.*, **18**, 2339 (1964).
42. S. Andersson, *Acta Chem. Scand.*, **19**, 1401 (1965).
43. K. M. Alexander and F. Fairbrother, *J. Chem. Soc.*, **1949**, S223.
44. P. Sue, *Compt. Rend.*, **208**, 814 (1939).
45. P. Sue, *Bull. Chim. Soc. France* (*Memoirs*), **6**, 830 (1939).
46. F. Fairbrother, A. H. Cowley and N. Scott, *J. Less-Common Metals*, **1**, 206 (1959).
47. T. E. Austin and S. Y. Tyree, *J. Inorg. Nucl. Chem.*, **14**, 141 (1960).
48. O. Ruff and F. Thomas, *Z. anorg. allgem. Chem.*, **156**, 213 (1926).
49. H. Schafer and C. Pietruck, *Z. anorg. allgem. Chem.*, **267**, 174 (1951).
50. H. Funk and W. Weiss, *Z. anorg. allgem. Chem.*, **295**, 327 (1958).
51. M. Chaigneau, *Compt. Rend.*, **243**, 957 (1956).
52. V. I. Spitzin and L. Kushtanov, *Z. anorg. allgem. Chem.*, **182**, 207 (1929).
53. R. C. Young and C. H. Brubacker, *J. Am. Chem. Soc.*, **74**, 4967 (1952).
54. A. Cowley, F. Fairbrother and N. Scott, *J. Chem. Soc.*, **1958**, 3133.
55. D. J. Bettinger, *J. Sci. Lab. Denison Univ.*, **45**, 162 (1961).
56. K. Knox, S. Y. Tyree, R. D. Srivastava, V. Norman, J. Y. Bassett and J. H. Holloway, *J. Am. Chem. Soc.*, **79**, 3358 (1957).
57. Z. G. Namoradze and O. E. Zvyagintsev, *J. Appl. Chem. USSR*, **12**, 603 (1939).

58. F. Fairbrother, J. F. Nixon and H. Prophet, *J. Less-Common Metals*, **9**, 434 (1965).
59. B. A. Voitovich and A. S Barabanova, *Russ. J. Inorg. Chem.*, **6**, 1073 (1961).
60. H. Schafer, L. Bayer and H. Lehmann, *Z. anorg. allgem. Chem.*, **268**, 268 (1952).
61. M. A. Opichtina and N. A. Fleischer, *Zh. Obshch. Khim.*, **7**, 2016 (1937).
62. J. B. Ainscough, R. J. W. Holt and F. W. Trowse, *J. Chem. Soc.*, **1957**, 1034.
63. D. N. Tarasenkow and A. V. Komandin, *Zh. Obshch. Khim.*, **10**, 1319 (1940).
64. H. Schafer and F. Kahlenberg, *Z. anorg. allgem. Chem.*, **305**, 291 (1960).
65. L. A. Nisel'son and A. I. Pustil'nik, *Izv. Akad. Nauk SSSR, Otd. Tekhn. Nauk., Met. i Gorn. Delo*, **1963**, 110.
66. L. A. Nisel'son, A. I. Pustil'nik and T. D. Sokolova, *Russ. J. Inorg. Chem.*, **9**, 574 (1964).
67. A. P. Palkin and N. D. Chikanov, *Russ. J. Inorg. Chem.*, **4**, 407 (1959).
68. G. Meyer, J. F. Oosterom and W. J. van Oeveren, *Rec. Trav. Chim.*, **80**, 502 (1961).
69. L. A. Nisel'son, *Zh. Neorg. Khim.*, **3**, 2603 (1958).
70. H. Schafer and F. Kahlenberg, *Z. anorg. allgem. Chem.*, **294**, 242 (1958).
71. V. M. Amosov, *Izv. Vysskikh Uchebn. Zavedenii, Tsvetn. Met.*, **6**, 103 (1963).
72. P. Gross, C. Hayman, D. L. Levi and G. L. Wilson, *Trans. Faraday Soc.*, **56**, 318 (1960).
73. S. A. Shchukarev, M. A. Oranskaya and T. S. Shemyakina, *Russ. J. Inorg. Chem.*, **5**, 1036 (1960).
74. L. A. Nisel'son and G. L. Perekhrest, *Zh. Neorg. Khim.*, **3**, 2150 (1958).
75. H. Schafer and F. Kahlenberg, *Z. anorg. Chem.*, **305**, 178 (1960).
76. S. A. Shchukarev, E. K. Smirnova, I. V. Vasil'kova and L. I. Lappo, *Vestn. Leningr. Univ.*, **15**, *Ser. Fiz. i Khim.*, 113 (1960).
77. S. A. Shchukarev and A. R. Kurbanov, *Vestn. Leningr. Univ.*, **17**, *Ser. Fiz. i Khim.*, 144 (1962).
78. A. Zalkin and D. E. Sands, *Acta Cryst.*, **11**, 615 (1958).
79. R. M. Douglass and E. Saritzky, *Anal. Chem.*, **29**, 315 (1957).
80. H. A. Skinner and L. E. Sutton, *Trans. Faraday Soc.*, **36**, 668 (1940).
81. J. Gaunt and J. B. Ainscough, *Spectrochim. Acta*, **10**, 52 (1957).
82. H. Moureu, P. Sue and M. Magat, *Contrib. Etude Struct. Mol., Vol. Commem. Victor Henri*, **1947**, 125.
83. G. L. Carlson, *Spectrochim. Acta*, **19**, 1291 (1963).
84. D. L. Kepert and R. S. Nyholm, *J. Chem. Soc.*, **1965**, 2871.
85. W. Bader and A. D. Westland, *Can. J. Chem.*, **39**, 2306 (1961).
86. P. Spacu, *Z. anorg. allgem. Chem.*, **232**, 225 (1937).
87. H. Moureu and C. H. Hamblet, *J. Am. Chem. Soc.*, **59**, 33 (1937).
88. H. Moureu and C. Hamblet, *Compt. Rend.*, **200**, 2184 (1935).
89. R. E. McCarley, B. G. Hughes, J. C. Boatman and B. A. Torp, *Advan. Chem. Ser.*, **37**, 243 (1963).
90. G. W. A. Fowles and C. M. Pleass, *J. Chem. Soc.*, **1957**, 2078.
91. P. J. H. Carnell and G. W. A. Fowles, *J. Chem. Soc.*, **1959**, 4113.

92. P. J. H. Carnell and G. W. A. Fowles, *J. Less-Common Metals*, **4**, 40 (1962).
93. M. Allbutt, K. Feenan and G. W. A. Fowles, *J. Less-Common Metals*, **6**, 299 (1964).
94. D. C. Bradley and I. M. Thomas, *Can. J. Chem.*, **40**, 449 (1962).
95. M. A. Glushkova and M. M. Evteeva, *Russ. J. Inorg. Chem.*, **6**, 9 (1961).
96. M. A. Glushkova, M. M. Ershova and Y. A. Buslaev, *Russ. J. Inorg. Chem.*, **10**, 1290 (1965).
97. *U.S. Patent* 2,921,948 (1960).
98. G. L. Juvinall, *J. Am. Chem. Soc.*, **86**, 4202 (1964).
99. E. Wiberg and H. Neumaier, *Z. anorg. allgem. Chem.*, **340**, 189 (1965).
100. D. B. Copley, F. Fairbrother, K. H. Grundy and A. Thompson, *J. Less-Common Metals*, **6**, 407 (1964).
101. D. B. Copley, F. Fairbrother and A. Thompson, *J. Less-Common Metals*, **8**, 256 (1965).
102. H. Funk and K. Niederlander, *Ber.*, **62**, 1688 (1929).
103. G. C. Kleinkopf and J. M. Shreeve, *Inorg. Chem.*, **3**, 607 (1964).
104. E. Hayek, J. Puschmann and A. Czaloun, *Monatsh. Chem.*, **85**, 359 (1954).
105. I. A. Sheka, B. A. Voitovich and L. A. Nisel'son, *Russ. J. Inorg. Chem.*, **4**, 813 (1959).
106. I. A. Sheka, *Chem. Zvesti*, **13**, 656 (1959).
107. L. A. Nisel'son, *Zh. Neorg. Khim.*, **2**, 816 (1957).
108. R. Gut and G. Schwarzenbach, *Helv. Chim. Acta*, **42**, 2156 (1959).
109. A. S. Barabanova and B. A. Voitovich, *Ukr. Khim. Zh.*, **30**, 1298 (1964).
110. D. B. Copley, F. Fairbrother and A. Thompson, *J. Chem. Soc.*, **1964**, 315.
111. K. Feenan and G. W. A. Fowles, *J. Chem. Soc.*, **1965**, 2449.
112. F. Fairbrother and J. F. Nixon, *J. Chem. Soc.*, **1962**, 150.
113. J. Desnoyers and R. Rivest, *Can. J. Chem.*, **43**, 1879 (1965).
114. R. J. H. Clark, D. L. Kepert and R. S. Nyholm, *J. Chem. Soc.*, **1965**, 2877.
115. K. Feenan and G. W. A. Fowles, *J. Chem. Soc.*, **1964**, 2842.
116. V. Gutmann, M. Baaz and O. Kunze, *Monatsh. Chem.*, **93**, 1142 (1962).
117. V. I. Spitsyn and N. A. Preobrazhenskii, *J. Gen. Chem. USSR*, **10**, 655 (1940).
118. S. A. Shchukarev, E. K. Smirnova, T. S. Shemyakina and A. N. Ryabov, *Russ. J. Inorg. Chem.*, **7**, 626 (1962).
119. H. Schafer and F. Kahlenberg, *Z. anorg. allgem. Chem.*, **305**, 326 (1960).
120. C. Djordjevic and V. Katovic, *J. Inorg. Nucl. Chem.*, **25**, 1099 (1963).
121. H. Hecht, G. Jander and H. Schlapmann, *Z. anorg. allgem. Chem.*, **254**, 255 (1947).
122. W. t'Hart and G. Meyer, *Rev. Trav. Chim.*, **84**, 1155 (1965).
123. H. Schafer, *Z. anorg. allgem. Chem.*, **317**, 321 (1962).
124. W. t'Hart and G. Meyer, *Rev. Trav. Chim.*, **83**, 1233 (1964).
125. Y. Saeki and T. Matsushima, *Denki Kagaku*, **32**, 667 (1964).
126. Y. Saeki, T. Suzuki and T. Matsushima, *Denki Kagaku*, **32**, 671 (1964).
127. M. Gloor and K. Wieland, *Helv. Chim. Acta*, **44**, 1098 (1961).
128. D. E. Sands, A. Zalkin and R. E. Elson, *Acta Cryst.*, **12**, 21 (1959).
129. D. Brown, *J. Chem. Soc.*, **1964**, 4944.
130. C. Djordjevic, *Spectrochim. Acta*, **21**, 301 (1965).
131. C. Djordjevic and V. Katovic, *Chem. Ind.* (*London*), **1963**, 411.
132. K. Dehnicke, *Naturwiss.*, **52**, 58 (1965).

133. H. Schafer and E. Sibbing, *Z. anorg. allgem. Chem.*, **305**, 341 (1960).
134. K. Huber and I. Baunok, *Chimica (Switz).*, **15**, 365 (1961).
135. H. Schafer, E. Sibbing and R. Gerken, *Z. anorg. allgem. Chem.*, **307**, 163 (1961).
136. H. G. Schnering and W. Merten, *Naturwiss.*, **51**, 522 (1964).
137. R. F. Rolsten, *J. Phys. Chem.*, **62**, 126 (1958).
138. S. S. Berdonosov, A. V. Lapitskii and L. G. Vlasov, *Russ. J. Inorg. Chem.*, **7**, 1125 (1962).
139. W. Barr, *J. Am. Chem. Soc.*, **30**, 1668 (1908).
140. S. A. Shchukarev, E. K. Smirnova, I. V. Vasil'kova and N. I. Borovkova, *Russ. J. Inorg. Chem.*, **7**, 625 (1962).
141. R. E. McCarley and J. C. Boatman, *Inorg. Chem.*, **4**, 1486 (1965).
142. S. S. Berdonosov, A. V. Lapitskii and L. G. Vlasov, *Vestn. Mosk. Univ., Ser. II, Khim.*, **18**, 57 (1963).
143. W. K. van Haagen, *J. Am. Chem. Soc.*, **32**, 729 (1910).
144. M. Chaigneau, *Compt. Rend.*, **248**, 3173 (1959).
145. S. S. Berdonosov, A. V. Lapitskii and E. K. Bakov, *Russ. J. Inorg. Chem.*, **10**, 173 (1965).
146. E. L. Wiseman and N. W. Gregory, *J. Am. Chem. Soc.*, **71**, 2344 (1949).
147. L. A. Nisel'son and T. D. Sokolova, *Russ. J. Inorg. Chem.*, **9**, 1117 (1964).
148. P. Gross, C. Hayman, D. L. Levi and G. L. Wilson, *Trans. Faraday Soc.*, **58**, 890 (1962).
149. S. S. Berdonosov, A. V. Lapitskii, D. G. Berdonosova and L. G. Vlasov, *Russ. J. Inorg. Chem.*, **8**, 1315 (1963).
150. G. Wilkinson and F. A. Cotton, *Chem. Ind. (London)*, 307 (1954).
151. D. M. Chizhikov and A. M. Grin'ko, *Russ. J. Inorg. Chem.*, **4**, 444 (1959).
152. K. M. Alexander and F. Fairbrother, *J. Chem. Soc.*, **1949**, 2472.
153. R. F. Rolsten, *J. Am. Chem. Soc.*, **79**, 5409 (1957).
154. L. A. Nisel'son and I. V. Petrusevich, *Russ. J. Inorg. Chem.*, **5**, 120 (1960).
155. W. Littke and G. Brauer, *Z. anorg. allgem. Chem.*, **325**, 122 (1963).
156. F. Korosy, *Technikai Kurir*, **9**, 81 (1938).
157. F. Korosy, *J. Am. Chem. Soc.*, **61**, 838 (1939).
158. R. F. Rolsten, *J. Am. Chem. Soc.*, **80**, 2952 (1958).
159. M. Chaigneau, *Bull. Soc. Chim. France*, **1957**, 886.
160. M. Chaigneau, *Compt. Rend.*, **242**, 263 (1956).
161. H. Schafer and R. Gerken, *Z. anorg. allgem. Chem.*, **317**, 105 (1962).
162. H. Schafer and L. Zylka, *Z. anorg. allgem. Chem.*, **338**, 309 (1965).
163. H. Schafer, C. Groser and L. Bayer, *Z. anorg. allgem. Chem.*, **265**, 258 (1951).
164. C. H. Brubaker and R. C. Young, *J. Am. Chem. Soc.*, **74**, 3690 (1952).
165. *German Patent*, 903,034 (1954).
166. R. E. McCarley and B. A. Torp, *Inorg. Chem.*, **2**, 540 (1963).
167. H. Schafer and C. Pietruck, *Z. anorg. allgem. Chem.*, **266**, 151 (1951).
168. H. Schafer and L. Bayer, *Z. anorg. allgem. Chem.*, **277**, 140 (1954).
169. V. Gutmann and H. Tannenberger, *Monatsh. Chem.*, **87**, 769 (1956).
170. P. Frere, *Ann. Chim. (Paris)*, **7**, 85 (1962).
171. H. Schafer and L. Grau, *Z. anorg. allgem. Chem.*, **275**, 198 (1964).
172. S. A. Shchukarev and A. R. Kurbanov, *Izv. Akad. Nauk Tadzh. SSR, Otd. Geol. Khim. i Tekhn. Nauk*, **1962**, 56.

173. O. Ruff and F. Thomas, *Ber.*, **55**, 1466 (1922).
174. H. Schafer, *Angew. Chem.*, **67**, 748 (1955).
175. R. E. McCarley and J. C. Boatman, *Inorg. Chem.*, **2**, 547 (1963).
176. H. G. Schnering and K. Wohrle, *Angew. Chem.*, **75**, 684 (1963).
177. H. Schafer, H. Scholz and R. Gerken, *Z. anorg. allgem. Chem.*, **331**, 154 (1964).
178. B. A. Torp, *Diss. Abs.*, **25**, 2751 (1964).
179. R. J. H. Clark, D. L. Kepert, J. Lewis and R. S. Nyholm, *J. Chem. Soc.*, **1965**, 2865.
180. H. Schafer and F. Liedmeier, *J. Less-Common Metals*, **6**, 307 (1964).
181. H. Schafer and F. Liedmeier, *Z. anorg. allgem. Chem.*, **329**, 225 (1964).
182. H. Schafer and K. D. Dohmann, *Z. anorg. allgem. Chem.*, **311**, 139 (1961).
183. H. Schafer, R. Gerken and H. Scholz, *Z. anorg. allgem. Chem.*, **335**, 96 (1965).
184. S. S. Berdonosov and A. V. Lapitskii, *Russ. J. Inorg. Chem.*, **9**, 152 (1964).
185. S. S. Berdonosov, A. V. Lapitskii and D. G. Berdonosova, *Russ. J. Inorg. Chem.*, **9**, 1388 (1964).
186. J. D. Corbett and P. W. Seabaugh, *J. Inorg. Nucl. Chem.*, **6**, 207 (1958).
187. P. W. Seabaugh and J. D. Corbett, *Inorg. Chem.*, **4**, 176 (1965).
188. L. F. Dahl and D. L. Wampler, *Acta Cryst.*, **15**, 903 (1962).
189. E. L. Muetterties and J. E. Castle, *J. Inorg. Nucl. Chem.*, **18**, 148 (1961).
190. P. Ehrlich, F. Ploger and G. Pietzka, *Z. anorg. allgem. Chem.*, **282**, 19 (1955).
191. V. Gutmann and K. H. Jack, *Acta Cryst.*, **4**, 244 (1951).
192. H. Schafer and K. D. Dohmann, *Z. anorg. allgem. Chem.*, **300**, 1 (1959).
193. C. H. Brubaker and R. C. Young, *J. Am. Chem. Soc.*, **73**, 4179 (1951).
194. A. R. Kurbanov, A. V. Suvorov, S. A. Shchukarev and G. I. Novikov, *Russ. J. Inorg. Chem.*, **9**, 289 (1964).
195. R. C. Young and T. J. Hastings, *J. Am. Chem. Soc.*, **64**, 1740 (1942).
196. P. Frere and A. Micheal, *Compt. Rend.*, **252**, 740 (1961).
197. I. D. Efros and M. F. Lantratov, *Zh. Prikl. Khim.*, **37**, 2521 (1964).
198. A. Mukhtar and R. Winand, *Compt. Rend.*, **260**, 3674 (1965).
199. J. L. Hoard, W. J. Martin, M. E. Smith and J. F. Whitney, *J. Am. Chem. Soc.*, **76**, 3820 (1954).
200. P. H. Ts'ui, N. P. Luzhnaya and I. V. Konstantinov, *Russ. J. Inorg. Chem.*, **8**, 201 (1963).
201. J. S. Fordyce and R. L. Baum, *J. Chem. Phys.*, **44**, 1166 (1965).
202. A. G. Sharpe, *Advances in Fluorine Chemistry*, Vol. 1, Butterworths, London, 1960.
203. V. I. Konstantinov and P. H. Ts'ui, *Russ. J. Inorg. Chem.*, **8**, 23 (1963).
204. J. L. Hoard, *J. Am. Chem. Soc.*, **61**, 1252 (1939).
205. O. L. Keller, *Inorg. Chem.*, **2**, 783 (1963).
206. H. Funk and H. Bohland, *Z. anorg. allgem. Chem.*, **334**, 155 (1964).
207. H. Bode and H. von Dohren, *Naturwiss.*, **44**, 179 (1957).
208. H. Bode and H. von Dohren, *Acta Cryst.*, **11**, 80 (1958).
209. J. S. Fordyce and R. L. Baum, *J. Phys. Chem.*, **69**, 4335 (1965).
210. R. D. W. Kemmitt and D. W. A. Sharp, *J. Chem. Soc.*, **1961**, 2496.
211. R. D. W. Kemmitt, D. R. Russell and D. W. A. Sharp, *J. Chem. Soc.*, **1963**, 4408.

212. B. Cox, *J. Chem. Soc.*, **1956**, 876.
213. R. D. Peacock and D. W. A. Sharp, *J. Chem. Soc.*, **1959**, 2762.
214. A. E. Baker and H. M. Haendler, *Inorg. Chem.*, **1**, 127 (1962).
215. J. L. Hoard and W. J. Martin, *J. Am. Chem. Soc.*, **63**, 11 (1941).
216. M. B. Williams and J. L. Hoard, *J. Am. Chem. Soc.*, **64**, 1139 (1942).
217. B. O. Field and C. J. Hardy, *Proc. Chem. Soc.*, **1963**, 11.
218. F. Galasso and W. Darby, *J. Phys. Chem.*, **66**, 1318 (1962).
219. A. Magneli and S. Nord, *Acta Chem. Scand.*, **19**, 1510 (1965).
220. M. Lundberg and S. Andersson, *Acta Chem. Scand.*, **19**, 1376 (1965).
221. M. Lundberg, *Acta Chem. Scand.*, **19**, 2274 (1965).
222. S. Andersson, *Acta Chem. Scand.*, **19**, 2285 (1965).
223. I. S. Morozov and A. T. Simonich, *Russ. J. Inorg. Chem.*, **6**, 477 (1961).
224. K. Huber and E. Jost, *Congr. Intern. Chim. Pure Appl.*, 16th, *Paris*, 1957, *Mem. Sect. Chim. Minerale*, 1958, p. 47.
225. I. S. Morozov, B. G. Korshunov and A. T. Simonich, *Zh. Neorg. Khim.*, **1**, 1646 (1956).
226. I. Zvarev and L. K. Tarasov, *Russ. J. Inorg. Chem.*, **7**, 1388 (1962).
227. I. S. Morozov and A. T. Simonich, *Zh. Neorg. Khim.*, **2**, 1907 (1957).
228. I. S. Morozov and D. Y. Toptygin, *Zh. Neorg. Khim.*, **3**, 1637 (1958).
229. K. Huber, E. Jost, E. Neuenschwander, M. Studer and B. Roth, *Helv. Chim. Acta*, **41**, 2411 (1958).
230. V. Gutmann, *Z. anorg. allgem. Chem.*, **264**, 151 (1951).
231. K. W. Bagnall and D. Brown, *J. Chem. Soc.*, **1964**, 3021.
232. T. S. Shemyakina, E. K. Smirnova, T. I. Popova and V. M. Kuptsova, *Russ. J. Inorg. Chem.*, **9**, 1291 (1964).
233. A. I. Efimov, *Khim. Redkikh Elementov*, *Leningr. Gos. Univ.*, **1964**, 38.
234. E. K. Smirnova, I. V. Vasil'kova and N. F. Kudryashova, *Russ. J. Inorg. Chem.*, **9**, 268 (1964).
235. S. A. Shchukarev, E. K. Smirnova, I. V. Vasil'kova and M. S. Kotova, *Vestn. Leningr. Univ.*, **18**, *Ser. Fiz. i Khim.*, 174 (1963).
236. A. P. Palkin and N. D. Chikanov, *Russ. J. Inorg. Chem.*, **7**, 705 (1962).
237. A. P. Palkin and N. D. Chikanov, *Russ. J. Inorg. Chem.*, **7**, 1239 (1962).
238. I. S. Morozov and B. G. Korshunov, *Zh. Neorg. Khim.*, **1**, 145 (1956).
239. D. M. Adams, J. Chatt, J. M. Davidson and J. Gerratt, *J. Chem. Soc.*, **1963**, 2189.
240. E. K. Smirnova and I. V. Vasil'kova, *Vestn. Leningr. Univ.*, **19**, *Ser. Fiz. i Khim.*, 164 (1964).
241. I. S. Morozov and V. A. Krokhin, *Russ. J. Inorg. Khim.*, **8**, 1244 (1963).
242. S. A. Shchukarev, E. K. Smirnova and I. V. Vasil'kova, *Vestn. Leningr. Univ.*, **18**, *Ser. Fiz. i Khim.*, 132 (1963).
243. S. A. Shchukarev, T. S. Shemyakina and E. K. Smirnova, *Russ. J. Inorg. Chem.*, **9**, 304 (1964).
244. S. A. Shchukarev, E. K. Smirnova and T. S. Shemyakina, *Russ. J. Inorg. Chem.*, **7**, 1147 (1962).
245. H. Funk, W. Weiss and K. P. Roethe, *Z. anorg. allgem. Chem.*, **301**, 271 (1959).
246. N. P. Lipatova and I. S. Morozov, *Russ. J. Inorg. Chem.*, **10**, 231 (1965).
247. R. F. Weinland and L. Storz, *Ber.*, **39**, 3057 (1906).
248. J. E. Guerchais, B. Spinner and R. Rohmer, *Bull. Soc. Chim. France*, 55 (1965).

249. N. P. Lipatova and I. S. Morozov, *Russ. J. Inorg. Chem.*, **10**, 1528 (1965).
250. A. Sabatini and I. Bertini, *Inorg. Chem.*, **5**, 204 (1966).
251. J. Dehand, J. E. Guerchais and R. Rohmer, *Bull. Soc. Chim. France*, **1966**, 346.
252. W. Ruedorff and D. Krug, *Z. anorg. allgem. Chem.*, **329**, 211 (1964).
253. B. G. Korshunov and V. V. Safonov, *Russ. J. Inorg. Chem.*, **6**, 383 (1961).
254. V. V. Safonov, B. G. Korshunov and Z. N. Shevtsova, *Russ. J. Inorg. Chem.*, **7**, 1021 (1962).
255. E. K. Smirnova and I. V. Vasil'kova, *Vestn. Leningr. Univ.*, **20**, *Ser. Fiz. i Khim.*, 161 (1965).
256. V. V. Safonov, B. G. Korshunov, Z. N. Shevtsova and L. G. Shadrova, *Russ. J. Inorg. Chem.*, **9**, 763 (1964).
257. V. V. Safonov, B. G. Korshunov, Z. N. Shevtsova and L. G. Shadrova, *Russ. J. Inorg. Chem.*, **10**, 359 (1965).
258. B. G. Korshunov and V. V. Safonov, *Russ. J. Inorg. Chem.*, **7**, 1019 (1962).
259. V. V. Safonov, B. G. Korshunov, Z. N. Shevtsova and S. I. Bakum, *Russ. J. Inorg. Chem.*, **9**, 914 (1964).
260. A. Astrom, *Acta Chem. Scand.*, **21**, 915 (1967).
261. L. Janhberg and S. Andersson, *Acta Chem. Scand.*, **21**, 615 (1967).
262. H. Preiss, *Z. anorg. allgem. Chem.*, **346**, 272 (1966).
263. H. Schafer and W. Polert, *Z. anorg. allgem. Chem.*, **353**, 78 (1967).
264. L. A. Reznitskii, *Zh. Fiz. Khim.*, **41**, 1482 (1967).
265. G. L. Gal'chenko, D. A. Gedakyan, B. I. Timofeev, S. M. Skuratov, T. I. Serebryakova and G. V. Samsonov, *Dokl. Akad. Nauk SSSR*, **170**, 132 (1966).
266. R. A. Walton and B. J. Brisdon, *Spectrochim. Acta*, **23A**, 2489 (1967).
267. W. t'Hart and G. Meyer, *Rev. Trav. Chim.*, **86**, 85, (1967).
268. D. Brown, J. F. Easey and J. G. H. du Preez, *J. Chem. Soc.*, **1966**, *A*, 258.
269. W. t'Hart and G. Meyer, *Rec. Trav. Chim.*, **86**, 1191 (1967).
270. A. V. Leshchenko, V. T. Panyushkin, A. D. Garnovskii and O. A. Osipov, *Zh. Obshch. Khim.*, **37**, 1069 (1967).
271. A. V. Leshchenko, V. T. Panyushkin, A. D. Garnovskii and O. A. Osipov, *Russ. J. Inorg. Chem.*, **11**, 1155 (1966).
272. A. V. Leshchenko and O. A. Osipov, *Zh. Obshch. Khim.*, **37**, 534 (1967).
273. I. S. Morozov and A. I. Morozov, *Russ. J. Inorg. Chem.*, **11**, 182 (1966).
274. P. M. Druce, M. F. Lappert and P. N. K. Riley, *Chem. Commun.*, **1967**, 486.
275. H. Schafer and H. Heine, *Z. anorg. allgem. Chem.*, **352**, 258 (1967).
276. V. P. Spiridonov and G. V. Romanov, *Vestn. Mosk. Univ. Ser. II*, **21**, 109 (1966).
277. R. Dorschner and J. Dehand, *Bull. Soc. Chim. France*, **1967**, 2056.
278. N. Brnicevic and C. Djordjivic, *J. Less-Common Metals*, **13**, 470 (1967).
279. S. M. Horner, F. N. Collier and S. Y. Tyree, *J. Less-Common Metals*, **13**, 85 (1967).
280. I. S. Morozov and N. P. Lipatova, *Russ. J. Inorg. Chem.*, **11**, 550 (1966).
281. T. M. Brown and G. S. Newton, *Inorg. Chem.*, **5**, 1117 (1966).
282. E. I. Krylov, A. V. Lapitskii, M. M. Pinaeva and S. S. Berdonosov, *Russ. J. Inorg. Chem.*, **11**, 541 (1966).
283. G. M. Brown and L. A. Walker, *Acta Cryst.*, **20**, 220 (1966).
284. O. L. Keller and A. Chetham-Strode, *Inorg. Chem.*, **5**, 367 (1966).

285. N. K. Jha, Ph. D. Thesis, University of British Columbia, 1965.
286. D. Grandjean and R. Weiss, *Bull. Soc. Chim. France*, **1967**, 3040.
287. J. Fischer, A. DeCain and R. Weiss, *Bull. Soc. Chim. France*, **1966**, 2646.
288. Z. G. Pinsker, *Soviet Physics-Crystallography*, **11**, 634 (1967).
289. S. Andersson, *Acta Chem. Scand.*, **21**, 1777 (1967).
290. J. MacCordick and R. Rohmer, *Compt. Rend.*, **263C**, 1369 (1966).
291. C. Furlani and E. Zinato, *Z. anorg. allgem. Chem.*, **351**, 210 (1967).
293. E. Wendling, *Bull. Soc. Chim. France*, **1967**, 5.
294. D. Brown and P. T. Jones, *J. Chem. Soc.*, **1966**, *A*, 247.
295. E. K. Smirnova and I. V. Vasil'kova, *Zh. Neorg. Khim.*, **12**, 566 (1967).
296. V. V. Safonov, B. G. Korshunov, T. N. Zimina and Z. N. Shevtsova, *Russ. J. Inorg. Chem.*, **11**, 1146 (1966).
297. V. V. Safonov, B. G. Korshunov and A. A. Yarovoi, *Russ. J. Inorg. Chem.*, **11**, 918 (1966).
298. V. A. Safonov, B. G. Korshunov and T. N. Zimina, *Russ. J. Inorg. Chem.*, **11**, 488 (1966).

Chapter 6

Molybdenum and Tungsten

Binary halides and complex halides of both molybdenum and tungsten are known for all oxidation states between II and VI, while oxide halides are mainly restricted to oxidation states V and VI.

HALIDES AND OXIDE HALIDES

The known halides and oxide halides are given in Tables 6.1 and 6.2.
The significant absences are tungsten pentafluoride, molybdenum hexachloride and molybdenum oxide tetrabromide. It is not clear why tungsten

TABLE 6.1

Binary Halides of Molybdenum and Tungsten

Oxidation state	Fluoride	Chloride	Bromide	Iodide
VI	MoF_6, WF_6	WCl_6	WBr_6	
V	MoF_5	$MoCl_5$, WCl_5	WBr_5	
IV	MoF_4, WF_4	$MoCl_4$, WCl_4	$MoBr_4$, WBr_4	
III	MoF_3	$MoCl_3$, WCl_3	$MoBr_3$, WBr_3	MoI_3, WI_3
II		$MoCl_2$, WCl_2	$MoBr_2$, WBr_2	MoI_2

pentafluoride has not been prepared; certainly attempts have been made to prepare it; reactions which lead to molybdenum pentafluoride either do not occur for tungsten or produce the tetrafluoride. The absence of

TABLE 6.2

Oxide Halides of Molybdenum and Tungsten

Oxidation state	Fluoride	Chloride	Bromide
VI	$MoOF_4$, WOF_4	$MoOCl_4$, $WOCl_4$	$WOBr_4$
	MoO_2F_2, WO_2F_2	MoO_2Cl_2, WO_2Cl_2	MoO_2Br_2, WO_2Br_2
V		$MoOCl_3$, $WOCl_3$	$MoOBr_3$
		MoO_2Cl	
IV		$MoOCl_2$	

molybdenum hexachloride and molybdenum oxide tetrabromide is more compatible with the systematic trends in the stabilities of the halides and oxide halides of the second- and third-row transition metals. However, these trends suggest that molybdenum hexachloride should be capable of existence if some route could be found avoiding intermediate formation of the pentachloride which appears to be thermodynamically and chemically very stable.

Oxidation State VI

Molybdenum and tungsten hexafluoride. A wide variety of methods is available for the preparation of both molybdenum and tungsten hexafluoride; but direct fluorination of the metal in a flow system at atmospheric pressure, and at a temperature of 150–300°, is the easiest and most convenient procedure[1-3]. O'Donnell[1] has described a simple glass apparatus incorporating metal valves for handling molybdenum hexafluoride, although later techniques using Kel-F are superior[4]. The technique can be used equally well for the tungsten compound. Other fluorinating agents that have been used directly on the metals include the nitrosyl fluoride–hydrogen fluoride adduct[5], chlorine trifluoride[6] and bromine trifluoride[2]. The product obtained by using chlorine trifluoride must be washed with anhydrous hydrogen fluoride to remove the excess of reagent. A disadvantage of using bromine trifluoride is that the hexafluoride has to be separated from elementary bromine which is soluble in the hexafluoride.

Under fairly specific conditions both molybdenum and tungsten hexafluoride can be prepared by the action of fluorine in excess on the corresponding hexacarbonyl. For molybdenum hexafluoride the reaction must be carried out at a temperature of not less than 50°, otherwise some pentafluoride is formed[7]; with tungsten carbonyl room temperature is sufficient to give pure tungsten hexafluoride[8], which perhaps reflects the instability of tungsten pentafluoride and the ease of oxidation of tungsten tetrafluoride. Iodine pentafluoride may be used as an alternative fluorinating agent on the carbonyls[8,9].

The more reactive halogen fluorides, namely, chlorine trifluoride, bromine trifluoride and iodine pentafluoride, react with anhydrous molybdenum or tungsten trioxide to give the metal hexafluoride[10]. Under more vigorous conditions, at 350° in a bomb, sulphur tetrafluoride also produces the metal hexafluorides from the trioxides[11].

Dry hydrogen fluoride at temperatures greater than 550° reacts in a flow system with both molybdenum and tungsten dibromide to give the metal hexafluorides[2,12]. It was suggested that the reaction proceeded through the initial formation of the metal difluoride which then dissociated to give the hexafluoride and the metal, the latter being identified in the residue.

$$2MBr_2 + 4HF \rightleftarrows 2MF_2 + 4HBr$$

$$3MF_2 \rightarrow 2M + MF_6$$

Bromine trifluoride also reacts with molybdenum dibromide to give molybdenum hexafluoride[2].

Other specific and less important methods of preparation include thermal disproportionation of molybdenum pentafluoride[13], proposed as:

$$2MoF_5 \rightarrow MoF_6 + MoF_4$$

and the action of fluorinating agents such as anhydrous hydrogen fluoride[14], arsenic trifluoride and antimony pentafluoride[15] on tungsten hexachloride:

$$WCl_6 + 6HF \rightarrow WF_6 + 6HCl$$

$$WCl_6 + 2AsF_3 \rightarrow WF_6 + 2AsCl_3$$

$$WCl_6 + 3SbF_5 \rightarrow WF_6 + 3SbF_3Cl_2$$

Both hexafluorides are colourless in the solid, liquid and gaseous states. Molybdenum hexafluoride[1,16] melts at 17.4° and boils at 34.0°, whereas tungsten hexafluoride[3,16] melts at 2.0° and boils at 17.1°. It is interesting that tungsten hexafluoride is more volatile than its molybdenum analogue, as pointed out in Chapter 1.

As with most other transition-metal hexafluorides, the molybdenum and tungsten compounds both exhibit a phase change from ortho-rhombic (with a slight tetragonal distortion of individual octahedra) at low temperatures, to a body-centred cubic lattice just below the melting point[17,18]. The unit-cell size for the cubic lattice of molybdenum hexa-fluoride is given[18] as 6.23 Å, and the densities for the two modifications of this compound are 3.27 g/cm³ at −46° (orthorhombic) and 2.88 g/cm³ at 5° (cubic).

The vapour pressure of molybdenum hexafluoride has been studied in detail by Cady and Hargreaves[16] and by Osborne and coworkers[18]. The results obtained are as follows:

Solid

$$\log p_{mm} = 10.216 - 2166.5/T \quad (-60° \text{ to } -8.7°)[16]$$
$$\log p_{mm} = 8.533 - 1722.9/T \quad (-8.7° \text{ to } 17.4°)[16]$$

Liquid

$$\log p_{mm} = 7.766 - 1499.9/T \quad (17.4° \text{ to } 34°)[16]$$
$$\log p_{mm} = 20.19354 - 2047.15/T - 4.28004 \log_{10} T \quad (18.0° \text{ to } 47°)[18].$$

The two separate determinations of the vapour pressure of liquid molyb-denum hexafluoride agree within 0.6% at 300°K. The vapour pressure of tungsten hexafluoride has been examined by Ruff and Ascher[19] and by Barber and Cady[3], who used the experimental values obtained by Ruff and Ascher for the solid hexafluoride to deduce the following equations:

$$(\text{below } -8.2°) \quad \log p_{mm} = 10.0682 - 2032.2/T;$$
$$(-8.2° \text{ to } 2.3°) \quad \log p_{mm} = 8.1847 - 1533.1/T.$$

Subsequently Cady and Hargreaves[16] remeasured the vapour pressure of solid tungsten hexafluoride and obtained the following results:

$$(-60° \text{ to } -8.2°) \quad \log p_{mm} = 9.951 - 2006.0/T;$$
$$(-8.2° \text{ to } 2.0°) \quad \log p_{mm} = 8.758 - 1689.9/T.$$

These sets of results differ from those of Ruff and Ascher by about 20% at 250°K and by about 2% at 270°K. The vapour pressure of liquid tungsten hexafluoride has also been measured twice:

$$(11° \text{ to } 31°) \quad \log p_{mm} = 6.88699 - \frac{928.58}{T} - \frac{67942.9}{T^2} \quad \text{(Barber and Cady)}$$

$$(2.0° \text{ to } 17.1°) \quad \log p_{mm} = 7.635 - \frac{1380.5}{T} \quad \text{(Cady and Hargreaves)}$$

These results agree to within 0.5 mm pressure at 17°C. In view of the remarkable level of agreement between these sets of results it appears that the results of Cady and Hargreaves for solid tungsten hexafluoride are likely to be more accurate than the early data of Ruff and Ascher.

Thermodynamic parameters for both hexafluorides has been calculated from the vapour-pressure measurements, from fluorine bomb calorimetry[20,21] and from solution calorimetry[22,23] and are given in Table 6.3.

Sundarum[24] has calculated the heat capacities, heat contents, free energies and entropies for both hexafluorides in the temperature range 100–1300°K. Heat capacities for molybdenum hexafluoride[18] and tungsten hexafluoride[17] have been measured over the range 4–300°K.

Early electron-diffraction studies[25] of the vapours of the hexafluorides suggested that they possessed rhombohedral symmetry, whereas infrared evidence indicates O_h symmetry. Subsequently it was suggested[26] that the method of analysis of the electron-diffraction data was inadequate.

The infrared and Raman spectra of both hexafluorides in the vapour phase have been recorded several times and unambiguously demonstrate the O_h symmetry of the molecules. The results are given in Table 6.4, and it is clear that quite good agreement is obtained between various authors except for the assignment of ν_6. It is to be noted that ν_6 has not been observed directly and that its value is deduced from a consideration of overtone bands. Osborne and coworkers[18] have pointed out that because it is three-fold degenerate and low, ν_6 makes an important contribution to the standard entropy of molybdenum hexafluoride at 298°K. They have compared the calculated entropies of formation of molybdenum hexafluoride using the various infrared data in Table 6.4 and by comparing the

TABLE 6.3

Thermodynamic Parameters[a] for Molybdenum and Tungsten Hexafluoride

Property	MoF_6	Ref.	WF_6	Ref.
ΔH°_{298} (l)	−388.6	23	−422.0	23
			−417.7	21
ΔH°_{298} (g)	−382.0	23	−416.0	23
	−372.4	20	−411.5	21
ΔH°_{298}(s)			−418.2	21
ΔH_{fusion}	0.92	16	0.42	16
	1.034	18	0.50	3
ΔH_{trans}	1.957	22	1.600	3
	1.953	18	1.400	16
	1.960	16		
ΔH_{vap}	6.940	16	6.330	16
	6.630	18	6.245	3
ΔH_{sub} (cubic)	7.850	16	7.750	16
(ortho)	9.810	16	9.150	16
ΔS°_{298}	72.13	20	71.67	21
	68.41	18		
ΔS_{fusion}	3.15	16	1.45	16
	3.557	18		
ΔS_{trans}	7.40	16	5.28	16
ΔS_{vap}	22.5	16	21.8	16

[a] ΔH in kcal mole^{-1}; ΔS in cal deg^{-1} mole^{-1}.

calculated results with their experimental values of the standard entropy they concluded that the assignment by Weinstock and Goodman[27] of ν_6 as 122 cm^{-1} is probably the most reliable.

Force constants have been calculated for both hexafluorides[32–36] but, because different fundamental vibrational assignments have been used, the results are somewhat variable. However, in all cases it has been found that the bonds in the tungsten compound are stronger than those in molybdenum hexafluoride. Mean square amplitudes of vibration have also been calculated by various groups[24,37–39].

Nikolaev and coworkers[40] have determined the solubilities of molybdenum and tungsten hexafluoride in anhydrous hydrogen fluoride at −5° as 18.5% and 11.52% (by weight), respectively. On a qualitative basis the acid strength of both hexafluorides in this medium has been shown to be moderate[10]. Cady and coworkers have studied the solubility of tungsten hexafluoride in perfluoropentane[41] and perfluorocyclopentane[42]. In a study to investigate the removal of fission-product molybdenum from uranium, Mears and coworkers[43] found that molybdenum hexafluoride is soluble in uranium hexafluoride and behaves as an ideal solute.

TABLE 6.4

Vapour-phase Infrared and Raman Spectra of MoF_6 and WF_6 (cm^{-1})

Molybdenum Hexafluoride

	IR[28]	Raman[29]	IR + Raman[30]	IR + Raman[31]	IR + Raman[27]
ν_1		736	741	741	741
ν_2		641	643	645	643
ν_3	742		741	741	741
ν_4	269		264	260	262
ν_5		319	306	322	312
ν_6	240		190	234	122

Tungsten Hexafluoride

	IR[28]	Raman[29]	IR + Raman[31]
ν_1		769	772
ν_2		760	672
ν_3	712		712
ν_4	256		258
ν_5		322	316
ν_6	261		215

Nikolaev and coworkers[40] have studied the controlled hydrolysis of the hexafluorides and found the equilibrium constants for the reaction

$$MF_6 + 2H_2O \rightleftarrows MO_2F_2 + 4HF$$
$$K = 3 \times 10^3 \text{ (Mo)}$$
$$K = 6 \times 10^2 \text{ (W)}$$

As a direct result of the lack of investigation of the chemical properties of the two hexafluorides, it had become an accepted belief that they were chemically very similar[44,45]. Recent investigations have shown that, whilst this is true for their reaction with water, there are in fact significant differences in their chemical reactivities.

The results of O'Donnell and Stewart[4,46] admirably illustrate the marked difference in the reactivity of the hexafluorides, as shown in Table 6.5 where only the molybdenum- and tungsten-containing products are shown.

TABLE 6.5

Reactions of Molybdenum and Tungsten Hexafluoride

Reagent	Products from MoF_6	Products from WF_6
PF_3	MoF_5	WF_4
CS_2	MoF_5	No reaction
PCl_3 (excess of MoF_6)	$Mo_2Cl_3F_6$ and MoF_5	No reaction
(excess of PCl_3)	$MoCl_5$	No reaction
$AsCl_3$, $SbCl_3$ (excess of MoF_6)	$Mo_2Cl_3F_6$	No reaction
(excess of XCl_3)	$MoCl_5$	No reaction
$TiCl_4$ (excess of MF_6)	$Mo_2Cl_3F_6$	WCl_6
(excess of $TiCl_4$)	$MoCl_5$	WCl_6
CCl_4, $SiCl_4$	$Mo_2Cl_3F_6$	No reaction
BCl_3 (excess of MF_6)	$Mo_2Cl_3F_6$	WCl_3F_3
(excess of BCl_3)	$MoCl_5$	WCl_6
PBr_3	$MoBr_3$	WBr_5

The most important features to be noted from this Table are the differing products obtained from the reactions of the hexafluorides with phosphorus trifluoride and the common occurrence of the compound $Mo_2Cl_3F_6$. Molybdenum hexafluoride is reduced to the pentafluoride by phosphorus trifluoride at room temperature, whereas tungsten hexafluoride is not reduced at room temperature to an appreciable extent, except in the presence of liquid anhydrous hydrogen fluoride, and even then shaking for several days is required. The different products obtained from the hexafluorides is also noteworthy. The compound $Mo_2Cl_3F_6$ has been formulated[47] as a trinuclear cluster compound, $(Mo_3Cl_9)^{3+}(MoF_6^-)_3$ and its properties are discussed in detail in Chapter 3. For all the reactions in Table 6.5 by which it is produced it is supposed[47] that molybdenum pentachloride is the initial product and that this then reacts with an excess of molybdenum hexafluoride.

Geichman and coworkers[48-50] have studied the reactions of nitric oxide, nitrosyl fluoride, nitryl fluoride and nitrosyl chloride with both hexafluorides. The reactions serve to emphasize the difference in reactivity between the hexafluorides noted above. The products are given in Table 6.6.

TABLE 6.6

Reactions of MoF_6 and WF_6 with Various Nitrogen Compounds

Reagent	MoF_6	WF_6	Ref.
NO	$NO \cdot MoF_6$	No reaction	49
NOF	$NOF \cdot MoF_6$	$NOF \cdot WF_6$	48, 50
NO_2F	$NO_2F \cdot MoF_6$	$NO_2F \cdot WF_6$	48, 50
NOCl	$NO \cdot MoF_6$	No reaction	48

$NO \cdot MoF_6$ is a rusty-orange solid melting at approximately 190° and it has a pseudo-cubic cell ($a = 5.080$ Å). Its infrared spectrum shows bands as 2333 and 615 cm^{-1} which are attributed to the NO^+ and MoF_6^- ion, respectively, and the compound is regarded as ionic. The reaction between nitric oxide and molybdenum hexafluoride is thus an oxidation–reduction reaction and it is worth noting that tungsten hexafluoride does not react. The following mechanistic path has been suggested[49] for the molybdenum reaction:

$$NO(g) + MoF_6(g) \rightarrow MoF_5(s) + NOF(g)$$
$$MoF_5(s) + NOF(g) \rightarrow NO^+(MoF_6)^-(s)$$

It would be interesting to investigate the magnetic properties and ESR spectrum of this compound to determine the location of the unpaired electron.

TABLE 6.7

Addition Compounds of Tungsten Hexafluoride

Reagent	Product	Properties
SO_3	$WF_6 \cdot 4.5SO_3$	Colourless, viscous liquid
NH_3	$WF_6(NH_3)_4$	Hygroscopic orange solid
Pyridine	$WF_6(C_5H_5N)_3$	Hygroscopic white solid
Methylamine	$WF_6(CH_3NH_2)_3$	Hygroscopic white solid

The compounds $NOF \cdot MF_6$ and $NO_2F \cdot MF_6$ are white solids having relatively high dissociation pressures at room temperature[48].

The reactions of tungsten hexafluoride with several donor molecules have been investigated[51] and the results are given in Table 6.7. The structures of these compounds have not been investigated.

Tungsten hexafluoride dissolves and reacts in a variety of organic solvents; coloured solutions are frequently formed. Although some attempt has been made[52] to correlate the colours of the solutions with the nature of the functional groups in the solvent, there is no information on the nature of the species in solution.

Tungsten pentafluoride chloride. A reaction between titanium tetrachloride and an excess of tungsten hexafluoride at 5° yields a red solid and a red liquid[53]. The solid has not been identified with certainty but it may be a mixture of tungsten fluoride pentachloride and difluoride tetrachloride. Low-temperature distillation of the liquid led to the isolation of tungsten pentafluoride chloride. This is a yellow liquid, freezing at −33.7° and volatilizing to give a colourless monomeric vapour. At 25° it slowly decomposes to tungsten hexafluoride and an unidentified solid fluoride chloride. The infrared spectrum of the pentafluoride chloride at 3 mm showed absorptions at 744, 700 and 655 cm^{-1}, tentatively assigned to metal–fluorine stretches. The ^{19}F-NMR spectrum showed two peaks in the ratio 1:4 at, respectively, 126.5 and 182.0 ppm downfield from CCl$_3$F, suggesting that the compound is octahedral with four equivalent fluorine atoms *cis* to the chlorine atom[53].

Molybdenum and tungsten oxide tetrafluoride. Ruff *et al.*[15] claimed to have prepared both oxide tetrafluorides by the action of anhydrous hydrogen fluoride on the corresponding oxide tetrachloride. However, the most convenient synthesis of both compounds is by the action, under controlled conditions, of an oxygen–fluorine mixture on the metal at elevated temperatures[54]. Tungsten oxide tetrafluoride has been prepared[55] by the action of dichlorodifluoromethane on tungsten dioxide at 525°. Both oxide tetrafluorides are white crystalline solids.

TABLE 6.8

Thermodynamic Parameters^a for
MoOF$_4$ and WOF$_4$

Property	MoOF$_4$	WOF$_4$
B.p.	186.0°	185.9°
Triple point	97.2°	104.7°
ΔH_{fusion}	1.020	2.260
ΔH_{vap}	12.090	14.230
ΔH_{sub}	13.110	16.490
ΔS_{fus}	2.768	5.981
ΔS_{vap}	26.3	31.0

^{a} ΔH in kcal mole^{-1};
ΔS in cal deg^{-1} mole^{-1}.

The vapour pressures of both compounds have been measured over a wide temperature range and the variation with temperature is given by the following equations[54]:

Solid MoOF$_4$ (40–95°) $\log p_{mm} = 9.21 - 2854/T$.

Liquid MoOF$_4$ (95–185°) $\log p_{mm} = 8.716 - 2671/T$.

Solid WOF$_4$ (50–104°) $\log p_{mm} = 10.96 - 3605/T$.

Liquid WOF$_4$ (105–186°) $\log p_{mm} = 9.69 - 3125/T$.

From these results various thermodynamic parameters have been calculated and are given in Table 6.8. The values of the Trouton constants suggest that some association occurs in the liquid state in each case.

Very little is known of the chemical properties of the oxide tetrafluorides, but the available evidence suggests that they are less reactive than the hexafluorides; for instance, they do not attack glass below their boiling points[54]. Several adducts of tungsten oxide tetrafluoride have been prepared indirectly by the action of iodine pentafluoride and selenium tetrafluoride on tungsten trioxide[56], as shown in the equations:

$$WO_3 + 2IF_5 \rightarrow WOF_4 \cdot IF_5 + IO_2F$$

$$WO_3 + 2SeF_4 \rightarrow WOF_4 \cdot SeOF_2 + SeOF_2$$

$$WO_3 + 3SeF_4 \rightarrow WOF_4 \cdot SeF_4 + 2SeOF_2$$

Molybdenum and tungsten dioxide difluoride. There has been remarkably little investigation into the preparation and chemical properties of the dioxide difluorides of molybdenum and tungsten[57]. Both have been prepared by the controlled hydrolysis of the hexafluorides[40]. The molybdenum compound was originally prepared by the interaction of anhydrous hydrogen fluoride and molybdenum dioxide dichloride, while the tungsten compound was prepared by the careful hydrolysis of the oxide tetrafluoride[15]. Both are white solids. Nothing is known of their chemistry except for the two adducts of molybdenum dioxide difluoride formed by interaction of molybdenum trioxide and iodine pentafluoride and selenium tetrafluoride[56]:

$$2MoO_3 + 3IF_5 \rightarrow 2MoO_2F_2 \cdot 2IF_5 + IO_2F$$

$$MoO_3 + 2SeF_4 \rightarrow MoO_2F_2 \cdot SeF_4 + SeOF_2$$

Tungsten hexachloride. Chlorination of the metal at 600° gives tungsten hexachloride[58-60]. Recently, considerable interest has been shown in the use of carbon tetrachloride as a chlorinating agent for the preparation of transition-metal chlorides. Tungsten hexachloride has been prepared by the action of this reagent on tungsten trioxide[60-62] and on the trisulphide[63]. These reactions are carried out in a bomb between 300° and 400°.

Tungsten hexachloride in its usual form is a blue-black crystalline solid[59]. If the vapours are quenched a red form is obtained, but this rapidly reconverts to the usual form on gentle heating. There is also a phase change at about 230°. Tungsten hexachloride is soluble in carbon tetrachloride, carbon disulphide and phosphorus oxide trichloride[59]. The density of liquid tungsten hexachloride over a considerable temperature range is given by the expression[64]:

$$\rho = 2.721 - 1.964 \times 10^{-3}\Delta t - 1.90 \times 10^{-6}\Delta t^2$$

Δt apparently being measured from the melting point.

Ketelaar and van Oosterhant[65] reported that the X-ray diffraction data of solid tungsten hexachloride could be indexed on the basis of either a rhombohedral or a hexagonal unit cell, with the following lattice parameters:

$$\text{Rhombohedral:} \quad a = 6.58 \text{ Å}, \qquad \alpha = 55.0°$$
$$\text{Hexagonal:} \quad a = 6.088 \text{ Å}, \qquad c = 16.68 \text{ Å}$$

They suggested that solid tungsten hexachloride consists of discrete octahedra of chlorine atoms about the central tungsten atom. However, this proposed structure does not account for the low volatility of tungsten hexachloride and further investigation of the crystal structure seems justified.

Electron-diffraction studies of the vapour of tungsten hexachloride show the molecule to be a perfect octahedron with a tungsten–chlorine distance of 2.26 ± 0.02 Å[66].

The vapour pressure of tungsten hexachloride has been measured by Vernon[58] between 20° and 150° and by Stevenson and coworkers[67] between 185° and 325°. The following equations were obtained:

Solid (α form) (25–150°) $\log p_{mm} = 3.1 - 1198/T$ (Vernon)

      (α form) (185–230°) $\log p_{mm} = 9.615 - 3996/T$ (Stevenson)

      (β form) (230–281.5°) $\log p_{mm} = 8.794 - 3588/T$ (Stevenson)

Liquid (281.5–325°) $\log p_{mm} = 8.194 - 3253/T$ (Stevenson)

At 160°, between the stated ranges of applicability of the two equations for α-WCl_6, the calculated vapour pressures are 2.153 mm (Vernon) and 2.427 mm (Stevenson), suggesting that both sets of data are reliable. On the other hand, Shchukarev and Novikov[68] have reported the vapour pressure of tungsten hexachloride at 215° as 43 mm, but the calculated result from Stevenson's formula is 26.55mm.

Thermodynamic parameters have been calculated from the vapour-pressure measurements and from calorimetry and are given in Table 6.9.

Interaction of tungsten hexachloride and tungsten trioxide gives both tungsten oxide tetrachloride and dioxide dichloride[76]. The phase diagram of the WCl_6–WO_2 system showed the presence of tungsten oxide trichloride[76].

Rideal[77] reported a remarkable reaction between gaseous ammonia and tungsten hexachloride at room temperature to give the nitride W_2N_3. With liquid ammonia at −33° two products were obtained and, although their analyses approximated to $WCl_6 \cdot 6NH_3$ and $WCl_6 \cdot 4NH_3$, both were

TABLE 6.9

Thermodynamic Parameters[a] for Tungsten
Hexachloride

Property		Value	Ref.
M.p.		281.5°	67
		280.0°	60
		275°	68
B.p.		348°	68
Transition point		227°	69
		230°	70
ΔH°_{form}	α	−163	71, 72
	β	−157	72
	(g)	−140	72
ΔH_{sub}	α	22.9	72
		20.1	73
ΔH_{sub}	β	17.3	72
		16.7	73
ΔH_{vap}		14.5	72
ΔS°_{form}	α	107	72
	β	94	72
	(g)	68	72
ΔS_{sub}	α	34.3	73
		38.9	72
		27.5	73
	β	28.0	72
ΔS_{vap}		24.0	73
		23.2	72

For the reaction $WCl_6(g) \rightleftarrows WCl_5(s) + \frac{1}{2}Cl_2(g)$

ΔH_{diss}		24.2	73
		24.0	74
ΔS_{diss}		30.8	73
		31.0	74

For the reaction $WCl_6(g) \rightleftarrows WCl_4(s) + Cl_2(g)$

ΔH_{diss}		43.0	73
		47.0	74
ΔS_{diss}		51.0	73, 74

Average bond energy W–Cl (kcal mole^{-1})	69	75

[a] ΔH in kcal mole^{-1}; ΔS in cal deg^{-1} mole^{-1}.

believed[78] to be mixtures containing ammonium chloride and amido complexes of somewhat uncertain composition. Heating these crude products gave a compound thought to be $WCl_2(NH_2)_2$.

A number of donor molecules react with tungsten hexachloride and in many cases complexes of a lower oxidation state are formed. Some of these reactions are given in Table 6.10.

Tungsten hexachloride dissolves in phosphorus oxide trichloride, and potentiometric titrations suggest[84] the formation of $[POCl_3]^+[WCl_7]^-$. With pentacarbonyliron, tungsten hexachloride reacts in a bomb, to give a yield of up to 85% of hexacarbonyltungsten[85].

Both 2,2'-bipyridyl and 1,10-phenanthroline reduce tungsten hexachloride to compounds of empirical formula $WCl_5 \cdot L$. On the basis of conductivity measurements these compounds have been formulated[86] as $[WCl_4L]^+Cl^-$.

TABLE 6.10

Some Reactions of Tungsten Hexachloride

Reagent	Product	Ref.
Amines	$[W(Amine)_6]Cl_6$	79, 80
Benzamide	$[W(C_6H_5CONH_2)_2]Cl_6$	80
Pyridine	$[W(C_5H_5N)_2]Cl_6$	81
Thiocyanates	$W(CNS)_6 \cdot 2Solvate$	82
Phenols	$W(OR)_6$	83
Dihydric phenols	$W(OR)_3$	83
Trihydric phenols	$W(OR)_2$	83

Molybdenum oxide tetrachloride.   Puttbach[87] first reported the preparation of molybdenum oxide tetrachloride, but Nordenskjold[88] claimed that Puttbach's compound was really a mixture of the pentachloride and dioxide dichloride. In the course of an investigation into the extraction of molybdenum from sulphide ores, Glukhov and Bekhtle[89] passed a mixture of chlorine and oxygen over heated molybdenum disulphide. The major product was molybdenum dioxide dichloride, but in oxygen-deficient systems some oxide tetrachloride was formed. Glukhov and Rodionova[90] subsequently obtained larger amounts of the compound by passing chlorine, saturated with sulphur chloride vapour, over molybdenum dioxide dichloride at 100–120°, the product being purified by repeated sublimation in a stream of dry chlorine.

Glukhov and Eliseev[91] showed that molybdenum oxide tetrachloride could, in fact, be prepared in good yield by the action of molybdenum pentachloride on molybdenum dioxide dichloride as suggested by Puttbach:

$$MoCl_5 + MoO_2Cl_2 \rightarrow MoOCl_4 + MoOCl_3$$

The major difficulty with this method lies in the separation of the product from unchanged starting materials. An additional disadvantage is that it involves handling the extremely reactive pentachloride, and that even traces of moisture would be sufficient to reduce the yield drastically.

Molybdenum oxide tetrachloride has been prepared by the action of sulphuryl chloride on the metal in a sealed tube at 200°. An approximately six-fold excess of sulphuryl chloride was used and the reaction took two days to approach completion[92]. An interesting observation was that if a deficiency of sulphuryl chloride was used, a brown product, which could be sublimed, was obtained, analysing as $Mo_2O_3Cl_5$. Unfortunately no further details of this product were given.

The easiest method of preparing and isolating molybdenum oxide tetra-chloride is by reaction of thionyl chloride with molybdenum trioxide[93]. On refluxing, the thionyl chloride rapidly becomes a very deep red, and from the solution molybdenum oxide tetrachloride is isolated by evaporation of the solvent followed by vacuum-sublimation. A major advantage of this method is that no precaution is necessary against moisture so long as the compound remains in the thionyl chloride solution. Hecht and co-workers[94] claimed to have isolated the addition compound $MoCl_5 \cdot MoO_2Cl_2$ from the vapour-phase reaction of thionyl chloride on molybdenum tri-oxide, but the description of their compound fits the oxide tetrachloride. Siefert and Quak[95] claimed to have obtained molybdenum pentachloride by heating molybdenum trioxide in thionyl chloride in a nitrogen stream, but no evidence was presented.

Molybdenum dioxide dichloride also reacts readily at room temperature with thionyl chloride to give the oxide tetrachloride[96]. Although the dioxide dichloride is not a convenient starting material, this is a significant reaction because here oxygen is being replaced by chlorine whereas, with the hydrate of molybdenum trioxide, chlorine may be thought of as replacing hydroxyl groups. The deep red solution obtained by dissolving molybdenum pentachloride in thionyl chloride also contains the oxide tetrachloride; presumably aerial oxidation to molybdenum(VI) occurs.

Molybdenum oxide tetrachloride forms green crystals which appear red in thin films. It is rapidly hydrolysed in moist air; water instantly causes hydrolysis to molybdate, although occasionally a transient blue colour is observed. The oxide tetrachloride is very soluble in dry chlorinated organic solvents; between 25° and 50° the solubilities in dichloroethane, carbon tetrachloride and chloroform vary from approximately 19 to 32, from 7 to 10, and from 13 to 15.5 g/100 g of solvent, respectively[97].

Molybdenum oxide tetrachloride melts[91] at 102° and boils[98] at 159° to give a heavy brown vapour which was shown to be monomeric by the Victor Meyer method[90]. The compound is best purified by vacuum-sublimation; this can be done at a temperature as low as 60° in a horizontal tube[93]. Molybdenum oxide tetrachloride can be slowly decomposed to molybdenum oxide trichloride by vigorous boiling in a nitrogen atmos-phere[96], and recently this decomposition has been shown to proceed smoothly in refluxing chlorobenzene[99]. Shchukarev and Suvorov[73,74] have estimated the heat of reaction for the decomposition of the oxide tetra-chloride to be 11.5 kcal mole^{-1} with an entropy change of 14.5 cal deg^{-1} mole^{-1}. They say that the compound decomposes to the oxide trichloride at 25°, but the reaction is very slow indeed at this temperature. By dis-solving molybdenum oxide tetrachloride in a standard sodium hydroxide solution its heat of formation was found[100] to be -153.43 kcal mole^{-1}.

The infrared spectrum of molybdenum oxide tetrachloride in thionyl chloride solution shows an intense, strong band at 1005 cm^{-1} which was attributed to the metal–oxygen stretching frequency[96]. A similar band has been reported at 1010 cm^{-1} for a carbon tetrachloride solution[99] and at 1015 cm^{-1} in the vapour phase[101].

Few chemical reactions of molybdenum oxide tetrachloride have been reported. It dissolves in concentrated hydrochloric acid solution to give the oxopentachloromolybdate(v) ion, as proved by isolation of the caesium salt, and not the oxohexachloromolybdate(vi) ion[93]. It is reported[102] to react with liquid ammonia at $-33°$ to give a dark amorphous solid formu-lated as $MoOCl(NH_2)_2$. Larsen and Moore[99] have recently found that the oxide tetrachloride reacts with a number of organic donor ligands; in each case a complex of the oxide trichloride was obtained, confirming the ready reduction of this molybdenum(vi) compound. The complexes obtained were paramagnetic and oxidative titration confirmed the presence of molybdenum(v). Their infrared spectra confirmed the presence of a $Mo{=}O$ bond. With acetylacetone the complex $MoOCl_3 \cdot C_5H_8O_2$, con-taining neutral acetylacetone as a ligand, was obtained. Benzophenone gave the complex $MoOCl_3 \cdot (C_6H_5)_2CO$ which molecular weight deter-minations showed to be partially associated in solution[99].

Tungsten oxide tetrachloride. Several methods of preparing tungsten oxide tetrachloride have been reported but most of them involve some degree of practical inconvenience. Tungsten trioxide reacts with carbon tetrachloride in a sealed ampoule at 250–320° to give tungsten oxide tetrachloride[61,103]:

$$WO_3 + 2CCl_4 \rightarrow WOCl_4 + 2COCl_2$$

The oxide tetrachloride is formed by interaction of tungsten trioxide and tungsten hexachloride[76]:

$$WCl_6 + WO_3 \rightarrow WOCl_4 + WO_2Cl_2$$

This is not a convenient method of preparation as the product has to be repeatedly sublimed to separate it from the other components of the system. Sulphuryl chloride in a sealed tube at 300° reacts over a period of a few days with tungsten metal to give the oxide tetrachloride[104].

The action of refluxing thionyl chloride on tungsten trioxide is the quickest and most convenient method of preparing the oxide tetrachloride. No precaution against moisture need be taken until the product is isolated from solution[96]. The red solution is evaporated to dryness under a vacuum and the compound is purified by sublimation in a horizontal tube at 100–120°. This reaction also proceeds[94] when the vapour of thionyl chloride is passed over the trioxide at 200°.

Tungsten oxide tetrachloride is formed by thermal decomposition of tungsten dioxide dichloride[105] and by the action of dichlorodifluoromethane on tungsten dioxide[55], but these methods are of minor importance.

Tungsten oxide tetrachloride is an orange or red crystalline solid[106] which melts at 209° and boils at 227°. The compound is best purified by vacuum sublimation at 100–120°. It is instantly hydrolysed by water, to give a colourless solution of tungstate ion, and all manipulations must be carried out in a dry box or vacuum line[96].

The crystals of tungsten oxide tetrachloride are of body-centred tetragonal symmetry with $a = 8.48$ and $c = 3.99$ Å. The space group was found to be $I4$. The structure consists of chains of slightly distorted octahedra parallel to the c-axis with oxygen bridges. The metal–halogen distance is 2.29 Å and the metal–oxygen distance is 2.20 Å. The angle O–W–Cl was found[107,108] to be 97.9°.

Various thermodynamic properties of tungsten oxide tetrachloride have been determined and these are given in Table 6.11.

The sublimation pressure is given by the equation[106]:

$$\log p_{mm} = 11.76 - 4400/T,$$

and the vapour pressure is given by the equation[106]:

$$\log p_{mm} = 9.53 - 3300/T.$$

The infrared spectrum of tungsten oxide tetrachloride shows an absorption assigned to a metal–oxygen double-bond stretching frequency at 1019 cm^{-1} in thionyl chloride solution[96] and at 1030 cm^{-1} in carbon disulphide solution[104].

Gaseous ammonia at room temperature reacts[77] with tungsten oxide tetrachloride to give the nitride W_2N_3. Various donor molecules have been found to form adducts or substitution compounds with the oxide tetrachloride and some of these are given in Table 6.12.

Molybdenum and tungsten dioxide dichloride. A large number of preparative methods for these two very similar compounds have been reported and some of these are summarized in Table 6.13.

16

TABLE 6.11

Thermodynamic Properties[a] of Tungsten Oxide Tetrachloride

Property		Value	Ref.
M.p.		209°	106
		204°	68
B.p.		227°	106
		224°	68
$\Delta H^{\circ}_{\text{form}}$	(s)	−177.5	71
		−178.0	72
	(g)	−159	72
$\Delta S^{\circ}_{\text{form}}$	(s)	130	72
	(g)	94	72
ΔG_{sub}		$20.14 - 0.040/T$	106
ΔH_{sub}		20.14	106
		21.7	73
		18.9	68
		18.3	72
ΔS_{sub}		40.43	106
		44.2	73
		38.0	68
		36.3	72
ΔG_{fusion}		$4.98 - 10.11/T$	106
ΔH_{fusion}		4.98	106
ΔS_{fusion}		10.11	106
ΔG_{vap}		15.16	106
ΔH_{vap}		15.16	106
		16.2	68
		16.5	72
ΔS_{vap}		30.32	106
		32.6	68
		32.8	72
For the reaction $2WOCl_4 \rightleftarrows WCl_6 + WO_2Cl_2$ (200–500°)			
ΔH_{diss}		11	74
		15.1	72
ΔS_{diss}		6	74
		13.4	72

[a] ΔH and ΔG in kcal mole^{-1}; ΔS in cal deg^{-1} mole^{-1}.

TABLE 6.12

Reactions with Tungsten Oxide Tetrachloride

Reagent	Product	Remarks	Ref.
Diethyl ether	$WOCl_4 \cdot O(C_2H_5)_2$	M.p. 54–57°	109
Methyl cyanide	$WOCl_4 \cdot MeCN$	M.p. 133–135°	109
Pyridine	$WOCl_4 \cdot (C_5H_5N)_2$	Decomposes	109
Aniline	$WO(C_6H_5NH_2)_4Cl_4$	Yellow-green	110
Phenol	$WO(C_6H_5OH)_4$		111

The dioxide dichlorides are volatile white solids, that are readily hydrolysed in air. The tungsten compound is thermally less stable than its molybdenum analogue, giving unspecified decomposition products[117]; it is quite insoluble in dry organic solvents, whereas molybdenum dioxide dichloride is soluble in many organic solvents to the extent of about 1 % w/w[97,117].

TABLE 6.13

Preparation of the Dioxide Dichlorides

Reaction	Conditions	Ref.
Cl_2–O_2 mixture on Mo	Flow system, 250–350°	96
Cl_2 on MoO_2	350–550°	112, 113
O_2–CCl_4 mixture on MoO_2	360°	114
NaCl and MoO_3	400–700°	115
$MoCl_5$ and MoO_3	120–130°	91
Cl_2 on MoO_3	Flow system, 650°	96
Cl_2–O_2 mixture on MoS_2		89
O_2–CCl_4 mixture on WO_2		114
Cl_2–N_2 mixture on WO_2	500–550°	105
CCl_4 on WO_2	Bomb, 250°	103
CCl_4 on WO_3	Bomb, 310–370°	61
Cl_2 on WO_3–C mixture	600°	106
HCl–CCl_4 mixture on WO_3	600°	116

Despite the ready hydrolysis of the dioxide dichlorides, they are stabilized in aqueous solution in a high concentration of hydrochloric acid, as shown by extraction studies[118,119].

The vapour-pressure equation for solid molybdenum dioxide dichloride is[120]:

$$\log p_{atm} = 9.84 - 4270/T.$$

The vapour pressure of the dioxide dichloride has been reported at several temperatures by other workers[121], and the two sets of results differ markedly, for example, at 142.5° the values are 276 mm[120] and 314 mm[121].

Tungsten dioxide dichloride sublimes and decomposes simultaneously at 260°, according to the equation[122];

$$2WO_2Cl_2(g) \rightleftarrows WO_3(s) + WOCl_4(g)$$

and the overall vapour pressure is given by the expression:

$$\log p_{mm} = 13.55 - 6750/T.$$

Thermodynamic measurements on the dioxide dichlorides are numerous and the results are given in Table 6.14.

TABLE 6.14

Thermodynamic Parameters^a for MoO_2Cl_2 and WO_2Cl_2

Property		MoO_2Cl_2	Ref.	WO_2Cl_2	Ref.
M.p.		170°	120		
		175°	98		
B.p.		250°	98		
ΔH°_{form}	(s)	−169.8	112	−200	72
		−173.1	100		
		−173.0	72		
	(g)			−179	72
ΔH_{sub}				26.3	122
				21	72
ΔS°_{form}	(s)			96	72
	(g)			67	72
ΔS_{sub}				39.6	122
				29	72

^{a} ΔH in kcal mole^{-1}; ΔS in cal deg^{-1} mole^{-1}.

For the reaction $2WO_2Cl_2(s) \rightleftarrows WOCl_4(g) + WO_3(s)$

ΔH_{diss} 36.0 kcal mole^{-1} (references 73, 74)

              30.5 kcal mole^{-1} (reference 122)

              29   kcal mole^{-1} (reference 72)

ΔS_{diss} 56.2 cal deg^{-1} mole^{-1} (references 73, 74)

              47.3 cal deg^{-1} mole^{-1} (reference 122)

              43   cal deg^{-1} mole^{-1} (reference 72)

For the reaction $3WO_2Cl_2 \rightleftarrows WCl_6 + 2WO_3(s)$

ΔH_{diss} 56.0 kcal mole^{-1} (references 73, 74)

ΔS_{diss} 82.0 cal deg^{-1} mole^{-1} (references 73, 74)

Tungsten dioxide dichloride crystallizes in an orthorhombic lattice[116] with unit-cell dimensions $a = 3.87$, $b = 3.892$ and $c = 13.882$ Å.

Much structural information on both dioxide dichlorides has been obtained from a study of their infrared spectra in the solid, solution and gas phases[117]. The infrared data to 300 cm^{-1} are given in Tables 6.15 and 6.16, where they are compared with the spectra of the trioxides.

The absence in the solid state of stretching frequencies that can be assigned to metal–oxygen double bonds leads to the suggestion that the structure consists of an infinite lattice containing bridging oxygen atoms.

TABLE 6.15

Infrared Spectra[a] of MoO_2Cl_2 and MoO_3

$MoO_3(s)$	$MoO_2Cl_2(s)$	MoO_2Cl_2 (acetone soln.)	$MoO_2Cl_2(g)$	Assignment
992s		963	992	M=O Stretch
			972	
	910m	926s		⎫
868s	864s			⎬ Mo–O–Mo–O
822sh	827sh	821w		⎬ stretches
	781s	763m		⎭
590s				
487sh				
	401m		453	Mo–Cl stretch
		342s	437	

[a] s = strong, m = medium, w = weak, sh = shoulder.

TABLE 6.16

Infrared Spectra[a] of WO_2Cl_2 and WO_3

$WO_3(s)$	$WO_2Cl_2(s)$	$WO_2Cl_2(g)$	Assignment
		984	W=O stretch
		972	
	843sh		⎫
860sh	819s		⎬ W–O–W–O
820s	767s		⎬ stretches
760s	638m		⎭
	403w		W–Cl stretch

[a] s = strong, m = medium, w = weak, sh = shoulder.

With the additional evidence that there is only one type of environment for chlorine atoms, deduced from nuclear quadrapole spectroscopy[123], the annexed structure has been suggested for these isostructural compounds[117], rather than the alternative chlorine-bridged structure proposed earlier[124].

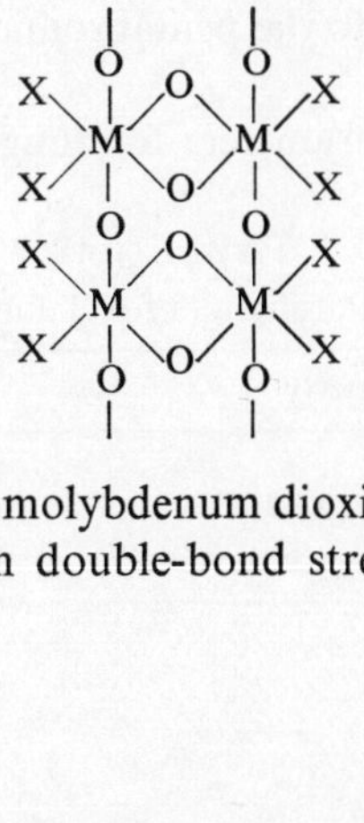

The solution spectrum of molybdenum dioxide dichloride shows a band assigned to a metal–oxygen double-bond stretching frequency, and the suggestion has been made[117] that in solution the compound exists predominantly as dimers. In the vapour phase the compounds are predominantly monomeric; some confirmatory evidence is provided for these ideas by a mass spectrometric study[117] which shows the compounds to be mainly monomeric with a small proportion of dimer.

Gaseous ammonia reacted with tungsten dioxide dichloride at room temperature to give tungsten dioxide[77]. Molybdenum dioxide dichloride reacted with liquid ammonia at −33°, and the product[102] appeared to be a mixture of ammonium chloride and $MoO_2(NH_2)_2$.

A number of donor molecules form adducts with molybdenum and tungsten dioxide dichloride, and some of these are given in Table 6.17. It appears that the adducts are all likely to be six-coordinate monomeric species.

TABLE 6.17

Reactions of the Dioxide Dichlorides

Reagent	Product	Ref.
Triphenylphosphine oxide	$MoO_2Cl_2 \cdot 2(C_6H_5)_3PO$	125
Ethers and nitriles	$MoO_2Cl_2 \cdot xL$ ($x = 1$ or 2)	126
Dimethylformamide	$MoO_2Cl_2 \cdot 2DMF$	99
Tributyl phosphate	$WO_2Cl_2 \cdot 2TBP$	119
Pyridine	$MoO_2Cl_2 \cdot 2py$	127

Tungsten hexabromide. This compound can be prepared by the action of bromine vapour, carried in a stream of nitrogen, on gently heated tungsten metal[128]. It has also been prepared by the action of liquid bromine on tungsten carbonyl at room temperature[70]. Tungsten hexabromide is one of a number of products obtained[129] by the action of carbon tetrabromide on the trioxide in a sealed tube at 200°.

Tungsten hexabromide is a blue-black lustrous solid, which on careful sublimation forms long needles. It is very sensitive to moisture and reacts slowly with oxygen at room temperature to give oxide bromides. Above 200° it begins to dissociate to the pentabromide; the reaction is reversible on cooling[70].

Some thermodynamic parameters for tungsten hexabromide are given in Table 6.18.

TABLE 6.18

Thermodynamic Parameters for Tungsten Hexabromide

Property	Value	Ref.
M.p.	309°	130
ΔH°_{form} (kcal mole^{-1})	−92	131
ΔH_{diss} (to WBr$_5$) (kcal mole^{-1})	11.2	70

Tungsten oxide tetrabromide. This compound has been prepared by the action of carbon tetrabromide on the dioxide[103] at 250° and on the trioxide[129,132] at between 200° and 490°.

It forms long black needles[130], melting at 321°, which are instantly hydrolysed in air. It may be purified by vacuum-sublimation[132]. The heat of formation has been given[132] as −139.2 kcal mole⁻¹.

Tungsten oxide tetrabromide is isostructural[107,108] with the corresponding oxide tetrachloride, consisting of chains of metal–oxygen linkages parallel to the *c*-axis. The tetragonal cell has $a = 8.96$ and $c = 3.93$ Å. The tungsten–bromine distance is 2.54 Å.

Molybdenum and tungsten dioxide dibromide. Molybdenum dioxide dibromide is best prepared[96] by passing a mixture of oxygen and bromine, diluted with nitrogen, over the metal at 300°. A similar method has been used for the corresponding tungsten compound[117]. Tungsten dioxide dibromide has also been prepared by the action of carbon tetrabromide on tungsten trioxide[129] in a bomb at 200° and by the action of bromine on tungsten dioxide[132] in a sealed tube at 440–490°.

Both dioxide dibromides are relatively stable, although some decomposition of the tungsten compound has been noted during purification by sublimation[117]. The compounds form purple-brown crystals which are hydrolysed in air[96].

The heats of formation of the dioxide dibromides are −148.6 and −179.7 kcal mole⁻¹ for molybdenum and tungsten, respectively[132,133].

Barraclough and Stals[117] showed that the dioxide dibromides are isostructural with the corresponding dioxide dichlorides, and their infrared spectra in the solid, solution, and gas phases are very similar to those of the chlorides.

Oxidation State V

Molybdenum pentafluoride. The best method of preparing molybdenum pentafluoride is by the reduction of molybdenum hexafluoride with an excess of phosphorus trifluoride at room temperature[46]. Several other methods have been reported in the literature and these are summarized in Table 6.19.

Molybdenum pentafluoride was first prepared by the interaction of fluorine and hexacarbonylmolybdenum at −75°. The initial product isolated is an olive-green solid of approximate composition Mo_2F_9, and heating this product under a vacuum at 170° produces the volatile yellow pentafluoride, the involatile light green tetrafluoride remaining behind[7]. Nothing is known of the constitution of the residue reported as Mo_2F_9 and it may be merely a mixture of the tetra- and penta-fluoride.

TABLE 6.19

Preparation of Molybdenum Pentafluoride

Method	Conditions	Ref.
$Mo(CO)_6$ and F_2	$-75°$	7
MoF_6 and $Mo(CO)_6$	Excess of MoF_6	13
MoF_6 and $W(CO)_6$		13
Mo and MoF_6	Flow system, 300–400°	13
F_2/N_2 mixture over Mo	400°	13
$Mo(CO)_6$ and ReF_6		134

Molybdenum pentafluoride undergoes irreversible disproportionation above 165° according to the equation[54]:

$$2MoF_5 \rightarrow MoF_4 + MoF_6$$

It forms a very viscous liquid and there is evidence for both association and dissociation in the liquid state[54].

The vapour pressure in the range 70–160° is given by the expression[54]:

$$\log p_{mm} = 8.58 - 2772/T,$$

and the resulting thermodynamic parameters are given in Table 6.20.

X-ray diffraction studies on a single crystal have established that molybdenum pentafluoride exists as a tetramer in the solid state[13]. The four molybdenum atoms and the four bridging fluorine atoms are coplanar, as described in Chapter 1. The structure is monoclinic with the following unit-cell characteristics: $a = 9.61$, $b = 14.22$, $c = 5.16$ Å and $\beta = 94.35°$. There are eight molecules in the unit cell.

Nothing has been reported on the chemistry of this interesting compound, except that acid–base studies in anhydrous hydrogen fluoride show

TABLE 6.20

Thermodynamic Properties of Molybdenum
Pentafluoride

Property	Value	Ref.
M.p.	64°	7
B.p. (extrapolated)	214°	54
Triple point	67°	54
ΔH_{vap} (kcal mole^{-1})	12.37	54
ΔS_{vap} (cal deg^{-1} mole^{-1})	24.4	54

it to be a very much weaker fluoride ion acceptor (Lewis acid) than antimony pentafluoride and arsenic pentafluoride[135].

Molybdenum pentachloride. The usual and most convenient method[96] of preparation of molybdenum pentachloride is chlorination of the metal at 400°. The impurity of oxide tetrachloride, which is responsible for the greenish colour described by earlier workers, is readily removed by sublimation at a temperature below the melting point of the pentachloride. Other less convenient methods of preparation include the action of carbon tetrachloride in a bomb at 400° on the trioxide[62] and on the trisulphide[63].

Molybdenum pentachloride is a black, shiny, crystalline solid, which melts at 194.4° to a dark, almost black liquid[64]. The vapour is reddish-brown. The compound is instantly hydrolysed by water and reacts slowly with oxygen at room temperature. It is soluble to the extent of 1–4% by weight in dichloroethane, carbon tetrachloride or chloroform to give red solutions[97], but air must be rigorously excluded to avoid instant oxidation to the oxide tetrachloride[96].

Russian work[64] shows the density of liquid molybdenum pentachloride from the melting point to 400° is given by the expression:

$$\rho = 2.196 - 2.11 \times 10^{-3}\Delta t.$$

In the vapour phase molybdenum pentachloride is monomeric and is probably a trigonal bipyramid[67] with a mean molybdenum–chlorine distance of 2.27 Å. However, in the solid state molybdenum pentachloride assumes the dimeric niobium pentachloride structure[136]. The crystals are monoclinic and the unit-cell parameters are $a = 17.31$, $b = 17.81$, $c = 6.097$ Å and $\beta = 95.7°$. The space group is $C2/m$ and there are twelve $MoCl_5$ units in the unit cell. The molybdenum–chlorine bond distances are 2.24 Å (terminal) and 2.53 Å (bridge).

The magnetic properties of molybdenum pentachloride have been examined over a wide temperature range. A Curie law is obeyed and the magnetic moment[96] is 1.67 BM. This figure is somewhat higher than previous values, probably because earlier samples contained variable amounts of the diamagnetic oxide tetrachloride[137,138]. Nevertheless, the result is higher than expected because, if no magnetic interaction occurred between the molybdenum atoms, a lower value should result from spin-orbit coupling, as is observed for the hexachloromolybdate(v) anion.

It is remarkable that the temperature variation of the vapour pressure of molybdenum pentachloride has not been reported in detail. However, a considerable number of thermodynamic data have been accumulated, as shown in Table 6.21.

The absorption spectrum of molybdenum pentachloride has been measured in solution and in the gas phase[139]. Only charge-transfer bands were observed, so no detailed information could be obtained. However, it was noted that in solution a band attributable to free chlorine was observed, suggesting some reduction to lower chlorides had occurred. The solution spectrum was similar to that of the gas phase, suggesting that molybdenum pentachloride is perhaps monomeric in solution[139].

TABLE 6.21

Thermodynamic Properties[a] of
Molybdenum Pentachloride

Property	Value	Ref.
ΔH°_{form}	−126.6	100
ΔH_{sub}	21.7	73
	22	74
	18.3	72
ΔH_{vap}	13.9	73
	14	74
ΔS°_{form}	77	72
ΔS_{sub}	43.5	73
	43	74
	35.6	72
ΔS_{vap}	25.3	73
	25	74
For the reaction $MoCl_5 \rightarrow MoCl_4 + \frac{1}{2}Cl_2$		
ΔH_{diss}	12.8	73
	13	74
	12.3	72
ΔS_{diss}	14.8	73
	15	74
	14.6	72

[a] ΔH in kcal mole^{-1}; ΔS in cal deg^{-1} mole^{-1}.

It is reported that molybdenum pentachloride is reduced in carbon tetrachloride at room temperature to give the tetrachloride[140], but this does not agree with other observations[96,97] and it is possible that oxygen was present and produced the oxide tetrachloride. Pentacarbonyliron reacts with molybdenum pentachloride in a bomb at 190° under a carbon monoxide pressure, to give hexacarbonylmolybdenum in fairly low yield[141]. Rather ill-defined compounds are produced by the action of liquid ammonia at −33° or at room temperature in a sealed tube[142]. At −33° a product analysing close to $MoCl_3 \cdot (NH_2)_2 \cdot NH_3$ was obtained, whose magnetic moment indicated that the metal was still pentavalent.

The authors suggest the compound is polymeric but it is not clear why this should be so since the complex is already six coordinate. At room temperature, the product formulated on the basis of analyses as $MoCl(NH)(NH_2)_2$ was formed[142]. Ammonium chloride was observed to react with molybdenum pentachloride very readily[143]; free chlorine was evolved, and it was suggested that the initial product was $(NH_4)_2MoCl_6$, analogous to the alkali-metal chloride reactions (see complexes, p. 250). However, the ammonium salt is thermally unstable and at 400° the final product analysed as MoNCl.

TABLE 6.22

Some Reactions of Molybdenum Pentachloride

Reagent	Product	Ref.
Diethyl ether	$MoCl_5 \cdot O(C_2H_5)_2$	145
Pyridine	$MoCl_5 \cdot xC_5H_5N$ (x = 3, 4 or 5)	145
Phosphorus pentachloride	$MoCl_5 \cdot PCl_5$	146
Phosphorus oxide trichloride	$MoCl_5 \cdot POCl_3$	147
Alkyl cyanides	$MoCl_4 \cdot 2RCN$ (R = Me, Et, or *n*-Pr)	148
Thiocyanates	$Mo(NCS)_5 \cdot 2Solvate$	
	(Solvate = acetone, ethyl methyl ketone)	83

An excess of disulphur dichloride reacted with molybdenum penta-chloride slowly at 250° and gave a solid which analysed as MoS_2Cl_3, but the authors suggested that this was in fact a dimeric molecule $Mo_2S_4Cl_6$, presumably containing a sulphur–sulphur linkage[144].

A number of donor molecules react with molybdenum pentachloride and some of these reactions are reported in Table 6.22.

Several investigators have attempted to prepare complexes of molybdenum pentachloride, but they obtained derivatives of molybdenum oxide trichloride which arose from the presence of oxygen or water in the system[125,145,149]. The products of reaction between molybdenum penta-chloride and monocarboxylic acids were formulated as $MoCl_3 \cdot 2L$, but the description of their properties strongly suggests[150] that they should be formulated as $MoOCl_3 \cdot 2L$.

Tungsten pentachloride. Until recently, the usual method of preparation of tungsten pentachloride was reduction of the hexachloride with hydrogen[151]. However, this method is not easy to control because of further reduction to lower chlorides. A much more convenient and efficient method is to reduce the hexachloride with red phosphorus[152].

Tungsten pentachloride is a black crystalline solid, which is extremely sensitive to moisture and oxygen. It may be sublimed in a vacuum or in

TABLE 6.23

Thermodynamic Data[a] for Tungsten
Pentachloride

Property	Value	Ref.
M.p.	244°	60
	230°	69
B.p.	286°	69
ΔH°_{form}	−137	72
ΔH_{sub}	18.5	72, 122
	16.7	69
ΔH_{vap}	13.6	72, 122
	15.7	69
ΔS°_{form}	71	72
ΔS_{sub}	33.1	72, 122
	30.3	69
ΔS_{vap}	23.9	72, 122
	28.3	69

For the reaction $2WCl_5 \rightarrow WCl_4 + WCl_6$
(250–800°)

ΔH_{diss}	6	72, 154
ΔS_{diss}	5	72, 154

[a] ΔH in kcal mole^{-1}; ΔS in cal deg^{-1} mole^{-1}.

pure nitrogen[153]. The structure of solid tungsten pentachloride is unknown, but its magnetic properties suggest that it is different from the molybdenum compound and that it may contain trinuclear clusters of tungsten atoms. The magnetic moment is 1.00 BM per tungsten atom, independent of temperature[138,153].

Thermodynamic data for tungsten pentachloride are listed in Table 6.23.

Tungsten pentachloride forms an adduct, $WCl_5 \cdot PCl_5$ when treated with phosphorus pentachloride in phosphorus oxide trichloride as solvent[146]. Alkyl cyanides cause reduction of tungsten pentachloride to compounds of the general type[148] $WCl_4 \cdot 2RCN$. These dark brown compounds are non-electrolytes, and the *n*-propyl cyanide complex is monomeric in benzene solution. The magnetic moments of the cyanide complexes are severely depressed from the spin-only values, and this is ascribed to spin–orbit coupling. These complexes are good starting materials for the preparation of other tungsten derivatives since the RCN group is readily replaced by other ligands.

It is reported that trimethylamine reacts with tungsten pentachloride to give $NHMe_3(WCl_5 \cdot NMe_3)$ since a nitrogen–hydrogen stretching frequency was observed in its infrared spectrum[155]. Tungsten pentachloride undergoes ready methanolysis to a series of mixed chloride methoxides[156].

Molybdenum and tungsten oxide trichloride. Tungsten oxide trichloride has only very recently been prepared by the reaction[157] of the oxide tetrachloride with aluminium powder in a sealed tube at 100–140°. It is an olive-green solid which is only slightly paramagnetic ($\chi'_m = 60 \times 10^{-6}$), and its infrared spectrum shows a strong band at 796 cm^{-1} assigned to a metal–oxygen single-bond stretch. The authors suggest that the compound has the NbOCl$_3$ structure, with magnetic interaction between the tungsten atoms; indeed, the X-ray powder diffraction pattern can be indexed on the basis of a tetragonal cell ($a = 10.7$ and $c = 3.8$ Å) similar to that of niobium oxide trichloride.

Molybdenum oxide trichloride was first isolated after reaction of molybdenum pentachloride with molybdenum trioxide or of molybdenum pentachloride with molybdenum dioxide dichloride[91,158]. An interesting method of preparation is by the slow action of liquid sulphur dioxide on molybdenum pentachloride in a sealed tube at room temperature[159]. A similar reaction occurs slowly with thionyl chloride[96]. Molybdenum oxide tetrachloride has been thermally decomposed, quantitatively, to the oxide trichloride[96]. Care must be taken not to heat the oxide trichloride above 200°, otherwise disproportionation occurs[96] (see below). It has recently been shown that molybdenum oxide tetrachloride can be smoothly reduced in refluxing chlorobenzene[99]. Wardlaw and Webb[145] were the first to state clearly that if molybdenum pentachloride is placed in wet solvents then molybdenum oxide trichloride is formed in solution. This has since been confirmed inadvertently by several groups of workers.

Molybdenum oxide trichloride is a black crystalline solid, instantly hydrolysed in moist air. It dissolves in hydrochloric acid to give a solution of the oxopentachloromolybdate(v) anion[96,159]. The magnetic moment at room temperature is 1.62 BM and it has been suggested that the compound has the NbOCl$_3$ structure[159]. Molybdenum oxide trichloride is thermally unstable, and decomposes according to the equation[98]:

$$3MoOCl_3 \rightarrow MoCl_3 + MoOCl_4 + MoO_2Cl_2$$

The vapour pressure of molybdenum oxide trichloride varies with temperature according to the equation[98]:

$$\log p_{atm} = 8.764 - 5484/T.$$

Decomposition was found to begin at 215° and the extrapolated boiling point[98] is 352°. From the vapour-pressure measurements the heat of sublimation was found to be 25 kcal mole^{-1} and the entropy of sublimation 40 cal deg^{-1} mole^{-1}.

A large number of adducts with donor molecules have been characterized. Some were prepared directly by reaction with molybdenum oxide trichloride, others from molybdenum pentachloride by oxygen abstraction from the ligand or from wet solvents. Some of these adducts are given in Table 6.24. Most of the adducts are green crystalline solids. Molybdenum oxide trichloride is reported[102] to react with liquid ammonia at $-33°$ to give $MoOCl \cdot (NH_2)_2 \cdot NH_3$ which is thought to contain molybdenum–oxygen chains.

TABLE 6.24

Some Adducts of Molybdenum Oxide Trichloride

Adduct	Properties	Ref.
$MoOCl_3 \cdot 2C_4H_8O$	$\mu = 1.73$ BM	160
$MoOCl_3 \cdot 2C_4H_8S$	$\mu = 1.75$ BM	160
$MoOCl_3 \cdot 2RCN$	$\mu = 1.7$ BM, very sensitive to moisture	161
$MoOCl_3 \cdot 2PPh_3$	$\nu_{M=O}$ 920 cm^{-1}	161
$MoOCl_3 \cdot Bipy$	$\nu_{M=O}$ 920 cm^{-1}	161
$MoOCl_3 \cdot (C_6H_5)_2CO$	M.p. = 156–161°, associated in soln.	99
$MoOCl_3 \cdot 2C_5H_5N$	$\nu_{M=O}$ 966 cm^{-1}	99
$MoOCl_3 \cdot 2(C_6H_5)_3PO$	$\mu = 1.65$ BM	125

Tungsten pentabromide. Tungsten pentabromide is prepared by the action of bromine vapour on tungsten metal at 450–500°; the reaction is slow but quantitative[70,153]. However, it is recommended that, before bromination, the metal be refluxed with thionyl chloride to remove oxide film from the metal since as little as 3% of oxygen in the metal suffices to lead to tungsten oxide tetrabromide instead of the pentabromide[153].

Tungsten pentabromide is a black crystalline solid, which is extremely sensitive to moisture. It is thermally stable and may be readily purified by vacuum-sublimation[153].

The magnetic properties of tungsten pentabromide have been examined over a wide temperature range, and the results have been interpreted as evidence for the presence of trinuclear clusters of tungsten atoms in the solid[153].

Thermodynamic properties have not been reported for tungsten pentabromide.

Tungsten pentabromide reacts with alkyl cyanides[148] to give dark brown complexes of tungsten(IV) of the general type $WBr_4 \cdot 2RCN$. With trimethylamine[155], it forms $NHMe_3(WBr_5NMe_3)$.

Molybdenum oxide tribromide. This compound has been prepared[96] by reaction of molybdenum dioxide dibromide with phosphorus pentabromide in refluxing carbon tetrachloride. The product was washed with hot carbon tetrachloride several times and then purified by vacuum-sublimation at 270–300°.

Oxidation State IV

Molybdenum and tungsten tetrafluoride. These two tetrafluorides are not well characterized. None of the methods of preparation reported and listed in Table 6.25 is fully satisfactory.

TABLE 6.25

Preparation of Molybdenum and Tungsten Tetrafluorides

Method	Conditions	Ref.
$MoF_5 \rightarrow MoF_4 + MoF_6$	>170°	7, 13
MoS_2–SF_4	Bomb, 350°	11
WF_6–HF–PF_3	Room temp., low yield	4
WF_6–Benzene	Bomb, 110°	162

Molybdenum tetrafluoride is reported as a pale green solid and the tungsten compound is red brown. Both are hygroscopic and non-volatile. The molybdenum compound has been found to react with organic bases[163].

Tungsten oxide difluoride. This compound has been briefly mentioned[162] as a product of the action of anhydrous hydrogen fluoride on tungsten dioxide at 500°. It is a grey, very inert solid, but no other information is available.

Molybdenum tetrachloride. Molybdenum tetrachloride has been prepared[164] in 100% yield by interaction of molybdenum trichloride and a slight excess of molybdenum pentachloride in a sealed tube at 250°. Alternatively, carbon tetrachloride[63] may be treated with molybdenum dioxide in a sealed tube at 250°. Another method of preparation involves refluxing molybdenum pentachloride in benzene[165]. It was claimed that the action of chlorine dissolved in refluxing hexachlorobutadiene on molybdenum dioxide gave molybdenum tetrachloride[166], but it was later stated[167] that the method is not completely reliable.

The standard heat of formation is given[72] as −114 kcal mole^{-1} and the corresponding entropy is estimated[72] as 65 cal deg^{-1} mole^{-1}.

Tungsten tetrachloride. Early methods of preparation of the tetrachloride included reduction of the hexachloride with hydrogen and chlorination of the dioxide with carbon tetrachloride in a sealed tube. More recently, tungsten tetrachloride has been prepared[152] by reduction of tungsten hexachloride with phosphorus trichloride at 250°. Traces of tungsten oxide tetrachloride are of no consequence in this preparation because of the additional reaction:

$$WOCl_4 + PCl_3 \rightarrow WCl_4 + POCl_3$$

Finally, aluminium foil has been used[168] to reduce the hexachloride to the tetrachloride. The aluminium was placed at one end of an evacuated tube and maintained at 475° and the hexachloride at the other end at 225°. The tetrachloride was formed as a coarse crystalline deposit at the cool end of the tube.

TABLE 6.26

Thermodynamic Data for Tungsten Tetrachloride

Property	Value (kcal mole^{-1})	Property	Value (cal deg^{-1} mole^{-1})	Ref.
ΔH_{form}°	−121	ΔS_{form}°	65	72
ΔH_{sub}	39	ΔS_{sub}	50	72
ΔH_{diss}	66	ΔS_{diss}	90	72, 154

Tungsten tetrachloride is diamagnetic and it is believed to be isostructural with niobium and tantalum tetrachloride[168].

Tungsten tetrachloride is thermally unstable, disproportionating according to the equation[72,169]:

$$3WCl_4 \rightarrow WCl_2 + 2WCl_5$$

Thermodynamic data are noted in Table 6.26.

Adducts of tungsten tetrachloride have been prepared only indirectly. Potassium hexachlorotungstate(IV) reacts[170] with pyridine to give $WCl_4 \cdot 2C_5H_5N$. Tungsten hexachloride is reduced by pyridine to the same compound[168].

Molybdenum oxide dichloride. This compound has been prepared by the temperature-gradient method in several ways[171], for example:

$$MoO_3 + 2MoCl_3 \rightarrow 3MoOCl_2$$
$$5MoO_3 + 6MoCl_5 + 4Mo \rightarrow 15MoOCl_2$$

It is diamagnetic and isostructural with the corresponding niobium and tantalum compounds. The monoclinic lattice has the unit-cell parameters $a = 12.77$, $b = 3.759$, $c = 6.54$ Å and $\beta = 104.8°$. There are four molecular units in the unit cell.

Molybdenum tetrabromide. Reaction of liquid bromine at room temperature on hexacarbonyl molybdenum yields the tetrabromide[172], and the compound has also been prepared[173] by the disproportionation of molybdenum dibromide at 900–1100°:

$$2MoBr_2 \rightarrow MoBr_4 + Mo$$

Molybdenum tetrabromide itself is thermally unstable, decomposing according to the equation:

$$2MoBr_4 \rightarrow 2MoBr_3 + Br_2$$

so it must be removed from the reaction zone quickly.

The magnetic moment of molybdenum tetrabromide[138] varies from 1.02 BM at 90°K to 1.28 BM at 293°K.

Tungsten tetrabromide. Tungsten tetrabromide was first prepared by reduction of tungsten pentabromide with tungsten metal by the temperature-gradient method[174]. The pentabromide was placed at one end of an evacuated tube and maintained at 340°, and tungsten metal at the other end was held at 630°. The method gives a pure product but is very slow. Subsequently, it was found that aluminium is a much more efficient reducing agent than tungsten, and the conditions used are very similar to those described for tungsten tetrachloride[168].

Adducts of tungsten tetrabromide have only been prepared by indirect methods, as for the tetrachloride; for example, potassium hexabromotungstate(IV) reacts with pyridine[170] to give $WBr_4 \cdot 2C_5H_5N$.

Oxidation State III

Molybdenum trifluoride. This compound was first prepared by passing anhydrous hydrogen fluoride over molybdenum tribromide at 600°, the product being a dark pink powder[2]. It may also be prepared in small amounts by heating molybdenum powder with anhydrous hydrogen fluoride in a bomb at 225° for 24 hours[175]. LaValle and coworkers[176] reinvestigated the preparation and properties of molybdenum trifluoride and found that it could be prepared by reduction of molybdenum pentafluoride with molybdenum metal at 400° or with antimony trifluoride at 200°. They found that the colour of the product varied considerably with the experimental conditions.

LaValle and coworkers[176] found molybdenum trifluoride to be stable to 520° in vacuum, but it decomposed at 600° to the metal and higher fluorides. On the other hand, Eméleus and Gutmann[2] found their product to be stable up to 800°. There is evidently some disagreement on the physical properties of this trifluoride and this situation is made worse by conflicting structural data.

Samples prepared by hydrofluorination of the tribromide have been stated[177] to have a simple ReO_3 cubic lattice with $a = 3.899$ Å whereas LaValle and coworkers found their sample to be rhombohedral with $a = 5.78$ Å and $\alpha = 54.72°$. They concluded that a cubic form of the trifluoride may exist, but found that the presence of small amounts of oxygen or water led to the formation of an oxide fluoride which in fact had a cubic lattice with a unit cell close to that reported by Gutmann and Jack[177] for the trifluoride. It is probable that there is a range of non-stoichiometric oxide fluorides of similar types to those well-established for niobium.

Wilkinson and coworkers[178] have studied the magnetic ordering in the molybdenum trifluoride lattice using NMR techniques; they found that the compound was antiferromagnetic below 185°K.

Nothing is known of the chemistry of molybdenum trifluoride.

Molybdenum trichloride. The best methods of preparation of molybdenum trichloride are by the hydrogen reduction of molybdenum pentachloride[164] in a bomb at 125° and by thermal decomposition of molybdenum pentachloride in a stream of nitrogen[179]. In the latter process, care must be taken to ensure that the trichloride is not overheated, otherwise some molybdenum dichloride is formed. Less satisfactory methods include reaction between molybdenum metal and mercurous chloride[180], hydrogen reduction of a mixture of molybdenum pentachloride and calcium oxide at 140° in an autoclave[181] and chlorination of molybdenum disulphide[89]. A hydrated soluble form of molybdenum trichloride has been prepared by electrolytic reduction of molybdenum trioxide in hydrochloric acid solutions[182].

One polymorph of molybdenum trichloride forms a unique stratified lattice with layers parallel to the (001) plane[183]. The monoclinic unit cell has the parameters $a = 6.065$, $b = 9.760$, $c = 7.250$ Å and $\beta = 124°$. The molybdenum atoms occur in pairs, 2.77 Å apart, and the shortest distance between layers is 3.70 Å. Each molybdenum atom is surrounded by a distortion octahedron of chlorine atoms, the molybdenum–chlorine distances falling into three pairs: two at 2.40 Å, two at 2.45 Å and the remaining two at 2.55 Å. This form of molybdenum trichloride is diamagnetic[183]. A different form is obtained by thermal decomposition of molybdenum pentachloride. This polymorph is paramagnetic and, from a detailed study of its magnetic behaviour over a wide temperature range, together with spectral and mass-spectral evidence, it has been suggested that this form contains trinuclear clusters of molybdenum atoms[179].

Few thermodynamic properties has been reported for molybdenum trichloride. The heat of formation has been given[72] as -94 kcal mole^{-1}, and the corresponding entropy as 43 cal deg^{-1} mole^{-1}. From the reaction[72]

$$2MoCl_3 \rightarrow MoCl_2 + MoCl_4$$

the heat of dissociation is 28 kcal mole^{-1} and the entropy of dissociation is 23 cal deg^{-1} mole^{-1}.

With pyridine, molybdenum trichloride gives[184] the yellow-brown adduct $MoCl_3 \cdot 3C_5H_5N$ which has a room temperature magnetic moment of 3·79 BM.

Molybdenum tribromide. Molybdenum tribromide has been prepared by thermal decomposition of the tetrabromide[173]. A more direct and rather general method involves reaction of molybdenum metal with bromine in ether solution at room temperature[185]. Direct bromination of the metal at 650–700° produces involatile molybdenum dibromide and the comparatively volatile molybdenum tribromide, but the reaction is slow[186].

Molybdenum tribromide forms fibrous dark green needles; although the structure is unknown, its physical properties strongly suggest some sort of chain structure. It is insoluble in, and unaffected by, water.

Molybdenum tribromide is antiferromagnetic[138], the effective magnetic moment varying from 0.39 BM at 90°K to 1.24 BM at 293°K.

Few chemical properties of molybdenum tribromide have been reported. It does not react with liquid ammonia at $-33°$, but at room temperature one molybdenum–bromine bond is ammonolysed[184] to give a product close to $MoBr_2 \cdot NH_2 \cdot 3NH_3$. With methylamine the product was formulated as $BrMo{=}NMe$ and with pyridine the compound $MoBr_3 \cdot 3C_5H_5N$ was obtained[184].

Tungsten tribromide. The preparation of this compound has been reported only comparatively recently; it was made[174] by the action of bromine on tungsten dibromide in a sealed tube at 50°; the reaction is slow, taking about two weeks. Tungsten tribromide is a black powder; it is insoluble in water but slightly soluble in some polar solvents to give wine-red solutions. At 80° it slowly decomposes to the dibromide and bromine but at higher temperatures small amounts of tungsten penta-bromide are formed[174].

Molybdenum and tungsten triiodide. Molybdenum triiodide can be prepared[187] by direct interaction of the metal and iodine in a sealed tube at 300°. It has been reported that it can also be prepared by the action of dry gaseous hydrogen iodide on a carbon disulphide solution of molybdenum pentachloride[188]. Both hexacarbonylmolybdenum and hexacarbonyltungsten react with iodine in a sealed tube (Mo at 105° and W at 120°), to give the respective triiodides[189].

Molybdenum triiodide closely resembles the tribromide in physical form, consisting of fibrous needles and like the tribromide is antiferromagnetic[187].

Both triiodides react with *o*-phenylenebis(dimethylarsine) (D) to give $[MI_2D_2]$, but surprisingly only the molybdenum compound reacts with pyridine[189], the product being $MoI_3 \cdot 3C_5H_5N$.

Oxidation State II

Molybdenum and tungsten dichloride. These two compounds and many of their derivatives have a hexameric structure and are discussed in Chapter 3.

Molybdenum dichloride may be prepared by passing carbonyl chloride over the metal at 600° but the method is inefficient[190]. An alternative route[191] utilizes the thermal disproportionation of molybdenum trichloride at 340°. Tungsten dichloride has been prepared by hydrogen reduction of tungsten hexachloride, but more recent methods have made use of the thermal disproportionation of tungsten tetrachloride[152].

Molybdenum dichloride begins to undergo disproportionation at 530° to give the metal and molybdenum tetrachloride. Very few thermodynamic properties are known but Shchukarev and coworkers[72] have given heats of formation as −69 and −60 kcal mole^{-1} for molybdenum and tungsten dichloride, respectively, and 29 and 30 cal deg^{-1} mole^{-1} for the respective entropies of formation.

Molybdenum dibromide. Molybdenum dibromide was prepared[192] by passing a bromine–nitrogen mixture over molybdenum metal at 600–700°. The heat of formation of the compound has been reported[93] to be −62.4 kcal mole^{-1}. Molybdenum dibromide disproportionates at 900° to give the metal and the tetrabromide.

Molybdenum diiodide. Molybdenum diiodide may be prepared[194] by the action of aluminium iodide on molybdenum trioxide in a sealed tube at 230°. It is also formed by the thermal disproportionation of molybdenum triiodide at 100° in a vacuum[188].

From a study of the reaction of iodine vapour on molybdenum metal in the temperature range 800–1600°K, the heat of formation and the entropy of formation were reported[195] as −25.0 kcal mole^{-1} and 9.5 cal deg^{-1} mole^{-1}, respectively.

COMPLEX HALIDES AND OXIDE HALIDES

A large number of complex halides and oxide halides of molybdenum and tungsten have been reported, but in many cases the compounds have been referred to only once or twice in the literature and it is difficult to judge the credibility of some of the claims. Another difficulty arises in the consideration of complex peroxide fluorides and oxide fluorides. In some cases it is not even clear to which class a particular compound belongs; we have therefore grouped all compounds of this type together at the end of this chapter.

Oxidation State VI

Octafluoromolybdates(VI) and octafluorotungstates(VI). Under strictly anhydrous conditions, alkali-metal fluorides do not react with molybdenum or tungsten hexafluorides[51]. However, in the presence of traces of moisture[51] or in a halogen fluoride solvent[8,9,196] reaction occurs as shown in Table 6.27.

TABLE 6.27

Preparation of Octafluoromolybdates(VI) and
Octafluorotungstates(VI)

Reaction	Solvent	Ref.
KF and $MF_6 \rightarrow K_2MF_8$ (M = Mo or W)	IF_5	8, 9
KI and $WF_6 \rightarrow K_2WF_8$	IF_5	8
KI and $W(CO)_6 \rightarrow K_2WF_8$	IF_5	8
Metal and $CsF \rightarrow Cs_2MF_8$ (M = Mo or W)	BrF_3	196

Sodium octafluorotungstate(VI) has been prepared[11] by heating a mixture of tungstic oxide, sodium fluoride and sulphur tetrafluoride in a bomb at 350°.

In the reaction between gaseous molybdenum or tungsten hexafluoride with sodium fluoride, the method of preparation of the sodium fluoride is critical in determining the reaction product. If sodium fluoride is prepared by thermal decomposition of the sodium fluoride–hydrogen fluoride adduct, then reaction occurs with the hexafluoride at temperatures between 160° and 350° and the octafluoro complexes are formed[197]. However, the reaction is not complete and the complexes are found to dissociate. Sodium fluoride prepared by the thermal decomposition of sodium octafluoro-uranate(VI) and then treated with molybdenum or tungsten hexafluoride gives the heptafluoro anions, and only at higher temperatures are the octafluoromolybdate(VI) and octafluorotungstate(VI) complexes formed[198].

The octafluoro salts are white solids which are easily hydrolysed. They are thermally stable to about 150°. Both potassium salts are cubic with $a = 10.01$ and 10.03 Å for the molybdenum and the tungsten compound, respectively[8,9].

Heptafluoromolybdates(VI) and heptafluorotungstates(VI). As noted above, the sodium heptafluoro complexes can be prepared[198] by the action of the metal hexafluoride vapour at 80° on sodium fluoride prepared from sodium octafluorouranate(VI). The rubidium and caesium heptafluoro salts of both metals have been prepared by interaction of the alkali-metal fluoride and the metal hexafluorides in iodine pentafluoride[8,9]. It is to be noted that if potassium fluoride is substituted for the heavier alkali-metal fluorides the octafluoro salts are obtained.

The heptafluoro complexes are white moisture-sensitive solids, stable to 150° in a vacuum. Both the caesium and the rubidium salts are cubic, but they are obviously not isostructural, as the unit-cell dimensions demonstrate[8,9]:

$RbMoF_7$	$a = 10.25$ Å;	$CsMoF_7$	$a = 5.36$ Å;
$RbWF_7$	$a = 10.27$ Å;	$CsWF_7$	$a = 5.49$ Å.

Oxopentafluoromolybdates(VI) and oxopentafluorotungstates(VI). Rubidium and caesium oxopentafluoromolybdates(VI) and -tungstates(VI) have been prepared by interaction of moist alkali-metal fluoride and the transition-metal hexafluorides in the presence of such solvents as iodine pentafluoride, sulphur dioxide and arsenic trifluoride[8,9]. Sodium oxopentafluorotungstate(VI) has been isolated after reaction between moist sodium iodide and hexacarbonyltungsten in iodine pentafluoride[8].

The oxopentafluoromolybdates(VI) and -tungstates(VI) are white solids. Sodium oxopentafluorotungstate(VI) appears from X-ray powder diffraction measurements to be cubic, with $a = 8.17$ Å. The rubidium and caesium salts are rhombohedral with unit-cell dimensions as shown[8,9]:

$RbMoOF_5$	$a = 5.12$ Å	$\alpha = 96.5°$
$CsMoOF_5$	$a = 5.29$ Å	$\alpha = 96.0°$
$CsWOF_5$	$a = 5.31$ Å	$\alpha = 95.5°$

A number of oxofluoro anions of molybdenum(VI) and tungsten(VI) have been claimed to result from the action of aqueous hydrogen fluoride on the respective trioxides, but few chemical or physical data is available. Those reported are the $[MO_2F_4]^{2-}$ anions[199–202], $[MoO_3F_3]^{3-}$ anions[199,203], $[WO_3F_2 \cdot H_2O]^{2-}$ [203] and $[WO_3F]^-$ anions[202].

Oxochloromolybdates(VI) and oxochlorotungstates(VI). Oxopentachlorotungstates(VI), $MWOCl_5$ [$M = (C_2H_5)_4N^+$ and $C_9H_8N^+$] have been prepared by causing MCl to react with tungsten oxide tetrachloride in chloroform solution. The compounds are soluble in methyl cyanide, and the conductivity of the resulting solution is consistent with the formulation of these compounds as 1:1 electrolytes. Strong absorption bands in their infrared spectra between 960 and 970 cm^{-1} are attributed to metal–oxygen double-bond stretching frequencies. The compounds are diamagnetic and from X-ray powder diffraction patterns, orthorhombic structures have been deduced with the following unit-cell dimensions[204]:

$(C_2H_5)_4N[WOCl_5]$ $a = 11.7$, $b = 12.3$, $c = 21.5$ Å

$C_9H_8N[WOCl_5]$ $a = 11.4$, $b = 12.2$, $c = 21.9$ Å

A series of salts of the dioxotetrachloromolybdate(VI) anion was prepared from a solution of molybdenum trioxide in hydrochloric acid, saturated with the appropriate alkali-metal chloride. The ammonium and potassium salts were obtained as the yellowish dihydrates, the rubidium and caesium salts as yellow anhydrous compounds. These are all readily hydrolysed by water but no further information is available[205]. It was also claimed that salts of the general type $K[MoO_2Cl_3 \cdot H_2O]$ could be obtained from the mother liquor after the dioxotetrachloromolybdates(VI) had been isolated from the potassium, rubidium and caesium systems[205].

Sodium and potassium salts of the trioxochlorotungstate(VI) anion are said[206] to be formed by the interaction of tungstic oxide and the alkali-metal chloride at 600°.

Oxopentabromotungstate(VI). Tetraethylammonium oxopentabromotungstate(VI) has been prepared by interaction of tetraethylammonium bromide with tungsten oxide tetrabromide in chloroform, in a preparation analogous to that of the corresponding chloro compound[204].

Oxidation State V

Octafluoromolybdate(V) and octafluorotungstate(V). The potassium salts of these anions have been prepared by the action of potassium iodide on the metal hexacarbonyl in iodine pentafluoride[8,9]. Potassium octafluoromolybdate(V) has also been prepared by interaction of potassium fluoride and molybdenum hexafluoride in liquid sulphur dioxide[9].

The white solids are stable in dry air, but readily hydrolyse in water to give coloured solutions[8,9]. The molybdenum compound has a magnetic moment at room temperature of 1.23 BM and it has a cubic structure[9], with $a = 14.1$ Å. The tungsten compound, however, appears[8] to be rhombohedral, with $a = 9.75$ Å and $\alpha = 86.4°$.

Hexafluoromolybdates(V) and hexafluorotungstates(V). The best general method of preparation is by reaction of an alkali-metal iodide with the transition-metal hexafluoride in liquid sulphur dioxide[207,208]. All alkali-metal salts except lithium hexafluoromolybdate(V) were prepared by this method. An alternative solvent for the preparation of the molybdenum compounds is iodine pentafluoride[9]. A large number of hexafluoro-molybdates(v) and -tungstates(v) have been prepared by the action of sulphur tetrafluoride on mixtures of alkali-metal fluoride and the transition-metal carbonyl in a bomb at elevated temperatures[209].

The hexafluoromolybdates(v) are white solids, and the corresponding tungstates are slightly brown[208]. The compounds are thermally stable to 200° in a vacuum; but above this temperature they attack glass and the thermal stability was not studied further. They all react violently with water to give blue solutions.

TABLE 6.28

Powder Diffraction Data for MoF_6^- and WF_6^-

Cation	Symmetry	Hexafluoromolybdate(v)	Hexafluorotungstate(v)
Li	Rhombohedral (LiSbF$_6$ type)	$a = 5.43$ Å $\alpha = 57.1°$	$a = 5.45$ Å $\alpha = 57.4°$
Na	Cubic (NaSbF$_6$ type)	$a = 8.15$ Å	$a = 8.18$ Å
K	Tetragonal (KNbF$_6$ type)	$a = 5.88$ Å $c = 9.98$ Å	$a = 5.85$ Å $c = 10.08$ Å
Tl	Rhombohedral (KOsF$_6$ type)	$a = 5.135$ Å $\alpha = 96.13°$	
Rb	Rhombohedral (KOsF$_6$ type)	$a = 5.11$ Å $\alpha = 96.5°$	$a = 5.14$ Å $\alpha = 97.6°$
Cs	Rhombohedral (KOsF$_6$ type)	$a = 5.29$ Å $\alpha = 96.0°$	$a = 5.31$ Å $\alpha = 95.5°$

The infrared spectra of the potassium salts show absorptions assigned to metal–fluorine stretches at 623 cm^{-1} for the hexafluoromolybdate(v) anion and 594 cm^{-1} for the corresponding tungstate(v) anion[210]. The X-ray powder diffraction patterns of the various salts have been examined[207] and the results are given in Table 6.28.

The magnetic properties of the hexafluoromolybdate(v) salts have been examined over a wide temperature range and have been found to conform to Curie–Weiss behaviour as follows[211]:

$$NaMoF_6 \qquad \mu = 1.66 \text{ BM} \qquad \theta = 218°$$
$$KMoF_6 \qquad \mu = 1.51 \text{ BM} \qquad \theta = 66°$$
$$RbMoF_6 \qquad \mu = 1.75 \text{ BM} \qquad \theta = 158°$$
$$CsMoF_6 \qquad \mu = 1.66 \text{ BM} \qquad \theta = 224°$$

The hexafluorotungstates(v) all exhibit antiferromagnetic behaviour[211].

Oxopentafluoromolybdates(v). Potassium oxopentafluoromolybdate(v) has been prepared as a green solid by fusing potassium hexafluoromolybdate(v) with potassium hydrogen fluoride in a carbon dioxide atmosphere and then extracting the melt with moist acetone[208].

The ESR spectra of several oxopentafluoromolybdates(v) have been examined in aqueous hydrogen fluoride solution and showed hyperfine structure attributed to four equivalent fluorine atoms, presumably *cis* to the oxygen atom in an octahedral arrangement[212].

Heptachlorotungstates(v). Heptachlorotungstates(v) have been prepared by the action of alkali-metal chlorides (K, Rb or Cs) on tungsten pentachloride[60,213]. The potassium salt is a dark green crystalline compound, which melts at 386° and begins to evolve tungsten pentachloride at 300° in a vacuum[214]. It is readily hydrolysed in moist air. Its heat of formation has been estimated[214] to be -12.7 kcal mole^{-1}.

Hexachloromolybdates(v). The only well-substantiated preparation of hexachloromolybdate(v) compounds is by interaction of quaternary ammonium chlorides (NMe_4^+ and NEt_4^+) and molybdenum pentachloride in dichloromethane at 70° in a sealed tube[215]. The black crystalline compounds dissolve in methyl cyanide to give conducting solutions. The magnetic moments of the compounds are severely depressed from the spin-only value because of spin-orbit coupling effects.

Hexachlorotungstates(v). Two general methods of preparation of salts of the hexachlorotungstate(v) anion have been reported. Solutions of tungsten hexachloride[216] or tungsten oxide chlorides[217] have been treated with quaternary ammonium chlorides in thionyl chloride solution to give these complexes. Direct interaction of an alkali-metal chloride[60] or iodide[218] with tungsten chlorides has led to the isolation of alkali-metal hexachlorotungstates(v).

A most remarkable observation is that tungsten hexachloride reacts with potassium hexachlorotungstate(IV) when they are ground together at room temperature, to form the hexachlorotungstate(v) salt, although heating to 100° is necessary for the reaction to be quantitative[218]. A rather indirect method[218] for preparing the potassium salt is to fuse tungsten trioxide with potassium carbonate and treat the mixture with carbon tetrachloride in a bomb at 400°.

The hexachlorotungstates(v) are generally green, although the caesium salt is claimed as dark blue[216]. They are hydrolysed in moist air, the potassium salt instantly and the caesium salt more slowly[218]. In the case of the caesium salt, the hydrolysis product has been variously identified as caesium oxopentachlorotungstate(v)[216] and as caesium hexachlorotungstate(IV)[218].

The metal–chlorine stretching frequency[216,217] is in the region 300–330 cm^{-1}. All the hexachlorotungstates(v) are antiferromagnetic[216] with Neél temperatures of 105°K (Cs$^+$), 100°K (NEt$_4^+$) and 140°K (NMe$_4^+$).

The heat of formation of potassium hexachlorotungstate(v) has been estimated[214] as -11.3 kcal mole^{-1}.

Oxopentachloromolybdates(v). The oxopentachloromolybdate(v) anion is the stable form of molybdenum(v) in chloride media. Two general methods of preparing this anion have been used. The first involves reduction of molybdenum(vi) in hydrochloric acid, either chemically[85,219–221] or electrolytically[222,223]. Alternatively, dissolution of molybdenum pentachloride in hydrochloric acid solution followed by addition of alkali-metal chloride leads to the isolation of salts of this anion[224]. Wardlaw and Webb[145] were the first to state clearly that when molybdenum pentachloride is placed into wet solvents or alcohol then the oxopentachloromolybdate(v) anion is formed, as proved by the isolation of various salts.

The oxopentachloromolybdates(v) are green crystalline solids, which are stable indefinitely in dry air. In moderately acid solution they dissolve to give green solutions that are thought to contain the unchanged anion, but as the acidity is decreased the solution assumes a dark colour and polymerization occurs. This phenomenon is discussed in more detail below.

Only a little information is available on the structures of these compounds. The caesium salt is reported[225] to be cubic with the K_2PtCl_6 structure and $a = 10.24$ Å, but the ammonium and rubidium salts are reported to be rhombohedral[221]. The magnetic susceptibility of caesium oxopentachloromolybdate(v) obeys the Curie–Weiss law with $\theta = 10°$ and the magnetic moment was found[225] to be 1.65 BM.

The ultraviolet spectrum of the oxopentachloromolybdate(v) ion has been the subject of some considerable study and controversy[226–229]. Gray and Hare[226] suggested that the ion was formally similar to the vanadyl ion which had been treated successfully in an earlier publication[230]. Their treatment allowed for strong π-bonding between the molybdenum and oxygen atoms, but it neglected any π-bonding between molybdenum and halogen atoms. Subsequent work[229], which dealt with the spectra of the ions MOX_5^{2-} (M = Mo or W; X = Cl or Br), revealed shifts in the positions of the bands that could be explained only on the assumption that metal-to-halogen π-bonding in fact occurs.

The ESR spectrum of the oxopentachloromolybdate(v) anion has been recorded several times[231–234]. Kon and Sharpless[234] commented specifically on the fact that the anomalous situation arises that $g_{\parallel}$ is greater than $g_{\perp}$ and they attributed this to strong metal-to-ligand π-bonding.

The infrared spectra of rubidium and caesium oxopentachloromolybdates(v) have been examined in detail[235], and the results and assignments are given in Table 6.29. Metal–oxygen frequencies for the other salts of this anion have been recorded and fall into the range 950–975 cm^{-1} [221,236].

In recent years there has been considerable interest in the behaviour of molybdenum(v) in solutions of varying hydrochloric acid concentration. In fairly concentrated acid ($> 8M$ HCl) the solutions are green, and all

TABLE 6.29

Infrared Spectra (cm^{-1}) of Rb_2MoOCl_5 and Cs_2MoOCl_5

Rb_2MoOCl_5	Cs_2MoOCl_5	Assignment
967vs	952vs	Mo=O stretch
339sh	329s	Mo–Cl stretch
327s	320sh	
230m	227m	Mo–O rock
219m		
187sh	178m	
177m		Cl–Mo–Cl vib
88m	86m	

vs = very strong, s = strong, m = medium, sh = shoulder.

investigators agree that they contain the monomeric $MoOCl_5^{2-}$ ion. On decreasing the acid concentration the solution becomes dark and almost opaque (5–6M HCl), and finally at less than 4M HCl a red-brown species is formed. These colour changes can be reversed by increasing the acid concentration.

Several investigations have been made of the species formed at low acidities, but in most cases measurements have been made on the solutions only and no product has been isolated. Sacconi and Cini[237] showed that the magnetic susceptibility of the molybdenum species in solution dropped from $1,284 \times 10^{-6}$ cgs in 10M acid ($MoOCl_5^{2-}$) to zero in 2.45M acid, and they concluded that a dimer was formed at low acidities.

In an elegant spectrophotometric study, Haight[238] showed that there were in fact two dimers present in the system. The first (5–6M acid) is responsible for the enhanced absorption in the visible region and was shown to have one of the annexed structures. Haight favoured the oxo-bridged formulation because it gave six-coordination to the molybdenum atoms. He also showed that in the solutions of lower acidity (1–3M acid) no further polymerization occurred; but he suggested no structure for this second dimer.

```
   Cl    Cl  Cl    Cl              Cl Cl OH₂  Cl Cl
    \   /    \   /                  \ | /     | /
    O=Mo----O----Mo=O    or        O=Mo       Mo=O
    /   \    /    \                  / | \    /| \
   Cl    Cl  Cl    Cl              Cl Cl OH₂ Cl Cl
```

In their ESR study of the system, Hare and coworkers[232] confirmed that two dimers exist, the first formed in 5–6M acid being paramagnetic and the second formed at low acidities being diamagnetic.

A major difficulty in isolating the polymerized species is that the salts are remarkably soluble; the usual method of preparation of the brown species is simple dilution of acid solutions of the green monomer, inevitably resulting in large volumes of low molybdenum content. By dissolving molybdenum pentachloride in concentrated hydrochloric acid and adding solid sodium hydroxide, it was found that the colour changes noted above were faithfully reproduced. By this method, solutions containing as much as 2–4 g of molybdenum in 10–15 ml of solution were readily obtained[239]. Addition of powdered caesium chloride caused slow separation of $Cs_4[Mo_2O_3Cl_8]$. This salt was diamagnetic and its visible spectrum was identical with that given by Haight for solutions of molybdenum(v) in 1M acid, thus confirming that the salt corresponds to Haight's second dimer.

The isolation and characterization of the diamagnetic dimer allows correlation and interpretation of the results obtained from measurements on the solutions. Haight showed that the first dimer was either $[Mo_2O_3Cl_8]^{4-}$ or $[Mo_2O_2(OH)_2Cl_8]^{4-}$ but, since the first of these is now known to be the second dimer, we may assume that the equilibria in the solutions of varying acid concentrations are as illustrated

```
              Cl Cl OH₂  Cl Cl      Cl        Cl  Cl       Cl
               \ | /     | /         \       /     \      /
MoOCl₅²⁻ ⇌     O=Mo       Mo=O  ⇌    O=Mo----O----Mo=O
               / | \     /| \        /       \     /      \
              Cl Cl OH₂ Cl Cl      Cl        Cl  Cl       Cl
  >8M acid        5–6M acid              1–3M acid
```

Oxopentachlorotungstates(v). This anion is prepared by reduction of tungstate(VI) in hydrochloric acid media, chemically[240] or electrolytically[241], or by dissolving tungsten pentachloride in hydrochloric acid solution[224]. The oxopentachlorotungstate(v) salts are green or bluish-green crystalline solids, which are stable in a dry atmosphere.

Caesium oxopentachlorotungstate(v) is cubic (K_2PtCl_6 structure)[225]

with $a = 10.24$ Å. The magnetic moment of this salt is 1.56 BM, the Curie–Weiss law is obeyed with $\theta = 30°$.

The infrared spectra of the rubidium and the caesium salt have been studied in detail[235]; the results are given in Table 6.30.

TABLE 6.30

Infrared Spectra (cm^{-1}) of Rb_2WOCl_5 and Cs_2WOCl_5

Rb_2WOCl_5	Cs_2WOCl_5	Assignment
960vs	957vs	W=O stretch
339sh	333w	W–Cl stretch
317s	309s	
229m	203m	W–O rock
177m	174m	
164w	164m	Cl–W–Cl def
85m	84m	

vs = very strong, s = strong, m = medium, w = weak,
sh = shoulder.

Oxotetrachloromolybdates(v) and oxotetrachlorotungstates(v). The reaction between molybdenum pentachloride and quaternary ammonium chlorides in liquid sulphur dioxide leads to isolation of oxotetrachloromolybdates(v), and the corresponding tungstates(v) can be prepared in a similar manner[224]. The tungsten compounds have been precipitated from solutions of tungsten(v) in hydrochloric acid by using large cations, whereas small cations gave the oxopentachlorotungstate(v) anion[222,240,241]. The rubidium and caesium salts were also prepared by treating alkali-metal chlorides with molybdenum pentachloride in liquid sulphur dioxide[242]. The compounds are brown solids.

Hexabromotungstates(v). Interaction of quaternary ammonium bromide and tungsten pentabromide in boiling chloroform in a sealed tube led to isolation of quaternary ammonium hexabromotungstates(v). The black, easily hydrolysed crystals are soluble in methyl cyanide, and the conductivity of the solution was as expected for a 1:1 electrolyte. In the ultraviolet spectra, three peaks were observed instead of the single absorption expected for O_h symmetry, and it was suggested that there is perhaps a Jahn–Teller distortion[243]. The magnetic moments of these compounds were of the order of 1.2–1.3 BM at room temperature[243].

Oxopentabromomolybdates(v) and oxopentabromotungstates(v). These compounds are prepared by dissolving molybdenum or tungsten pentachloride in hydrobromic acid and then adding a quaternary ammonium bromide[224]. Ammonium oxopentabromomolybdate(v) has also been prepared by dissolving ammonium molybdate in fuming hydrobromic acid and evaporating the solution to dryness[244].

The infrared spectra of the rubidium and caesium salts of both the molybdenum and the tungsten complexes have been examined[235]; the results are listed in Table 6.31.

TABLE 6.31

Infrared Spectra (cm^{-1}) of Rb_2MOBr_5 and Cs_2MOBr_5

Rb_2MoOBr_5	Cs_2MoOBr_5	Rb_2WOBr_5	Cs_2WOBr_5	Assignment
972sh	948vs	968vs	960vs	M=O stretch
962vs				
253m	246vs	224s	220s	M–Br stretch
244vs				
207m	209m	203s	202s	M–O rock
187m	195m			
132m	136w	142w	143w	
128w	125w	120m	119m	Br–M–Br def
119m	118w			

vs = very strong, s = strong, m = medium, w = weak, sh = shoulder.

Oxotetrabromomolybdate(v). Quinolinium oxotetrabromomolybdate(v) was prepared by dissolving molybdenum trioxide in fuming hydrobromic acid and adding quinoline to the hot solution. The dark red needles were recrystallized from hydrobromic acid[244].

Oxidation State IV

Hexafluoromolybdate(iv). Reaction of an excess of sodium iodide on molybdenum hexafluoride in liquid sulphur dioxide gave sodium hexafluoromolybdate(iv). This product is a dark brown powder which is hydrolysed only slowly in air[245].

From X-ray powder diffraction data it was thought to be cubic[245], with $a = 10.00$ Å, but reinvestigation[246] led to the conclusion that it is orthorhombic with $a = 5.76$, $b = 4.48$ and $c = 10.14$ Å.

Hexachloromolybdates(iv) and hexachlorotungstates(iv). These salts are usually prepared by reaction of molybdenum pentachloride or tungsten hexachloride with an alkali-metal chloride, either in the melt[213,247,248] or in liquid sulphur dioxide[224,242]. An alternative method[249] for the hexachloromolybdates(iv) is to heat the alkali-metal chloride and molybdenum pentachloride in iodine monochloride solution in a tube at 150°. The hexachlorotungstates(iv) have been prepared[170] by reaction of alkali-metal iodides with tungsten hexachloride in a sealed tube at 200°. Potassium hexachlorotungstate(IV) has been prepared[218] by thermal disproportionation of potassium hexachlorotungstate(V):

$$2KWCl_6 \rightleftarrows K_2WCl_6 + WCl_6$$

The hexachloromolybdates(IV) and hexachlorotungstates(IV) are green crystalline solids, sensitive to moisture, and decomposed by water and acids[249].

TABLE 6.32

Infrared Spectra (cm^{-1}) of $MoCl_6^{2-}$ and WCl_6^{2-}

Compound	v_3 (M–Cl stretch)	v_4 (M–Cl bend)	Lattice mode
K_2MoCl_6	340	174	74
Rb_2MoCl_6	334	172	70
Cs_2MoCl_6	325	170	70
K_2WCl_6	324	165	77
Rb_2WCl_6	306	160	66
Cs_2WCl_6	308	166	71

The compounds are all cubic, with the K_2PtCl_6 structure and the following unit cell parameters[170,225,249]:

K_2MoCl_6	$a = 9.85$ Å	K_2WCl_6	$a = 9.88$ Å
Tl_2MoCl_6	$a = 9.84$ Å	Tl_2WCl_6	$a = 9.87$ Å
Rb_2MoCl_6	$a = 9.99$ Å	Rb_2WCl_6	$a = 10.00$ Å
Cs_2MoCl_6	$a = 10.27$ Å	Cs_2WCl_6	$a = 10.27$ Å

The magnetic properties of these molybdates and tungstates are somewhat irregular; the results cannot be accounted for by Kotani's theory, and the high values of the Curie–Weiss constant suggests strong interaction between magnetic centres[218,249].

The infrared spectra of a number of hexachloromolybdates(IV) and hexachlorotungstates(IV) have been investigated[250], with the results given in Table 6.32. All the spectra are similar to those of the corresponding M_2PtCl_6 compounds.

Hydroxopentachlorotungstate(IV). A compound formulated as potassium hydroxopentachlorotungstate(IV) can be prepared by reduction of tungstate(VI) in hydrochloric acid with tin. Addition of potassium chloride after complete reduction leads to the isolation of small quantities of a green compound[251]. Little investigation has been made of this compound, but it appears likely that it should in fact be formulated as potassium μ-oxodecachloroditungstate(IV), $K_4[W_2OCl_{10}]$.

Hexabromomolybdates(IV) and hexabromotungstates(IV). Hexabromomolybdates(IV) have been prepared[249] from molybdenum tribromide, alkali-metal bromide and iodine monobromide in a sealed tube at 200°. Alkali-metal hexabromotungstates(IV) have been prepared[170] by interaction of the alkali-metal iodide and tungsten hexabromide in a sealed tube at 130°.

All the hexabromomolybdates(IV) and hexabromotungstates(IV) are cubic[170,249] except for potassium hexabromotungstate(IV) which is tetragonal.

Rb_2MoBr_6	cubic	$a = 10.50$ Å	
Cs_2MoBr_6	cubic	$a = 10.70$ Å	
K_2WBr_6	tetragonal	$a = 7.22$ Å,	$c = 10.64$ Å
Rb_2WBr_6	cubic	$a = 10.50$ Å	
Cs_2WBr_6	cubic	$a = 10.70$ Å	

The magnetic moments of all the hexabromotungstates(IV) are strongly depressed and the salts are probably antiferromagnetic[170].

Oxidation State III

Hexafluoromolybdate(III) and hexafluorotungstate(III). Potassium hexafluoromolybdate(III) and -tungstate(III) have recently been prepared by interaction of the trioxide, potassium fluoride and potassium tetrafluoroborate at 900–995° in an argon atmosphere[252]. Potassium hexafluoromolybdate(III) has also been prepared by fusion of potassium hexachloromolybdate(III) and potassium hydrogen fluoride. This brown compound is reported to have a cubic lattice and a magnetic moment of 3.2 BM at room temperature[253].

Hexachloromolybdates(III). The hexachloromolybdates(III) are prepared by electrolytic reduction of molybdate(VI); when the reduction is complete, an excess of alkali-metal chloride is added to precipitate the salts[191,254,255]. The brick-red compounds are stable in air and can be heated to 600° in a vacuum without decomposition[191].

The magnetic moment of potassium hexachloromolybdate(III) is about the spin-only value; a Curie–Weiss constant of 11° was observed[256,257], and the effective magnetic moment at 300° is 3.79 BM.

Electrolysis of potassium hexachloromolybdate(III) in a fused KCl–NaCl eutectic[258] gives pure metallic molybdenum with a current efficiency of 100%.

Pentachloromolybdates(III). Anions formulated as $MoCl_5^{2-}$ or $(MoCl_5 \cdot H_2O)^{2-}$ are frequently isolated as second products in the preparation of the hexachloromolybdate(III) salts if the hydrogen chloride concentration is low[254,255,259].

Nonachloroditungstates(III). This interesting anion is formed under conditions when one might expect to produce the hexachlorotungstate(III)

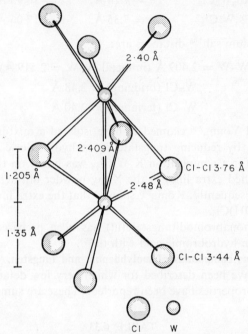

Figure 6.1 The $W_2Cl_9^{3-}$ ion.

anion. Reduction of tungstate(VI) in hydrochloric acid media by chemical[251,260,261] or electrolytic[262] methods to tungsten(III), followed by saturation of the solution with gaseous hydrogen chloride and addition of alkali-metal halide led to the isolation of nonachloroditungstates(III).

The structure of this anion was first deduced by Brosset from X-ray powder diffraction results[263,264] and this has since been confirmed by a single-crystal study[265]. The anion, illustrated in Figure 6.1, consists of two octahedra sharing a face, the triangles formed by terminal chlorine atoms being rotated by 60° relative to the triangle formed by the bridging chlorine atoms. The tungsten–chlorine terminal bonds are shorter than the tungsten–chlorine bridging bonds, and the tungsten–tungsten bond is less than that in tungsten metal and corresponds to a double bond[265].

18

The alkali-metal salts are all tetragonal with the following dimensions[263,264]:

$K_3W_2Cl_9$	$a = 7.16$ Å,	$c = 16.16$ Å
$(NH_4)_3W_2Cl_9$	$a = 7.16$ Å,	$c = 16.17$ Å
$Tl_3W_2Cl_9$	$a = 7.15$ Å,	$c = 16.33$ Å
$Rb_3W_2Cl_9$	$a = 7.24$ Å,	$c = 16.95$ Å
$Cs_3W_2Cl_9$	$a = 7.35$ Å,	$c = 17.06$ Å

For the potassium salt[265] distances are:

$$W–W = 2.409 \text{ Å (in metal W–W} = 2.519 \text{ Å)}$$
$$W–Cl \text{ (bridging)} = 2.48 \text{ Å}$$
$$W–Cl \text{ (terminal)} = 2.40 \text{ Å}$$

Laudise and Young[266] claimed to have isolated a mixture of $K_3W_2Cl_9$ and $K_5W_3Cl_{14}$ by reducing tungstate(VI) in hydrochloric acid with tin. The evidence for a composition $K_5W_3Cl_{14}$ was based on the presence of some unidentified extra lines in the X-ray powder diffraction pattern of $K_3W_2Cl_9$. Subsequently, König[267] showed that the extra lines were in fact due to $K_2W(OH)Cl_5$.

Potassium nonabromoditungstate(III) has been prepared by reducing tungstate(VI) in hydrobromic acid with tin[268].

Miscellaneous compounds of molybdenum and tungsten. A number of compounds have been described for which very few details of chemical and physical properties have been reported. These are summarized below in Table 6.33.

TABLE 6.33

Miscellaneous Compounds of Molybdenum and Tungsten

Compound	Ref.	Compound	Ref.
$MoOF \cdot 4H_2O$	269	K_3WO_3F	272
$MoOCl \cdot 4H_2O$	270, 271	Na_3WO_4F	274
$K_2MoO_3F_4$	200, 272, 273	$Mo_2Cl_9^{3-}$	249
$K_2MoO_5F_2$	272	$Mo_2Br_9^{3-}$	249
$K_3Mo_2O_4F_7$	201	$Na_5Mo_3F_{14}$	275
$K_{10}Mo_6O_{11}F_{24}$	201		

ADDENDA

Halides and Oxide Halides

Nitrogen trifluoride has been used to prepare molybdenum hexafluoride and tungsten hexafluoride from molybdenum disulphide and tungsten metal, respectively[276], the reactions being carried out in a flow system at 280°. Reaction of nitrogen trifluoride with tungsten trioxide at 430° gave tungsten hexafluoride and NO[WOF$_5$], whilst the analogous reaction at the same temperature with molybdenum trioxide gave only small amounts of molybdenum hexafluoride, the main products being molybdenum dioxide difluoride and NO[MoO$_2$F$_3$][276].

X-ray powder diffraction studies on both molybdenum and tungsten hexafluoride have been reported[277]. As noted earlier, each has a cubic high-temperature form and a lower-symmetry (probably orthorhombic) low-temperature form. The data are summarized in Table 6.34.

TABLE 6.34

Crystallographic Data for Molybdenum and Tungsten Hexafluoride

Property	MoF$_6$	WF$_6$
M.p.	17.4°	1.9°
Transition temperature	−9.6°	−8.5°
Cubic form (Å)	$a = 6.23$	$a = 6.28$
Orthorhombic form (Å)	$a = 9.61$	$a = 9.68$
	$b = 8.75$	$b = 8.81$
	$c = 5.07$	$c = 5.09$

The infrared spectrum of molybdenum hexafluoride has been observed at −180° and the results interpreted on the basis of D_{4h} symmetry[278]. The vibration-rotation spectrum of tungsten hexafluoride has been studied in the gas phase[279].

Electron diffraction by molybdenum hexafluoride and tungsten hexafluoride has been re-examined[280]. It was concluded that the molecules possess O_h symmetry and the mean metal–fluorine bond lengths are Mo–F = 1.820 Å and W–F = 1.832 Å.

The solubilities of molybdenum and tungsten hexafluoride in anhydrous hydrogen fluoride at room temperature have been given as 1.50 and 3.14 moles per 1000 g of hydrogen fluoride, respectively[281]. The Raman spectra of these solutions showed only very small shifts from those observed in the gas phase. The solutions were non-conducting and it therefore appears as though the hexafluorides dissolve without reaction. A cryoscopic method for determining small quantities of anhydrous hydrogen fluoride in tungsten hexafluoride has been developed[282].

A thorough study of the reaction between tungsten hexafluoride and titanium tetrachloride has been made[283]. The existence of tungsten pentafluoride chloride has been confirmed and, in addition, tungsten difluoride tetrachloride and fluoride pentachloride were isolated. The compounds were separated by very careful vacuum-sublimation. Unstable tungsten tetrafluoride dichloride is one of the products[283] of treating tungsten hexachloride with fluorine at 25°. The infrared spectrum of tungsten pentafluoride chloride showed very strong absorptions at 743, 703, 667, 400, and 254 cm^{-1}. Weaker bands were observed at 302, 278, and 228 cm^{-1}. Tungsten pentafluoride chloride does not react with nitric oxide or phosphorus trifluoride, but with pyridine the adduct $WF_5Cl \cdot 2py$ was isolated[283].

The crystal structure of molybdenum oxide tetrafluoride has been determined by Edwards and coworkers[284]. The compound has a monoclinic cell of the same type as found for the pentafluorides of vanadium, chromium, and rhenium. The unit cell parameters are $a = 7.84$, $b = 16.98$, $c = 5.49$ Å, and $\beta = 92.5°$. The space group is $P2_1/a$ and there are eight molecules in the cell. The structure is the same as that given for the above pentafluorides in Figure 1.7 (page 19). The important feature is that there are bridging *fluorine* atoms, the $MoOF_5$ octahedra are arranged such that the terminal oxygen atom is *trans* to one of the bridging fluorines. The angle at the bridging fluorine is 151°. The bond lengths are:

Mo=O 1.65 Å
Mo–F (bridge *trans* to oxygen) 2.29 Å
Mo–F (bridge *cis* to oxygen) 2.00 Å
Remaining Mo–F (mean) 1.84 Å

Tungsten oxide tetrafluoride is not isostructural with its molybdenum analogue[284]; instead it adopts the tetrameric structure for niobium pentafluoride (Figure 1.6, page 18). The monoclinic cell has $a = 9.65$, $b = 14.42$, $c = 5.15$ Å, and $\beta = 95.4°$. The space group is $C2/m$ and there are eight molecules in the unit cell. No further detail of this structure has been published. The vapour-phase infrared spectrum of both molybdenum and tungsten oxide tetrafluoride have been reported twice[284,285]. The spectra are very similar and good agreement was obtained between the two groups of workers. Blanchard[285] has assigned some of the bands on the basis of a monomeric species with C_{4v} symmetry as follows (cm^{-1}).

	ν_1	ν_7	ν_3	ν_8
$MoOF_4$	1045	720	680	530
WOF_4	1055	700	735	560

It has been claimed[286] that molybdenum hexachloride is one of the products formed when molybdenum trioxide is refluxed with thionyl chloride for a long period. This result could not be confirmed[287].

Tungsten hexachloride is reported[288] to show a very strong, very broad tungsten–chlorine stretching mode between 270 and 290 cm^{-1}.

The vapour pressure of liquid molybdenum oxide tetrachloride over the temperature range 97–160° is given by the expression[289]

$$\log p_{mm} = 10.418 - 3540/T$$

The boiling point is 197° and the heat of vaporization is 16.19 kcal mole^{-1}.

The density of liquid tungsten oxide tetrachloride from the melting point to 440° is given by the expression[290]

$$\rho = 3.2189 - 0.16 \times 10^{-2}T - 0.264 \times 10^{-5}T^2$$

Further 1:1 adducts between tungsten oxide tetrachloride and pyridine, alkyl cyanides, and cyclic ethers have been reported[291].

The vapour pressure of molybdenum dioxide dichloride has been measured again[292], but the results are not in good agreement with either of the measurements reported previously. The variation of vapour pressure with temperature over the temperature range 50–157° is given by the expression[292]

$$\log p_{mm} = 11.747 - 3830/T$$

Tungsten dioxide dichloride has been prepared by subliming tungsten hexachloride is a stream of pure dry oxygen[293], and by interaction of tungsten hexachloride and tungsten trioxide in a sealed tube at 410° [294]. More adducts of the types $WO_2Cl_2 \cdot 2L$, where L is a monodentate donor ligand, and $WO_2Cl_2 \cdot L$ where L is bipyridyl or *o*-phenanthroline, have been reported[293,295].

Tungsten hexabromide has been prepared by the action of boron tribromide on tungsten hexachloride at room temperature[296]. The following thermodynamic functions have been measured for tungsten oxide tetrabromide[297]:

M.p.	322.4°
B.p.	331°
ΔH_{vap}	13 kcal mole^{-1}
ΔH_{fus}	14.7 kcal mole^{-1}

A number of simple adducts of tungsten dioxide dibromide, similar to those previously reported for the dioxide dichloride, have been prepared[295].

Molybdenum trifluoride dichloride has been prepared by Kolditz and Calov[298] by the interaction of molybdenum pentachloride and arsenic trifluoride. It is an orange compound that is thermally unstable above 90°. It is very sensitive to moisture.

The vapour pressure of molybdenum pentachloride is given by the expressions[299]

$$\text{Solid} \quad \log p_{\text{mm}} = 9.465 - 3504/T$$

$$\text{Liquid} \quad \log p_{\text{mm}} = 8.186 - 2880/T$$

The dissociation pressure over molybdenum pentachloride due to the reaction

$$2\text{MoCl}_5 \rightarrow 2\text{MoCl}_4 + \text{Cl}_2$$

is given by the expression

$$\log p_{\text{mm}} = 13.611 - 5530/T$$

Rinke and Schafer[300] have shown by mass-spectrometric studies that molybdenum pentachloride is monomeric in the gas phase.

The far-infrared spectrum of tungsten pentachloride has been recorded[288] and it appears to be similar to that of molybdenum pentachloride, consistent with D_{2h} symmetry. Bands were observed at 460, 395, 380, 340, and 235 cm^{-1}.

Adducts of the type $\text{MoCl}_5 \cdot \text{L}_2$ and $\text{WCl}_5 \cdot \text{L}_2$ have been prepared by reaction of the pentachlorides with 2,4,6-trimethylpyridine or benzonitrile[301]. Conductivities suggested that they should be formulated as $[\text{MCl}_4\text{L}_2]^+ \text{X}^-$. Molybdenum pentachloride reacts with $\text{Al}(\text{C}_6\text{H}_5)_3$ in tetrahydrofuran (THF) to give $\text{MoCl}_4 \cdot 2\text{THF}$[302].

The general features of the magnetic properties of tungsten pentachloride[303,304] and tungsten pentabromide[303] have been confirmed. Although it is now clear that the pentahalides are not trimeric, it has been admitted that the magnetic properties are anomalous and, as yet, inexplicable[303].

Greenwood and coworkers[304] have carried out a two-dimensional single-crystal X-ray diffraction study on tungsten pentachloride. They found the compound to be almost isodimensional with molybdenum pentachloride with $a = 17.3$, $b = 17.6$, $c = 6.07$ Å, and $\beta = 95.5°$. It was concluded that the compounds are isostructural.

Complexes of the type $\text{WOCl}_3 \cdot 2\text{L}$ have been prepared by reaction of the ligand with tungsten hexachloride in acetone[293]. A number of tungsten oxide trichloride adducts have also been prepared by reaction of the donor ligand with tungsten oxide tetrachloride[291].

Molybdenum dioxide chloride has been prepared[305] by dissolving molybdenum pentachloride in absolute ethanol, evaporating the solution, and finally drying the residue at about 150°. Molybdenum dioxide chloride has a temperature-independent magnetic moment of about 0.8 BM and its infrared spectrum indicates the presence of both bridging and terminal oxygen atoms.

Schafer and coworkers[306] have prepared crystalline molybdenum tetrachloride by the reduction of the pentachloride with molybdenum metal, using the thermal gradient technique. Molybdenum tetrachloride obeys the Curie–Weiss law with a Weiss constant of 38°K and a magnetic moment of about 2.4 BM. This form of molybdenum tetrachloride has a trigonal unit cell of space group $P\bar{3}1c$, containing three formula units, with $a = 6.06$ and $c = 11.67$ Å. The structure is of the layer lattice type with a hexagonal close-packed chlorine sequence. Mass-spectrometric studies[300] show that molybdenum tetrachloride is monomeric in the gas phase. Adducts of molybdenum tetrachloride[307] and molybdenum tetrabromide[308] have been prepared.

Molybdenum trichloride has been prepared by the reduction of the pentachloride with phosphorus in a sealed tube[309] at 200° and with stannous chloride in a nitrogen stream[310] at 290–300°. Schafer and coworkers[306] made a very detailed study of the preparation and physical and chemical properties of molybdenum trichloride. They found that there are two forms of molybdenum trichloride, the β-form being in fact $MoCl_{3.08}$. They discussed the structures of both forms of molybdenum trichloride in detail.

Molybdenum tribromide is formed by the interaction of molybdenum pentachloride and boron tribromide at room temperature[296]. Schafer and coworkers[311] have prepared tungsten trichloride by the action of liquid chlorine on tungsten dichloride, as described in Chapter 3.

Molybdenum dibromide, molybdenum diiodide, tungsten dichloride, tungsten dibromide, and tungsten diiodide have been shown[306] to be cluster compounds, isotypic with Mo_6Cl_{12}.

Complex Halides and Oxide Halides

One of the products of the interaction[276] of nitrogen trifluoride and tungsten trioxide at 430° in $NO[WOF_5]$, whereas the analogous reaction with molybdenum trioxide gives $NO[MoO_2F_3]$. The latter compound can also be prepared by the reaction of nitrosyl fluoride with molybdenum dioxide difluoride. Both complexes appear to contain the NO^+ ion. The major absorptions in the infrared spectra (cm^{-1}) are[276]

$NO[MoO_2F_3]$	$NO[WOF_5]$	Assignment
2320	2330	N=O stretch
980, 930	1005	M=O stretch
640	625–450	M–F stretch

Weiss and coworkers have confirmed the existence of dioxotetrafluoro-molybdates(VI) and -tungstates(VI) and examined the crystal structure of a number of these complexes.

$K_2MoO_2F_4 \cdot H_2O$ is monoclinic with $a = 6.214$, $b = 6.192$, $c = 18.079$ Å, and $\beta = 96.2°$. The space group is $P2_1/c$ and there are four formula units in the cell[312,313]. The dioxotetrafluoromolybdate anion is a slightly distorted octahedron with the oxygen atoms in a *cis*-arrangement. The bond distances are: molybdenum–oxygen, 1.71 Å; molybdenum–fluorine (*trans* to O) 2.0 Å, and molybdenum–fluorine (*trans* to F), 1.94 Å. The water molecules are hydrogen bonded to fluorine atoms of two MoO_2F_4 octahedra and effectively link chains of anions together. The infrared spectrum of $K_2MoO_2F_4 \cdot H_2O$ shows absorptions at 940 and 905 cm^{-1} assigned to the metal–oxygen double-bond stretching frequencies[313].

Copper(II) dioxotetrafluorotungstate(VI) tetrahydrate, $CuWO_2F_4 \cdot 4H_2O$, is monoclinic with $a = 5.545$, $b = 9.88$, $c = 7.492$ Å, and $\beta = 103.5°$. There are two formula units in the cell[314] of space group $P2_1/c$. The structure contains WO_2F_4 octahedra and planar $Cu(H_2O)_4$ cations, although long copper–fluorine interactions, which give a chain structure, complete a distorted octahedron about the copper atoms.

The complex $NH_4CuWO_2F_5 \cdot 4H_2O$ has been shown[315] to be in fact $Cu(H_2O)_4WO_2F_4 \cdot NH_4F$ with a structure containing $Cu(H_2O)_4$ cations, WO_2F_4 anions, and free NH_4F, the whole structure being held together by hydrogen bonding and copper–fluorine interactions. The compound is orthorhombic with $a = 7.707$ and $c = 8.419$ Å and has the space group $P4/n$.

French workers[316,317] have characterized a number of oxoperoxotetrafluoromolybdates(VI), and the crystal structure of the complex $K_2[MoO(O_2)F_4] \cdot H_2O$ has been examined. This hydrate is monoclinic and isomorphous with potassium dioxotetrafluoromolybdate hydrate, with $a = 6.308$, $b = 6.274$, $c = 18.166$ Å, and $\beta = 98.3°$. The molybdenum atom is effectively seven-coordinate in this complex, although the anion could be regarded as octahedral with the O_2 group occupying one coordination site. The orientation of the O_2 molecule is at right angles to the metal–peroxide bond. The peroxo group and the terminal oxygen atom occupy *cis*-positions in the psuedo-octahedral anion. The bond distances are: Mo=O (terminal), 1.642 Å; Mo–O (peroxo), 1.949 and 1.935 Å; O–O, 1.44 Å, and Mo–F approximately 2.0 Å. The role of the water molecule is to link the anions by hydrogen bonding; it is coordinated to a fluorine of one anion and of the peroxo oxygens of another.

Wendling[318] has confirmed the existence of the dioxotetrachloro-molybdates(VI) and has also prepared some oxoperoxotetrachloro-molybdates(VI). All these compounds are isostructural and cubic with the cubic K_2PtCl_6 type lattice. The unit-cell parameters are:

$(NH_4)_2MoO_2Cl_4$	$a = 9.76$ Å	$(NH_4)_2MoO(O_2)Cl_4$	$a = 9.77$ Å
$Rb_2MoO_2Cl_4$	$a = 9.77$ Å	$Rb_2MoO(O_2)Cl_4$	$a = 9.84$ Å
$Cs_2MoO_2Cl_4$	$a = 10.11$ Å	$Cs_2MoO(O_2)Cl_4$	$a = 10.18$ Å

Caesium oxoperoxotetrachlorotungstate(vi) has been prepared[319]. Its infrared spectrum shows bands at 948, 899, 603, and 543 cm^{-1}, the last of these being assigned to a peroxo group vibration.

Hydrazinium fluoride, $N_2H_6F_2$, reacts with molybdenum hexafluoride to give, among other products[320], hydrazinium hexafluoromolybdate(v) $N_2H_6[MoF_6]_2$, and it is interesting that tungsten hexafluoride does not react with reagent. The molybdenum–fluorine stretching frequency occurs at 620 cm^{-1} as a broad absorption, and the magnetic moment of the compound is 2.54 BM per molecule (1.79 BM per molybdenum atom).

Potassium oxopentafluoromolybdate(v) hydrate, $K_2MoOF_5 \cdot H_2O$, is monoclinic[316,321,322] with $a = 8.533$, $b = 8.508$, $c = 9.107$ Å, and $\beta = 100.0°$. The octahedral anion is slightly distorted and the bond distances are: molybdenum–oxygen, 1.66 Å; molybdenum–fluorine (*trans* to O), 2.03 Å; and molybdenum–fluorine (*cis* to O), between 1.66 and 1.93 Å. There are different environments for the potassium atoms, one type is six-coordinate with interaction between six $MoOF_5$ groups forming anion–potassium–anion chains parallel to the three principal axes. The remaining potassium atoms are twelve-coordinate, lying between the planes. The water molecules form hydrogen bonds between the chains. The metal–oxygen stretching frequency occurs[322] at 980 cm^{-1}.

The magnetic and spectral properties of a number of oxopentachloro- and oxotetrachloromolybdates(v), and the corresponding tungsten complexes, have been examined in some detail[303]. In general, the magnetic behaviour is not in accord with theory.

Piovesana and Furlani[323] showed that the size of the cation is the major factor in determining whether oxopentachloromolybdates(v) or oxotetra-chloromolybdates(v) are obtained from aqueous solution. Most quaternary ammonium salts give the oxotetrachloro complexes. The preparative methods used were: (*a*) molybdenum pentachloride and cation chloride in concentrated hydrochloric acid saturated with gaseous hydrogen chloride; (*b*) electrolytic reduction of molybdenum trioxide in hydrochloric acid in the presence of cation chloride; and (*c*) oxidation of hexachloro-molybdates(iv) in methanol.

The ESR spectrum of molybdenum(v) in hydrobromic acid gave evidence of two monomeric species[324], one of which was identified as oxopenta-bromomolybdate(v).

Tetraphenylarsonium oxotetrabromomolybdate(v) hydrate,

$$[Ph_4As][MoOBr_4(H_2O)],$$

is tetragonal with $a = 13.14$ and $c = 7.89$ Å. The space group is $P4/n$ and there are 2 molecules in the unit cell[325]. The anion is basically square-pyramidal with the water molecule weakly held in the sixth octahedral position *trans* to the oxygen atom. The bond distances are: molybdenum–bromine, 2.516 Å; molybdenum–oxygen (H_2O), 2.39 Å; and molybdenum–oxygen (terminal), 1.78 Å. The structure of the anion is very similar to that of the corresponding rhenium complex.

The second major product of the reaction[320] between molybdenum hexafluoride and hydrazinium fluoride is hydrazinium hexafluoromolybdate(iv), $N_2H_6(MoF_6)$. It has a body-centred cubic lattice with $a = 10.55$ Å and it gives molybdenum–fluorine stretching frequencies at 540 and 600 cm^{-1}.

The interaction[309] of molybdenum pentachloride or tungsten hexachloride and caesium chloride with phosphorus gives the appropriate caesium hexachlorometallate(iv). X-ray powder diffraction studies have been reported on some alkali-metal hexachloromolybdates(iv) and -tungstates(iv). All are cubic with the K_2PtCl_6 type lattice[318]. The unit cell parameters are:

Rb_2MoCl_6	$a = 9.99$ Å	Rb_2WCl_6	$a = 10.00$ Å
Cs_2MoCl_6	$a = 10.27$ Å	Cs_2WCl_6	$a = 10.27$ Å

Potassium nonachloroditungstate(iii) has been prepared by reduction of tungsten(vi) with tin in a cooled hydrochloric acid solution[326]. Reaction with pyridine gave $W_2Cl_6(py)_4$ and the previously reported compound $W_2Cl_6(py)_3$ could not be confirmed.

REFERENCES

1. T. A. O'Donnell, *J. Chem. Soc.*, **1956**, 4681.
2. H. J. Emeléus and V. Gutmann, *J. Chem. Soc.*, **1949**, 2979.
3. E. J. Barber and G. H. Cady, *J. Phys. Chem.*, **60**, 505 (1956).
4. T. A. O'Donnell and D. F. Stewart, *Inorg. Chem.*, **5**, 1434 (1966).
5. *Dutch* Pat. Appl. 6,400–628 (1964).
6. N. S. Nikolaev, Y. A. Buslaev and A. A. Opalovskii, *Zh. Neorg. Khim.*, **3**, 1731 (1958).
7. R. D. Peacock, *Proc. Chem. Soc.*, **1957**, 59.
8. G. B. Hargreaves and R. D. Peacock, *J. Chem. Soc.*, **1958**, 2170.
9. G. B. Hargreaves and R. D. Peacock, *J. Chem. Soc.*, **1958**, 4390.
10. N. S. Nikolaev and V. F. Sukhoverkhov, *Bul. Inst. Politeh Iasi* [*NS*] **3**, 61 (1957).
11. A. L. Oppegard, W. C. Smith, E. L. Muetterties and V. A. Engelhardt, *J. Am. Chem. Soc.*, **82**, 2835 (1960).

12. H. J. Emeleus and V. Gutmann, *J. Chem. Soc.*, **1950**, 2115.
13. A. J. Edwards, R. D. Peacock and R. W. H. Small, *J. Chem. Soc.*, **1962**, 4486.
14. O. Ruff and F. Eisner, *Ber.*, **38**, 742 (1905).
15. O. Ruff, F. Eisner and W. Heller, *Z. anorg. allgem. Chem.*, **52**, 256 (1907).
16. G. H. Cady and G. B. Hargreaves, *J. Chem. Soc.*, **1961**, 1563.
17. B. Weinstock, E. F. Westrum and G. L. Goodman, *Proc. 8th Intern. Conf. Low Temp. Physics, London*, **1962**, p. 405.
18. D. W. Osborne, F. Schreiner, J. G. Malm, H. Selig and L. Rochester, *J. Chem. Phys.*, **44**, 2802 (1966).
19. O. Ruff and E. Ascher, *Z. anorg. allgem. Chem.*, **196**, 413 (1931).
20. J. L. Settle, H. M. Feder and W. N. Hubbard, *J. Phys. Chem.*, **65**, 1337 (1961).
21. P. A. G. O'Hare and W. N. Hubbard, *J. Phys. Chem.*, **70**, 3353 (1966).
22. A. P. Brady, O. E. Meyers and J. K. Clauss, *J. Phys. Chem.*, **64**, 588 (1960).
23. O. E. Meyers and A. P. Brady, *J. Phys. Chem.*, **64**, 591 (1960).
24. S. Sundaram, *Z. Physik. Chem.* (Frankfurt) **34**, 225 (1962).
25. H. Braune and R. Pinnow, *Z. Physik*, **B35**, 239 (1937).
26. R. T. Glauber and V. Schomaker, *Phys. Rev.*, **89**, 667 (1953).
27. B. Weinstock and G. L. Goodman, *Advan. Chem. Phys.*, **9**, 197 (1965).
28. J. Gaunt, *Trans. Faraday Soc.*, **49**, 1122 (1953).
29. K. N. Tanner and A. B. F. Duncan, *J. Am. Chem. Soc.*, **73**, 1164 (1951).
30. H. H. Claassen, H. Selig and J. G. Malm, *J. Chem. Phys.*, **36**, 2888 (1962).
31. T. G. Burke, D. F. Smith and A. H. Nielsen, *J. Chem. Phys.*, **20**, 447 (1952).
32. J. Gaunt, *Trans. Faraday Soc.*, **50**, 546 (1954).
33. C. W. F. T. Pistorius, *J. Chem. Phys.*, **29**, 1328 (1958).
34. J. W. Linnett and C. J. M. Simpson, *Trans. Faraday Soc.*, **55**, 857 (1959).
35. H. H. Claassen, *J. Chem. Phys.*, **30**, 968 (1959).
36. R. B. Singh and D. K. Rai, *Can. J. Phys.*, **43**, 167 (1965).
37. M. Kimura and K. Kimura, *J. Mol. Spectr.*, **11**, 368 (1963).
38. O. N. Singh and D. K. Rai, *Can. J. Phys.*, **43**, 378 (1965).
39. E. Meisingseth and S. J. Cyrin, *Acta Chem. Scand.*, **16**, 2452 (1962).
40. N. S. Nikolaev, S. V. Vlasov, Y. A. Buslaev and A. A. Opalovskii, *Izv. Sibirsk. Otd. Akad. Nauk SSSR*, **1960**, 47.
41. E. J. Barber and G. H. Cady, *J. Am. Chem. Soc.*, **73**, 4247 (1951).
42. G. H. Rohrback and G. H. Cady, *J. Am. Chem. Soc.*, **73**, 4250 (1951).
43. W. S. Mears, R. V. Townend, R. D. Broadley, A. D. Turissini and R. F. Stahl, *Ind. Eng. Chem.*, **50**, 1771 (1958).
44. N. V. Sidgwick, *The Chemical Elements and Their Compounds*, Oxford Univ. Press, London, 1950, p. 1034.
45. A. B. Burg in *Fluorine Chemistry* (Ed. J. H. Simons) Academic Press, New York, Vol. 1, 1950, p. 112.
46. T. A. O'Donnell and D. F. Stewart, *J. Inorg. Nucl. Chem.*, **24**, 309 (1962).
47. D. F. Stewart and T. A. O'Donnell, *Nature*, **210**, 836 (1966).
48. J. R. Geichman, E. A. Smith and P. R. Ogle, *Inorg. Chem.*, **2**, 1012 (1963).
49. J. R. Geichman, E. A. Smith, S. S. Trond and P. R. Ogle, *Inorg. Chem.*, **1**, 661, (1962).
50. J. R. Geichman, P. R. Ogle and L. R. Swaney, *U.S.A.E.C. Report* GAT-T-809 (1961).

51. H. C. Clark and H. J. Eméleus, *J. Chem. Soc.*, **1957**, 4778.
52. H. F. Priest and W. C. Schumb, *J. Am. Chem. Soc.*, **70**, 2291 (1948).
53. B. Cohen, A. J. Edwards, M. Mercer and R. D. Peacock, *Chem. Commun.*, **1965**, 322.
54. G. H. Cady and G. B. Hargreaves, *J. Chem. Soc.*, **1961**, 1568.
55. A. D. Webb and H. A. Young, *J. Am. Chem. Soc.*, **72**, 3356 (1950).
56. N. Bartlett and P. L. Robinson, *J. Chem. Soc.*, **1961**, 3549.
57. R. D. Peacock, Progress in Inorganic Chemistry (ed. F. A. Cotton), Interscience, N.Y., Vol. 2, 1960, p. 228.
58. A. A. Vernon, *J. Am. Chem. Soc.*, **59**, 1832 (1937).
59. M. H. Lietzke and M. L. Holt, *Inorg. Syn.*, **3**, 163 (1950).
60. I. V. Vasil'kova, N. D. Zaitseva and P. S. Shapkin, *Russ. J. Inorg. Chem.*, **8**, 1237 (1963).
61. S. A. Shchukarev, G. I. Novikov, A. V. Suvorov and A. K. Baev, *Zh. Neorg. Khim.*, **3**, 2630 (1958).
62. K. Knox, S. Y. Tyree, R. D. Srivastava, V. Norman, J. Y. Bassett and J. H. Holloway, *J. Am. Chem. Soc.*, **79**, 3358 (1957).
63. A. B. Bardawil, F. N. Collier and S. Y. Tyree, *Inorg. Chem.*, **3**, 149 (1964).
64. L. A. Nisel'son and T. D. Sokolova, *Russ. J. Inorg. Chem.*, **10**, 9 (1965).
65. J. A. A. Ketelaar and G. W. van Oosterhant, *Rev. Trav. Chim.*, **62**, 197 (1943).
66. R. V. G. Ewens and M. W. Lister, *Trans. Faraday Soc.*, **34**, 1358 (1938).
67. F. D. Stevenson, C. E. Wicks and F. E. Block., *U.S. Bur. Mines Dept. Invest.* No 6367 (1964).
68. S. A. Shchukarev and G. I. Novikov, *Zh. Neorg. Khim.*, **1**, 357 (1956).
69. J. A. A. Ketelaar, G. W. van Oosterhant and P. B. Braun, *Rec. Trav. Chim.*, **62**, 597 (1943).
70. S. A. Shchukarev and G. A. Kokovin, *Russ. J. Inorg. Chem.*, **9**, 715 (1964).
71. S. A. Shchukarev, I. V. Vasil'kova and G. I. Novikov, *Zh. Neorg. Khim.*, **3**, 2642 (1958).
72. S. A. Shchukarev, G. I. Novikov and I. V. Vasil'kova, *Russ. J. Inorg. Chem.*, **5**, 802 (1960).
73. S. A. Shchukarev and A. V. Suvorov, *Vestn. Leningr. Univ.* **16**, Ser. Fiz. i Khim., 87 (1961).
74. S. A. Shchukarev and A. V. Suvorov, *Russ. J. Inorg. Chem.*, **6**, 763 (1961).
75. T. L. Allen, *J. Chem. Phys.*, **26**, 1644 (1957).
76. S. A. Shchukarev, G. I. Novikov, A. V. Suvorov and V. K. Maksimov, *Russ. J. Inorg. Chem.*, **4**, 935 (1959).
77. S. Rideal, *J. Chem. Soc.*, **55**, 41 (1889).
78. G. W. A. Fowles and B. P. Osborne, *J. Chem. Soc.*, **1959**, 2275.
79. S. Prasad and K. S. R. Krishnaiah, *J. Indian Chem. Soc.*, **37**, 588 (1960).
80. S. Prasad and K. S. R. Krishnaiah, *J. Indian Chem. Soc.*, **38**, 177 (1961).
81. S. Prasad and K. S. R. Krishnaiah, *J. Indian Chem. Soc.*, **38**, 182 (1961).
82. H. Funk and H. Bohland, *Z. anorg. allgem. Chem.*, **324**, 168 (1963).
83. S. Prasad and K. S. R. Krishnaiah, *J. Indian Chem. Soc.*, **37**, 681 (1960).
84. M. Baaz, V. Gutmann and M. Y. A. Talaat, *Monatsh. Chem.*, **92**, 714 (1961).
85. A. N. Nesmeyanov, K. N. Anisimov, E. P. Mikheev, V. L. Volkov and Z. P. Valueva, *Russ. J. Inorg. Chem.*, **4**, 107 (1959).

86. P. M. Boorman, N. N. Greenwood, M. A. Hildon and R. V. Parish, *Inorg. Nucl. Chem. Letters*, **2**, 377 (1966).
87. W. Puttbach, *Ann. Chem.*, **201**, 128 (1880).
88. I. Nordenskjold, *Ber.*, **34**, 1572 (1901).
89. I. A. Glukhov and G. A. Bekhtle, *Trudy Akad. Nauk Tadzh. SSR*, **84**, 35 (1958).
90. I. A. Glukhov and I. A. Rodionova, *Dokl. Akad. Nauk Tadzh. SSR*, **2**, 15 (1959).
91. I. A. Glukhov and S. S. Eliseev, *Russ. J. Inorg. Chem.*, **7**, 40 (1962).
92. D. A. Edwards and A. A. Woolf, *J. Chem. Soc.*, **1966**, *A*, 91.
93. R. Colton, I. B. Tomkins and P. W. Wilson, *Australian J. Chem.*, **17**, 496 (1964).
94. H. Hecht, G. Jander and H. Schlapmann, *Z. anorg. allgem. Chem.*, **254**, 255 (1947).
95. H. J. Seifert and H. P. Quak, *Angew. Chem.*, **73**, 621 (1961).
96. R. Colton and I. B. Tomkins, *Australian J. Chem.*, **18**, 447 (1965).
97. I. A. Glukhov and L. A. Tikhimirov, *Dokl. Akad. Nauk Tadzh. SSR*, **4**, 13 (1961).
98. I. A. Glukhov and S. S. Eliseev, *Russ. J. Inorg. Chem.*, **8**, 50 (1963).
99. M. L. Larson and F. W. Moore, *Inorg. Chem.*, **5**, 801 (1966).
100. S. A. Shchukarev, I. V. Vasil'kova and B. N. Sharupin, *Vestn. Leningr. Univ.* **14**, *Ser. Fiz. i Khim.*, 73 (1959).
101. T. V. Iorns and F. E. Stafford, *J. Am. Chem. Soc.*, **88**, 4819 (1966).
102. Y. A. Buslaev, A. A. Kuznetsova and L. F. Goryacheva, *Izvt. Akad. Nauk SSSR, Neorgan. Materialy*, **1**, 142 (1965).
103. E. R. Epperson and H. Frye, *Inorg. Nucl. Chem. Letters*, **2**, 223 (1966).
104. D. A. Edwards and A. A. Woolf, *J. Chem. Soc.*, **1966**, A, 91.
105. A. V. Komandin and D. N. Tarasenkov, *J. Gen. Chem. USSR*, **10**, 1333 (1940).
106. K. Funaki and K. Uchimura, *Denki Kagaku*, **30**, 35 (1962).
107. H. Hartung, *Z. Chem.*, **4**, 232 (1964).
108. H. Hess and H. Hartung, *Z. anorg. allgem. Chem.*, **344**, 157 (1966).
109. H. Funk and G. Mohaupt, *Z. anorg. allgem. Chem.*, **315**, 204 (1962).
110. S. Prasad and K. S. R. Krishnaiah, *J. Indian. Chem., Soc.*, **38**, 352 (1961).
111. S. Prasad and K. S. R. Krishnaiah, *J. Indian Chem. Soc.*, **38**, 400 (1961).
112. R. L. Graham and L. G. Helper, *J. Phys. Chem.*, **63**, 723 (1959).
113. H. M. Neumann and N. C. Cook, *J. Am. Chem. Soc.*, **79**, 3026 (1957).
114. F. Zado, *J. Inorg. Nucl. Chem.*, **25**, 1115 (1963).
115. A. N. Zelikman and N. N. Gorovits, *Zh. Obshsh. Khim.*, **24**, 1916 (1954).
116. F. Schroeder, *Naturwissenschaften*, **52**, 389 (1965).
117. C. G. Barraclough and J. Stals, *Australian J. Chem.*, **19**, 741 (1966).
118. E. N. Nenarokomov and I. G. Shepchenko, *Russ. J. Inorg. Chem.*, **8**, 1459 (1963).
119. K. H. Arend and H. Specker, *Z. anorg. allgem. Chem.*, **333**, 18 (1964).
120. S. A. Shchukarev, I. V. Vasil'kova and B. N. Sharupin, *Vestn. Leningr. Univ.* **16**, *Ser. Fiz. i Khim.*, 130 (1961).
121. S. M. Batisova, R. M. Davydovskaya and G. A. Bekhtle, *Izv. Otd. Estestv. Nauk, Akad. Nauk Tadzh. SSR*, **1957**, 35.
122. K. Funaki and K. Uchimura, *Denki Kagaku*, **30**, 106 (1962).

123. H. G. Dehmelt, *J. Chem. Phys.*, **21**, 380 (1953).
124. E. M. Shustorovich and L. O. Atovnyan, *Zh. Strukt. Khim.*, **4**, 273 (1963).
125. S. M. Horner and S. Y. Tyree, *Inorg. Chem.*, **1**, 122 (1962).
126. H. L. Krauss and W. Huber, *Chem. Ber.*, **94**, 2864 (1961).
127. J. Bernard and M. Camelot, *Compt. Rend.*, **263**, 1068 (1966).
128. H. A. Schaffer and E. F. Smith, *J. Am. Chem. Soc.*, **18**, 1098 (1896).
129. M. Pourand and M. Chaigneau, *Compt. Rend.* **249**, 2568 (1959).
130. S. A. Shchukarev, G. I. Novikov and G. A. Kokovin, *Russ. J. Inorg. Chem.*, **4**, 995 (1959).
131. S. A. Shchukarev and G. A. Kokovin, *Russ. J. Inorg. Chem.*, **5**, 241 (1960).
132. S. A. Shchukarev and G. A. Kokovin, *Russ. J. Inorg. Chem.*, **9**, 849 (1964).
133. I. V. Vasil'kova, N. D. Zaitseva and Y. S. Svalov, *Vestn. Leningr. Univ.* **16**, *Ser. Fiz. i Khim.*, 140 (1962).
134. G. B. Hargreaves and R. D. Peacock, *J. Chem. Soc.*, **1960**, 1099.
135. H. H. Hyman, T. J. Lane and T. A. O'Donnell, *Abstr.* 145th *Nat. Meeting Amer. Chem. Soc.*, New York, N.Y., September 1963, 63T.
136. D. E. Sands and A. Zalkin, *Acta Cryst.*, **12**, 723 (1959).
137. K. Knox and C. E. Coffey, *J. Am. Chem. Soc.*, **81**, 5 (1959).
138. W. Klemm and H. Steinberg, *Z. anorg. allgem. Chem.*, **227**, 193 (1936).
139. R. F. W. Bader and A. D. Westland, *Can. J. Chem.*, **39**, 2306 (1961).
140. I. M. Pearson and C. S. Garner, *J. Phys. Chem.*, **65**, 690 (1961).
141. A. N. Nesmeyanov, E. P. Mikheev, K. N. Anisimov, V. L. Volkov and Z. P. Valueva, *Russ. J. Inorg. Chem.*, **4**, 228 (1959).
142. D. A. Edwards and G. W. A. Fowles, *J. Less-Common Metals*, **3**, 181 (1961).
143. M. A. Glushkova, *Russ. J. Inorg. Chem.*, **6**, 7 (1961).
144. N. S. Fortunatov and N. I. Timoshchenko, *Ukr. Khim. Zh.*, **31**, 1078 (1965).
145. W. Wardlaw and H. Webb, *J. Chem. Soc.*, **1930**, 2100.
146. W. L. Groeneveld, *Rec. Trav. Chim.*, **71**, 1152 (1952).
147. V. Gutmann, *Z. anorg. allgem. Chem.*, **269**, 279 (1952).
148. E. A. Allen, B. J. Brisdon and G. W. A. Fowles, *J. Chem. Soc.*, **1964**, 4531.
149. P. C. H. Mitchell, *J. Inorg. Nucl. Chem.*, **25**, 963 (1963).
150. M. L. Larson, *J. Am. Chem. Soc.*, **82**, 1223 (1960).
151. W. Biltz and C. Fendius, *Z. anorg. allgem. Chem.*, **172**, 385 (1928).
152. G. I. Novikov, N. V. Andreeva and O. G. Polyachenok, *Russ. J. Inorg. Chem.*, **6**, 1019 (1961).
153. R. Colton and I. B. Tomkins, *Australian J. Chem.*, **19**, 759 (1966).
154. S. A. Shchukarev, G. I. Novokov and N. V. Andreeva, *Zh. Obshch. Khim.*, **28**, 1998 (1958).
155. B. J. Brisdon and G. W. A. Fowles, *J. Less-Common Metals*, **7**, 102 (1964).
156. H. Funk and H. Naumann, *Z. anorg. allgem. Chem.*, **343**, 294 (1966).
157. G. W. A. Fowles and J. L. Frost, *Chem. Commun.*, **1966**, 252.
158. I. A. Glukhov and S. S. Eliseev, *Izv. Akad. Nauk Tadzh. SSR, Otd. Geol. Khim. i Tekh. Nauk*, **1959**, 79.
159. D. A. Edwards, *J. Inorg. Nucl. Chem.*, **25**, 1198 (1963).
160. K. Feenan and G. W. A. Fowles, *Inorg. Chem.*, **4**, 310 (1965).
161. D. A. Edwards, *J. Inorg. Nucl. Chem.*, **27**, 303 (1965).
162. H. F. Priest and W. C. Schumb, *J. Am. Chem. Soc.*, **70**, 3378 (1948).
163. E. L. Muetterties, *J. Am. Chem. Soc.*, **82**, 1082 (1960).

164. D. E. Couch and A. Brenner, *J. Res. Nat. Bur. Std.*, **63A**, 185 (1959).
165. M. L. Larson and F. W. Moore, *Inorg. Chem.*, **3**, 285 (1964).
166. T. E. Austin and S. Y. Tyree, *J. Inorg. Nucl. Chem.*, **14**, 141 (1960).
167. S. M. Horner and S. Y. Tyree, *Inorg. Chem.*, **1**, 947 (1962).
168. R. E. McCarley and T. M. Brown, *Inorg. Chem.*, **3**, 1232 (1964).
169. S. A. Shchukarev, G. I. Novikov and N. V. Andreeva, *Vestn. Leningr. Univ.* **14,** *Ser. Fiz. i Khim.*, 120 (1959).
170. C. D. Kennedy and R. D. Peacock, *J. Chem. Soc.*, **1963**, 3392.
171. H. Schafer and J. Tillack, *J. Less-Common Metals*, **6**, 152 (1964).
172. W. Hieber and E. Romberg, *Z. anorg. allgem. Chem.*, **221**, 321 (1935).
173. I. V. Vasil'kova, A. I. Efimov and B. Z. Pitirimov, *Khim. Redkikh Elementov, Leningr. Gos. Univ.*, **1964**, 44.
174. R. E. McCarley and T. M. Brown, *J. Am. Chem. Soc.*, **84**, 3216 (1962).
175. E. L. Muetterties and J. E. Castle, *J. Inorg. Nucl. Chem.*, **18**, 148 (1961).
176. D. E. LaValle, R. M. Steele, M. K. Williamson and H. L. Yakel, *J. Am. Chem. Soc.*, **82**, 2433 (1960).
177. V. Gutmann and K. H. Jack, *Acta Cryst.*, **4**, 244 (1951).
178. M. K. Wilkinson, E. O. Wollan, H. R. Child and J. W. Cable, *Phys. Rev.*, **121**, 74 (1961).
179. R. Colton and R. L. Martin, *Nature*, **207**, 141 (1965).
180. D. J. Bettinger, *J. Sci. Lab. Denison Univ.*, **45**, 162 (1962).
181. *U.S. Pat.* 3,057,697.
182. W. Wardlaw and R. L. Wormell, *J. Chem. Soc.*, **1927**, 1087.
183. H. G. Schnering and H. Woehrle, *Naturwissenschaften*, **50**, 91 (1963).
184. D. A. Edwards and G. W. A. Fowles, *J. Less-Common Metals*, **4**, 512 (1962).
185. J. R. M. Fernadez and A. B. Duran, *Anales Real Soc. Espan. Fis. Quim.* (*Madrid*) **55B**, 823 (1959).
186. C. Durand, R. Schaal and P. Souchay, *Compt. Rend.*, **248**, 979 (1959).
187. J. Lewis, D. J. Machin, R. S. Nyholm, P. Pauling and P. W. Smith, *Chem. Ind.* (*London*), **1960**, 159.
188. F. Klanberg and H. W. Kohlschutter, *Z. Naturforsch.*, **15b**, 616 (1960).
189. C. Djordjevic, R. S. Nyholm, C. S. Pande and M. H. B. Stiddard, *J. Chem. Soc.*, **1966**, A, 16.
190. L. Lindner, E. Haller and H. Helwig, *Z. anorg. allgem. Chem.*, **130**, 209 (1923).
191. S. Senderoff and A. Brenner, *J. Electrochem. Soc.*, **101**, 28 (1954).
192. K. Lindner and H. Helwig, *Z. anorg. allgem. Chem.*, **142**, 180 (1925).
193. S. A. Shchukarev, I. V. Vasil'kova, D. V. Kovol'kov and S. S. Nikol'skii, *Vestn. Leningr. Univ.* **17,** *Ser. Fiz. i Khim.*, 148 (1962).
194. M. Chaigneau, *Bull. Soc. Chim. France*, 1957, 886.
195. T. L. Allen and D. M. Yost, *J. Chem. Phys.*, **22**, 855 (1954).
196. B. Cox, D. W. A. Sharp and A. G. Sharpe, *J. Chem. Soc.*, **1956**, 1242.
197. S. Katz, *Inorg. Chem.*, **3**, 1598 (1964).
198. S. Katz, *Inorg. Chem.*, **5**, 666 (1966).
199. N. V. Sidgwick, *The Chemical Elements and their Compounds*, Oxford Univ. Press, London, 1950, p. 1044.
200. R. Weiss, D. Grandjean and B. Metz, *Compt. Rend.*, **260**, 3969 (1965).
201. Y. A. Busleav and R. L. Davidovich, *Dokl. Akad. Nauk SSSR*, **164**, 1296 (1965).

202. Y. A. Busleav and R. L. Davidovich, *Russ. J. Inorg. Chem.*, **10**, 1014 (1965).
203. O. Schmitz-Dumont and P. Opgenhoff, *Z. anorg. allgem. Chem.*, **275**, 21 (1954).
204. G. W. A. Fowles and J. L. Frost, *J. Chem. Soc.*, **1966**, *A*, 1631.
205. E. Weinland and W. Knoll, *Z. anorg. allgem. Chem.*, **44**, 81 (1905).
206. J. Prigent and P. Caillet, *Compt. Rend.*, **256**, 2184 (1963).
207. R. D. W. Kemmitt, D. R. Russell and D. W. A. Sharp, *J. Chem. Soc.*, **1963**, 4408.
208. G. B. Hargreaves and R. D. Peacock, *J. Chem. Soc.*, **1957**, 4212.
209. R. D. W. Kemmitt and D. W. A. Sharp, *J. Chem. Soc.*, **1961**, 2496.
210. R. D. Peacock and D. W. A. Sharp, *J. Chem. Soc.*, **1959**, 2762.
211. G. B. Hargreaves and R. D. Peacock, *J. Chem. Soc.*, **1958**, 3776.
212. N. S. Garif'yanov, V. N. Fedotov and N. S. Kucheryavenko, *Izv. Akad. Nauk SSSR, Ser. Khim.*, **1964**, 743.
213. A. I. Efimov, I. V. Vasil'kova, E. K. Smirnova, N. D. Zaitseva, T. S. Shemyakina and I. L. Perfilova, *Khim. Redkikh Elementov, Leningr. Gos. Univ.*, **1964**, 38.
214. N. D. Zaitseva, *Russ. J. Inorg. Chem.*, **8**, 1239 (1963).
215. B. J. Brisdon and R. A. Walton, *J. Inorg. Nucl. Chem.*, **27**, 1101 (1965).
216. K. W. Bagnall, D. Brown and J. G. H. Du Preez, *J. Chem. Soc.*, **1964**, 2603.
217. D. M. Adams, J. Chatt, J. M. Davidson and J. Gerratt, *J. Chem. Soc.*, **1963**, 2189.
218. R. N. Dickinson, S. E. Feil, F. N. Collier, W. W. Horner, S. M. Horner and S. Y. Tyree, *Inorg. Chem.*, **3**, 1600 (1964).
219. J. P. Simon and P. Souchay, *Bull. Chim. Soc. France*, 1402 (1956).
220. P. Klasen, *Ber.*, **34**, 148 (1901).
221. E. Wendling, R. Rohmer and R. Weiss, *Compt. Rend.*, **256**, 1117 (1963).
222. R. G. James and W. Wardlaw, *J. Chem. Soc.*, **1927**, 2145.
223. F. Foerster and E. Fricke, *Angew. Chem.*, **36**, 458 (1923).
224. E. A. Allen, B. J. Brisdon, D. A. Edwards, G. W. A. Fowles and R. G. Williams, *J. Chem. Soc.*, **1963**, 4649.
225. D. Brown, *J. Chem. Soc.*, **1964**, 4944.
226. H. B. Gray and C. R. Hare, *Inorg. Chem.*, **1**, 363 (1962).
227. C. K. Jorgensen, *Acta Chem. Scand.*, **11**, 73 (1957).
228. R. A. D. Wentworth and T. S. Piper, *J. Chem. Phys.*, **41**, 3884 (1964).
229. S. M. Horner and S. Y. Tyree, *Inorg. Nucl. Chem. Letters*, **1**, 43 (1965).
230. C. J. Balhausen and H. B. Gray, *Inorg. Chem.*, **1**, 111 (1962).
231. N. S. Garif'yanov and V. N. Fedotov, *Zh. Strukt. Khim.*, **3**, 711 (1962).
232. C. R. Hare, I. Bernal and H. B. Gray, *Inorg. Chem.*, **1**, 831 (1962).
233. K. DeArmond, B. B. Garrett and H. S. Gutowsky, *J. Chem. Phys.*, **42**, 1019 (1965).
234. H. Kon and N. E. Sharpless, *J. Phys. Chem.*, **70**, 105 (1966).
235. A. Sabatini and I. Bertini, *Inorg. Chem.*, **5**, 204 (1966).
236. C. G. Barraclough, J. Lewis and R. S. Nyholm, *J. Chem. Soc.*, **1959**, 3552.
237. L. Sacconi and R. Cini, *J. Am. Chem. Soc.*, **76**, 4239 (1954).
238. G. P. Haight, *J. Inorg. Nucl. Chem.*, **24**, 663 (1963).
239. R. Colton and G. G. Rose, *Australian J. Chem.* **21**, 883 (1968).
240. O. Collenberg, *Z. anorg. allgem. Chem.*, **102**, 259 (1918).
241. O. Collenberg and A. Guthe, *Z. anorg. allgem. Chem.*, **134**, 317 (1924).

242. E. Allen, D. A. Edwards and G. W. A. Fowles, *Chem. Ind. (London)*, **1962**, 1026.
243. B. J. Brisdon and R. A. Walton, *J. Chem. Soc.*, **1965**, 2274.
244. J. F. Allen and H. M. Neumann, *Inorg. Chem.*, **3**, 1612 (1964).
245. A. J. Edwards and R. D. Peacock, *Chem. Ind. (London)*, **1960**, 1441.
246. D. H. Brown, K. R. Dixon, R. D. W. Kemmitt and D. W. A. Sharp, *J. Chem. Soc.*, **1965**, 1559.
247. A. I. Efimov, L. P. Belorukova and A. M. Ryndina, *Russ. J. Inorg. Chem.*, **8**, 605 (1963).
248. I. V. Vasil'kova and A. I. Efimov, *J. Gen. Chem. USSR*, **32**, 2699 (1962).
249. A. J. Edwards, R. D. Peacock and A. Said, *J. Chem. Soc.*, **1962**, 4643.
250. D. M. Adams, H. A. Gebbie and R. D. Peacock, *Nature*, **199**, 278 (1963).
251. O. Olsson, *Ber.*, **46**, 566 (1913).
252. S. Aleonard, *Compt. Rend.*, **260**, 1977 (1965).
253. R. D. Peacock, *Progress in Inorganic Chemistry* (ed. F. A. Cotton), Interscience, N.Y., Vol. 2, 1960, p. 205.
254. W. R. Bucknell, S. R. Carter and W. Wandlaw, *J. Chem. Soc.*, **1927**, 512.
255. K. H. Lohmann and R. C. Young, *Inorg. Syn.*, **4**, 97 (1953).
256. B. N. Figgis, J. Lewis and F. E. Mabbs, *J. Chem. Soc.*, **1961**, 3138.
257. P. C. H. Mitchell and R. J. P. Williams, *J. Chem. Soc.*, **1962**, 4570.
258. S. Senderoff and A. Brenner, *J. Electrochem. Soc.*, **101**, 16 (1954).
259. T. Komorita, S. Miki and S. Yamada, *Bull. Chem. Soc. Japan*, **38**, 123 (1965).
260. H. B. Jonassen and S. Cantor, *Rec. Trav. Chim.*, **75**, 609 (1956).
261. R. A. Laudise and R. C. Young, *Inorg. Syn.*, **6**, 153 (1960).
262. H. B. Jonassen, A. R. Tarsey, S. Cantor and G. F. Helfrich, *Inorg. Syn.*, **5**, 139 (1957).
263. C. Brossett, *Nature*, **135**, 874 (1935).
264. C. Brossett, *Arkiv Kemi Min. Geol.*, **1935**, No. 12A.
265. W. H. Watson and J. Waser, *Acta Cryst.*, **11**, 689 (1958).
266. R. A. Laudise and R. C. Young, *J. Am. Chem. Soc.*, **77**, 5288 (1955).
267. E. König, *Inorg. Chem.*, **2**, 1238 (1963).
268. R. C. Young, *J. Am. Chem. Soc.*, **54**, 4515 (1932).
269. W. Wardlaw and R. L. Wormell, *Nouveau Traité de Chimie Minérale* (Ed. P. Pascal) Masson Paris, Vol. 14, 1959, p. 644.
270. W. Wardlaw and R. L. Wormell, *J. Chem. Soc.*, **1927**, 130.
271. W. Wardlaw and R. L. Wormell, *J. Chem. Soc.*, **1924**, 2370.
272. W. P. Griffith, *J. Chem. Soc.*, **1964**, 5248.
273. D. Grandjean and R. Weiss, *Acta Cryst.*, **16**, 1180 (1963).
274. Z. Mateiko and G. A. Bukhalova, *Russ. J. Inorg. Chem.*, **4**, 743 (1959).
275. *U.S. Pat.* 2,945,744 (1960).
276. O. Glemser, J. Wegner and R. Mews, *Chem. Ber.*, **100**, 2474 (1967).
277. S. Siegel and D. A. Northrup, *Inorg. Chem.*, **5**, 2187 (1966).
278. K. H. Hellberg, A. Muller and O. Glemser, *Z. Naturforsch.*, **21b**, 118 (1966).
279. S. Abramowitz and I. W. Lewin, *Inorg. Chem.*, **6**, 538 (1967).
280. H. M. Siep and R. Siep, *Acta Chem. Scand.*, **20**, 2698 (1966).
281. B. Frlec and H. H. Hyman, *Inorg. Chem.*, **6**, 1596 (1967).

19

282. W. D. Hedge, U.S.A.E.C. Report K-1699 (1967).
283. G. W. Fraser, M. Mercer and R. D. Peacock, *J. Chem. Soc.*, **1967**, *A*, 1091.
284. A. J. Edwards, G. R. Jones and B. R. Steventon, *Chem. Commun.*, **1967**, 462.
285. S. Blanchard, French Atomic Energy Commission Report, C.E.A.-R3194 (1967).
286. M. Mercer, *Chem. Commun.*, **1966**, 119.
287. J. H. Canterford, R. Colton and I. B. Tomkins, *Australian J. Chem.*, in the press.
288. R. A. Walton and B. J. Brisdon, *Spectrochim. Acta*, **23A**, 2489 (1967).
289. Y. Sacki and R. Matsuzaki, *Denki Kagaku*, **34**, 455 (1966).
290. L. A. Nisel'son, R. K. Nikolaev and Z. N. Orshanskayer, *Zh. Neorg. Khim.*, **12**, 860 (1967).
291. G. W. A. Fowles and J. L. Frost, *J. Chem. Soc.*, **1967**, *A*, 671.
292. Y. Sacki and R. Matsuzaki, *Denki Kagaku*, **34**, 504 (1966).
293. B. J. Brisdon, *Inorg. Chem.*, **6**, 1791 (1967).
294. H. Funk and F. Modry, *Z. Chem.*, **7**, 27B (1967).
295. W. M. Carmicheal, D. A. Edwards, G. W. A. Fowles and P. R. Marshall, *Inorg. Chim. Acta*, **1**, 93 (1967).
296. P. M. Druce, M. F. Lappert and P. N. K. Riley, *Chem. Commun.*, **1967**, 486.
297. G. A. Kokovin, *Zh. Neorg. Khim.*, **12**, 15 (1967).
298. L. Kolditz and U. Calov, *Z. Chem.*, **6**, 431A (1966).
299. Y. Sacki and R. Matsuzaki, *Denki Kagaku*, **33**, 151 (1966).
300. K. Rinke and H. Schafer, *Angew. Chem.*, **79**, 650 (1967).
301. T. M. Brown and B. Ruble, *Inorg. Chem.*, **6**, 1335 (1967).
302. B. Heyn, *Z. Chem.*, **7**, 280B (1967).
303. B. J. Brisdon, D. A. Edwards, D. J. Machin, K. S. Murray and R. A. Walton, *J. Chem. Soc.*, **1967**, *A*, 1825.
304. P. M. Boorman, N. N. Greenwood, M. A. Hildon and H. J. Whitfield, *J. Chem. Soc.*, **1967**, *A*, 2017.
305. R. Colton and I. B. Tomkins, *Australian J. Chem.*, in the press.
306. H. Schafer, H. G. Schnering, J. Tillack, F. Kuhnen, H. Woehrle and H. Baumann, *Z. anorg. allgem. Chem.*, **353**, 281 (1967).
307. W. M. Carmicheal, D. A. Edwards and R. A. Walton, *J. Chem. Soc.*, **1967**, *A*, 97.
308. T. M. Brown, D. K. Pungs, L. R. Lieto and D. S. Delong, *Inorg. Chem.*, **5**, 1695 (1966).
309. S. M. Horner, F. N. Collier and S. Y. Tyree, *J. Less-Common Metals*, **13**, 85 (1967).
310. A. K. Mallock, *Inorg. Nucl. Chem. Letters*, **3**, 441 (1967).
311. R. Siepman, H. G. Schnering and H. Schafer, *Angew. Chem. Internat. Edit., Engl.*, **6**, 637 (1967).
312. D. Grandjean and R. Weiss, *Compt. Rend.*, **262C**, 1864 (1966).
313. D. Grandjean and R. Weiss, *Bull. Soc. Chim. France*, **1967**, 3049.
314. J. Fischer, A. DeCian and R. Weiss, *Bull. Soc. Chim. France*, **1966**, 2646.
315. A. DeCian, J. Fischer and R. Weiss, *Bull. Soc. Chim. France*, **1966**, 2647.
316. D. Grandjean and R. Weiss, *Bull. Soc. Chim. France*, **1967**, 3040.
317. D. Grandjean and R. Weiss, *Bull. Soc. Chim. France*, **1967**, 3044.

318. E. Wendling, *Bull. Soc. Chim. France*, **1967**, 5.
319. J. E. Guerchais and M. T. Youinou, *Compt. Rend.*, **264C,** 1389 (1967).
320. B. Frlec, H. Selig and H. H. Hyman, *Inorg. Chem.*, **6,** 1775 (1967).
321. D. Grandjean and R. Weiss, *Compt. Rend.*, **263C,** 58 (1966).
322. D. Grandjean and R. Weiss, *Bull. Soc. Chim. France*, **1967,** 3054.
323. O. Piovesana and C. Furlani, *Inorg. Nucl. Chem. Letters*, **3,** 535 (1967).
324. R. D. Dowsing and J. F. Gibson, *J. Chem. Soc.*, **1967,** *A*, 655.
325. J. G. Scane, *Acta Cryst.*, **23,** 85 (1967).
326. R. Saillant, J. L. Hayden and R. A. D. Wentworth, *Inorg. Chem.*, **6,** 1497 (1967).

Chapter 7

Technetium and Rhenium

Binary halides of rhenium are known for all oxidation states from I to VII; oxide halides are mainly restricted to oxidation states V to VII. The chemistry of technetium has not been well explored so far, but potentially it is as interesting as that of rhenium.

A dramatic development in rhenium chemistry in recent years has been the emergence of the fascinating chemistry of rhenium(III). Two distinct types of chemistry are observed; one, based on compounds of the type $Re_2X_8^{2-}$ will be discussed in this chapter, but the second type, involving compounds of the general formula $Re_3X_{12}^{3-}$ have been discussed in Chapter 3.

HALIDES AND OXIDE HALIDES

The known halides and oxide halides of technetium and rhenium are listed in Tables 7.1 and 7.2. However, it is not always certain that the absence of a specific compound from these tables is significant: it may often be that no one has seriously attempted to prepare it. Nevertheless this latter is certainly not true in the case of technetium heptafluoride; concerted efforts have been made by the group at the Argonne National Laboratory to prepare this compound, but without success.

TABLE 7.1

Binary Halides of Technetium and Rhenium

Oxidation state	Fluoride	Chloride	Bromide	Iodide
VII	ReF_7			
VI	TcF_6, ReF_6	$TcCl_6, ReCl_6$		
V	TcF_5, ReF_5	$ReCl_5$	$ReBr_5$	
IV	ReF_4	$TcCl_4, ReCl_4$	$ReBr_4$	ReI_4
III		$ReCl_3$	$ReBr_3$	ReI_3
II				ReI_2
I				ReI

Chlorination of pure metallic technetium produces predominantly technetium tetrachloride, with a small amount of technetium hexachloride. Under similar conditions pure metallic rhenium gives predominantly the hexachloride; however, if the rhenium metal has been produced by reduction of potassium perrhenate the pentachloride is the major product. This effect has been ascribed to the presence of large amounts of potassium

TABLE 7.2

Oxide Halides of Technetium and Rhenium

Oxidation state	Fluoride	Chloride	Bromide
VII	$ReOF_5$		
	ReO_2F_3		
	TcO_3F, ReO_3F	TcO_3Cl, ReO_3Cl	ReO_3Br
VI	$TcOF_4$, $ReOF_4$	$TcOCl_4$, $ReOCl_4$	$ReOBr_4$
V	$ReOF_3$	$TcOCl_3$, $ReOCl_3$	$TcOBr_3$, $ReOBr_3$

in the rhenium; perhaps one should use impure technetium metal to obtain technetium pentachloride. The absence of technetium pentachloride is important because, by analogy with rhenium and molybdenum chemistry, it should decompose thermally to the unknown technetium trichloride, which would then open the way to exploring the preparation of trinuclear complexes of technetium(III).

Oxidation State VII

Rhenium heptafluoride. It has been shown that rhenium heptafluoride is formed by the action of fluorine at 250 mm pressure on rhenium metal at 300–400° [1,2]. The product is always a mixture of the heptafluoride and the hexafluoride, in proportions depending on the experimental conditions. Low temperatures favour formation of the hexafluoride. As it was almost impossible to separate the two fluorides, the mixture was heated with fluorine at 3 atm pressure at 400° for several hours, the hexafluoride being thus converted quantitatively into the heptafluoride.

Rhenium heptafluoride is a yellow solid very similar in appearance to the hexafluoride, a fact which no doubt delayed its discovery. Malm and Selig[2] studied the physical properties of both halides and showed conclusively that almost all the earlier samples of the hexafluoride were contaminated with the higher fluoride.

Rhenium heptafluoride is thermally stable and can be kept indefinitely in dry Pyrex glass. It is instantly hydrolysed by water to perrhenic and hydrofluoric acid. It is reduced by rhenium metal to the hexafluoride

TABLE 7.3

Thermodynamic Properties of
Rhenium Heptafluoride

Property	Value
Triple point	48.3°
B.p.	73.72°
Liquid density (52°) g cm^{-3}	3.65
ΔH_{fus} (kcal mole^{-1})	1.799
ΔH_{vap} (kcal mole^{-1})	9.154
ΔS_{fus} (cal deg^{-1} mole^{-1})	5.60

but, rather remarkably, it does not react with oxygen even when heated to 500° for several hours.

The vapour pressure of rhenium heptafluoride has been measured over a fairly wide temperature range[1,2]. The following equations were deduced from the experimental results:

Solid ReF$_7$ (−14.47–48.3°)

$$\log p_{mm} = 13.043 - 1.470 \log T - 2206/T$$

Liquid ReF$_7$ (48.3–74.61°)

$$\log p_{mm} = -21.584 + 9.908 \log T - 244.3/T$$

The thermodynamic properties shown in Table 7.3 have been calculated from the vapour pressure measurements.

The infrared spectrum of rhenium heptafluoride[3] is shown in Figure 7.1.

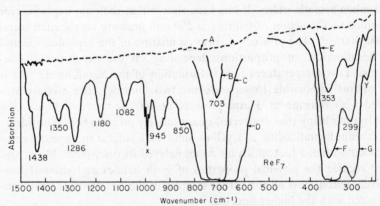

Figure 7.1 Infrared spectrum of ReF$_7$. Sample pressures were: A (background), B (unknown, <1 mm, path length 60 cm), C (3 mm, path length 60 cm), D (87 mm, path length 60 cm), E (9 mm, path length 10 cm), F (25 mm, path length 10 cm), G (97 mm, path length 10 cm).

The Raman spectrum[3] shows peaks at the following frequencies: 351m, 485s, 590m, 650w, 737vs cm^{-1}. Use of this information and of the infrared spectrum suggests that rhenium heptafluoride is a pentagonal bipyramid but, as Claassen and Selig[3] pointed out, this evidence is not conclusive.

The ^{19}F-NMR spectrum of rhenium heptafluoride is not very informative since there appears to be very rapid intramolecular exchange of fluorine that results in one resonance peak only[4,5]. Bartlett and coworkers[4] give the position of this peak as 510 ppm downfield from that of silicon tetrafluoride.

Rhenium oxide pentafluoride. Rhenium oxide pentafluoride is one of the products[6] of the action of fluorine on potassium perrhenate at about 100°. Once the reaction has begun the potassium perrhenate melts owing to the heat evolved. The other product is rhenium dioxide trifluoride, in the approximate ratio of, usually, $ReOF_5 : ReO_2F_3 = 1:10$. The action of fluorine on rhenium dioxide gives the same products but usually in the ratio $ReOF_5 : ReO_2F_3 = 1:3$.

At room temperature rhenium oxide pentafluoride is a cream-coloured crystalline solid. It melts at 34.5° to a colourless liquid that boils at 55°. In the absence of moisture it does not etch glass. It gives white fumes in moist air and is instantly hydrolysed by water, giving perrhenic and hydrofluoric acid.

The vapour pressure of rhenium oxide pentafluoride has been measured over a wide temperature range[7]. There is a solid–solid transition at 30°, the vapour-pressure equations deduced from the experimental data being as follows:

$$\text{Solid } ReOF_5 \ (0\text{--}30°): \log p_{mm} = 9.581 - 2250/T$$
$$\text{Solid } ReOF_5 \ (30\text{--}41°): \log p_{mm} = 8.620 - 1958.9/T$$
$$\text{Liquid } ReOF_5 \ (41\text{--}73°): \log p_{mm} = 7.727 - 1678.6/T$$

Some thermodynamic properties of rhenium oxide pentafluoride are given in Table 7.4.

The ^{19}F-NMR spectrum of the oxide pentafluoride shows unequivocally that the molecule possesses C_{4v} symmetry[4]. The spectrum consists of a weak quartet at 159.6 ppm from the axial fluorine atom and a strong doublet at 361.9 ppm from four equivalent fluorine atoms, the positions of the resonances being downfield relative to silicon tetrafluoride[4].

Rhenium dioxide trifluoride. This is the second product resulting from the action of fluorine on potassium perrhenate or rhenium dioxide[6]. Rhenium dioxide trifluoride is a pale yellow solid which melts at 90°.

The liquid solidifies to a glass but the compound may be obtained crystalline by slow sublimation in a vacuum. Rhenium dioxide trifluoride does not attack glass up to 300°; it is easily hydrolysed by water to perrhenic and hydrofluoric acid.

The vapour pressure of rhenium dioxide trifluoride has been measured only for the liquid phase[7]. The vapour pressure equation is

$$\log p_{mm} = 10.36 - 3437/T \quad (90\text{–}170°)$$

Cady and Hargreaves[7] found the triple point to be 90° and estimated the boiling point as 185.4°. The heat and entropy of vaporization were calculated to be 15.7 kcal mole^{-1} and 34.3 cal deg^{-1} mole^{-1}, respectively.

TABLE 7.4

Thermodynamic Properties of
Rhenium Oxide Pentafluoride

Property	Value
Triple point	40.8°
B.p.	73.0°
Transition point	30.0°
ΔH_{trans} (kcal mole^{-1})	1.339
ΔH_{vap} (kcal mole^{-1})	7.720
ΔH_{sub} (above 30°) (kcal mole^{-1})	8.940
(below 30°) (kcal mole^{-1})	10.280
ΔS_{trans} (cal deg^{-1} mole^{-1})	3.868
ΔS_{vap} (cal deg^{-1} mole^{-1})	22.3

Technetium trioxide fluoride (pertechnyl fluoride). The existence of technetium trioxide fluoride was suspected some years ago from a mass-spectroscopic examination of the products obtained on reaction between technetium heptaoxide and uranium tetrafluoride[8].

Technetium trioxide fluoride has since been isolated after fluorine has been passed over heated technetium dioxide[9]. It is surprising that a molecule containing three oxygen atoms per technetium atom should be obtained from a material containing only two oxygen atoms per technetium atom. Obviously some type of disproportionation must occur, giving an oxygen-deficient product as well as technetium trioxide fluoride. It was, in fact, reported that a grey residue remained in the reaction vessel but this was not identified. The difference between this reaction and that between fluorine and rhenium dioxide is also noteworthy.

Technetium trioxide fluoride is a yellow crystalline compound which melts at 18.3° to a yellow liquid. The boiling point obtained by extrapolation from vapour-pressure measurements is about 100°. It is stable at room temperature in nickel or Monel metal but it attacks Pyrex glass. Water causes hydrolysis to pertechnetic and hydrofluoric acid. With an excess of fluorine at 400° and 4 atm pressure the compound gives technetium hexafluoride[9].

The vapour pressure of technetium trioxide fluoride is given by the following equations:

Solid TcO_3F (−8.78–18.28°): $\log p_{mm} = 12.448 - 3239.4/T$

Liquid TcO_3F (18.28–51.82°): $\log p_{mm} = 8.417 - 2064.6/T$

Thermodynamic data have been calculated[9] and are given in Table 7.5.

TABLE 7.5

Thermodynamic Data for
Technetium Trioxide Fluoride

Property	Value
M.p.	18.3°
B.p.	about 100°
ΔH_{sub} (kcal mole^{-1})	14.83
ΔH_{vap} (kcal mole^{-1})	9.453
ΔH_{fus} (kcal mole^{-1})	5.377

Rhenium trioxide fluoride (perrhenyl fluoride). The existence of rhenium trioxide fluoride was suspected by Ruff but he did not isolate the compound. It was first prepared by interaction of rhenium trioxide chloride, ReO_3Cl, and anhydrous hydrogen fluoride[10]. The excess of hydrogen fluoride was pumped away and the product was purified by vacuum-sublimation.

Rhenium trioxide fluoride has also been prepared in good yield by the reaction of iodine pentafluoride on finely divided potassium perrhenate[11]. Reaction was only slight at room temperature, but, on refluxing, the potassium perrhenate dissolved to give a deep yellow solution, from which a yellow solid separated on cooling. The excess of iodine pentafluoride was pumped off and the product purified by vacuum-sublimation at 140°.

Rhenium trioxide fluoride is a yellow solid melting at 147° to a very viscous yellow liquid which boils at 164° with slight decomposition[10]. The liquid usually solidifies to a glass, but the compound can be obtained crystalline by slow sublimation in a vacuum. Like the other heptavalent rhenium fluorides, rhenium trioxide fluoride does not attack glass, but it is very reactive towards moisture. It fumes in moist air and in water is instantly hydrolysed to produce perrhenic and hydrofluoric acid.

The microwave spectrum of rhenium trioxide fluoride has been observed[12], the molecule being found to be a symmetrical top, like rhenium trioxide chloride. The following parameters were obtained: Re–O = 1.692 Å; Re–F = 1.859 Å; F–Re–O = 109°31′.

The dipole moment was found to be 0.85 D.

Technetium trioxide chloride (pertechnyl chloride). Technetium trioxide chloride, TcO_3Cl, was said to have been formed on treatment of potassium pertechnetate dissolved in 18M sulphuric acid with 12M hydrochloric acid[13]. It was found that the compound could be extracted into chloroform, carbon tetrachloride or hexane; although its vibrational spectrum was recorded, there is no account of its having been isolated and characterized.

More recently however, technetium trioxide chloride has been isolated by heating technetium tetrachloride gently in a stream of oxygen[14]. Technetium trioxide chloride, like its rhenium analogue, is a colourless liquid. It is less stable, however, than the rhenium compound; gentle heating caused some decomposition to a red solid although the bulk of the liquid distilled unchanged. Heating the red solid in a stream of chlorine gave technetium trioxide chloride again, and it was thought that the solid was technetium trioxide. The decomposition of technetium trioxide chloride thus resembles that of rhenium trioxide bromide (see below).

Rhenium trioxide chloride (perrhenyl chloride). Rhenium trioxide chloride was first prepared by Bruckl and Ziegler[15] by chlorinating rhenium metal to give a volatile chloride which was then allowed to react with rhenium heptaoxide. By fractionating the products in nitrogen they were able to separate rhenium trioxide chloride as a colourless, highly refractive liquid from rhenium oxide tetrachloride, the other product of the reaction. The same two chlorides are also formed by the action of oxygen on rhenium trichloride[16,17]. It has been claimed[18] that oxygen and rhenium pentachloride give rhenium dioxide trichloride, but it has recently been shown that the products of the reaction are, in fact, rhenium trioxide chloride and rhenium oxide tetrachloride[14]. The supposed ReO_2Cl_3 was probably a mixture of the two compounds. Rhenium trioxide chloride is also formed by the action of oxygen on either rhenium hexachloride or rhenium oxide tetrachloride[14]. Possibly the best method of preparation is to chlorinate rhenium trioxide at 160–190°; this method is said to give a very pure product on removal of dissolved chlorine by vacuum-distillation[19].

Rhenium trioxide chloride is a colourless compound, m.p. 4.5°, the boiling point having been given as 131° (reference 15) and 128° (reference 19). The compound is stable in dry air but is instantly hydrolysed by water to give only perrhenic and hydrochloric acid[15]. It is very reactive and is decomposed by mercury, silver or stopcock grease to give rhenium trioxide[19]. The infrared spectrum of rhenium trioxide chloride shows a band at 10.4 μ attributed to the Re=O double-bond stretch. From a study of the microwave spectrum of rhenium trioxide chloride, Amble and co-workers[20] were able to show that the molecule was a symmetrical top and they derived the parameters: Re–O = 1.761 Å; Re–Cl = 2.230Å; Cl–Re–O = 108°20′.

Rhenium trioxide bromide (perrhenyl bromide). Rhenium trioxide bromide may be prepared by the action of bromine vapour on potassium perrhenate[21], or by the action of liquid bromine on rhenium trioxide[20] or heptaoxide[22]. It is a colourless compound which is readily decomposed thermally to the trioxide[21], a very unusual type of decomposition which has also been observed for technetium trioxide chloride[14].

The infrared spectrum of rhenium trioxide bromide has been observed; it is very similar to that of rhenium trioxide chloride and the following assignments were made[23]: $\nu_6 = 168$, $\nu_2 = 195$, $\nu_5 = 332$, $\nu_2 = 350$, $\nu_4 = 963$, and $\nu_1 = 997$ cm^{-1}.

Oxidation State VI

Technetium hexafluoride. Technetium hexafluoride has been prepared by the action of fluorine on technetium metal[24]; the metal, prepared by reduction of ammonium pertechnetate with hydrogen at 600°, was treated with an excess of fluorine in a nickel reactor for two hours at 400°; the volatile product was purified by fractional sublimation. It was characterized as the hexafluoride in several ways and there was no evidence of formation of the heptafluoride. Measurement of the fluorine consumption during the reaction showed that 3 moles of fluorine were used for every mole of technetium. Vapour-density determinations gave values for the molecular weights agreeing with that required for the hexafluoride, whilst chemical analysis gave an empirical formula of TcF$_{5.8}$. Technetium hexafluoride is also produced as the major product when fluorine is passed over technetium metal at 350° in a flow system[25].

Technetium hexafluoride is a golden-yellow solid[26] at room temperature, melting to a yellow liquid at 37.4°. The boiling point has been calculated to be 55.3° and the vapour is colourless and monomeric[24]. As with other transition-metal hexafluorides there is a phase transition in the solid, marking the change from the cubic high-temperature form to the orthorhombic low-temperature form; with technetium hexafluoride this change[26] occurs at −4.54°, as calculated from vapour-pressure data although it was actually observed at −5.3°.

The vapour pressure of technetium hexafluoride is described by the following equations[26]:

Solid TcF_6 (orthorhombic) ($-16.32°$ to $-5.3°$)

$$\log p_{mm} = 41.1252 - 10.787 \log T - 3564.8/T$$

Solid TcF_6 (cubic) ($-5.3°$ to $37.4°$)

$$\log p_{mm} = 15.33427 - 2.295 \log T - 2178.0/T$$

Liquid TcF_6 (37.4–$51.67°$)

$$\log p_{mm} = 24.8087 - 5.8036 \log T - 2404.9/T$$

Thermodynamic parameters were calculated from the vapour-pressure measurements and are recorded in Table 7.6.

TABLE 7.6

Thermodynamic Properties of
Technetium Hexafluoride

	Property	Value
ΔH_{sub}	(cubic 37.4°) (kcal mole^{-1})	8.555
ΔH_{sub}	(orthorhombic $-5.3°$) (kcal mole^{-1})	10.577
ΔH_{sub}	(cubic $-5.3°$) (kcal mole^{-1})	8.750
ΔH_{vap}	(cubic 37.4°) (kcal mole^{-1})	7.427
ΔH_{fus}	(cubic 37.4°) (kcal mole^{-1})	1.128
ΔH_{trans}	(kcal mole^{-1})	1.827
ΔS_{fus}	(cubic 37.4°) (cal deg^{-1} mole^{-1})	3.63
ΔS_{trans}	(cal deg^{-1} mole^{-1})	6.82
Trouton constant (liquid)		22.0

The infrared spectrum of technetium hexafluoride shows only two sharp bands; the others are either missing or are broad[27]. A similar situation occurs for rhenium and tungsten hexafluoride and suggests that, like these compounds, technetium hexafluoride has O_h symmetry. The following assignments were made: v_1 705, v_2 551, v_3 748, v_4 265 and v_5 255 cm^{-1}.

Force constants and mean square amplitudes of vibration have been calculated for technetium hexafluoride[28-30].

The magnetic moment[31] of technetium hexafluoride is very low (0.45 BM at 300°K), and peculiar behaviour is observed below 14°K.

Rhenium hexafluoride. Rhenium hexafluoride is always formed together with the heptafluoride when fluorine reacts with heated rhenium metal. It was first investigated by Ruff and coworkers[32-34] although Malm and Selig[2] suggest, that judged by its vapour pressure, Ruff's material contained much heptafluoride. The best way to obtain the hexafluoride is to heat the reaction mixture obtained from heated fluorine and rhenium with an excess of rhenium metal. Under these conditions any hepta-fluoride is quantitatively reduced to the hexafluoride[2]. Rhenium hexa-fluoride can also be made[35] by the action of chlorine trifluoride vapour on rhenium metal at 300°; the mixture of chlorine trifluoride and rhenium hexafluoride collected in a cooled trap was dissolved in hydrogen fluoride, and the solution was cooled in solid carbon dioxide. Large yellow crystals of an adduct $ReF_6 \cdot xClF_3$ were obtained and were decomposed by dis-tillation in a platinum tube at 50° under hydrogen; the rhenium hexa-fluoride was purified by pumping at −70° for 4 hours; its melting point was 18.7°, in agreement with the values given below.

Rhenium hexafluoride is a yellow solid which melts at 18.5°. It is very reactive towards water, giving the usual disproportionation reaction for Re(VI) compounds:

$$3Re(\text{VI}) \rightarrow 2Re(\text{VII}) + Re(\text{IV})$$

In contrast to the early reports of Ruff and coworkers, later investigators have found that rhenium hexafluoride does not attack dried Pyrex glass or silica. Malm and Selig[2] found that, like the heptafluoride, it does not react with oxygen at 500°. This behaviour is in contrast to that of the binary compounds of rhenium with the other halogens; these all react very readily with oxygen. It is interesting that Ruff and Kwasnik[34] claimed to have prepared rhenium oxide tetrafluoride by the action of oxygen on the hexafluoride. Later workers have since made this compound and it is quite different from Ruff's material which was probably a hydrolysis product.

The vapour pressure of rhenium hexafluoride has been measured by Malm and Selig[2] and by Cady and Hargreaves[36]. The vapour pressures obtained by the two groups agreed quite well and the equations deduced from the experimental data are:

Solid (−50° to −1.9°)

$\log p_{\text{mm}} = 10.110 - 2151.2/T$ (Cady and Hargreaves)

Solid ReF_6 (−10.47° to −3.45°)

$\log p_{\text{mm}} = 12.70721 - 0.8327 \log T - 2303.6/T$ (Malm and Selig)

Solid ReF_6 (−3.45° to 18.5°)

$\log p_{\text{mm}} = 9.12298 - 0.1790 \log T - 1765.4/T$ (Malm and Selig)

Liquid ReF_6 (18.5–48.06°)

$\log p_{\text{mm}} = 18.20814 - 3.599 \log T - 1956.7/T$ (Malm and Selig)

Thermodynamic properties calculated from the vapour-pressure meas-urements are shown in Table 7.7. Various other thermodynamic properties of rhenium hexafluoride have been calculated for the temperature ranges 4–300°K (reference 37) and 100–1500°K (reference 38).

The solid–solid transition for rhenium hexafluoride was observed by both groups of workers, and Malm and Selig confirmed the change by X-ray diffraction studies[2]. They found that the high-temperature phase (−3.45° to 18.5°) has a body-centred cubic lattice isostructural with that of other metal hexafluorides. The low-temperature form is again like the low-temperature form of other metal hexafluorides and so is probably orthorhombic.

TABLE 7.7

Thermodynamic Properties of Rhenium Hexafluoride

	Value reported by	
Property	Malm and Selig[2]	Cady and Hargreaves[36]
M.p.	18.5°	18.7°
B.p.	33.68°	33.8°
Solid–solid transition	−3.45°	−1.9°
ΔH_{trans} (kcal mole^{-1})	2.027	2.090
ΔH_{fus} (kcal mole^{-1})	1.107	0.940
ΔH_{vap} (kcal mole^{-1})	6.867	
ΔS_{trans} (cal deg^{-1} mole^{-1})	7.52	7.71
ΔS_{fus} (cal deg^{-1} mole^{-1})	3.80	3.21

The infrared spectra of rhenium heptafluoride and hexafluoride provide a sensitive way of detecting an impurity of one in the other. Both spectra show a strong fundamental vibration at 715 cm^{-1} attributed to the metal–fluorine bond-stretching motion, but the heptafluoride shows additional peaks. The spectra in the range 600–1600 cm^{-1} are shown in Figure 7.2. The infrared spectrum obtained by Guant[39] for rhenium hexafluoride shows quite clearly that his sample contained some rhenium heptafluoride, but this does not affect his conclusion that the molecule is a perfect octahedron.

The infrared and Raman spectra of rhenium hexafluoride, rigorously purified from the heptafluoride, have been obtained[40]. The fundamentals were assigned as follows: ν_1 755, ν_2 596, ν_3 715, ν_4 257, ν_5 246 and ν_6 193(?) cm^{-1} (octahedral symmetry; point group O_h).

Force constants and mean-square amplitudes of vibration of rhenium hexafluoride have been calculated by various groups of workers[28,29,38,41–43].

The magnetic properties[44] of rhenium hexafluoride have been measured over the temperature range 14–296°K and the molar susceptibility is given by

$$\chi_M = 0.87 \times 10^{-4} + (78 \times 10^{-4}/T),$$

from which $\mu = 0.25$ BM. This low moment is attributed to spin-orbit coupling.

Rhenium hexafluoride reacts with nitric oxide and with nitrosyl fluoride to form $NOReF_6$ and $(NO)_2ReF_8$, respectively[45].

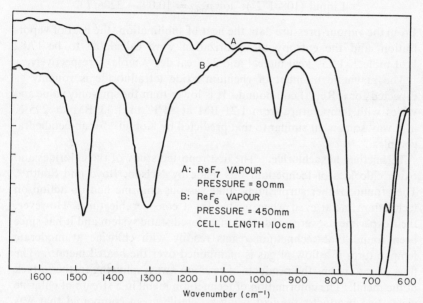

A: ReF₇ VAPOUR
   PRESSURE = 80mm
B: ReF₆ VAPOUR
   PRESSURE = 450mm
   CELL LENGTH 10cm

Wavenumber (cm⁻¹)

Figure 7.2   Infrared spectra of ReF_6 and ReF_7.

Technetium oxide tetrafluoride. The blue oxide tetrafluoride has been briefly reported[25,46] as being a minor product of the fluorination of technetium metal in a flow system, the oxygen presumably coming from oxide films on the metal. It is very similar to its rhenium analogue; its magnetic moment (1.76 BM at 25°, $\theta = 9°$) is as expected for a d^1-compound.

Rhenium oxide tetrafluoride. The preparation of rhenium oxide tetrafluoride was claimed by Ruff who described it as a colourless compound, but this can no longer by sustained in the light of present knowledge.

Rhenium oxide tetrafluoride is one of the major products of the reaction of rhenium hexafluoride and metal carbonyls[47], as noted below in the sections on rhenium pentafluoride and tetrafluoride. It is a blue crystalline solid which melts at 108° to give a blue liquid that boils at 171° under atmospheric pressure, forming a colourless vapour. At 250° the vapour attacks Pyrex glass to give a non-volatile product that is rhenium oxide trifluoride. It is rapidly hydrolysed by water.

The vapour pressure of rhenium oxide tetrafluoride has been measured[7]; and the equations deduced from the data are:

$$\text{Solid } (50\text{--}107^\circ): \quad \log p_{mm} = 11.88 - 3888/T$$

$$\text{Liquid } (108\text{--}172^\circ): \quad \log p_{mm} = 10.09 - 3206/T$$

From the vapour-pressure data the heat of sublimation, the heat of vaporization, and the entropy of vaporization were calculated to be 17.82 kcal mole^{-1}, 14.59 kcal mole^{-1} and 32.7 cal deg^{-1} mole^{-1}, respectively.

The magnetic moment of rhenium oxide tetrafluoride is roughly as expected for a Re(VI) compound. It is lower than the spin-only value and varies with temperature from 1.21 BM at 84°K to 1.33 BM at 295°K in a way somewhat similar to that predicted by Kotani[48] for an octahedral complex.

Technetium hexachloride. The first reported study of the chlorides and oxide chlorides of technetium was made by Nelson, Boyd and Smith[49]. They found, rather surprisingly, that gaseous chlorine had no action on technetium metal even when heated for a considerable time. However, their experiments were conducted in a closed static system and it has since been found that technetium reacts readily with chlorine at moderate temperatures if a flow of gas is maintained over the heated metal[50]. The flow of gas sweeps the products of reaction away, allowing further attack of the metal. The chlorination of technetium metal in a stream of chlorine yields two products, the first being a volatile green compound that was shown to be technetium hexachloride, and the second being technetium tetrachloride.

Technetium hexachloride is extremely unstable, decomposing to the tetrachloride even on very gentle warming. Samples sealed in an atmosphere of chlorine gas decomposed completely to the tetrachloride in 24 hours. Technetium hexachloride melts at about 25° and it is quite volatile. It was possible to separate it from the tetrachloride, also formed during the chlorination of the metal, by distilling it at room temperature in a rapid stream of nitrogen and collecting it in a tube cooled in ice. Several distillations were necessary to remove dissolved chlorine which appears to be quite soluble in the liquid hexachloride. Technetium hexachloride was characterized[50] by analysis, which showed a ratio of technetium to chlorine of 1:6 and also by demonstrating that the compound was hydrolysed in the manner expected for a compound of Tc(VI).

Rhenium hexachloride. There are reports in the literature of a volatile green chloride of rhenium which was thought to be the heptachloride or the hexachloride, but it was never characterized[51,52]. No more was heard of the supposed green chloride after Geilmann and coworkers[16] announced the discovery of the brown pentachloride. After the discovery of technetium hexachloride it became apparent that pure rhenium metal was required if rhenium hexachloride was to be prepared.

Accordingly rhenium metal was prepared[53] by reduction of ammonium perrhenate with hydrogen at 600°. After the apparatus had been flushed with purified nitrogen, chlorine was passed over the heated metal at 600°. On the small scale no rhenium pentachloride was observed, but a dark solid was obtained that melted very readily and gave a green vapour. It could be readily distilled in the chlorine stream into a U-tube cooled in an ice–water mixture. Analysis showed the substance to be rhenium hexachloride.

The reaction of chlorine on a film of rhenium metal is thus similar to that on technetium metal and is in contrast to that on commercial rhenium powder (made from potassium perrhenate). However, it has also been shown[53] that, although the pentachloride is the major product of the reaction of chlorine with rhenium powder (previously heated in hydrogen to reduce the surface oxides), some hexachloride is also formed. It appears that some hexachloride has been present in most samples of rhenium pentachloride.

The best way to prepare large amounts of rhenium hexachloride is to absorb ammonium perrhenate solution into porous brick material, dry the particles, reduce the salt to the metal by hydrogen at 600°, and to treat with a 1:1 mixture of chlorine and nitrogen at 650°.

Rhenium hexachloride forms long needles which are dichroic, appearing red-brown by transmitted light and dark green by reflected light. The crystals melt at 25° to give a dark brown liquid, which volatilizes on gentle heating to a green vapour. In contrast to technetium hexachloride, the compound is thermally stable in both nitrogen and chlorine, and there is no decomposition to the tetrachloride at 300°. It is readily hydrolysed by moist air or water.

When rhenium hexachloride is warmed in an atmosphere of oxygen the only product observed is rhenium trioxide chloride[53]. In the rhenium–fluorine system, all three possible Re(VII) oxide fluorides are known, but the only known oxide chloride of Re(VII) is rhenium trioxide chloride. The difference in reactivity of rhenium hexachloride and rhenium hexafluoride towards oxygen is noteworthy; rhenium hexafluoride can be heated in oxygen to 400° without reaction[2].

Rhenium hexachloride obeys the Curie–Weiss law closely[54] over the range 98–300°K. The value of θ is 28° and the magnetic moment is 2.07 BM; this value is to be compared with that of 0.25 BM obtained for the hexafluoride.

20

Technetium oxide tetrachloride. Two products that were thought to have been oxide chlorides of technetium were observed during the reaction between chlorine and technetium dioxide[49]. The first product sublimed at 80–90°, and the second brown product could be sublimed at 500°. Neither of them was characterized at that time, although it was noted that both were paramagnetic. It has since been suggested[55] that the brown compound was technetium oxide trichloride. This has been confirmed[14] and it appears very likely that the blue compound is technetium oxide tetrachloride.

Rhenium oxide tetrachloride. Little fresh information on rhenium oxide tetrachloride has been published since soon after its discovery by Bruckl and Ziegler[15] who obtained it from the reaction between a rhenium chloride and rhenium heptaoxide. Other methods of preparation are mentioned in the section on rhenium trioxide chloride.

The melting point of the compound seems to be a matter of some doubt; Bruckl and Ziegler[15] reported that it melts at 29–30.5°, whilst Kolling[17], who made it by the action of oxygen on rhenium trichloride, observed a melting point of 34°. Determination of the boiling point by the same workers gave values of 223° and 225°, respectively.

Rhenium oxide tetrachloride is a brown crystalline solid which melts to give a brown liquid. The vapour is greenish-brown, intermediate between the colours of the vapours of rhenium pentachloride (brown) and rhenium hexachloride (green). The compound fumes in air and is instantly hydrolysed by water.

Rhenium oxide tetrachloride has been shown to be monomeric in the vapour phase[56]. The variation of vapour pressure with temperature is given by the expression:

$$\log p_{mm} = 7.63 - 2380/T$$

over the whole liquid range[56]. From these measurements the heat of vaporization was found[56] to be 10.9 kcal mole^{-1} and the extrapolated boiling point 228°.

The magnetic moment of rhenium oxide tetrachloride was measured some years ago and a value of $\mu_{eff} = 1.5$ BM was obtained[57].

Bruckl and Ziegler[15] reported that rhenium oxide tetrachloride dissolved in cold concentrated hydrochloric acid to give a brown solution which may contain the complex acid H_2ReOCl_6, since they claimed to have isolated potassium oxohexachlororhenate(VI) from the solution.

Some interesting, but unconfirmed, observations of the behaviour of rhenium oxide tetrachloride in carbon tetrachloride solution have been reported by Bruckl and Plettinger[58]. They found that on careful addition of water to these solutions a blue precipitate was formed which had a

Re:Cl ratio of 1:2 with varying numbers of oxygen and hydroxyl groups; but the product was never properly characterized. These workers also claimed that cold dry ammonia gas reacted with rhenium oxide tetrachloride to give $ReO(NH_2)_2Cl_2$.

Rhenium oxide tetrabromide. The blue compound formulated as rhenium dioxide dibromide has been shown to be, in fact, rhenium oxide tetrabromide[59]. It is made by any of several reactions, for example, rhenium metal heated in a bromine–oxygen stream, rhenium heptaoxide and bromine vapour, rhenium tetrabromide and oxygen or, best of all, anhydrous rhenium dioxide and bromine vapour. Rhenium oxide tetrabromide is a blue solid with a low melting point and, on heating, it is thermally decomposed to rhenium oxide tribromide.

Oxidation State V

Technetium pentafluoride. It has recently been reported[46] that technetium pentafluoride is a by-product of the fluorination of technetium metal. Technetium pentafluoride is a yellow solid, melting at 50° and having an orthorhombic lattice with $a = 7.6$, $b = 5.8$ and $c = 16.6$ Å which is isostructural with that of chromium pentafluoride. The compound is readily hydrolysed and begins to decompose in glass at about 60°.

Rhenium pentafluoride. In an unsuccessful attempt to prepare rhenium carbonyl fluoride, Hargreaves and Peacock[47] isolated rhenium pentafluoride, rhenium tetrafluoride and rhenium oxide tetrafluoride. The experimental conditions and the products formed are displayed in Table 7.8.

TABLE 7.8

Reaction of Rhenium Hexafluoride with Carbonyls

Reactants	Products
$ReF_6 + Re_2(CO)_{10}$	$ReOF_4$ + residue
ReF_6 (large excess) + $W(CO)_6$	$ReOF_4$, WF_6 + impure ReF_4
ReF_6 (small excess) + $W(CO)_6$	$ReOF_4$, ReF_5, WF_6 + impure ReF_4
ReF_6 (small excess) + WF_6 (large excess) + $W(CO)_6$	ReF_5 + impure ReF_4

Rhenium pentafluoride is a green solid which melts at 48° to a yellow viscous liquid which is difficult to crystallize on cooling. Above about 140° it undergoes an apparently irreversible disproportionation to the hexafluoride and tetrafluoride. Rhenium pentafluoride is rapidly hydrolysed by moist air.

The vapour pressure of rhenium pentafluoride has been measured[7]; the equation deduced from the experimental data is:

$$\log p_{mm} = 9.024 - 3037/T \quad (48.0–140°)$$

Certain thermodynamic properties have been calculated: triple point 48°; b.p. 221.3°; heat of vaporization 13.88 kcal mole^{-1}; and entropy of vaporization 28.1 cal deg^{-1} mole^{-1}. The high Trouton constant and the viscosity of liquid rhenium pentafluoride suggests that there is association in the liquid.

The magnetic susceptibility of rhenium pentafluoride has been measured over a wide temperature range[47]. Detailed interpretation of the results is difficult because the structure of the solid is unknown, but it is possible that a polymeric structure with metal–metal bonds can accommodate the results.

Rhenium oxide trifluoride. Pyrex glass is slowly attacked at 250° by rhenium oxide tetrafluoride to give a black non-volatile compound which is rhenium oxide trifluoride[47]. The compound has a tetragonal unit cell with $a = 8.54$ and $c = 8.21$ Å. It is very hygroscopic and gives a blue aqueous solution which presumably contains a complex oxide fluoride ion.

Rhenium pentachloride. The pentachloride is the major product[16,53] when chlorine reacts with rhenium powder (previously heated in hydrogen to reduce oxide films) at 500–700°. The small amount of rhenium hexachloride also formed can be readily distilled out at a temperature lower than the melting point of the pentachloride.

Rhenium pentachloride is formed, together with the trichloride, on thermal decomposition of silver hexachlororhenate(IV). There is no evidence for the formation of the tetrachloride which might be expected from this reaction[16].

Rhenium pentachloride is a deep brown or black crystalline solid, melting at 220°, which volatilizes easily to give a red-brown vapour. It is instantly hydrolysed by water.

The magnetic properties of rhenium pentachloride have been investigated several times. Schuth and Klemm[57] found a moment of 2.3 BM for the solid compound on the basis of three measurements. Knox and Coffey[60] found that the pentachloride obeyed a Curie–Weiss law to below 150°K, giving $\mu_{eff} = 2.21$ BM and $\theta = 164°$. More recently[54] the susceptibility was measured for a sample that had been carefully freed from hexachloride, and this gave a value for θ of 266°, agreeing precisely with that obtained by Schuth and Klemm although the actual susceptibilities were higher. It has been suggested[54] that the sample used by Knox and Coffey may have contained some rhenium hexachloride which would have lowered the value of θ observed. On the other hand, Knox and Coffey reported a divergence from the Curie–Weiss law below 150°K and this was confirmed by Brown and Colton[54] who were able to show that the divergence occurred at about 110°K, in a region where Knox and Coffey reported no results.

Rhenium pentachloride is a very reactive compound, although comparatively little use has been made of it as an intermediate or starting material in the preparative chemistry of rhenium. It reacts readily with oxygen to give oxide chlorides (above) and when heated with potassium chloride, it forms the hexachlororhenate(IV) ion[61]:

$$2ReCl_5 + 4KCl \rightarrow 2K_2ReCl_6 + Cl_2$$

Technetium oxide trichloride. Technetium oxide trichloride is rather involatile, subliming at about 500° in a vacuum. This low volatility is a common feature of this type of pentavalent compound and it appears likely that this substance has a structure similar to that of niobium oxide trichloride.

Rhenium oxide trichloride. Preparation of the pure compound has not been reported, but a number of its adducts have been prepared indirectly. Thus, Chatt and Rowe[62] prepared complexes of the type $ReOCl_3(PR_3)_2$ by interaction of alkali-metal perrhenate and the phosphine in a mixture of concentrated hydrochloric acid and ethanol. Oxotrichlorobis(triphenylphosphine)rhenium(V) reacts with 2,2'-bipyridyl to give $ReOCl_3 \cdot bipy$[63].

Rhenium pentabromide. Rhenium pentabromide is the major product[59] if bromine vapour is carried in a stream of nitrogen over rhenium at 650°, although a previous report[64] claimed that the tribromide was the product formed at 450°. There is a no evidence of the formation of a hexabromide even if a freshly reduced film of rhenium metal is used. Rhenium pentabromide is a dark blue solid which melts a little above room temperature to give a bluish-green liquid, the vapour being blue. When heated in vacuum or in nitrogen, rhenium pentabromide decomposes in the same way as the pentachloride, although more readily, to give the tribromide[59].

Technetium oxide tribromide. Only one oxide bromide of technetium has been prepared so far. Bromine vapour reacts with technetium dioxide at about 350° to give a black sublimate of technetium oxide tribromide[14]. Technetium oxide tribromide is rather involatile but quite stable thermally. It is instantly hydrolysed by water and alkali.

Oxidation State IV

Rhenium tetrafluoride. Hargreaves and Peacock[47] prepared rhenium tetrafluoride as a pale blue powder by the thermal decomposition of the pentafluoride at about 150°. Previously, Ruff[32-34] had claimed to have prepared rhenium tetrafluoride by the reduction of the hexafluoride with hydrogen at 200°, with carbon monoxide at 300° and with sulphur dioxide at 400°. The properties of his material, however, were not the same as those described by Hargreaves and Peacock who suggest that Ruff obtained a mixture of the tetrafluoride and the pentafluoride. Another method[65] of preparing the tetrafluoride is by reduction of rhenium hexafluoride with an excess of rhenium metal at 550°.

Rhenium tetrafluoride is not very volatile but it can be sublimed without decomposition at about 300° in a vacuum. It is hydrolysed by water, giving rhenium dioxide and hydrofluoric acid[47].

X-ray diffraction data for powdered specimens of rhenium tetrafluoride have been indexed[65] on the basis of a tetragonal lattice with unit-cell parameters $a = 10.12$ and $c = 15.95$ Å.

Technetium tetrachloride. The major product of the chlorination of technetium metal is the tetrachloride. This red compound is quite stable and it is easily purified by sublimation at about 300° in a gentle stream of chlorine or nitrogen[50]. Technetium tetrachloride was first prepared[66], however, by the interaction of technetium heptaoxide and carbon tetrachloride in a sealed tube at about 400°.

The crystal structure of technetium tetrachloride has recently been determined by Elder and Penfold[67,68]. The crystals are orthorhombic, of space group *Pbca*, and have the unit-cell parameters: $a = 11.65$, $b = 14.06$ and $c = 6.03$ Å. The structure represents a new type for AB_4 compounds and is shown in Figure 7.3. Distorted octahedral units of composition $TcCl_6$ are linked to form a polymeric chain. The repeating unit of the chain is a Tc_2Cl_8 unit made up of two $TcCl_4$ planar asymmetric units related to each other by a glide plane. There are three chemically distinct Tc–Cl bonds in the polymer. The shortest bonds (2.24 Å) involve the non-bridging chlorine atoms Cl(4) and Cl(5). The longest bonds (2.49 Å) are to bridging chlorines, Cl(2) and Cl(3), aligned perpendicularly to the chain length. Intermediate in length (2.38 Å) is the third pair of bonds to the bridging chlorines Cl(2′) and Cl(3′), parallel to the chain length. The differences in length between these three types are highly significant, the smallest difference (0.11 Å) being much greater than the standard deviation. All bond angles are within 6° of the 90° that would be expected for a regular octahedron. The angle of 94° between the two short bonds will reduce electrostatic repulsion between the two chlorine atoms, and there is a corresponding reduced angle of 86.5° between the two longest Tc–Cl bonds. An attempt has been made to explain these different Tc–Cl bond lengths in terms of their relative π-bonding.

The magnetic behaviour of technetium tetrachloride has been studied over a temperature range, but only five measurements were recorded[60]. The plot of the reciprocal of the corrected molar susceptibility against the absolute temperature was not linear. The three points at the higher temperatures were taken to give a crude Curie–Weiss plot from which the values of $\mu = 3.14$ BM and $\theta = -57°$ were obtained. Whilst it would be desirable for a more detailed study of the magnetic properties of technetium tetrachloride to be made, the published results appear to be in qualitative agreement with those expected from the structure of the compound.

Technetium tetrachloride dissolves in hydrochloric acid to give yellow solutions containing the hexachlorotechnetate(IV) anion. Its behaviour

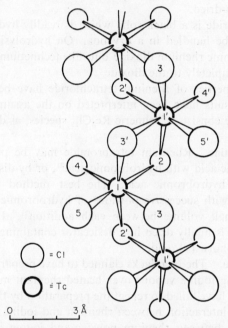

Figure 7.3   A section of a $(TcCl_4)_n$ chain viewed normal to the *a*-axis.

in water and alkaline solutions is similar to that of rhenium tetrachloride in that it is not instantly hydrolysed: indeed, it is difficult to hydrolyse technetium and rhenium tetrachloride completely.

Rhenium tetrachloride.   There are claims in the early literature to the preparation of rhenium tetrachloride but none has been substantiated. It is noteworthy that reactions such as thermal decomposition of silver hexachlororhentate(IV), that might be expected to give the tetrachloride, actually give mixtures of the pentachloride and trichloride.

Rhenium tetrachloride has been prepared by the action of thionyl chloride on hydrated rhenium dioxide[69]. It was necessary to prepare the dioxide by hydrolysis of rhenium pentachloride in water, since hydrolysis of ammonium hexachlororhenate(IV) and other salts of this anion always gave dioxide containing large amounts of cationic impurities which in turn gave impure rhenium tetrachloride. The pure dioxide prepared in this way was separated, washed with water and acetone, and vacuum-dried.

After the dry oxide had been refluxed with thionyl chloride for several hours the supernatant liquid had a very dark green colour, but the bulk of the product was formed as a black insoluble solid. After centrifuging, the solid was vacuum-dried.

Rhenium tetrachloride is a black solid which is readily hydrolysed by moist air and must be handled in a dry box. On hydrolysis, rhenium tetrachloride forms some rhenium dioxide but, like technetium dioxide, it is not hydrolysed completely to the dioxide.

The magnetic properties of rhenium tetrachloride have been investigated[54,69] and the results have been interpreted on the assumption that rhenium tetrachloride consists of trimeric Re_3Cl_{12} species, as described in Chapter 3.

Rhenium tetrabromide. Rhenium tetrabromide may be prepared by reduction of perrhenic acid with hydrobromic acid[21], or by dissolution of rhenium dioxide in hydrobromic acid. The best method is to treat rhenium tetraiodide with successive portions of hydrobromic acid, with evaporation to a small volume between each addition[21]. In all these methods the product is finally dried in a desiccator containing potassium hydroxide and phosphorus(v) oxide.

Rhenium tetraiodide. The Noddacks claimed to have prepared rhenium tetraiodide by passing iodine vapour over heated rhenium metal; however, other workers[70] have failed to repeat the preparation by this method. The latter found no interaction between rhenium and iodine in a sealed tube at 170–180° or between rhenium powder and iodine in refluxing carbon tetrachloride. It is now known that rhenium tetraiodide is thermally unstable, and hence none of these methods could be expected to give the desired compound.

Rhenium tetraiodide was finally prepared by the reduction of perrhenic acid with hydriodic acid at room temperature[71]. Iodine is released in the reaction and an intermediate, which is probably a hydrate of hexaiodorhenic acid, is the first product obtained as the solution is evaporated to dryness. The intermediate compound loses water and hydriodic acid when kept in a desiccator with alkali and phosphorus(v) oxide, to give rhenium tetraiodide.

Rhenium tetraiodide is a rather unstable compound, losing iodine slowly in a vacuum at room temperature and rapidly on heating. It is very hygroscopic and dissolves in water, to give a brown solution in which it is rapidly hydrolysed to rhenium dioxide. However, rather more stable brown solutions can be prepared in acetone and ether.

Although rhenium tetraiodide appears to be crystalline, it is almost amorphous, no X-ray diffraction pattern being obtained from the compound. The magnetic moment has been reported[72] as 0.9 BM, the susceptibility and θ value were not given.

Oxidation State III

Rhenium trichloride. Rhenium trichloride is best prepared by thermal decomposition of rhenium pentachloride in nitrogen[16], a suitable apparatus being described by Hurd and Brimm[73]. Other methods of preparation are known, but none is so convenient or so efficient. Sulphuryl chloride was found to react with rhenium powder, with or without the addition of aluminium chloride, to give very small amounts of rhenium trichloride[70]. The fact that yields were not increased by prolonged treatment suggests that it was in fact an oxide film which reacted with the sulphuryl chloride. Rhenium trichloride is also formed by thermal decomposition of salts of hexachlororhenic(IV) acid[61,74].

Rhenium trichloride is a red crystalline compound. It has been shown to exist in the solid state, in solution and even in the vapour phase in the form of trinuclear clusters, Re_3Cl_9. These clusters and many of their derivatives are discussed in detail in Chapter 3.

Schuth and Klemm[57] found that rhenium trichloride had a very small temperature-independent paramagnetism; but a later determination by Knox and Coffey[60] gave higher values of the susceptibility which varied slightly with temperature. It had been noticed[14] that rhenium trichloride prepared from rhenium pentachloride and used without further treatment was chemically reactive, but if it were vacuum-sublimed at 500° it became comparatively unreactive. It has recently been shown[75] that the low-temperature form of rhenium trichloride has a molar susceptibility corresponding to that measured by Schuth and Klemm ($\approx 20 \times 10^{-6}$ cgs), and the vacuum-sublimed material (high-temperature form) has a susceptibility corresponding to that measured by Knox and Coffey ($\approx 495 \times 10^{-6}$ cgs). However, no detectable structure difference between the two forms could be observed by X-ray diffraction techniques[75].

Rhenium trichloride is reduced by hydrogen to the metal at 250–350° and with oxygen it gives rhenium trioxide chloride and rhenium oxide tetrachloride. In water, rhenium trichloride gives a red solution and is slowly hydrolysed. Conductivity experiments[16] showed that the final hydrolysis product was $Re_2O_3 \cdot xH_2O$.

Rhenium trichloride solutions in hydrochloric acid are very stable. Wrigge and Biltz suggested that the tetrachlororhenate(III) ion is formed and they claimed to have isolated salts containing the ion[76]. However recent work has shown that the situation is more complicated than this and involves the formation of trinuclear clusters (see Chapter 3).

Rhenium tribromide. Rhenium tribromide may be prepared by the thermal decomposition of the pentabromide[59] or silver hexabromo-rhenate(IV)[77]. It has also been reported[78] that rhenium tribromide is isolated when the mixture of rhenium bromides formed by reaction of rhenium metal and liquid bromine at 500° is dissolved in benzene and the solution is evaporated at 80°.

Rhenium tribromide is a red-brown solid. It is soluble in hydrobromic acid to form trinuclear complexes, as described in Chapter 3.

A solution of rhenium tribromide in benzene was saturated with dry ammonia at 5–6 atmospheres pressure at 20°. The dark brown product was thought to be $ReBr_3 \cdot 4NH_3$ contaminated with some ammonium bromide.

Rhenium triiodide. Rhenium triiodide was first prepared by thermal decomposition of the tetraiodide in a sealed tube at 350°. It may also be prepared[71] by the thermal decomposition of ammonium hexaiodo-rhenate(IV) at 325° in a vacuum and subsequent heating of the residue with iodine in a sealed tube at 200°. A recent, and more direct, method is the reduction of perrhenic acid with hydriodic acid and alcohol at elevated temperatures[79], the crystals being washed with alcohol and carbon tetra-chloride.

Rhenium triiodide is only slightly soluble in water or dilute acids and almost insoluble in alcohol, acetone or ether. It slowly loses iodine in a vacuum, especially if heated.

Oxidation State II

Rhenium diiodide. Rhenium diiodide was prepared by heating the triiodide for 6 hours in a sealed tube at 350° in an atmosphere of carbon dioxide[72]. The iodine was extracted with carbon tetrachloride. The magnetic moment was given as 0.5 BM and it is likely that rhenium–rhenium interaction occurs in this compound.

Oxidation State I

Rhenium monoiodide. Rhenium monoiodide was first prepared by heating rhenium tetraiodide to constant weight in a stream of nitrogen in the presence of a little iodine at 200°. More recently, the thermal decomposition of ammonium hexaiodorhenate(IV) at 440° in a vacuum has been used to prepare rhenium monoiodide[80].

An X-ray powder diffraction study of rhenium monoiodide revealed a simple cubic lattice with $a = 9.33$ Å. Rhenium monoiodide combines with iodine in a sealed tube at 200° to give the triiodide. In a vacuum it is thermally decomposed to the metal. The magnetic moment is given[72] as 0.6 BM.

COMPLEX HALIDES AND OXIDE HALIDES

A feature of rhenium chemistry is the large number of complex halides and oxide halides which have been prepared. In recent years the application of X-ray crystallography to some of these compounds has revealed hitherto unsuspected structural features which have shown rhenium to be one of the most interesting and versatile elements in the Periodic Table. The extensive and unique chemistry of trinuclear compounds based on the rhenium(III) halides has already been discussed in Chapter 3, but there is a distinct chemistry of rhenium(III) based on dinuclear complexes, and it is remarkable that the two series of compounds appear to be non-inter-convertable except in melts. Yet another feature to emerge in recent years is the existence of rhenium(V) oxide halide complexes of the general formula ReX_4O^- in which the complex assumes a square-pyramidal arrangement.

In contrast to the definite results of X-ray crystallographic analysis, there is considerable confusion concerning the nature of the obviously numerous products obtained by reduction of the perrhenate ion in hydrochloric acid solutions.

Comparatively few complexes of technetium have so far been prepared, but the existence of the unusual $[Tc_2Cl_8]^{3-}$ anion suggests that potentially it may be as interesting as rhenium.

Oxidation State VII

Dioxotetrafluororhenates(VII). This is the only example of a complex halide or oxide halide of oxidation state VII. It was prepared by dissolving potassium perrhenate in bromine trifluoride, oxygen and bromine being evolved. After reaction had ceased the excess of bromine trifluoride was removed under a vacuum, leaving a cream residue which analysis showed[81] to be potassium dioxotetrafluororhenate(VII), $KReO_2F_4$. Other alkali-metal dioxotetrafluororhenates(VII) may be made in an analogous manner[81]. The complexes are very hygroscopic, rapidly hydrolysing in moist air and water.

Oxidation State VI

Octafluororhenates(VI). Eight-coordinate fluoro complexes have recently been obtained by the interaction of rhenium hexafluoride and potassium fluoride[82]. Addition of potassium fluoride to rhenium hexafluoride cooled to 0° in a Teflon tube caused considerable evolution of heat. After all the fluoride had dissolved the tube was sealed and heated to 20°, and after several hours the excess of hexafluoride was pumped off, leaving a residue of potassium octafluororhenate(VI). The rubidium and caesium salts have also been prepared by this method[83].

The potassium compound is an orange crystalline solid which has an orthorhombic lattice with the following unit-cell parameters: $a = 8.70$, $b = 6.03$ and $c = 12.50$ Å. There are four molecules per unit cell. The octafluororhenate(VI) ion adopts a square-antiprismatic configuration[84].

The octafluororhenates(VI) have magnetic moments in the range 1.6–1.7 BM. This comparatively high moment is to be compared with the severely depressed moment observed for rhenium hexafluoride; apparently the lower symmetry of the anion diminishes the effects of spin–orbit coupling.

Heptafluororhenates(VI). Nikolaev and Ippolitov[83] have shown that the octafluororhenates(VI) react with rhenium hexafluoride to give a series of heptafluororhenates(VI):

$$M_2ReF_8 + ReF_6 \rightarrow 2MReF_7$$

The thermal stability of the series of heptafluororhenates(VI) is in the order: $Cs > Rb > K > Na$.

Oxopentafluororhenates(VI). The octafluororhenates(VI) gradually become blue in air or water; the blue compounds have been shown[82] to be oxopentafluororhenates(VI):

$$M_2ReF_8 + H_2O \rightarrow MReOF_5 + MF \cdot 2HF$$

The oxopentafluororhenates(VI) were best prepared by grinding the octafluororhenates(VI) in a platinum dish, the moisture in the air causing the partial hydrolysis. The caesium salt rapidly became blue and viscous, but as the potassium and rubidium salts were rather more stable it was necessary to add 99% hydrofluoric acid to them. When they were blue, the products were washed with methanol and extracted with ethyl methyl ketone. The evaporated solutions yielded the crystalline oxopentafluororhenates(VI). They were all soluble in water and organic solvents although the aqueous solutions rapidly became brown owing to hydrolysis. The valency of rhenium in caesium oxopentafluororhenate(VI) was shown to be six, and the magnetic moment was given as 1.48 BM.

Oxohexachlororhenates(VI). It has been claimed[15] that when rhenium oxide tetrachloride is dissolved in concentrated hydrochloric acid and potassium chloride is added, the red salt, potassium oxohexachloro-rhenate(VI) is precipitated. The complex has also been prepared by the aerial oxidation of solutions of rhenium pentachloride in hydrochloric acid and was then precipitated by alkali-metal chloride[85]. A similar reaction occurs when rhenium pentachloride is dissolved in a mixture of thionyl chloride and iodine monochloride[85].

Oxopentachlororhenates(VI). Compounds of the type $MReOCl_5$ [M = $(C_6H_5)_4As^+$, $(C_2H_5)_4N^+$, etc.] have been prepared by the reaction of the chlorides of large organic cations with rhenium oxide tetrachloride in chloroform solution[86]. The complexes are soluble in nitromethane and give a molar conductance consistent with their formulation as 1:1 electrolytes. The magnetic moments of the complexes at room temperature are reported to be in the range 1.5–1.6 BM and the lack of spin–orbit coupling effects is attributed to the axial asymmetry associated with the oxygen atom.

Oxidation State V

Hexafluorotechnetates(V). Salts of this anion have been prepared by reaction of alkali-metal chlorides with technetium hexafluoride in iodine pentafluoride solution[25,46]. The yellow crystalline salts are of rhombohedral symmetry and the lattice parameters are as follows:

$NaTcF_6$ $a = 5.77$ Å, $\alpha = 55.8°$. $RbTcF_6$ $a = 5.09$ Å, $\alpha = 95.5°$.

$KTcF_6$ $a = 4.97$ Å, $\alpha = 97.0°$. $CsTcF_6$ $a = 5.25$ Å, $\alpha = 96.2°$.

It is clear that, whilst the last three compounds may be isostructural, the sodium salt obviously assumes a different structure.

The magnetic moments of the hexafluorotechnetates(V) fall in the range 2.25–2.51 BM at room temperature[25]. The variation of magnetic susceptibility with temperature does not conform to the predictions of the Kotani theory, and detailed interpretation of the magnetic behaviour has not been effected.

Hexafluororhenates(V). The hexafluororhenate(V) ion has been prepared by reduction of rhenium hexafluoride with potassium iodide in liquid sulphur dioxide[87]; an excess of hexafluoride was used so that potassium hexafluororhenate(V) was the only involatile product of the reaction and it could be purified by pumping. The hexafluororhenates(V) are white crystalline solids and attack glass at 300°. They are very sensitive to moisture and darken on exposure to air. Water and alkalis cause vigorous hydrolysis[87], giving precipitates of hydrated rhenium dioxide; the supernatant solutions contain fluoride, perrhenate and hexafluororhenate(IV).

The lattice symmetries of a number of hexafluororhenates(V) have been determined[88], as shown in Table 7.9. It is notable that sodium and potassium hexafluororhenates(v) are not isostructural with the corresponding hexafluorotechnetates(v).

The rhenium–fluorine stretching frequency in potassium hexafluororhenate(v) has been reported[89] to be 627 cm^{-1}.

The magnetic properties of the alkali-metal hexafluororhenates(v) have been studied over a wide temperature range[90]. The compounds do not behave as predicted by the Kotani theory for a d^2-system, and considerable antiferromagnetic interactions may occur in the solid. Although no Néel points were observed for these compounds in the temperature range studied, the corresponding tungsten compounds did show Néel

TABLE 7.9

Crystallographic Data for the Hexafluororhenates(v)

Compound	Symmetry and lattice type	Unit-cell parameters
LiReF$_6$	Rhombohedral (LiSbF$_6$)	$a = 5.43$ Å, $\alpha = 55.5°$
NaReF$_6$	Cubic (NaSbF$_6$)	$a = 8.18$ Å
KReF$_6$	Tetragonal (KNbF$_6$)	$a = 5.044$ Å, $c = 10.09$ Å
RbReF$_6$	Rhombohedral (KOsF$_6$)	$a = 5.11$ Å, $\alpha = 96.7°$
CsReF$_6$	Rhombohedral (KOsF$_6$)	$a = 5.28$ Å, $\alpha = 95.9°$

points, confirming the view that antiferromagnetic interactions are possible in this type of compound. The magnetic moments (at 300°K) obtained were:

NaReF$_6$ $\mu = 1.57$ BM, $\theta = 100°$. RbReF$_6$ $\mu = 1.56$ BM, $\theta = 50°$.

KReF$_6$ $\mu = 2.05$ BM, $\theta = 58°$. CsReF$_6$ $\mu = 1.53$ BM, $\theta = 35°$.

Oxopentachlorotechnetates(v). Chloro complexes of technetium(v) were first observed in solution[91]. In 12M hydrochloric acid, potassium pertechnetate was reduced directly to technetium(v) without the formation of detectable intermediate compounds, and it was suggested that the oxotetrachlorotechnetate(v) ion was formed although no derivatives were isolated. Further reduction to hexachlorotechnetate(IV) occurred only slowly. The technetium(v) complex, whilst stable in 3M hydrochloric acid, disproportionated to pertechnetate and the hydrolysis products of hexachlorotechnetate(IV) in 1M acid[91]. It would be interesting to isolate this complex because, on the one hand, it is analogous to the oxotetrahalorhenates(v), but the method of preparation is essentially identical with that later reported to yield the oxopentachlorotechnetate(v) anion[92,93].

Oxopentachlororhenate(v). Rhenium pentachloride dissolves in 12M hydrochloric acid, to give a red-brown solution from which caesium oxopentachlororhenate(v) was precipitated on addition of caesium chloride[94].

The magnetic properties of caesium oxopentachlororhenate(v) are remarkably simple. The compound obeys the Curie–Weiss law accurately with a value of 20° for θ. The magnetic moment is 2.85 BM, almost exactly the spin-only value for a d^2-system, indicating that the effects of spin–orbit coupling are nullified by distortion of the complex to a symmetry lower than octahedral.

Oxotetrahalorhenates(v). In the last two years Cotton and coworkers have characterized a series of oxotetrahalorhenates(v), mainly chloro and

TABLE 7.10

Some Oxotetrahalorhenates(v)

Compound	Preparation	Remarks
$(C_2H_5)_4N[ReOBr_4(H_2O)]$	Oxidn. of Re_3Br_9	Sol. in acetone or acetonitrile
$Cs[ReOBr_4]$	Oxidn. of Re_3Br_9	Insol. in non-aqueous solvents
$(C_6H_5)_4As[ReOBr_4]$	Redn. of $KReO_4$ in HBr	Sol. in acetone or chloroform
$(C_6H_5)_4As[ReOCl_4]$	Redn. of $KReO_4$ in HCl or halogen exchange with $[ReOBr_4]^-$ salt	Sol. in acetone or chloroform
$[(n\text{-}C_4H_9)_4N][ReOI_4]$	Redn. of $KReO_4$ in HI	Sol. in acetone or ether

bromo complexes[95-98]. These are the same compounds that were briefly mentioned and thought to be monomeric $ReBr_4^-$ and $[ReBr_4(OH)_2]^-$ in an early review of the halogen chemistry of rhenium[99].

Two general methods of preparation have been used; the first is partial oxidation of the Re_3Br_9 entity in hydrobromic acid by air, and the second is reduction of potassium perrhenate with zinc in the presence of an excess of the appropriate halogen acid.

Two types of complexes have been isolated; those of the type exemplified by the compound $Cs[ReOBr_4]$, and those of the type exemplified by $[(C_6H_5)_4As][ReOBr_4(CH_3CN)]$ in which a molecule of a strong donor molecule is weakly bound to the rhenium atom.

Some of the compounds characterized are given in Table 7.10.

The infrared absorption attributed to the rhenium–oxygen double bond of all oxotetrahalogenorhenates(v) fall in the range 1000–1010 cm^{-1}, except for the caesium salts, in which it occurs at 955 cm^{-1}.

The structures of

$$[(C_6H_5)_4As][ReOBr_4(CH_3CN)] \quad \text{and} \quad [(C_2H_5)_4N][ReOBr_4(H_2O)]$$

have been determined by X-ray diffraction studies on single crystals[96,98]. In both cases the anion consists of a basic square-pyramidal arrangement of the doubly bound oxygen atom and the four bromine atoms with the solvent molecule weakly held in the sixth position. Although to date no structure determination has been reported on one of the anions without a

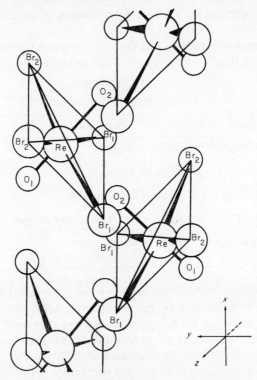

Figure 7.4   Molecular structure, packing, and labelling scheme of the [ReOBr$_4$(H$_2$O)]$^-$ anion.

coordinated solvent molecule, there is no doubt from spectral evidence that, in these anions also, the rhenium adopts a square-pyramidal structure.

The structure of the oxotetrabromoaquorhenate(v) ion is shown in Figure 7.4. The compound crystallizes in the orthorhombic system with the unit cell parameters $a = 11.14$, $b = 11.54$ and $c = 12.90$ Å. The space group is *Pnam* and there are four molecular entities per unit cell. The numbering of the atoms in Figure 7.4 is taken from Cotton and Lippard[96]. Oxygen atoms designated O$_1$ are the terminal oxygens, and those designated O_2 are the oxygen atoms of the coordinated water molecules. The basic structure of the methyl cyanide complex of the oxo-tetrabromorhenate(v) anion is very similar to that of the aquo complex. The compound crystallizes in the triclinic system with $a = 8.47$, $b = 12.90$, $c = 13.82$ Å, $\alpha = 104.7°$, $\beta = 98.8°$ and $\gamma = 90.1°$. The space group is $P\bar{1}$ and there are two molecular units in the cell[96].

The important interatomic distances for both compounds are given in Table 7.11.

TABLE 7.11

Interatomic Distances (Å) in $[\text{ReOBr}_4(\text{H}_2\text{O})]^-$
and $[\text{ReOBr}_4(\text{CH}_3\text{CN})]^-$

Distance	Aquo complex	Methyl cyanide complex
Re–Br	2.51	2.48
Re=O	1.71	1.73
Re–OH$_2$	2.32	
Re–N		2.31

An interesting suggestion which has arisen from the characterization of these compounds is that perhaps the oxopentachloromolybdates(v) and -tungstates(v) have a distorted octahedral configuration which would be best described in terms of a basic square pyramid with the fifth chlorine atom loosely bound.

When $[(\text{C}_2\text{H}_5)_4\text{N}][\text{ReOBr}_4(\text{H}_2\text{O})]$ was heated to constant weight in air at 150°, an orange product was obtained whose analyses were close to those of $[(\text{C}_2\text{H}_5)_4\text{N}][\text{ReO}_2\text{Br}_2]$. No further property of this compound was reported.

Neutral rhenium(v) complexes of the type ReOX_3L_2 [L = $(\text{C}_6\text{H}_5)_3\text{P}$, $(\text{C}_6\text{H}_5)_3\text{As}$] are readily prepared from the oxotetrahalorhenates(v)[97].

Oxidation State IV

Hexafluorotechnetates(iv). Pink potassium hexafluorotechnetate(iv) has been obtained by the reaction of both potassium hexachlorotechnetate(iv)[65] or hexabromotechnetate(iv)[100] with potassium hydrogen fluoride melts. The fluorotechnetate anion, like its rhenium analogue, is quite resistant to hydrolysis and may be purified by recrystallization from water. The complex must be heated in concentrated alkaline solution to bring about hydrolysis[100]. Solutions of the free acid and of other hexafluorotechnetates(iv) have been prepared from the potassium salt by ion-exchange procedures. The sodium and ammonium salts are very soluble and the barium salt, again like its rhenium analogue, becomes less soluble on ageing.

Potassium and rubidium hexafluorotechnetate(IV) have hexagonal lattices (K_2GeF_6 type) with the following unit cell parameters:

K_2TcF_6　$a = 5.807$ Å,　$c = 4.645$ Å　(references 100, 101).

Rb_2TcF_6　$a = 5.986$ Å,　$c = 4.798$ Å　(reference 101).

The infrared spectrum of potassium hexafluorotechnetate(IV) shows a band at 574 cm^{-1} which has been assigned to the metal–fluorine stretch[100]. The magnetic moment[102] of this salt is 3.95 BM with a Weiss constant of 28°.

Hexafluororhenates(IV). Ruff and Kwasnik[103] claimed to have prepared the hexafluororhenate(IV) ion by the action of hydrogen fluoride on potassium perrhenate in the presence of potassium iodide. This is a general method for the preparation of the other hexahalogenorhenates(IV), but later workers have failed to prepare the complex fluoride by this method[104,105].

Weise[104] prepared the potassium salt by treating the corresponding hexabromorhenate(IV) with hydrogen fluoride at 450°. It was found that the compound had a tetragonal structure, and not the cubic K_2PtCl_6 structure as reported by Ruff and Kwasnik[103].

Potassium hexafluororhenate(IV) may also be prepared[105] by the interaction of ammonium hexaiodorhenate(IV) and potassium hydrogen fluoride at 250°; the crude salt, after separation from the more soluble potassium fluoride and potassium iodide, was recrystallized from hot water. The potassium salt was also been obtained from potassium perrhenate by reduction with potassium iodide in a potassium hydrogen fluoride melt[65].

Other salts of the hexafluororhenate(IV) ion have been prepared by neutralizing the free acid, prepared from the potassium salt by ion exchange[83]. The hexafluororhenates(IV) are generally resistant to hydrolysis,

TABLE 7.12

Crystallographic Data for the Hexafluororhenates(IV)

Compound	Symmetry	Unit-cell parameters		Ref.
Na_2ReF_6	Orthorhombic	$a = 5.81$,	$b = 4.49, c = 10.10$ Å	106
K_2ReF_6	Hexagonal	$a = 5.86$,	$c = 4.60$ Å	101, 107
Rb_2ReF_6	Hexagonal	$a = 6.01$,	$c = 4.77$ Å	101, 107
$(NH_4)_2ReF_6$	Hexagonal	$a = 6.06$,	$c = 4.77$ Å	101, 107
Cs_2ReF_6	Hexagonal	$a = 6.32$,	$c = 4.99$ Å	101, 107
$BaReF_6$	Rhombohedral	$a = 4.92$ Å,	$\alpha = 97.4°$	101, 107

although the silver and copper salts decompose if their solutions are evaporated to dryness.

The lattice symmetries of a number of hexafluororhenates(IV) have been determined and are given in Table 7.12.

The magnetic properties of potassium and caesium hexafluororhenates(IV) have been studied over a wide temperature range[108]. The compounds obey the Curie–Weiss law with $\theta = 40°$ and $\mu_{300} = 3.30$ BM for the potassium salt, and $\theta = 24°$ and $\mu_{300} = 3.32$ BM for the caesium salt. In aqueous solution potassium hexafluororhenate(IV) has a magnetic moment of 3.43 BM at room temperature.

It has been reported[65] that thermal decomposition of ammonium hexafluororhenate(IV) in an argon atmosphere, or in a vacuum, at 300° gives a black solid formulated as ReNF.

Hexachlorotechnetates(IV). Potassium hexachlorotechnetate(IV) has been prepared by reduction of potassium pertechnetate by hydrochloric acid alone[91]; but it is usual to add some potassium iodide to facilitate the reaction[109].

Potassium hexachlorotechnetate(IV) forms golden-yellow octahedra and is isostructural[49] with the corresponding rhenate and platinate, the lattice being cubic with $a = 9.89$ Å. The magnetic properties of the solid compound have been studied[49] over a wide temperature range: it obeys the Curie–Weiss law with $\theta = 87°$ and has an effective magnetic moment of 4.3 BM. The magnetic moment of the compound in hydrochloric acid solution has been measured twice, a value of 4.05 BM being obtained by the Gouy method[109] and a value of 3.83 BM by the NMR method[110]. In both cases measurements were made at room temperature only and the Curie law was assumed to hold, that is, $\theta = 0°$.

The hexachlorotechnetate(IV) ion is not as stable as its rhenium analogue. Thus, the silver salt cannot be prepared by the action of silver nitrate on a neutral solution of the potassium salt because of rapid hydrolysis of the complex anion, although this method can be used for preparing silver hexachlororhenate(IV). Even qualitative observation shows that potassium hexachlorotechnetate(IV) is hydrolysed in dilute hydrochloric acid; a more detailed study indicated that the potassium salt is unstable in 1M hydrochloric acid, decomposing to an unidentified oxygenated species with the ultimate formation of the pertechnetate ion[91].

Heating ammonium hexachlorotechnetate(IV) to red heat in an inert atmosphere gives technetium metal[111].

Hexachlororhenates(IV). The hexachlororhenate(IV) ion is probably the best known and most studied complex of rhenium. It is usually made by reduction of perrhenate in hydrochloric acid with one of several possible reducing agents or, alternatively, by dissolving rhenium dioxide in hydrochloric acid solution[112-115]. The reduction of perrhenate is very complicated. There is strong evidence that the first stage involves rapid reduction to Re(v), followed by comparatively slow reduction to oxo and hydroxo compounds of Re(IV) and finally complete replacement by chlorine to give potassium hexachlororhenate(IV). The successive colour changes which accompany the rather lengthy reduction suggest that the reaction is very complex. Several oxo and hydroxo compounds which must be regarded as intermediates between the perrhenate and hexachlororhenate(IV) ions have actually been isolated from such reaction mixtures under various conditions, as described below. However, repeated evaporation of the reaction mixture with concentrated hydrochloric acid yields an emerald-green solution of potassium hexachlororhenate(IV) which can be recovered in high yield on evaporation. Some of the early workers claimed that further reaction with hydrochloric acid led to further reduction to Re(III), but this is contrary to the experience of later workers.

Rulfs and Meyer[116] developed what is probably the most convenient preparation of the hexachlororhenate(IV) ion, using hypophosphorous acid to reduce potassium perrhenate in hydrochloric acid solution.

Rhenium dioxide dissolves readily in concentrated hydrochloric acid to give, first, a brown solution which probably contains hydroxochloro complexes; but, when the solution is boiled, its colour rapidly changes to the characteristic green of the hexachlororhenate(IV) ion, and addition of potassium chloride then leads to precipitation of the potassium salt. Schweitzer and Wilhelm[117] prepared their dioxide by the reduction of potassium perrhenate in alkaline solution with hydrazine sulphate and used this general method to prepare the complex bromides and iodides as well as the chloride.

Tetramethylammonium and tetraethylammonium hexachlororhenate(IV) have been prepared by interaction of the alkylammonium chloride and rhenium oxide tetrachloride in thionyl chloride solution[85].

Hexachlororhenates(IV) may also be prepared[118] by reaction of perrhenates with carbon tetrachloride in a bomb at 400°; rhenium pentachloride is also produced in the reaction.

The hexachlororhenates(IV) that have been studied are all cubic with the K_2PtCl_6 structure[101,119,120]: K_2ReCl_6 $a = 9.84$ Å; Rb_2ReCl_6 $a = 9.97$ Å; Cs_2ReCl_6 $a = 10.26$ Å.

The heat capacity of solid potassium hexachlororhenate(IV) over the range 7.09–300°K exhibits four cooperative transitions with maxima at 11.9°, 76.05°, 103.4°, and 110.9°K; but only the transition at 11.9°K is associated with a magnetic transition[121].

The infrared and Raman spectra of the hexachlororhenate(IV) ion have been observed[122]. The observed absorption bands and their assignments are given below:

$$\nu_1 \ 346 \quad (R) \qquad \nu_5 \qquad 159 \quad (R)$$
$$\nu_2 \ — \qquad\qquad \nu_6 \qquad\quad —$$
$$\nu_3 \ 313 \quad (IR) \qquad \nu_3 + \nu_5 \quad 473 \quad (IR)$$
$$\nu_4 \ 172 \quad (IR) \qquad \nu_2 + \nu_3 \quad 588 \quad (IR)$$

Force constants have been determined for the hexachlororhenate(IV) anion by several groups of workers[123-126].

TABLE 7.13

Magnetic Properties of Some Hexachlororhenates(IV)

Complex	μ_{300} (BM)	θ
K_2ReCl_6	3.25	88°
Cs_2ReCl_6	3.35	45°
$(pyH)_2ReCl_6$	3.58	14°
$(QH)_2ReCl_6$	3.54	13°
$(TH)_2ReCl_6$	3.50	35°

pyH^+ = pyridinium; QH^+ = quinolinium;
TH^+ = toluidinium.

The magnetic properties of the hexachlororhenate(IV) anion have been the subject of several investigations. The earlier measurements[108] showed that the anion obeyed the Curie–Weiss law, and some values for different cations are shown in Table 7.13. However, the nature of the susceptibility variations with temperature suggested that there was considerable anti-ferromagnetic interaction in these complexes. In an attempt to reduce the interaction the salts of large cations were prepared as shown in Table 7.13. For the pyridinium and quinolinium salts, θ is small, but for the potassium and toluidinium salts it is rather high. The latter pair were shown to be isostructural, but the first two have different structures[127].

In another effort to make samples more magnetically dilute Westland and Bhiwandker[128] measured the susceptibility of pure potassium hexachlororhenate(IV) and mixtures of this compound with potassium hexachloroplatinate(IV). However, the results showed that significant super-exchange still occurred, causing a lowering of the magnetic moment. They obtained a room temperature moment of 3.72 BM ($\theta = 90°$) for the pure compound and a moment of 3.76 BM ($\theta = 26°$) for mixtures with the platinum salt.

The suggestion that these compounds are antiferromagnetic has been confirmed by recent susceptibility measurements extending down to liquid-helium temperatures[129]. The Curie temperature was found to be 12.4°K, and at higher temperatures it was found that the Curie–Weiss law was obeyed with $\theta = 55°$. The large discrepancy between this θ value and those noted above is rather curious; it suggests that perhaps some of the samples were not completely pure.

Other chloro complexes of rhenium(IV). Krauss and Dahlmann[114] claimed to have isolated green potassium hydroxopentachlororhenate(IV) as one of the products of the reduction of potassium perrhenate by potassium iodide in hydrochloric acid solution. This was later confirmed by Jezowska-Trzebiatowska[115,130] who also isolated μ-oxodecachloro-dirhenate(IV), $K_4[Re_2OCl_{10}]$. It was further shown[130] that $K_2[Re(OH)Cl_5]$ and $K_4[Re_2OCl_{10}]$ are in equilibrium with each other in solution. The absorption spectrum of the reaction mixture showed that the hydroxo compound was the primary product and that it gradually changed to the oxo binuclear species which is the more stable entity below 18°. Measurements of molar conductance confirmed the formulation as 2:1 and 4:1 electrolytes, respectively. The mononuclear hydroxo compound had a magnetic susceptibility corresponding to three unpaired electrons, but the binuclear compound had only a very small temperature-independent paramagnetism.

The crystal structure of potassium μ-oxodecachlorodirhenate(IV) has been determined from single-crystal studies[131]. It was found that the compound was dehydrated at 125°, losing one molecule of water. The X-ray studies showed that the compound should indeed be formulated as $K_4[Re_2OCl_{10}] \cdot H_2O$. The unit cell is tetragonal with $a = 7.070$ and $c = 17.719$ Å. The structure shows the presence of the

$$[Cl_5–Re–O–Re–Cl_5]^{4-}$$

anion formed by joining two octahedra by the common oxygen atom. The rhenium–chlorine bond distance is 2.38 Å and the rhenium–oxygen distance is 1.86 Å.

The treatment by Dunitz and Orgel[132] to explain the diamagnetism of the corresponding ruthenium compound has also been applied to this case[133].

Hexabromotechnetates(IV). Potassium hexabromotechnetate(IV) was prepared by treating the corresponding hexachlorotechnetate(IV) with successive portions of hydrobromic acid and repeatedly evaporating the solution to expel the hydrochloric acid formed in the exchange reaction[109].

Both potassium and rubidium hexabromotechnetate(IV) form dark red or black crystals which are cubic, having a lattice of the K_2PtCl_6 type. The unit-cell dimensions are $a = 10.37$ Å (references 101, 109) and $a = 10.46$ Å (reference 101) for the potassium and the rubidium salt, respectively.

The magnetic moment[102] of potassium hexabromotechnetate(IV) is 4.06 BM with a Curie–Weiss constant of 75° and this value has been confirmed[109] by measurements of hydrobromic acid solutions.

Potassium hexabromotechnetate(IV) is readily hydrolysed by water; but it may be recrystallized from concentrated hydrobromic acid.

Hexabromorhenates(IV). Only the hexabromorhenate(IV) ion is well established, although the hydroxopentabromorhenate(IV) ion was claimed[114] as a product of the reduction of potassium perrhenate with hydrobromic acid and potassium bromide.

Hexabromorhenic acid may be prepared in solution by reduction of perrhenic acid with hydrobromic acid[21] or by dissolution of rhenium dioxide in hydrobromic acid[117]. The potassium salt is prepared by addition of potassium bromide to solutions of the acid, or, directly, by reduction of potassium perrhenate by hypophosphorous acid in the presence of potassium bromide and hydrobromic acid[116], or, again, by evaporation of solid potassium hexachlororhenate(IV) with successive portions of hydrobromic acid[14,109].

Potassium hexabromorhenate(IV) is a dark red solid which gives yellow or red solutions in hydrobromic acid. It is rapidly hydrolysed, especially on warming, in water or alkaline solution, giving rhenium dioxide quantitatively.

Potassium and rubidium hexabromorhenate(IV) have been shown by X-ray powder diffraction patterns to be cubic with a structure of the K_2PtCl_6 type. The unit-cell parameters are $a = 10.387$ Å and 10.490 Å for the potassium[101,109] and the rubidium salt[101], respectively. A single-crystal examination of the potassium salt gave a value of 2.50 Å for the rhenium–bromine distance[134].

The magnetic properties of potassium hexabromorhenate(IV) have been examined over a temperature range[127]. The Curie–Weiss law is obeyed, with $\theta = 105°$ with a magnetic moment of 3.70 BM.

Hexaiodotechnetates(IV). Potassium hexaiodotechnetate(IV) is prepared by digesting the corresponding chloro- or bromo-technetate(IV) with successive portions of hydriodic acid[109]. The shiny black crystals produced give an X-ray powder diffraction pattern almost identical with that of potassium hexaiodorhenate(IV), but the compound is not isostructural with the chloro- and bromo-technetates(IV). The diffraction pattern has

been indexed[109] on the basis of a body-centered orthorhombic cell with
$a = 11.22$, $b = 8.00$ and $c = 8.87$ Å. The rubidium salt is, however,
cubic (K_2PtCl_6 type) with $a = 11.301$ Å.

The magnetic moment of potassium hexaiodotechnetate(IV) has been
found to be 4.14 BM in hydriodic acid by the Gouy method, the Curie
law being assumed to hold[109], whereas in the solid state[102] the magnetic
moment is 4.20 BM with a Weiss constant of 81°.

Hexaiodorhenates(IV). Potassium hexaiodorhenate(IV) may be prepared in a similar way to the corresponding chloride and bromide. The
earliest preparative method was the reduction of potassium perrhenate
with hydriodic acid and potassium iodide[114,135]. This salt has also been
prepared by dissolution of rhenium dioxide in hydriodic acid followed by
addition of potassium iodide[14], by reduction of potassium perrhenate by
hypophosphorous acid in the presence of hydriodic acid and potassium
iodide[117] and by evaporating the corresponding complex chloride or
bromide with successive portions of hydriodic acid[14,109].

Potassium hexaiodorhenate(IV) is a very dark red, or even black, solid
which is rapidly hydrolysed in water or alkaline solution with quantitative
precipitation of rhenium dioxide. It is soluble in hydriodic acid and also
gives moderately stable solutions in dry methanol and acetone. Potassium
hexaiodorhenate(IV) is not isostructural with the other halogen complexes
of this type[136]; It has an orthorhombic cell with $a = 11.07$, $b = 13.48$
and $c = 10.19$ Å. The rubidium salt[101] however, has a cubic K_2PtCl_6 type
structure with $a = 11.320$ Å.

The magnetic moment of the potassium salt has been found[127] to be
3.32 BM at 300°K with $\theta = 100°$.

Other Iodo Complexes of Rhenium(IV). Biltz and coworkers[137] observed
that when potassium hexaiodorhenate(IV) was dissolved in 20% sulphuric
acid the red colour could be extracted with ether. Furthermore, it was
shown that all the potassium and one-sixth of the iodine remained in the
aqueous phase and that all the rhenium and five-sixths of the iodine was
extracted into the ether layer. It was shown that the rhenium was still
in the quadrivalent state. On the basis of these observations they suggested
that the following reaction occurred:

$$K_2ReI_6 + H_2SO_4 \rightarrow K_2SO_4 + HI + HReI_5$$

but neither the complex acid nor its salts were isolated.

These observations have recently been confirmed[94]. By addition of an
alcoholic solution of tetraethylammonium chloride to the ether solution of
the complex rhenium acid, a salt has been isolated and shown to be
tetraethylammonium hydroxopentaiodorhenate(IV). Thus it becomes

apparent that in 20% sulphuric acid, potassium hexaiodorhenate(IV) is extensively hydrolysed to the hydroxopentaiodorhenate(IV) complex. That this is correct has been substantiated by the observation that in equimolar mixtures of water and sulphuric acid, the extraction by ether does not occur, presumably because the hydrolysis is suppressed and the hexaiodorhenate(IV) ion has no way of forming a hydrogen bond to the ether so as to facilitate extraction. Biltz *et al.* also observed that under the same conditions the corresponding complex bromide was not extracted into ether. This has also been confirmed; but it has been found that if the bromo complex is dissolved in very dilute alkaline solution and set aside for a few minutes hydrolysis does occur, since on acidification and shaking with ether partial extraction takes place. The fact that alkaline conditions are required for hydrolysis merely reflects that the complex bromide is more stable to hydrolysis than is the iodide.

Oxidation State III

Octahalodirhenates(III). A series of salts containing the octachloro- and octabromodirhenate(III) anion, $[Re_2X_8]^{2-}$, has been characterized by Cotton and coworkers[97,138].

Three methods of preparation of these dark blue or green salts have been reported:

(*a*) Reduction of potassium perrhenate in hydrochloric acid by hypophosphorous acid. The upper limit of the yield of the required anion appears to be about 40%, the major rhenium product being the hexachlororhenate(IV) anion. It is curious that, so far, no reducing agent other than hypophosphorous acid gives the dimeric rhenium(III) anion.

(*b*) Reduction at 290° of potassium perrhenate in hydrochloric acid by molecular hydrogen, initially at a pressure of 50 atmospheres. This was the original method of preparation of these salts as reported by Tronev and coworkers[139]; but the complex was incorrectly formulated by these workers as a compound of rhenium(II).

(*c*) Hydrochloric acid reacts with the dimeric chlorocarboxylate complexes of Re(III), to give the octachlorodirhenate(III) anion[140]:

$$ClRe(RCO_2)_4ReCl + 4HCl + 2Cl^- \rightarrow [Cl_4Re-ReCl_4]^{2-} + 4RCO_2H$$

This reaction is readily reversible[97,141] and provides evidence that both types of rhenium complex are similarly bonded.

The crystal structure of potassium octachlorodirhenate(III) dihydrate has been determined from a single-crystal X-ray diffraction study[138]. The crystal is triclinic with the unit cell parameters $a = 6.75$ Å, $b = 7.86$ Å, $c = 7.61$ Å, $\alpha = 102.0°$, $\beta = 109.0°$, and $\gamma = 105.0°$. There is a single molecular unit in the cell and the space group was found to be $P\bar{1}$. The structure of the dinuclear rhenium anion is shown in Figure 7.5. Each rhenium atom is essentially square-coordinated to four chlorine atoms. The rhenium–rhenium distance is exceedingly short at 2.24 Å, and the two sets of four chlorine atoms are in the eclipsed, rather than the staggered, rotomeric configuration. The positions involve slight distortion of the planar arrangement about each rhenium atom.

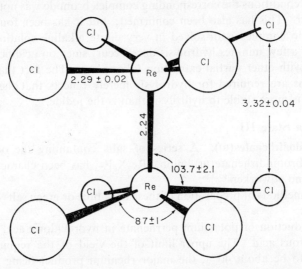

Figure 7.5   Structure of the $[Re_2Cl_8]^{2-}$ ion in $K_2Re_2Cl_8 \cdot 2H_2O$.

Russian workers[142] reported the structure of the compound previously formulated as $(C_5H_5N)H(ReCl_4)$ to be dimeric with a rhenium–rhenium distance of 2.22 Å and a rhenium–chlorine distance of 2.43 Å. Cotton and Harris[138] have reinvestigated the Russian data and have shown the dimensions of the anion to be identical with those found in $K_2ReCl_8 \cdot 2H_2O$.

Cotton[143] has considered the bonding in the octachlorodirhenate(III) anion. It is clear that any satisfactory theory of the bonding must explain the extremely short metal–metal distance and also the eclipsed configuration of the two approximately planar $ReCl_4$ groups. A simple molecular-orbital treatment has been used and it is clear that the two rhenium atoms are joined by a quadrupole bond, consisting of one σ-, two π- and one δ-bond. An estimate of the minimum value of the δ-bond can in principle be obtained merely by considering the electrostatic repulsion between the chlorine atoms, since it is only the δ-bond which maintains this configuration. There are, nevertheless, some difficulties in this calculation and only an estimated value of about 7 kcal mole^{-1} could be obtained, whereas a tentative assignment of the spectrum of this complex suggests that the strength of the δ-bond may be of the order of 100 kcal mole^{-1}.

The octahalodirhenate(III) anions react with acetic acid[141] to give the chloroacetates of rhenium(III) and with phosphine[144] to give a variety of products.

The Hexachlororhenate(III) Ion. There have been several attempts to prepare salts of the hexachlororhenate(III) anion, but the ion has probably not been isolated. Krauss and Dahlmann[114] claimed that potassium hexachlororhenate(III) was the ultimate reduction product of potassium perrhenate in hydrochloric acid solution, but this is not in accord with more recent work.

Manchot and Dusing[145] reduced solutions of potassium perrhenate electrolytically at a mercury cathode. They observed that the solution became first dark green and then brown, supposedly owing to hydrolysis. It was shown that oxygen equivalent to the oxidation of Re(III) to Re(VII) was absorbed on storage, thus strongly suggesting that a Re(III) species existed in solution; but no compound was actually isolated. The same method has been used by Russian workers[146] who claimed the isolation of caesium hexachlororhenate(III) as fine green crystals. Unfortunately the claim was not substantiated by magnetic evidence and only rhenium analyses were reported. One of us has repeated these experiments[14] and, on adding caesium chloride to the reduced solution, obtained a buff precipitate which had approximately the rhenium analysis reported by the Russians. However, caesium and chlorine analyses showed that the product was an ill-defined mixture and not caesium hexachlororhenate(III).

Other Russian workers[139] have claimed the preparation of the hexachlororhenate(III) ion by hydrogenation of ammonium or potassium perrhenate in concentrated hydrochloric acid solution at pressures of about 100 lb in^{-2}. Ammonium perrhenate was said to give green ammonium hexachlororhenate(IV) and yellow ammonium hexachlororhenate(III), while potassium perrhenate was said to give either blue-black potassium tetrachlororhenate(II) or a mixture of potassium hexachlororhenate(IV) and yellow potassium hexachlororhenate(III). However, Cotton and Johnson[147] have reinvestigated these systems and shown that the reported hexachlororhenates(III) are, in fact, hexachlororhenates(IV). It seems, therefore, that the hexachlororhenate(III) ion does not exist.

The Ion [Tc$_2$Cl$_8$]$^{3-}$. The ammonium salt of the [Tc$_2$Cl$_8$]$^{3-}$ ion, formally containing technetium in oxidation states II and III, was first prepared by Eakins and coworkers[148] by reduction of ammonium hexachlorotechnetate(IV) by zinc in hydrochloric acid.

Cotton and Bratton[149] determined the structure of this compound by applying X-ray diffraction techniques to a single crystal. The lattice is trigonal with $a = 13.30$ Å and $c = 8.40$ Å, and the anion was essentially isostructural with the octahalodirhenate(III) ion with technetium–technetium and technetium–chlorine distances of 2.21 Å, and 2.35 Å, respectively. The compound should, of course, be paramagnetic and Cotton and Bratton[149] report that it has a susceptibility corresponding to one unpaired electron per two technetium atoms.

ADDENDA

Halides and Oxide Halides

Rhenium heptafluoride is cubic with $a = 6.26$ Å at room temperature, but at very low temperatures there is a phase change to a lattice of lower symmetry[150]. The cubic form of rhenium hexafluoride[150] also has $a = 6.26$ Å and below the transition temperature ($-3.5°$) it is orthorhombic with $a = 9.61$, $b = 8.76$, and $c = 5.06$ Å. For technetium hexafluoride[150] the corresponding lattice parameters are $a = 6.16$ Å (cubic) and $a = 9.55$, $b = 8.74$, and $c = 5.02$ Å below the transition temperature of $-5.3°$.

The solubility of rhenium hexafluoride in anhydrous hydrogen fluoride is 1.75 moles per 1000 g solvent at room temperature[151]. The Raman-active ν_1 frequency of rhenium hexafluoride in these solutions was almost the same as that in the gas phase, indicating that reaction with the solvent does not occur. Conductivity measurements[151] are in accord with this.

Rhenium pentafluoride chloride is one of the products formed[152] by the action of fluorine on rhenium pentachloride at 30°. Strict control of the temperature is necessary. It is a red solid, melting at $-2°$ to a red liquid. The monomeric vapour is yellow and at room temperature the vapour pressure is about 300 mm. Rhenium pentafluoride chloride is unstable, decomposing rapidly at room temperature and even slowly at $-30°$, to rhenium hexafluoride and rhenium chlorides. The infrared spectrum[152] in the vapour phase is very similar to that of tungsten pentafluoride chloride and shows bands at 732, 689, 640, 389, 330, 278, 250, and 227 cm^{-1}. Rhenium pentafluoride chloride obeys the Curie–Weiss law with a Weiss constant of 203° and $\mu = 1.11$ BM.

Both technetium and rhenium oxide tetrafluoride are isostructural with molybdenum oxide tetrafluoride although their unit-cell parameters are quite different from those of the molybdenum compound. The monoclinic cells have the dimensions:

$$\text{TcOF}_4 \quad a = 18.83 \text{ Å}, \quad b = 5.49 \text{ Å}, \quad c = 14.43 \text{ Å}, \quad \beta = 114.0°$$
$$\text{ReOF}_4 \quad a = 19.01 \text{ Å}, \quad b = 5.57 \text{ Å}, \quad c = 14.72 \text{ Å}, \quad \beta = 114.0°$$

The space group is $C2/c$ and there are sixteen molecular units in the cell. The structure consists of chains of octahedra joined through *cis* bridging fluorine atoms, the geometry being the same as that for the pentafluorides of chromium, vanadium, and rhenium (Figure 1.7, page 19). The angle at the bridging fluorine atom in rhenium oxide tetrafluoride is 139°.

The density of liquid rhenium oxide tetrachloride is given by the expression[153]

$$\rho = 3.3090 - 0.23 \times 10^{-2}T^2 - 0.114 \times 10^{-5}T^2$$

from the melting point to 280°.

The structure of rhenium pentafluoride has not been elucidated in detail; however, it is reported to be of the same type as that of rhenium oxide tetrafluoride though no further detail is available[154].

Rhenium pentachloride is isostructural[155] with the pentachlorides of molybdenum and niobium (Figure 5.1, page 154). The monoclinic cell has $a = 9.24$, $b = 11.54$, $c = 12.03$ Å, and $\beta = 109.1°$. The unit cell contains eight molecular units and the space group is $P2_1/c$. Two octahedral $ReCl_6$ units share an edge to give dimeric Re_2Cl_{10}. The rhenium–chlorine bond lengths are 2.465 Å (bridging) and 2.244 Å (terminal). The rhenium–rhenium distance is 3.74 Å.

Technetium oxide trichloride has been definitely characterized as the major product of the chlorination of technetium dioxide[156]. It is a brown, thermally stable compound. Its infrared spectrum has a band at 1017 cm^{-1} assigned as a metal–oxygen double bond stretching frequency.

Technetium oxide tribromide is the only product of the bromination of technetium dioxide in a flow system[156]. It is a black, thermally stable compound, and its infrared spectrum shows a band at 770 cm^{-1} which has been assigned to a metal–oxygen–metal bridging system. Thus the compound cannot be isostructural with technetium oxide trichloride.

A curious situation has occurred with rhenium tetrachloride. A commercial sample of alleged rhenium trichloride was found to be a new form of rhenium tetrachloride[157], but its preparation could not be repeated. This form of rhenium tetrachloride reacts with chloride ion to give $[Re_2Cl_8]^{2-}$ and it is not stable in solution, giving, usually, rhenium(III) and rhenium(V) complexes.

The crystal structure of the new form of rhenium tetrachloride has been determined[158]. The monoclinic lattice has $a = 6.366$, $b = 6.282$, $c = 12.165$ Å, and $\beta = 93.17°$. The structure is similar to that of the $[W_3Cl_9]^{3-}$ ion (Figure 6.1, page 253) in that the rhenium atoms are arranged in pairs with three bridging chlorine atoms. However, an infinite chain structure is generated by one of the remaining chlorine atoms bridging to another rhenium atom in the next pair. In Schafer's notation the structure is described as $(Re_2Cl_7)Cl_{2/2}$.

We have found[159] that this form of rhenium tetrachloride is readily prepared by the interaction of rhenium trichloride and rhenium pentachloride in a sealed tube at about 300°.

Mass-spectrometric studies[160] have provided indirect evidence that technetium cluster compounds exist. The method used was to reduce a mixture of ammonium perrhenate and ammonium pertechnetate to the mixed metals and then these were treated with chlorine over a thermal gradient of 600–450°. The mass spectrum of the product, $(Re, Tc)_3Cl_9$, showed the presence of the following ions: $TcCl_4^+$, $ReCl_5^+$, $Tc_3Cl_9^+$, $Tc_2ReCl_9^+$, $TcRe_2Cl_9^+$, $Re_3Cl_9^+$, $Tc_3Cl_{12}^+$, and $Tc_2ReCl_{12}^+$, thus providing evidence that technetium clusters exist and also that trinuclear clusters can exist for technetium(IV) and rhenium(IV).

Mixed halides clusters $Re_3(Cl, Br)_9$ have been prepared[160] by interaction of rhenium trichloride and rhenium tribromide in a thermal gradient of 500–200° or by subliming rhenium trichloride in an atmosphere of hydrogen bromide. The mass spectrum of the products showed the presence of all intermediates between rhenium trichloride and rhenium tribromide.

The crystal structure of the adduct $Re_2Cl_6[P(C_6H_5)_3]_2$ has been determined[158]. The monoclinic unit cell has $a = 7.644$, $b = 10.985$, $c = 14.206$ Å, and $\beta = 96.5°$. The space group is $P2_1/n$ and there are two formula units in the cell. The compound is prepared by the interaction of $[Re_2Cl_8]^{2-}$ and triphenylphosphine and the eclipsed configuration of this ion is retained (Figure 7.5, page 310). One triphenylphosphine group is coordinated to each rhenium atom in place of a chlorine atom and the phosphine molecules are arranged in a *trans* configuration across the molecule. The bond distances are: rhenium–rhenium, 2.222 Å; rhenium–chlorine (*trans* to P), 2.35 Å; rhenium–chlorine (*cis* to P), 2.30 Å, and rhenium–phosphorus, 2.46 Å.

A most interesting complex, $Re_2Cl_5(DTH)_2$ (DTH = dithiahexane), has been prepared by the interaction of tetra-*n*-butyl octachlorodirhenate(III) and dithiahexane[161]. The crystals are monoclinic with $a = 8.023$, $b = 14.355$, $c = 8.243$ and $\beta = 105.5°$. The space group is $P2_1/m$ and there are two molecules in the unit cell. The compound contains both rhenium(II) and rhenium(III). The rhenium(III) atom has four chlorine atoms coordinated to it, as in the $[Re_2Cl_8]^{2-}$ ion (Figure 7.5, page 310). The other rhenium atom has four sulphur atoms arranged in a square about it, and the orientation of the two coordination planes is similar to that in $[Re_2Cl_8]^{2-}$ except that the *staggered* rotomeric configuration is assumed.

The remaining chlorine atom is coordinated to the rhenium(II) atom *trans* to the metal–metal bond and is weakly bonded to the rhenium(III) atom of the next molecule. As a direct consequence of the relative orientation of the planes, there can be no δ bond, and the overall rhenium–rhenium bonding is one σ and two π, which is reflected in a slightly longer metal–metal distance of 2.29 Å.

Complex Halides and Oxide Halides

Hydrazinium fluoride reacts[162] with both technetium hexafluoride and rhenium hexafluoride in anhydrous hydrogen fluoride to give yellow hydrazinium hexafluorometallates(V). The rhenium compound has a metal–fluorine stretching frequency at 627 cm^{-1} and its magnetic moment is 2.13 BM at room temperature.

A number of oxopentachlororhenates(V) have been isolated[163] by reduction of potassium perrhenate in hydrochloric acid by hydrogen iodide, followed by addition of the appropriate chloride. Salts of organic cations, such as 2,2'-bipyridinium, were converted into the neutral ReOCl$_3$·L type complexes when heated in hydrochloric acid solution[164].

Grove and Wilkinson[165] found that the magnetic properties of the oxopentachlororhenate(V) ion varied with the method of preparation and they reported magnetic moments ranging from 1.0 to 2.0 BM. However, in all cases the g value was 2.01 and the variation of magnetic moment with constant g value was not explained. The obvious explanation is that variable amounts of a diamagnetic impurity were present in the samples. It is interesting that none of the reported magnetic moments agreed with those previously reported, but the value of g for all the samples is exactly that expected on the basis of the earlier magnetic results.

A second product of the interaction[162] of hydrazinium fluoride and the hexafluorides of technetium and rhenium in anhydrous hydrogen fluoride is the hydrazinium hexafluorometallate(IV). Both compounds are cubic with $a = 10.48$ Å (technetium) and 10.49 Å (rhenium). Metal–fluorine stretching frequencies occur at 545 cm^{-1} for the technetium compound, and at 540 cm^{-1} in the rhenium complex. Both compounds obey the Curie–Weiss law as follows:

$$N_2H_6TcF_6 \quad \mu = 3.79 \text{ BM} \quad \theta = 52°$$
$$N_2H_6ReF_6 \quad \mu = 3.27 \text{ BM} \quad \theta = 90°$$

The crystal structure of bis(toluidinium) hexachlororhenate(IV) has been investigated[166]. The crystals are monoclinic with $a = 7.01$, $b = 25.04$, $c = 11.54$ Å, and $\beta = 90.0°$. The space group is $P2_1/c$ and there are four molecular units in the cell. The structure consists of regular $ReCl_6$ octahedra which form layers that alternate with the organic cations.

The red crystals which are sometimes isolated as an intermediate in the reduction of potassium pertechnetate to potassium hexachloro-technetate(IV) have been shown[167] to be pentachloroaquotechnetate(IV). The crystals are cubic with $a = 9.829$ Å and are isomorphous with potassium hexachlorotechnetate(IV). The compound obeys the Curie–Weiss law with a Weiss constant of 50° and a magnetic moment of 3.6 BM. The infrared spectrum shows a technetium–chlorine stretching frequency of 332 cm^{-1} and a technetium–oxygen stretching frequency of 427 cm^{-1}.

Bonati and Cotton[168] have shown that $[Re_2X_8]^{2-}$ ions, where X = Cl or Br, may be oxidized by chlorine and bromine to give dinuclear rhenium complexes $[Re_2X_9]^-$. In addition, the intermediate complexes $[Re_2X_9]^{2-}$ have been obtained. These latter compounds at room temperature have magnetic moments close to the spin-only value for one unpaired electron per dimer. The actual structures of these interesting complexes have not yet been reported.

A detailed molecular-orbital calculation on the bonding in the $[Re_2X_8]^{2-}$ ion has been given[169] which confirms the previously suggested importance of the δ-bond. The total rhenium–rhenium bond strength was found to be 366 kcal $mole^{-1}$ and the relative contributions of each type of bond was estimated as $\pi : \sigma : \delta = 2.2 : 1.5 : 1$.

Sodium thiocyanate reacts with $[Re_2Cl_8]^{2-}$ to give either $[Re_2(CNS)_8]^{2-}$ or $[Re(CNS)_6]^{2-}$ depending on the experimental conditions. The presence of acid favours formation of the dimeric species[170].

Both $[Re_2Cl_8]^{2-}$ and $[Re_2(CNS)_8]^{2-}$ undergo one- and two-electron reduction in acetonitrile[171]. It was suggested that the electrons are accommodated in empty σ-orbitals on the metal atoms *trans* to the metal–metal bond.

The reaction of the $[Re_2X_8]^{2-}$ ions with a number of carboxylic acids and sulphur ligands have been investigated[172]. In most cases the dimeric unit was retained.

REFERENCES

1. J. G. Malm, H. Selig and S. Fried, *J. Am. Chem. Soc.*, **82**, 1510 (1960).
2. J. G. Malm and H. Selig, *J. Inorg. Nucl. Chem.*, **20**, 189 (1961).
3. H. H. Claassen and H. Selig, *J. Chem. Phys.*, **43**, 103 (1965).
4. N. Bartlett, S. Beaton, L. W. Reeves and E. J. Wells, *Can. J. Chem.*, **42**, 2531 (1964).
5. E. L. Muetterties and K. J. Packer, *J. Am. Chem. Soc.*, **86**, 293 (1964).
6. E. E. Aynsley, R. D. Peacock and P. L. Robinson, *J. Chem. Soc.*, **1950**, 1622.
7. G. H. Cady and G. B. Hargreaves, *J. Chem. Soc.*, **1961**, 1568.

8. J. R. Sites, C. R. Baldock and L. O. Gilpatrick, *U.S.A.E.C. Report* ORNL 1327 (1952).
9. H. Selig and J. G. Malm, *J. Inorg. Nucl. Chem.*, **25**, 349 (1963).
10. A. Engelbrecht and A. V. Grosse, *J. Am. Chem. Soc.*, **76**, 2042 (1954).
11. E. E. Aynsley and M. L. Hair, *J. Chem. Soc.*, **1958**, 3747.
12. J. F. Lotspeich, A. Javan and A. Engelbrecht, *J. Chem. Phys.*, **31**, 633 (1959).
13. R. H. Busey and Q. V. Larson, *U.S.A.E.C. Report* ORNL 2584 (1959).
14. R. Colton, unpublished observations (1961).
15. A. Bruckl and K. Ziegler, *Chem. Ber.*, **65**, 916 (1932).
16. W. Geilmann, F. W. Wrigge and W. Biltz, *Z. anorg. allgem. Chem.*, **214**, 248 (1933).
17. O. W. Kolling, *Trans. Kansas Acad. Sci.*, **56**, 378 (1953).
18. H. V. A. Briscoe, P. L. Robinson and A. J. Rudge, *J. Chem. Soc.*, **1932**, 1104.
19. C. J. Wolf, A. F. Clifford and W. H. Johnston, *J. Am. Chem. Soc.*, **79**, 4257 (1957).
20. E. Amble, S. L. Miller, A. L. Schawlaw and C. H. Townes, *J. Chem. Phys.*, **20**, 192 (1952).
21. R. Colton and G. Wilkinson, *Chem. Ind. (London)*, **1959**, 1314.
22. A Bruckl and K. Ziegler, *Monatsh. Chem.*, **63**, 329 (1933).
23. F. A. Miller and J. L. Carlson, *Spectrochim. Acta*, **16**, 1148 (1960).
24. H. Selig, C. H. Chernick and J. G. Malm, *J. Inorg. Nucl. Chem.*, **19**, 377 (1961).
25. D. Hugill and R. D. Peacock, *J. Chem. Soc.*, **1966**, *A*, 1339.
26. H. Selig and J. G. Malm, *J. Inorg. Nucl. Chem.*, **24**, 641 (1962).
27. H. H. Claassen, H. Selig and J. G. Malm, *J. Chem. Phys.*, **36**, 2288 (1962).
28. R. B. Singh and D. K. Rai, *Can. J. Phys.*, **43**, 167 (1965).
29. O. N. Singh and D. K. Rai, *Can. J. Phys.*, **43**, 378 (1965).
30. G. Nagarajan, *Indian J. Pure Appl. Phys.*, **1**, 232 (1963).
31. H. Selig and J. G. Malm, personnal communication quoted by R. Colton and R. D. Peacock, *Quart. Rev. (London)*, **16**, 310 (1962).
32. O. Ruff, W. Kwasnik and E. Ascher, *Z. anorg. allgem. Chem.*, **209**, 113 (1932).
33. O. Ruff, *Angew. Chem.*, **46**, 239 (1933).
34. O. Ruff and W. Kwasnik, *Z. anorg. allgem. Chem.*, **220**, 96 (1934).
35. N. S. Nikolaev and E. G. Ippolitiv, *Dokl. Akad. Nauk SSSR*, **134**, 358 (1960).
36. G. H. Cady and G. B. Hargreaves, *J. Chem. Soc.*, **1961**, 1563.
37. B. Weinstock, E. F. Westrum and G. L. Goodman, *Proc. 8th Intern. Conf. Low Temp. Physics, London*, 1962, p. 405.
38. S. Sundaram, *Z. physik. Chem. (Frankfurt)*, **34**, 225 (1962).
39. J. Gaunt, *Trans. Faraday Soc.*, **50**, 209 (1954).
40. H. H. Claassen, J. G. Malm and H. Selig, *J. Chem. Phys.*, **36**, 2890 (1962).
41. M. Kimura and K. Kimura, *J. Mol. Spectr.* **11**, 368 (1963).
42. H. H. Claassen, *J. Chem. Phys.*, **30**, 968 (1959).
43. G. Nagarajan, *Australian J. Chem.*, **16**, 906 (1963).
44. H. Selig, F. A. Cafasso, D. N. Gruen and J. G. Malm, *J. Chem. Phys.*, **36**, 3440 (1962).

45. N. Bartlett, S. P. Beaton and N. K. Jha, *Chem. Commun.*, **1966**, 168.
46. A. J. Edwards, D. Hugill and R. D. Peacock, *Nature*, **200**, 672 (1963).
47. G. B. Hargreaves and R. D. Peacock, *J. Chem. Soc.*, **1960**, 1099.
48. M. Kotani, *J. Phys. Soc. Japan*, **4**, 293 (1949).
49. C. M. Nelson, G. E. Boyd and W. T. Smith, *J. Am. Chem. Soc.*, **76**, 348 (1954).
50. R. Colton, *Nature*, **193**, 872 (1962).
51. W. Noddack, *Z. Elektrochem.*, **34**, 627 (1928).
52. F. Schacheral, *Chem. Listy*, **23**, 632 (1929).
53. R. Colton, *Nature*, **194**, 374 (1962).
54. D. Brown and R. Colton, *J. Chem. Soc.*, **1964**, 714 (1964).
55. G. E. Boyd, *J. Chem. Educ.*, **36**, 7 (1959).
56. N. V. Baryshnikov, A. N. Zelikman and M. V. Teslitskaya, *Russ. J. Inorg. Chem.*, **7**, 1368 (1962).
57. W. Schuth and W. Klemm, *Z. anorg. allgem. Chem.*, **220**, 193 (1934).
58. A. Bruckl and E. Plettinger, *Chem. Ber.*, **65**, 971 (1933).
59. R. Colton, *J. Chem. Soc.*, **1962**, 2078.
60. K. Knox and C. E. Coffey, *J. Am. Chem. Soc.*, **81**, 5 (1959).
61. H. V. A. Briscoe, P. L. Robinson and C. M. Stoddart, *J. Chem. Soc.*, **1931**, 2263.
62. J. Chatt and G. A. Rowe, *Chem. Ind.* (*London*), **1962**, 92.
63. F. A. Cotton and R. A. Walton, *Inorg. Chem.*, **5**, 1802 (1966).
64. H. Hagan and A. Sieverts, *Z. anorg. allgem. Chem.*, **215**, 111 (1933).
65. D. E. LaValle, R. M. Steele and W. T. Smith, *J. Inorg. Nucl. Chem.*, **28**, 260 (1966).
66. K. Knox, S. Y. Tyree, R. D. Srivastava, V. Norman, J. Y. Bassett and J. H. Holloway, *J. Am. Chem. Soc.*, **79**, 3358 (1957).
67. M. Elder and B. R. Penfold, *Chem. Commun.*, **1965**, 308.
68. M. Elder and B. R. Penfold, *Inorg. Chem.*, **5**, 1197 (1966).
69. D. Brown and R. Colton, *Nature*, **198**, 1300 (1963).
70. C. L. Rulfs and P. J. Elving, *J. Am. Chem. Soc.*, **72**, 3304 (1950).
71. R. D. Peacock, A. J. E. Welch and L. F. Wilson, *J. Chem. Soc.*, **1958**, 2901.
72. J. E. Fergusson, B. H. Robinson and W. R. Roper, *J. Chem. Soc.*, **1962**, 2113.
73. L. C. Hurd and E. Brimm, *Inorg. Syn.*, **1**, 182 (1939).
74. T. Mao and V. G. Tronev, *Zh. Neorg. Khim.*, **4**, 1768 (1959).
75. D. Brown and R. Colton, *Australian J. Chem.*, **18**, 441 (1965).
76. F. W. Wrigge and W. Biltz, *Z. anorg. allgem. Chem.*, **228**, 372 (1936).
77. J. P. King and J. W. Cobble, *J. Am. Chem. Soc.*, **82**, 2111 (1960).
78. V. G. Tronev and R. A. Dovlyatshina, *Russ. J. Inorg. Chem.*, **10**, 160 (1965).
79. L. Malatesta, *Inorg. Syn.* **7**, 185 (1963).
80. V. G. Tronev and R. A. Dovlyatshina, *Azerb. Khim. Zh.*, **1965**, No. 4, 116.
81. R. D. Peacock, *J. Chem. Soc.*, **1955**, 601.
82. E. G. Ippolitov, *Russ. J. Inorg. Chem.*, **7**, 485 (1962).
83. N. S. Nikolaev and E. G. Ippolitov, *Dokl. Akad. Nauk SSSR*, **140**, 129 (1961).
84. P. A. Koz'min, *Zh. Strukt. Khim.*, **5**, 70 (1964).

85. K. W. Bagnall, D. Brown and R. Colton, *J. Chem. Soc.*, **1964**, 3017.
86. B. J. Brisdon and D. A. Edwards, *Chem. Commun.*, **1966**, 278.
87. R. D. Peacock, *J. Chem. Soc.*, **1957**, 467.
88. R. D. W. Kemmitt, D. R. Russell and D. W. A. Sharp, *J. Chem. Soc.*, **1962**, 4408.
89. R. D. Peacock and D. W. A. Sharp, *J. Chem. Soc.*, **1959**, 2762.
90. G. B. Hargreaves and R. D. Peacock, *J. Chem. Soc.*, **1958**, 3776.
91. R. H. Busey, *U.S.E.A.C. Report* ORNL 2782 (1959).
92. B. Jezowska-Trzebiatowska and M. Baluka, *Bull. Acad. Polon. Sci., Ser. Sci. Chim.*, **13**, 1 (1965).
93. L. Ossicini, F. Saracino and M. Lederer, *J. Chromatog.*, **16**, 524 (1964).
94. R. Colton, *Australian J. Chem.*, **18**, 435 (1965).
95. F. A. Cotton and S. J. Lippard, *Inorg. Chem.*, **5**, 9 (1966).
96. F. A. Cotton and S. J. Lippard, *Inorg. Chem.*, **4**, 1621 (1965).
97. F. A. Cotton, N. F. Curtis, B. F. G. Johnson and W. R. Robinson, *Inorg. Chem.*, **4**, 326 (1965).
98. F. A. Cotton and S. J. Lippard, *Inorg. Chem.*, **5**, 416 (1966).
99. F. A. Cotton, N. F. Curtis, C. B. Harris, B. F. G. Johnson, S. J. Lippard, J. T. Mague, W. R. Robinson and J. S. Wood, *Science*, **145**, 1305 (1964).
100. K. Schwochau and W. Herr, *Angew. Chem., Intern. Ed. Engl.*, **2**, 97 (1963).
101. K. Schwochau, *Z. Naturforsch.*, **19a**, 1237 (1964).
102. K. Schwochau, A. Knappwost, E. Burkard and T. S. B. N. Raju, *Z. Naturforsch.*, **19a**, 1128 (1964).
103. O. Ruff and W. Kwasnik, *Z. anorg. Chem.*, **219**, 65 (1943).
104. E. Weise, *Z. anorg. Chem.*, **283**, 337 (1956).
105. R. D. Peacock, *Chem. Ind. (London)*, **1955**, 1453.
106. D. H. Brown, K. R. Dixon, R. D. W. Kemmitt and D. W. A. Sharp, *J. Chem. Soc.*, **1965**, 1559.
107. R. D. Peacock, *J. Chem. Soc.*, **1956**, 1291.
108. B. N. Figgis, J. Lewis and F. E. Mabbs, *J. Chem. Soc.*, **1961**, 3138.
109. J. Dalziel, N. S. Gill, R. S. Nyholm and R. D. Peacock, *J. Chem. Soc.*, **1958**, 4012.
110. D. F. Evans, *J. Chem. Soc.*, **1959**, 2003.
111. J. D. Eakins and D. G. Humphries, *J. Inorg. Nucl. Chem.*, **25**, 737 (1963).
112. E. Enk, *Chem. Ber.*, **64**, 791 (1931).
113. F. Krauss and H. Steinfeld, *Chem. Ber.*, **64**, 2552 (1931).
114. F. Krauss and H. Dahlmann, *Chem. Ber.*, **65**, 877 (1932).
115. B. Jezowska-Trzebiatowska, *Trav. Soc. Sci. Lettres Wroclaw, Ser. B*, **39**, 5 (1953).
116. C. L. Rulfs and R. J. Meyer, *J. Am. Chem. Soc.*, **77**, 4505 (1955).
117. G. K. Schweitzer and D. L. Wilhelm, *J. Inorg. Nucl. Chem.*, **3**, 1 (1956).
118. W. W. Horner, F. N. Collier and S. Y. Tyree, *Inorg. Chem.*, **3**, 1388 (1964).
119. B. Aminoff, *Z. Krist.*, **94**, 246 (1936).
120. H. J. Berthold and G. Jakobson, *Angew. Chem.*, **76**, 497 (1964).
121. R. H. Busey, H. H. Dearman and R. B. Bevan, *J. Phys. Chem.*, **66**, 82 (1962).
122. L. A. Woodward and M. J. Ware, *Spectrochim. Acta*, **20**, 711 (1964).
123. G. N. Krynauw and C.W.F.T. Pitorius, *Z. phys. Chem. (Frankfurt)*, **43**, 113 (1964).

124. G. Nagarajan, *Bull. Soc. Chim. Belges*, **73**, 799 (1964).
125. W. A. Yeranos, *Bull. Soc. Chim. Belges*, **74**, 5 (1965).
126. W. A. Yeranos, *Z. Phys. Chem. (Frankfurt)*, **45**, 77 (1965).
127. B. N. Figgis, J. Lewis, R. S. Nyholm and R. D. Peacock, *Disc. Faraday Soc.*, **26**, 103 (1958).
128. A. D. Westland and N. C. Bhiwandker, *Can. J. Chem.*, **39**, 1284 (1961).
129. R. H. Busey and E. H. Sondar, *J. Chem. Phys.*, **36**, 93 (1962).
130. B. Jezowska-Trzebiatowska and S. Wajda, *Bull. Acad. Polon. Sci.*, *Classe III*, **2**, 249 (1954).
131. J. C. Morrow, *Acta Cryst.*, **15**, 851 (1962).
132. J. D. Dunitz and L. E. Orgel, *J. Chem. Soc.*, **1953**, 2594.
133. B. Jezowska-Trzebiatowska and W. Wojciechowski, *J. Inorg. Nucl. Chem.*, **25**, 1477 (1963).
134. D. H. Templeton and C. H. Dauben, *J. Am. Chem. Soc.*, **73**, 4492 (1951).
135. H. V. A. Briscoe, P. L. Robinson and A. J. Rudge, *J. Chem. Soc.*, **1931**, 3218.
136. J. C. Morrow, *J. Phys. Chem.*, **60**, 19 (1956).
137. W. Biltz, F. W. Wrigge, E. Prange and G. Lange, *Z. anorg. allgem. Chem.*, **234**, 142 (1933).
138. F. A. Cotton and C. B. Harris, *Inorg. Chem.*, **4**, 330 (1965).
139. V. G. Tronev and S. M. Bondin, *Khim. Redkikh. Elementov, Akad. Nauk SSR, Inst. Obshch. i Neorgan. Khim.*, **1**, 40 (1954).
140. F. Taha and G. Wilkinson, *J. Chem. Soc.*, **1963**, 5406,
141. F. A. Cotton, C. Oldham and W. R. Robinson, *Inorg. Chem.*, **5**, 1798 (1966).
142. P. A. Koz'min, V. G. Kuznetsov and Z. V. Popova, *Zh. Strukt. Khim.*, **6**, 651 (1965).
143. F. A. Cotton, *Inorg. Chem.*, **4**, 334 (1965).
144. F. A. Cotton, N. F. Curtis and W. R. Robinson, *Inorg. Chem.*, **4**, 1696 (1965).
145. W. Manchot and J. Dusing, *Z. anorg. allgem. Chem.*, **212**, 21 (1933).
146. D. I. Ryabchikov, V. A. Zarinskii and I. I. Nazarenko, *Zh. Neorg. Khim.*, **6**, 1138 (1961).
147. F. A. Cotton and B. F. G. Johnson, *Inorg. Chem.*, **3**, 780 (1964).
148. J. D. Eakins, D. G. Humphries and C. E. Mellish, *J. Chem. Soc.*, 1963, 6012.
149. F. A. Cotton and W. K. Bratton, *J. Am. Chem. Soc.*, **87**, 921 (1965).
150. S. Siegel and D. A. Northrup, *Inorg. Chem.*, **5**, 2187 (1966).
151. B. Frlec and H. H. Hyman, *Inorg. Chem.*, **6**, 1596 (1967).
152. R. D. Peacock and D. F. Stewart, *Inorg. Nucl. Chem. Letters*, **3**, 255 (1967).
153. L. A. Nisel'son, R. K. Nikolaev and Z. N. Orshanskaya, *Zh. Neorg. Khim.*, **12**, 860 (1967).
154. A. J. Edwards, G. R. Jones and B. R. Steventon, *Chem. Commun.*, **1967**, 462.
155. K. Mucker, G. S. Smith and Q. Johnson, U.S.A.E.C. Report UCRL-70509 (1967).
156. R. Colton and I. B. Tomkins, *Australian J. Chem.*, in the press.
157. F. A. Cotton, W. R. Robinson and R. A. Walton, *Inorg. Chem.*, **6**, 223 (1967).

158. M. J. Bennett, F. A. Cotton, B. M. Fuxman and P. F. Stokels, *J. Am. Chem. Soc.*, **89**, 2759 (1967).
159. J. H. Canterford and R. Colton, *Australian J. Chem.*, in the press.
160. K. Rinke, M. Klein and H. Schafer, *J. Less-Common Metals*, **12**, 497 (1967).
161. M. J. Bennett, F. A. Cotton and R. A. Walton, *J. Am. Chem. Soc.*, **88**, 3865 (1966).
162. B. Frlec, H. Selig and H. H. Hyman, *Inorg. Chem.*, **6**, 1775 (1967).
163. B. N. Ivanov-Emin, K. C. Dipak and A. I. Ezhov, *Russ. J. Inorg. Chem.*, **11**, 733 (1966).
164. K. C. Dipak and B. N. Ivanov-Emin, *Russ. J. Inorg. Chem.*, **11**, 736 (1966).
165. D. E. Grove and G. Wilkinson, *J. Chem. Soc.*, **1966**, A, 1224.
166. E. Adman and T. N. Margulis, *Inorg. Chem.*, **6**, 210 (1967).
167. M. Elder, J. E. Fergusson, G. J. Gainsford, J. H. Hickford and B. R. Penfold, *J. Chem. Soc.*, **1967**, A, 1423.
168. F. Bonati and F. A. Cotton, *Inorg. Chem.*, **6**, 135 (1967).
169. F. A. Cotton and C. B. Harris, *Inorg. Chem.*, **6**, 924 (1967).
170. F. A. Cotton, W. R. Robinson, R. A. Walton and R. Whyman, *Inorg. Chem.*, **6**, 929 (1967).
171. F. A. Cotton, W. R. Robinson and R. A. Walton, *Inorg. Chem.*, **6**, 1257 (1967).
172. F. A. Cotton, C. Oldham and R. A. Walton, *Inorg. Chem.*, **6**, 214 (1967).

Chapter 8

Ruthenium and Osmium

Despite the fact that halides and oxide halides are known for all oxidation states between VIII and I, it is true to say that the chemistry of osmium, and also of ruthenium, has not been studied adequately.

HALIDES AND OXIDE HALIDES

The known halides and oxide halides of ruthenium and osmium are given in Table 8.1. An interesting feature is the lack of chlorides higher

TABLE 8.1

Halides and Oxide Halides of Ruthenium and Osmium

Oxidn. state	Fluoride		Chloride	Bromide	Iodide
VIII		OsO_3F_2			
VII		OsF_7			
		$OsOF_5$			
VI	RuF_6,	OsF_6		$OsOCl_4$	
	$RuOF_4$				
V	RuF_5,	OsF_5			
IV	RuF_4,	OsF_4	$RuCl_4(?)$, $OsCl_4$	$OsBr_4$	
			Os_2OCl_6		
III	RuF_3		$RuCl_3$, $OsCl_3$	$RuBr_3$, $OsBr_3$	RuI_3, OsI_3
II					OsI_2
I					OsI

than ruthenium trichloride or osmium tetrachloride. When the multiplicity of higher chlorides for the previous groups is recalled, this absence becomes even more puzzling. The lack of oxide halides is especially noteworthy.

A great deal of work was reported on the halides of these elements before 1930. Much of it is obviously incorrect, and we have neglected work that has not been confirmed by subsequent investigations. Typical compounds coming under this classification are osmium octafluoride, osmium octachloride, and ruthenium difluoride[1].

Oxidation State VIII

Osmium trioxide difluoride. This is the only compound of osmium in oxidation state eight containing a halogen. It is prepared by the action of bromine trifluoride on osmium tetraoxide at about 50° and by the action of a 2:1 mixture of oxygen and fluorine on heated osmium metal[2].

Osmium trioxide difluoride is an orange powder, melting at 170–172° and is instantly hydrolysed by water. No other detail of the physical or chemical properties of this compound is available.

Oxidation State VII

Osmium heptafluoride. Osmium heptafluoride has been prepared by Glemser and coworkers[3] from osmium metal under the extraordinary conditions of 350–400 atmospheres of fluorine at 500–600° in a nickel bomb.

Osmium heptafluoride is only stable under a high pressure of fluorine. In the absence of an excess of fluorine it dissociates above −100° to osmium hexafluoride and fluorine. The magnetic moment at 90°K is about 1.08 BM. The infrared spectrum[3] shows absorptions at 715, 550 483, 366, 336 and 282 cm^{-1}.

Osmium oxide pentafluoride. Osmium oxide pentafluoride has been prepared[4] by passing a 1:2 mixture of oxygen and fluorine over osmium metal at 250° or fluorine over osmium dioxide at 250°; some osmium hexafluoride is also produced in these reactions and may be separated from the less volatile oxide pentafluoride by trap-to-trap distillation. Osmium oxide pentafluoride is an emerald-green crystalline solid, melting at 59.8° and boiling at 100.5° to give a colourless vapour[4,5]. It is hydrolysed violently by water. The heat of fusion and heat of vaporization are 2.20 kcal mole^{-1} and 8.60 kcal mole^{-1}, respectively[5].

Osmium oxide pentafluoride is orthorhombic with $a = 9.540$, $b = 8.669$ and $c = 5.019$ Å, with four formula units in the unit cell[4]. It appears to be isostructural with the orthorhombic (low-temperature) form of the transition-metal hexafluorides.

The ^{19}F-NMR spectrum of osmium oxide pentafluoride in tungsten hexafluoride showed only one band at 215 ppm downfield relative to silicon tetrafluoride[6]. At room temperature the magnetic moment[5] of osmium oxide pentafluoride is 1.45 BM.

Oxidation State VI

Ruthenium hexafluoride. Ruthenium hexafluoride is prepared by induction heating of ruthenium metal in fluorine at 300 mm Hg pressure in a quartz reactor equipped with a cold finger to cool the product rapidly, as it is thermally unstable[7]. The product always contains some ruthenium pentafluoride which can be removed by fractional distillation.

Ruthenium hexafluoride is a deep red brown solid[7], melting at 54°. Its boiling point cannot be determined accurately because of dissociation to the pentafluoride and fluorine; but it is known to form a red-brown vapour. As with the more stable hexafluorides, there is a solid-state transition, occurring at 2.5°, from the low-temperature orthorhombic form to the high-temperature cubic form.

The infrared spectrum of ruthenium hexafluoride has been observed by Weinstock, Claassen and Chernick[8], and the following fundamentals were assigned, on the assumption of O_h symmetry:

$$\nu_1 \; 675, \; \nu_2 \; 575^*, \; \nu_3 \; 735, \; \nu_4 \; 275, \text{ and } \nu_5 \; 262 \text{ cm}^{-1}$$

*Estimated.

Ruthenium hexafluoride is extraordinarily reactive and even attacks glass, dried by flaming-out under a high vacuum, at room temperature[7]. It reacts[9] with nitric oxide to give $NO^+RuF_6^-$, which has a cubic lattice with $a = 10.087$ Å. It is also reported to react non-stoichiometrically with xenon but details are not available[10].

Osmium hexafluoride. Osmium hexafluoride is, in fact, the compound which Ruff and Tschirch[11] claimed as the octafluoride. It was first shown to be the hexafluoride by Weinstock and Malm[12] who realized that the melting and boiling points were in the hexafluoride range and that the reported "osmium hexafluoride" was too involatile. These workers used chemical analysis and vapour-density measurements to establish the identity of the hexafluoride and this was quickly confirmed by Hargreaves and Peacock who studied its magnetic properties[13].

Osmium hexafluoride is prepared[12-14] by direct fluorination of the metal in a flow system at 200–300°. It is a pale yellow solid which is instantly hydrolysed by moisture.

Below −0.4° osmium hexafluoride adopts an orthorhombic lattice[14,15] and above the transition temperature it is cubic with $a = 6.23$ Å.

The vapour pressure of osmium hexafluoride has been determined by Cady and Hargreaves[14] over a wide temperature range and it varies according to the following equations:

Solid orthorhombic OsF_6 (−40° to −0.4°)

$$\log p_{mm} = 10.290 - 2284/T$$

Solid cubic OsF_6 (−0.4° to 33.4°)

$$\log p_{mm} = 8.726 - 1858/T$$

Liquid OsF_6 (34–47.5°)

$$\log p_{mm} = 7.470 - 1473/T$$

Various thermodynamic parameters have been determined for osmium hexafluoride from the vapour-pressure data and these and the melting and boiling points are given in Table 8.2.

The infrared spectrum of osmium hexafluoride has been observed by Weinstock, Claassen, and Malm[17] who deduced the following fundamentals, assuming octahedral symmetry:

$$\nu_1 \; 733, \; \nu_2 \; 632, \; \nu_3 \; 720, \; \nu_4 \; 268, \; \nu_5 \; 252, \; \text{and} \; \nu_6 \; 220 \; \text{cm}^{-1}$$

Mean-square amplitudes of vibration and force constants for osmium hexafluoride have been calculated[18,19].

TABLE 8.2

Thermodynamic Data for Osmium Hexafluoride

Property	Value	Ref.
M.p.	32.1°	12, 16
	33.4°	14
B.p.	45.9°	12, 16
	47.5°	14
ΔH_{fus} (kcal mole^{-1})	1.76	14
ΔH_{trans} (kcal mole^{-1})	1.97	14
ΔH_{sub} (cubic) (kcal mole^{-1})	8.48	14
ΔH_{sub} (ortho) (kcal mole^{-1})	10.45	14
ΔH_{vap} (kcal mole^{-1})	6.72	14
ΔS_{fus} (cal deg^{-1} mole^{-1})	5.72	14
ΔS_{trans} (cal deg^{-1} mole^{-1})	7.20	14
ΔS_{vap} (cal deg^{-1} mole^{-1})	21.0	14

The magnetic susceptibility of osmium hexafluoride has been determined over a wide temperature range[13]. It obeys the Curie–Weiss law with a Weiss constant of 66°, and the effective magnetic moment at room temperature is 1.50 BM.

Osmium hexafluoride is readily reduced by selenium tetrafluoride to give the adduct $OsF_5 \cdot SeF_4$ and selenium hexafluoride[20]. Both nitric oxide and nitrosyl fluoride react with osmium hexafluoride to give $NO^+OsF_6^-$, but with nitrosyl fluoride some $NO^+OsF_7^-$ is also formed[21]. Both these fluoroosmates are cubic, with $a = 10.126$ Å for $NO^+OsF_6^-$ (references 9, 21) and $a = 5.14$ Å for $NO^+OsF_7^-$ (reference 21).

Ruthenium oxide tetrafluoride. Ruthenium oxide tetrafluoride has been prepared by the action of bromine trifluoride on ruthenium metal. This is a violent reaction, the metal burns and the reaction bulb must be cooled with liquid air to control the reaction. Obviously the oxide tetrafluoride is formed from an oxide film on the metal and this is confirmed since the major product of the reaction is ruthenium pentafluoride[22].

Ruthenium oxide tetrafluoride is colourless when completely purified by vacuum-sublimation. It is extremely susceptible to hydrolysis, but with small amounts of water it forms a red liquid of unknown constitution. Ruthenium oxide tetrafluoride melts at 115° and its estimated boiling point is 184°. The vapour is colourless.

The vapour pressure of ruthenium oxide tetrafluoride as a function of temperature is given by the expressions:

$$\text{Solid RuOF}_4 \quad \log p_{mm} = 9.82 - 2857/T \quad (20\text{–}110°)$$
$$\text{Liquid RuOF}_4 \quad \log p_{mm} = 8.60 - 2616/T \quad (120\text{–}160°)$$

The heat and entropy of vaporization are 11.97 kcal mole^{-1} and 26.1 cal deg^{-1} mole^{-1}, respectively[22].

The magnetic moment of ruthenium oxide tetrafluoride is about 2.8 BM at room temperature.

Osmium oxide tetrachloride. This compound has been prepared by passing a 1:8 oxygen–chlorine mixture over osmium metal at 400° in a flow system[2]. It forms diamagnetic, needle-shaped crystals which melt at 32°. It gives a dark yellow vapour and boils above 200°.

Oxidation State V

Ruthenium pentafluoride. Ruthenium pentafluoride is prepared by direct fluorination of the metal above 300° in a flow system[22,23]. It has also been prepared by the thermal decomposition of the adduct $BrF_3 \cdot RuF_5$ which is formed by the interaction of ruthenium metal and bromine trifluoride at room temperature. Heating the adduct causes decomposition and removal of any ruthenium oxide tetrafluoride which may be present[24].

Thermal decomposition of barium hexafluororuthenate(v) above 400° also results in the formation of ruthenium pentafluoride[24].

Ruthenium pentafluoride is a dark green solid, melting at 86.5° to a very dark green viscous liquid which does not crystallize readily on cooling. It forms a colourless vapour and the estimated boiling point is 227°. It is extremely reactive; for example, it attacks dry glass above 100°, and at 180° is reacts further with glass to form a black solid and a red liquid which have not been identified[22].

The vapour pressure of liquid ruthenium pentafluoride has been determined[22] over the temperature range 90–160°, and the variation with temperature is given by the equation:

$$\log p_{mm} = 9.54 - 3329/T$$

The heat and entropy of vaporization are 15.23 kcal mole^{-1} and 30.5 cal deg^{-1} mole^{-1}, respectively[22]. The heat of formation of ruthenium pentafluoride has been determined by Hubbard and coworkers[25] using fluorine bomb calorimetry to be -213.4 kcal mole^{-1}.

Holloway and coworkers[23] have shown that ruthenium pentafluoride adopts a tetrameric configuration with a distorted version of the molybdenum pentafluoride structure (see Chapter 1). The crystals are monoclinic with $a = 12.47$, $b = 10.01$, $c = 5.42$ Å and $\beta = 99.8°$.

The magnetic moment of ruthenium pentafluoride is close to the spin-only value as expected for a d^3-octahedral configuration[22].

Ruthenium pentafluoride reacts with sulphur tetrafluoride to give the adduct $SF_4 \cdot RuF_5$ which is a pale pink solid, melting at 150° to give a red liquid[26]. In view of the low melting point of this adduct it is possible that it is a covalent compound with fluorine bridges rather than a compound containing discrete ions.

Osmium pentafluoride. Hargreaves and Peacock[27] have shown that the compound claimed by Ruff and Tschirch[11] as osmium hexafluoride is, in fact, the pentafluoride.

Reaction of an excess of osmium hexafluoride with hexacarbonyltungsten at 0° gives a mixture of osmium pentafluoride, osmium metal and tungsten hexafluoride[27]. Osmium pentafluoride is purified by fractional sublimation at 120°. It has also been prepared by the interaction of an excess of osmium hexafluoride with iodine in iodine pentafluoride solution[27]; it is essential to use an excess of osmium hexafluoride since if sufficient iodine is present, further reaction occurs to produce black non-volatile osmium iodide tetrafluoride. Osmium hexafluoride may be decomposed to the pentafluoride by irradiation with ultraviolet light; however, the reaction must be carried out in a flow system since it appears that an equilibrium is established in a closed vessel[27].

Osmium pentafluoride is a blue-grey solid,[27,28] melting at 70° to a green viscous liquid. The estimated boiling point is 226° and the vapour is colourless. It is extremely reactive towards moisture, and disproportionates above 180° giving the hexafluoride and the tetrafluoride[28].

The vapour pressure of liquid osmium pentafluoride over the temperature range 75–180° is given by the expression[28]:

$$\log p_{mm} = 9.75 - 3429/T$$

The heat of vaporization of osmium pentafluoride is 15.68 kcal mole^{-1}.

Osmium pentafluoride is reported to be monoclinic and isostructural with ruthenium pentafluoride; but no unit cell parameter has been given so far[23].

The magnetic moment of osmium pentafluoride is 2.06 BM at room temperature[27]. This value is to be compared with that of its ruthenium analogue which was about the spin-only value. It may be that some weak metal–metal interaction within the tetrameric unit is responsible for the lower moment.

The adduct $OsF_5 \cdot SeF_4$ is formed indirectly by the interaction of selenium tetrafluoride and osmium hexafluoride[20]. It is a pale blue solid melting at 150°, which suggests the possibility of its being a covalent fluorine-bridged compound. The corresponding sulphur tetrafluoride adduct, $OsF_5 \cdot SF_4$, is isomorphous with the cubic $SF_4 \cdot SbF_5$ adduct and a preliminary structural analysis[5] suggests that it may be $SF_3^+ OsF_6^-$.

Oxidation State IV

Ruthenium tetrafluoride. Ruthenium tetrafluoride has been prepared by reduction of ruthenium pentafluoride with iodine, in iodine pentafluoride as the reaction medium[29]. It is essential that an excess of ruthenium pentafluoride be used, otherwise further reduction to the trifluoride occurs. Removal of the excess of ruthenium pentafluoride and iodine pentafluoride leaves a yellow residue of the relatively involatile ruthenium tetrafluoride. Its melting point is above 280°, and at higher temperatures it attacks glass, leaving a black residue. Ruthenium tetrafluoride is readily attacked by moist air and reacts violently with water.

The effective magnetic moment[29] at room temperature is 3.04 BM and the Curie–Weiss law is obeyed with a Weiss constant of 74°.

Osmium tetrafluoride. Osmium tetrafluoride, a yellow solid, is one of the products of the reaction between osmium hexafluoride and hexacarbonyltungsten[27]. It has also been prepared[28] by thermal decomposition of osmium pentafluoride at temperatures in excess of 180°.

Ruthenium tetrachloride. Ruthenium tetrachloride has never been isolated, but vapour-pressure measurements of the reaction between chlorine and ruthenium suggest the possibility that ruthenium tetrachloride exists in the vapour[30,31]. The following vapour-state equilibrium has been postulated:

$$RuCl_3 + \tfrac{1}{2}Cl_2 \rightleftarrows RuCl_4$$

Osmium tetrachloride. Osmium tetrachloride is formed together with a considerable amount of the trichloride when the metal is chlorinated at 600° in a flow system[32]. The reaction rate varies from batch to batch of the metal but it is always slow. Osmium tetrachloride may also be prepared by direct interaction of the elements under somewhat different experimental conditions[33]. The apparatus consists of a thick U-tube containing liquid chlorine at one end and osmium metal at 600° at the other. The reaction is slow but it is claimed that only the tetrachloride is formed.

Osmium tetrachloride is a black solid which is insoluble in organic solvents, water and dilute sulphuric acid. However, it is rapidly hydrolysed by aqueous alkaline solutions[33].

The heat of formation[34] of osmium tetrachloride is -60.9 kcal mole^{-1} and its entropy of formation is 37.0 cal deg^{-1} mole^{-1}. Osmium tetrachloride is thermally unstable above 350°, dissociating to the trichloride and chlorine[33,34].

Diosmium oxide hexachloride. It has been claimed that reduction of osmium tetraoxide in concentrated hydrochloric acid, followed by evaporation to dryness in hydrogen chloride vapour, gives osmium oxide-trichloride[35] or osmium hydroxotrichloride[33]. However, it has been demonstrated recently that the product from this reaction is, in fact, diosmium oxide hexachloride[32]. It was shown by determination of the oxidation state that the osmium in this oxide chloride is quadrivalent. An osmium–oxygen stretching frequency was observed at 460 cm^{-1} and assigned to a bridging oxygen group. Conclusive proof of an osmium–oxygen–osmium linkage was obtained from a mass-spectrometric examination of the compound which showed the presence of this fragment[32].

Osmium tetrabromide. Osmium tetrabromide has been prepared by direct interaction of the elements in a sealed tube. The end of the tube containing the osmium metal was maintained at a temperature in excess of 450° and the tetrabromide sublimed from the hot zone[36]. It is a black non-hygroscopic solid, insoluble in water and in liquid bromine. Osmium tetrabromide decomposes to the tribromide and bromine at 350° in a vacuum[36].

Oxidation State III

Ruthenium trifluoride. Ruthenium trifluoride may be prepared[37] by reduction of ruthenium pentafluoride with iodine at 150°, or with sulphur at 200°. X-ray powder diffraction studies have shown that ruthenium trifluoride adopts a rhombohedral lattice, but the unit-cell parameters vary according to the experimental conditions of preparation[38], as shown in Table 8.3. Whilst the variations between individual values are small, they are nevertheless significant overall and it is considered[38] that the variation is caused by the presence in the lattice of cations with oxidation states other than III. On the basis of the X-ray powder diffraction data it has been suggested that ruthenium trifluoride consists of almost regular octahedra of fluorine atoms about each ruthenium atom, the octahedra being joined by sharing of all corners.

Ruthenium trichloride. The only method of preparation of ruthenium trichloride is direct chlorination of the metal; but this apparently simple reaction has led to several products whose constitution has only recently been established. Hill and Beamish[39] obtained shiny black inert plates and a brown solid that was soluble in ethanol and water. They suggested two forms of ruthenium trichloride had been prepared, but Fletcher and coworkers[40,41] subsequently showed that the soluble form is probably the oxide chloride Ru_2OCl_6. It is somewhat ironical that Fletcher and coworkers[40,41] have demonstrated that there are, in fact, two forms of

TABLE 8.3

Lattice Parameters of Ruthenium Trifluoride

Method of Prepn.	a (Å)	α
Excess of RuF_5	5.386	54.79°
Excess of RuF_5	5.392	54.78°
Small excess of I_2	5.403	54.67°
Large excess of I_2	5.408	54.67°
Large excess of S	5.407	54.66°

ruthenium trichloride. The α-form, contaminated with oxide chlorides, may be prepared as described by Hill and Beamish. The β-form, a brown powder, insoluble in water, is prepared[40,41] by passing a 1:3 mixture of carbon monoxide and chlorine over the metal at 340°. The β-form is converted irreversibly into the α-form at 460°; but the temperature must not exceed 500°, otherwise dissociation of the α-form occurs. In a chlorine stream, however, the β-form is converted into the α-form at 650° and this may be sublimed in chlorine at 750° (references 40, 41). The conversion of β-ruthenium trichloride is probably the best method of preparing the α-form.

Both forms of ruthenium trichloride adopt a hexagonal lattice with the following unit-cell parameters:

$$\alpha\text{-RuCl}_3 \quad a = 5.99 \text{ Å} \quad c = 17.22 \text{ Å} \quad \text{(reference 42)}$$

$$\alpha\text{-RuCl}_3 \quad a = 5.96 \text{ Å} \quad c = 17.2 \text{ Å} \quad \text{(reference 43)}$$

$$\beta\text{-RuCl}_3 \quad a = 6.125 \text{ Å} \quad c = 5.653 \text{ Å} \quad \text{(references 42, 44)}$$

Stroganov and Ouchinnikov[43] suggest that α-RuCl₃ is isomorphous with the violet form of chromium trichloride, consisting of a cubic close packed array of chlorine atoms with the ruthenium atoms in layers alternating with layers of octahedral holes.

At high temperatures, ruthenium trichloride dissociates into the metal and chlorine, and there is no evidence to suggest the formation of lower chlorides in this dissociation. The equilibrium dissociation pressure of chlorine in the temperature range 650–840° is given by the expression[45]:

$$\log p_{\text{atm}} = 12.61 - 1.510 \log T - 9005/T$$

The heat and entropy of formation of ruthenium trichloride have been redetermined by Bell and coworkers[45] as -60.5 kcal mole^{-1} and 56.4 cal deg^{-1} mole^{-1}, respectively. They suggested that earlier determinations, for example those by Shchukarev and coworkers[46], were erroneous for a variety of reasons.

The α-form of ruthenium trichloride is paramagnetic[41,44,47], although at very low temperatures it becomes antiferromagnetic[40]. The magnetic moment at room temperature is about 2.2 BM. The β-form has a small temperature-independent paramagnetism[40].

Osmium trichloride. Kolbin and coworkers[33] were unable to prepare osmium trichloride directly from the elements. However, it can be prepared in good yield by the thermal decomposition of osmium tetrachloride at 470° in a flow system with a low pressure of chlorine. In the absence of chlorine, osmium metal is produced and no evidence for the presence of lower osmium chlorides could be detected[33,48]. The dissociation pressure of chlorine is reported[49] to be one atmosphere at 600°.

Osmium trichloride is a dark grey, non-hydroscopic solid which is insoluble in water although it is hydrolysed by aqueous alkaline solutions[33]. Its heat of formation and entropy of formation are -45.5 kcal mole^{-1} and 56.6 cal deg^{-1} mole^{-1}, respectively[48].

Ruthenium tribromide. Shchukarev and coworkers[50,51] have prepared ruthenium tribromide by interaction of the elements at 450° under a high pressure of carbon dioxide. Direct bromination of ruthenium metal at 500° also gives ruthenium tribromide. It is a dark brown, inert powder which is insoluble in water. These properties are quite different from those of the product obtained by the interaction of ruthenium tetraoxide and hydrobromic acid[1]. It is likely that the latter, water-soluble compound is an oxide bromide.

Ruthenium tribromide is non-volatile, but it dissociates into the metal and bromine, with no evidence for the formation of lower bromides[50,51]. The equilibrium dissociation pressure of bromine over ruthenium tribromide in the temperature range 360–620° is given by the expression[51]:

$$\log p_{\text{atm}} = 2.524 - 2584/T$$

The heat and entropy of formation of ruthenium tribromide are -44 kcal mole^{-1} and 48 cal deg^{-1} mole^{-1}, respectively[51].

The X-ray powder diffraction pattern of ruthenium tribromide shows it to be hexagonal with $a = 12.924$ and $c = 5.860$ Å. There are eight molecular units in the cell[44].

Osmium tribromide.   The product obtained when osmium and bromine react together at high temperatures and pressures was found to be inter-mediate between osmium tribromide and tetrabromide[52]. This product was heated at 350° in bromine vapour at 160 mm Hg pressure. The resultant black insoluble compound was said to be osmium tribromide, but the analyses reported showed between 3% and 7% of unidentified impurity. It is possible that the product contains some oxide bromides, the oxygen being derived from oxide film on the metal.

Ruthenium triiodide.   Schnering and coworkers[44] prepared ruthenium triiodide by direct interaction of the elements at 350° but, on the other hand, Shchukarev and coworkers[53] have claimed that iodine does not react with ruthenium metal. The Russians prepared the triiodide by treating potassium iodide with the product obtained by the reduction of ruthenium tetraoxide in hydrochloric acid[53]. It is a black, non-hygroscopic solid.

Ruthenium triiodide dissociates at elevated temperatures to give the metal and iodine[53]. The heat and entropy of formation, as determined by calorimetry, are -38.3 kcal mole^{-1} and 59 cal deg^{-1} mole^{-1}, respectively[53].

Ruthenium triiodide is hexagonal with $a = 6.982$ and $c = 6.231$ Å. There are two molecular units in the cell[44].

Osmium triiodide.   Fergusson and coworkers[54] have prepared osmium triiodide indirectly. Osmium diiodide was refluxed with concentrated hydriodic acid, the solution evaporated to dryness to yield $(H_3O)_2OsI_6$, which was then decomposed by heating it in a sealed tube at 250°. The triiodide is a black solid with a room temperature magnetic moment of 1.8 BM[54].

Oxidation States II and I

Osmium diiodide has been prepared by reducing osmium tetraoxide with a hot solution of concentrated hydriodic acid[54]. The addition of ethanol led to the separation of the black diiodide. Prolonged heating of the solution of osmium tetraoxide in concentrated hydriodic acid resulted in the formation of osmium monoiodide[54].

COMPLEX HALIDES AND OXIDE HALIDES

Complex halides of both ruthenium and osmium are mainly restricted to compounds of oxidation states V and IV.

Oxidation State VIII

Trioxotrifluoroosmates(VIII).   These orange salts have been reported to be formed by the action of an excess of bromine trifluoride on a mixture of osmium tetraoxide and an alkali-metal bromide or, in the case of the silver salt, silver iodate[2]. Nothing is known of the chemical or physical properties of these compounds.

Oxidation State VI

Dioxotetrachlororuthenates(VI) and -osmates(VI). Rubidium and caesium dioxotetrachlororuthenates(VI) are prepared by addition of the alkali-metal chloride to a solution of ruthenium tetraoxide in very concentrated hydrochloric acid[55-57]. Potassium dioxotetrachloroosmate(VI) has been prepared from a solution of potassium dioxotetrahydroxoosmate(VI) in dilute hydrochloric acid[58].

Caesium dioxotetrachlororuthenate(VI) is diamagnetic with a cubic lattice $(a = 10.07 \text{ Å})^2$. Powder and single-crystal X-ray studies[58,59] have shown that potassium dioxotetrachloroosmate(VI) has a tetragonal unit cell with $a = 6.991$ and $c = 8.752$ Å. The space group is $I4/mmm$ and there are two molecular units in the cell. The anion is octahedral with the two oxygen atoms in the *trans*-position to each other[58]. The osmium–oxygen bond distance[58] is 1.750 Å and the osmium–chlorine distance is 2.379 Å.

The infrared spectrum of solid caesium dioxotetrachlororuthenate(VI) shows two strong absorptions at 814 and 824 cm^{-1}, which have been assigned to the asymmetric stretching frequencies of the O–Ru–O group[56].

Oxidation State V

Hexafluororuthenates(V) and -osmates(V). The methods of preparing hexafluororuthenates(V) and -osmates(V) are summarized in Table 8.4. The nitrosyl salts have already been discussed in the sections on the appropriate hexafluoride.

The hexafluororuthenates(V) are pale pink and the corresponding osmates(V) are pale cream-coloured[24,61]. Both series of salts dissolve slowly in water, a complicated reaction occurring with the appropriate

TABLE 8.4

Preparation of Hexafluororuthenates(V) and -osmates(V)

Method	Product	Ref.
KBr, CsCl or AgBr, Ru metal and BrF$_3$	MRuF$_6$	24
M(BrO$_3$)$_2$, Ru metal and BrF$_3$ (M = Ca, Sr, or Ba)	M(RuF$_6$)$_2$	24
TlF, RuF$_5$ and SeF$_4$	TlRuF$_6$	24
MCl, RuCl$_3$ and F$_2$ (flow system at 350°) (M = K, Rb, or Cs)	MRuF$_6$	60
MBr, OsBr$_4$ and BrF$_3$ (M = Na, K, Cs, or Ag)	MOsF$_6$	61

23

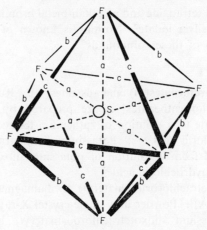

Figure 8.1   The hexafluoroosmate(v) anion. Atomic distances:
a = 1.82 Å, b = 2.48 Å, c = 2.66 Å.

tetraoxide and oxygen among the products.   The hexafluororuthenate(IV) and -osmate(IV) may be recovered from solution[24,61].

A single crystal X-ray study of potassium hexafluoroosmate(v) has revealed the presence of discrete OsF_6^- ions[62]; and, although all of the fluorine atoms are 1.82 Å from the osmium atom, there is distinct distortion of the octahedron, as shown in Figure 8.1.   The lattice parameters of this compound are given in Table 8.5, together with those of other

TABLE 8.5

Lattice Parameters of Hexafluororuthenates(v) and -osmates(v)

Compound	Symmetry and lattice type	Unit-cell parameters	Ref.
$LiRuF_6$	Rhombohedral; $LiSbF_6$	$a = 5.30$ Å, $\alpha = 56.3°$	63, 64
$NaRuF_6$	Rhombohedral; $LiSbF_6$	$a = 5.80$ Å, $\alpha = 55.2°$	63
		$a = 5.80$ Å, $\alpha = 54.32°$	64
$AgRuF_6$	Tetragonal; $KNbF_6$	$a = 4.85$ Å, $c = 9.54$ Å	63
$KRuF_6$	Rhombohedral; $KOsF_6$	$a = 4.95$ Å, $\alpha = 97.4°$	60, 62, 63
$TlRuF_6$	Rhombohedral; $KOsF_6$	$a = 5.09$ Å, $\alpha = 96.6°$	63
$RbRuF_6$	Rhombohedral; $KOsF_6$	$a = 5.07$ Å, $\alpha = 96.9°$	60, 62, 63
$CsRuF_6$	Rhombohedral; $KOsF_6$	$a = 5.25$ Å, $\alpha = 96.3°$	60, 62, 63
$LiOsF_6$	Rhombohedral; $LiSbF_6$	$a = 5.43$ Å, $\alpha = 55.5°$	63
		$a = 5.41$ Å, $\alpha = 56.2°$	64
$NaOsF_6$	Rhombohedral; $LiSbF_6$	$a = 5.80$ Å, $\alpha = 55.2°$	63
	Monoclinic	$a = 4.88$ Å, $c = 2.68$ Å	62
		$c = 4.41$ Å, $\beta = 93.4°$	
$AgOsF_6$	Tetragonal; $KNbF_6$	$a = 4.92,$ Å, $c = 9.58$ Å	63
$KOsF_6$	Rhombohedral	$a = 4.991$ Å, $\alpha = 97.18°$	61–63
$RbOsF_6$	Rhombohedral; $KOsF_6$	$a = 5.106$ Å, $\alpha = 96.74°$	63
$CsOsF_6$	Rhombohedral; $KOsF_6$	$a = 5.28$ Å, $\alpha = 96.1°$	61–63

hexafluororuthenates(v) and -osmates(v) that have been determined from X-ray powder diffraction studies.

The metal–fluorine stretching frequency occurs in the range 625–640 cm⁻¹ for the hexafluororuthenates(v) and in the range 616–630 cm⁻¹ for the hexafluoroosmates(v)[64,65].

Both potassium and caesium hexafluoroosmate(v) obey the Curie–Weiss law and the magnetic moments were found to be 3.34 and 3.23 BM, respectively[66]. Hexafluororuthenates(v) have been found to have room-temperature magnetic moments in the range 3.6–3.8 BM and other hexa-fluoroosmates(v) in the range 2.95–3.2 BM.

Oxidation State IV

Hexafluororuthenates(IV) and -osmates(IV). Both series of salts are generally prepared from the corresponding hexafluororuthenates(v) and -osmates(v) by reaction with water. After evolution of oxygen and metal tetraoxide has ceased, the solution is cooled and the salts crystal-lize[24,61]. Other methods include fusion[68] of a ruthenium nitrosyl nitrate complex with potassium hydrogen fluoride at 250° and fluorination[60] of a equimolar mixture of ruthenium trichloride and barium chloride at 350°. Both series of salts are yellow.

A large number of hexafluororuthenates(IV) and -osmates(IV) have been examined by X-ray powder diffraction techniques; the results are summarized in Table 8.6.

The metal–fluorine stretching frequency[65] in potassium hexafluoro-ruthenate(IV) occurs at 581 cm⁻¹ and for the corresponding osmate(IV) at 548 cm⁻¹.

The room-temperature magnetic moments[67,71] of the hexafluororuth-enates(IV) are about 2.90 BM and for the hexafluoroosmates(IV) in the range 1.35–1.50 BM.

TABLE 8.6

Lattice Parameters of Hexafluororuthenates(IV) and -osmates(IV)

Compound	Symmetry	Unit-cell parameters	Ref.
Na_2RuF_6	Hexagonal	$a = 9.32$ Å, $c = 5.15$ Å	69
K_2RuF_6 (α)	Cubic	$a = 8.37$ Å	67
(β)	Hexagonal	$a = 5.76$ Å, $c = 4.64$ Å	67
Rb_2RuF_6	Cubic	$a = 8.51$ Å	67
Cs_2RuF_6	Hexagonal	$a = 6.23$ Å, $c = 5.00$ Å	67
$BaRuF_6$	Rhombohedral	$a = 4.88$ Å, $\alpha = 98.0°$	60, 62
Na_2OsF_6 (α)	Hexagonal	$a = 9.36$ Å, $c = 5.11$ Å	69
(β)	Orthorhombic	$a = 5.80$ Å, $b = 4.50$ Å, $c = 10.14$ Å	69
K_2OsF_6	Hexagonal	$a = 5.80$ Å, $c = 4.62$ Å	70
Cs_2OsF_6	Hexagonal	$a = 6.26$ Å, $c = 5.00$ Å	70

Hexachlororuthenates(IV) and -osmates(IV). Both the hexachlororuthenates(IV) and -osmates(IV) are well-established anions; some of the best known methods of preparation are given in Table 8.7.

Both series of salts are partially hydrolysed in hydrochloric acid solutions of moderate strength, to give the oxo-bridged $Ru(Os)_2OCl_{10}^{4-}$ salts.

Puche[76] has studied the thermal decomposition of the hexachloroosmates(IV). At elevated temperatures they all decompose to alkalimetal chloride, osmium and chlorine. There was no evidence for the formation of lower binary osmium chlorides[76].

TABLE 8.7

Preparation of Hexachlororuthenates(IV) and -osmates(IV)

Method	Ref.
Oxidn. with Cl_2 of $M_2RuCl_5 \cdot H_2O$ in conc. HCl	55, 56
Recrystn. of $Ru_2OCl_{10}^{4-}$ from conc. HCl	55, 72
Redn. of RuO_4 in conc. HCl and addn. of KCl	73
Dil. HCl on K_2RuO_4 melt	55
Redn. of OsO_4 with $FeCl_2$ in conc. HCl	74, 75
Chlorination of mixtures of osmium and alkali-metal chloride	76

X-ray powder diffraction patterns have shown that both potassium hexachlororuthenate(IV) and -osmate(IV) have the cubic $(NH_4)_2PtCl_6$ structure with $a = 10.26$ Å and $a = 9.73$ Å, respectively[73,77].

The metal–chlorine stretching frequency[78,79] has been observed in the range 332–346 cm^{-1} for the hexachlororuthenates(IV) and in the range 304–328 cm^{-1} for the hexachloroosmates(IV). In addition, the Raman spectrum of hexachloroosmic(IV) acid has been observed[80]: two bands assigned as ν_5 (314 cm^{-1}) and ν_4 (177 cm^{-1}) were detected.

The magnetic moments[71] of the hexachlororuthenates(IV) lie in the range 2.70–3.01 BM at room temperature, and the corresponding moments for the hexachloroosmates(IV) are in the range 1.5–1.7 BM.

μ-Oxodecachlorodiruthenates(IV) and -osmates(IV). The compounds reported in the early literature as pentachlorohydroxoruthenates(IV) and -osmates(IV) have been shown to be, in fact, oxygen-bridged binuclear compounds.

Potassium μ-oxodecachlorodiruthenate(IV) may be prepared by first reducing ruthenium tetraoxide in 3M hydrochloric acid at room temperature and then adding potassium chloride dissolved in hydrochloric acid[55,56]. Howe[55] has also reported that this binuclear anion is formed when alkalimetal hexachlororuthenates(IV) are recrystallized from dilute hydrochloric acid. The corresponding osmium complexes have been prepared by the slow reduction of osmium tetraoxide in hydrochloric acid with ferrous sulphate[74,81]. Addition of ammonium chloride gave ammonium μ-oxodecachlorodiosmate(IV).

The first suggestion that the compound "K_2RuCl_5OH" was not a simple octahedral complex of ruthenium(IV) was made by Mellor[82], who found that the solid was diamagnetic. The problem was resolved by Mathieson, Mellor and Stephenson[83], who determined the structure of a single crystal using X-ray diffraction techniques. The potassium salt

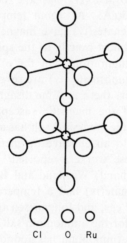

Cl   O   Ru

Figure 8.2   Configuration of the $Ru_2OCl_{10}^{4-}$ anion.

is tetragonal with $a = 7.10$ and $c = 16.95$ Å. The structure of the anion is shown in Figure 8.2. It contains a linear Ru–O–Ru linkage and each ruthenium atom achieves octahedral coordination. The octahedra are joined by sharing a corner. The ruthenium–oxygen distance is short at 1.80 Å, and the ruthenium–chlorine distance is normal at 2.34 Å.

Dunitz and Orgel[84] considered the bonding in the μ-oxodecachloro-diruthenate(IV) anion on a molecular-orbital basis. They showed that there is considerable π-bonding between the oxygen and the two ruthenium atoms, and furthermore that the π-bonding is greatest in the linear configuration.

The infrared spectrum[56] of the ruthenium anion shows a sharp absorption at 888 cm^{-1} which may be attributed to the ruthenium–oxygen stretching frequency. The corresponding osmium complex[81] shows a similar band at 870 cm^{-1} and this constitutes the most direct evidence to date that the osmium compound also has the μ-oxo configuration.

Hexabromoruthenates(IV) and -osmates(IV). Hexabromoruthenates(IV) may be prepared by addition of alkali-metal bromides to solutions of ruthenium tetraoxide in concentrated hydrobromic acid[85]. The hexabromoosmates(IV) have been prepared in an analogous manner[86] and also by the action of hydrobromic acid on hexachloroosmates(IV)[87]. The hexabromoruthenates(IV) and -osmates(IV) are dark red or black solids which are more easily hydrolysed than the corresponding chloro complexes.

Potassium hexabromoosmate(IV) has the cubic $(NH_4)_2PtCl_6$ type structure[77] with $a = 10.30$ Å. At room temperature potassium and rubidium hexabromoruthenates(IV) have magnetic moments[71] of about 2.8 BM, corresponding almost exactly to the spin-only value for a spin-paired d^4 octahedral configuration. On the other hand, the magnetic moments of the hexabromoosmates(IV) are severely depressed from the spin-only value. However, there is some disagreement in the literature over the actual value of the magnetic susceptibility. Earnshaw and coworkers[71] reported that the potassium salt has a susceptibility of 6.09×10^{-4} cgs, corresponding to an effective magnetic moment of 1.21 BM. For the caesium salt these workers reported[71] a magnetic moment of 1.76 BM. On the other hand, Westland and Bhiwandker[88] found that potassium hexabromoosmate(IV) had a temperature-independent paramagnetism of 9.86×10^{-4} cgs, and Johannesen and Lindberg[89] reported a value of 9.80×10^{-4} cgs for the ammonium salt.

Hexaiodoosmates(IV). Ammonium hexaiodoosmate(IV) has been prepared by refluxing the corresponding hexachloroosmate(IV) in hydriodic acid in the presence of ammonium iodide[54]. The corresponding potassium salt has been isolated from the mixture formed when osmium tetraoxide is reduced in 2M hydriodic acid in the presence of an excess of potassium iodide[90]. The free acid, $(H_3O)_2OsI_6$, has been isolated as a blue-black solid from a solution of osmium dioxide in concentrated hydriodic acid[54].

The potassium salt is cubic[90] with $a = 9.87$ Å. The magnetic moments of the hexaiodoosmates(IV) vary between 1.3 and 1.65 BM at room temperature. The variation of the effective magnetic moment with the size of the cation suggests a decreasing interaction by super-exchange[54,71].

Oxidation State III

Hexafluororuthenate(III). Potassium hexafluororuthenate(III) has been prepared by the fusion of ruthenium triiodide or trichloride with potassium hydrogen fluoride in the absence of oxygen[68,91]. It is a brown solid, having[91] a tetragonal unit cell and a magnetic moment of 1.25 BM. It is unstable in water.

Pentachlororuthenates(III). Although several types of chloro complexes of ruthenium(III) were reported in the early literature, the only type which has been confirmed recently is the pentachloroaquoruthenate(III) ion. The complex may be prepared by reduction of the corresponding hexachlororuthenate(IV) in hydrochloric acid by many reducing agents, for example, stannous chloride or oxalic acid[55,56]. An alternative procedure is to reduce potassium μ-oxodecachlorodiruthenate(IV) in a refluxing mixture of hydrochloric acid and ethanol[56].

Oxidation State II

Tetrachlororuthenates(II). Tetrachlororuthenates(II) are prepared by reduction of ruthenium trichloride in hydrochloric acid solution[92] or by electrolytic reduction of hexachlororuthenates(IV)[93]. The complexes are very unstable and are readily oxidized.

ADDENDA

Halides and Oxide Halides

The existence of osmium trioxide difluoride has been confirmed by Jha[94]. When freshly prepared, this compound is orange-yellow but it slowly becomes red. The red form, which is the low-temperature form, can be converted into the orange-yellow form by heating to approximately 90°. The high-temperature form has a monoclinic unit cell with $a = 5.571$, $b = 5.555$, $c = 5.571$ Å, and $\beta = 93°$. The red form has a more complex X-ray diffraction pattern. Jha[94] suggested that the red form has six-coordinate osmium atoms in a tetrameric arrangement as there are similarities between the X-ray diffraction patterns of this compound and of the pentafluorides of ruthenium, rhodium, iridium, and platinum. He also suggested that the yellow form has a dimeric structure.

The variation of vapour pressure of osmium oxide pentafluoride with temperature is given by the expressions[94]:

$$\log p_{mm} = 9.064 - 2266/T \quad (32\text{–}59°)$$
$$\log p_{mm} = 7.994 - 1911/T \quad (59\text{–}105°)$$

The heat of sublimation, the entropy of fusion, and the entropy of vaporization are 10.37 kcal mole^{-1}, 5.29 cal deg^{-1} mole^{-1}, and 23.4 cal deg^{-1} mole^{-1}, respectively[94].

Like the transition-metal hexafluorides, osmium oxide pentafluoride is dimorphic, having an orthorhombic low-temperature form and a cubic high-temperature modification[94]. The transition temperature[94] is $32.5°$. The cubic form has $a = 6.143$ Å and unpublished data[95], obtained from a single crystal X-ray diffraction study of the orthorhombic form of osmium oxide pentafluoride, show the presence of discrete, slightly distorted $OsOF_5$ octahedra.

The infrared, visible, and ultraviolet spectra of osmium oxide penta-fluoride have been recorded[94]. The infrared spectrum of the vapour was roughly assigned on the basis of C_{4v} symmetry and the following fundamentals were deduced v_1 960, v_2' 640, v_2'' 650, v_3' 700, v_3'' 710, and v_4' 440 cm^{-1}.

Jha[94] showed by means of chemical reactions that osmium oxide penta-fluoride is more like osmium hexafluoride than like iridium hexafluoride in its behaviour. With nitric oxide, the pale lilac complex $NO^+OsOF_5^-$ is formed[94].

TABLE 8.8

Some Properties of Ruthenium and Osmium Hexafluorides

Property	RuF_6	OsF_6
M.p.	54.0°	33.2°
Transition temperature	2.5°	1.4°
Cubic form	$a = 6.11$ Å	$a = 6.25$ Å
Orthorhombic form	$a = 9.44$ Å	$a = 9.59$ Å
	$b = 8.59$ Å	$b = 8.75$ Å
	$c = 4.98$ Å	$c = 5.04$ Å

The structures of the two crystal modifications of ruthenium and osmium hexafluoride have been investigated[96]. The structural values obtained, and some closely related thermodynamic parameters are summarized in Table 8.8.

Frlec and Hyman[97] have determined the solubility of osmium hexa-fluoride in anhydrous hydrogen fluoride to be 0.97 mole per 1000 g of solvent at room temperature. The solution so formed has a very low conductivity, indicating only a very small amount of ionization in anhydrous hydrogen fluoride. It was found[97] that solutions of osmium hexafluoride in anhydrous hydrogen fluoride react quite readily with Kel-F.

The infrared spectrum of osmium hexafluoride at $-180°$ has been recorded and shown to be consistent with a tetragonally distorted octa-hedral configuration[98].

Nitric oxide reacts[94] with osmium hexafluoride to give $NO^+OsF_6^-$. This compound obeys the Curie–Weiss law with $\mu = 3.36$ BM and a Weiss constant of 22°. Cubic ($a = 11.162$ Å) $OsF_5 \cdot SF_4$ is formed[94] as a white solid by the reaction of osmium hexafluoride with sulphur tetrafluoride; it has a magnetic moment of 3.46 BM at room temperature[94].

Osmium tetrachloride has been shown to be the major product when osmium tetraoxide is reduced by thionyl chloride[32,99]. This form of osmium tetrachloride is chemically more reactive and is probably a different polymorph from that prepared by chlorination of the metal.

μ-Oxohexachlorodiosmium(IV) has been prepared by Schafer and Hunelse[100] by the interaction of osmium, chlorine, and oxygen in a temperature gradient. Its reported chemical properties were similar to those noted previously[32]. An additional product of the thermal-gradient preparation was Os_2Cl_7.

The structures of both forms of ruthenium trichloride have been re-investigated[101]. The unit-cell parameters for both forms agree well with those previously reported, although it was suggested[101] that previous samples of β-RuCl$_3$ were not pure. The magnetic properties of ruthenium trichloride have also been discussed[101].

Complex Halides and Oxide Halides

Interaction[94] of osmium tetraoxide, nitrosyl chloride, and bromine trifluoride leads to the formation of yellow, diamagnetic $NO^+OsO_3F_3^-$.

Frlec and coworkers[102] have studied the reaction between osmium hexafluoride and hydrazinium fluoride in anhydrous hydrogen fluoride. They isolated a pale violet substance $N_2H_6(OsF_6)_2$. Osmium–fluorine stretching frequencies were observed at 640 and 570 cm^{-1}.

The structure of sodium hexafluoroosmate(V) has been studied by single crystal X-ray diffraction techniques[103]. The structure, which has a rhombohedral unit cell with $a = 5.803$ Å and $\alpha = 55.17°$, consists of sodium and hexafluoroosmate(V) ions in a distorted sodium chloride type lattice. The osmium–fluorine bond distance is 1.84 Å.

Hydrazinium hexafluoroosmate(IV) has been prepared[102] as a beige solid which has a strong metal–fluorine stretching frequency at 550 cm^{-1}. Its effective magnetic moment is 2.29 BM at room temperature[102].

The unit-cell parameters and metal–halogen stretching frequencies of a number of hexachloro- and hexabromoosmates(IV) have been reported[104] and are summarized in Table 8.9.

TABLE 8.9

Lattice Parameters and Stretching Frequencies of OsX_6^{2-}

Compound	a (Å)	ν (cm^{-1})	Compound	a (Å)	ν (cm^{-1})
K_2OsCl_6	9.76	327	K_2OsBr_6		224
Rb_2OsCl_6	9.95	317	Rb_2OsBr_6	10.39	221
Cs_2OsCl_6	10.21	312	Cs_2OsBr_6	10.71	216

The relationship between observed stretching frequency and the size of the counter-ion has also been discussed[104].

Hirashi and Shimanouchi[105] have studied the infrared spectrum of potassium hexachloroosmate(IV) and reported the following assignments:

Osmium–chlorine stretch   326 cm^{-1}
Deformation mode   176 cm^{-1}
Lattice mode   85 cm^{-1}

REFERENCES

1. J. W. Mellor, *A Comprehensive Treatise on Inorganic and Theoretical Chemistry*, Vol. XV, Longmans, London, 1936.
2. M. A. Hepworth and P. L. Robinson, *J. Inorg. Nucl. Chem.*, **4**, 24 (1957).
3. O. Glemser, H. W. Roesky, K. H. Hellberg and H. W. Werther, *Chem. Ber.*, **99**, 2652 (1966).
4. N. Bartlett, N. K. Jha and J. Trotter, *Proc. Chem. Soc.*, **1962**, 277.
5. N. Bartlett, in *Preparative Inorganic Reactions* (ed. W. L. Jolly), Vol. 2, Interscience, New York, 1965.
6. N. Bartlett, S. Beaton, L. W. Reeves and E. J. Wells, *Can. J. Chem.*, **42**, 2531 (1964).
7. H. H. Claassen, H. Selig, J. G. Malm, C. L. Chernick and B. Weinstock, *J. Am. Chem. Soc.*, **83**, 2390 (1961).
8. B. Weinstock, H. H. Claassen and C. L. Chernick, *J. Chem. Phys.*, **38**, 1470 (1963).
9. N. Bartlett and D. H. Lohmann, *J. Chem. Soc.*, **1962**, 5253.
10. N. Bartlett and N. K. Jha, in *Noble Gas Compounds* (ed. H. H. Hyman), University of Chicago Press, Chicago, 1963.
11. O. Ruff and F. W. Tschirch, *Ber.*, **46**, 929 (1913).
12. B. Weinstock and J. G. Malm, *J. Am. Chem. Soc.*, **80**, 4466 (1958).
13. G. B. Hargreaves and R. D. Peacock, *Proc. Chem. Soc.*, **1959**, 85.
14. G. H. Cady and G. B. Hargreaves, *J. Chem. Soc.*, **1961**, 1563.
15. B. Weinstock, E. F. Westrum and G. L. Goodman, *Proc. 8th Intern. Conf. Low Temp. Physics, London*, 1962, p. 405.
16. B. Weinstock and J. G. Malm, *Proc.* 2nd *U.N. Intern. Conf. Peaceful Uses At. Energy, Geneva*, **28**, 125 (1958).
17. B. Weinstock, H. H. Claassen and J. G. Malm, *J. Chem. Phys.*, **32**, 181 (1960).
18. M. Kimura and K. Kimura, *J. Mol. Spectr.*, **11**, 368 (1963).
19. H. Claassen, *J. Chem. Phys.*, **30**, 968 (1959).
20. M. A. Hepworth, P. L. Robinson and G. Westland, *Chem. Ind. (London)*, **1955**, 1516.
21. N. Bartlett, S. P. Beaton and N. K. Jha, *Chem. Commun.*, **1966**, 16.
22. J. H. Holloway and R. D. Peacock, *J. Chem. Soc.*, **1963**, 527.
23. J. H. Holloway, R. D. Peacock and R. W. H. Small, *J. Chem. Soc.*, **1964**, 644.
24. M. A. Hepworth, R. D. Peacock and P. L. Robinson, *J. Chem. Soc.*, **1954**, 1197.
25. H. A. Porte, E. Greenberg and W. N. Hubbard, *J. Phys. Chem.*, **69**, 2308 (1965).

26. N. Bartlett and P. L. Robinson, *J. Chem. Soc.*, **1961**, 3417.
27. G. B. Hargreaves and R. D. Peacock, *J. Chem. Soc.*, **1960**, 2618.
28. G. H. Cady and G. B. Hargreaves, *J. Chem. Soc.*, **1961**, 1568.
29. J. H. Holloway and R. D. Peacock, *J. Chem. Soc.*, **1963**, 3892.
30. S. A. Shchukarev, N. I. Kolbin and A. N. Ryabov, *Russ. J. Inorg. Chem.*, **4**, 763 (1959).
31. W. E. Bell, M. C. Garrison and U. Merten, *J. Phys. Chem.*, **65**, 517 (1961).
32. R. Colton and R. H. Farthing, *Australian J. Chem.*, **21**, 589 (1968).
33. N. I. Kolbin, I. N. Semenov and Y. M. Shutov, *Russ. J. Inorg. Chem.*, **8**, 1270 (1963).
34. N. I. Kolbin and I. N. Semenov, *Russ. J. Inorg. Chem.*, **9**, 108 (1964).
35. R. Charonnet, in *Nouveau Traité de Chimie Mineral* (ed. P. Pascal), Vol. XIX, Paris, 1958, p. 266.
36. I. N. Semenov and N. I. Kolbin, *Russ. J. Inorg. Chem.*, **7**, 111 (1962).
37. E. E. Aynsley, R. D. Peacock and P. L. Robinson, *Chem. Ind. (London)*, **1952**, 1002.
38. M. A. Hepworth, K. H. Jack, R. D. Peacock and G. J. Westland, *Acta Cryst.*, **10**, 63 (1957).
39. M. A. Hill and F. E. Beamish, *J. Am. Chem. Soc.*, **72**, 4855 (1950).
40. J. M. Fletcher, W. E. Gardner, E. W. Hooper, K. R. Hyde, F. H. Moore and J. L. Woodhead, *Nature*, **199**, 1089 (1963).
41. K. R. Hyde, E. W. Hooper, J. Waters and J. M. Fletcher, *J. Less-Common Metals*, **8**, 428 (1965).
42. N. I. Kolbin and A. N. Ryabov, *Vestn. Leningr. Univ.*, **14**, *Ser. Fiz. i Khim.*, 121 (1959).
43. E. V. Stroganov and K. V. Ouchinnikov, *Vestn. Leningr. Univ.*, **12**, *Ser. Fiz. i Khim.*, 152 (1957).
44. H. G. Schnering, K. Brodersen, F. Moers, H. K. Breitbach and G. Thiele, *J. Less-Common Metals*, **11**, 288 (1966).
45. W. E. Bell, M. C. Garrison and U. Merten, *J. Phys. Chem.*, **64**, 145 (1960).
46. S. A. Shchukarev, N. I. Kolbin and A. N. Ryabov, *Zh. Neorg. Khim.*, **3**, 1721 (1958).
47. C. Epstein and N. Elliot, *J. Chem. Phys.*, **22**, 634 (1954).
48. N. I. Kolbin, I. N. Semenov and Y. M. Shutov, *Russ. J. Inorg. Khim.*, **9**, 563 (1964).
49. U. Merten, W. D. Bell and J. D. Hale, *U.S.A.E.C. Report* G.A. 2512 (1961).
50. S. A. Shchukarev, N. I. Kolbin and A. N. Ryabov, *Russ. J. Inorg. Chem.*, **5**, 923 (1960).
51. S. A. Shchukarev, N. I. Kolbin and A. N. Ryabov, *Vestn. Leningr. Univ.*, **16**, *Ser. Fiz. i Khim.*, 100 (1961).
52. S. A. Shchukarev, N. I. Kolbin and I. N. Semenov, *Russ. J. Inorg. Chem.*, **6**, 638 (1961).
53. S. A. Shchukarev, N. I. Kolbin and A. N. Ryabov, *Russ. J. Inorg. Chem.*, **6**, 517 (1961).
54. J. E. Fergusson, B. H. Robinson and W. R. Roper, *J. Chem. Soc.*, **1962**, 2113.
55. J. L. Howe, *J. Am. Chem. Soc.*, **49**, 2381 (1927).
56. J. L. Woodhead and J. M. Fletcher, *U.K.A.E.A. Research Report* R-4123.
57. J. L. Howe, *J. Am. Chem. Soc.*, **23**, 775 (1901).

58. F. H. Kruse, *Acta Cryst.*, **14**, 1035 (1961).
59. J. L. Hoard and J. D. Grenko, *Z. Krist.*, **87**, 100 (1934).
60. E. Weise and W. Klemm, *Z. anorg. allgem. Chem.*, **279**, 74 (1955).
61. M. A. Hepworth, P. L. Robinson and G. J. Westland, *J. Chem. Soc.*, **1954**, 4269.
62. M. A. Hepworth, K. H. Jack and G. J. Westland, *J. Inorg. Nucl. Chem.*, **2**, 79 (1956).
63. R. D. W. Kemmitt, D. R. Russell and D. W. A. Sharp, *J. Chem. Soc.*, **1963**, 4408.
64. J. C. Boston and D. W. A. Sharp, *J. Chem. Soc.*, **1960**, 907.
65. R. D. Peacock and D. W. A. Sharp, *J. Chem. Soc.*, **1959**, 2762.
66. B. N. Figgis, J. Lewis and F. E. Mabbs, *J. Chem. Soc.*, **1961**, 3138.
67. R. D. Peacock, *Rec. Trav. Chim.*, **75**, 576 (1956).
68. R. D. Peacock, *Chem. Ind. (London)*, **1956**, 1391.
69. D. H. Brown, K. R. Dixon, R. D. W. Kemmitt and D. W. A. Sharp, *J. Chem. Soc.*, **1965**, 1559.
70. M. A. Hepworth, P. L. Robinson and G. J. Westland, *J. Chem. Soc.*, **1958**, 611.
71. A. Earnshaw, B. N. Figgis, J. Lewis and R. D. Peacock, *J. Chem. Soc.*, **1961**, 3132.
72. N. K. Pshenitskaya and N. A. Ezerskaya, *Russ. J. Inorg. Chem.*, **6**, 312 (1961).
73. S. Forcheri, V. Lungagnani, S. Martini and G. Sibona, *Energia Nucl. (Milan)*, **7**, 537 (1960).
74. F. P. Dwyer and J. W. Hogarth, *J. Proc. Roy. Soc. N.S. Wales*, **84**, 194 (1951).
75. L. L. Larson and C. S. Garner, *J. Am. Chem. Soc.*, **76**, 2180 (1954).
76. F. Puche, *Ann. Chim. (Paris)*, **9**, 233 (1938).
77. J. D. McCullough, *Z. Krist.*, **94**, 143 (1936).
78. D. M. Adams, J. Chatt, J. M. Davidson and J. Gerratt, *J. Chem. Soc.*, **1963**, 2189.
79. D. M. Adams and H. A. Gebbie, *Spectrochim. Acta*, **19**, 925 (1963).
80. L. A. Woodward and M. J. Ware, *Spectrochim. Acta*, **20**, 711 (1964).
81. B. Jezowska-Trzebiatowska, J. Hanuza and W. Wojciechowski, *J. Inorg. Nucl. Chem.*, **28**, 2701 (1966).
82. D. P. Mellor, *Proc. Roy. Soc. N.S. Wales*, **77**, 145 (1944).
83. A. McL. Mathieson, D. P. Mellor and N. C. Stephenson, *Acta Cryst.*, **5**, 185 (1952).
84. J. D. Dunitz and L. E. Orgel, *J. Chem. Soc.*, **1953**, 2594.
85. J. L. Howe, *J. Am. Chem. Soc.*, **26**, 942 (1904).
86. R. Gilchrist, *J. Res. Nat. Bur. Stds.*, **9**, 279 (1932).
87. A. Gutbier, *Ber.*, **46**, 2098 (1913).
88. A. D. Westland and N. C. Bhiwandker, *Can. J. Chem.*, **39**, 1284 (1961).
89. R. D. Johannesen and A. R. Lindberg, *J. Am. Chem. Soc.*, **76**, 5349 (1954).
90. E. Fenn, R. S. Nyholm, P. G. Owston and A. Turco, *J. Inorg. Nucl. Chem.*, **17**, 387 (1961).
91. R. D. Peacock, in *Progress in Inorganic Chemistry* (ed. F. A. Cotton, Vol. 2, Interscience, N.Y., 1960.
92. L. W. N. Godward and W. Wardlaw, *J. Chem. Soc.*, **1938**, 1422.

93. G. A. Rechnitz, *Inorg. Chem.*, **1**, 953 (1962).
94. N. K. Jha, Ph.D. Thesis, University of British Columbia, 1965.
95. N. Bartlett and J. Trotter, unpublished observation, quoted in reference 94.
96. S. Siegel and D. A. Northrup, *Inorg. Chem.*, **5**, 2187 (1966).
97. B. Frlec and H. H. Hyman, *Inorg. Chem.*, **6**, 1596 (1967).
98. K. H. Hellberg, A. Muller and O. Glemser, *Z. Naturforsch.*, **21b,** 118 (1966).
99. P. Machmer, *Chem. Commun.*, **1967,** 610.
100. H. Schafer and K. A. Hunelse, *J. Less-Common Metals*, **12,** 331 (1967).
101. J. M. Fletcher, W. E. Gardner, A. C. Fox and G. Topping, *J. Chem. Soc.*, **1967,** A, 1038.
102. B. Frlec, H. Selig and H. H. Hyman, *Inorg. Chem.*, **6,** 1775 (1967).
103. K. H. Jack, personal communication.
104. D. H. Brown, K. R. Dixon, C. M. Livingston, R. H. Nuttall and D. W. A. Sharp, *J. Chem. Soc.*, **1967,** A, 100.
105. J. Hirashi and T. Shimanouchi, *Spectrochim. Acta*, **22,** 1483 (1966).

Chapter 9

Rhodium and Iridium

By comparison with molybdenum, tungsten, technetium, rhenium and, to a small extent, with ruthenium and osmium, there is a marked decrease in the number of oxidation states which are found for rhodium and iridium. Apart from the fluorides where the metal is in the hexavalent or pentavalent state, the metal is found in oxidation states IV or III in all the halides and complex halides. It is remarkable that there is not a single, well-established oxide halide or complex oxide halide that is stable at room temperature, for either element.

HALIDES

There are various references in the early literature to halides of rhodium and iridium in oxidation states less than III, but these reports are not in

TABLE 9.1
Binary Halides of Rhodium and Iridium

Oxidation state	Fluoride	Chloride
VI	RhF_6, IrF_6	
V	RhF_5, IrF_5	
IV	RhF_4	
III	RhF_3, IrF_3	$RhCl_3$, $IrCl_3$

accord with more recent data and they have not been confirmed. There also appears to be a total lack of binary bromides and iodides of both rhodium and iridium. The known halides of these elements are given in Table 9.1.

Oxidation State VI

Rhodium hexafluoride. Rhodium hexafluoride has been prepared by Chernick, Claassen and Weinstock[1] by burning rhodium metal in fluorine gas in close proximity to a surface cooled by liquid nitrogen. The yields are small and it is essential to use a silica reaction vessel rather than a Pyrex one, since the hexafluoride appears to react with borosilicate glass.

Rhodium hexafluoride is a black crystalline solid and it gives a deep red-brown monomeric vapour. It is thermally unstable at room temperature, dissociating to fluorine and the pentafluoride[1]. As a result of this instability, the melting point and the temperature of the usual solid-phase transition found in hexafluorides cannot be determined accurately, but they are approximately 70° and 7°, respectively[1].

The infrared spectrum of rhodium hexafluoride has been observed and the absorptions have been assigned as follows on the basis of O_h symmetry[2]: ν_1 634, ν_2 595, ν_3 724, ν_4 283, ν_5 269 and ν_6 192 cm^{-1}.

Rhodium hexafluoride has been reported to react with xenon at room temperature, to give a deep red solid which tensimetric measurements suggest is $XeRhF_6^3$.

Iridium hexafluoride. Iridium hexafluoride may be prepared by the more conventional technique of passing fluorine over iridium metal at 300–400° [4,5]. It is a yellow, reactive solid.

Cady and Hargreaves[6] have measured the variation of vapour pressure of iridium hexafluoride over a wide temperature range and their results are summarized in the expressions:

Solid (-50 to 0.4°) $\log p_{mm} = 10.00 - 2246/T$

Solid (0.4–44°) $\log p_{mm} = 8.618 - 1868/T$

Liquid (44–54°) $\log p_{mm} = 7.952 - 1657/T$

Thermodynamic properties derived from the vapour-pressure measurements are given in Table 9.2.

TABLE 9.2

Thermodynamic Data for Iridium Hexafluoride

Property	Value
M.p.	43.8°
B.p.	53.6°
Transition point	0.4°
ΔH_{fus} (kcal mole^{-1})	1.19
ΔH_{vap} (kcal mole^{-1})	7.38
ΔH_{trans} (kcal mole^{-1})	1.70
ΔH_{sub} (kcal mole^{-1})	8.57 (above 0.4°)
	10.27 (below 0.4°)
ΔH_{fus} (cal deg^{-1} mole^{-1})	3.74
ΔS_{vap} (cal deg^{-1} mole^{-1})	22.6
ΔS_{trans} (cal deg^{-1} mole^{-1})	6.21

As usual with transition-metal hexafluorides, there is a solid-phase transition from the low-temperature orthorhombic lattice to the high-temperature cubic form[7]. For iridium hexafluoride, this transition[6] takes place at 0.4°.

The infrared spectrum of iridium hexafluoride has been recorded and on the basis of assumed O_h symmetry the bands were assigned as[5,8]: v_1 696, v_2 643, v_3 718, v_4 272, v_5 260 and v_6 205 cm^{-1}. Mean-square amplitudes of vibration and force constants have been calculated for iridium hexafluoride by various groups[9-12].

The variation with temperature of the magnetic susceptibility[13] of iridium hexafluoride obeys the Curie–Weiss law with a Weiss constant of 30° and a magnetic moment of 2.9 BM.

Iridium hexafluoride reacts with nitric oxide[4,14] to give a mixture of $NOIrF_6$ and $(NO)_2IrF_6$. With nitrosyl fluoride it also gives $NOIrF_6$, fluorine and nitrogen oxide trifluoride[14]. X-ray powder diffraction studies have revealed that these products adopt the following lattices[14]: $NOIrF_6$, cubic, $a = 10.114$ Å; $(NO)_2IrF_6$, hexagonal, $a = 10.01$ Å, $c = 3.53$ Å. It is also reported that dinitrogen tetraoxide reacts with iridium hexafluoride to form $(NO_2)_2IrF_6$, and with sulphur tetrafluoride the adduct $SF_4 \cdot IrF_5$ is formed[4].

Oxidation State V

Rhodium pentafluoride. Rhodium pentafluoride is prepared[15] by the action of fluorine at 90 p.s.i. on rhodium trifluoride at 400°. It has also been observed as the product of the thermal decomposition of rhodium hexafluoride[1].

It is a dark red solid, melting at 95.5°, and it reacts violently with water. It has been established[15] that rhodium pentafluoride is isomorphous with the tetrameric pentafluorides of ruthenium, osmium and iridium, although a detailed structural analysis has not as yet been reported. The unit cell is monoclinic with $a = 12.28$, $b = 9.95$, $c = 5.48$ Å, and $\beta = 99.2°$. There are eight molecular units in the cell.

The magnetic properties of rhodium pentafluoride show that there is little interaction between the metal atoms in the tetrameric unit. A magnetic susceptibility close to that expected for the two unpaired electrons per rhodium atom was observed[15].

Rhodium pentafluoride is an extremely powerful oxidizing and fluorinating agent; it reacts with carbon tetrachloride and chlorine monofluoride has been identified as one of the products[15].

Iridium pentafluoride. It has now been established that the compound reported[4] about 1956 as iridium tetrafluoride is, in fact, the pentafluoride[16].

Bartlett and Rao have shown that the reaction of iridium hexafluoride and powdered glass at 350° yields the pentafluoride[16]. However, it is best prepared[16] by the interaction of iridium metal and fluorine in stoichiometric amounts in a Monel bomb at 350–380°. Iridium pentafluoride is a yellowish-green, readily hydrolysed solid, which melts at 104–105°.

Iridium pentafluoride is isostructural and almost isodimensional with tetrameric ruthenium pentafluoride. The monoclinic unit cell[16] has the dimensions $a = 12.5$, $b = 10.0$, $c = 5.4$ Å and $\beta = 99.8°$. The magnetic properties of iridium pentafluoride have been measured over a wide temperature range[16]. The susceptibility is almost independent of temperature as is typical for octahedral d^4 complexes of the third-row transition elements with high spin–orbit coupling constants.

Very little is known of the chemistry of iridium pentafluoride but its adducts with sulphur dioxide and sulphur tetrafluoride[4] and with selenium tetrafluoride[17] have been prepared indirectly from iridium hexafluoride.

Oxidation State IV

Rhodium tetrafluoride. Ruff and Ascher[18] obtained a small amount of a reddish-brown sublimate from the reaction of fluorine with rhodium metal, rhodium trichloride or rhodium trifluoride at 500–600° and they suggested that this was the tetrafluoride or possibly the pentafluoride. Subsequently, it was proved by Sharpe[19] to be the tetrafluoride. The tetrafluoride is best prepared, however, by thermal decomposition of the product formed by the action of bromine trifluoride on "rhodium tribromide"[19].

Rhodium tetrafluoride is a purple-red solid which is readily hydrolysed. Its magnetic moment[20] at room temperature is 1.1 BM.

Oxidation State III

Rhodium trifluoride. Rhodium trifluoride may be prepared[18,21] by the action of fluorine on rhodium trihalides at temperatures less than 500°. It is reported to be formed in very small amounts when rhodium wire is burned in fluorine[15]. Rhodium trifluoride is a red solid, insoluble in water. X-ray powder diffraction studies[21] have shown that it is rhombohedral with $a = 5.330$ Å and $\alpha = 54.42°$; the lattice consists of almost regular octahedra of fluorine atoms joined by sharing corners.

The nonahydrate, $RhF_3 \cdot 9H_2O$, has been reported to result from the treatment of potassium hexafluororhodate(III) with cold 40% hydrofluoric acid solution[22].

Iridium trifluoride. Iridium trifluoride is prepared by the reduction of iridium pentafluoride (which before 1965 was thought to be the tetrafluoride) with sulphur tetrafluoride or iridium metal[4]. It is a black solid, insoluble in water, and is reported[4] to dissociate into fluorine and iridium metal above 250°.

It is isostructural[21] with the trifluoride of rhodium, having a rhombohedral unit cell with $a = 5.418$ Å and $\alpha = 54.3°$.

Rhodium trichloride. Rhodium trichloride is prepared[23] by direct chlorination of the metal at temperatures between 300° and 800°. It is a red solid which is insoluble in water and dissociates at high temperatures to the metal and chlorine[24].

Rhodium trichloride adopts a monoclinic lattice[25] isostructural with that of aluminium trichloride. The unit cell has the parameters $a = 5.95$, $b = 10.30$, $c = 6.03$ Å and $\beta = 109.2°$. There are four molecular units in the cell.

Adducts of rhodium trichloride of the general formula $RhCl_3 \cdot 3L$ have been prepared by using alkyl cyanides[26] and dialkyl sulphides and selenides[27].

Iridium trichloride. Iridium trichloride is prepared[28-30] by direct chlorination of the metal at temperatures exceeding 600°. The reaction is very slow, probably owing to formation of a film of the involatile trichloride on the metal. Stepin and Chernyak[31] found that a small proportion of carbon monoxide in the chlorine stream acted as an efficient catalyst in the chlorination in much the same way as has been noted for ruthenium. Iridium trichloride dissociates above 775° to the metal and chlorine, and there is no evidence of the formation of any lower chloride[30].

There are two crystalline modifications of iridium trichloride [28,32,33] although it is not clear under what conditions each modification is formed

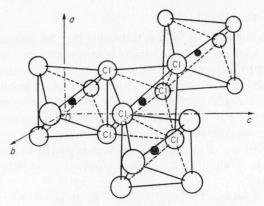

Figure 9.1 $IrCl_6$ octahedra in β-$IrCl_3$.

preferentially. The α-form is monoclinic with $a = 5.99$, $b = 10.37$, $c = 5.99$ Å and $\beta = 109.4°$. There are four formula units in the cell and the structure closely resembles that of aluminium trichloride[32,33]. The β-form is orthorhombic[28] with $a = 6.59$, $b = 9.81$ and $c = 20.82$ Å. The structure is shown in Figure 9.1; it consists of $IrCl_6$ octahedra and the Ir–Ir–Ir angle is 120°.

The heat of formation and entropy of formation of iridium trichloride have been given[30] as -60.8 kcal mole^{-1} and 61 cal deg^{-1} mole^{-1}, respectively.

The adduct $IrCl_3 \cdot 3(C_5H_5N)$ has been prepared indirectly by treating pyridine with the hexahydrate of hexachloroiridic(IV) acid[34]. Adducts of the type $IrCl_3 \cdot 3SR_2$ and $IrCl_3 \cdot 2SeR_2$ have also been reported[27].

COMPLEX HALIDES

Complex halides of rhodium and iridium are known for oxidation states V, IV and III. Although the tetrachlorides are not known, the hexachlororhodate(IV) and hexachloroiridate(IV) ions are known. However, the rhodium complex is rather unstable.

Oxidation State V

Hexafluororhodate(v). Interaction of an equimolar mixture of caesium fluoride and rhodium pentafluoride in iodine pentafluoride solution has led to the preparation of caesium hexafluororhodate(v)[15]. The red brown salt, obtained by removal of the solvent, is reported to be isomorphous and almost isodimensional with rhombohedral caesium hexafluoro-platinate(v).

Hexafluoroiridates(v). Hexafluoroiridates(v) have been prepared by the interaction, in bromine trifluoride solution, of alkali-metal bromides and the compound said to be iridium tribromide[35]. This latter compound was prepared by repeated evaporation of ammonium hexachloroiridate(IV) with hydrobromic acid. Barium hexafluoroiridate(IV) has been prepared in a similar fashion by using barium bromate[35].

The hexafluoroiridates(v) are white crystalline solids which react with water to give oxygen and the corresponding hexafluoroiridates(IV)[35].

The structures of the hexafluoroiridates(v) have been examined by X-ray powder diffraction techniques and the lattice parameters are given in Table 9.3.

The iridium–fluorine stretching frequency in the hexafluoroiridate(v) ion occurs[37,39] at about 667 cm^{-1}. The magnetic moments of several hexafluoroiridates(v) have been determined[40,41] at room temperature and they fall in the range 1.2–1.3 BM.

TABLE 9.3

Lattice Parameters of Hexafluoroiridates(v)

Compound	Symmetry	Unit-cell parameters	Ref.
$LiIrF_6$	Rhombohedral; $LiSbF_6$ type	$a = 5.41$ Å, $\alpha = 56.0°$	36, 37
$NaIrF_6$	Rhombohedral; $LiSbF_6$ type	$a = 5.80$ Å, $\alpha = 55.2°$	36, 37
$AgIrF_6$	Tetragonal; $KNbF_6$ type	$a = 4.85$ Å, $c = 9.70$ Å	36
$KIrF_6$	Rhombohedral; $KOsF_6$ type	$a = 4.98$ Å, $\alpha = 97.4°$	35, 36, 38
$RbIrF_6$	Rhombohedral; $KOsF_6$ type	$a = 5.105$ Å, $\alpha = 97.0°$	36
$CsIrF_6$	Rhombohedral; $KOsF_6$ type	$a = 5.27$ Å, $\alpha = 96.2°$	35, 36, 38

Oxidation State IV

Heptafluororhodate(iv). Sodium heptafluororhodate(iv) has been prepared by Sharpe[19] by the interaction of a 3:1 molar ratio of sodium chloride and rhodium trichloride in bromine trifluoride solution. The pale blue complex has a magnetic moment of 1.74 BM at room temperature[20].

Hexafluororhodates(iv). Hexafluororhodates(iv) may be prepared[42] by fluorination of a 2:1-molar mixture of an alkali-metal chloride and rhodium trichloride at 320°. An alternative method is to use bromine trifluoride as the fluorinating agent[43]. The complexes are pale yellow crystalline solids which are hydrolysed by water.

The hexafluororhodates(iv) have been examined by X-ray powder diffraction techniques, and the lattice parameters are given in Table 9.4.

TABLE 9.4

Lattice Parameters of Hexafluororhodates(iv)

Compound	Symmetry	Unit-cell parameters	Ref.
Na_2RhF_6	Hexagonal	$a = 9.32$ Å, $c = 5.32$ Å	44
K_2RhF_6	Hexagonal	$a = 5.73$ Å, $c = 4.64$ Å	42
Rb_2RhF_6	Hexagonal	$a = 5.90$ Å, $c = 4.80$ Å	42
Cs_2RhF_6	Hexagonal	$a = 6.28$ Å, $c = 10.11$ Å	42, 43

The rhodium–fluorine stretching frequency in potassium hexafluororhodate(iv) was observed[39] at 589 cm^{-1}. The magnetic moments[42] of the hexafluororhodates(iv) at room temperature are about 2.0 BM.

Hexafluoroiridates(iv). Hexafluoroiridates(iv) have been prepared, as mentioned earlier, by the action of water on the corresponding hexafluoroiridate(v) complex[35,45]. The potassium salt may also be prepared by fusing $K_3Ir(NO_2)_6$ with potassium hydrogen fluoride[22] or by fusing a mixture of iridium metal, potassium hydrogen fluoride and lead tetrafluoride[46]. In each case, the hexafluoroiridate(iv) is recrystallized as a pink solid from aqueous solution.

The hexafluoroiridates(IV) have been examined by X-ray powder diffraction techniques, and the lattice parameters of a number of these complexes are given in Table 9.5.

The iridium–fluorine stretching frequency in potassium hexafluoroiridate(IV) occurs[39] at 568 cm^{-1}. The magnetic moment of the caesium salt is 1.42 BM at room temperature[45].

TABLE 9.5

Lattice Parameters of Hexafluoroiridates(IV)

Compound	Symmetry	Unit-cell parameters	Ref.
Na_2IrF_6	Hexagonal	$a = 9.34$ Å, $c = 5.14$ Å	44,45
K_2IrF_6	Hexagonal	$a = 5.80$ Å, $c = 4.63$ Å	45
$(NH_4)_2IrF_6$	Hexagonal	$a = 5.98$ Å, $c = 4.79$ Å	45
Rb_2IrF_6	Hexagonal	$a = 5.97$ Å, $c = 4.79$ Å	45
Cs_2IrF_6	Hexagonal	$a = 6.24$ Å, $c = 5.00$ Å	45
$(NMe_4)_2IrF_6$	Cubic	$a = 11.41$ Å	45
$BaIrF_6$	Rhombohedral	$a = 4.90$ Å, $\alpha = 97.8°$	35

Hexachlororhodate(IV). Caesium hexachlororhodate(IV) was first prepared by Dwyer, Nyholm and Rogers[47,48] by oxidation of the corresponding hexachlororhodate(III) salt. The ion could not be made in solution by chlorine oxidation since it was essential to maintain a high concentration of hydrochloric acid to ensure that all the rhodium(III) was converted into hexachlororhodate(III). The oxidation potential of chlorine decreases as the acid concentration increases and is not high enough to oxidize the rhodium(III). Therefore, the sparingly soluble caesium hexachlororhodate(III) was precipitated. It was then suspended in ice cold 1M nitric acid in the presence of ceric ions and chlorine was passed through the suspension. The initially pink precipitate became green and analysis showed it to be caesium hexachlororhodate(IV). Subsequently, Nyholm and coworkers[49] developed a more efficient method of preparing the salt directly from rhodium trichloride. It reacts readily with water, chlorine and caesium pentachloroaquorhodate(III) being the products[48].

Caesium hexachlororhodate(IV) is cubic, with a lattice of the K_2PtCl_6 type and $a = 10.20$ Å[47,48]. At room temperature the effective magnetic moment was found to be 1.78 BM, falling to 1.4 BM at 78°K[49].

Hexachloroiridates(IV). The usual method[23,50] of preparation of the hexachloroiridates(IV) is by direct chlorination of a mixture of iridium metal and alkali-metal chloride at about 400°. Alternatively, carbon tetrachloride vapour may be used[51] as the chlorinating agent at 500–600°.

It is interesting that both these methods, when used with rhodium, give hexachlororhodates(III).

Puche[23] has shown that the hexachloroiridates(IV) decompose at high temperatures to give iridium metal, chlorine and alkali-metal chloride, although there is some evidence that the hexachloroiridate(III) complexes are formed as intermediates in the decomposition.

The iridium–chlorine stretching frequency in several hexachloroiridates(IV) has been found to occur at about 330 cm^{-1}, although in some cases the band is split into a doublet[52].

Hexabromoiridates(IV). These blue compounds have been isolated by addition of an alkali-metal bromide to a solution of hydrated iridium dioxide in concentrated hydrobromic acid[53]. No recent investigation of the chemistry of these compounds has been reported.

Oxidation State III

Hexafluororhodate(III). Potassium hexafluororhodate(III) has been prepared[22] by the fusion of potassium hexanitritorhodate(III) with potassium hydrogen fluoride at 500°. The buff-coloured crystalline solid is reported to be tetragonal and diamagnetic[54].

Hexachlororhodates(III). The normal method of preparing hexachlororhodates(III) is to pass chlorine over a mixture of rhodium metal and the appropriate chloride or carbonate at high temperatures[23,47,48,55-57]. Alternatively, carbon tetrachloride may be used at 600° as the chlorinating agent[51].

The hexachlororhodates(III) are thermally unstable, decomposing at about 700° to give rhodium metal, chlorine and the appropriate metal halide. There is no evidence for the formation of lower rhodium chlorides[23,55].

The hexachlororhodate(III) anion reacts slowly with water, to form the pentachloroaquorhodate(III) ion[48].

Hexachloroiridates(III). Hexachloroiridates(III) may be prepared by reduction of the corresponding hexachloroiridates(IV). The reduction may be carried out by using hydrogen at 190° but it is far more conveniently done in solution with mild reductants such as hydrogen sulphide or oxalate.

The iridium–chlorine stretching frequency[52] in potassium hexachloroiridate(III) occurs at 296 cm^{-1}.

Like the rhodium analogue, the hexachloroiridate(III) ion in water is slowly converted into the pentachloroaquoiridate(III) ion.

Complex bromides of rhodium(III). A number of compounds of the types $RhBr_6^{3-}$, $Rh_2Br_9^{3-}$, $Rh_2Br_{10}^{4-}$ and $Rh_2Br_{11}^{5-}$ have been isolated by

Poulenc by the interaction of alkali-metal bromides and a rhodium complex in hydrobromic acid solution[58,59]. Nothing is known of the constitution of these compounds and they may well merit further study.

Hexabromoiridates(III). Salts of the hexabromoiridate(III) ion have been prepared by reduction of the corresponding hexabromoiridate(IV), and, as for the latter, very little is known about their chemical properties[53].

Hexaiodoiridates(III). Hexaiodoiridates(III) may be prepared by treating the hexachloroiridates(III) with alkali-metal iodide in hydriodic acid solution[53].

ADDENDA

X-ray powder diffraction data for both modifications of rhodium and iridium hexafluoride have been reported[60]. The results are summarized below.

RhF_6 Cubic, $a = 6.13$ Å;
    Orthorhombic, $a = 9.40$, $b = 8.54$, $c = 4.96$ Å
IrF_6 Cubic, $a = 6.23$ Å;
    Orthorhombic, $a = 9.58$, $b = 8.73$, $c = 5.04$ Å

Iridium hexafluoride is reduced[61] by chlorine to iridium pentafluoride and by sulphur tetrafluoride to $IrF_5 \cdot SF_4$. This yellow compound, which is thought to be ionic, has a magnetic moment of 1.51 BM at room temperature[61]. The compound $NO^+IrF_6^-$ has a magnetic moment of 1.23 BM at room temperature, but the susceptibility is almost independent of temperature[61].

The infrared spectrum of potassium hexachloroiridate(IV) shows three bands at 332, 182, and 86 cm^{-1}, severally, assigned to the metal–chlorine stretch, metal–chlorine deformation, and lattice mode, respectively[62].

Several alkali-metal hexabromoiridates(IV) have been shown to be cubic with the K_2PtCl_6 type lattice[63]. The unit-cell dimensions and also the metal–bromine stretching frequencies are:

K_2IrBr_6 $a = 10.19$ Å $v = 230$ cm^{-1}
Rb_2IrBr_6 $a = 10.42$ Å $v = 227$ cm^{-1}
Cs_2IrBr_6 $a = 10.53$ Å $v = 223$ cm^{-1}

It has been reported[64] that chlorine does not react with rhodium below 500° in a flow system. Above this temperature rhodium trichloride is formed. The compound begins to sublime at about 800° and at 920° begins to decompose to the metal without evidence for the formation of lower chlorides.

Iridium tribromide has been prepared by the interaction of the elements in a sealed tube at about 600°. It is a yellow crystalline solid[65].

REFERENCES

1. C. L. Chernick, H. H. Claassen and B. Weinstock, *J. Am. Chem. Soc.*, **83**, 3165 (1961).
2. B. Weinstock, H. H. Claassen and C. L. Chernick, *J. Chem. Phys.*, **38**, 1470 (1963).
3. N. Bartlett and N. K. Jha, in *Noble Gas Compounds* (ed. H. H. Hyman), University of Chicago Press, Chicago, 1963.
4. P. L. Robinson and G. J. Westland, *J. Chem. Soc.*, 1956, 4481.
5. H. C. Mattraw, N. J. Hawkins, D. R. Carpenter and W. W. Sabol, *J. Chem. Phys.*, **23**, 985 (1955).
6. G. H. Cady and G. B. Hargreaves, *J. Chem. Soc.*, **1961**, 1563.
7. B. Weinstock, E. E. Westrum and G. L. Goodman, *Proc. 8th Intern. Conf. Low Temp. Physics*, London, 1962, p. 405.
8. H. H. Claassen and B. Weinstock, *J. Chem. Phys.*, **33**, 436 (1960).
9. M. Kimura and K. Kimura, *J. Mol. Spectr.*, **11**, 368 (1963).
10. H. H. Claassen, *J. Chem. Phys.*, **30**, 968 (1959).
11. O. N. Singh and D. K. Rai, *Can. J. Phys.*, **43**, 378 (1965).
12. S. Sundaram, *Z. Physik. Chem. (Frankfurt)*, **34**, 225 (1962).
13. B. N. Figgis, J. Lewis and F. E. Mabbs, *J. Chem. Soc.*, **1961**, 3138.
14. N. Bartlett, S. P. Beaton and N. K. Jha, *Chem. Commun.*, **1966**, 168.
15. J. H. Holloway, P. R. Rao and N. Bartlett, *Chem. Commun.*, **1965**, 306.
16. N. Bartlett and P. R. Rao, *Chem. Commun.*, **1965**, 252.
17. M. A. Hepworth, P. L. Robinson and G. Westland, *Chem. Ind. (London)*, **1955**, 1576.
18. O. Ruff and E. Ascher, *Z. anorg. allgem. Chem.*, **183**, 193 (1929).
19. A. G. Sharpe, *J. Chem. Soc.*, **1950**, 3444.
20. R. S. Nyholm and A. G. Sharpe, *J. Chem. Soc.*, **1952**, 3579.
21. M. A. Hepworth, K. H. Jack, R. D. Peacock and G. J. Westland, *Acta Cryst.*, **10**, 63 (1957).
22. R. D. Peacock, *J. Chem. Soc.*, **1955**, 3291.
23. F. Puche, *Ann. Chim. (Paris)*, **9**, 233 (1938).
24. U. Merten, W. E. Bell and J. D. Hale, *U.S.A.E.C. Report* G.A.-2512 (1961).
25. H. Baerniglausen and B. K. Handa, *J. Less-Common Metals*, **6**, 226 (1964).
26. B. F. G. Johnson and R. A. Walton, *J. Inorg. Nucl. Chem.*, **28**, 1901 (1966).
27. E. K. Fritsman and V. V. Krinitskii, *J. Appl. Chem. USSR*, **11**, 1610 (1938).
28. D. Babel and P. Deigner, *Z. anorg. allgem. Chem.*, **339**, 57 (1965).
29. W. E. Bell and M. Tagami, *J. Phys. Chem.*, **70**, 640 (1966).
30. W. E. Bell and M. Tagami, *J. Phys. Chem.*, **70**, 3736 (1966).
31. B. D. Stepin and A. I. Chernyak, *Russ. J. Inorg. Chem.*, **5**, 1047 (1960).
32. K. Brodersen, *Angew. Chem. Intern. Ed. Engl.* **3**, 579 (1964).
33. K. Brodersen, F. Moers and H. G. Schnering, *Naturwissenschaften*, **52**, 205 (1965).
34. E. Ogawa, *J. Chem. Soc. Japan*, **51**, 189 (1930).
35. M. A. Hepworth, P. L. Robinson and G. J. Westland, *J. Chem. Soc.*, **1954**, 4269.

36. R. D. W. Kemmitt, D. R. Russell and D. W. A. Sharp, *J. Chem. Soc.*, **1963**, 4408.
37. J. L. Boston and D. W. A. Sharp, *J. Chem. Soc.*, **1960**, 907.
38. M. A. Hepworth, K. H. Jack and G. J. Westland, *J. Inorg. Nucl. Chem.*, **2**, 79 (1956).
39. R. D. Peacock and D. W. A. Sharp, *J. Chem. Soc.*, **1959**, 2762.
40. A. Earnshaw, B. N. Figgis, J. Lewis and R. D. Peacock, *J. Chem. Soc.*, **1961**, 3132.
41. R. D. Peacock, *Rec. Trav. Chim.*, **75**, 576 (1956).
42. E. Weise and W. Klemm, *Z. anorg. allgem. Chem.*, **272**, 211 (1953).
43. B. Cox, D. W. A. Sharp and A. G. Sharpe, *J. Chem. Soc.*, **1956**, 1242.
44. D. H. Brown, K. R. Dixon, R. D. W. Kemmitt and D. W. A. Sharp, *J. Chem. Soc.*, **1965**, 1559.
45. M. A. Hepworth, P. L. Robinson and G. J. Westland, *J. Chem. Soc.*, **1958**, 611.
46. H. I. Schlesinger and M. W. Tapley, *J. Am. Chem. Soc.*, **46**, 276 (1924).
47. F. P. Dwyer and R. S. Nyholm, *Nature*, **160**, 502 (1947).
48. F. P. Dwyer, R. S. Nyholm and L. E. Rogers, *Proc. Roy. Soc. N.S. Wales*, **81**, 267 (1947).
49. I. Feldman, R. S. Nyholm and E. Watton, *J. Chem. Soc.*, **1965**, 4724.
50. D. P. Mellor, *Proc. Roy. Soc. N.S. Wales*, **77**, 145 (1943).
51. M. Delepine, *Bull. Soc. Chim. France*, **1956**, 282.
52. D. M. Adams and H. A. Gebbie, *Spectrochim. Acta*, **19**, 925 (1963).
53. J. W. Mellor, *A Comprehensive Treatise on Inorganic and Theoretical Chemistry*, Vol. XV, Longmans, London, 1936.
54. R. D. Peacock, in *Progress in Inorganic Chemistry* (ed. F. A. Cotton) Vol. 2. Interscience, New York.
55. G. Gire and F. Puche, *Compt. Rend.*, **200**, 670 (1935).
56. *Jap. Pat.* 19,823 (1961).
57. G. B. Kauffman and J. H. S. Tsa, *J. Less-Common Metals*, **4**, 519 (1962).
58. P. Poulenc, *Compt. Rend.*, **190**, 639 (1930).
59. P. Poulenc, *Ann. chim. (Paris)*, **4**, 567 (1935).
60. S. Siegel and D. A. Northrup, *Inorg. Chem.*, **5**, 2187 (1966).
61. N. K. Jha, Ph. D. Thesis, University of British Columbia, 1965.
62. J. Hirashi and T. Shimanouchi, *Spectrochim. Acta*, **22**, 1483 (1966).
63. D. H. Brown, K. R. Dixon, C. M. Livingston, R. H. Nuttall and D. W. A. Sharp, *J. Chem. Soc.*, **1967**, *A*, 100.
64. Y. I. Ivashentsev and R. I. Timonova, *Russ. J. Inorg. Chem.*, **11**, 1173 (1966).
65. N. I. Kolbin and V. M. Samoilov, *Zh. Neorg. Khim.*, **12**, 2526 (1967).

Chapter 10

Palladium and Platinum

With the exception of platinum hexafluoride, platinum pentafluoride, the poorly characterized platinum oxide trifluoride and platinum triiodide, the binary halides of palladium and platinum are restricted to oxidation states IV and II. The compound of empirical formula PdF_3 has been shown to contain palladium(IV) and palladium(II). Much of the chemistry of palladium and platinum fluorides and their derivatives has been investigated by Bartlett and coworkers. With the sole exception of the above-mentioned platinum oxide trifluoride there is no oxide halide. There is some indirect evidence that several platinum trihalides and mono-halides may exist in the vapour phase, but they have never been isolated.

HALIDES

The known halides of palladium and platinum are given in Table 10.1.

TABLE 10.1
Halides of Palladium and Platinum

Oxidation state	Fluoride	Chloride	Bromide	Iodide
VI	PtF_6			
V	PtF_5			
IV	PdF_4, PtF_4	$PtCl_4$	$PtBr_4$	PtI_4
III				PtI_3
II	PdF_2	$PdCl_2, PtCl_2$	$PdBr_2, PtBr_2$	PdI_2, PtI_2

Oxidation State VI

Platinum hexafluoride. Thermally unstable platinum hexafluoride is prepared by burning platinum wire in fluorine in close proximity to a surface cooled by liquid nitrogen[1,2]; the platinum wire is electrically heated to initiate the vigorous reaction. Even with these special techniques some lower fluorides of platinum are invariably formed. The hexafluoride is purified by vacuum-distillation.

Platinum hexafluoride is a dark red-black solid melting at 61.3° to give a dark red liquid[2]. This boils at 69.14° to give a monomeric brown vapour[1,2]. As is usually found with transition-metal hexafluorides there is a solid-state phase transition between the low-temperature orthorhombic form and the high-temperature cubic modification[2,3]. The transition temperature[2] is 0°. The cubic form[2] has $a = 6.209$ Å.

TABLE 10.2

Thermodynamic Data for Platinum Hexafluoride

Property	Value[a]
M.p.	61.3°
B.p.	69.14°
Transition temperature	0°
Liquid density (g/cc)	3.826
ΔH_{sub} (0°, orthorhombic)	11.44
ΔH_{sub} (0°, cubic)	9.30
ΔH_{sub} (61.3°, cubic)	8.59
ΔH_{vap}	7.51
ΔH_{fus}	1.08
ΔH_{trans}	2.14
ΔS_{sub} (0°, orthorhombic)	41.4
ΔS_{sub} (0°, cubic)	33.7
ΔS_{sub} (61.3°, cubic)	25.7
ΔS_{vap}	22.5
ΔS_{fus}	3.2
ΔS_{trans}	7.8

[a] ΔH in kcal mole^{-1}; ΔS in cal deg^{-1} mole^{-1}.

The vapour pressure of platinum hexafluoride has been measured over a temperature range and the vapour pressure is given by the expressions[2]:

Orthorhombic solid $\log p_{mm} = 27.776 - 6.09 \log T - 3148/T$
(−23 to 0°)

Cubic solid $\log p_{mm} = 20.628 - 4.08 \log T - 2529/T$
(0–61.3°)

Liquid $\log p_{mm} = 89.15 - 27.49 \log T - 5686/T$
(61.3–81.7°)

The thermodynamic properties of platinum hexafluoride that have been calculated[2] from the vapour-pressure measurements are given in Table 10.2.

The infrared spectrum of platinum hexafluoride has been observed and interpreted on the basis of octahedral symmetry[4]. The following assignments were made: ν_1 655, ν_2 601, ν_3 705, ν_4 273, ν_5 242 and ν_6 211 cm^{-1}.

Mean-square amplitudes of vibration[5,6] and heat capacities, heat contents and entropies[5] in the temperature range 100–1500°K have been calculated for platinum hexafluoride.

Platinum hexafluoride is an extremely reactive compound and this is no doubt in part due to its thermal instability[1,2]. Platinum pentafluoride and fluorine are the initial products of this decomposition, but the penta-fluoride itself is also thermally unstable, disproportionating to the hexa-fluoride and the tetrafluoride. Thus the final products of decomposition

TABLE 10.3

Physical Properties of Some Complex Platinum Fluorides

Compound	Property	Value	Ref.
$NOPtF_6$	Cubic symmetry	$a = 10.112$ Å	8
		$a = 10.135$ Å	9
	N–O stretches	2327, 2316 cm^{-1}	9
	Pt–F stretch	567 cm^{-1}	9
	Magnetism	$g = 2.0$	9
NO_2PtF_6	Cubic symmetry	$a = 10.344$ Å	9
	N–O stretch	2595 cm^{-1}	9
	Pt–F stretches	583, 567 cm^{-1}	9
	Magnetism	$g = 1.75$	9
$(NO)_2PtF_6$	Cubic symmetry	$a = 10.468$ Å	9
	Hexagonal symmetry	$a = 10.01, c = 3.53$ Å	8
	Magnetism	Diamagnetic	9
$N_2O_3PtF_6$	Cubic symmetry	$a = 10.605$ Å	9
	N–O stretches	2391, 2364, 2319, 2310 cm^{-1}	9
	Pt–F stretch	573 cm^{-1}	9
	Magnetism	Diamagnetic	9

are fluorine and platinum tetrafluoride. Platinum hexafluoride reacts with bromine trifluoride, plutonium tetrafluoride and lower neptunium fluorides to form the corresponding highest fluoride[2]. It reacts with bromine penta-fluoride to form fluorine and a black viscous liquid mixture containing platinum, bromine and fluorine[7]. Reaction with chlorine trifluoride[7] affords fluorine and the adduct $ClF_3 \cdot PtF_5$.

With nitrosyl fluoride, platinum hexafluoride forms $NO^+PtF_6^-$, although with an excess of nitrosyl fluoride some $(NO)_2PtF_6$ is also formed[8,9]. Both these salts may also be formed by the interaction of nitric oxide and platinum hexafluoride[8,9]. Platinum hexafluoride reacts[9] with nitryl fluoride to give $NO_2^+PtF_6^-$ and with dinitrogen tetraoxide to give $N_2O_3PtF_6$. On the basis of its infrared spectrum, a structure $(NO^+NO_2^+)PtF_6^{2-}$ is suggested for the last-mentioned compound. X-ray powder diffraction data, infrared absorption bands and magnetic data for these compounds are given in Table 10.3.

Platinum hexafluoride reacts with oxygen at room temperature[10], to give dioxygenyl hexafluoroplatinate(v). This compound is indentical with the supposed platinum oxide tetrafluoride which had previously been prepared by the fluorination of platinum dichloride at 350°, the oxygen resulting from the attack of fluorine on the Pyrex or silica reaction vessel[11]. Subsequently it was shown by chemical and magnetic studies that there were six fluorine atoms bound to platinum[12]. After the preparation of dioxygenyl hexafluoroplatinate(v), Bartlett considered the possible oxidation of xenon on the basis of the similar ionization potentials of the oxygen molecule and xenon. This led to the now famous reaction between xenon and platinum hexafluoride. The physical and chemical properties of dioxygenyl hexafluoroplatinate(v) and the products of the reaction between xenon and platinum hexafluoride are discussed in detail in the section on hexafluoroplatinates(v) (p. 370).

Oxidation State V

Platinum pentafluoride. Platinum pentafluoride is best prepared[13] by fluorination of platinum dichloride at about 350°. It is a deep red solid, melting at 80° to a viscous red liquid[13]. Platinum pentafluoride readily disproportionates into the hexafluoride and tetrafluoride, thus making a direct determination of the boiling point extremely difficult.

Platinum pentafluoride is reported to be isostructural with tetrameric ruthenium pentafluoride, but details are not available[14]. It is paramagnetic[14] with a magnetic moment of 2.05 BM.

Xenon reacts with platinum pentafluoride in the presence of an excess of fluorine at 80 p.s.i. and 200° to give a yellow compound[14] of empirical formula $XePtF_{11}$. This was shown by a single-crystal X-ray diffraction study to be $XeF_5^+PtF_6^-$, but the details of this structure will be discussed in the section on hexafluoroplatinates(v) (p. 373).

Platinum pentafluoride dissolves in bromine trifluoride to give a deep red solution. Removal of the excess of solvent under a vacuum leads to the isolation[13] of the compound $(BrF_3)_2PtF_4$. With iodine pentafluoride under reflux, a deep red solution is obtained from which a pale yellow solid could be isolated. Analysis[13] showed the compound to have the empirical formula $PtF_5 \cdot IF_5$, and the same complex has been prepared by dissolving dioxygenyl hexafluoroplatinate(v) in iodine pentafluoride[10]. The adduct melts at 140°, begins to decompose at 180°, and at 300° the residue is platinum tetrafluoride. It has been suggested that the comparatively low melting point is indicative of a fluorine-bridged covalent structure rather than an ionic compound[13]. $PtF_5 \cdot IF_5$ is paramagnetic with an effective magnetic moment of 0.65 BM at room temperature[10,13].

Chlorine trifluoride reacts with platinum hexafluoride[7], platinum pentafluoride and dioxygenyl hexafluoroplatinate(v)[13] to give the adduct $PtF_5 \cdot ClF_3$. Reaction with platinum tetrafluoride at 300° gives the same product[13]. The adduct is a pale orange solid, melting at about 170° and may be sublimed in a vacuum at 100°. The melting point suggests a possible covalent structure[10] but its infrared spectrum[7] favours the ionic formulation $ClF_2^+PtF_6^-$.

Platinum oxide trifluoride. This compound is a light brown solid prepared[13] by the fluorination of platinum dioxide at 200°. It is also formed as one of the products when fluorine, diluted with nitrogen, is passed over a heated mixture of powdered glass and platinum[13]. There is a second unidentified product in the latter reaction, and it has been suggested that it may be a non-stoichiometric oxide fluoride of the type PtO_xF_{3-x}, similar to the niobium series[13].

Oxidation State IV

Palladium tetrafluoride. This compound has been prepared by the action of fluorine on palladium(II) hexafluoropalladate(IV) ("palladium trifluoride") in a flow system at 150–300°; but it is best prepared[15] by fluorination under a pressure of 100 p.s.i. The brick red solid has a tetragonal unit cell with $a = 6.585$ and $c = 5.835$ Å. There are four formula units in the cell[15]. Palladium tetrafluoride is structurally similar to platinum tetrafluoride.

The tetrafluoride is easily reduced, either chemically or merely by thermal decomposition, to palladium(II) hexafluoropalladate(IV). It reacts violently with water.

Platinum tetrafluoride. Platinum tetrafluoride is usually made by the thermal decomposition at 180° of the adduct $(BrF_3)_2PtF_4$, which is obtained by the interaction of bromine trifluoride and platinum dichloride or dibromide[16,17]. The product obtained in this manner contains a small amount of bromine trifluoride which is best removed by fluorination with a nitrogen–fluorine stream at 250°. Other methods of preparation include fluorination of platinum dichloride[11] at less than 200°, interaction of platinum metal and chlorine trifluoride in a bomb[18] and the action[19] of sulphur tetrafluoride at 5–50 atmospheres pressure on platinum disulphide at 150–350°. Platinum tetrafluoride is also formed whenever platinum hexafluoride is prepared.

Platinum tetrafluoride[13] is a yellowish-brown crystalline solid which is hydrolysed only slowly in water, and it may be reduced to the metal with hydrogen at temperatures as low as 100°. X-ray powder diffraction patterns indicate that it adopts a monoclinic unit cell with $a = 6.68$, $b = 6.68$,

$c = 5.71$ Å and $\gamma = 92.02°$. There are four molecular units in the cell and the structure is similar to that of uranium tetrachloride in which the uranium is eight-coordinate[13].

The infrared spectrum[13] of platinum tetrafluoride shows two strong absorptions at 675 and 576 cm⁻¹. The first investigation of the magnetic properties of the tetrafluoride suggested that it was paramagnetic with an effective magnetic moment of 1.1 BM at room temperature[20]. However, reinvestigation of the magnetic properties by Bartlett and Lohmann[13] showed that the compound is in fact diamagnetic. These authors suggested that the earlier samples contained a bromine trifluoride–platinum trifluoride adduct analogous to the well-known palladium compound, although it should be pointed out that, so far, platinum trifluoride has not been prepared.

Platinum tetrafluoride dissolves in selenium tetrafluoride to give a pale yellow solution which[13,21] on refluxing and subsequent removal of the excess of solvent yields the yellow adduct $PtF_4 \cdot 2SeF_4$. The same adduct may be prepared from dioxygenyl hexafluoroplatinate(v)[10] or platinum pentafluoride[13]. It is diamagnetic and it decomposes without melting at about 350° to give platinum metal and selenium hexafluoride. The X-ray powder diffraction data show that the adduct adopts a hexagonal lattice with $a = 15.74$ and $c = 4.93$ Å with four molecules in the cell[10]. The adduct has been formulated as $(SeF_3)_2PtF_6$ and some evidence for this postulate is the relatively high decomposition temperature and the fact that it is isomorphous with the corresponding palladium compound. The palladium compound is almost certainly ionic since addition of alkali-metal fluoride gives the alkali-metal hexafluoropalladate(IV)[22].

Platinum tetrafluoride dissolves in bromine trifluoride on refluxing, to give a deep red solution from which the reddish-brown adduct $PtF_4 \cdot 2BrF_3$ was isolated[13]. This compound was, in fact, first prepared by Sharpe[16] by the action of bromine trifluoride on platinum dichloride or dibromide. The adduct may also be prepared from platinum pentafluoride[13] and from dioxygenyl hexafluoroplatinate(v)[10]. The diamagnetic solid melts at 136° and decomposes between 180° and 200°, to give platinum tetrafluoride. It is most important to note the marked differences in the modes of decomposition of the selenium tetrafluoride and bromine trifluoride adducts of platinum tetrafluoride. Bartlett and Lohmann[13] have suggested that the difference is mainly due to the facts that selenium tetrafluoride is a stronger fluoride-ion donor than bromine trifluoride, and that the selenium tetrafluoride adduct is ionic whilst the other is probably covalent.

Platinum tetrachloride. Platinum tetrachloride may be prepared by chlorinating either platinum metal[23] or platinum dichloride[24] at elevated temperatures. Alternatively, hexachloroplatinic acid may be heated alone, or in a chlorine atmosphere, to give platinum tetrachloride[25].

The tetrachloride forms reddish-brown crystals which are readily soluble in water and in polar organic solvents such as acetone and alcohol. Platinum tetrachloride is thermally unstable[24,26,27], decomposing to the dichloride above about 350°. In a detailed study of this thermal decomposition, Shchukarev and coworkers[27] suggested that platinum trichloride may be formed as an intermediate in the gas phase, but it could not be isolated.

It is remarkable that the structure of platinum tetrachloride is unknown. The only data[25] available are from a powder X-ray diffraction study which showed it to be cubic with $a = 10.45$ Å. The somewhat unexpected assumption was made that the platinum is tetrahedrally coordinated and on this basis a platinum–chlorine bond distance of 2.26 Å was obtained. However, it is clear that such a coordination would give a paramagnetic molecular compound which would be expected to be volatile. It should be noted that, if the tetrahedral coordination were correct, then platinum tetrachloride would be the first tetrahedral platinum compound.

A few adducts of platinum tetrachloride are known; it forms 1:2 adducts with dithiane $(C_4H_4S_2)$[28], alkyl sulphides and pyridine[29]. With arenediazonium compounds, platinum tetrachloride is claimed to form 1:1 adducts[30,31]. A number of hydrates of platinum tetrachloride have been isolated, the most common being $PtCl_4 \cdot 5H_2O$. These hydrates are likely to be complex acids of platinum(IV).

Platinum tetrabromide. Platinum tetrabromide may be prepared by direct bromination of platinum metal at 150° in a flow system, although the reaction is reported to be very slow[32]. A better method of preparation is to dissolve platinum metal in concentrated hydrobromic acid, containing free bromine, in a sealed tube at 150°.

The tetrabromide is a very dark red solid which is only slightly soluble in water. It is thermally less stable that the tetrachloride[32,33], decomposition to the dibromide beginning at about 180°. It has been suggested that platinum tribromide is formed as a highly unstable intermediate product in this decomposition.

Platinum tetrabromide forms a 1:2 adduct with dimethyl sulphide[34].

Platinum tetraiodide. Platinum tetraiodide is prepared by the interaction of platinum metal with either the stoichiometric amount of iodine at 150° in a sealed tube[35] or an excess of iodine at 240° in a sealed tube[36]. Interaction of potassium iodide and hexachloroplatinic acid in solution at room temperature is claimed to produce platinum tetraiodide, although the product decomposes on drying at 80°, platinum triiodide being the product[35,36]. The decomposition is quantitative at 200° in an argon stream and there is some evidence that the tetraiodide decomposes slowly even at room temperature[36]. The heat of dissociation[36] is given as only 4.3 kcal mole^{-1}.

The magnetic properties of platinum tetraiodide have been investigated[35]; the compound has a temperature-independent paramagnetism of about 200×10^{-6} cgs.

Oxidation State III

A compound of empirical formula PdF_3 is known, but it has been shown to be palladium(II) hexafluoropalladate(IV). It is therefore discussed with other hexafluoropalladates(IV) below.

Attempts have been made to prepare platinum trifluoride by the reduction of the tetrafluoride. A black solid, isomorphous with other trifluorides in the platinum group is formed during the fluorination of platinum in the presence of powdered glass but, in view of the oxygen-rich environment, this compound is considered to be an oxide fluoride[13].

Platinum triiodide. Platinum triiodide is best prepared[35,36] by adding potassium iodide to a solution of hexachloroplatinic acid and heating the resulting precipitate to 200°. It is important that the temperature be strictly controlled since the triiodide itself is thermally unstable, giving the diiodide and iodine at about 230°. The dissociation pressure of iodine is 1 atmosphere at 277°, and the variation of the dissociation pressure of iodine over the temperature range 230–250° is given by the expression[36]:

$$\log p_{atm} = 3.652 - 1895/T$$

The heat of dissociation is 12.5 kcal mole^{-1}.

Platinum triiodide is a black solid which has been shown by X-ray powder diffraction studies to be a true compound and not a mixture[35,36]. Argue and Banewicz[35] interpreted the X-ray diffraction data on the basis of a cubic lattice with $a = 11.3$ Å. The magnetic susceptibility varies from 90 to 143×10^{-6} cgs in the temperature range 83–400°K, the decreasing susceptibility with decreasing temperature suggesting antiferromagnetic interactions.

Oxidation State II

Palladium difluoride. Palladium difluoride was first prepared by Ruff and Ascher by fluorination of palladium dichloride at about 500° or by reduction of the "trifluoride" with hydrogen or iodine at elevated temperatures[37]. However, the product from these reactions was not pure and contained some palladium metal. Also, Bartlett and Hepworth[38] found

25

that when sulphur tetrafluoride vapour was passed over "palladium tri-fluoride" at 250–300°, palladium difluoride contaminated with the free metal was formed. They prepared the pure violet difluoride, however, by the following reaction sequence:

$$PdI_2 + BrF_3 \xrightarrow[\text{temp}]{\text{Room}} PdF_3 \cdot BrF_3$$

$$PdF_3 \cdot BrF_3 + SeF_4 \xrightarrow{\text{Reflux}} PdF_4 \cdot 2SeF_4$$

$$PdF_4 \cdot 2SeF_4 \xrightarrow[\text{excess SeF}_4]{\text{Reflux in}} PdF_2$$

A more direct synthesis is to reflux the "trifluoride" with selenium tetra-fluoride[22]. The interaction of palladium disulphide and sulphur tetra-fluoride at 150–300° in a bomb at 5–50 atmospheres pressure may also be used[19]. A most interesting method of preparing palladium difluoride is by thermal decomposition of palladium(II) hexafluorogermanate(IV) at 350° in a vacuum[15].

The structure of palladium difluoride has been investigated by X-ray powder diffraction studies[38,39]. It is tetragonal with $a = 4.956$ and $c = 3.389$ Å. It adopts the rutile structure and is isostructural with the di-fluorides of manganese, iron, cobalt, nickel and zinc[39]. The effective magnetic moment[39] of palladium difluoride at room temperature is 1.84 BM.

Palladium dichloride. Palladium dichloride is best prepared by direct chlorination of the metal at 300° in a flow system[40]. It is a red solid which decomposes at elevated temperatures to the metal and chlorine[26,40–42]. The dissociation pressure[41] of chlorine is one atmosphere at 980°. The equilibrium dissociation pressure of chlorine is given by the following expressions[43]:

Solid $\log p_{\text{mm}} = 8.63 - 6729/T$ (610–680°)

Liquid $\log p_{\text{mm}} = 7.26 - 5423/T$ (680–857°)

The true vapour pressure of palladium dichloride, corrected for the dis-sociation pressure of chlorine, is given by the expressions[43]:

Solid $\log p_{\text{mm}} = 8.86 - 7453/T$ (610–680°)

Liquid $\log p_{\text{mm}} = 6.32 - 5032/T$ (680–857°)

Thermodynamic parameters, calculated from the vapour-pressure meas-urements and other sources, are given in Table 10.4.

X-ray diffraction studies indicate that there are at least three polymorphs of palladium dichloride, the actual modification obtained depending critically on the mode of preparation. Differential thermal analysis[44] indicated that transitions take place at 401° and 504°.

TABLE 10.4

Thermodynamic Properties of Palladium Dichloride

Property	Value	Ref.
M.p.	678°	40
	680°	41, 43
$\Delta H^{\circ}_{\text{form}}$ (kcal mole^{-1})	-33.0	43
$\Delta S^{\circ}_{\text{form}}$ (cal deg^{-1} mole^{-1})	28.0	43
ΔH_{fus} (kcal mole^{-1})	4.4	41
	9.7	40
	11.5	43
ΔH_{vap} (kcal mole^{-1})	33.5	43
ΔS_{vap} (cal deg^{-1} mole^{-1})	27.0	43

The best-known form of palladium dichloride is orthorhombic with $a = 3.81$, $b = 3.34$ and $c = 11.0$ Å, and there are two formula units in the cell[45]. The structure is shown in Figure 10.1 and consists of infinite chains in which each palladium atom is surrounded by four coplanar bridging chlorine atoms at a uniform distance of 2.31 Å.

A second polymorph has also been studied by single-crystal techniques and has been shown to be hexameric and contain octahedral clusters of palladium atoms[46]. This form of palladium dichloride has been discussed in Chapter 3. It is interesting that vapour-pressure measurements by Bell and coworkers[41] suggest that below 980° the major species in the vapour phase is $(PdCl_2)_5$.

No structural information is available so far for the third polymorph of palladium dichloride.

The infrared spectrum of solid palladium dichloride has been investigated by Adams and coworkers[47] who observed absorptions at 348, 340, 297, 187 and 174 cm^{-1}.

It is well known that an enormous number of square-planar complexes of palladium(II) of the general type $PdCl_2L_2$ exist, particularly with amines, and these may be regarded as adducts of palladium dichloride. In fact, many of these complexes are prepared from tetrachloropalladates(II) and not from the dichloride itself. Much work has been done of

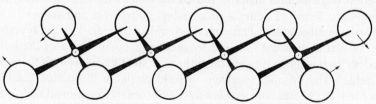

Figure 10.1   The chain form of palladium dichloride.

the preparation and properties of these compounds and they are fully discussed elsewhere[48-51].

Platinum dichloride. Platinum dichloride may be prepared by direct chlorination of the metal at elevated temperatures[23], by chlorination of platinum dioxide[52] at 550°, by thermal decomposition of platinum tetrachloride[23,24,27] or by passing chlorine over hexachloroplatinic acid[52] at 500°. It is to be noted that several of these reactions have been previously given as methods of preparation of the tetrachloride. In all cases low temperatures favour the tetrachloride and the higher temperatures, above the decomposition temperature of the tetrachloride, naturally favour the dichloride.

Platinum dichloride itself is decomposed thermally at even higher temperatures, to give the metal and chlorine[26,53] although Shchukarev and coworkers[27] have suggested that above 330° platinum monochloride exists in the vapour phase.

The dichloride is a green-brown solid which is insoluble in water. A single crystal X-ray study by Brodersen and coworkers[54,55] shows that the dichloride is hexameric and isostructural with palladium dichloride. The details of this structure are given in Chapter 3. Falqui and Rollier[56] examined platinum dichloride by power diffraction techniques and concluded that it was isostructural with the infinite-chain form of palladium dichloride. It is not clear at this stage whether or not platinum dichloride is polymorphic.

The infrared spectrum of solid platinum dichloride[47] shows absorptions at 318 and 200 cm^{-1}.

A most interesting adduct[57] of platinum dichloride is formed when phosphorus trifluoride is passed over the dichloride at 200°. The white solid, $PtCl_2 \cdot 2PF_3$, melts at 102° and decomposes between 240° and 285° to form the red dimeric adduct $(PtCl_2 \cdot PF_3)_2$. Heating it to still higher temperatures yields platinum metal.

Palladium dibromide. There appears to be very little information in the literature on palladium dibromide. The only methods of preparation are direct bromination of palladium metal, which is extremely slow, and dissolution of palladium metal in nitric acid containing free bromine. It is reported to form 1:2 adducts with trialkyl phosphines and arsines[58].

Platinum dibromide. Platinum dibromide is prepared by the bromination of platinum metal followed by thermal decomposition of the initial product[32]. It is difficult to obtain in the pure state since it is itself thermally unstable. The infrared spectrum of solid platinum dibromide has been recorded by Adams and coworkers[47] who observed absorptions at 242 and 230 cm^{-1}.

Palladium diiodide. Palladium diiodide has been prepared by dissolving palladium dichloride in hydrochloric acid and then adding potassium iodide[59]. The black precipitate is insoluble in water, alcohol and ethers, but it dissolves readily in potassium iodide, presumably forming the tetraiodopalladate(II) ion.

Palladium diiodide does not melt or develop a significant vapour pressure up to 740°, although it dissociates quite readily above 350°. The equilibrium dissociation pressure of iodine over the temperature range 360–640° is given by the expression[59]:

$$\log p_{mm} = 6.66 - 6140/T$$

The heat and entropy of formation are given[59] as -14.0 kcal mole^{-1} and 33 cal deg^{-1} mole^{-1}, respectively.

A 1:2 adduct with diethyl sulphide has been reported for palladium diiodide[58].

Platinum diiodide. Platinum diiodide is prepared[35,36] by the thermal decomposition of platinum triiodide at 270°, while at 500° the diiodide decomposes to platinum metal[35]. The black solid has a temperature-independent paramagnetism[35] of about 100×10^{-6} cgs.

COMPLEX HALIDES

All the complex chlorides, bromides and iodides of palladium and platinum are either octahedral complexes of oxidation state IV or square-planar complexes of oxidation state II. Complex fluorides of platinum(V) and platinum(IV) are known, whilst for palladium, the known oxidation states in complex fluorides are IV and II.

Oxidation State V

Alkali-metal hexafluoroplatinates(v). Impure hexafluoroplatinates(v) may be prepared[60] by the action of fluorine on mixtures of platinum halides and alkali-metal halides at 300°. The reaction product is contaminated with hexafluoroplatinate(IV), thus indicating the difficulty of oxidizing that complex. Pure hexafluoroplatinates(v) are best prepared from adducts derived by reduction of platinum hexafluoride.

Potassium hexafluoroplatinate(v) may be prepared by the interaction of potassium fluoride and dioxygenyl hexafluoroplatinate(v) in liquid iodine pentafluoride[10,12,13]. It was found that a cloudy red solution was formed upon refluxing the mixture, and on removal of the solvent the yellow crystalline complex was obtained.

Rubidium and caesium hexafluoroplatinate(v) have been prepared by mixing platinum hexafluoride, xenon and alkali-metal fluoride in a silica vessel at room temperature. The platinum hexafluoride reacts with the xenon to form a xenon hexafluoroplatinate salt. Iodine pentafluoride is then distilled on to the mixture, and subsequent reaction to give the alkali-metal hexafluoroplatinate(v) occurred in this solvent[61].

The alkali-metal hexafluoroplatinates(v) are all rhombohedral and isostructural with the corresponding hexafluoroosmates(v) and hexafluoroiridates(v)[12,13,61]. The lattice parameters are:

$$KPtF_6 \quad a = 4.96 \text{ Å} \quad \alpha = 97.4°$$
$$RbPtF_6 \quad a = 5.08 \text{ Å} \quad \alpha = 97.0°$$
$$CsPtF_6 \quad a = 5.27 \text{ Å} \quad \alpha = 96.3°$$

Potassium hexafluoroplatinate(v) is paramagnetic and the effective magnetic moment[13] at room temperature is 0.87 BM.

The hexafluoroplatinates(v) all react violently with water, the major products including platinum dioxide, hexafluoroplatinate(IV) and ozone[13].

Dioxygenyl hexafluoroplatinate(v). Dioxygenyl hexafluoroplatinate(v) was first prepared by Bartlett and Lohmann who found that a deep red solid was formed when fluorine was passed over platinum dichloride at 350° in silica apparatus[11]. Initially it was thought that the red solid was platinum oxide tetrafluoride, but it was subsequently established[12] that the compound had an empirical formula of PtO_2F_6. Bartlett and Lohmann[10] then made an extensive study of the preparation and properties of this compound and showed by various techniques, such as magnetism, structure determination, and chemical properties, that the compound should be formulated as $O_2^+PtF_6^-$.

It has been found that dioxygenyl hexafluoroplatinate(v) is formed when platinum halides are fluorinated at temperatures greater than 400° in the presence of oxygen[10]. The attack of fluorine on Pyrex glass or silica at this temperature is a sufficiently good source of oxygen. Other methods of preparation[10] include the action of a mixture of fluorine and oxygen on platinum sponge at 450°, the reaction of platinum hexafluoride with oxygen at room temperature and, thirdly, the passage of oxygen difluoride over platinum sponge at 400°.

Dioxygenyl hexafluoroplatinate(v) is a very dark red solid which gives an orange vapour. The solid is easily purified by vacuum-sublimation above 90° and it melts at 219° with some decomposition. It is readily hydrolysed by water vapour, oxygen being evolved[10].

X-ray powder diffraction studies showed dioxygenyl hexafluoroplatinate(v) to be cubic with $a = 10.032$ Å. There are eight formula units in the cell[10,12] and the space group is *Ia*3. The following internuclear distances were deduced from the data:

Pt–F	1.74 Å
F–F	2.57 Å and 2.99 Å
O_2–F	2.71 Å and 3.74 Å
O–O	1.13 Å

The structure of $O_2^+PtF_6^-$ is illustrated in Figure 10.2 which shows that the O_2^+ ion has twelve near neighbours at the corners of icosahedron which

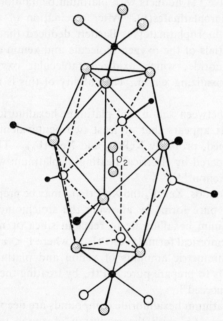

Figure 10.2   Structure of dioxygenyl hexafluoroplatinate(v), $O_2^+PtF_6^-$.

is elongated along its three-fold axis. A neutron diffraction study by Ibers and Hamilton[62] confirmed the geometry of the complex as determined by X-ray diffraction[10] but failed to fix unambiguously the oxygen–oxygen distance in the cation. The platinum–fluorine distance was refined to a value of 1.82 Å.

The magnetic properties of dioxygenyl hexafluoroplatinate(v) have been measured[10] over the temperature range 88–294°K and the susceptibility conforms to a Curie–Weiss law with a Weiss constant of 45° and a magnetic moment of 2.57 BM. The results are compatible with a localized un-paired electron on the oxygenyl cation and on the hexafluoroplatinate(v) anion.

Dioxygenyl hexafluoroplatinate(v) is an extremely reactive compound. It reacts with bromine trifluoride at room temperature, the products including oxygen and the bromine trifluoride–platinum tetrafluoride adduct[10,13]. Selenium tetrafluoride is oxidized to the hexafluoride, oxygen being evolved, and the platinum tetrafluoride–selenium tetrafluoride adduct may be isolated from the reaction mixture. Both iodine penta-fluoride and chlorine trifluoride react with the dioxygenyl compound to form the respective 1:1 adducts with platinum pentafluoride[10,13].

Xenon hexafluoroplatinates(v). After elucidation of the structure of dioxygenyl hexafluoroplatinate(v), Bartlett deduced that, since the first ionization potentials of the oxygen molecule and xenon are very similar, platinum hexafluoride, which oxidized molecular oxygen, should be capable also of oxidizing xenon. The validity of this is now a matter of chemical history.

The reaction between xenon and platinum hexafluoride is quite com-plicated[14,61,63]. It appears that at least two pentavalent platinum com-pounds are formed, probably $XePtF_6$ and $Xe(PtF_6)_2$. These compounds may also be prepared by electrical heating of platinum wire in a mixture of fluorine and xenon[64,65].

The two compounds, $XePtF_6$ and $Xe(PtF_6)_2$, may be prepared separately, in a reasonably pure form, by allowing the stoichiometric amounts of xenon and platinum hexafluoride to react in silica or nickel apparatus. Compounds of empirical formula $Xe(PtF_6)_x$, where $1 < x < 2$, are formed when non-stoichiometric amounts of xenon and platinum hexafluoride react[61]. Attempts to prepare pure $XePtF_6$ by treating these products with xenon did not succeed[61].

The xenon–platinum hexafluoride compounds are deep red solids which decompose above 165° with the evolution of xenon tetrafluoride[61]. A brick-red diamagnetic solid, of empirical formula $XePt_2F_{10}$, is the other product of the thermal decomposition, and chemical tests indicate the presence of platinum in oxidation state IV.

The compound $XePtF_6$ has been formulated as $Xe^+PtF_6^-$ on the basis of its infrared spectrum, which shows strong absorptions at 652 and 550 cm^{-1} indicative of the presence of the hexafluoroplatinate(v) ion, and on the basis of its chemical reactions[61]. The second compound, $Xe(PtF_6)_2$, contains pentavalent platinum and it has been suggested that it may be xenon(II) hexafluoroplatinate(v)[61]. Whilst these formulations have not been proved beyond doubt, they do account for the chemical properties of the compounds. Further studies, particularly structural and magnetic, will be of importance in establishing the correctness of these formulations.

A compound of empirical formula Xe_2PtF_{17} is formed[14] when a mixture of xenon and a molar excess of platinum pentafluoride reacts with fluorine at 80 p.s.i. and 200°. The structure of this compound is not known, but it would be of the greatest interest if it were one of the three most obvious possibilities. It could be $[Xe_2F_{11}^+]PtF_6^-$ which presumably would involve a single xenon–fluorine bridging atom with two octahedrally coordinated xenon atoms; but no other dinuclear xenon compounds have been reported. On the other hand, the second formulation, $(XeF_5^+)_2PtF_7^{2-}$, contains the known pentafluoroxenon(VI) cation (see next section), but the so far unknown heptafluoroplatinate(V) ion. It appears from the evidence so far presented that platinum is reluctant to adopt a coordination number greater than six with fluorine. The third possibility, which overcomes the objections raised with the first two, is a structure formulated as $(XeF_5^+)_2PtF_6^-F^-$, containing equal numbers of free fluoride ions and hexafluoroplatinate(V) ions. There are precedents for the presence of free fluoride ions in lattices of transition-metal complex fluorides. For example, Decain, Fischer and Weiss[66,67] have shown by three-dimensional single-crystal X-ray diffraction studies that the compounds $NH_4CuTiF_7 \cdot 4H_2O$ and $NH_4CuWO_2F_5 \cdot 4H_2O$ contain free fluoride ions. It is possible that this problem can be resolved by a study of the infrared spectrum of this compound since the absorptions associated with XeF_5^+ and PtF_6^- can be determined from pentafluoroxenon(VI) hexafluoroplatinate(V). If the heptafluoroplatinate(V) anion is formed, there should be additional observable platinum–fluorine stretches. Similarly, if a dinuclear $Xe_2F_{11}^+$ cation exists it should show an infrared spectrum different to that of XeF_5^+.

Pentafluoroxenon(VI) hexafluoroplatinate(V). As stated above, a yellow crystalline compound, melting at about 100° and of empirical formula $XePtF_{11}$, is formed[14] when equimolar amounts of xenon and platinum pentafluoride react with fluorine at 80 p.s.i. in a bomb at about 200°.

A single-crystal X-ray diffraction study by Bartlett, Einstein, Stewart and Trotter[14] showed the compound to be orthorhombic with $a = 8.16$, $b = 16.81$ and $c = 5.73$ Å. There are four formula weights in the unit cell and the space group is *Pmnb*. The structure, shown in Figure 10.3, consists of well-defined pentafluoroxenon(VI) groups and hexafluoroplatinate(V) groups which are weakly held together by a single xenon–fluorine bond. The anion is almost a regular octahedron with a mean platinum–fluorine bond distance of 1.91 Å. The stereochemistry of the cation is a slightly distorted, square pyramid, almost identical with that of the isoelectronic iodine pentafluoride molecule. The xenon-to-bridging-fluorine distance is long, at 2.62 Å, and the presence of this fluorine atom appears to have negligible influence of the stereochemistry of the cation compared with the lone pair of electrons on the xenon atom.

The magnetic properties of this interesting compound have been investigated[14] over the temperature range 80–290°K; it obeys the Curie–Weiss law with a Weiss constant of 35°. The magnetic moment is 1.97 BM.

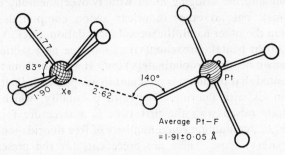

Figure 10.3   Structure of pentafluoroxenon(VI) hexafluoroplatinate(V).

The infrared spectrum[14] shows a broad intense absorption at about 645 cm^{-1} with a weak band at 545 cm^{-1}, attributed to the platinum–fluorine stretching frequencies.

Oxidation State IV

Palladium(II) hexafluoropalladate(IV).   This compound has the empirical formula PdF$_3$, but Bartlett and Rao[15] have shown conclusively that the metal is in a mixed oxidation state and the compound should be formulated as Pd^{2+}(PdF$_6$)$^{2-}$.

It was first prepared by Ruff and Ascher[37] by fluorination of palladium dihalides at 200–250° in a flow system. Preparation by fluorination of palladium diiodide at 400° has also been reported[68], although Bartlett and Hepworth[38] report that this reaction can occur at room temperature. Bromine trifluoride may be used instead of fluorine with palladium di-halides[15,16,38]; the initial product is an adduct, PdF$_3 \cdot$BrF$_3$, which may be thermally decomposed at 180° in a vacuum.

Palladium(II) hexafluoropalladate(IV) is a black crystalline solid and, unlike rhodium and iridium trifluorides, it is rapidly hydrolysed by water. Chemical evidence that it should be formulated as a mixed oxidation state compound comes from the general behaviour of palladium dihalides in bromine trifluoride in the presence of fluoride ion acceptors. A series of compounds of the general formula Pd^{2+}(MF$_6$)$^{2-}$ with M = Ge, Pt or Sn, has been prepared[15] and they are isostructural with Pd(PdF$_6$). Although the room temperature magnetic moment of 2.05 BM was originally interpreted as being consistent with the low-spin d^7-configuration for palladium trifluoride[20], a more detailed subsequent study by Bartlett and Rao[15] has been interpreted as showing a moment due to two unpaired electrons associated with the Pd^{2+} cation in the formula unit $Pd^{2+}(PdF_6)^{2-}$. It should be noted that the actual susceptibilities in both studies are very similar. Support for the latter interpretation comes from the fact that similar magnetic moments are found for the compounds $Pd(GeF_6)$ and $Pd(SnF_6)$, where the magnetic properties can only be associated with the cation. Palladium(II) hexafluoropalladate(IV) is rhombohedral[15,68] with $a = 5.523$ Å and $\alpha = 53.93°$.

Hexafluoropalladates(IV). Potassium, rubidium and caesium hexafluoropalladates(IV) have been prepared from the corresponding hexachloropalladates(IV) by the action of fluorine[69] at 200–300° or by dissolution in bromine trifluoride[70]. The products obtained by the latter method must be heated to about 150° to remove the excess of bromine trifluoride and bromine. Potassium hexafluoropalladate(IV) has also been prepared by Bartlett and Quail[22] by the following reaction sequence:

$$\left. \begin{array}{l} KBr \xrightarrow{\text{BrF}_3} KBrF_4 \xrightarrow{\text{SeF}_4} KSeF_5 \\ PdBr_2 \xrightarrow{\text{BrF}_3} PdF_3 \cdot BrF_3 \xrightarrow{\text{SeF}_4} PdF_4 \cdot 2SeF_4 \end{array} \right\} \xrightarrow[\text{in SeF}_4]{\text{Reflux}} K_2PdF_6$$

The hexafluoropalladates(IV) are yellow diamagnetic solids which, unlike the corresponding platinates(IV), are sensitive to moisture[69,70]. An interesting reaction occurs with hydrochloric acid solution, to give the corresponding hexachloropalladate(IV)[70].

The X-ray powder diffraction patterns for a number of hexafluoropalladates(IV) have been observed. A feature of the hexafluoropalladates(IV) and most other hexafluorometallates(IV) is the variety of phases which may be obtained according to the method of preparation. The available results are given in Table 10.5.

TABLE 10.5
Lattice Parameters of the Hexafluoropalladates(IV)

Compound	Symmetry	Unit-cell parameters	Ref.
Na_2PdF_6	Hexagonal	$a = 9.23$ Å, $c = 5.25$ Å	71
K_2PdF_6	Hexagonal	$a = 5.717$ Å, $c = 4.667$ Å	69
	Hexagonal	$a = 5.75$ Å, $c = 9.51$ Å	22
	Rhombohedral	$a = 4.88$ Å, $\alpha = 98.4°$	72
Rb_2PdF_6	Cubic	$a = 8.57$ Å	69
Cs_2PdF_6	Cubic	$a = 9.00$ Å	69, 70
Ag_2PdF_6	Rhombohedral	$a = 4.72$ Å, $\alpha = 98.2°$	72

The infrared spectrum of potassium hexafluoropalladate(IV) shows a strong absorption at 602 cm^{-1} attributed to the palladium–fluorine stretching frequency[73].

The adduct $PdF_4 \cdot 2SeF_4$ may be prepared[13,22] by the action of selenium tetrafluoride on $PdF_3 \cdot BrF_3$. It is hydrolysed violently by water; but, when it is dissolved in hydrochloric acid and potassium chloride is added, red potassium hexachloropalladate(IV) is precipitated. The adduct is a yellow diamagnetic solid which rapidly decomposes at 155° to give palladium difluoride[22]. The decomposition has led Bartlett and coworkers[13,22] to suggest that, since selenium tetrafluoride is a relatively strong fluoride ion donor, the compound should perhaps be formulated as trifluoroselenium(IV) hexafluoropalladate(IV), $(SeF_3)_2PdF_6$. Additional evidence for this formulation is obtained by the formation of potassium hexafluoropalladate(IV) on addition of potassium fluoride dissolved in selenium tetrafluoride[22].

Hexafluoroplatinates(IV). These complexes may be prepared by two basic methods. Dry methods involve reaction of fluorine, bromine trifluoride or chlorine trifluoride with the corresponding hexachloroplatinates(IV)[70,74,75]. Hexafluoroplatinates(IV) may be prepared from aqueous solution by neutralization of hexafluoroplatinic acid by various bases[76], or by interaction of alkali-metal nitrate or hydroxide with lanthanum hexafluoroplatinate(IV)[77]. More specific examples of the preparation of particular hexafluoroplatinates(IV) are exemplified by the reaction of platinum tetrafluoride and potassium fluoride in bromine trifluoride solution[78], the action of chlorine trifluoride on a mixture of platinum and potassium hydrogen fluoride[75] and the fluorination of mixtures of platinum and rare-earth trifluorides[79] at 525°. Finally, potassium hexafluoroplatinate(IV) has been prepared by the reaction of potassium hexafluoroplatinate(V) with water[13].

The hexafluoroplatinates(IV) are usually pale yellow diamagnetic solids which, in marked contrast to the corresponding palladium salts, are hydrolytically stable and may even be recrystallized from water. The salts of sodium, magnesium, calcium and strontium are thermally unstable. The sodium salt is reported to decompose in air just above room temperature[74], whilst the alkaline-earth salts are reported to decompose at 600° to platinum metal and the alkaline-earth difluoride[76].

Structural data derived from X-ray powder diffraction studies are given in Table 10.6.

The infrared spectrum of potassium hexafluoroplatinate(IV)[73] shows a strong absorption at 583 cm^{-1}, and the sodium salt[74] shows strong absorptions at 571 and 287 cm^{-1}. The Raman spectrum of an aqueous solution of sodium hexafluoroplatinate(IV)[74] showed absorptions at 600, 576 and 210 cm^{-1}.

There is evidence[13] (melting point and mode of decomposition) to suggest that the adduct $PtF_4 \cdot 2SeF_4$ should be formulated as trifluoroselenium(IV) hexafluoroplatinate(IV), $(SeF_3)_2PtF_6$, as for the corresponding palladate(IV).

TABLE 10.6

Lattice Parameters of the Hexafluoroplatinates(IV)

Compound	Symmetry	Unit-cell parameters	Ref.
Na_2PtF_6	Hexagonal	$a = 9.41$ Å, $c = 5.16$ Å	70, 71
K_2PtF_6	Hexagonal	$a = 5.76$ Å, $c = 4.64$ Å	80
	Rhombohedral	$a = 4.88$ Å, $\alpha = 98.0°$	72
Rb_2PtF_6	Hexagonal	$a = 5.96$ Å, $c = 4.83$ Å	70
Cs_2PtF_6	Hexagonal	$a = 6.22$ Å, $c = 5.01$ Å	70
Ag_2PtF_6	Rhombohedral	$a = 4.74$ Å, $\alpha = 97.8°$	72
$PdPtF_6$	Rhombohedral	$a = 5.55$ Å, $\alpha = 54.0°$	15

Trifluorotrichloroplatinates(IV). These interesting compounds have been prepared by the interaction of bromine trifluoride with the alkali-metal hexachloroplatinates(IV)[81] under controlled conditions. The potassium salt has also been prepared by the action of bromine trifluoride on potassium tetrachloroplatinate(II) at room temperature. Attempts to prepare the corresponding fluorobromo- and fluoroiodoplatinates(IV) by similar methods were unsuccessful[81].

The trifluorotrichloroplatinates(IV) are stable, non-hygroscopic orange solids which decompose only slowly in aqueous solution to give the hexafluoro- and hexachloroplatinates(IV).

X-ray powder diffraction studies showed conclusively that the products were genuine compounds and not intimate mixtures of hexafluoro- and hexachloroplatinates(IV). The lattice parameters of the trifluorotrichloroplatinates(IV) are:

$K_2PtCl_3F_3$ Orthorhombic $a = 7.58$ Å, $b = 9.70$ Å, $c = 7.80$ Å

$Rb_2PtCl_3F_3$ Cubic $a = 9.50$ Å

$Cs_2PtCl_3F_3$ Cubic $a = 9.79$ Å

Rubidium and caesium trifluorotrichloroplatinate(IV) are isostructural with the corresponding hexachloroplatinates(IV)[81].

The infrared spectra of the trifluorotrichloroplatinates(IV) are given in Table 10.7; both of the platinum–halogen stretching frequencies show very significant shifts from the values observed in the hexafluoro- and hexachloroplatinates(IV), as shown in the Table.

TABLE 10.7

Infrared Spectra of Trifluorotrichloroplatinates(IV)

Compound	Pt–F stretch	Pt–Cl stretch
$K_2PtCl_3F_3$	566m, 520vs	415w, 373s
$Rb_2PtCl_3F_3$	564m, 518vs	415w, 370s
$Cs_2PtCl_3F_3$	560m, 515vs	415w, 367s
K_2PtF_6	583vs	—
K_2PtCl_6	—	340vs

Hexachloropalladates(IV) and -platinates(IV). The hexachloropalladates(IV) and -platinates(IV) may both be prepared by wet or dry methods. Dissolution of either metal in aqua regia or in concentrated hydrochloric acid saturated with chlorine leads to the formation of the hexachloro anions which may be isolated by the addition of alkali-metal chlorides[40,82]. Hexachloroplatinates(IV) may be isolated readily by dissolving platinum tetrachloride in hydrochloric acid solution and adding an alkali-metal chloride[83]. Passing chlorine or carbon tetrachloride vapour over a heated intimate mixture of platinum metal and alkali-metal chloride gives the corresponding hexachloroplatinates(IV)[84]. More specific methods of preparing potassium hexachloropalladate(IV) are dissolution of potassium hexafluoropalladate(IV) in hydrochloric acid[70], or of trifluoroselenium(IV) hexafluoropalladate(IV) in a hydrochloric acid solution of potassium chloride[22].

The hexachloropalladates(IV) and -platinates(IV) are dark red crystalline solids. The palladium salts are thermally unstable, decomposing above about 200°, losing chlorine to give the corresponding tetrachloropalladates(II)[40,42,85]. The heat of formation of ammonium hexachloropalladate(IV)[86] is given as −244.2 kcal mole⁻¹.

Most alkali-metal hexachloropalladates(IV) and -platinates(IV) are isostructural with ammonium hexachloroplatinate(IV) whose structure has been determined by single-crystal diffraction measurements[87]. This structure determination by Wyckoff and Posnjak was one of the first performed on a complex compound. The body-centred, cubic unit cell, shown in Figure 10.4, has the ammonium ion at the centre of the cube and four platinum atoms tetrahedrally arranged around it. The chlorine atoms are centred at the mid-point of each edge of the cube. The platinum–chlorine distance is 2.44 Å. The lattice parameters of a number of hexachloropalladates(IV) and -platinates(IV) are given in Table 10.8. Vaughan and coworkers[89] studied the X-ray scattering pattern of a solution of hexachloroplatinic acid and deduced that the ion is octahedral with a mean, but rather uncertain, platinum–chlorine distance of 2.39 Å. This can be

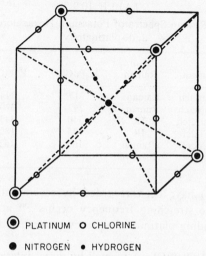

⊙ PLATINUM ○ CHLORINE

● NITROGEN • HYDROGEN

Figure 10.4 The basic structural unit in ammonium hexachloroplatin-
ate(IV).

compared with a value of 2.33 Å found in solid potassium hexachloro-
platinate(IV)[90].

Hiraishi and coworkers[91] observed the infrared and Raman spectra of
potassium hexachloropalladate(IV), and they and Woodward and Creighton[92] studied potassium hexachloroplatinate(IV) also. There is almost
exact agreement for the hexachloroplatinate(IV) ion between the two
groups. The absorptions have been assigned on the basis of O_h symmetry
and are given in Table 10.9. The relative intensities of ν_1 and ν_2 in the
hexachloroplatinate(IV) ion compared with the intensities found in the
corresponding fluoro complex and the implication of these with regard to
π-bonding between platinum and chlorine have been discussed in Chapter
2. The metal–chlorine stretching frequencies in hexachloropalladates(IV)

TABLE 10.8

Lattice Parameters of Some Hexachloropalladates(IV)
and -platinates(IV)

Compound	Parameter	Ref.	Compound	Parameter	Ref.
K_2PdCl_6	9.74 Å	99	K_2PtCl_6	9.755 Å	88
$(NH_4)_2PdCl_6$	9.81 Å	99	$(NH_4)_2PtCl_6$	9.843 Å	87
Rb_2PdCl_6	9.87 Å	88	Rb_2PtCl_6	9.901 Å	88
Cs_2PdCl_6	10.16 Å	99	Cs_2PtCl_6	10.215 Å	88

TABLE 10.9

Infrared and Raman Spectra of Potassium Hexachloropalladate(IV)
and -platinate(IV)

Vibrational mode	Assignment	IR or Raman	K$_2$PdCl$_6$[91]	K$_2$PtCl$_6$[91]	K$_2$PtCl$_6$[92]
ν_1 (a_{1g})	M–Cl stretch	Raman	317	344	344
ν_2 (e_g)	M–Cl stretch	Raman	292	320	320
ν_3 (f_{1a})	M–Cl stretch	IR	340	343	340
ν_4 (f_{1a})	ClMCl def	IR	175	182	—
ν_5 (f_{2g})	ClMCl def	Raman	164	162	162
ν_6 (f_{2u})	—	Inactive	—	—	—

and -platinates(IV) have been recorded by several other groups. The palladium–chlorine stretching frequency occurs[93,94] at about 357 cm^{-1}, and the corresponding platinum frequency occurs[93–95] in the range 330–345 cm^{-1}.

The complex, (NO)$_2$PtCl$_6$, is formed by direct interaction of platinum tetrachloride and nitrosyl chloride[96] and when platinum metal is dissolved in aqua regia[49]. It has a cubic lattice[97] with $a = 11.27$ Å.

Hexabromopalladates(IV). Hexabromopalladates(IV) are usually prepared by the action of bromine on the corresponding tetrabromopalladate(II) in hydrobromic acid solution[49,98]. The black solids give dark red solutions in hydrobromic acid.

Most of the alkali-metal hexabromopalladates(IV) are cubic with the K$_2$PtCl$_6$ structure. Some typical values of the lattice constants are given in Table 10.10. There is some disagreement between the two sets of data.

TABLE 10.10

Lattice Parameters of Hexabromopalladates(IV)

Compound	Wyckoff[88]	Ketelaar and van Walsem[99]
K$_2$PdBr$_6$	10.27 Å	9.92 Å
(NH$_4$)$_2$PdBr$_6$	10.33 Å	9.95 Å
Rb$_2$PdBr$_6$	10.38 Å	10.25 Å
Cs$_2$PdBr$_6$	10.62 Å	10.64 Å

Hexabromoplatinates(IV). Hexabromoplatinates(IV) have been frequently prepared from solutions of hexabromoplatinic acid[49,100,101], which is itself prepared by dissolution of platinum in hydrobromic acid containing free bromine[101] or merely by dissolving platinum tetrachloride in hydrobromic acid[49].

X-ray powder diffraction studies have shown that most of the alkali-metal hexabromoplatinates(IV) adopt the cubic K_2PtCl_6 structure. Lattice constants[88] of several hexabromoplatinates(IV) are:

K_2PtBr_6	10.27 Å	Rb_2PtBr_6	10.41 Å
$(NH_4)_2PtBr_6$	10.37 Å	Cs_2PtBr_6	10.63 Å

In solution the hexabromoplatinate(IV) ion has been shown[89] to constitute a regular octahedron with a platinum–bromine bond distance of 2.43 Å.

Hiraishi and coworkers[91] and Woodward and Creighton[92] have made a detailed study of the infrared and Raman spectra of potassium hexabromo-platinate(IV) and they observed a number of absorptions which were assigned on the basis of O_h symmetry as follows: v_1 207, v_2 190, v_3 244, v_4 90 and v_5 97 cm^{-1}. Adams and Gebbie[93] observed a platinum–bromine stretching frequency at 240 cm^{-1} in the infrared spectrum of potassium hexabromoplatinate(IV).

Hexaiodoplatinates(IV). Hexaiodoplatinates(IV) may be prepared from hexachloroplatinic acid by reaction with an excess of potassium iodide[102] or by treatment with hydriodic acid followed by addition of an alkali-metal iodide[49,103]. Alternatively, the action of alkali-metal iodide on platinum tetraiodide in hydriodic acid may be used[49].

The hexaiodoplatinates(IV) are not isostructural with the corresponding hexachloroplatinates(IV). The available results[81] are given in Table 10.11. The platinum–iodine stretching frequency[93] occurs at 186 cm^{-1}.

TABLE 10.11

Lattice Parameters of Hexaiodoplatinates(IV)

Compound	Symmetry	Unit-cell parameters
K_2PtI_6	Orthorhombic	$a = 10.73$, $b = 8.10$, $c = 7.65$ Å
Rb_2PtI_6	Tetragonal	$a = 5.58$, $c = 6.45$ Å
Cs_2PtI_6	Tetragonal	$a = 5.68$, $c = 6.55$ Å

Oxidation State II

Trifluoropalladate(II). The interaction of an equimolar mixture of caesium fluoride and palladium difluoride in refluxing selenium tetra-fluoride produces a pink-brown solid on removal of the solvent[22]. The compound is paramagnetic with a magnetic moment of 1.60 BM. The structure of caesium trifluoropalladate(II) is not known, so that a detailed interpretation of the magnetic data is not possible. It was not possible to prepare the potassium analogue and no further information is available on this interesting compound.

Tetrachloropalladates(II). The interaction of palladium dichloride and an alkali-metal chloride in hydrochloric acid solution leads to the formation of the yellowish alkali-metal tetrachloropalladates(II)[49]. All other reported methods of preparing these complexes involve reduction of the corresponding hexachloropalladate(IV). Reduction may be achieved simply by thermal decomposition[40,42] or with palladium sponge in hydrochloric acid solution[104].

The standard heats of formation of the potassium[105] and ammonium salts[86,105] have been determined as −261.6 and −204.8 kcal mole^{-1}, respectively.

Potassium and ammonium tetrachloropalladates(II) are isostructural with the corresponding platinum salts, the tetragonal unit cells having the following parameters[106]:

$$K_2PdCl_4 \qquad a = 9.96 \text{ Å} \qquad c = 4.10 \text{ Å}$$
$$(NH_4)_2PdCl_4 \qquad a = 10.20 \text{ Å} \qquad c = 4.26 \text{ Å}$$

Tetrachloroplatinates(II). Platinum dichloride dissolves in hydrochloric acid to form the tetrachloroplatinate(II) ion, and addition of an alkali-metal chloride or carbonate gives the corresponding tetrachloroplatinate(II)[49]. Alternatively, the salts may be prepared by reducing the corresponding hexachloroplatinate(IV) with the stoichiometric amount of hydrazine hydrochloride[107] or by bubbling hydrogen sulphide through the solution[49].

Dickinson[106] has examined the crystal structure of potassium tetrachloroplatinate(II). The compound has a tetragonal unit cell with $a = 9.87$ and $c = 4.13$ Å. The structure, shown in Figure 10.5, consists of alternate layers of square-planar $PtCl_4$ units and potassium ions. The platinum–chlorine distance is 2.33 Å.

The infrared spectra of several tetrachloroplatinates(II) have been studied by a number of groups and the observed absorptions are given in

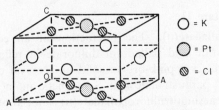

Figure 10.5　Structure of potassium tetrachloroplatinate(II).

Table 10.12. Stammreich and Forneris[110] have studied the Raman spectrum of the tetrachloroplatinate(II) ion. Three Raman-active bands were observed and these were assigned as follows: ν_1 335, ν_3 164 and ν_5 304 cm^{-1}.

TABLE 10.12

Infrared Spectra of Tetrachloroplatinates(II)

Assignment	K_2PtCl_4[108]	K_2PtCl_4[109]	Rb_2PtCl_4[108]	Cs_2PtCl_4[108]
ν_2	175	172	167	160
ν_6	325	322	320	316
ν_7	193	195	190	185

Tetrabromopalladates(II). Tetrabromopalladates(II) have been prepared by halogen exchange with the corresponding tetrachloropalladate(II) or by reducing the corresponding hexabromopalladate(IV) with the calculated amount of oxalic acid[100].

Tetrabromoplatinates(II). Tetrabromoplatinates(II) may be prepared by treating the corresponding tetrachloroplatinates(II) with sodium bromide in hydrobromic acid solution[100]. Shagisultanova[103] reduced the hexabromoplatinate(IV) to the corresponding tetrabromoplatinate(II) with the stoichiometric amount of hydrazine sulphate. Oxalates may be used alternatively as reductant[100].

The platinum–bromine stretching frequency[93] in potassium hexabromoplatinate(II) has been observed at 233 cm^{-1}.

Hexahalodipalladates(II) and -diplatinates(II). A number of compounds having the stoichiometry $(NR_4)MX_3$ (M = Pd or Pt; X = Cl, Br or I; R = CH_3, C_2H_5, etc.) may be prepared by interaction of aqueous solutions of the tetrahalometallate(II) and the quaternary ammonium salts, or, for the iodide, by treating the transition-metal diiodide in aqueous alcohol with an excess of sodium iodide containing the quaternary ammonium iodide[111]. Conductivity measurements suggested that these compounds are ionic and should be formulated as $(NR_4)_2M_2X_6$. This formulation has been confirmed by a single crystal X-ray diffraction study[112] of the compound $[N(C_2H_5)_4]_2Pt_2Br_6$. The compound is triclinic, with a = 7.60, b = 8.38, c = 12.34 Å, α = 105.6°, β = 84.0° and γ = 112.8°. The space group is $P\bar{1}$ and a single formula weight comprises the unit cell. The anion, shown in Figure 10.6, consists of a planar Pt_2Br_6 unit with slightly distorted square-planar coordination about each platinum atom.

It would be interesting to determine whether caesium trifluoropalladate(II), which is formally analogous to the hexabromodiplatinate(II), is similar.

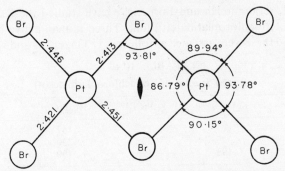

Figure 10.6   Structure of the hexabromodiplatinate(II) ion.

ADDENDA

Halides

The transition temperature[113] for platinum hexafluoride is 3.0°. The high-temperature cubic form has $a = 6.21$ Å and the low-temperature orthorhombic form has $a = 9.55$, $b = 8.71$, and $c = 5.03$ Å.

The magnetic moment of platinum hexafluoride is 1.30 BM at room temperature[114] but the susceptibility is almost independent of temperature as expected for a d^4 octahedral complex with a high spin–orbit coupling constant. Carbon monoxide and hexafluorobenzene both reduce platinum hexafluoride violently to platinum tetrafluoride, chlorine gives the adduct $PtF_5 \cdot ClF_3$ and sulphur tetrafluoride gives platinum tetrafluoride and the adduct $PtF_5 \cdot SF_4$ [114].

It was claimed that platinum difluoride is formed when a platinum wire was electrically exploded in sulphur hexafluoride vapour[115]. The product was insoluble in water and, since the compound could not be analysed satisfactorily, the formulation as the difluoride was based on the fact that its properties differ from those of the known platinum fluorides. In view of Bartlett's work on platinum fluorides, it is probable that the formulation as the difluoride is incorrect.

A thermogravimetric study of the platinum–chlorine reaction has been carried out[116]. It was found that even at 300° the reaction was not complete. The thermal decomposition of platinum tetrachloride was also studied[116] and thermal effects were noted as follows: 370° $PtCl_3$, 428° $PtCl_2$, 578° PtCl, and 583° Pt metal.

Platinum tetrachloride reacts with boron tribromide to give platinum tetrabromide[117].

Single crystals of palladium dibromide were grown[118] in a thermal gradient at about 700°. The compound is monoclinic with $a = 6.59$, $b = 3.96$, $c = 25.22$ Å, and $\beta = 92.6°$. The space group is $P2_1/c$ and there are eight formula units in the cell. The compound is isostructural with palladium dichloride (Figure 10.1, page 367), although the coordination of the four bromine atoms about the palladium atom is not exactly square.

Complex Halides

Contrary to earlier reports $NO^+PtF_6^-$ has a rhombohedral unit cell[114] with $a = 5.03$ Å and $\alpha = 97.6°$.

Refined data for the structure of pentafluoroxenon(vi) hexafluoroplatinate(v) (Figure 10.3, page 374) are now available[119]. The bond distances are xenon–fluorine (2.52–2.65) × 4 and 2.95 Å, platinum–fluorine 1.80–1.95 Å, and the angle F–Pt–F is 90°.

Further powder X-ray diffraction results have been reported for the cubic hexachloroplatinates(iv).

K_2PtCl_6	$a = 9.73$ Å	(reference 120)
$(NH_4)_2PtCl_6$	$a = 9.84$ Å	(reference 121)
Rb_2PtCl_6	$a = 8.88$ Å	(references 120, 121)
Cs_2PtCl_6	$a = 10.19$ Å	(references 120, 121)
Ag_2PtCl_6	$a = 9.93$ Å	(reference 122)
Tl_2PtCl_6	$a = 9.97$ Å	(reference 122)
$(NMe_4)_2PtCl_6$	$a = 12.66$ Å	(reference 122)
$(NEt_4)_2PtCl_6$	$a = 14.07$ Å	(reference 122)

The infrared spectra of a number of hexachloroplatinates have been observed[120,122,123], but by far the most detailed study is that by Adams and Morris[122] who also examined the Raman spectra of the complexes. They examined the spectra of ten hexachloroplatinates(iv) and, in general, the fundamentals fall in the following ranges (cm^{-1}):

ν_1 335–350	ν_2 312–320	ν_3 325–340
ν_4 181–187	ν_5 166–177	ν_6 65–90

Adams and Morris[122] also examined the infrared and the Raman spectra of potassium hexabromoplatinate(iv) and made the following assignments: ν_1 217, ν_2 195, ν_3 243, ν_4 78, ν_5 115, and ν_6 100 cm^{-1}.

The palladium–chlorine and palladium–bromine stretching frequencies[120] for a number of alkali-metal hexahalopalladates(iv) fall in the ranges 344–355 and 254–261 cm^{-1}, respectively.

Both the infrared[124,126] and the Raman[125] spectra of a number of tetrahalopalladates(ii) and -platinates(ii) have been observed. The

Raman-active and infrared-active metal–halogen stretching frequencies (in cm^{-1}) are:

	IR^{124}	R^{125}		IR^{126}	R^{125}
K_2PdCl_4	336	310	K_2PtCl_4	321	333
Rb_2PdCl_4	331		Rb_2PtCl_4	320	
Cs_2PdCl_4	328		Cs_2PtCl_4	313	
K_2PdBr_4	260	192	K_2PtBr_4	232	205
Rb_2PdBr_4	258		Rb_2PtBr_4	237	
Cs_2PdBr_4	249		Cs_2PtBr_4	229	

In addition, Hendra[125] has observed both the infrared and the Raman spectrum of potassium tetraiodoplatinate(IV), the metal–iodine stretching frequencies being 180 and 142 cm^{-1}, respectively. This observation is interesting in view of the conclusion by Corain and Pöe[127], who made a thorough study of the platinum–iodine system, that the tetraiodo-platinate(IV) ion cannot be isolated.

Adams and coworkers[128] have made an extensive study of the infrared spectra of the hexahalodipalladates(II) and -diplatinates(II).

REFERENCES

1. B. Weinstock, H. H. Claassen and J. G. Malm, *J. Am. Chem. Soc.*, **79**, 5832 (1957).
2. B. Weinstock, J. G. Malm and E. E. Weaver, *J. Am. Chem. Soc.* **83**, 4310 (1961).
3. B. Weinstock, E. F. Westrum and G. L. Goodman, *Proc. 8th Intern. Conf. Low Temp. Physics, London*, 1962, p. 405.
4. B. Weinstock, H. H. Claassen and J. G. Malm, *J. Chem. Phys.*, **32**, 181 (1960).
5. S. Sundaram, *Z. Physik. Chem. (Frankfurt)*, **34**, 225 (1962).
6. M. Kimura and K. Kimura, *J. Mol. Spectr.*, **11**, 368 (1963).
7. F. P. Gortsema and R. H. Toeniskoetter, *Inorg. Chem.*, **5**, 1925 (1966).
8. N. Bartlett, S. P. Beaton and N. K. Jha, *Chem. Commun.*, **1966**, 168.
9. F. P. Gortsema and R. H. Toeniskoetter, *Inorg. Chem.*, **5**, 1217 (1966).
10. N. Bartlett and D. H. Lohmann, *J. Chem. Soc.*, **1962**, 5253.
11. N. Bartlett and D. H. Lohmann, *Proc. Chem. Soc.*, **1960**, 14.
12. N. Bartlett and D. H. Lohmann, *Proc. Chem. Soc.*, **1962**, 115.
13. N. Bartlett and D. H. Lohmann, *J. Chem. Soc.*, **1964**, 619.
14. N. Bartlett, F. Einstein, D. F. Stewart and J. Trotter, *Chem. Commun.*, **1966**, 550.
15. N. Bartlett and P. R. Rao, *Proc. Chem. Soc.*, **1964**, 393.
16. A. G. Sharpe, *J. Chem. Soc.*, **1950**, 3444.
17. M. L. Hair and P. L. Robinson, *J. Chem. Soc.*, **1960**, 3419.
18. W. Hückel, *Nachr. Akad. Wiss. Goettingen Math.-Physik. Kl.*, **1946**, 36.
19. U.S. Pat. 2,952,514.
20. R. S. Nyholm and A. G. Sharpe, *J. Chem. Soc.*, **1952**, 3579.

21. N. Bartlett and P. L. Robinson, *J. Chem. Soc.*, **1961**, 3417.
22. N. Bartlett and J. W. Quail, *J. Chem. Soc.*, **1961**, 3728.
23. L. Wohler and S. Streicher, *Ber.*, **46**, 1591 (1913).
24. V. P. Kazakov and B. I. Peshchevitskii, *Radiokhimiya*, **4**, 509 (1962).
25. M. T. Faliqui, *Ann. Chim. (Rome)*, **48**, 1160 (1958).
26. J. Krustinsons, *Z. Elektrochem.*, **44**, 537 (1938).
27. S. A. Shchukarev, M. A. Oranskaya and T. S. Shemyakina, *Zh. Neorg. Khim.*, **1**, 17 (1956).
28. J. W. Bourknight and G. McP. Smith, *J. Am. Chem. Soc.*, **61**, 28 (1939).
29. P. C. Ray and P. C. Mukherjee, *J. Indian Chem. Soc.*, **6**, 885 (1929).
30. A. N. Nesmeyanov, K. A. Kockeshkov, V. A. Klimova and N. K. Gipp, *Ber.*, **68**, 1877 (1935).
31. K. A. Kocheshkov and A. N. Nesmeyanov, *J. Gen. Chem. USSR*, **6**, 144 (1936).
32. L. Wohler and F. Muller, *Z. anorg. allgem. Chem.*, **149**, 377 (1925).
33. S. A. Shchukarev, T. A. Tolmacheva, M. A. Oranskaya and L. V. Komandroskaya, *Zh. Neorg. Khim.*, **1**, 8 (1956).
34. P. Spinoglio and M. De Gasperi, *Gazz. Chim. Ital.*, **67**, 318 (1937).
35. G. R. Argue and J. J. Banewicz, *J. Inorg. Nucl. Chem.*, **25**, 923 (1963).
36. S. A. Shchukarev, T. A. Tolmacheva and G. M. Shavutskaya, *Russ. J. Inorg. Chem.*, **9**, 1351 (1964).
37. O. Ruff and E. Ascher, *Z. anorg. allgem. Chem.*, **183**, 204 (1929).
38. N. Bartlett and M. A. Hepworth, *Chem. Ind. (London)*, **1956**, 1425.
39. N. Bartlett and R. Maitland, *Acta Cryst.*, **11**, 747 (1958).
40. F. Puche, *Ann. Chim. (Paris)*, **9**, 233 (1938).
41. W. E. Bell, U. Merten and M. Tagami, *J. Phys. Chem.*, **65**, 510 (1961).
42. F. Puche, *Compt. Rend.*, **200**, 1206 (1935).
43. M. A. Oranskaya and N. A. Mikhailova, *Russ. J. Inorg. Chem.*, **5**, 5 (1960).
44. J. R. Soulen and P. Saumagne, *J. Phys. Chem.*, **69**, 3669 (1965).
45. A. F. Wells, *Z. Krist.*, **100**, 189 (1938).
46. H. Schafer, U. Wiesse, K. Rinke and K. Brendel, *Angew. Chem.*, **79**, 244 (1967).
47. D. M. Adams, M. Goldstein and E. F. Mooney, *Trans. Faraday Soc.*, **59**, 2228 (1963).
48. J. W. Mellor, *A Comprehensive Treatise on Inorganic and Theoretical Chemistry*, Vol. XV, Longmans, London, 1936.
49. *Nouveau Traité de Chimie Minerale* (ed., P. Pascal), Vol. XIX, Masson, Paris, 1958.
50. A. E. Martell and M. Calvin, *Structure of Chelate Compounds*, Prentice-Hall, N.J., 1952.
51. F. Basolo and R. G. Pearson, *Mechanisms of Inorganic Reactions*, Wiley, New York, 1958.
52. J. M. Lutton and R. W. Parry, *J. Am. Chem. Soc.*, **76**, 4272 (1954).
53. J. Krustinsons, *Z. Elektrochem.*, **45**, 83 (1939).
54. K. Brodersen, G. Thiele and H. G. Schnering, *Z. anorg. allgem. Chem.*, **337**, 120 (1965).
55. K. Brodersen, *Angew. Chem. Intern. Ed. Engl.*, **3**, 519 (1964).
56. M. T. Falqui and M. A. Rollier, *Ann. Chim. (Rome)*, **48**, 1154 (1958).
57. J. Chatt, *Nature*, **165**, 637 (1950).

58. F. G. Mann and D. Purdie, *J. Chem. Soc.*, **1935**, 1549.
59. S. A. Shchukarev, T. A. Tolmacheva and Y. L. Pazukhina, *Russ. J. Inorg. Chem.*, **9**, 1354 (1964).
60. N. Bartlett, in *Preparative Inorganic Reactions* (ed. W. L. Jolly), Vol. 2, Interscience, New York, 1965.
61. N. Bartlett and N. K. Jha, in *Noble Gas Compounds* (ed. H. H. Hyman), Univ. Chicago Press, Chicago, 1963.
62. J. A. Ibers and W. C. Hamilton, *J. Chem. Phys.*, **44**, 1748 (1965).
63. N. Bartlett, *Proc. Chem. Soc.*, **1962**, 218.
64. F. Mahieux, *Compt. Rend.*, **257**, 1683 (1963).
65. F. Mahieux, *Compt. Rend.*, **258**, 3497 (1964).
66. A. Decain, J. Fischer and R. Weiss, *Bull. Soc. Chim. France*, **1966**, 2647.
67. A. Decain, J. Fischer and R. Weiss, *Acta Cryst.*, **22**, 340 (1967).
68. M. A. Hepworth, K. H. Jack, R. D. Peacock and G. J. Westland, *Acta Cryst.*, **10**, 63 (1957).
69. R. Hoppe and W. Klemm, *Z. anorg. allgem. Chem.*, **268**, 364 (1952).
70. A. G. Sharpe, *J. Chem. Soc.*, **1953**, 197.
71. D. H. Brown, K. R. Dixon, R. D. W. Kemmitt and D. W. A. Sharp, *J. Chem. Soc.*, **1965**, 1559.
72. B. Cox, *J. Chem. Soc.*, **1956**, 876.
73. R. D. Peacock and D. W. A. Sharp, *J. Chem. Soc.*, **1959**, 2762.
74. L. A. Woodward and M. J. Ware, *Spectrochim. Acta*, **19**, 775 (1963).
75. I. I. Chernyaev, N. S. Nikolaev and E. G. Ippolitov, *Dokl. Akad. Nauk SSSR*, **132**, 378 (1960).
76. M. K. Norr, T. P. Perros and C. R. Naeser, *J. Am. Chem. Soc.*, **80**, 5053 (1958).
77. T. E. Wheeler, T. P. Perros and C. R. Naeser, *J. Am. Chem. Soc.*, **77**, 3488 (1955).
78. I. I. Chernyaev, N. S. Nikolaev and E. G. Ippolitov, *Dokl. Akad. Nauk SSSR*, **130**, 1041 (1960).
79. T. P. Perros and C. R. Naeser, *J. Am. Chem. Soc.*, **75**, 2516 (1953).
80. D. P. Mellor and N. C. Stephenson, *Australian J. Sci. Res.*, A, **4**, 406 (1951).
81. D. H. Brown, K. R. Dixon and D. W. A. Sharp, *J. Chem. Soc.*, **1966**, A, 1244.
82. N. V. Sidgwick, *The Elements and Their Chemical Compounds*, Oxford Univ. Press, London, 1950.
83. N. S. Kurnakov and E. A. Nikitina, *J. Gen. Chem. USSR*, **10**, 577 (1940).
84. M. Delépine, *Bull. Soc. Chim. France*, **1956**, 282.
85. K. Watanabe, *Nippon Kagaku Zasshi*, **77**, 1675 (1956).
86. A. A. Shidlovskii, *Theoriya Vzrvchatykh Veshchestv, Sb. Statei*, **1963**, 543.
87. R. W. G. Wyckoff and E. Posnjak, *J. Am. Chem. Soc.*, **43**, 2292 (1921).
88. R. W. G. Wyckoff, *Crystal Structures*, Vol. 3, Interscience, New York, 1965.
89. P. A. Vaughan, J. H. Studivant and L. Pauling, *J. Am. Chem. Soc.*, **72**, 5477 (1950).
90. F. J. Ewing and L. Pauling, *Z. Krist.*, **68**, 223 (1928).
91. J. Hiraishi, I. Nakagawa and T. Shimanouchi, *Spectrochim. Acta*, **20**, 819 (1964).
92. L. A. Woodward and J. A. Creighton, *Spectrochim. Acta*, **17**, 594 (1961).

93. D. M. Adams and H. A. Gebbie, *Spectrochim. Acta*, **19**, 925 (1963).
94. D. M. Adams, *Proc. Chem. Soc.*, **1961**, 335.
95. D. M. Adams, J. Chatt, J. M. Davidson and J. Gerratt, *J. Chem. Soc.*, **1963**, 2189.
96. J. R. Partington and A. L. Whynes, *J. Chem. Soc.*, **1948**, 1952.
97. D. W. A. Sharp and J. Thorley, *J. Chem. Soc.*, **1963**, 3557.
98. A. Gutbier and A. Krell, *Ber.*, **38**, 2385 (1905).
99. J. A. A. Ketelaar and J. F. van Walsem, *Rec. Trav. Chim.*, **57**, 964 (1938).
100. E. Biilmann and A. C. Anderson, *Ber.*, **36**, 1565 (1903).
101. A. Gutbier and F. Bauriedel, *Ber.*, **42**, 4244 (1909).
102. R. L. Datta, *J. Am. Chem. Soc.*, **35**, 1186 (1913).
103. G. A. Shagisultanova, *Russ. J. Inorg. Chem.*, **6**, 904 (1961).
104. *Brit. Pat.*, 879,074 (1959).
105. A. A. Shidlovskii, *Russ. J. Phys. Chem.*, **36**, 957 (1962).
106. R. G. Dickinson, *J. Am. Chem. Soc.*, **44**, 2404 (1922).
107. N. G. Klyuchnikov and R. N. Savel'eva, *Zh. Neorg. Khim.*, **1**, 2764 (1956).
108. A. Sabatini, L. Sacconi and V. Schettino, *Inorg. Chem.*, **3**, 1775 (1964).
109. H. Poulet, P. Delorme and J. P. Mathieu, *Spectrochim. Acta*, **20**, 1855 (1964).
110. H. Stammreich and R. Forneris, *Spectrochim. Acta*, **16**, 363 (1960).
111. C. M. Harris, S. E. Livingstone and N. C. Stephenson, *J. Chem. Soc.*, **1958**, 3697.
112. N. C. Stephenson, *Acta Cryst.*, **17**, 587 (1964).
113. S. Siegel and D. A. Northrup, *Inorg. Chem.*, **5**, 2187 (1966).
114. N. K. Jha, Ph. D. Thesis, University of British Columbia, 1965.
115. E. Cooke and B. Siegel, *J. Inorg. Nucl. Chem.*, **29**, 2739 (1967).
116. Y. I. Ivashentsev and R. I. Timonova, *Zhur. Ves. Khim. Obshch.* **12**, 109 (1967).
117. P. M. Druce, M. F. Lappert and P. N. K. Riley, *Chem. Commun.*, **1967**, 486.
119. N. Bartlett, F. Einstein, D. F. Stewart and J. Trotter, *J. Chem. Soc.*, **1967**, *A*, 1190.
118. K. Brodersen, G. Thiele and H. Gaedcke, *Z. anorg. allgem. Chem.*, **348**, 162 (1966).
120. D. H. Brown, K. R. Dixon, C. M. Livingston, R. H. Nuttall and D. W. A. Sharp, *J. Chem. Soc.*, **1967**, *A*, 100.
121. E. Wendling, *Bull. Soc. Chim. France*, **1967**, 5.
122. D. M. Adams and D. M. Morris, *J. Chem. Soc.*, **1967**, *A*, 1666.
123. J. Hirashi and T. Shimanouchi, *Spectrochim. Acta*, **22**, 1483 (1966).
124. C. H. Perry, D. P. Athans, E. F. Young, J. R. Dusing and B. R. Mitchell, *Spectrochim. Acta*, **23A**, 1137 (1967).
125. P. J. Hendra, *J. Chem. Soc.*, **1967**, *A*, 1298.
126. J. H. Fertel and C. H. Perry, *J. Phys. Chem. Solids*, **26**, 1773 (1965).
127. B. Corain and A. J. Pöe, *J. Chem. Soc.*, **1967**, *A*, 1318.
128. D. M. Adams, P. J. Chandler and R. G. Churchill, *J. Chem. Soc.*, **1967**, *A*, 1272.

Chapter 11

Silver and Gold

This group is unique in that the two elements of the second- and third-row transition series exhibit different oxidation states rather than a mere difference in degree of stability of the same oxidation states. Thus, most silver compounds are of oxidation state I. Silver difluoride appears to be a true bivalent silver compound and the only halide compound of silver(III) is the tetrafluoroargentate(III) ion. In contrast, most gold compounds are of oxidation state III, and few compounds of univalent gold exist. No example of bivalent gold is known. There is no oxide halide or complex oxide halide known for either element.

HALIDES

The known binary halides of silver and gold are given in Table 11.1.

TABLE 11.1
Binary Halides of Silver and Gold

Oxidation State	Fluoride	Chloride	Bromide	Iodide
III	AuF_3	$AuCl_3$	$AuBr_3$	
II	AgF_2			
I	AgF	$AgCl, AuCl$	$AgBr, AuBr$	AgI, AuI
	Ag_2F			

Oxidation State III

Gold trifluoride. Gold trifluoride was first prepared by the action of bromine trifluoride on the metal or on gold trichloride[1]. The product obtained from this reaction is a yellow adduct $AuF_3 \cdot BrF_3$. When heated to temperatures between 180° and 300°, this adduct undergoes thermal decomposition to give gold trifluoride. It has been shown subsequently that the material so prepared contains some bromine as an impurity[2]. Alternative procedures are the direct fluorination of gold monochloride,

390

monoiodide or cyanide, although the products always contain some metallic gold[2]. The most satisfactory method[2] of preparation of gold trifluoride is direct fluorination of gold trichloride at 200°.

Gold trifluoride may be sublimed in a vacuum at 300°, to yield orange-yellow crystals, but at temperatures in excess of 500° it decomposes to the metal[1]. The heat of formation of gold trifluoride has been determined[3] indirectly from heats of solution to be −83.3 kcal mole⁻¹.

The molecular configuration of gold trifluoride is unknown, but the lattice is hexagonal[2] with $a = 5.149$ and $c = 16.26$ Å. There are six molecular entities in the unit cell. Gold trifluoride is not isostructural with any other transition-metal trifluoride, but it has been suggested that it consists essentially of a square-planar arrangement about each metal atom, the planar units building up into a spiral. Such a structure would have equal numbers of terminal and bridging fluorine atoms. The magnetic moment has been measured only at room temperature; the reported value[4] is 0.5 BM. A truly square-planar arrangement as suggested above would be expected to be diamagnetic, but until the variation of magnetic susceptibility with temperature has been investigated it would be unwise to speculate on possible structures from the magnetic evidence.

Gold trifluoride is reported to be a vigorous fluorinating agent; for example, it reacts with carbon tetrachloride and causes alcohol and benzene to burn[1]. The gold trifluoride-bromine trifluoride adduct reacts with selenium tetrafluoride at room temperature to give the adduct $AuF_3 \cdot SeF_4$[5]. At 300° this adduct decomposes to give some gold trifluoride, gold metal and selenium hexafluoride[5]. When gold is dissolved in bromine trifluoride, and nitrosyl chloride is passed into the solution, a pale yellow solid is formed, which has been formulated as $NOAuF_4$[6].

Gold trichloride. Gold trichloride is best prepared[7] by direct chlorination of the metal at 200°. An interesting but indirect method of preparing gold trichloride is the reported action of arsenic trichloride on gold metal at room temperature[8].

Gold trichloride is a red crystalline solid which has been shown by a single-crystal X-ray diffraction study[9] to be monoclinic with $a = 6.57$, $b = 11.04$, $c = 6.44$ Å and $\beta = 110.3°$. The structure is shown in Figure 11.1 and consists of planar molecules of composition Au_2Cl_6 in which each gold atom has four neighbouring chlorine atoms, two of which are terminal and the other two are bridging atoms. The important molecular dimensions of the dimer are also shown in Figure 11.1. Gold trichloride is also dimeric in the vapour state[10].

The heat of formation of gold trichloride has been found[11] to be −27 kcal mole⁻¹ and the corresponding entropy is 52 cal deg⁻¹ mole⁻¹.

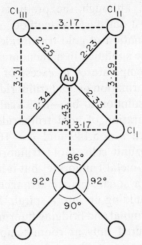

Figure 11.1　Molecular dimensions of Au_2Cl_6.

Gold trichloride dissociates at high temperatures to give gold monochloride and chlorine. The equilibrium pressure of chlorine over the temperature range 420–520° is given by the expression

$$\log p_{\text{atm}} = 8.73 - 4547/T$$

The pressure of chlorine is one atmosphere at 253°. The heat and entropy of dissociation are 18.5 kcal mole^{-1} and 38.5 cal deg^{-1} mole^{-1}, respectively[11].

A number of square-planar adducts of gold trichloride have been prepared and some of these are summarized in Table 11.2. The compound formed between gold trichloride and $(C_7H_7)_2S$ and formulated as $(C_7H_7)_2S \cdot AuCl_2$ has been shown[14] to consist of equimolar amounts of linear $(C_7H_7)_2S \cdot AuCl$ and square-planar $(C_7H_7)_2S \cdot AuCl_3$.

TABLE 11.2

Some Adducts of Gold Trichloride

Compound	Ref.	Compound	Ref.
$AuCl_3 \cdot R_2S$	12–14	$AuCl_3 \cdot POCl_3$	17
$AuCl_3 \cdot (CH_2)_5S$	15	$AuCl_3 \cdot NOCl$	18
$AuCl_3 \cdot C_4H_8O_2$	16		

Gold tribromide. Gold tribromide may be prepared by direct bromination of the metal[19] at approximately 150° or by treating gold(III) oxide with molten arsenic tribromide[20].

Only a few adducts of gold tribromide have been reported; but in each case they are identical with the corresponding gold trichloride compounds. Thus $(C_7H_7)_2S$ reacts[14] with gold tribromide to give $(C_7H_7)_2S \cdot AuBr_2$, and $(CH_2)_5S$ reacts[15] to give $(CH_2)_5S \cdot AuBr_3$.

Oxidation State II

Silver difluoride. Silver difluoride is the only halide of oxidation state II for both silver and gold and may be prepared by direct fluorination of silver at 200–250° in a flow system[21-24]. Alternatively, chlorine trifluoride may be used with the metal at elevated temperatures[25]. Reaction of other silver halides or silver nitrate with either fluorine or chlorine trifluoride at temperatures between 150° and 250° also leads to the formation of silver difluoride. An unusual reaction is the oxidation of silver monofluoride dissolved in anhydrous hydrogen fluorine by gaseous fluorine[26].

Silver difluoride is a brown crystalline solid which melts[21] at approximately 690°. It is instantly hydrolysed by moist air. It appears to be relatively stable to heat and the dissociation pressure at 700° is less than atmosphere[21].

The heat of formation of silver difluoride is -84.5 kcal mole^{-1}. Its magnetic moment[24,27] has been measured twice at room temperature; the results suggest that considerable interaction between magnetic centres occurs and this problem merits further study; in particular, an investigation of the magnetic properties over a wide temperature range.

Silver difluoride is a useful fluorinating agent and is used particularly for the preparation of fluorocarbons[28] and in the preparation of sulphur fluorides[29].

Oxidation State I

Silver monofluoride. Silver monofluoride is usually prepared by dissolving silver carbonate or silver oxide in aqueous hydrogen fluoride and evaporating the solution to dryness in the absence of light[30,31]. It may also be prepared in small quantities by thermal decomposition of silver tetrafluororoborate[32] at 200°.

Silver fluoride is a yellow crystalline solid which is extremely soluble in water and aqueous hydrogen fluoride. It is soluble in anhydrous hydrogen fluoride to the remarkable extent[26] of 83 g in 100 g of solvent at 12°. The silver fluoride–hydrogen fluoride–water system has been studied in detail at 0° and $-15°$ by Jache and coworkers[33,34], and the following solid phases were isolated: $AgF \cdot 4H_2O$, $AgF \cdot 2H_2O$, $AgF \cdot HF$, $AgF \cdot 2HF$, $AgF \cdot 3HF$, $AgF \cdot 5HF$, $3AgF \cdot 2HF$ and $6AgF \cdot 7HF \cdot H_2O$.

Silver fluoride adopts the sodium chloride cubic lattice[32] with $a = 4.94$ Å. It is a mild fluorinating agent, reacting with selenium at 180–200° to form selenium tetrafluoride and silver selenide[35].

Silver monochloride. Silver chloride is, of course, produced as a flocculent white precipitate when sufficiently concentrated solutions of its constituent ions are mixed. It may be produced in a more crystalline form by dissolving the initial precipitate in dilute ammonia solution and allowing the ammonia to evaporate from the hot solution in the dark[36].

Silver chloride is a light-sensitive compound and there is a vast area of specialized literature, which is beyond the scope of this work, on the theory and application of this phenomenon to photography. Related to this, there has been considerable study of the electronic properties of silver chloride[37-39].

The vapour pressure of silver chloride has been measured between 755° and 987° and was found to conform to the expression[40]:

$$\log p_{mm} = 8.5974 - 10{,}385/T$$

The boiling point of silver chloride obtained by extrapolation[40] was found to be 1818°. The heat and entropy of vaporization were calculated[40] to be 47.5 kcal mole^{-1} and 26.1 cal deg^{-1} mole^{-1}, respectively. The heat of formation of silver chloride[41] is -30.1 kcal mole^{-1}.

Under normal conditions silver chloride adopts a cubic sodium lattice, but at very high pressures it is converted into a tetragonal polymorph[42] with $a = 3.92$ and $c = 9.03$ Å.

The mass spectrum of silver chloride vapour shows the surprising presence of trimeric species[43,44]. The microwave spectrum of silver chloride vapour has been observed and an internuclear distance of 2.28 Å deduced[45].

Silver chloride is soluble in a variety of media. This is attributed to complex formation, but in no case has a complex been isolated and the formulae of the proposed species have been deduced from potentiometric measurements, colligative properties, or solubility studies. For instance, Tien and Harrington[46] postulated that, in the lithium nitrate–potassium nitrate eutectic and in the presence of an excess of chloride ion, the complex ion $AgCl_2^-$ is formed, although the quantitative aspects of the treatment are of doubtful validity[47]. Silver chloride dissolves in aqueous silver nitrate and it has been suggested that the complex ion Ag_2Cl^+ is formed[48]. Similarly, silver chloride is soluble in potassium chloride solution, but in this case the ions $AgCl_2^-$ and $AgCl_4^{3-}$ have been postulated[49]. It appears that some of these systems might repay further study, especially if efforts were made to isolate the complexes.

Gold monochloride. Gold monochloride is prepared by thermal decomposition of gold trichloride[7] at 160°. However, it is thermally unstable, and at high temperatures dissociates into the metal and chlorine[10,11]. The equilibrium dissociation pressure of chlorine over the temperature range 420–520° is given by the expression[11]:

$$\log p_{atm} = 6.23 - 3483/T$$

The heat and entropy of dissociation[11] are 16 kcal mole^{-1} and 30 cal deg^{-1} mole^{-1}, respectively. The heat and entropy of formation of gold chloride are −8 kcal mole^{-1} and 15 cal deg^{-1} mole^{-1}, respectively[11].

Gold chloride is a yellow powder which adopts an orthorhombic lattice[7] with $a = 6.41$, $b = 3.36$ and $c = 9.48$ Å.

Few derivatives of gold chloride are known. The adduct $AuCl \cdot 2P(C_6H_5)_3$ was prepared indirectly by treating the ligand with an acid solution containing the trachloroaurate(III) ion[50]. Similarly, an excess of tetrahydrothiapyran or dialkyl sulphide with gold trichloride in hydrochloric acid give complexes[13,15] of the type $AuCl \cdot L$.

Silver monobromide. Silver bromide is invariably prepared by the interaction of the constituent ions in aqueous solution. Like silver chloride, silver bromide is widely used for photographic purposes and its electronic properties have been investigated extensively.

The vapour pressure of silver bromide over the temperature range 696–951° is given by the expression[40]:

$$\log p_{mm} = 8.7141 - 10,367/T$$

The boiling point obtained by extrapolations is 1778° and the heat and entropy of vaporization are respectively 47.4 kcal mole^{-1} and 26.7 cal deg^{-1} mole^{-1}. The heat of formation[41] is −27.5 kcal mole^{-1}.

The presence of trimeric species in the vapour of silver bromide has been established by mass-spectrometric studies[43]. An internuclear distance of 2.39 Å was deduced from the microwave spectrum of silver bromide vapour[51].

Silver bromide is soluble in a variety of aqueous solutions of ionic salts and also in melts, as a result of the formation of complex compounds. Typical solutions and melts are aqueous ammonium bromide[52,53], aqueous silver fluoride[54] and a melt composed of equimolar amounts of potassium and sodium nitrate[55,56].

Silver monoiodide. Silver iodide is precipitated when aqueous solutions of its constituent ions are mixed. It is a pale yellow, light-sensitive solid.

Silver iodide has been reported to exhibit a rather remarkable number of solid phases according to experimental conditions, as listed in Table

TABLE 11.3

Polymorphs of Silver Iodide

Phase	Conditions	Ref.
Exact wurtzite	$-196°$	57
Distorted wurtzite	Normal temp., 1 atm	57, 58
Zinc blende	Sublimed	59
Metastable sphalerite	$80-140°$, 1 atm	58
Body-centred cubic	Above $146°$, 1 atm	58
Caesium chloride	Above 3 kbar pressure	58
Sodium chloride	Above 97 kbar pressure	58

11.3. The phase change from the wurtzite to the body-centred cubic form of silver iodide occurs at approximately 150° at atmospheric pressure[60-62]. The structure of the room-temperature form[63] of silver iodide is hexagonal with $a = 4.592$ and $c = 7.510$ Å and the silver–iodine bond distance is 2.814 Å.

Silver iodide melts[62] at 555.5°, and its heat of formation has been determined[41] as -15.3 kcal mole^{-1}.

Silver iodide is soluble in many iodide-containing solutions as a result of the formation of complex ions, both cationic and anionic[64]. However there appears to be considerable confusion concerning the conditions of formation and the actual constitution of these complexes. Some of the anionic complexes have been tentatively identified[65-73] as AgI_2^-, AgI_3^{2-}, $Ag_2I_6^{4-}$, AgI_4^{3-} and $Ag_4I_6^{2-}$. Only the $Ag_2I_3^-$ complex appears to have been isolated as a solid[68-70].

The structure of caesium triiododiargentate(I), $CsAg_2I_3$, has been studied by single-crystal X-ray diffraction techniques[70]. It forms an orthorhombic lattice with $a = 11.08$, $b = 13.74$ and $c = 6.23$ Å. There are four molecular units in the cell. The structure, shown in Figure 11.2,

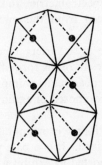

Figure 11.2   Double chain of tetrahedra in $CsAg_2I_3$.

consists of double chains of composition Ag_2I_3 ions parallel to the c axis which are formed by sharing edges of the tetrahedra. The caesium atoms are accommodated in the lattice between the chains.

The constitution of the ions AgI_2^- and AgI_6^{2-} have been studied in solution by X-ray diffraction techniques[71]. The AgI_2^- ion is non-linear, with the silver–iodine distance 2.85 Å, and the angle I–Ag–I 111°. The $Ag_4I_6^{2-}$ anion is based on a tetrahedron of silver atoms with an iodine atom above each edge; the silver–silver distance is 4.55 Å and the silver–iodine distance is 5.43 Å.

The complex ion $Ag_2I^+F^-$ resulting from dissolution of silver iodide in silver fluoride solution has been isolated[54]; it has a monoclinic lattice with $a = 4.72$, $b = 7.66$, $c = 6.36$ Å and $\alpha = 86.5°$.

Gold monoiodide. Gold iodide has been prepared[74] by heating the metal and iodine in a sealed tube at 120° for four months! It is a light yellow powder with a tetragonal lattice[75] for which $a = 4.35$ and $c = 13.73$ Å. The structure consists of chains of alternate gold and iodine atoms with a very short internuclear distance of 2.62 Å.

Silver subfluoride. Silver subfluoride is best prepared by the electrolysis of a saturated silver fluoride solution at a silver anode[76]. It forms yellow-green plates which have a metallic appearance.

Silver subfluoride has a hexagonal lattice of the cadmium iodide type, but there is a discrepancy in the unit-cell parameters reported by two groups. Ott and Seyfarth[77] gave $a = 3.0$ and $c = 5.14$ Å, whereas Terry and Diamond[78] gave $a = 2.99$ and $c = 5.71$ Å.

Above 200° silver subfluoride decomposes to give the metal and silver monofluoride[79]. This reaction has been exploited in radiotracer experiments to confirm the non-equivalence of the two silver atoms in the molecule[80].

COMPLEX HALIDES

Almost all the complexes of silver and gold halides to be discussed in this section are ions of the type MX_4^-. The few complexes based on the general formula MX_2^- have already been discussed under the headings of the appropriate halide.

Tetrafluoroargentates(III). Salts of the tetrafluoroargentate(III) anion have been prepared[81] by direct fluorination of equimolar mixtures of silver nitrate and the appropriate alkali-metal chloride at 200–400°. The compounds are hydrolysed violently by water but no further physical or chemical property of any of these salts has been reported.

Tetrafluoroaurates(III). Tetrafluoroaurates(III) have been prepared in two major ways; by the action of fluorine[82] or bromine trifluoride[1]

27

TABLE 11.4
Infrared and Raman Spectra of Tetrachloroaurates(III)

Infrared[85]			Raman[86]	
$RbAuCl_4$	$CsAuCl_4$	Assignment	$AuCl_4^-$	Assignment
358	365	ν_6	347	ν_1
175, 171	179, 168	ν_7	324	ν_5
144	143	ν_2	171	ν_3

on alkali-metal tetrachloroaurates(III), or by the action of bromine trifluoride on a mixture of silver and gold[1,83] to give $AgAuF_4$ or on gold and potassium chloride[1] to give potassium tetrafluoroaurate(III).

The tetrafluoroaurate(III) anion is, of course, diagmagnetic[4] and the infrared spectrum[84] shows two absorptions, at 477 and 585 cm^{-1}.

Tetrachloroaurates(III).   The tetrachloroaurate(III) ion is formed when gold trichloride is dissolved in hydrochloric acid or when gold metal is dissolved in aqua regia. Addition of an alkali-metal chloride leads to the isolation of well-defined solid compounds.

Potassium tetrachloroaurate(III) decomposes thermally to potassium

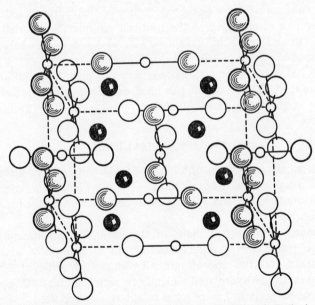

Figure 11.3   Atomic arrangements in $Cs_2AgAuCl_6$ and $Cs_2AuAuCl_6$. Large full circles represent caesium atoms, large open circles chlorine atoms, and small circles gold and silver atoms.

chloride, gold metal and chlorine, and there is no evidence for the formation of any intermediate chlorine-containing gold compound[10].

Both the infrared and the Raman spectrum of the tetrachloroaurate(III) anion have been reported and the results are given in Table 11.4.

The compounds $Cs_2AgAuCl_6$ and $CsAuCl_3$ ($Cs_2AuAuCl_6$) were originally reported to be cubic[87] but a later single-crystal study[88] revealed that they are isostructural with a body-centred tetragonal lattice with the following unit-cell parameters:

$$Cs_2AgAuCl_6 \quad a = 7.38 \text{ Å}, \quad c = 11.01 \text{ Å}.$$
$$Cs_2AuAuCl_6 \quad a = 7.49 \text{ Å}, \quad c = 10.87 \text{ Å}.$$

The structure of the two complexes is shown in Figure 11.3 and consists essentially of equal numbers of dichlorometallate(I) anions and tetrachloroaurate(III) anions arranged perpendicularly to each other.

Tetrabromoaurates(III). These complexes may be isolated from solutions of gold tribromide in hydrobromic acid. The infrared and Raman spectra of typical salts have been recorded[85,86] and show the same general pattern as those of the tetrachloroaurates(III).

ADDENDA

Halides

Bartlett and coworkers[89] have determined the full crystal structure of gold trifluoride. The lattice dimensions are as noted earlier and the space group is $P6_122$. The compound is a polymer with each gold atom in a square of fluorine atoms. Each square is linked to the next by two *cis*-bridges, giving an infinite hexagonal helix. The bond lengths are 2.04 Å (bridging) and 1.91 Å (terminal). The Au–F–Au angle is 116°. In addition, weak cross-linking occurs between chains to give effectively a distorted octahedron about the metal atom with a long gold–fluorine bond of 2.69 Å.

Silver difluoride is weakly ferrimagnetic[90] with a critical temperature of 163°K. The magnetic moment at room temperature is 2.0 BM. There have been two reports of X-ray powder diffraction results of silver difluoride, but they do not agree. Charpin and coworkers[91] find it to be orthorhombic with $a = 5.813$, $b = 5.529$, and $c = 5.073$ Å. Russian workers[92] find silver difluoride to be monoclinic with $a = 3.34$, $b = 4.57$, $c = 4.65$ Å, and $\beta = 84.5°$.

The vapour pressure of silver monofluoride is given by the expressions[93]:

$$\log p_{atm} = 10.7 - 10,230/T \quad \text{(less than 435°)}$$
$$\log p_{atm} = 4.78 - 9370/T \quad \text{(581–751°)}$$

The heats of formation, vaporization, sublimation, and fusion were determined as -48.5, 42.8 at $935°K$, 50.9 at $298°K$, and 4.0 kcal mole^{-1}, respectively.

Moore and Skelly[94] found that at high pressures (>4 kbar) the triiodide ion is formed in silver iodide crystals.

Another X-ray powder diffraction study[95] of silver subfluoride has confirmed the data of Terry and Diamond[78]. The compound was found[95] to be hexagonal with $a = 2.996$ and $c = 5.691$ Å.

Complex Halides

Hoppe and Homann[96] have prepared potassium dicaesium hexafluoro-argentate(III) by passing fluorine over the correct mixture of caesium chloride, potassium chloride, and silver nitrate at $300°$. The salt is cubic with $a = 9.175$ Å.

The crystal structure of sodium tetrachloroaurate(III) dihydrate has been determined[97]. The crystals are orthorhombic with $a = 12.818$, $b = 7.067$, and $c = 8.993$ Å. The space group is *Pnma*. The structure contains discrete $AuCl_4$ units in a square-planar configuration with a gold–chlorine bond length of 2.28 Å. Both the potassium and the ammonium tetrachloroaurate(III) are monoclinic[97]:

$KAuCl_4$ $a = 8.671$ Å, $b = 6.386$ Å, $c = 12.268$ Å

$NH_4AuCl_4 \cdot xH_2O$ $a = 14.054$ Å, $b = 11.519$ Å, $c = 14.496$ Å

The Raman spectra of potassium tetrabromo- and tetraiodoaurate(III) have been observed[98]. The principal absorptions occurred at 214, 196, and 102 cm^{-1} for the bromo complex, and at 148, 110, and 75 cm^{-1} for the iodo complex.

REFERENCES

1. A. G. Sharpe, *J. Chem. Soc.*, **1949**, 2901.
2. L. B. Asprey, F. H. Kruse, K. H. Jack and R. Maitland, *Inorg. Chem.*, **3**, 602 (1964).
3. A. A. Woolf, *J. Chem. Soc.*, **1964**, 4694.
4. R. S. Nyholm and A. G. Sharpe, *J. Chem. Soc.*, **1952**, 3579.
5. N. Bartlett and P. L. Robinson, *J. Chem. Soc.*, **1961**, 3417.
6. A. A. Woolf, *J. Chem. Soc.*, **1950**, 1053.
7. L. Capella and C. Schwab, *Compt. Rend.*, **260**, 4337 (1965).
8. E. Montignie, *Bull. Soc. Chim. France*, **3**, 190 (1936).
9. E. S. Clark, D. H. Templeton and C. H. MacGillavry, *Acta Cryst.*, **11**, 284 (1958).
10. W. Fischer and W. Biltz, *Z. anorg. allgem. Chem.*, **176**, 81 (1928).
11. S. A. Shchukarev, M. A. Oranskaya and V. M. Tsintsius, *Zh. Neorg. Khim.*, **1**, 881 (1956).
12. J. P. Teresa, *Anales Real Soc. Espan. Fis Quim.* (*Madrid*), **40**, 222 (1944).
13. P. C. Ray and D. C. Sen, *J. Indian Chem. Soc.*, **7**, 67 (1930).
14. F. H. Brain, C. S. Gibson, J. A. J. Jarvis, R. F. Phillips, H. M. Powell and A. Tyabji, *J. Chem. Soc.*, **1952**, 3686.

15. H. J. Worth and H. H. Haendler, *J. Am. Chem. Soc.*, **64**, 1232 (1942).
16. H. Funk and H. Kohler, *Z. anorg. allgem. Chem.*, **294**, 233 (1958).
17. V. Gutmann and F. Mairinger, *Monatsh. Chem.*, **89**, 724 (1958).
18. J. R. Partington and A. L. Whynes, *J. Chem. Soc.*, **1949**, 3135.
19. N. V. Sidgwick, *The Chemical Elements and Their Compounds*, Oxford Univ. Press, London, 1950, p. 180.
20. G. Jander and K. Gunter, *Z. anorg. allgem. Chem.*, **302**, 155 (1959).
21. H. von Wartenberg, *Z. anorg. allgem. Chem.*, **242**, 406 (1939).
22. H. Jockrush, *Naturwiss.*, **22**, 561 (1934).
23. O. Ruff and M. Giese, *Z. anorg. allgem. Chem.*, **219**, 143 (1934).
24. O. Ruff and M. Giese, *Angew. Chem.*, **47**, 480 (1934).
25. W. Hückel, *Nachr. Akad. Wiss. Göttingen Math.-Phys. Klasse*, **1946**, 36.
26. A. W. Jache and G. H. Cady, *J. Phys. Chem.*, **56**, 1106 (1952).
27. E. Gruner and W. Klemm, *Naturwissenschaften*, **25**, 59 (1937).
28. M. Stacy and J. C. Tatlow, *Advances in Fluorine Chemistry*, Vol. 1, Butterworths, London, 1960, p. 187.
29. O. Glemser and H. Richert, *Z. anorg. allgem. Chem.*, **307**, 313 (1961).
30. S. T. Talipov and D. A. Abdullaev, *Trudy Sredneaz. Univ.*, No. 40, *Khim. Nauk*, **1953**, 65.
31. A. G. Sharpe, *Advances in Fluorine Chemistry*, Vol. 1, Butterworths, London, 1960.
32. A. G. Sharpe, *J. Chem. Soc.*, **1952**, 4538.
33. H. J. Thomas and A. W. Jache, *J. Inorg. Nucl. Chem.*, **13**, 54 (1960).
34. J. P. Buettner and A. W. Jache, *J. Inorg. Nucl. Chem.*, **19**, 376 (1961).
35. O. Glemser, F. Meyer and A. Haas, *Naturwissenschaften*, **52**, 130 (1965).
36. W. Zimmerman, *J. Am. Chem. Soc.*, **74**, 852 (1952).
37. F. C. Brown, *J. Phys. Chem.*, **66**, 2368 (1962).
38. P. M. Scop, *Phys. Rev.*, **A139**, 934 (1965).
39. F. Bassani, R. S. Knox and W. B. Fowler, *Phys. Rev.*, **A137**, 1217 (1965).
40. H. Bloom, J. O'M. Bockris, N. E. Richards and R. G. Taylor, *J. Am. Chem. Soc.*, **80**, 2044 (1958).
41. A. Bertram and W. A. Roth, *Z. Physik. Chem.*, **A178**, 227 (1937).
42. J. L. Jamieson and A. W. Lawson, *J. Applied Phys.*, **33**, 776 (1962).
43. H. M. Rosenstock, J. R. Walton and L. K. Brice, *U.S.A.E.C. Report* ORNL 2772 (1959).
44. A. V. Gusarov and L. N. Gorokhov, *Vestn. Mosk. Univ. Ser. II Khim.*, **17**, 14 (1962).
45. L. C. Krisher and W. G. Norris, *J. Chem. Phys.*, **44**, 391 (1966).
46. H. T. Tien and G. W. Harrington, *Inorg. Chem.*, **3**, 215 (1964).
47. G. W. Harrington and H. T. Tien, *Inorg. Chem.*, **3**, 1333 (1964).
48. R. Jacoud, V. C. Reinsborough and F. E. W. Wetmore, *Australian J. Chem.*, **19**, 1597 (1966).
49. H. Chateau and B. Hervier, *J. Chim. Phys.*, **54**, 637 (1957).
50. I. Collamati, *Ric. Sci. Rend.*, *Sez. A*, **6**, 363 (1964).
51. L. C. Krisher and W. G. Norris, *J. Chem. Phys.*, **44**, 974 (1966).
52. K. S. Lyalikov, *Dokl. Akad. Nauk SSSR*, **65**, 171 (1949).
53. J. Poradier, A. M. Venet and H. Chateau, *J. Chim. Phys.*, **51**, 375 (1954).
54. K. H. Lieser, *Z. anorg. allgem. Chem.*, **305**, 133 (1960).
55. R. Cigen and N. Mannerstrand, *Acta Chem. Scand.*, **18**, 1755 (1964).
56. R. Cigen and N. Mannerstrand, *Acta Chem. Scand.*, **18**, 2203 (1964).

57. L. Helmholz, *J. Chem. Phys.*, **3**, 740 (1935).
58. B. L. Davis and L. Adams, *Science*, **146**, 519 (1964).
59. L. Sieg, *Naturwissenschaften*, **40**, 439 (1953).
60. G. Burley, *J. Phys. Chem.*, **68**, 1111 (1964).
61. K. H. Lieser, *Z. Physik. Chem. (Frankfurt)*, **2**, 238 (1954).
62. J. Noelting, *Ber. Bunsenges. Physik. Chem.*, **67**, 172 (1963).
63. G. Burley, *J. Chem. Phys.*, **38**, 2807 (1963).
64. E. L. King, H. J. Krall and M. L. Pandow, *J. Am. Chem. Soc.*, **74**, 3492 (1952).
65. G. Burley and H. E. Kissinger, *J. Res. Nat. Bur. Std.*, **64A**, 403 (1960).
66. E. L. Mackor, *Rec. Trav. Chim.*, **70**, 457 (1951).
67. H. Chateau and M. C. Moncet, *J. Chim. Phys.*, **60**, 1060 (1963).
68. H. J. Meyer, *Acta Cryst.*, **16**, 788 (1963).
69. J. E. Marsh and W. C. Rhymes, *J. Chem. Soc.*, **103**, 782 (1913).
70. C. Brink, N. F. Binnendijk and J. van de Linde, *Acta Cryst.*, **7**, 176 (1954).
71. G. Dallinga and E. L. Mackor, *Rec. Trav. Chim.*, **75**, 796 (1956).
72. A. M. Golub, *Ukr. Khim. Zh.*, **19**, 467 (1953).
73. I. Leden, *Acta Chem. Scand.*, **10**, 812 (1956).
74. A. Weiss and A. Weiss, *Z. Naturforsch.*, **11b**, 604 (1956).
75. H. Jagodzinski, *Z. Krist.*, **112**, 80 (1959).
76. R. Hilsch, G. V. Minnigerode and H. von Wartenberg, *Naturwissenschaften*, **44**, 463 (1957).
77. H. Ott and H. Seyfarth, *Z. Krist.*, **67**, 430 (1928).
78. H. Terry and H. Diamond, *J. Chem. Soc.*, 2820 (1928).
79. L. Poyer, M. Fielder and B. E. Bryant, *Inorg. Syn.*, **5**, 18 (1957).
80. M. Bruno and U. Santoro, *Gazz. Chim. Ital.*, **86**, 1095 (1956).
81. R. Hoppe, *Z. anorg. allgem. Chem.*, **292**, 28 (1957).
82. R. Hoppe and W. Klemm, *Z. anorg. allgem. Chem.*, **268**, 364 (1952).
83. A. G. Sharpe, *J. Chem. Soc.*, **1950**, 2907.
84. R. D. Peacock and D. W. A. Sharp, *J. Chem. Soc.*, **1959**, 2762.
85. A. Sabatini, L. Sacconi and V. Schettino, *Inorg. Chem.*, **3**, 1775 (1964).
86. H. Stammreich and R. Forneris, *Spectrochim. Acta*, **16**, 363 (1960).
87. N. Elliot, *J. Chem. Phys.*, **2**, 419 (1934).
88. N. Elliot and L. Pauling, *J. Am. Chem. Soc.*, **60**, 1846 (1938).
89. F. W. B. Einstein, P. R. Rao, J. Trotter and N. Bartlett, *J. Chem. Soc.*, **1967**, *A*, 478.
90. P. Charpin, A. J. Dianoux, H. Marquet-Ellis and N. Nguyen, *Compt. Rend.*, **264C**, 1108 (1967).
91. P. Charpin, A. J. Dianoux, H. Marquet-Ellis and N. Nguyen, *Compt. Rend.*, **263C**, 1359 (1966).
92. E. A. Baturina, V. A. Luk'yanychev and L. N. Rastorguev, *Zh. Strukt. Khim.*, **7**, 627 (1966).
93. K. F. Zmbov and J. L. Margrave, *J. Phys. Chem.*, **71**, 446 (1967).
94. M. J. Moore and D. W. Skelly, *J. Chem. Phys.*, **46**, 3676 (1967).
95. G. Argay and I. Naray-Szabo, *Acta Chim. Acad. Sci. Hung.*, **49**, 329 (1966).
96. R. Hoppe and R. Homann, *Naturwissenschaften*, **53**, 501A (1966).
97. M. Bonamico, G. Dessy and A. Vaciago, *Atti Acad. Nazl. Lincei, Rend. Classe Sci. Fis. Mat. Nat.*, **39**, 504 (1965).
98. P. Hendra, *J. Chem. Soc.*, **1967**, *A*, 1298.

Index

403